Lecture Notes in Computer Science

Lecture Notes in Artificial Intelligence   14304

Founding Editor

Jörg Siekmann

Series Editors

Randy Goebel, *University of Alberta, Edmonton, Canada*
Wolfgang Wahlster, *DFKI, Berlin, Germany*
Zhi-Hua Zhou, *Nanjing University, Nanjing, China*

The series Lecture Notes in Artificial Intelligence (LNAI) was established in 1988 as a topical subseries of LNCS devoted to artificial intelligence.

The series publishes state-of-the-art research results at a high level. As with the LNCS mother series, the mission of the series is to serve the international R & D community by providing an invaluable service, mainly focused on the publication of conference and workshop proceedings and postproceedings.

Fei Liu · Nan Duan · Qingting Xu · Yu Hong
Editors

Natural Language Processing and Chinese Computing

12th National CCF Conference, NLPCC 2023
Foshan, China, October 12–15, 2023
Proceedings, Part III

Editors
Fei Liu
Emory University
Atlanta, GA, USA

Nan Duan
Microsoft Research Asia
Beijing, China

Qingting Xu
Soochow University
Suzhou, China

Yu Hong
Soochow University
Suzhou, China

ISSN 0302-9743   ISSN 1611-3349 (electronic)
Lecture Notes in Artificial Intelligence
ISBN 978-3-031-44698-6   ISBN 978-3-031-44699-3 (eBook)
https://doi.org/10.1007/978-3-031-44699-3

LNCS Sublibrary: SL7 – Artificial Intelligence

This Springer imprint is published by the registered company Springer Nature Switzerland AG
The registered company address is: Gewerbestrasse 11, 6330 Cham, Switzerland

Paper in this product is recyclable.

Preface

Welcome to NLPCC 2023, the twelfth CCF International Conference on Natural Language Processing and Chinese Computing. Following the success of previous conferences held in Beijing (2012), Chongqing (2013), Shenzhen (2014), Nanchang (2015), Kunming (2016), Dalian (2017), Hohhot (2018), Dunhuang (2019), Zhengzhou (2020), Qingdao (2021), and Guilin (2022), this year's NLPCC will be held in Foshan. As a premier international conference on natural language processing and Chinese computing, organized by the CCF-NLP (Technical Committee of Natural Language Processing, China Computer Federation, formerly known as Technical Committee of Chinese Information, China Computer Federation), NLPCC serves as an important forum for researchers and practitioners from academia, industry, and government to share their ideas, research results, and experiences, and to promote their research and technical innovations.

The fields of natural language processing (NLP) and Chinese computing (CC) have boomed in recent years. Following NLPCC's tradition, we welcomed submissions in ten areas for the main conference: Fundamentals of NLP; Machine Translation and Multilinguality; Machine Learning for NLP; Information Extraction and Knowledge Graph; Summarization and Generation; Question Answering; Dialogue Systems; Large Language Models; NLP Applications and Text Mining; Multimodality and Explainability. This year, we received 478 valid submissions to the main conference on the submission deadline.

After a thorough reviewing process, including meta reviewing, out of 478 valid submissions (some of which were withdrawn by authors or desk-rejected due to policy violations), 134 papers were finally accepted as regular papers to appear in the main conference, resulting in an acceptance rate of 29.9%. Among them, 64 submissions will be presented as oral papers and 79 as poster papers at the conference. 5 papers were nominated by our area chairs for the best paper award. An independent best paper award committee was formed to select the best papers from the shortlist. This proceeding includes only the accepted English papers; the Chinese papers will appear in the ACTA Scientiarum Naturalium Universitatis Pekinensis. In addition to the main proceedings, 3 papers were accepted to the Student workshop, 32 papers were accepted to the Evaluation workshop.

We are honored to have four internationally renowned keynote speakers, Denny Zhou (Google Deepmind), Xia (Ben) Hu (Rice University), Arman Cohan (Yale University), and Diyi Yang (Stanford University), sharing their findings on recent research progress and achievements in natural language processing.

We would like to thank all the people who have contributed to NLPCC 2023. First of all, we would like to thank our 21 area chairs for their hard work recruiting reviewers, monitoring the review and discussion processes, and carefully rating and recommending submissions. We would like to thank all 322 reviewers for their time and efforts to review the submissions. We are also grateful for the help and support from the general chairs,

Rada Mihalcea and Hang Li, and from the organization committee chairs, Biqin Zeng, Yi Cai and Xiaojun Wan. Special thanks go to Yu Hong and Qingting Xu, the publication chairs. We greatly appreciate all your help!

Finally, we would like to thank all the authors who submitted their work to NLPCC 2023, and thank our sponsors for their contributions to the conference. Without your support, we could not have such a strong conference program.

We are happy to see you at NLPCC 2023 in Foshan and hope you enjoy the conference!

August 2023   Fei Liu
                                                                   Nan Duan

Organization

NLPCC 2023 is organized by China Computer Federation (CCF), and hosted by South China Normal University. Publishers comprise Lecture Notes on Artificial Intelligence (LNAI), Springer Verlag, and ACTA Scientiarum Naturalium Universitatis Pekinensis.

Organization Committee

General Chairs

Rada Mihalcea   University of Michigan
Hang Li   ByteDance Technology

Program Committee Chairs

Fei Liu   Emory University
Nan Duan   Microsoft Research Asia

Student Workshop Chairs

Jing Li   The Hong Kong Polytechnic University
Jingjing Wang   Soochow University

Evaluation Chairs

Yunbo Cao   Tencent
Piji Li   Nanjing University of Aeronautics and
                                        Astronautics

Tutorial Chairs

Zhongyu Wei   Fudan University
Zhaochun Ren   Shandong University

Publication Chairs

Yu Hong	Soochow University
Qingting Xu	Soochow University

Journal Coordinator

Yunfang Wu	Peking University

Conference Handbook Chair

Leixin Du	South China Normal University

Sponsorship Chairs

Min Zhang	Harbin Institute of Technology (Shenzhen)
Haofen Wang	Tongji University
Ruifeng Xu	Harbin Institute of Technology (Shenzhen)

Publicity Chairs

Benyou Wang	The Chinese University of Hong Kong (Shenzhen)
Shen Gao	Shandong University
Xianling Mao	Beijing Institute of Technology

Organization Committee Chairs

Biqin Zeng	South China Normal University
Yi Cai	South China University of Technology
Xiaojun Wan	Peking University

Treasurer

Yajing Zhang	Soochow University
Xueying Zhang	Peking University

Webmaster

Hui Liu   Peking University

Program Committee

Xiang Ao   Institute of Computing Technology, Chinese
                                       Academy of Sciences, China
Jiaxin Bai   Hong Kong University of Science and
                                       Technology, China
Xinyi Bai   Google, USA
Junwei Bao   JD AI Research, China
Qiming Bao   The University of Auckland, New Zealand
Xiangrui Cai   Nankai University, China
Shuyang Cao   Univerisity of Michigan, USA
Zhangming Chan   Alibaba Group, China
Yufeng Chen   Beijing Jiaotong University, China
Yulong Chen   Zhejiang University, Westlake University, China
Bo Chen   Minzu University of China, China
Jianghao Chen   CASIA, China
Wenhu Chen   University of Waterloo & Google Research,
                                       Canada
Yubo Chen   Institute of Automation, Chinese Academy of
                                       Sciences, China
Xuelu Chen   UCLA, USA
Yidong Chen   Department of Artificial Intelligence, School of
                                       Informatics, Xiamen University, China
Chen Chen   Nankai University, China
Guanyi Chen   Utrecht University, Netherlands
Qi Chen   Northeastern University, China
Wenliang Chen   Soochow University, China
Xinchi Chen   Amazon AWS, USA
Muhao Chen   USC, USA
Liang Chen   The Chinese University of Hong Kong,
                                       Hong Kong Special Administrative Region
                                       of China
Jiangjie Chen   Fudan University, China
Leshang Chen   Oracle America, Inc., USA
Sihao Chen   University of Pennsylvania, USA
Wei Chen   School of Data Science, Fudan University, China
Kewei Cheng   UCLA, USA
Cunli Mao   Kunming University of Science and Technology,
                                       China

Xiang Deng	The Ohio State University, USA
Chenchen Ding	NICT, Japan
Qianqian Dong	ByteDance AI Lab, China
Yue Dong	University of California Riverside, USA
Zi-Yi Dou	UCLA, USA
Rotem Dror	University of Pennsylvania, Israel
Xinya Du	University of Texas at Dallas, USA
Junwen Duan	Central South University, China
Chaoqun Duan	JD AI Research, China
Nan Duan	Microsoft Research Asia, China
Xiangyu Duan	Soochow University, China
Alex Fabbri	Salesforce AI Research, USA
Zhihao Fan	Fudan University, China
Tianqing Fang	Hong Kong University of Science and Technology, Hong Kong Special Administrative Region of China
Zichu Fei	Fudan University, China
Shi Feng	Northeastern University, China
Jiazhan Feng	Peking University, China
Yang Feng	Institute of Computing Technology, Chinese Academy of Sciences, China
Zhangyin Feng	Harbin Institute of Technology, China
Yansong Feng	Peking University, China
Xingyu Fu	Upenn, USA
Guohong Fu	Soochow University, China
Yi Fung	University of Illinois at Urbana Champaign, USA
Shen Gao	Shandong University, China
Heng Gong	Harbin Institute of Technology, China
Yeyun Gong	Microsoft Research Asia, China
Yu Gu	The Ohio State University, USA
Yi Guan	School of Computer Science and Technology, Harbin Institute of Technology, China
Tao Gui	Fudan University, China
Daya Guo	Sun Yat-Sen University, China
Shaoru Guo	Institute of Automation, Chinese Academy of Sciences, China
Yiduo Guo	Peking University, China
Jiale Han	Beijing University of Posts and Telecommunications, China
Xudong Han	The University of Melbourne, Australia
Lifeng Han	The University of Manchester, UK
Xianpei Han	Institute of Software, Chinese Academy of Sciences, China

Tianyong Hao	School of Computer Science, South China Normal University, China
Hongkun Hao	Shanghai Jiao Tong University, China
Ruifang He	Tianjin University, China
Xudong Hong	Saarland University/MPI Informatics, Germany
I-Hung Hsu	USC Information Sciences Institute, USA
Zhe Hu	Baidu, China
Junjie Hu	University of Wisconsin-Madison, USA
Xiaodan Hu	University of Illinois at Urbana-Champaign, USA
Minghao Hu	Information Research Center of Military Science, China
Shujian Huang	National Key Laboratory for Novel Software Technology, Nanjing University, China
Fei Huang	Tsinghua University, China
Baizhou Huang	Peking University, China
Junjie Huang	The Chinese University of Hong Kong, Hong Kong Special Administrative Region of China
Yueshan Huang	University of California San Diego, China
Qingbao Huang	Guangxi University, China
Xin Huang	Institute of Automation, Chinese Academy of Sciences, China
James Y. Huang	University of Southern California, USA
Jiangping Huang	Chongqing University of Posts and Telecommunications, China
Changzhen Ji	Hithink RoyalFlush Information Network, China
Chen Jia	Fudan University, China
Tong Jia	Northeastern University, China
Hao Jia	School of Computer Science and Technology, Soochow University, China
Hao Jiang	University of Science and Technology of China, China
Wenbin Jiang	Baidu Inc., China
Jingchi Jiang	Harbin Institute of Technology, China
Huiming Jin	Apple Inc., USA
Feihu Jin	Institute of Automation, Chinese Academy of Sciences, China
Peng Jin	Leshan Normal University, China
Zhu Junguo	Kunming University of Science and Technology, China
Lingpeng Kong	The University of Hong Kong, Hong Kong Special Administrative Region of China
Fajri Koto	MBZUAI, United Arab Emirates

Tuan Lai	University of Illinois at Urbana-Champaign, USA
Yuxuan Lai	Peking University, China
Yuanyuan Lei	Texas A&M University, USA
Maoxi Li	School of Computer Information Engineering, Jiangxi Normal University, China
Zekun Li	University of Minnesota, USA
Bei Li	Northeastern University, China
Chenliang Li	Wuhan University, China
Piji Li	Nanjing University of Aeronautics and Astronautics, China
Zejun Li	Fudan University, China
Yucheng Li	University of Surrey, UK
Yanran Li	The Hong Kong Polytechnic University, China
Shasha Li	College of Computer, National University of Defense Technology, China
Mingda Li	University of California, Los Angeles, USA
Dongfang Li	Harbin Institute of Technology, Shenzhen, China
Zuchao Li	Wuhan University, China
Mingzhe Li	Peking University, China
Miao Li	The University of Melbourne, Australia
Jiaqi Li	iFlytek Research (Beijing), China
Chenxi Li	UCSD, USA
Yanyang Li	The Chinese University of Hong Kong, China
Fei Li	Wuhan University, China
Jiajun Li	Shanghai Huawei Technology Co., Ltd., China
Jing Li	Department of Computing, The Hong Kong Polytechnic University, Hong Kong Special Administrative Region of China
Fenghuan Li	Guangdong University of Technology, China
Zhenghua Li	Soochow University, China
Qintong Li	The University of Hong Kong, Hong Kong Special Administrative Region of China
Haonan Li	MBZUAI, United Arab Emirates
Zheng Li	Stockton University, USA
Bin Li	Nanjing Normal University, China
Yupu Liang	University of Chinese Academy of Sciences, China
Yaobo Liang	Microsoft, China
Lizi Liao	Singapore Management University, Singapore
Ye Lin	Northeastern University, China
Haitao Lin	National Laboratory of Pattern Recognition, Institute of Automation, CAS, China
Jian Liu	Beijing Jiaotong University, China

Xianggen Liu	Sichuan University, China
Fei Liu	Emory University, USA
Yuanxing Liu	Harbin Institute of Technology, China
Xuebo Liu	Harbin Institute of Technology, Shenzhen, China
Pengyuan Liu	Beijing Language and Culture University, China
Lemao Liu	Tencent AI Lab, China
Chunhua Liu	The University of Melbourne, Australia
Qin Liu	University of Southern California, USA
Tianyang Liu	University of California San Diego, USA
Puyuan Liu	University of Alberta, Canada
Qian Liu	Sea AI Lab, Singapore
Shujie Liu	Microsoft Research Asia, Beijing, China, China
Kang Liu	Institute of Automation, Chinese Academy of Sciences, China
Yongbin Liu	School of Computer Science, University of South China, China
Zhenhua Liu	School of Computer Science and Technology, Soochow University, China, China
Xiao Liu	Microsoft Research Asia, China
Qun Liu	Chongqing University of Posts and Telecommunications, China
Yunfei Long	University of Essex, UK
Renze Lou	Pennsylvania State University, USA
Keming Lu	University of Southern California, USA
Jinliang Lu	National Laboratory of Pattern Recognition, CASIA, Beijing, China, China
Jinzhu Lu	Fudan University, China
Xin Lu	Harbin Institute of Technology, China
Shuai Lu	Microsoft, China
Hengtong Lu	Beijing University of Posts and Telecommunications, China
Minghua Ma	Microsoft, China
Cong Ma	Institute of Automation, Chinese Academy of Sciences; University of Chinese Academy of Sciences, China
Mingyu Derek Ma	UCLA, USA
Yinglong Ma	North China Electric Power University, China
Yunshan Ma	National University of Singapore, Singapore
Xianling Mao	Beijing Institute of Technology, China
Zhao Meng	ETH Zurich, Switzerland
Xiangyang Mou	Meta, USA
Minheng Ni	Microsoft Research, China
Yasumasa Onoe	The University of Texas at Austin, USA

Zhufeng Pan	Google, USA
Xutan Peng	Huawei, China
Ehsan Qasemi	University of Southern California, USA
Weizhen Qi	University of Science and Technology of China, China
Tao Qian	Hubei University of Science and Technology, China
Yanxia Qin	School of Computing, National University of Singapore, Singapore
Zixuan Ren	Institute of Automation, China
Stephanie Schoch	University of Virginia, USA
Lei Sha	Beihang University, China
Wei Shao	City University of Hong Kong, China
Zhihong Shao	Tsinghua University, China
Haoran Shi	Amazon Inc., USA
Xing Shi	Bytedance Inc., China
Jyotika Singh	Placemakr, USA
Kaiqiang Song	Tencent AI Lab, USA
Haoyu Song	Harbin Institute of Technology, China
Zhenqiao Song	UCSB, China
Jinsong Su	Xiamen University, China
Dianbo Sui	Harbin Institute of Technology, China
Zequn Sun	Nanjing University, China
Kexuan Sun	University of Southern California, USA
Chengjie Sun	Harbin Institute of Technology, China
Kai Sun	Meta, USA
Chuanyuan Tan	Soochow University, China
Zhixing Tan	Zhongguancun Laboratory, China
Minghuan Tan	Shenzhen Institutes of Advanced Technology, Chinese Academy of Sciences, China
Ping Tan	Universiti Malaysia Sarawak, Malaysia
Buzhou Tang	Harbin Institute of Technology (Shenzhen), China
Rongchuan Tang	Institute of Automation, Chinese Academy of Sciences, China
Xiangru Tang	Yale University, USA
Duyu Tang	Tencent, China
Xunzhu Tang	University of Luxembourg, Luxembourg
Mingxu Tao	Peking University, China
Zhiyang Teng	Nanyang Technological University, Singapore
Xiaojun Wan	Peking University, China
Chen Wang	National Laboratory of Pattern Recognition, Institute of Automation, CAS, China

Lijie Wang	Baidu, China
Liang Wang	Microsoft Research, China
Xinyuan Wang	University of California, SanDiego, USA
Haoyu Wang	University of Pennsylvania, USA
Xuesong Wang	Harbin Institute of Technology, China
Hongwei Wang	Tencent AI Lab, USA
Hongling Wang	Soochow University, China
Ke Wang	Huawei Technologies Ltd., China
Qingyun Wang	University of Illinois at Urbana-Champaign, USA
Yiwei Wang	Amazon, USA
Jun Wang	University of Melbourne, Australia
Jingjing Wang	Soochow University, China
Ruize Wang	Academy for Engineering and Technology, Fudan University, China
Zhen Wang	The Ohio State University, USA
Qiang Wang	Hithink RoyalFlush AI Research Institute, China, China
Lingzhi Wang	The Chinese University of Hong Kong, China
Yufei Wang	Macquaire University, Australia
Xun Wang	Microsoft, USA
Sijia Wang	Virginia Tech, USA
Yaqiang Wang	Chengdu University of Information Technology, China
Siyuan Wang	Fudan University, China
Xing Wang	Tencent, China
Fei Wang	University of Southern California, USA
Gengyu Wang	Columbia University, USA
Tao Wang	Department of Biostatistics & Health Informatics, King's College London, UK
Bo Wang	Tianjin University, China
Wei Wei	Huazhong University of Science and Technology, China
Bingbing Wen	The University of Washington, USA
Lianwei Wu	School of Software Engineering, Xi'an Jiaotong University, China
Chenfei Wu	Microsoft, China
Ting Wu	Fudan University, China
Yuxia Wu	Xi'an Jiaotong University, China
Sixing Wu	School of Software, Yunnan University, China
Junhong Wu	Cognitive Computing Lab, Peking University, China
Shuangzhi Wu	Bytedance, China
Lijun Wu	Microsoft Research, China

Tengxiao Xi	University of Chinese Academy of Sciences School of Artificial Intelligence, China
Yang Xiang	Peng Cheng Laboratory, China
Tong Xiao	Northeastern University, China
Min Xiao	State Key Laboratory of Multimodal Artificial Intelligence Systems, Institute of Automation, CAS, China
Ye Xiao	Hunan University, China
Jun Xie	Alibaba DAMO Academy, China
Yuqiang Xie	Institute of Information Engineering, Chinese Academy of Sciences, China
Qingting Xu	Soochow University, China
Jinan Xu	Beijing Jiaotong University, China
Yiheng Xu	Microsoft Research Asia, China
Chen Xu	Northeastern University, China
Kang xu	Nanjing University of Posts and Telecommunications, China
Wang Xu	Harbin Institute of Technology, China
Jiahao Xu	Nanyang Technological University, Singapore
Nan Xu	University of Southern California, USA
Yan Xu	Hong Kong University of Science and Technology, Hong Kong Special Administrative Region of China
Hanzi Xu	Temple University, USA
Zhixing Xu	Nanjing Normal University, China
Jiacheng Xu	Salesforce AI Research, USA
Xiao Xu	Harbin Institute of Technology, China
Rui Yan	Renmin University of China, China
Kun Yan	Beihang University, China
Lingyong Yan	Baidu Inc., China
Baosong Yang	Alibaba Damo Academy, Alibaba Inc., China
Shiquan Yang	The University of Melbourne, Australia
Haoran Yang	The Chinese University of Hong Kong, Hong Kong Special Administrative Region of China
Liang Yang	Dalian University of Technology, China
Jun Yang	Marcpoint Co., Ltd., China
Muyun Yang	Harbin Institute of Technology, China
Kai Yang	Zhongguancun Laboratory, China
Zhiwei Yang	College of Computer Science and Technology, Jilin University, China
Ziqing Yang	CISPA Helmholtz Center for Information Security, Germany

Jianmin Yao	Soochow University, China
Shengming Yin	University of Science and Technology of China, China
Wenpeng Yin	Pennsylvania State University, USA
Pengfei Yu	Department of Computer Science, University of Illinois at Urbana Champaign, USA
Botao Yu	Nanjing University, China
Donglei Yu	Institute of Automation, Chinese Academy of Sciences, China
Dong Yu	Beijing Language and Culture University, China
Tiezheng Yu	The Hong Kong University of Science and Technology, Hong Kong Special Administrative Region of China
Junjie Yu	Soochow University, China
Heng Yu	Shopee, China
Chunyuan Yuan	Institute of Information Engineering, Chinese Academy of Sciences, China
Xiang Yue	The Ohio State University, USA
Daojian Zeng	Hunan Normal University, China
Qi Zeng	University of Illinois at Urbana-Champaign, USA
Shuang	(Sophie)University of Oklahoma Zhai, USA
Yi Zhang	University of Pennsylvania, USA
Qi Zhang	Fudan University, China
Yazhou Zhang	Zhengzhou University of Light Industry, China
Zhuosheng Zhang	Shanghai Jiao Tong University, China
Weinan Zhang	Harbin Institute of Technology, China
Shuaicheng Zhang	Virginia Polytechnic Institute and State University, USA
Xiaohan Zhang	Institute of Automation, Chinese Academy of Sciences, China
Jiajun Zhang	Institute of Automation Chinese Academy of Sciences, China
Zhihao Zhang	Beihang University, China
Zhiyang Zhang	National Laboratory of Pattern Recognition, Institute of Automation, CAS, China
Dakun Zhang	SYSTRAN, France
Zixuan Zhang	University of Illinois Urbana-Champaign, USA
Peng Zhang	Tianjin University, China
Wenxuan Zhang	DAMO Academy, Alibaba Group, Singapore
Yunhao Zhang	National Laboratory of Pattern Recognition, Institute of Automation, Chinese Academy of Sciences, China
Xingxing Zhang	Microsoft Research Asia, China

Yuanzhe Zhang	Institute of Automation, Chinese Academy of Sciences, China
Zhirui Zhang	Tencent AI Lab, China
Xin Zhao	Fudan University, China
Zhenjie Zhao	Nanjing University of Information Science and Technology, China
Yanyan Zhao	Harbin Institute of Technology, China
Mengjie Zhao	Center for Information and Language Processing, LMU Munich, Germany
Xinpei Zhao	CASIA, China
Sanqiang Zhao	University of Pittsburgh, Department of Informatics and Networked Systems, School of Computing and Information, USA
Wanjun Zhong	Sun Yat-Sen University, China
Ben Zhou	University of Pennsylvania, USA
Weikang Zhou	Fudan University, China
Peng Zhou	Kuaishou, China
Xin Zhou	Fudan University, China
Xiabing Zhou	Soochow University, China
Guangyou Zhou	School of Computer Science, Central China Normal University, China
Wangchunshu Zhou	ETH Zurich, Switzerland
Tong Zhu	Soochow University, China
Jie Zhu	Soochow University, China
Conghui Zhu	Harbin Institute of Technology, China
Yaoming Zhu	ByteDance AI lab, China
Muhua Zhu	Meituan Group, China

Organizers

Organized by

China Computer Federation, China

Hosted by

Guilin University of Electronic Technology

In Cooperation with

Lecture Notes in Computer Science

Springer

ACTA Scientiarum Naturalium Universitatis Pekinensis

Sponsoring Institutions

Diamond Sponsors

China Mobile

KuaiShou

OPPO

Baidu

Platinum Sponsors

GTCOM

HUAWEI

Douyin Group

Golden Sponsors

Microsoft

TRS

BaYou

NiuTrans

DATAOCEAN AI

Tencent AI Lab

Vivo

Contents – Part III

Evaluation Workshop: Multi-perspective Scientific Machine Reading Comprehension

Evaluation Workshop: Math Word Problem Solving

Evaluation Workshop: Conversational Aspect-Based Sentiment Quadruple Analysis

Evaluation Workshop: Chinese Medical Instructional Video Question Answering

Evaluation Workshop: Chinese Few-Shot and Zero-Shot Entity Linking

Evaluation Workshop: Chinese Essay Discourse Coherence Evaluation

**Evaluation Workshop: Learn to Watch TV: Multimodal Dialogue
Understanding and Response Prediction**

Poster: Summarization and Generation

Fantastic Gradients and Where to Find Them: Improving Multi-attribute Text Style Transfer by Quadratic Program

Qian Qu, Jian Wang, Kexin Yang, Hang Zhang, and Jiancheng Lv[✉]

No.24, South Section of 1st Ring Road, Chengdu, China
kylinaive77@gmail.com

Abstract. Unsupervised text style transfer (TST) is an important task with extensive implications in natural language generation (NLG). A prevalent approach involves editing the latent representations of text, guided by gradients from an attribute classifier. However, in multi-attribute TST, the simultaneous satisfaction of all required attributes remains challenging. In this paper, we unveil that the gradient direction during editing might conflict with certain attribute representations through empirical analysis. To tackle this problem, we introduce a mathematical programming method to impose constraints on the editing direction of multiple attributes, effectively mitigating potential attribute conflicts during the inference stage. Our proposed method considers the potential conflict between different attributes for the first time. Experimental results from the YELP benchmark showcase that our method can effectively improve the multi-attribute-transfer accuracy and quality without compromising single attribute performance. Moreover, our method can be readily integrated with pre-trained auto-encoders, providing an effective and scalable solution for multi-attribute scenarios.

Keywords: Text Style Transfer · Multiple-Attribute Text Generation · Auto-Encoder · Quadratic Program

1 Introduction

Text style transfer (TST) seeks to rephrase the source text in a language style specific to certain attributes while preserving content that is independent of these style attributes. As depicted in Table 1, the *style* in TST could be any attribute requiring modification, such as sentiment, topic, gender, writing style, or a combination thereof [7,23]. Although substantial strides have been made in multi-attribute text generation [6,9], much of the existing research concentrates on achieving a balance between content preservation and style manipulation constraints, often ignoring the challenges inherent in satisfying multiple attributes simultaneously. In light of this, we turn to an approach that modifies the latent representations of texts without disentanglement, guided by classifier gradients [12,26]. This method offers both training efficiency and flexibility in text transformation [12,19], making it an attractive choice for our exploration of multi-attribute TST. Our empirical study reveals that, during the editing

Table 1. Several common TST tasks with example sentences.

Task	Attribute	Example
Sentiment	Positive	This movie is really meaningful and I learned a lot from it
	Negative	This movie is really meaningless and I don't get anything from it
Gender	Male	My wife likes the fried chicken here
	Female	My husband likes the fried chicken here
Formality	Formal	I can't eat another bite. I proceed to chew and explode
	Informal	Ooh, I can't eat another bite (munch munch, explode)
Author styles	Shakespearean	I saw thee late at the Count Orsino's
	Modern	I saw you at Count Orsino's recently

process, the gradient direction may contradict the representations of certain attributes. This could potentially lead to the generation of attribute-incomplete text.

To address this, we introduce a novel method grounded in mathematical programming for constrained multi-attribute text style transfer, based on a latent representation editing model. Specifically, our approach starts with an auto-encoder for sentence self-representation, which could also be a pre-trained model. It then establishes constraints on the editing direction of multiple attributes by guiding modifications to the latent representation via a classifier. Our method, for the first time, considers potential conflicts between different attributes, ensuring that generated text satisfies the required attributes to the greatest extent possible during the editing process. Experimental results on the widely-recognized YELP benchmark [10] demonstrate the efficacy of our method in enhancing text-transfer accuracy across multiple attributes. Our main contributions include:

- We identify the limitations and possible reasons for the suboptimal performance of existing latent representation editing methods in multi-attribute scenarios.
- We propose a novel, flexible multi-attribute TST model based on the latent variable editing method, which first takes into account the conflict and satisfaction between multiple attributes of generated text.
- By utilizing Quadratic Programming (QP) with inequality constraints, we can modify the gradient while preserving its key attributes, resulting in improved overall accuracy for multiple attributes.

2   Related Work

For the disentanglement-based methods [5,15,22], its main idea is to separate the style and content of the original text, then generate the new text with the target style and content representation. The key lies include adversarial learning methods [5,17,22], attention mechanism [27,29], or other method such as Levenshtein Editing [11,20]. Instead of performing a disentanglement of content and style, entanglement-based methods rewrite the entangled representations directly in a specific manner, such as reinforcement learning [14], back-translation technique [1,2,21], and latent vector editing method [12,19,26].

Multi-attribute style transfer is an extension of single attribute but is more difficult. There are also studies that focus specifically on multiple attributes. [9] proposed an adversarial training model using word-level conditional architecture and a two-stage training program for multi-attribute generation. [10] implemented multi-attribute style transfer by adjusting the average embedding of each target attribute and using a combination of DAE and back translation techniques. [6] use multiple style-aware language models as discriminators in combination with transformer-based encoder-decoders to enhance their rewriting capabilities.

3   Methodology

We start with a dataset $\mathcal{D} = (x^i, s^i)_{i=1}^n$, wherein each unit (x, s) denotes a sentence x together with its corresponding attribute vector s. This attribute vector might cover multiple attributes, such as *sentiment* and *gender*, which can be represented as $s = \{s_{sent}, s_{gend}\}$. The main aim is to transform a given sentence x^i, accompanied by its associated attribute s^i, into a new sentence $\hat{x}$ that aligns with a target attribute $\hat{s}$.

3.1   Preliminary

In pursuing this aim, we turn our attention to the latent representation revision method. The fundamental concept here involves fine-tuning the entangled latent representation of the input sentence to align with the desired attribute. As depicted in Fig. 1(A), the model typically integrates three core components: an encoder G_{enc}, a decoder G_{dec}, and an attribute classifier C. It's noteworthy that some studies [12] prefer to utilize multiple classifiers. The process begins with the encoder, which translates a given input sentence x into a latent representation z. This representation integrates both the attribute and the content in a tangled manner. Following this, z is modified to match the target attribute, under the guidance of the classifier. Ultimately, the decoder converts z back into a sentence $\hat{x}$, embodying the desired attribute.

The modification of z using the gradient provided by C [12,26] is merely one among a host of potential strategies. Another option suggested by [19] involves steering z directly across the surface of the decision boundary. In this work, we have chosen to adhere to the gradient modification approach to execute multi-attribute style transfer.

3.2   Problem Analysis

Our approach modifies the latent representation z of the input sentence to incorporate the target attribute by using the gradient from the attribute classifier C.

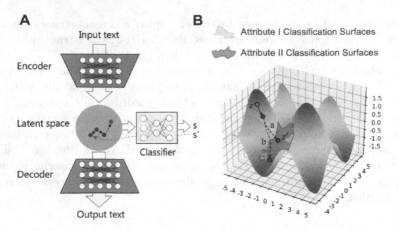

Fig. 1. Overview of Latent representation revision method. (A) Model architecture. (B) Latent representation editing for multi-attribute TST. Given a sentence, the objective of the model is to rephrase it such that it incorporates both Attribute I and Attribute II.

This gradient guides the search for a new representation z' that satisfies the desired attribute s' while staying close to the original sentence:

$$z' = z - \omega_i \nabla_z \mathcal{L}_C(C_{\theta_C}(z), s'), \tag{1}$$

where θ_C and ω_i are the parameters of the classifier C and the adjustment factor, respectively. This process is repeated until the classifier C confirms that z' matches the target style.

However, this method may compromise the generation quality when transferring multiple attributes. The attribute classifier provides a joint gradient on all labels s' to update the latent representation, i.e.,

$$\sum_{s'} \nabla_z \mathcal{L}_C(C_{\theta_C}(z), s'). \tag{2}$$

Given that the decision surfaces for each attribute in the classification may not completely overlap under multi-attribute style transfer, conflicts might arise between the gradient orientations of different attributes when modifying the latent representation along a specific gradient path. For example, certain steps might draw z' nearer to attribute s_1 while distancing it from attribute s_2. As depicted in Fig. 1 (B), adjusting the latent representation along the gradient direction of path b, leading to a lower final loss, only meets the target attribute s_2 criteria. Conversely, path a, despite a higher loss value, accommodates two attributes and thus produces a more desirable outcome. Our experiments confirmed this phenomenon by identifying instances of conflict between the editing gradient orientation and the single-attribute gradient orientation during the transfer process, as discussed in Sect. 4.4.

3.3   Model Architecture

Our framework is designed to be compatible with any auto-encoder (AE) and multi-attribute classifier, making it agnostic to the specific neural network architecture employed. In this work, we employed a transformer-based auto-encoder [24] in conjunction with an MLP-based classifier.

Transformer-Based Auto-Encoder G. Given an input sentence $x = \{x_1, x_2, ..., x_m\}$, the encoder $G_{enc}(\theta_{enc}; x)$ transforms it into a continuous latent representation: $z \sim G_{enc}(\theta_{enc}; x) = q(z|x)$, while the decoder $G_{dec}(\theta_{dec}; z)$ maps the latent representation z back to the sentence, reconstructing it: $x \sim G_{dec}(\theta_{dec}; z) = p(x|z)$. During training, the objective of G is to minimize the reconstruction error. The reconstruction loss is defined as:

$$\mathcal{L}_G(\theta_{enc}, \theta_{dec}; x) = -\frac{1}{|s|} \sum_{i=1}^{|s|} q(z|x) \log p(x|z), \tag{3}$$

where $|s|$ denotes the number of attributes.

Multiple-Attribute Classifier C. Our classifier is implemented as an MLP consisting of two linear layers and a sigmoid activation function. Specifically, it is defined as $C(z) = MLP(z) = p(s|z)$. The attribute classification loss is:

$$\mathcal{L}_C(\theta_C; z, s) = -\frac{1}{|s|} \sum_{i=1}^{|s|} [s_i \log(p(s_i|z)) + (1 - s_i) \log(1 - p(s_i|z))],$$

where $|s|$ is the number of attributes and s_i is the ground truth label for the i-th attribute.

3.4   Multiple-Attributes Gradient Iterative Modification

Conflict Resolution in Modification. To align z' with all target attributes, we adopt a gradient direction detection and conflict resolution strategy inspired by GME [13] when modifying z. We consider not only the gradient conflict of classifiers over z, but also the conflict that arises during the intermediate gradient propagation in C. Therefore, during the inference stage, we detect the gradient direction by computing the inner product of the gradient vectors in each linear layer as the gradient backpropagates in C. This enables us to identify potential directional conflicts between the gradient of any single attribute g_i and the overall gradient g^1. The constraint is satisfied when the gradient g agrees with all desired attribute directions, expressed as follows:

$$\langle g_i, g \rangle := \langle \nabla_z \mathcal{L}_C(C_{\theta_C}(z), s_i'), \nabla_z \mathcal{L}_C(C_{\theta_C}(z), s') \rangle \geq 0. \tag{4}$$

In cases where a conflict arises, modifying the gradient in question could potentially cause z to deviate from the target property associated with the conflicting

---

[1] For simplicity, we denote all the gradients to be detected in C by $\nabla_z \mathcal{L}_C(C_{\theta_C}(z), s')$.

direction. To tackle this, we project the gradient g onto the nearest gradient $\tilde{g}$ that fulfills all attributes:

$$\text{minimize}_{\tilde{g}} \frac{1}{2} \| g - \tilde{g} \|_2^2 \quad s.t. \langle g_i, \tilde{g} \rangle \geq 0. \tag{5}$$

To address Eq. 5, which presents a Quadratic Program (QP) with inequality constraints [4,13], it is useful to return to the primal form:

$$\text{minimize}_r \frac{1}{2} r^\top H r + p^\top r \quad s.t. \ Ar \geq b, \tag{6}$$

where $H \in \mathbb{R}^{p \times p}$ is a symmetric, positive semi-definite matrix, $p \in \mathbb{R}^p$, $A \in \mathbb{R}^{|s| \times p}$, $b \in \mathbb{R}^{|s|}$. The dual problem of inequality [3] (Eq. 6) is:

$$\text{minimize}_{u,v} \frac{1}{2} u^\top H u - b^\top v \quad s.t. \ A^\top v - H u = p, v \geq 0. \tag{7}$$

Drawing from Dorn's duality theorem [3], if a solution u^* and v^* is obtained from Eq. 7, then there exists a solution r^* to Eq. 6, which satisfies $Hr^* = Hr^*$.

On this basis, the original QP (Eq. 5) can be expressed as:

$$\text{minimize}_w \frac{1}{2} r^\top r - g^\top r + \frac{1}{2} g^\top g \quad s.t. \ Gr \geq 0, \tag{8}$$

where $G = (g, g_1, ..., g_{|s|})$. The dual problem of (Eq. 8) is:

$$\text{minimize}_v \frac{1}{2} v^\top G G^\top v + g^\top G^\top v \quad s.t. \ v \geq 0, \tag{9}$$

where $u = G^\top v + g$ and $g^\top g$ is the constant term. This is a QP on $|s|$ attributes. Then once we solve the problem (9) for v^*, we can get the adjusted new gradient $\tilde{g} = G^\top v^* + g$.

Following the resolution of conflicts, the adjusted gradient $\tilde{g}$ is propagated to the subsequent layer of the network. This gradient then steers the modifications applied to the latent representation z'. The detail of this process is outlined in Algorithm 1.

To preserve the attribute-independent content and linguistic integrity of the latent representation, we confine gradient modifications to large-step gradients. This approach mitigates potential negative impacts on the linguistic fluency and coherence of the decoded text that may result from insignificant style category changes induced by small gradients. It is crucial to note that this procedure is strictly implemented during the inference stage and does not come into play during training.

4   Experiments

4.1   Dataset

We evaluated our approach on the Yelp Review Dataset (YELP) [10], which contains complete reviews along with review sentiment, gender and restaurant category information. We conducted multi-attribute style transfer experiments on the three attributes of sentiment, gender, and restaurant categories. The restaurants here we choose three types: Asian, American, and Mexican.

Algorithm 1: Multiple-Attributes Fast Gradient Iterative Modification Algorithm.

Input: Auto-encoder latent representation z; Target attribute $s' = (s_i', ..., s_k')$;
         Well-trained attribute classifier C_θ; Weights $\omega = \{\omega_i\}$

Output: A modified latent representation z'

$g \leftarrow \nabla_z \mathcal{L}_C(C_{\theta_C}(z), s')$;

$g_i \leftarrow \nabla_z \mathcal{L}_C(C_{\theta_C}(z), s_i')$ for all $i = 1, ..., k$;

if $|s' - C_{\theta_C}(z')| > t$ **then**

    for *each linear_layers* $\in C_\theta$ **do**

        if $\langle g, g_i \rangle \geq 0$ *for all* $i = 1, ..., k$; **then**

            | $\tilde{g} \leftarrow g$;

        else

            | $\tilde{g} \leftarrow \text{PROJECT}(g, g_1, ..., g_k)$, see (9) ;

        end

    end

    $z' = z - \omega_i \tilde{g}$;

else

    | reture z';

end

4.2 Baselines

We compare our model with the most relevant and state-of-the-art models as follows: 1) **StyIns** [28]. encodes sentences with a certain style to vectors as the style instances and uses the generative flow technique to construct style latent representation based on it, then decodes the input sentence along with the style representation to generate desired text. 2) **ControllableAttrTransfer (CAT)** [26]. edits the sentence latent representations guided by an attribute classifier until it is evaluated as the target style. 3) **MultipleAttrTransfer (MAT)** [10]. is based on the Denoising auto-encoding (DAE) [25] model and back translation strategy. 4) **MUCOCO** [8]. conducts controlled inference from the pre-trained model and formulates the decoding process as a multi-optimization problem. It then generates the target sentences using Lagrange multipliers and gradient-descent based techniques.

4.3 Evaluations Metrics

Automatic Evaluation. Following previous works [7,17,22,23], we use the automatic metrics as follows: 1) **Style transfer Accuracy.** We train an external classifier to measure the accuracy of the transferred sentences related to the required attribute. Here, we have trained a GPT-based [18] classifier on each attribute (sentiment, gender, category) using the training data. 2) **Content preservation.** We calculate the BLEU [16] score between the transferred sentence and the original input sentence (self-BLEU), with higher scores meaning more content retention. 3) **Fluency.** We calculate the perplexity of transferred

Table 2. Automatic and human evaluation results for multi-attribute transfer tasks on YELP. Notice that since there is a multi-attribute task, the accuracy here does not simply refer to the correct rate of one attribute, but to the overall attribute, that is, the generated sentence that satisfies all the target attributes.

	Automatic			Human			
	Acc	BLEU	PPL	Sty	Con	Flu	Avg
StyIns [28]	33.7	23.75	75.25	2.88	3.84	3.82	3.66
CAT [26]	37.5	20.53	52.77	3.21	3.92	4.15	3.76
MAT [10]	34.1	25.34	55.34	3.06	4.12	4.22	3.81
MUCOCO [8]	28.9	28.45	51.68	2.78	3.98	4.01	3.51
Our model	39.8	26.23	49.89	3.35	4.05	4.27	3.89

sentences by a Transformer-Based language model, which is trained with the Training data (the lower the better).

Human Evaluation. We further conduct the human evaluation for transfer results. Following some previous works [6,12,20], evaluators are asked to rate sentences according to the three criteria described above with each aspect rated on a 5-point Likert scale. Especially, for Style transfer strength, a score of five is given when the sentence satisfies all the attributes and makes sense, with an equal proportional reduction for missing attributes or not reasonable enough.

4.4 Main Results

Gradient Conflict Detection. Here, we verify our claim that editing z with a gradient direction may conflict with the gradient direction of some attributes. For the well-trained model, we randomly select 200 data from the test set to perform multi-attribute TST and detect the situation between the edit gradient direction and the single-attribute direction during the transfer process. The experimental results show that the gradient direction conflict occurred in 100% of the 200 texts. Notably, not every conflict will lead to an attribute-incomplete generation text, but increasing the corresponding possibility (we verify such a situation in Sect. 4.5).

Compare with Baselines. In Table 2, we present the automatic and human evaluation results of both our model and the baseline model. The results indicate that our model outperforms the baseline model in terms of style transfer accuracy, achieving the highest score with a significant improvement compared with baseline models (t-test, $p < 0.05$).

Notably, the automatic accuracy of all models is relatively low as it requires all target attributes to be satisfied in a single transferred sentence. In reality, the accuracy of satisfying just one of the attributes would be much higher, as will be demonstrated in detail in the ablation study below. Furthermore, the BLEU and PPL scores are within a normal range. Our model achieves the best results

Table 3. Ablation study results on YELP dataset, comparing the performance of our model without (w_o) and with ($w\_$) the implementation of the gradient conflict adjustment strategy. The accuracy for each target attribute, as well as the overall accuracy, is provided for both scenarios. The 'overall accuracy' refers to the percentage of the generated text that conforms to all of the requisite target attributes simultaneously. Best viewed in **bold**.

	Sentiment	Gender	Category	Overall
	$w\_o/w\_$	$w\_o/w\_$	$w\_o/w\_$	$w\_o/w\_$
Accuracy	0.98/0.98	0.58/0.58	0.69/**0.72**	0.38/**0.40**
F1-score	0.98/0.98	0.68/0.68	0.82/**0.84**	-/-
PPL	-/-	-/-	-/-	50.54/**49.90**

on PPL and the second-best score on BLEU, which could be due to the fact that slightly more of the original text was modified to satisfy additional properties.

In human evaluation, we selected ten sentences from each model for each multi-attribute task and asked five evaluators to rate each comparison sample. In total, we evaluated 70 sentences for each model, taking into account the transfer of each attribute to the other (e.g., positive → negative with any other gender and category transfer, positive → negative with any gender and category transfer, ...). Our model proved to be the unequivocal leader, surpassing all others in both accuracy scores and average scores. Furthermore, we observed that the accuracy of human ratings significantly exceeded that of automatic evaluations. This can be attributed to the fact that human ratings consider sentences that satisfy one or two target attributes, while automatic evaluations only account for the generation that fulfills all attributes when calculating accuracy. This fills a missing in the perspective of automated evaluation, as transfer results that satisfy two attributes are considered superior to results that satisfy only one or fewer attributes.

Moreover, to observe the characteristics of each model under the multi-attribute task more intuitively, we randomly sampled a set of output sentences and showed them in Table 4.

4.5   Ablation Study

To further validate the reliability of our approach, we conduct an extensive analysis of the key components of our model in this section. In Table 3 we show the comparison in performance of our model without and with implementing the gradient conflict adjustment strategy on the YELP dataset. It can be seen that after applying the gradient programming strategy, the overall accuracy improves by 2.3% points with a statistically significant (t-test, $p < 0.05$). And for every single attribute, the correct rate is equal to or greater than before. In particular, the category accuracy experiences a significant improvement (t-test, $p < 0.05$) as it is a multi-attribute scenario with three sub-attributes, therefore, our method can also be effective here This finding underscores the effectiveness

Table 4. Case study of generated text by all models. The blue word indicates relevant text in the output that contain the target sentiment attribute, the red words indicate the target gender attribute and green words indicate category attribute.

	Negative to Positive, Female to Male, Mexican to Others
Original text	awful! all i can say. horrible service for 1 and the food is nothing special and it's over priced !
Our model	wow! i can say that a good place. great service and the food. on top, my wife and i both chose the cheeseburger with turkey burgers and it is well made no longer like home fries. wouldn't be exceptional!
StyIns	wow! i can say that great service and all the food. we are allergic to the menu and we get the greenspsmyhummus without chips, while we ate there to enjoy our dinner, after we are served with several things that is
CAT	wow! i can say that all the good reviews. excellent food and service. this is a great place for sushi, and over spiced with clients the Hunan beef is amazing! they just feels like it's one of her favorite sushi restaurant.
MAT	wow ! i can say food was okay and service was awesome. i must say we really enjoyed it ! took my kids and wife, they were cooking the waffles with spices and had the best seasoning in what you can describe the place, had a great comfort food
MUCOCO	wow! i can say that's good. nice service and the food. i was excited to eat some Chinese dishes but just try to pick up our order and give it a long day of sitting down. obviously, we have been so far because the pork and avocado came delicious!

of our method in improving style transfer accuracy for transferred text in multi-attribute scenarios. Sentiment and gender are binary classes and just a transfer from one class to another, so there is no problem of multiple directions and thereby no improvement by our method. Moreover, the full model also achieves better scores on PPL. This result confirms that our method improves attribute accuracy without sacrificing sentence fluency and, in some cases, even leads to better outcomes.

In addition, we can see that even if we detect conflicts in almost every transfer process, there are still 38% of transferred sentences that satisfy all attributes. After conflict resolution, the overall accuracy has improved. This confirms that the conflicts in the directions of gradients indeed affect the satisfaction of different attributes, but not every conflict will lead to an attribute-incomplete generation text, it increases the corresponding possibility of such occurrences.

5   Conclusions

In this study, we presented a novel mathematical programming approach for coordinating and controlling multi-attribute style transfer, which we evaluated on the YELP dataset. Our experiments demonstrated that this method can effectively enhance the accuracy of multi-attribute transfer, while maintaining the accuracy of each individual attribute. Furthermore, this method allows pre-trained auto-encoders to efficiently transmit language attributes, eliminating the need for additional tuning and enabling faster and more scalable learning.

Moving forward, we plan to extend our approach to cross-lingual style transfer tasks and explore ways to optimize the algorithm's time efficiency.

References

1. Cheng, Y., Gan, Z., Zhang, Y., Elachqar, O., Li, D., Liu, J.: Contextual text style transfer. In: Findings of the Association for Computational Linguistics: EMNLP 2020, Online Event, 16–20 November 2020, vol. EMNLP 2020, pp. 2915–2924 (2020)
2. Dai, N., Liang, J., Qiu, X., Huang, X.: Style transformer: unpaired text style transfer without disentangled latent representation. In: Proceedings of the 57th Conference of the Association for Computational Linguistics, ACL 2019, Florence, Italy, July 28- August 2, 2019, Volume 1: Long Papers, pp. 5997–6007 (2019)
3. Dorn, W.S.: Duality in quadratic programming. Q. Appl. Math. **18**, 155–162 (1960)
4. Frank, M., Wolfe, P., et al.: An algorithm for quadratic programming. Naval Res. Logist. Q. **3**(1–2), 95–110 (1956)
5. Fu, Z., Tan, X., Peng, N., Zhao, D., Yan, R.: Style transfer in text: exploration and evaluation. In: Proceedings of the AAAI Conference on Artificial Intelligence, vol. 32 (2018)
6. Goyal, N., Srinivasan, B.V., Natarajan, A., Sancheti, A.: Multi-style transfer with discriminative feedback on disjoint corpus. In: Proceedings of the 2021 Conference of the North American Chapter of the Association for Computational Linguistics: Human Language Technologies, NAACL-HLT 2021, 6–11 June 2021, pp. 3500–3510 (2021)
7. Jin, D., Jin, Z., Hu, Z., Vechtomova, O., Mihalcea, R.: Deep learning for text style transfer: a survey. Comput. Linguist. **48**, 155–205 (2022)
8. Kumar, S., Malmi, E., Severyn, A., Tsvetkov, Y.: Controlled text generation as continuous optimization with multiple constraints. Adv. Neural Inf. Process. Syst. **34**, 14542–14554 (2021)
9. Lai, C.T., Hong, Y.T., Chen, H.Y., Lu, C.J., Lin, S.D.: Multiple text style transfer by using word-level conditional generative adversarial network with two-phase training. In: Proceedings of the 2019 Conference on Empirical Methods in Natural Language Processing and the 9th International Joint Conference on Natural Language Processing (EMNLP-IJCNLP), pp. 3579–3584 (2019)
10. Lample, G., Subramanian, S., Smith, E.M., Denoyer, L., Ranzato, M., Boureau, Y.: Multiple-attribute text rewriting. In: 7th International Conference on Learning Representations, ICLR 2019, New Orleans, LA, USA, 6–9 May 2019 (2019)
11. Li, J., Jia, R., He, H., Liang, P.: Delete, retrieve, generate: a simple approach to sentiment and style transfer. In: Proceedings of the 2018 Conference of the North American Chapter of the Association for Computational Linguistics: Human Language Technologies, NAACL-HLT 2018, New Orleans, Louisiana, USA, 1–6 June 2018, Volume 1 (Long Papers), pp. 1865–1874 (2018)
12. Liu, D., Fu, J., Zhang, Y., Pal, C., Lv, J.: Revision in continuous space: Unsupervised text style transfer without adversarial learning. In: Proceedings of the AAAI Conference on Artificial Intelligence, vol. 34, pp. 8376–8383 (2020)
13. Lopez-Paz, D., Ranzato, M.: Gradient episodic memory for continual learning. In: Advances in Neural Information Processing Systems, vol. 30 (2017)
14. Luo, F., et al.: A dual reinforcement learning framework for unsupervised text style transfer. In: Proceedings of the Twenty-Eighth International Joint Conference on

Artificial Intelligence, IJCAI 2019, Macao, China, 10–16 August 2019, pp. 5116–5122 (2019)

15. Malmi, E., Severyn, A., Rothe, S.: Unsupervised text style transfer with padded masked language models. arXiv preprint arXiv:2010.01054 (2020)

16. Papineni, K., Roukos, S., Ward, T., Zhu, W.J.: Bleu: a method for automatic evaluation of machine translation. In: Proceedings of the 40th annual meeting of the Association for Computational Linguistics, pp. 311–318 (2002)

17. Prabhumoye, S., Tsvetkov, Y., Salakhutdinov, R., Black, A.W.: Style transfer through back-translation. In: Gurevych, I., Miyao, Y. (eds.) Proceedings of the 56th Annual Meeting of the Association for Computational Linguistics, ACL 2018, Melbourne, Australia, 15–20 July 2018, Volume 1: Long Papers, pp. 866–876 (2018)

18. Radford, A., Wu, J., Child, R., Luan, D., Amodei, D., Sutskever, I., et al.: Language models are unsupervised multitask learners. OpenAI blog 1, 9 (2019)

19. Raedt, M.D., Godin, F., Buteneers, P., Develder, C., Demeester, T.: A simple geometric method for cross-lingual linguistic transformations with pre-trained autoencoders. In: Proceedings of the 2021 Conference on Empirical Methods in Natural Language Processing, EMNLP 2021, Virtual Event/Punta Cana, 7–11 November 2021, pp. 10108–10114 (2021)

20. Reid, M., Zhong, V.: LEWIS: levenshtein editing for unsupervised text style transfer. In: Findings of the Association for Computational Linguistics: ACL/IJCNLP 2021, Online Event, 1–6 August 2021, vol. ACL/IJCNLP 2021, pp. 3932–3944 (2021)

21. dos Santos, C.N., Melnyk, I., Padhi, I.: Fighting offensive language on social media with unsupervised text style transfer. In: Proceedings of the 56th Annual Meeting of the Association for Computational Linguistics, ACL 2018, Melbourne, Australia, 15–20 July 2018, Volume 2: Short Papers, pp. 189–194 (2018)

22. Shen, T., Lei, T., Barzilay, R., Jaakkola, T.: Style transfer from non-parallel text by cross-alignment. In: Advances in Neural Information Processing Systems, vol. 30 (2017)

23. Toshevska, M., Gievska, S.: A review of text style transfer using deep learning. IEEE Trans. Artif. Intell. 3, 669–684 (2021)

24. Vaswani, A., et al.: Attention is all you need. In: Advances in Neural Information Processing Systems, vol. 30 (2017)

25. Vincent, P., Larochelle, H., Bengio, Y., Manzagol, P.A.: Extracting and composing robust features with denoising autoencoders. In: Proceedings of the 25th International Conference on Machine Learning, pp. 1096–1103 (2008)

26. Wang, K., Hua, H., Wan, X.: Controllable unsupervised text attribute transfer via editing entangled latent representation. In: Advances in Neural Information Processing Systems, vol. 32 (2019)

27. Xu, J., et al.: Unpaired sentiment-to-sentiment translation: a cycled reinforcement learning approach. In: Proceedings of the 56th Annual Meeting of the Association for Computational Linguistics, ACL 2018, Melbourne, Australia, 15–20 July 2018, Volume 1: Long Papers, pp. 979–988 (2018)

28. Yi, X., Liu, Z., Li, W., Sun, M.: Text style transfer via learning style instance supported latent space. In: Proceedings of the Twenty-Ninth International Conference on International Joint Conferences on Artificial Intelligence, pp. 3801–3807 (2021)

29. Zhang, Y., Xu, J., Yang, P., Sun, X.: Learning sentiment memories for sentiment modification without parallel data. In: Proceedings of the 2018 Conference on Empirical Methods in Natural Language Processing, Brussels, Belgium, October 31–November 4, 2018, pp. 1103–1108 (2018)

TiBERT: A Non-autoregressive Pre-trained Model for Text Editing

Baoxin Wang[1,2], Ziyue Wang[2], Wanxiang Che[1], Dayong Wu[2(✉)], Rui Zhang[3], Bo Wang[3], and Shijin Wang[2,3]

[1] Research Center for SCIR, Harbin Institute of Technology, Harbin, China
`car@ir.hit.edu.cn`
[2] State Key Laboratory of Cognitive Intelligence, iFLYTEK Research, Hefei, China
`{bxwang2,zywang27,dywu2,sjwang3}@iflytek.com`
[3] iFLYTEK AI Research (Hebei), Langfang, China
`{ruizhang19,bowang3}@iflytek.com`

Abstract. Text editing refers to the task of creating new sentences by altering existing text through methods such as replacing, inserting, or deleting. Two commonly used techniques for text editing are Seq2Seq and sequence labeling. The Seq2Seq method can be time-consuming, while the sequence labeling method struggles with multi-token insertion. To solve these issues, we propose a novel pre-trained model called TiBERT, which is specially designed for **T**ext Editing tasks. TiBERT addresses these challenges by adjusting the length of the hidden representation to insert and delete tokens. We pre-train our model using a denoising task on a large dataset. As a result, TiBERT provides not only fast inference but also an improvement in the quality of text generation. We test the model on grammatical error correction, text simplification, and Chinese spelling check tasks. The experimental results show that TiBERT predicts faster and achieves better results than other pre-trained models in these text editing tasks.

Keywords: Text Editing · Non-autoregressive Model · Pre-trained Language Model

1 Introduction

Text editing [12] is a form of text generation task, in which new sentences are created by replacing, inserting, or deleting words. The source and target sentences are often quite similar, making it appropriate to generate the target sentence by making modifications to only specific words. Typical text editing tasks include grammatical error correction (GEC) [2], text simplification (TS) [7], and Chinese spelling check (CSC) [3,8], etc.

Text editing is typically accomplished through the use of Seq2Seq and sequence labeling methods. Seq2Seq methods require the entire text to be regenerated, making them relatively slow and not fully utilizing the similarities between input and output. On the other hand, sequence labeling methods

F. Liu et al. (Eds.): NLPCC 2023, LNAI 14304, pp. 15–26, 2023.
https://doi.org/10.1007/978-3-031-44699-3_2

tend to be faster but often have difficulty handling multiple token insertions due to their limitation of inserting only one token at a time.

We propose a novel pre-trained model named TiBERT as an effective solution to enhance the performance of text editing tasks. This model is more powerful than sequence labeling methods and faster than Seq2Seq methods. Specifically, our model consists of three parts, namely, Encoder, Locator, and Editor. The Encoder is responsible for encoding the context information of the input. The Locator generates a sequence of numbers with the same length as the input. Each number of the sequence indicates the number of tokens to be generated at this position. The hidden representation of the last layer of the Encoder is edited (i.e., kept, inserted or deleted) according to the predicted editing number sequence. Then combined with a new position representation, the resulting representation is fed to the Editor. Finally, the output is generated by a non-autoregressive transformer. In this way, the problem that only one token can be added at a time for the sequence labeling method can be avoided. As shown in Fig. 1, the Locator predicts a "2" for the second input position, indicating there is one extra token to be inserted. While the "0" represents a deletion operation, meaning no token should be generated at this position.

We train our model on large-scale English and Chinese data by a denoising task. To test the effect of our model, we conduct experiments on four tasks, including English and Chinese GEC, text simplification, and CSC. The experimental results show that TiBERT runs faster and achieves better scores than other pre-trained models in all the text editing tasks.

The main contributions of this paper are as follows:

- We are the first to propose a novel pre-trained model for text editing tasks, which fills the gaps in the pre-trained model of text editing tasks.
- Our TiBERT model achieves the best results in both English and Chinese text editing tasks.
- We conduct a detailed experimental analysis and introduce application scenes for TiBERT.

2   Related Work

2.1   Text Editing Methods

Text editing methods are becoming popular solutions to natural language generation tasks with a large overlap between inputs and outputs, such as sentence fusion, style transfer, TS, and GEC. Most of these methods need to construct tag sets of editing operations before training. LaserTagger [12] and FELIX [11] employ three editing operations (the tags): token-independent *keep*, token-independent *delete* and token-dependent *add/insert*. GECToR [14] expands the tag set to 5000 token-level transformations, including basic transformations for *keep, delete, insert, replace,* and 29 task-specific grammatical transformations. EditNTS [7] is a two-stage method consisting of a programmer to generate an

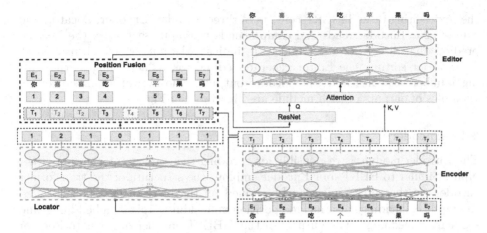

Fig. 1. The architecture of TiBERT. The input and output are translated as "Do you like apples?". The incorrect characters in the input and the corresponding corrections are shown in red. (Color figure online)

edit-operation sequence and an interpreter to recover the target text. It adds an extra operation, *stop*, to the interpreter to indicate the termination of the editing process.

Compared to other text editing models, our model can handle multi-word insertions without the need for iterative refinement. This allows our model to achieve better performance and faster prediction speed.

2.2 Pre-trained Language Models

Pre-trained language models promote the NLP tasks markedly since the presence of BERT [6]. BERT adopts the pre-training and fine-tuning mechanism. It has two pre-training tasks, next sentence prediction (NSP) and masked language model (MLM), and can be adapted to downstream tasks through task-specific fine-tuning. BERT belongs to the autoencoding model category which is better at natural language understanding (NLU) tasks such as text classification and information extraction. Contrarily, autoregressive pre-trained models, such as GPT [15] and BART [10], perform better on generation-based tasks. GPT and its improvements [16] are uni-directional models consisting of the decoder of transformers. BART includes both the encoder and the decoder. Its encoder introduces noise functions to interfere with the training data and its decoder learns to recover the original sequence. As far as we know, we are the first to pre-train a model specifically for text editing tasks.

3   Method

To enhance inference speed and tackle the challenge of inserting multiple tokens, we introduce a non-autoregressive pre-trained model, named TiBERT, to solve the text editing task. TiBERT consists of three modules: Encoder, Locator, and Editor. The Encoder reads and comprehends the input sentences; the Locator predicts the editing number sequence to indicate the number of tokens at each position for editing; the Editor generates edited tokens according to the editing number sequence and the Encoder outputs. The overall architecture and examples of outputs of each module are illustrated in Fig. 1.

3.1   Encoder

The Encoder module is responsible for encoding the context information of the input. Similar to BERT, our Encoder employs the structure of the transformer encoder, so that our model can be trained on the basis of BERT. Moreover, the input embeddings also include position embeddings, token embeddings, and segment embeddings. The outputs of the TiBERT encoder are sent to Locator and Editor modules respectively.

$$\mathbf{H} = \text{Transformer}(\mathbf{E_t} + \mathbf{E_p} + \mathbf{E_s}) \tag{1}$$

Here, $\mathbf{E_t}$, $\mathbf{E_p}$ and $\mathbf{E_s}$ represent the token embeddings, position embeddings and segment embeddings respectively; $\mathbf{H}$ denotes the hidden representation of Encoder outputs.

3.2   Locator

The output sentences of text editing tasks are usually similar to the input sentences. Consequently, we can obtain the output by several editing operations while leaving the rest input tokens unchanged. The editing operations involve keeping, replacement, insertion, and deletion. In addition, the lengths of output and input sentences are usually unequal. In this paper, we use Locator to predict the editing number for each token from the input. The editing number is a non-negative integer, indicating the number of tokens to be generated at the corresponding location. As shown in Fig. 1, the Locator predicts the number of output tokens at each input position. Concretely, if the editing number at a position is predicted to be 0, the hidden representation at this position will not participate in the subsequent process. If the number is 3, the hidden representation of the token at that position will be extended to three copies and will participate in the subsequent operation. The equations are as follows:

$$\begin{aligned}
\mathbf{H_l} &= \text{Transformer}(\mathbf{H}) \\
\mathbf{H_l'} &= \text{FFN}(\mathbf{H_l}) \\
\mathbf{P} &= \text{softmax}(\mathbf{W}\mathbf{H_l'}) \\
t_i &= \text{argmax}(p_i)
\end{aligned} \tag{2}$$

where $\mathbf{H}$ is the output of Encoder, FFN is a feed-forward network used by Vaswani et al. [18]. $\mathbf{W}$ is the trainable weight; p_i is the predicted probability of the editing number at position i, and t is the editing number, indicating the number of tokens to appear at position i in the output.

3.3   Editor

The input of the Editor module consists of three parts: the hidden representations of the last layer of the Encoder, the input embeddings, and the reordered position embedding. We feed the sum of the three representations into an attention layer and get the consequential hidden representation $\mathbf{H_i}$ as follows:

$$\mathbf{H_e} = \text{LayerNorm}(\mathbf{E_p'} + \mathbf{E'} + \mathbf{H'})$$
$$\mathbf{Q} = \mathbf{W_Q H_e}, \mathbf{K} = \mathbf{W_K H}, \mathbf{V} = \mathbf{W_V H} \qquad (3)$$
$$\mathbf{H_i} = \text{Attention}(\mathbf{Q}, \mathbf{K}, \mathbf{V})$$

where $\mathbf{E'}$ is the input embedding, which is the sum of token embedding, position embedding, and segment embedding. $\mathbf{E_p'}$ is the reordered position embedding ranging from 0 to T, T is the sum of editing numbers, $\mathbf{H'}$ is hidden representation of Encoder. $\mathbf{E'}$, $\mathbf{E_p'}$ and $\mathbf{H'}$ are transformed from $\mathbf{E}$, $\mathbf{E_p}$ and $\mathbf{H}$ respectively. Eventually, the output tokens are predicted through an n-layer transformer.

$$\mathbf{H_i'} = \text{FFN}(\mathbf{H_i})$$
$$\mathbf{H_o} = \text{Transformer}(\mathbf{H_i'}) \qquad (4)$$

where $\mathbf{H_o}$ is the output representation of Editor.

3.4   Pre-training

To acquire a language model with stronger modeling and understanding ability, we pre-train TiBERT by the denoising task [10]. The denoising task requires interfering with the original sentences via extra noises and then telling the language model to denoise them. The model is trained in a more challenging manner than trained using the original data. By this means, the language modeling ability of TiBERT is enhanced. The detailed noising process is as follows:

Step 1. Input the original sentence, and randomly stream the editing number of each position from 0 to 5 according to the following probabilities, 7.5%, 80%, 7.5%, 2.5%, 2%, 0.5%, until the sum of editing numbers is greater than or equal to the length of the original sentence. If the sum grows greater than the length, we reassign the editing number of the last token to ensure that the final sum equals to the length of the original sentence. In this situation, the editing number at the last position is calculated as subtracting the sum of previous positions from the length.

Step 2. For each position, tokens are generated randomly based on the editing number. If the editing number is 0, 30% of the tokens will come from the original sentence and 70% will be randomly selected from the vocabulary. If the editing number is 1 or higher, 80% of the tokens will remain the same, 15% will be randomly selected from the vocabulary, and 5% will be taken from the original sentence.

TiBERT needs to predict the editing numbers and the editing tokens at the same time, so the final loss is a combination of the two parts, Locator and Editor. The loss function of Locator and Editor are both cross-entropy loss.

$$Loss = \lambda Loss_{locator} + (1 - \lambda)Loss_{editor} \tag{5}$$

where λ is a hyper-parameter varying from 0 to 1. For pre-training stage, we set λ to 0.5.

3.5   Fine-Tuning

After the pre-training stage, we fine-tune TiBERT with four text editing tasks. First of all, we need to convert parallel sentence pairs into editing number sequences and editing tokens. We obtain the editing numbers and the corresponding tokens at each position by Levenshtein distance. For all the editing tasks, we fine-tune our model by the loss in Equation (5). For tasks with different input and output lengths such as GEC and TS, we first generate the editing numbers by Locator and then generate the editing tokens according to the editing numbers and input tokens. For the CSC task, whose input and output lengths are the same, we input the standard editing number (all "1"s) in the test stage.

4   Experiments

We conducted experiments on various types of text editing tasks, including English and Chinese GEC, TS, and CSC. In text editing tasks, our pre-trained model works better than the autoregressive pre-trained models such as BART, and also better than the non-autoregressive models such as BERT and RoBERTa.

4.1   Settings

We use a 6-layer transformer for Encoder, a 1-layer transformer for Locator, and a 6-layer transformer for Editor. The hidden layer dimension is 768, and the intermediate size of FFN is 3072. We restrict the editing number as an integer from 0 to 5. For English pre-training, we use Colossal Cleaned CommonCrawl Corpus (C4) dataset with a total size of 305GB. For Chinese pre-training, we use Wikipedia and Wudaocorpora [25] with a total size of 152GB after data cleaning. We perform further pre-training based on BERT for English TiBERT and based on RoBERTa-wwm [4] for Chinese TiBERT. Encoder is initialized with the first 6 layers, and Editor is initialized with the last 6 layers. TiBERTs for both languages are trained with 1 million steps using batch size 2048. For the fine-tuning, 10 epochs are trained and the hyper-parameter λ is set to 0.5.

4.2   Data Conversion

Conventionally, the training data for text editing tasks are often in the form of parallel sentence pairs. Therefore, we need to convert the paired sentences into the form required for TiBERT, i.e., input token sequence, editing numbers at each position, and output token sequence. The length of output tokens and

Table 1. Experimental results on CoNLL 2014 GEC dataset. All the results are from single models.

Model	P	R	$F_{0.5}$
CopyNet [28]	65.2	33.2	54.7
PIE [1]	66.1	**43.0**	59.7
GECToR$_{BERT}$ [14]	72.1	42.0	63.0
GECToR$_{RoBERTa}$ [14]	73.9	41.5	64.0
TiBERT	**74.5**	42.1	**64.6**

Table 2. Experimental results on NLPCC 2018 GEC dataset. The best results are **bolded**, and the second best results are <u>underlined</u>.

Model	P	R	$F_{0.5}$
BLCU [27]	**47.63**	12.56	30.57
HRG [27]	36.79	<u>27.82</u>	34.56
Seq2Edit [27]	39.83	23.01	34.75
Seq2Seq [27]	37.67	**29.88**	35.80
POL-Pc [23]	46.45	23.68	<u>38.95</u>
TiBERT	<u>47.21</u>	24.86	**40.02**

the sum of editing numbers should be the same. In this paper, we convert the data format by Levenshtein, which generates a transformation between input and output. For keeping and replacing operations, the edit numbers remain 1. For the insertion operation, we add the number of inserted tokens to the origin editing number "1". For example, if adding one token to a position, the editing number of that position will be added to 2. For deletion operation, the corresponding number is 0. By the above method, we can convert the paired data form into TiBERT's input form.

4.3   Grammatical Error Correction (GEC)

The GEC task takes an erroneous sentence as the input and produces a correct version without changing the meaning. For English GEC task, we use Lang-8 [17], NUCLE [5], FCE [24] and W&I+LOCNESS[1] [2] as our training set and CoNLL 2014 as the test data. For Chinese GEC task, we conduct experiments on the training set and test set from NLPCC 2018 GEC shared task. We filter out the sentences without corrections, and use OpenCC[2] to convert all traditional characters into simplified characters. The final training data includes 1,019,371 sentence pairs. We follow the previous work and adopt $F_{0.5}$ based on MaxMatch as our evaluation method.

---

[1] https://www.cl.cam.ac.uk/research/nl/bea2019st/data/wi+locness_v2.1.bea19.tar. gz.

[2] https://github.com/BYVoid/.

Table 3. Experimental results on WikiLarge of Text Simplification. The best results are **bolded**, and the second best results are <u>underlined</u>.

Model	SARI↑	ADD↑	DELETE↑	KEEP↑	FKGL↓
PBMT-R [22]	35.92	**5.44**	32.07	70.26	10.16
NTS [13]	33.97	3.57	30.02	68.31	9.63
DRESS-LS [26]	32.98	2.57	30.77	65.60	<u>8.94</u>
EditNTS [7]	34.94	3.23	32.37	69.22	9.42
FELIX [11]	<u>38.13</u>	3.55	**40.45**	<u>70.39</u>	8.98
TiBERT	**38.98**	<u>3.77</u>	<u>38.10</u>	**75.07**	**8.89**

We compare our models with selected models based on Seq2Seq and sequence labeling methods. From the experimental results for English GEC task in Table 1, we can see that the performance of our model is better than that of CopyNet. TiBERT achieves 4.9% higher than that of PIE, which is a BERT-based text editing method. GECToR has designed dozens of special heuristic transformations for English grammatical error correction and achieves good results. Even so, our TiBERT still achieves better performance than the single model of GEC-ToR based on BERT and RoBERTa.

Table 2 shows the experimental results of Chinese GEC. Seq2Edit is based on the sequence labeling method and trained from StructBERT [21]. Seq2Seq is a generation method based on BART. The effect of our model is higher than that of StructBERT and BART models, even though they are large models, whose parameters are much more than that of TiBERT. Experimental results show that our pre-trained model achieves better results than other generation methods and sequence labeling methods on the Chinese GEC task.

4.4 Text Simplification (TS)

Text simplification is a type of paraphrasing task. It reduces the content of the original text while preserving the key ideas and making it more concise. We use WikiLarge and WikiSmall [29] as our training set for the text simplification task. The test set consists of 359 source sentences taken from Wikipedia. Each source sentence contains eight references which are simplified using Amazon Mechanical Turkers. We utilize SARI and FKGL [9] as the evaluation metrics.

Table 3 shows the experimental results. EditNTS achieves good results by the editing-based method, and Felix achieves good scores based on BERT. TiBERT outperforms all the other models on the overall SARI score and the FKGL score. In addition, TiBERT performs better than FELIX on the SARI-ADD score, which implies that TiBERT has a stronger ability in adding operations.

4.5 Chinese Spelling Check (CSC)

Chinese spelling check is an important task in the field of Chinese proofreading. The numbers of input and output characters of this task are the same. We use the

Table 4. The performance on SIGHAN 2015. The best results are **bolded**, and the second best results are underlined.

Model	Detection-level			Correction-level		
	D-P	D-R	D-F	C-P	C-R	C-F
FASPell [8]	67.6	60.0	63.5	66.6	59.1	62.6
BERT [3]	73.7	78.2	75.9	70.9	75.2	73.0
SpellGCN [3]	74.8	<u>80.7</u>	77.7	<u>72.1</u>	**77.7**	<u>74.8</u>
RoBERTa [19]	74.7	77.3	76.0	<u>72.1</u>	74.5	73.3
DCN [19]	**76.6**	79.8	<u>78.2</u>	**74.2**	<u>77.3</u>	**75.7**
TiBERT	<u>76.3</u>	**81.8**	**79.0**	71.9	77.1	74.4

large automatically generated corpus [20][3] as our training data for CSC task. In addition, the training sets of SIGHAN 2013, SIGHAN 2014, and SIGHAN 2015 are included. We evaluate our proposed model on the test sets from SIGHAN 2015 benchmarks. Similar to the previous works, we convert the traditional characters to simplified characters by OpenCC. To compare with the state-of-the-art models, We use the widely adopted sentence-level precision, recall, and F1-score as our evaluation metrics, which have been used by Hong et al. [8][4].

We compared our model with other state-of-the-art models. As shown in Table 4, our model achieves the best performance on detection-level F1-score. TiBERT achieves 3 points higher than other pre-trained models such as BERT and RoBERTa on detection-level F1. Compared with SpellGCN and DCN models, our proposed model achieves higher detecting performance. This indicates that our model has strong detection capability in CSC tasks. However, the correction results are slightly lower than these two models'. This is because TiBERT does not use any Chinese phonetic and glyph information. As a result, TiBERT can properly detect the errors, while the predicted corrections are not the optimal answers. By contrast, SpellGCN and DCN use phonetic and glyph information to improve their performance. Even without the incorporation of additional phonetic and glyph information, TiBERT still achieves comparable performance on correction-level F1 against these models which depend on phonetic and glyph information.

5 Analysis

Generally, larger and more complex models tend to perform better. We evaluate the inference speed of several pre-trained models and find that TiBERT is slightly slower than BERT but much faster than BART. The detailed results are shown in Table 5. Additionally, our model can complete text editing tasks in a single inference, unlike other non-autoregressive models such as Levenshtein

---

[3] https://github.com/wdimmy/Automatic-Corpus-Generation.
[4] https://github.com/iqiyi/FASPell.

Table 5. Inference time (in ms) for BERT, BART and TiBERT on GPU (Nvidia Tesla M40). We get the average time across 100 runs.

batch size	BERT	BART	TiBERT
1	15	621	26
8	49	2480	76
32	189	5981	288

Table 6. Examples from TiBERT on text editing tasks.

Dataset	Source Sentence	TiBERT Results
CoNLL 2014	Although it looks like no laws and it is your own space to speak and do anything you want, you are actually wrong	Although it looks like **there are** no laws and it is your own space to speak and do anything you want, you are actually wrong
SIGHAN 2015	我真不好意可是今天不能参加。 Translation: I'm **sor**, but I can't attend today	我真不好意思是今天不能参加。 I'm **sorry**, I can't attend today

transformer and GECToR which require multiple iterations. This makes our model more efficient for text editing tasks in terms of inference speed.

We analyze the predicted results of TiBERT in the text editing task. We observe that TiBERT can effectively insert multiple tokens at a time. As shown in Table 6, for the CoNLL 2014 task, TiBERT can correctly predict that it is necessary to add two tokens and insert "there are" before "no laws" to make the sentence more fluent.

Since the SIGHAN 2015 dataset not only includes spelling errors, but also involves some extra missing errors, which may confuse TiBERT in certain situations. In Table 6, "不好意" (sor) should be changed to "不好意思" (sorry), but this will lead to the missing of "但" (but). Because SIGHAN 2015 strictly limits the consistency of input and output lengths, there are no better means to correct these two errors at the same time.

6   Conclusion

In this paper, we present a new pre-trained non-autoregressive model named TiBERT for text editing tasks. TiBERT not only guarantees the inference speed but also enhances the generation performance. It demonstrates superior performance in various text editing tasks, including GEC, text simplification, and CSC. We also conduct detailed experimental analysis and introduce application scenes for TiBERT. In the future, we will continue to explore the application of TiBERT in natural language understanding (NLU) tasks.

References

1. Awasthi, A., Sarawagi, S., Goyal, R., Ghosh, S., Piratla, V.: Parallel iterative edit models for local sequence transduction. In: Proceedings of the EMNLP-IJCNLP, pp. 4260–4270. Association for Computational Linguistics, Hong Kong, China (2019)
2. Bryant, C., Felice, M., Andersen, Ø.E., Briscoe, T.: The BEA-2019 shared task on grammatical error correction. In: Proceedings of the Fourteenth Workshop on Innovative Use of NLP for Building Educational Applications, pp. 52–75. Association for Computational Linguistics, Florence, Italy (2019)
3. Cheng, X., et al.: SpellGCN: incorporating phonological and visual similarities into language models for Chinese spelling check. In: Proceedings of the ACL, pp. 871–881. Association for Computational Linguistics, Online (2020)
4. Cui, Y., Che, W., Liu, T., Qin, B., Yang, Z.: Pre-training with whole word masking for Chinese BERT. IEEE/ACM Trans. Audio, Speech Lang. Process. **29**, 3504–3514 (2021)
5. Dahlmeier, D., Ng, H.T., Wu, S.M.: Building a large annotated corpus of learner English: the NUS corpus of learner English. In: Proceedings of the Eighth Workshop on Innovative Use of NLP for Building Educational Applications, pp. 22–31. Association for Computational Linguistics, Atlanta, Georgia (2013)
6. Devlin, J., Chang, M.W., Lee, K., Toutanova, K.: BERT: Pre-training of deep bidirectional transformers for language understanding. In: Proceedings of the NAACL, pp. 4171–4186. Association for Computational Linguistics, Minneapolis, Minnesota (2019)
7. Dong, Y., Li, Z., Rezagholizadeh, M., Cheung, J.C.K.: EditNTS: an neural programmer-interpreter model for sentence simplification through explicit editing. In: Proceedings of the ACL, pp. 3393–3402. Association for Computational Linguistics, Florence, Italy (2019)
8. Hong, Y., Yu, X., He, N., Liu, N., Liu, J.: FASPell: a fast, adaptable, simple, powerful Chinese spell checker based on DAE-decoder paradigm. In: Proceedings of the 5th Workshop on Noisy User-generated Text (W-NUT 2019), pp. 160–169. Association for Computational Linguistics, Hong Kong, China (2019)
9. Kincaid, J.P., Jr, R.P.F., Rogers, R.L., Chisson, B.S.: Derivation of new readability formulas (automated readability index, fog count and flesch reading ease formula) for navy enlisted personnel (1975)
10. Lewis, M., et al.: BART: denoising sequence-to-sequence pre-training for natural language generation, translation, and comprehension. In: Proceedings of the 58th Annual Meeting of the Association for Computational Linguistics, pp. 7871–7880. Association for Computational Linguistics, Online (2020)
11. Mallinson, J., Severyn, A., Malmi, E., Garrido, G.: FELIX: flexible text editing through tagging and insertion. In: Findings of the Association for Computational Linguistics: EMNLP 2020, pp. 1244–1255. Association for Computational Linguistics, Online (2020)
12. Malmi, E., Krause, S., Rothe, S., Mirylenka, D., Severyn, A.: Encode, tag, realize: high-precision text editing. In: EMNLP-IJCNLP (2019)
13. Nisioi, S., Štajner, S., Ponzetto, S.P., Dinu, L.P.: Exploring neural text simplification models. In: Proceedings of the ACL, pp. 85–91. Association for Computational Linguistics, Vancouver, Canada (2017)
14. Omelianchuk, K., Atrasevych, V., Chernodub, A., Skurzhanskyi, O.: GECToR - grammatical error correction: Tag, not rewrite. In: Proceedings of the Fifteenth

Workshop on Innovative Use of NLP for Building Educational Applications,. pp. 163–170. Association for Computational Linguistics, Seattle, WA, USA Online (2020)

15. Radford, A., Narasimhan, K.: Improving language understanding by generative pre-training (2018)

16. Radford, A., Wu, J., Child, R., Luan, D., Amodei, D., Sutskever, I.: Language models are unsupervised multitask learners (2019)

17. Tajiri, T., Komachi, M., Matsumoto, Y.: Tense and aspect error correction for ESL learners using global context. In: Proceedings of the ACL, pp. 198–202. Association for Computational Linguistics, Jeju Island, Korea (2012)

18. Vaswani, A., et al.: Attention is all you need. In: Guyon, I., et al. (eds.) Advances in Neural Information Processing Systems 30: Annual Conference on Neural Information Processing Systems 2017, December 4–9, 2017, Long Beach, CA, USA, pp. 5998–6008 (2017)

19. Wang, B., Che, W., Wu, D., Wang, S., Hu, G., Liu, T.: Dynamic connected networks for chinese spelling check. In: Findings of the Association for Computational Linguistics: ACL-IJCNLP 2021, pp. 2437–2446 (2021)

20. Wang, D., Song, Y., Li, J., Han, J., Zhang, H.: A hybrid approach to automatic corpus generation for Chinese spelling check. In: Proceedings of the EMNLP, pp. 2517–2527. Association for Computational Linguistics, Brussels, Belgium (2018)

21. Wang, W., et al.: StructBERT: incorporating language structures into pre-training for deep language understanding. In: 8th International Conference on Learning Representations, ICLR 2020, Addis Ababa, Ethiopia, April 26–30, 2020. OpenReview.net (2020)

22. Wubben, S., van den Bosch, A., Krahmer, E.: Sentence simplification by monolingual machine translation. In: Proceedings of the ACL, pp. 1015–1024. Association for Computational Linguistics, Jeju Island, Korea (2012)

23. Xie, H., Lyu, X., Chen, X.: String editing based Chinese grammatical error diagnosis. In: Proceedings of the 29th International Conference on Computational Linguistics, pp. 5335–5344. International Committee on Computational Linguistics, Gyeongju, Republic of Korea (2022)

24. Yannakoudakis, H., Briscoe, T., Medlock, B.: A new dataset and method for automatically grading ESOL texts. In: Proceedings of the ACL, pp. 180–189. Association for Computational Linguistics, Portland, Oregon, USA (2011)

25. Yuan, S., et al.: WuDaoCorpora: a super large-scale Chinese corpora for pre-training language models. AI Open **2**, 65–68 (2021)

26. Zhang, X., Lapata, M.: Sentence simplification with deep reinforcement learning. In: Proceedings of the EMNLP, pp. 595–605. Association for Computational Linguistics (2017)

27. Zhang, Y., et al.: MuCGEC: a multi-reference multi-source evaluation dataset for Chinese grammatical error correction. In: Proceedings of NAACL-HLT. Association for Computational Linguistics, Online (2022)

28. Zhao, W., Wang, L., Shen, K., Jia, R., Liu, J.: Improving grammatical error correction via pre-training a copy-augmented architecture with unlabeled data. In: Proceedings of the NAACL, pp. 156–165. Association for Computational Linguistics, Minneapolis, Minnesota (2019)

29. Zhu, Z., Bernhard, D., Gurevych, I.: A monolingual tree-based translation model for sentence simplification. In: Proceedings of the COLING, pp. 1353–1361. Coling 2010 Organizing Committee, Beijing, China (2010)

Student Workshop: Information Retrieval and Text Mining

A Study on the Classification of Chinese Medicine Records Using BERT, Chest Impediment as an Example

He Chen⬤, Donghong Qin$^{(\boxtimes)}$⬤, Xiaoyan Zhang, Hui Zhang, and Xiao Liang

School of Artificial Intelligence, Guangxi Minzu University, Nanning 530006, China
chenhe@stu.gxmzu.edu.cn, donghong_qin@163.com

Abstract. Traditional Chinese Medicine (TCM) is the treasure of Chinese civilization and plays an indispensable role in China's medical system, but the diagnosis of TCM relies heavily on doctors' experience, which can affect the accuracy of diagnosis in practice. With the development of natural language processing technology, its mechanism can learn from a large amount of unstructured text to obtain a comprehensive and unified classification model. In this paper, we take chest impediment disease (i.e. coronary heart disease in Western medicine) as an example and build a pre-training diagnostic model based on the BERT model for TCM texts to accomplish the text classification task for different types of chest impediment medical records. Its overall F1 value reached 0.851, which improved 0.096 compared with the model without TCM pre-training; it also explored the problem of long text truncation and stopwords removing of TCM cases, which improved 0.087 compared with no TCM stopwords removing. This paper introduces natural language processing into the TCM auxiliary diagnosis problem, in order to improve the informationization, standardization and intelligence of TCM in the new era.

Keywords: BERT · Text classification · Chest impediment · Unstructured data

1 Introduction

Traditional Chinese Medicine (TCM) is the treasure of China's medicine, and has played an important role in our medical system since ancient times, and in the treatment of chronic diseases such as chest impediment (i.e. coronary heart disease in Western medicine), it has unique advantages [1]. Chest impediment

---

D. Qin—Received his Ph.D. degree in Department of Computer Science and Technology, Tsinghua University, China in 2013. He has published more than 50 papers in refereed international conferences and journals. He is a professor in School of Artificial Intelligence, GuangXi Minzu University, Nanning, China. His current research interests focus on Natural Language Processing, Algorithm Design, etc.

F. Liu et al. (Eds.): NLPCC 2023, LNAI 14304, pp. 29–37, 2023.
https://doi.org/10.1007/978-3-031-44699-3_3

disease has a high prevalence in China with a high morbidity and mortality rate, which has become a major public health problem in China [2], needing better treatment methods. As a kind of empirical medicine, the personal experience and subjective judgment of doctors in TCM diagnosis has a large proportion, and moreover, there are many schools of TCM and the diagnostic system is not entirely consistent, which can affect the accuracy of diagnosis in clinical practice and even lead to bias in diagnosis. TCM medical records are a large amount of free text recorded by clinical personnel, containing the diagnosis, treatment and medication, and prognosis of patients [3], which is difficult to be processed by traditional expert systems or machine learning methods. Natural language processing (NLP) technology can be used to process a great deal of unstructured text to make unified informational decisions. Applying NLP to TCM medical records' text discernment processing can avoid the bias of human perception and produce the results with uniform standards and objective data support [4].

In TCM's diagnosis system, chest impediment can be divided into 8 types [5], giving a TCM medical record. Thus, the diagnosis question can be transformed to a discourse-level text classification task in NLP field. Pre-training language model is the most important progress of NLP in recent years, and some SOTA models for text classification are also based on pre-training models. Several of the most competitive pre-training language models include the dynamic word vector algorithm ELMo [6], the generative pre-training language model GPT [7], the masked pre-training language model BERT [8], seq2seq pre-training language model BART [9]. GPT is a one-way model and can only be combined with the above context, which makes it more appropriate for generative task rather than discriminative task in this paper. BART can take context into account, but its pre-training process is more cumbersome and it is not specifically designed for text classification tasks. The ELMo model combines the context to solve the problem of polysemy comparing one-hot and word2vec, which enhances its comprehending ability, but ELMo is a shallow bidirectional model with weak feature extraction ability and long training time. The BERT model comprehends the advantages of many existing language models and is a true deep bidirectional model. BERT is derived from the Encoder part of the Transformer [10], which uses the Multi-Head Attention mechanism to extract the features of each character in the sequence in parallel, with high computational efficiency and strong generalization alility. The unique input method also makes it better understand the text and can really solve the problem of polysemy. In summary, BERT is chosen as the base model for the experiments in this paper.

2   Data

2.1   Data Source

The data of this article were obtained from China National Knowledge Infrastructure (CNKI). According to the search formula TI= *'chest impediment'*+ *'coronary heart disease'*+ *'coronary atherosclerotic heart disease'* AND SU= *'medical cases'*+ *'disease cases'*+ *'test cases'*+ *'examples'*- *'data mining'*- *'big data*'- '*statistics*'- '*forensic*'- '*mental health*'- '*nursing*' (TI=Title, SU=Subject), 936 eligible chest impediment TCM medical records were retrieved. Each medical record is relatively sufficient, the minimum number of characters is 56, the maximum number is 5014, and the average number is 1021, which has enough information to be processed. The content is relatively complete, including the patient's personal information, chief complaint medical history, dialectical analysis, TCM prescriptions, etc. Dataset collection is extensive, there are not only the case studies of masters of TCM such as Shikui Guo, Tietao Deng, and Keji Chen, but also the clinical cases of many outstanding first-line doctors. The following (Fig. 1) is a case of the dataset:

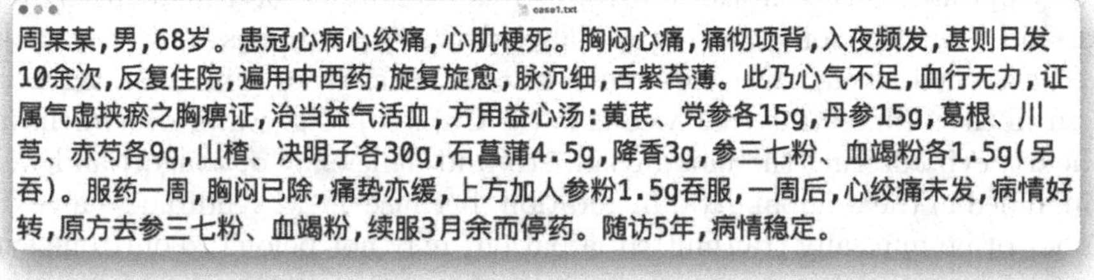

周某某，男，68岁。患冠心病心绞痛，心肌梗死。胸闷心痛，痛彻项背，入夜频发，甚则日发10余次，反复住院，遍用中西药，旋复旋愈，脉沉细，舌紫苔薄。此乃心气不足，血行无力，证属气虚挟瘀之胸痹证，治当益气活血，方用益心汤：黄芪、党参各15g，丹参15g，葛根、川芎、赤芍各9g，山楂、决明子各30g，石菖蒲4.5g，降香3g，参三七粉、血竭粉各1.5g（另吞）。服药一周，胸闷已除，痛势亦缓，上方加人参粉1.5g吞服，一周后，心绞痛未发，病情好转，原方去参三七粉、血竭粉，续服3月余而停药。随访5年，病情稳定。

Fig. 1. An example of the dataset

2.2 Data Labeling

Syndrome type is a unique concept of TCM, and it is a reflection of the pathological nature of a certain stage in the process of disease occurrence and evolution [11]. On the basis of identifying diseases, TCM further distinguishes syndromes, which embodies the idea of "seeking the root of disease" in TCM. Chest impediment can be divided into 8 syndromes in Chinese Internal Medicine (in Chinese) with different treatment ideas and methods [5], and an accurate classification is the premise and key to obtain good curative effect. In this supervised machine learning task, the features are free text in medical records (as shown in Fig. 1), and the labels are the potential syndrome one record belongs to, which displayed in Table 1. The standard of syndromes refers to the chapter Chest Impediment in the book Chinese Internal Medicine (in Chinese), 4th edition of China Press of Traditional Chinese Medice. The 8 syndromes defined in the book are: (1) heart-blood stasis syndrome, (2) syndrome of Qi stagnation in heart and chest, (3) phlegm blocking syndrome, (4) syndrome of cold clotting in heart and veins, (5) syndrome of deficiency of Qi and Yin, (6) syndrome of Yin deficiency in heart and kidney, (7) syndrome of Yang deficiency in heart and kidney, (8) Yang detachment syndrome.

The data labeling work was handled by two undergraduates majoring in Traditional Chinese Medicine and a medical doctor to confirm. Syndrome labeling processing is a complex task that requires dealing with a variety of situations. Among all the records, some of them are noted the corresponding syndrome and can be used directly. Some cases are ambiguous to recognize and need to be categorized with medical knowledge. For example, the term "Qi yu" was recorded, and the term derives from Plain Questions·Great Treatise on the Regular Principles of the Six Origins (in Chinese), which is mostly caused by emotional and mental discomfort and Qi stagnation [12], so it can be classified as "syndrome of Qi stagnation in heart and chest". Another term is "xin Yang bu zhen", which comes from the chapter Heart Palpitation in the Chinese Internal Medicine (in Chinese), and the clinical manifestations are palpitation, chest tightness and shortness of breath, especially when moving, pale face, cold form and cold limbs, pale tongue with white fur, weak or sunken and weak pulse [13]. According to those symptoms, this term can be grouped as "syndrome of Yang deficiency in heart and kidney". Some cases were labeled their syndromes, but they could not be classified as current syndromes due to inconsistency with the diagnostic system in the Chinese Internal Medicine (in Chinese) (e.g. water overwhelming the heart, evil entering the blood channels, and deficiency of zongqi) and were not included in the original data. In addition, because TCM syndromes can exist together or be mutually transmitted, a patient may not belong to only one syndrome, and multiple syndromes may occur. According to the idea of "treating both the surface symptoms and the root cause" in TCM, the model is expected to identify all syndromes occurring in a patient. In practice, up to two of the most prominent syndrome(s) of the current case were labeled. The specificity of the data also requirs that this model completes a multiple classification task rather than a single classification task.

Table 1. Example Data Set

	heart-blood stasis syndrome	syndrome of Qi stagnation in heart and chest	phlegm blocking syndrome	syndrome of cold clotting in heart and veins	syndrome of deficiency of Qi and Yin	syndrome of Yin deficiency in heart and kidney	syndrome of Yang deficiency in heart and kidney	Yang detachment syndrome
Case 1	1	0	0	0	1	0	0	0
Case 2	0	0	0	1	0	0	0	0
Case 3	0	1	1	0	0	0	0	0
Case 4	0	0	0	0	0	1	0	0
Case 5	1	0	0	0	0	0	1	0

3   Method

3.1   Pre-processing Stage

In this paper, we preprocessed data from raw medical cases by filter, truncation, and stopwords. The data set was first filtered to eliminate those invalid syndrome cases so that they would not adversely affect the model, which has been mentioned in data labeling chapter.

Secondly, truncation of the filtered dataset is performed. Discourse-level text classification requires the input of entire articles into the model, and the length of TCM case records is not uniform and the content is relatively free, which creates difficulties in the use of models with limited input size, such as BERT. Therefore, this experiment intercepts long cases based on the model size limitation and preserves as much important information as possible. The TCM case interception is divided into three steps: (1) Original case cutting: the original complete case is cut into several segments. (2) Case structuring: a case structure table is summarized based on medical knowledge, which specifies that the case contains different parts such as diagnostic part, medication part, and specifies the importance of different parts. This table allows each paragraph of the original case to be divided into one of these sections. (3)Structured case interception: In case the text is too long, the less important parts are deleted in turn.

Finally, stopwords removing of the cases was performed by applying the TCM stopwords table on basis of truncation, because the writing grammar and sentence structure of TCM cases are more literary oriented, and if there is no word segmentation or stopwords removing is not used by stopwords table after segmentation, it will adversely affect the prediction of the model, making the model focus on those prepositions and inflectional auxiliaries (which exist in abundance in ancient texts). This method enables the model to focus on the important words during pre-training, which both improves the accuracy and saves the time for training.

3.2   Pre-training Stage

The BERT model used in this paper was built by our team. In order to match the amount of data with the size of the model for better results, the BERT model was pre-trained with num_layers=4 and num_hiddens=512 for the pre-processed TCM cases and TCM texts. Both NSP_loss and MLM_loss metrics are not too high or too low.

Table 2. Pre-Training Losses

MLM_LOSS	NSP_LOSS
3.445	0.711

3.3   Model Fine-tuning Stage

After the pre-training is completed, fine-tuning begins. The dataset is divided into eight syndromes, and an eight classifier is constructed. Since the two most probable syndromes are to be output, the loss function and the labels need to be fine-tuned to some extent. When fine-tuning the model, a feed-forward neural network layer and a softmax layer are added to the model, and then the results of the case subscripts are put into the maximum probability category of the model output to obtain the type of chest impediment suffered by the case. The method of accuracy is judged as follows: when predicting, two syndromes with the highest probability are given, for only one syndrome, as long as it is among the two predicted syndromes, it is successful, if there are two syndromes, only if all of them are predicted correctly is considered successful. Table 3 shows a small selection from all the predictions: the first (2, -100): (2, 1) for example, the number in the first bracket represents the syndrome of this case, and -100 means there is no second syndrome (-100 will only appear in the second position). So (2, -100) has only one syndrome, and the second bracket is the predicted syndrome, (2, 1) means the prediction is 2 and 1 syndrome.

Table 3. Example of Forecast

Label 1	Label 2	Prediction 1	Prediction 2
2	-100	2	1
5	4	5	4
7	-100	7	5

4   Results

4.1   Experimental Results of BERT Model

Through the above data pre-processing and the two stages of BERT method, the results of the chest impediment category classification experiment are shown in Table 4.

Table 4. Experimental results of the model in this paper

Category	Precision P	Recall R	F1 value
Heart-blood Stasis Syndrome	0.979	0.6	0.744
Syndrome of Qi Stagnation in Heart and Chest	1.0	0.597	0.747
Phlegm Blocking Syndrome	1.0	0.776	0.873
Syndrome of Cold Clotting in Heart and Veins	0.909	0.769	0.833
Syndrome of Deficiency of Qi and Yin	0.985	0.945	0.964
Syndrome of Yin Deficiency in Heart and Kidney	0.957	0.697	0.806
Syndrome of Yang Deficiency in Heart and Kidney	0.947	0.849	0.895
Yang Detachment Syndrome	0.996	0.903	0.947

From the data results in Table 4, it can be seen that the Precision P, Recall R, and F1 values all reached good levels in this dataset, and from the F1 values, which show comprehensive performance, the model has good results for each classification. Among them, the recall rate R was low for syndrome of cold clotting in heart and veins, syndrome of Yang deficiency in heart and kidney and heart-blood stasis syndrome. From the data set, it is either because the number of positive cases is small and the positive and negative ratio is unbalanced, or because most of them have two labels and it is more difficult to complete two predictions at the same time.

4.2   Experimental Results of Multi-model Comparison

This experiment selects hfl's chinese-electra-small model for comparison, which is a full-task model for small dataset and low computing power in the NLP field released by iFlyTek Joint Lab of HIT in 2021. This model has achieved good performance on GLUE and other datasets, and has 43.8k downloads on Hugging Face, which is a very effective model with small dataset. The more common models, such as bert-base-chinese, hfl/chinese-roberta-wwm-ext, hfl/chinese-bert-wwm-ext, etc., do not have a good result in the case of small dataset and long sample length because they have too many parameters and layers. In addition, the decision tree algorithm was also chosen to classify the data, as it is a classical machine learning method and widely used in assisted diagnosis problem.

In order to further verify the performance of the BERT model and the feasibility and effectiveness of the adopted method, this experiment also selected hfl's chinese-electra-small model for experimental comparison, and the decision tree algorithm for classifying the data, in addition to comparing the effect of using stopwords or not on the model. The results of the experimental comparisons are shown in Table 5.

Table 5. Comparison results of multi-model experiments

Models	Precision P	Recall R	F1 value
BERT(this paper)	**0.972**	**0.767**	**0.851**
Chinese-electra-small	0.788	0.695	0.755
Decision Tree	0.538	0.547	0.565
BERT without Pro-processing	0.87	0.698	0.764

From the overall F1 values, the BERT model used in this experiment is improved over the hfl/chinese-electra-small and decision tree algorithms, and from the precision P and recall R of each category, the model used in this experiment is also improved, which is attributed to the preprocessing work of truncation, word segmentation, and stopwords in the previous stage, as well as to the use of texts related to TCM cases in the pre-training stage to improve the understanding of the model. In addition, the comparison results also show that the evaluation items of the model decrease without using the stopwords, which fully proves the effectiveness of the stopwords table used in this experiment and reflects that there are many words of little use in each data, and these words will make the attention mechanism to focus on those parts that have little effect on the classification, thus reducing the performance of the model.

5 Discuss

After a series of training, the experimental model has good performance on the collected chest impediment TCM case dataset, both in terms of overall F1 value and individual category precision and recall, which has some improvement compared with the common pre-training model chinese-electra-small or decision tree, which indicates that the experimental model has some practical value. However, because of the limited size of the training dataset and the single way of processing the original case data, further efforts are needed to make the model perform well on larger datasets. In general, the trend of applying deep learning knowledge to the field of TCM is irresistible. This experiment constructs a specific model for TCM diagnosis problem and achieves a certain accuracy, which has the potential to assist doctors in diagnosis and is expected to improve the standardization and accuracy of TCM diagnosis. This experiment tries to combine the emerging natural language processing technology with traditional TCM career, explores the related work of TCM case truncation and TCM stopwords list construction, and does some subsequent natural language processing for TCM. At the same time, the complex and ambiguous TCM diagnosis problems are solved by adopting a unified model, which is conducive to the progress of quantification, informatization and intelligence of TCM in the new era.

Acknowledgment. This work was supported by the Guangxi Science and Technology Base and Talent Project (No. 2022AC16002), Horizontal Scientific Research Project of Guangxi Minzu University (No. 2022450016000429).

References

1. Standardization project group of clinical application guidelines of proprietary Chinese medicines for the treatment of prevailing diseases: clinical application guidelines of proprietary Chinese medicines for the treatment of coronary heart disease (2020). Chinese J. Integrative Med. **41**(04), 391–417 (2021)
2. The writing committee of the report on cardiovascular health and diseases in China: summary of report on cardiovascular health and disease in China 2020. Chinese Circ. J. **37**(06), 553–578 (2022)
3. Candong, L.: Traditional Chinese Diagnostics. China Press of Traditional Chinese Medice, Beijng, China, pp. 206–207 (2016)
4. Zongyou, W.: A review of research on text mining of electronic medical records. Comput. Res. Dev. **58**(03), 513–527 (2021)
5. Boli, Z., Mianhua, W.: Chinese Internal Medicine. China Press of Traditional Chinese Medice, Beijng, China, pp. 93–100 (2017)

6. Peters, M.-M.: Deep contextualized word representations. In: Proceedings of the 2018 Conference of the North American Chapter of the Association for Computational Linguistics: Human Language Technologies, Volume 1 (Long Papers), pp. 2227–2237. New Orleans, Louisiana (2018)

7. Radford, A., et al.: Improving language understanding by generative pre-training. https://s3-us-west-2.amazonaws.com/openaiassets/research-covers/langua geunsupervised/languageunderstandingpaper.pdf (2018)

8. Jacob, D.-L.: BERT: pre-training of deep bidirectional transformers for language understanding. In: Proceedings of the 2019 Conference of the North American Chapter of the Association for Computational Linguistics: Human Language Technologies, Volume 1 (Long and Short Papers), pp. 4171–4186. Minneapolis, Minnesota (2019)

9. Mike, L.-L.: BART: denoising sequence-to-sequence pre-training for natural language generation, translation, and comprehension. In: Proceedings of the 58th Annual Meeting of the Association for Computational Linguistics, pp. 7871–7880. Online (2020)

10. Vaswani, A.-N.: Attention is all you need. In: 31st International Conference on Neural Information Processing Systems, pp. 6000–6010. Curran Associates Inc., Red Hook, NY, USA (2017)

11. Candong, L.: Traditional Chinese Diagnostics. China Press of Traditional Chinese Medice, Beijng, China, p. 4 (2016)

12. Boli, Z., Mianhua, W.: Chinese Internal Medicine. China Press of Traditional Chinese Medice, Beijng, China, pp. 289–285 (2017)

13. Boli, Z., Mianhua, W.: Chinese Internal Medicine. China Press of Traditional Chinese Medice, Beijng, China, pp. 87–93 (2017)

Student Workshop: Information Extraction and Knowledge Acquisition

Semantic Candidate Retrieval
for Few-Shot Entity Linking

Jianyong Chen, Jiangming Liu[✉], Jin Wang, and Xuejie Zhang

School of Information Science and Engineering, Yunnan University, Kunming City,
Yunnan Province, China
cjy@mail.ynu.edu.cn, {jiangmingliu,wangjin,xjzhang}@ynu.edu.cn

Abstract. Entity Linking (EL) is the task of automatically linking
entity mentions in texts to the corresponding entries in a knowledge
base. Current EL systems exhibit the great performances on the standard
datasets, but in real-world applications, they are computationally intensive and expensive in large-scale processing, and the entity entries are
limited to the knowledge bases. The newly-emerging entities may hinder
the generalization ability of the EL systems. To this end, we propose the
semantic candidate retrieval method for the few-shot entity linking task.
The semantic candidates corresponding to the mentions are selected by
inverted indexing, and then, the semantic ranker is proposed to choose
the top appropriate candidate to be linked. The proposed model achieves
the accuracy of 53.19% in the shared task 6 of NLPCC-2023.

Keywords: entity linking · semantic candidate · inverted index

1 Introduction

Entity Linking (EL) is the task of automatically connecting entities mentioned
in the text to their corresponding entries in a Knowledge Base (KB), such
as Wikipedia, which is a collection of facts relating to those entities. EL is
widely used in natural language processing (NLP) applications, including question answering [1], information extraction [2], and natural language understanding [3]. It is essential for connecting unstructured text with knowledge bases,
allowing access to a wealth of carefully selected material.

The entity mentions that appear in the context often pose ambiguity and
cannot be directly linked to the KB. Specifically, entity mentions in the text
invariably involve the inherent ambiguity of natural language expressions, where
the same entity has multiple mentions referring to multiple entities. As shown in
Fig. 1, the mention of *England* is attached to the entity *England Football Team*
instead of a country, a part of the United Kingdom. In real-world application,
the newly-emerging entities do not exist in the knowledge bases in the inference
stage, which is called zero-/few-shot entity linking [4].

To this end, existing EL methods apply the semantic retrieval in a Siamese
network with information stored in the knowledge base, such as textual entity
descriptions or fine-grained entity types. However, If these are billions of textual

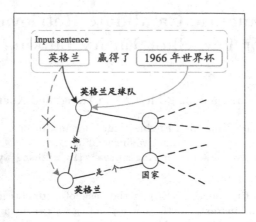

Fig. 1. An illustrated example of zero- and few-shot entity linking.

descriptions, these methods will be computationally intensive, resulting in the expensive computation.

To alleviate this problem, we propose a semantic candidate retrieval based on inverted indexing for zero- and few-shot entity linking. An inverted indexing is built to store the mappings from the mentions of entities to a set of relevant textual descriptions. Instead of all the entity candidates, we select several semantic-related entities candidates to be matched with the mentions by the inverted indexing with the highest scores of term frequency-inverse document frequency (TF-IDF). After that, the final entity linked to the mention is obtained by measuring the cosine similarity between the selected entity candidates and the context via the sentence-transformer [5].

The experiments are conducted on the development set released by the official organizers. The experimental results show that our model has a 23% improvement in Recall@10 over baseline, reaching 95.6%.

The rest of the paper is organized as follows. Section 2 introduces the related work. Section 3 presents the proposed semantic candidate retrieval based on an inverted index. Section 4 shows the experimental results and the ablation study. Conclusions are drawn in Sect. 5.

2   Related Work

EL usually consists of two basic stages, candidate entity generation and entity disambiguation. This section briefly summarizes the related work about the two stages.

2.1   Candidate Generation

Much prior work on candidate generation use a Dictionary-Based approach. This method is applied to almost all entity linking systems. The main idea is to make

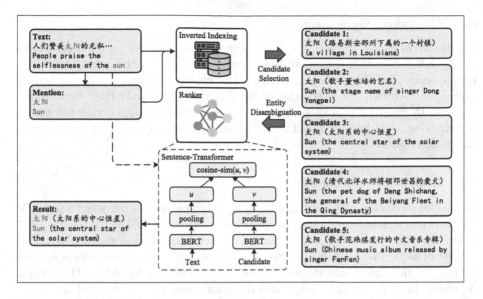

Fig. 2. Overall architecture of the proposed semantic candidate retrieval for zero- and few-shot entity linking.

full use of all kinds of information provided by Wikipedia, including redirection pages, disambiguation pages, anchor text, etc., to construct a mapping relationship dictionary between entity names and all linked entities, and then use the information in the dictionary to generate candidate entities gather.

2.2 Entity Disambiguation

Previous work focuses on designing effective artificial features and complex similarity measures to obtain better disambiguation performance. He et al. learn distributed representations of entities to measure similarity without human features by keeping words and entities in the joint semantic space and ranking candidate entities directly based on vector similarity [6]. Sun et al. propose the embedded representations of the entities and the contexts via convolutional neural networks [7]. Based on BERT [8], Chen et al. integrate the entity similarity into the local model of the latest model to capture the entity type information [9].

3 Semantic Candidate Retrieval

As shown in Fig. 2, the proposed semantic candidate retrieval consists of the inverted indexing module and the ranker. The candidate generation module is designed to select top-n candidate entities together with their descriptions in KB, and the ranker is designed to obtain final entity according to the cosine similarity between the entity descriptions and the context.

3.1　Candidate Generation

Given the entities in the KB, it is expensive to enumerate all entity descriptions in the KB for each mention. Instead, we aim to search the relevant entities by applying TF-IDF scoring method on the entity descriptions. In particular, given one mention, we select the entity descriptions in KB that contain the mention by inverted indexing. After that, we obtain the top-n relevant entity descriptions according to the TF-IDF score of the mention over the selected entity descriptions.

3.2　Entity Disambiguation

Given the context $u = [u_1, u_2, ..., u_m, ..., u_l]$, where u_i is the ith word and u_m is the mention, A set of candidates of entity descriptions, $V = \{v\}^n$, are generated, as described in Sect. 3.1. Each candidate of entity description $v = [v_1, v_2, ..., v_k]$ consist of sequence of words. The Simaese network with dual encoders is applied to project the entity descriptions v and the context u to obtain the hidden representations in a vector space, and the cosine similarity is computed,

$$\text{sim}(u, v) = \frac{\phi(u)^T \psi(v)}{\phi(u)\psi(v)}, \tag{1}$$

where ϕ and ψ are BERT encoders, and representations of [CLS] is used to be the representation of input texts.

　　In addition, we adopt the TF-IDF score calculated by the inverted indexing as the prior knowledge. The final score is produced with the cosine similarity as

$$score(u, v) = P(v|u) \cdot \text{sim}(u, v) \tag{2}$$

3.3　Post-processing

We define the function that returns the maximum frequency of the entity linked by the mention:

$$f(u_m) = \max_{e \in E} c(e, u_m), \tag{3}$$

where the function $c(e, u_m)$ returns the frequency of the entity e linked by the mention u_m. In the post-procerssing, we assign the mention u_m if $f(u_m) \leq 2$ with the entity $e = \arg max_{e \in E} c(e, u_m)$.[1]

4　Experiments

4.1　Dataset

Table 1 shows the data descriptions in Entity Linking, where each sample contains a *mention*, as well as a text. The *start* and *end* index indicate the starting

---

[1] The entity is chosen with random sampling if more than one entities satisfy the condition.

Table 1. An example in Entity Linking provided by the share task in NLPCC 2023.

Field	Description	Example
id	The id of this sample	hansel-eval-zs-1463
text	The text which contains the mention to be linked.	...吉尔莫·德尔·托罗的《匹诺曹》，在上个月...
start	Starting position of the mention in the text.	29
end	Ending position of the mention in the text.	32
mention	A word or phrase to be linked.	匹诺曹
gold_id	The id of the corresponding entity in the KB.	Q73895818
source	The source of text.	https://www.1905.com/news/20181107/1325389.shtml
domain	The field that the text is talking about.	news

and ending position of the mention in the text, respectively. We use the data provided from the shared task in NLPCC 2023 for the experiments. This task aims at testing the generalization of Chinese EL systems for infrequent and newly-emerging entities. The dataset is a human-calibrated and multi-domain Chinese EL benchmark with Wikidata as KB, consisting of 9,879,813 mentions with 541,058 entities for training and 9,674 mentions with 6,320 entities as a validation set. The evaluation metrics are recall and accuracy.

4.2 Baselines and Results

In order to investigate the modules in the proposed models, we take the two baseline models:

- FTS: search for entity candidates by matching the mention with the wiki titles. Then sort the candidates according to the number of mentions in the wiki.
- RIS: obtain the candidates using the elastic search only without additional selection strategy.

Table 2 shows the recall of the candidate generation in the second column. Since both RIS-ST and RIS use the elastic search algorithm, they have the same recall scores. The models equipped with the elastic search algorithm achieved the highest recall score of 0.94. Table 2 shows the accuracy of the entity linking. Compared to RIS, the proposed model achieves the best accuracy of 0.65 with considering the cosine similarity via the sentence-transformer.

4.3 Analysis

Indexing Option. The main difference between using *keyword* and *text* as index options in Elastic Search is that *keyword* is for the exact query on structured data, while *text* is for the full-text search on unstructured data. To investigate

Table 2. The recall of the candidate generation across models and the accuracy of the entity linking

Model	Recall(%)	Accuracy (%)
FTS	71.2	/
RIS	94.0	59.2
RIS-ST (ours)	94.0	65.4

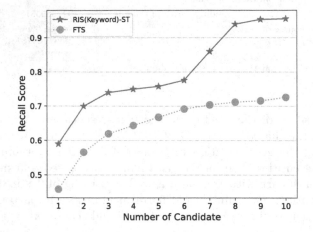

Fig. 3. The recall in choosing top-n candidates.

which indexing option is better for entity linking, we carry the comparative experiment, where one model uses the text option, and the other uses the keyword option. The experiments shows that the model using the keyword options can achieves the recall of 94.0% in the candidate generation, which is better than the model using the text option (86.6% recall).

Post-processing. In the test set, a total of about 900 entities or emerging entities were post-processed (described in Sect. 3.3), resulting that the accuracy improved by 3% points, compared to the models without post-processing.

Amount of Candidates. The top-n candidates are chosen as the results of the candidate generation. If the size of candidates is too small, the correct links will not appear in the list of candidates. In contrast, the more candidates there are, the more noisy links will be added. Therefore, it is important to make a trade-off. Figure 3 depicts the recall score of RIS-ST with different value of n. Based on the elbow approach, we optimize the n to be 8 in our final models.

Hand-off Test Results. Table 3 shows the test results provided by the all ablation models in the shared task of NLPCC 2023. We recommend the elastic search to obtain 8 high-quality candidate sets with indexing options using keywords. The sentence-transformer is used to make full use of the contextual information of wiki text to select reasonable hypotheses from the candidate sets. We also propose that post-processing for tail entities or emerging entities can also improve the overall performance of the model.

Table 3. The test results across different models.

Strategy	Accuracy (%)
RIS(Text)	48.59
RIS(Text)-ST	49.69
RIS(Keyword)-ST	50.18
RIS(Keyword)-ST-Post Processing	53.19

5 Conclusion

In this paper, the method based on inverted index and semantic analysis and sorting is proposed for Chinese entity linking. In addition, we discovered that the post-processing shows the significant improvement in the task of entity linking for the newly-emerging entities. Together with the modules and the strategies, our models achieved 53.19% in the share task 6 of NLPCC-2023 Accuracy, and the final model is ranked 3 among all the submission models.

References

1. Sorokin, D., Gurevych, I.: Mixing context granularities for improved entity linking on question answering data across entity categories, 4 (2018)
2. Shen, W., Wang, J., Han, J.: Entity linking with a knowledge base: issues, techniques, and solutions. IEEE Trans. Knowl. Data Eng. **27**, 443–460 (2015)
3. Neumann, M., King, D., Beltagy, I., Ammar, W.: Scispacy: fast and robust models for biomedical natural language processing, 2 (2019)
4. Xu, Z., Shan, Z., Li, Y., Hu, B., Qin, B.: Hansel: a Chinese few-shot and zero-shot entity linking benchmark. In: Proceedings of the Sixteenth ACM International Conference on Web Search and Data Mining, pp. 832–840. Association for Computing Machinery (2023)
5. Reimers, N., Gurevych, I.: Sentence-BERT: sentence embeddings using Siamese BERT-networks, 8 (2019)
6. He, Z., Liu, S., Li, M., Zhou, M., Zhang, L., Wang, H.: Learning entity representation for entity disambiguation (2013)
7. Sun, M., Guo, Z., Deng, X.: Intelligent BERT-BiLSTM-CRF based legal case entity recognition method. In Proceedings of the ACM Turing Award Celebration Conference - China, ACM TURC '21, pp. 186–191, New York, NY, USA, (2021). Association for Computing Machinery
8. Devlin, J., Chang, M.-W., Lee, K., Toutanova, K.: Google, and A I Language. BERT: pre-training of deep bidirectional transformers for language understanding (2018)
9. Chen, S., Wang, J., Jiang, F., Lin, C.-Y.: Improving entity linking by modeling latent entity type information, 1 (2020)

ERNIE-AT-CEL: A Chinese Few-Shot Emerging Entity Linking Model Based on ERNIE and Adversarial Training

Hongyu Zhou[ID], Chengjie Sun[✉], Lei Lin, and Lili Shan

Harbin Institute of Technology, Computer Science and Technology, Harbin, China
sunchengjie@hit.edu.cn

Abstract. This article proposes a Chinese few-shot emerging entity linking model based on ERNIE and adversarial training. The model utilizes ERNIE as the base model and achieves accurate linking of Chinese few-shot emerging entities by adding adversarial perturbations during the training process. Experimental results on standard entity linking evaluation datasets demonstrate significant performance improvements of our proposed model compared to baseline models. Moreover, we compare multiple candidate entity retrieval methods through comparative experiments to evaluate and compare their effectiveness in the entity linking task. The experimental results show that our appoarch achieved an F1 score of 0.60 and ranked second in the NLPCC 2023 Shared Task 6 (Chinese Few-shot and Zero-shot Entity Linking). Experimental results demonstrate that the model has high predictive performance and robustness in the Chinese few-shot emerging entity linking task, providing reference and inspiration for research and practice in related fields.

Keywords: Entity Linking · Candidate Entity Retrieval · Adversarial Training

1 Introduction

Entity linking (EL) is a fundamental task in natural language processing, which aims to establish links between entities mentioned in the text and entities in a knowledge base. Entity linking is widely applied in various domains, including question answering systems, information extraction, semantic search, and relation extraction. With the development of deep learning, significant progress has been made in the field of entity linking, particularly with the advent of pre-trained language models. Enhanced Representation through kNowledge IntEgration (ERNIE) [10] is a semantic representation model proposed by Baidu, which achieves state-of-the-art performance on various natural language understanding tasks. ERNIE is built upon techniques such as bidirectional Transformer encoders and masked language modeling. In comparison to Bidirectional Encoder Representations from Transformers (BERT), ERNIE 1.0 incorporates semantic knowledge from massive amounts of data, including words, entities, and entity relationships, to learn real-world semantic knowledge.

F. Liu et al. (Eds.): NLPCC 2023, LNAI 14304, pp. 48–56, 2023.
https://doi.org/10.1007/978-3-031-44699-3_5

In this paper, we propose CELAT, a Chinese entity linking model based on ERNIE and adversarial training, leveraging existing pre-trained models in the general domain. By constructing adversarial training examples and various retrieval strategies, CELAT aims to address the issues of poor performance in few-shot Chinese entity linking, as well as the popularity bias in tail and emerging entities.

2 Related Work

2.1 Pretrained Language Models

pretrained language models (PLMs) are a type of deep learning models that are trained on large-scale textual data to learn language features such as vocabulary, grammar, and semantics. These models learn in an unsupervised manner and can be trained on massive amounts of unlabeled text data, such as Wikipedia articles, web content, or extensive books. PLMs can be used for various natural language processing tasks, including text classification, named entity recognition, syntax analysis, machine translation, etc. By fine-tuning the pretrained models based on specific domains or tasks, their performance can be further improved. In recent years, renowned PLMs such as Generative Pretrained Transformer (GPT) and Bidirectional Encoder Representations from Transformers (BERT) have achieved tremendous success in the field of natural language processing (NLP), becoming foundational models for numerous tasks.

2.2 Candidate Entity Retrieval

Candidate entity retrieval is a metric used in IR (information retrieval) and NLP tasks to evaluate the effectiveness of a system in retrieving relevant entities. It measures the proportion of relevant entities that are successfully retrieved by the system among all the possible relevant entities. The goal of candidate entity retrieval is to assess the system's ability to recall all the relevant entities, ensuring that important information is not missed during the retrieval process. A common approach for candidate entity retrieval involves constructing an entity name mapping table, where each entity is represented as a key-value pair (entity-set of aliases). This table serves as an alias query table for the knowledge base. Additionally, a reverse index table (mention-set of entities) is maintained based on tne alias query table to facilitate querying entities by their aliases.

Candidate Entity Retrieval Based on Fuzzy String Matching. Entity aliases can be retrieved through methods such as prefix matching, suffix matching, and edit distance. Based on the inverted index table of entity aliases, each alias index field is treated as the query text, and upper-level indexes are built using algorithms such as trie and text inverted index.

Candidate Entity Retrieval Based on Semantic Vector Retrieval. Candidate Entity Retrieval based on Vector Retrieval requires encoding each entity semantically and mapping them to a vector space. During the retrieval process, the mention is also encoded and mapped to the same vector space. This process is known as text embedding. After text embedding, solving the Approximate Nearest Neighbor (ANN) problem regarding the semantic vector of the mention can complete the retrieval process [8].

Mention and Entity Encoding Methods. Traditional text embedding methods use one-hot method. Due to the often large size of the vocabulary, one-hot encoding results in a high-dimensional sparse vector space, which not only incurs high computational cost but also makes it difficult to obtain effective semantic information. Word2vec [6] method utilizes a low-dimensional dense vector space for text embedding. In the word2vec method, words with similar meanings tend to have higher vector similarity, and similar algorithms are referred to as static word embedding methods. Static word embedding methods face challenges such as polysemy and reliance on tokenization.

Nearest Neighbor Methods. K-Nearest Neighbor (KNN) is used to find k vectors that are most similar to the query, and Radius Nearest Neighbor (RNN) is used to find vectors that are within a distance smaller than d from the query. Commonly used distance metrics for vectors in machine learning include Euclidean distance, Cosine distance, and Hamming distance. Euclidean distance measures the straight-line distance between two vectors in Euclidean space.

$$d(\mathbf{p}, \mathbf{q}) = \sqrt{\sum_{i=1}^{n} (q_i - p_i)^2} \tag{1}$$

Cosine distance calculates the angle between two vectors in Euclidean space.

$$d(\mathbf{p}, \mathbf{q}) = \frac{\sum_{i=1}^{n} p_i q_i}{\sqrt{\sum_{i=1}^{n} p_i^2} \sqrt{\sum_{i=1}^{n} q_i^2}} \tag{2}$$

Hamming distance calculates the number of different characters at corresponding positions in two equally long strings. The computation complexity for solving exact KNN or RNN problems is high, therefore, an approximate solution method called Approximate Nearest Neighbor (ANN) has been proposed for vector retrieval. Faiss [4] is an open-source library developed by Facebook AI Research for efficient similarity search and vector retrieval, and aims to address large-scale vector retrieval problems. Faiss provides a range of highly optimized algorithms and data structures that enable fast approximate nearest neighbor search on large-scale datasets.

In the past two years, many researchers have proposed new methods for entity representation and entity retrieval. Ran et. al. propose a novel approach called STAMO to learn high-quality EL features for entitys automatically, as it could leverage the knowledge hidden in the unlabeled data [9]. Cho et. al. address two challenge in entity linking: how to leverage wider contexts surrounding a mention, and how to deal with limited training data [1].

3 Model Introduction

The structure of CELAT is shown in Fig. 1.

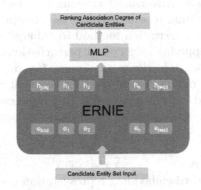

Fig. 1. Model structure of CELAT.

3.1 Task Definition

Given a document D, a mention set M in the document and a knowledge base KB, where document D is an ordered sequence of multiple words. Each mention $m \in M$ is composed of one or more adjacent words. The knowledge base KB is a collection of entities, each entity $e \in KB$ can unambiguously and uniquely describe a thing. The task goal of entity linking is to attempt to map each $mi \in M$ to an entity emi that is semantically consistent with it, and $emi \in KB$.

3.2 Model with ERNIE

CELAT consists of input layers, encoding layers, and output layers.

Input Layer. First, each sentence is tokenized. Then, each word or subword is transformed into a fixed-dimensional word vector through an embedding layer. These word vectors are then passed as inputs to the next layer.

Encoding Layer. ERNIE consists of 12 layers of bidirectional Transformer encoders. Each encoder in each layer includes two components: multi-head attention and feed forward neural network.

Output Layer. The output layer is a fully connected layer used to map the output of the encoding layer to the scores of candidate entities, we use a tanh activation function layer to map the input values to an output range of $[-1, 1]$. Output values represents the relevance between candidate entities and mentions.

3.3 Adversarial Training

In the candidate entity sorting of the model, we used adversarial training to enhance the training data. Adversarial training is a technique that improves model robustness by training it with adversarial examples. In NLP, adversarial training serves as a regularization method to enhance model generalization, and typically involves applying adversarial perturbations to the word embedding matrix, causing changes in the word vectors. Goodfellow et al. proposed a perturbation calculation method called the Fast Gradient Sign Method (FGSM) [3], and further improved it to introduce the Fast Gradient Method (FGM) [7]. For the input samples in entity linking, the formula for perturbation calculation can be written as

$$\Delta x = \epsilon \cdot \frac{\nabla_x L(\theta, x, y)}{\|\nabla_x L(\theta, x, y)\|}. \tag{3}$$

where x, y indicate the word embedding representation corresponds to the mention and the entity ID needs to be predicted.

4 Experiments

4.1 Preprocessing and Parameter Setting

The experiment uses a dataset from the NLPCC 2023 Technical Evaluation Task 6 (Chinese Few-shot and Zero-shot Entity Linking). The data is sourced from hansel, a high-quality human-annotated Chinese entity linking (EL) dataset. The training dataset consists of a total of 9,879,812 data points, including 541,058 entities. All mentions have corresponding entities. First, 10,000 data points were randomly selected from the original training set as the training set for the model, and candidate entity retrieval is performed based on the given 10,000 mentions. We employ the following methods for candidate entity retrieval.

Exact Matching. Exact matching is a string matching method that matches mentions with entity names. By constructing an inverted index table for entity names, we can quickly find the corresponding entity for a mention. The exact matching method may result in an empty candidate entity retrieval set.

Token Matching. Token matching is a method that involves tokenizing the mention to obtain a set of tokens. We constructs a token inverted index table to quickly search for entity sets corresponding to the tokens in the mention. The token matching method retrieves a larger number of entities in the retrieval set, which increases the recall rate of candidate entity retrieval in cases where the mention and entity names do not match exactly. However, it may lower the precision of candidate entity ranking.

Approximate Nearest Neighbor Matching. The ANN (Approximate Nearest Neighbor) method first encodes the entity names of each entity semantically, and uses the Locality Sensitive Hashing algorithm from the faiss library to project the entity name vectors into a 256-bit Hamming space. The candidate entity set consists of k entities that have a Hamming distance less than d and the highest similarity with the mention [5]. In the experiment, we set k to 50 and d to 3, which is a better value in our texts.

Jaro Similarity Matching. Jaro similarity is a measure used to compare the similarity between two strings. It is based on the matching of characters and the differences in their positions within the strings. Jaro similarity takes into account the number of character matches, the similarity of character order, and the differences in character positions [2]. We consider entities with the top 50 Jaro similarity as candidate entity sets.

$$Jaro\_sim = \frac{1}{3} \cdot \left(\frac{m}{l1} + \frac{m}{l2} + \frac{m - \frac{t}{2}}{m} \right) \tag{4}$$

where l1 and l2 are the lengths of the two strings, m is the number of matching characters between the two strings, and t is the number of transpositions (characters that are out of order) between the two strings. Both ANN matching method and Jaro similarity matching method require matching against the entire entity set, resulting in a high computational cost.

We encode the input text of the candidate entity ranking task using the ERNIE model. First, concatenate the mention feature text and the candidate entity feature text with [SEP] to obtain the mention-entity pair text. Then, add [CLS] and [SEP] tokens before and after the concatenated text to obtain the input text. We implemented the model based on ERNIE using the PaddlePaddle framework. During training, the text was cropped to a maximum length of 280 characters. The AdamW optimizer was used with a learning rate of 5e-5 and a batch size of 100. A linear decay learning rate was applied during the training process, gradually decreasing as the number of epochs increased. In the last epoch, the learning rate was reduced to 1e-6. To mitigate overfitting, L2 regularization was employed with a weight decay coefficient of 5e-6.

4.2 Evaluation Metrics

Entity linking (EL), as a fundamental task in NLP, is typically evaluated using precision, recall, and F1 score as the evaluation metrics.

4.3 Experimental Results

We first tested several methods for candidate entity retrieval, using the validation dataset from the Hansel dataset. The validation set consists of 9,673 data points,

Table 1. Entity Linking prediction performance of candidate entity retrieval methods using the validation dataset from Hansel

Method	F1 score
Exact Matching	0.8641
Token Matching	0.9119
ANN Matching	0.9092
Jaro Similarity Matching	0.9283

including 6,320 entities. Table 1 shows the performance of different candidate entity retrieval methods on the validation set.

As expected, the exact matching method has the worst results due to the small number of recalled entities, and the token matching method and the ANN matching method have similar effects. However, the token matching method retrievals more related entities, which takes much more time than other methods. The Jaro similarity method has the best effect, which may be due to the high character matching of entity results and mentions.

We conducted ablation experiments on adversarial training, and the results are shown in Table 2. The ERNIE model with adversarial training showed a significant improvement in F1 score compared to the ERNIE model without adversarial training. Therefore, introducing adversarial training during the training process can increase noise perturbation in the data and enhance the robustness of the model under perturbations.

Table 2. Entity Linking prediction performance of Adversarial Training for Candidate Entity Ranking using the validation dataset from Hansel

Model	F1 score
ERNIE	0.9283
ERNIE with Adversarial Training	0.9312

4.4 Analysis of Results

The final result of our model on the leaderboard is 0.6009, ranking second. Through data analysis of the given test dataset and validation dataset of NLPCC 2023 Task6, it can be seen in Table 3 that the number of mentions in the test dataset that cannot be excat matched with entity names is much larger than that in the validation dataset. This means that there is a higher similarity between the entity results and elements in the validation set, while there is a higher difference between the entity results and elements in the test set, which maximizes the impact of whether the entity results in the entity recall strategy exist in the entity recall set on the entity link results. Therefore, the effect of candidate entities retrieval has a greater impact on the prediction of entity linking by the model. This is also consistent with the fact that the entity names in the common sense knowledge base cannot cover a large number of mentions that exist in real life.

Table 3. The number of mentions in the validation dataset and the test dataset from Hansel

Dataset	Excat matched	Inexact matched	The proportion of inexact matches
Validation dataset	8555	1119	0.1157
Test dataset	3534	4466	0.5583

5 Conclusion

Entity linking is important as it associates entities in the text with entities in a knowledge base, providing support for semantic understanding, improving information retrieval, and facilitating knowledge graph construction and natural language processing tasks. In this paper, we proposed CELAT, an entity linking model that focuses on candidate entity retrieval and adversarial training. Our experiments demonstrate the effectiveness of our approach in improving the accuracy of entity linking. By leveraging advanced retrieval techniques, we achieved a higher recall rate in candidate entity retrieval, ensuring a more comprehensive coverage of potential entities. Additionally, the integration of adversarial training enhanced the model's robustness against noise and improved the precision of entity linking. The experimental results indicate that our model achieved an F1 value of 0.60 and a second place performance in NLPCC 2023 Task 6 (Chinese Few shot and Zero shot Entity Linking). Overall, our model presents a promising solution for accurate and reliable few-shot entity linking with tail and emerging entities.

Acknowledgements. This work is supported by the National Key Research and Development Program of China under Grant 2020YFB1406902 and State Key Laboratory of Communication Content Cognition, People's Daily Online (No. A12003).

References

1. Cho, Y.M., Zhang, L., Callison-Burch, C.: Unsupervised entity linking with guided summarization and multiple-choice selection. In: Goldberg, Y., Kozareva, Z., Zhang, Y. (eds.) Proceedings of the 2022 Conference on Empirical Methods in Natural Language Processing, EMNLP 2022, Abu Dhabi, United Arab Emirates, December 7–11, 2022, pp. 9394–9401. Association for Computational Linguistics (2022). https://aclanthology.org/2022.emnlp-main.638

2. Dreßler, K., Ngomo, A.N.: Time-efficient execution of bounded jaro-winkler distances. In: Shvaiko, P., Euzenat, J., Mao, M., Jiménez-Ruiz, E., Li, J., Ngonga, A. (eds.) Proceedings of the 9th International Workshop on Ontology Matching collocated with the 13th International Semantic Web Conference (ISWC 2014), Riva del Garda, Trentino, Italy, October 20, 2014. CEUR Workshop Proceedings, vol. 1317, pp. 37–48. CEUR-WS.org (2014). https://ceur-ws.org/Vol-1317/om2014_Tpaper4.pdf

3. Goodfellow, I.J., Shlens, J., Szegedy, C.: Explaining and harnessing adversarial examples. In: Bengio, Y., LeCun, Y. (eds.) 3rd International Conference on Learning Representations, ICLR 2015, San Diego, CA, USA, May 7–9, 2015, Conference Track Proceedings (2015). http://arxiv.org/abs/1412.6572

4. Johnson, J., Douze, M., Jégou, H.: Billion-scale similarity search with GPUs. CoRR abs/1702.08734 (2017). http://arxiv.org/abs/1702.08734

5. Kedzierski, A., Radoszewski, J.: k-approximate quasiperiodicity under hamming and edit distance. In: Gørtz, I.L., Weimann, O. (eds.) 31st Annual Symposium on Combinatorial Pattern Matching, CPM 2020, June 17–19, 2020, Copenhagen, Denmark. LIPIcs, vol. 161, pp. 18:1–18:15. Schloss Dagstuhl - Leibniz-Zentrum für Informatik (2020). https://doi.org/10.4230/LIPIcs.CPM.2020.18

6. Mikolov, T., Chen, K., Corrado, G., Dean, J.: Efficient estimation of word representations in vector space. In: Bengio, Y., LeCun, Y. (eds.) 1st International Conference on Learning Representations, ICLR 2013, Scottsdale, Arizona, USA, May 2–4, 2013, Workshop Track Proceedings (2013). http://arxiv.org/abs/1301.3781

7. Miyato, T., Dai, A.M., Goodfellow, I.J.: Adversarial training methods for semi-supervised text classification. In: 5th International Conference on Learning Representations, ICLR 2017, Toulon, France, April 24–26, 2017, Conference Track Proceedings. OpenReview.net (2017). https://openreview.net/forum?id=r1X3g2_xl

8. Ogita, T., Ichihashi, H., Notsu, A., Honda, K.: Improvement of PCA-based approximate nearest neighbor search using distance statistics. J. Adv. Comput. Intell. Intell. Inform. 18(4), 658–664 (2014). https://doi.org/10.20965/jaciii.2014.p0658

9. Ran, C., Shen, W., Gao, J., Li, Y., Wang, J., Jia, Y.: Learning entity linking features for emerging entities. CoRR abs/2208.03877 (2022). https://doi.org/10.48550/arXiv.2208.03877

10. Sun, Y., et al.: ERNIE: enhanced representation through knowledge integration. CoRR abs/1904.09223 (2019). http://arxiv.org/abs/1904.09223

Evaluation Workshop: Chinese Grammatical Error Correction

HWCGEC:HW-TSC's 2023 Submission for the NLPCC2023's Chinese Grammatical Error Correction Task

Chang Su[✉], Xiaofeng Zhao, Xiaosong Qiao, Min Zhang, Hao Yang,
Junhao Zhu, Ming Zhu, and Wenbing Ma

Huawei Translation Services Center, Shenzhen, China
suchang8@huawei.com

Abstract. Deep learning has shown remarkable effectiveness in various language tasks. This paper presents Huawei Translation Services Center's (HW-TSC's) work called HWCGEC which get the best performance among the seven submitted results in the NLPCC2023 shared task 1, namely Chinese grammatical error correction (CGEC). CGEC aims to automatically correct grammatical errors that violate language rules and converts the noisy input texts to clean output texts. This paper, through experiments, discovered that after model fine-tuning the BART a sequence to sequence (seq2seq) model performs better than the ChatGLM a large language model (LLM) in situations where training data is large while the LoRA mode has a smaller number of parameters for fine-tuning. Additionally, the BART model achieves good results in the CGEC task through data augmentation and curriculum learning methods. Although the performance of LLM is poor in experiments, they possess excellent logical abilities. With the training set becoming more diverse and the methods for training set data augmentation becoming more refined, the supervised fine-tuning (SFT) mode trained LLMs are expected to achieve significant improvements in CGEC tasks in the future.

Keywords: Natural Language Generation · Pre-trained Language Model · Grammatical Error Correction · Text Editing System

1 Introduction

Given a potentially noisy input sentence, grammatical error correction (GEC) aims to remove all underlying textual errors in a given sentence without changing its meaning [2]. Chinese Grammatical Error Correction (CGEC) aims to automatically correct grammatical errors that violate language rules and converts the noisy input texts to clean output texts. In recent years, CGEC has attracted more and more attention from NLP researchers due to its broader applications in all kinds of daily scenarios and downstream tasks [5,9].

NLPCC2023's task1, which is a Chinese Grammatical Error Correction (CGEC) task. In CGEC task, the widely used benchmarks are derived from the grammatical errors made by foreign Chinese learners (i.e., L2 learners). The gap

F. Liu et al. (Eds.): NLPCC 2023, LNAI 14304, pp. 59–68, 2023.
https://doi.org/10.1007/978-3-031-44699-3_6

between the language usage habits of L2 learners and Chinese native speakers makes the performance of the CGEC models in real scenarios unpredictable. This task focuses on correcting grammatical errors made by Chinese native speakers, which will be a challenging benchmark and a meaningful resource to facilitate further development of CGEC.

2   Related Work

With the progress of deep learning, data-driven methods based on neural networks, e.g., transformer [14], have become the mainstream for CGEC [6,13,19,22]. However, owing to the limited number of real sentences containing grammatical errors, the long-term lack of highquality annotated training corpora hinders many data-driven models from exercising their capabilities on the CGEC task. For Chinese GEC (CGEC), datasets are relatively scarce. The two publicly available CGEC evaluation datasets are NLPCC18 and CGED, contributed by the [21] and the series of CGED shared tasks [10], respectively.

For model evaluation, the widely used benchmarks such as NLPCC [21] and CGED [10,11] are all derived from the grammatical errors made by foreign Chinese learners (i.e., L2 learners) in their process of learning Chinese, the gap between the language usage habits of L2 learners and Chinese native speakers makes the performance of the CGEC models in real scenarios unpredictable. Besides, sentences in existing CGEC evaluation datasets usually have only one reference (i.e., 87% of the sentences inNLPCC18 and all in CGED). The model performance will be unfairly underestimated. There is great demand for correcting errors made by native speakers. For CGEC, such research has just begun. CCTC [15] is the first native CGEC dataset composed of web documents written by natives. Paper [17] collects sentences from the questions in Chinese examinations. Another work, [3,12] increase the number of references.

3   Data Description

3.1   Schema Definition

According to the authoritative linguistic papers [1,7], Chinese grammatical errors are categorized into 7 types: Structural Confusion, Improper Logicality, Missing Component, Redundant Component, Improper Collocation, Improper Word Order and Ambiguity. It is important to note that ambiguity errors are frequently caused by a lack of contextual information. six types grammatical errors are described as follows:

1. **Structural Confusion** refers to the mixing of two or more different syntactic structures within a single sentence, leading to a confusing sentence structure.
2. **Improper Logicality** signifies the inconsistency or lack of adherence to objective reasoning in the meaning of a sentence.
3. **Missing Component** indicates an incomplete sentence structure where certain grammatical components are absent.

4. **Redundant Component** refers to the unnecessary addition of words or phrases to a well-structured sentence.
5. **Improper Collocation** occurs when the collocation between sentence components violates the structural rules or grammatical conventions of Chinese.
6. **Improper Word Order** primarily refers to the ungrammatical arrangement of words or clauses within a sentence.

3.2   Training Set

The evaluation task provided some data sets, and we also utilized other Chinese monolingual data sets.

Lang8 [21] is a language learning platform, where native speakers voluntarily correct texts written by second-language learners. The NLPCC-2023 shared task organizers collect about 717K Chinese sentences with their corrections from Lang8 and encourage participants to use them as the training data.

HSK Dynamic Composition Corpus [18] has collected about 156K Chinese sentence pairs is a corpus of answers for foreign non-Chinese native speakers to take the higher Chinese proficiency test (HSK) composition exam. It collects the essay answers of some foreign candidates from 1992–2005. The corpus version 1.0 contains 10740 corpus articles, about 4 million words, and went live in December 2006. In July 2008, after revision and supplementation, the total number of corpus of version 1.1 reached 11569, with a total of 4.24 million words.

MuCGEC [19] is a multireference multi-source evaluation dataset for Chinese Grammatical Error Correction (CGEC), consisting of 7,063 sentences collected from three Chinese-as-a-Second-Language (CSL) learner sources. Each sentence is corrected by three annotators, and their corrections are carefully reviewed by a senior annotator, resulting in 2.3 references per sentence.

CGED [10,11] is the training data released by the Chinese Grammatical Error Diagnosis (CGED) evaluation task since the first CGED task was held in NLPCC2014. This data is for free use only for technical evaluation, academic research and public welfare goals.

News Crawl [16] is WMT2022 general MT task's monolingual training data, which updated large corpora of crawled news, collected since 2007. After using chinese grammatical error data generation method, we can generate CGEC pseudo-parallel data for model training.

4   Methodology

In this section, we will introduce the specific details of the system's method. We employ the mainstream seq2seq model in all experiments. We attempt two training approaches, namely the Encode-Decoder model and the Decoder-only model, and established two sets of experimental procedures.

4.1   Encoder-Decoder Model

The Encoder-Decoder model is based on the BART pre-training model, and its basic module is transformer, a model based on encoder and decoder. Its

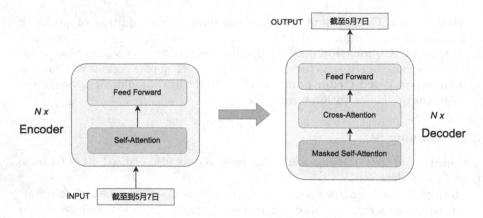

Fig. 1. Encoder-Decoder Model

structure is shown in the figure. Each Encoder module includes a Multi-Head Self-Attention layer and Feed Forward layer, and each Decoder includes a Masked Multi-Head Self-Attention layer, Multi-Head Cross-Attention layer and Feed Forward layer(Figs. 1 and 2)).

In the process of training the BART model, we used the training code of SynGEC, we only used stage 1, and did not train the GEC-Oriented Parser. Therefore, the BART model only relies on the understanding and learning of the training corpus to generate results, without incorporating syntactic information.

4.2 Decoder Only Model

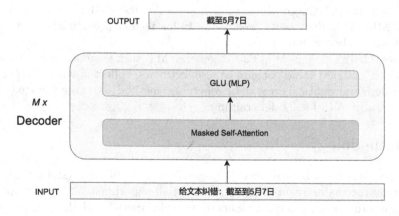

Fig. 2. Decoder Model

The Decoder model uses a chat language model based on ChatGLM-6B which based on many GLMBlocks. A GLMBlock can be regarded as a Decoder module.

A GLMBlock consists of a Multi-Head Self-Attention layer and a GLU layer. On the basis of pre-training, ChatGLM-6B also uses human intent alignment training, including Supervised Fine-Tuning, Feedback Bootstrap, Reinforcement Learning from Human Feedback, and performs well in Chinese understanding and generation.

We use the LoRA method to fine-tune ChatGLM. For details, please see [4]. LoRA is a training method that accelerates the training of large models while consuming less memory. It adds pairs of rank-decomposition weight matrices to existing weights, and only trains those newly added weights. We use PEFT [8] to add the LoRA matrix to the attention layer of the original model to obtain the fine-tuned Decode model.

4.3 Distantly Supervised Data Augmentation

We think there is a need to do data augmentation after observing training data and development data because we find that the sentence length and grammatical Error types are strongly different. The model will not perform very well when encountering a grammatical error if the model has never seen any similar types of errors during training.

We use two distantly supervised methods to augment data. One is to transform the correct sentences, for instance, using rules to generate some wrong sentences as pseudo training data, which is similar to Zhang's paper [20].

The other is a method proposed by us. We extract the type of errors that occur less frequently in the training set, especially errors related to conjunctions and prepositions. Then we use conjunctions and prepositions as keywords, retrieve the training set containing keywords from the training set, and manually modify them into corresponding error types. For details, you can see experiment.

5 Experiment

In this section, we will introduce the specific details of our experiment.

5.1 Setup

The basic settings of the experiment are as follows:

Model. Our benchmark models are based on the BART and ChatGLM. For BART, it is a pre-trained Encoder-Decoder seq2seq model that has recently achieved SOTA performance on mainstream CGEC datasets. For ChatGLM, it is a decoder-only auto-regressive large language model.

Baseline. We select Zhang's [19] real learner bart CGEC model[1] which has SOTA performance in multi-domain Chinese grammatical error correction as our baseline.

---

[1] https://github.com/HillZhang1999/NaSGEC.

Evaluation Metric. We use the character-based metric proposed by Zhang [19]. It is a consensus that a good model should correct errors accurately to ensure a positive user experience. Therefore, we use $F_{0.5}$ to place more emphasis on precision by weighting precision twice as recall. The evaluation metric can be described as follows:

1. Align the model's output and reference with the input sentence to extract two groups of character-based edits.
2. Merges them into spans based on rules.
3. Compares them to calculate the precision (P), recall (R), and $F_{0.5}$ score.

$$F_{0.5} = (1 + \alpha^2) \cdot \frac{precision \cdot recall}{\alpha^2 \cdot precision + recall}; \alpha = 0.5 \qquad (1)$$

5.2   Training Data

We use three kinds of data to train our models.

NLPCC2023's Training Data. We select 500k sentence pairs from the Lang8 data set, 100k sentence pairs from the HSK data set randomly, and select all of the sentence pairs from the MuCGEC data set.

Pseudo Training Data. We select 100k Chinese news sentences randomly from News Crawl mentioned in Sect. 3 and use a method called linguistic rules-based corpus generation which proposed by Ma [7] to generate 600k sentence pairs (a grammatical error sentence and a correct sentence).

Artificially Constructed Training Data. We select 100 Chinese sentences from HSK set and change them into one of six grammatical error types mentioned in Sect. 3 grammatical error sentences artificially.

5.3   Development Data

We find that there is a large gap between the training set and the development set. To compare our models more sufficiently, we select two kinds of development data to test our models' performance.

NLPCC2023's Development Data. The NLPCC2023 provides 500 CGEC sentence pairs of development data.

Self-collected Development Data. We select 100 CGEC sentence pairs from the ungrammatical sentence judgment questions in Chinese examinations. Those questions ask students to choose 1–3 ungrammatical sentences from 4 candidates. We get them from the website[2] and make the sentence pairs artificially.

---

[2] https://tiku.baidu.com.

5.4 Training Steps

We finetune BART and ChatGLM on different training data and compare the models' performance of different training stages.

Stage 1. Fine-tune the BART and the ChatGLM models on the NLPCC2023's training data. At the end of the training, we get the BART-FT1 and the ChatGLM-FT1 models.

Stage 2. Fine-tune the BART-FT1 model on the pseudo training data. As the ChatGLM-FT1's performance does not exceed the baseline, we are not going to continue fine-tuning the ChatGLM-FT1. At the end of the training, we get the BART-FT2 model.

Stage 3. Fine-tune the BART-FT2 model on the artificially constructed training data. At the end of the training, we get the BART-FT3 model.

5.5 Experimental Results

We compare the performance of these trained models according to the experiment procedure, and the performance on NLPCC2023's development data shown in the Table 1 can prove that the training data at different stages are valid. The baseline model's performance is not as high as described in the Zhang's paper [20]. It should be due to a large gap between the NLPCC2023's development set and the test set in the paper [20]. The ChatGLM basically can't handle CGEC tasks, this model can't understand Chinese grammatical error. As limited competition time and training resources, we use the fine-tune mode of LoRA to train ChatGLM with simple prompts. Even with the fine-tuning of the training data, it can't have a nice performance compared with the baseline model. This may be due to the fact that we are using the fine-tune mode of LoRA, which has a smaller number of parameters for fine-tuning. When the training data is large, the training performance of the model is poorer. Alternatively, it could be due to the overly simplistic design of the prompts. Therefore, it is crucial to focus on exploring these factors in the future. However, the BART-based baseline model's performance can be improved after stage 1 fine-tuning. So, we won't fine-tune the ChatGLM-based model in the next stages. Compared these BART-FT1, BART-FT2, and BART-FT3 models, with adding different c to the model training process, the performance of the models is improved gradually.

Obviously, the model's performance on the two development sets differs greatly, shown in the Table 1 and 2. This indicates that the GAP of the training set is different from that of the different development sets. However, the performance of the four models (Baseline, BART-FT1, BART-FT2, and BART-FT3) shows that the training data is valid. Constructing a better training set containing more types of Chinese grammatical errors, which is great helpful to improve the ability of solving CGEC task. So, we will focus on the training set augmentation in the future.

66   C. Su et al.

Table 1. The performance of each model on the NLPCC2023's development data.

Model	precision	recall	$F_{0.5}$
Baseline	0.3656	0.2429	0.3320
ChatGLM	0.0829	0.0791	0.1022
ChatGLM-FT1	0.2312	0.1773	0.2180
BART-FT1	0.3825	0.4375	0.2545
BART-FT2	0.5928	0.6120	0.5268
BART-FT3	**0.6823**	**0.6978**	**0.6268**

Finally, on the test set of the NLPCC2023's CGEC task, BART-FT3 get 0.5095 *precision* score, 0.3129 *recall* score and 0.4526 $F_{0.5}$ score[3], get the best performance among the seven submitted results.

Table 2. The performance of each model on the self-collected development data.

Model	precision	recall	$F_{0.5}$
Baseline	0.5177	0.5775	0.3661
ChatGLM	0.0892	0.0908	0.0832
ChatGLM-FT1	0.1501	0.1431	0.1863
BART-FT1	0.5542	0.6026	0.4196
BART-FT2	0.6851	0.6971	0.6411
BART-FT3	**0.7326**	**0.7339**	**0.7273**

6   Conclusion

This paper presents a system named HWCGEC to tackle the problem of Chinese grammatical error correction. We compared two types of seq2seq auto-regressive decoding models, one is a Encode-Decoder model called BART, the other is a Decoder-only large language model called ChatGLM. In the experiment, we find that compared with the model structure, the impact of the data domain similarity is obvious. Using CGEC data augmentation method, we generate a batch of training data rich in grammatical error types. According to the curriculum learning, we train the BART-based model in three stages, and at last, the model works well. Due to limitations in time and training resources, as well as the simplicity of our prompt design, fully experiment with the large language model is scarce. However, we believe that the large language model will work better, although it does not have a nice performance in our experiments.

[3] https://github.com/masr2000/NaCGEC.

References

1. Borong, H., Xudong, L.: Modern Chinese (updated five editions) (2011)
2. Bryant, C., Yuan, Z., Qorib, M.R., Cao, H., Ng, H.T., Briscoe, T.: Grammatical error correction: a survey of the state of the art. arXiv preprint arXiv:2211.05166 (2022)
3. Choshen, L., Abend, O.: Inherent biases in reference based evaluation for grammatical error correction and text simplification. arXiv preprint arXiv:1804.11254 (2018)
4. Hu, E.J., et al.: LoRA: low-rank adaptation of large language models. arXiv preprint arXiv:2106.09685 (2021)
5. Kubis, M., Vetulani, Z., Wypych, M., Zietkiewicz, T.: Open challenge for correcting errors of speech recognition systems. In: Vetulani, Z., Paroubek, P., Kubis, M. (eds.) Human Language Technology. Challenges for Computer Science and Linguistics - 9th Language and Technology Conference, LTC 2019, Poznan, Poland, May 17–19, 2019, Revised Selected Papers. Lecture Notes in Computer Science, vol. 13212, pp. 322–337. Springer (2019). https://doi.org/10.1007/978-3-031-05328-3_21
6. Li, J., et al.: Sequence-to-action: grammatical error correction with action guided sequence generation (2022)
7. Ma, S., et al.: Linguistic rules-based corpus generation for native Chinese grammatical error correction. arXiv preprint arXiv:2210.10442 (2022)
8. Mangrulkar, S., Gugger, S., Debut, L., Belkada, Y., Paul, S.: PEFT: state-of-the-art parameter-efficient fine-tuning methods (2022). https://github.com/huggingface/peft
9. Omelianchuk, K., Atrasevych, V., Chernodub, A., Skurzhanskyi, O.: GECToR - grammatical error correction: tag, not rewrite. In: Proceedings of the Fifteenth Workshop on Innovative Use of NLP for Building Educational Applications. pp. 163–170. Association for Computational Linguistics, Seattle, WA, USA Online (2020). https://doi.org/10.18653/v1/2020.bea-1.16, https://aclanthology.org/2020.bea-1.16
10. Rao, G., Gong, Q., Zhang, B., Xun, E.: Overview of NLPTEA-2018 share task Chinese grammatical error diagnosis. In: Proceedings of the 5th Workshop on Natural Language Processing Techniques for Educational Applications, pp. 42–51 (2018)
11. Rao, G., Yang, E., Zhang, B.: Overview of NLPTEA-2020 shared task for Chinese grammatical error diagnosis. In: Proceedings of the 6th Workshop on Natural Language Processing Techniques for Educational Applications, pp. 25–35 (2020)
12. Sakaguchi, K., Napoles, C., Post, M., Tetreault, J.: Reassessing the goals of grammatical error correction: fluency instead of grammaticality. Trans. Assoc. Comput. Linguist. 4, 169–182 (2016)
13. Tang, Z., Ji, Y., Zhao, Y., Li, J.: Chinese grammatical error correction enhanced by data augmentation from word and character levels. In: Proceedings of the 20th Chinese National Conference on Computational Linguistics, Hohhot, China, pp. 13–15 (2021)
14. Vaswani, A., et al.: Attention is all you need. In: Advances in Neural Information Processing Systems, vol. 30 (2017)
15. Wang, B., Duan, X., Wu, D., Che, W., Chen, Z., Hu, G.: CCTC: a cross-sentence Chinese text correction dataset for native speakers. In: Proceedings of the 29th International Conference on Computational Linguistics, pp. 3331–3341 (2022)
16. Weller-Di Marco, M., Fraser, A.: Findings of the WMT 2022 shared tasks in unsupervised MT and very low resource supervised MT. In: Proceedings of the Seventh Conference on Machine Translation (WMT), pp. 801–805 (2022)

17. Xu, L., Wu, J., Peng, J., Fu, J., Cai, M.: FCGEC: fine-grained corpus for Chinese grammatical error correction. arXiv preprint arXiv:2210.12364 (2022)
18. Zhang, B.: The characteristics and functions of the HSK dynamic composition corpus. Int. Chin. Lang. Educ. 4(11) (2009)
19. Zhang, Y., et al.: MuCGEC: a multi-reference multi-source evaluation dataset for Chinese grammatical error correction (2022)
20. Zhang, Y., et al.: NaSGEC: a multi-domain Chinese grammatical error correction dataset from native speaker texts. arXiv preprint arXiv:2305.16023 (2023)
21. Zhao, Y., Jiang, N., Sun, W., Wan, X.: Overview of the NLPCC 2018 shared task: grammatical error correction. In: Zhang, M., Ng, V., Zhao, D., Li, S., Zan, H. (eds.) NLPCC 2018. LNCS (LNAI), vol. 11109, pp. 439–445. Springer, Cham (2018). https://doi.org/10.1007/978-3-319-99501-4_41
22. Zhao, Z., Wang, H.: MaskGEC: improving neural grammatical error correction via dynamic masking. In: Proceedings of the AAAI Conference on Artificial Intelligence, vol. 34, pp. 1226–1233 (2020)

GrammarGPT: Exploring Open-Source LLMs for Native Chinese Grammatical Error Correction with Supervised Fine-Tuning

Yaxin Fan[1,2,3], Feng Jiang[1,3,4(✉)], Peifeng Li[2], and Haizhou Li[1,3]

[1] School of Data Science, The Chinese University of Hong Kong, Shenzhen, China
yxfansuda@stu.suda.edu.cn, haizhouli@cuhk.edu.cn
[2] School of Computer Science and Technology, Soochow University, Suzhou, China
pfli@suda.edu.cn
[3] Shenzhen Research Institute of Big Data, Shenzhen, Guangdong, China
[4] School of Information Science and Technology, University of Science and
Technology of China, Hefei, China
jeffreyjiang@cuhk.edu.cn

Abstract. Grammatical error correction aims to correct ungrammatical sentences automatically. Recently, some work has demonstrated the excellent capabilities of closed-source Large Language Models (LLMs, e.g., ChatGPT) in grammatical error correction. However, the potential of open-source LLMs remains unexplored. In this paper, we introduced GrammarGPT, an open-source LLM, to preliminary explore its potential for native Chinese grammatical error correction. The core recipe of GrammarGPT is to leverage the hybrid dataset of ChatGPT-generated and human-annotated. For grammatical errors with clues, we proposed a heuristic method to guide ChatGPT to generate ungrammatical sentences by providing those clues. For grammatical errors without clues, we collected ungrammatical sentences from publicly available websites and manually corrected them. In addition, we employed an error-invariant augmentation method to enhance the ability of the model to correct native Chinese grammatical errors. We ultimately constructed about 1k parallel data and utilized these data to fine-tune open-source LLMs (e.g., Phoenix, released by The Chinese University of Hong Kong, Shenzhen) with instruction tuning. The experimental results show that GrammarGPT outperforms the existing SOTA system significantly. Although model parameters are 20x larger than the SOTA baseline, the required amount of data for instruction tuning is 1200x smaller, illustrating the potential of open-source LLMs on native CGEC. Our GrammarGPT ranks 3rd on NLPCC2023 SharedTask1, demonstrating our approach's effectiveness. The code and data are available at https://github.com/FreedomIntelligence/GrammarGPT.

Keywords: Native Chinese grammatical error correction · Large language models · ChatGPT · Instruction tuning

F. Liu et al. (Eds.): NLPCC 2023, LNAI 14304, pp. 69–80, 2023.
https://doi.org/10.1007/978-3-031-44699-3_7

1 Introduction

Grammatical Error Correction (GEC) aims to automatically correct ungrammatical sentences without changing their meaning [10,26,27]. Previous works [13,14,26,28] in Chinese Grammatical Error Correction (CGEC) mainly study the errors from foreign Chinese learners, which are very obvious and naive. Therefore, recent works [10,27] shift to the grammatical errors made by native speakers, which are more subtle and challenging. Table 1 shows the six main types of grammatical errors made by native speakers, which can be divided into two types, e.g., with (w/) and without (w/o) clues. We can find that the incorrect sentences are fluent and in line with the habits of native Chinese. However, they do not conform to Chinese grammar, which is more difficult to correct.

Previous studies in GEC mainly adopted both Seq2edit [5,9,10,26] and Seq2seq [7,15,29] paradigms and have achieved impressive performance on various GEC benchmarks. With the emergence of LLMs, Fang et al. [4] evaluated the performance of closed-source LLMs (e.g., ChatGPT[1]) on GEC and revealed its excellent capabilities for error detection and correction. However, the potential of open-source LLMs remains unexplored.

In this paper, we introduce GrammarGPT, a novel model for studying the potential of open-source LLMs architectures in addressing Native Chinese Grammatical Error Correction (CGEC) through supervised fine-tuning. The key challenge in fine-tuning LLMs for CGEC is obtaining high-quality parallel data comprising grammatical errors made by native speakers. However, manually annotating such data is not only time-consuming but also expensive, necessitating the exploration of automatic data annotation methods. Recent works [22,25] have successfully leveraged distilled data from ChatGPT and real-world datasets to fine-tune LLMs for specific domains, effectively reducing costs while achieving superior performance. Inspired by this line of research, we propose a hybrid dataset that incorporates different types of native Chinese grammatical errors.

Specifically, we first proposed a heuristic method for the grammatical errors with clues as shown in Fig. 1 that guides ChatGPT to generate ungrammatical sentences by providing those clues. Then, for those errors without clues, we collected the ungrammatical sentences from the public website and corrected them manually. In addition, we proposed an error-invariant data augmentation method to enhance the diversity of the data by substituting the named entities in parallel data with similar ones, which can improve the ability of the model to correct native Chinese grammatical errors. We ultimately constructed 1k parallel data and utilized these data to fine-tune LLMs with instruction tuning. The experimental results show that GrammarGPT can significantly outperform state-of-the-art (SOTA) systems. Although the size of model parameters is 20x larger than the SOTA baseline, the data for fine-tuning is 1200x smaller, which demonstrated the potential of open-source LLMs on Chinese grammatical error correction.

---

[1] https://chat.openai.com/.

Table 1. Examples of sentences with various types of grammatical errors. For those errors with clues, we can easily detect and correct them. For example, the co-occurrence of (*more than*) and (*about*) lead to redundant component error and we can remove one of them to make the sentence conform to Chinese grammar. However, for those errors without clues, a deeper understanding of Chinese grammar is required to detect and correct.

w/ Clues	Redundant Component (RC)	**Incorrect:** The population of this satellite city is estimated to be more than about one million. **Correct:** The population of this satellite city is estimated to be over one million.
	Structural Confusion (SC)	**Incorrect:** The cause of this network failure is caused by the server failure. **Correct:** The cause of the network failure is the server failure.
	Improper Collocation (IC)	**Incorrect:** Xihu District is promoting the pace of integration of regional industry and city development. **Correct:** Xihu District is accelerating the pace of integration of regional industry and city development.
w/o Clues	Improper Word Order (IWO)	**Incorrect::** 20 The school in three months requires each student to complete 20 hours of volunteer service. **Correct:** 20 The school requires each student to complete 20 hours of volunteer service in three months.
	Improper Logicality (IL)	**Incorrect:** The group apologizes to people from all walks of life and villagers along the way. **Correct:** The group apologizes to people from all walks of life.
	Missing Component (MC)	**Incorrect:** (...) The report accused man of destroying nature. **Correct:** The report accused man the crime of destroying nature.

Our contributions are as follows:

- To the best of our knowledge, we are the first to explore the potential of open-source LLMs with instruction tuning for native Chinese grammatical error correction.
- We have constructed a hybrid dataset generated by ChatGPT and manual annotation, which can effectively cover native Chinese grammatical errors for taming the LLMs into an excellent grammar detector.
- We designed an error-invariant data augmentation method to substitute the named entities in parallel data with similar ones, making the model more accurate in correcting grammatical errors.
- The experimental results show that GrammarGPT can outperform the SOTA system significantly, and the data size for instruction tuning is only 1/1200 of the SOTA system.

2   Related Work

2.1   Grammatical Error Correction

The works in grammatical error correction can be divided into two paradigms: the Seq2edit paradigm and the Seq2seq paradigm.

Seq2edit Paradigm. Seq2edit paradigm aims to predict the modification label, including insertion, deletion, and substitution, for each position of the sentence iteratively. Hinson et al. [5] proposed a heterogeneous approach to CGEC, composed of a NMT-based model, a sequence editing model, and a spell checker. Liang et al. [9] introduced and transferred the BERT-fused NMT model and sequence tagging model into the CGEC field. Zhang et al. [26] proposed a multi-reference multi-source evaluation dataset for CGEC and adopted the seq2edit method that enhanced with large pre-trained language models. Ma et al. [10] propose a linguistic rules-based approach to construct large-scale CGEC training corpora with automatically generated grammatical errors and adopt the seq2edit method for evaluation.

Seq2seq Paradigm. This paradigm treats CGEC as a monolingual translation task. Katsumata and Komachi [7] explored the utility of bidirectional and auto-regressive transformers (BART) as a generic pre-trained encoder-decoder model for GEC. Zhao and Wang [29] proposed a simple yet effective method to improve the NMT-based GEC models by dynamic masking, which can generate more diverse instances to enhance model generalization. Rothe et al. [15] proposed a language-agnostic method to generate a large number of synthetic examples, and then fine-tune large-scale multilingual language models.

In addition, several works [5,8,9,26] observe the complementary power of the above two paradigms, thus promoting the performance through the model ensemble. In this paper, we adopt the Se2seq paradigm to fine-tune LLMs with instruction tuning.

2.2   Instruction Tuning for LLMs

Instruction tuning [16,21] can improve the ability of model generalization by learning from a large number of tasks guided by instruction, which has been successfully applied to fine-tune LLMs on some specific tasks. The work on task-specific instruction tuning can be categorized into three types by data sources: ChatGPT-generated, human-annotated, and hybrid dataset of ChatGPT and human.

ChatGPT-generated Data. Several works adopted the data generated by ChatGPT to fine-tune LLMs in the form of instructions. Ho et al. [6] proposed Fine-tune-CoT, a method that generates reasoning samples from LLMS to fine-tune smaller models, which enables substantial reasoning capability of small models. Wang et al. [19] proposed SCOTT, a faithful knowledge distillation method to

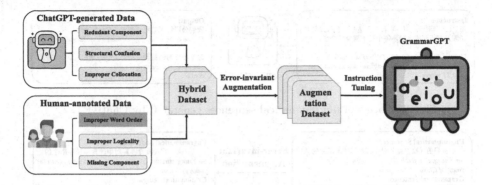

Fig. 1. The framework of our method.

learn a small, self-consistent CoT model from a teacher model that is orders of magnitude. Chen et al. [1] explored distilling the reasoning ability of LLMs into a more compact student model for multimodal named entity and multimodal relation extraction. Chen et al. [1] proposed a data synthesis framework built upon the data generation functions parameterized by LLMs and prompts and used synthesized data to fine-tune LLaMA.

Human-annotated Data. Some works directly convert the supervised data into the format of instructions to fine-tune LLMs. Zhang et al. [24] proposed to fine-tune LLaMA [18] on financial sentiment analysis with a small portion of supervised financial sentiment analysis data. Wang et al. [20] proposed a unified information extraction framework based on instruction tuning to model various information extraction tasks and capture the inter-task dependency.

Hybrid Dataset of ChatGPT and Human. Recently, some works utilized the hybrid data of humans and ChatGPT/GPT-4 to fine-tune LLMs. Zhang et al. [25] proposed to leverage both distilled data from ChatGPT and real-world data from doctors to fine-tune Bloom [17]. Yu et al. [22] adopted a hybrid data of Chinese education and general-domain instructions [12] generated by GPT-4 to fine-tune LLaMA [18]. In this paper, we follow this line and fine-tune LLMs on native CGEC with the hybrid dataset of ChatGPT-generated and human-annotated with instruction tuning.

3   Methods

Fig. 1 illustrates the framework of our method, which involves the construction of parallel data comprising six types of native Chinese grammatical errors to facilitate the fine-tuning of open-source Language Model (LLMs). While human-annotated data offer high-quality samples, the associated high cost remains a significant concern. To address this, we adopt a compromise approach. We first guide ChatGPT to generate ungrammatical sentences with clues by providing

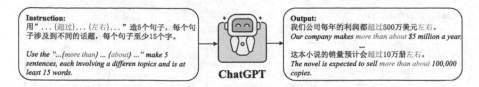

Fig. 2. Process of ungrammatical sentences generated by ChatGPT.

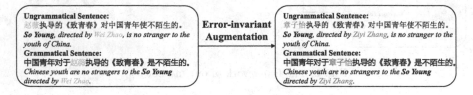

Fig. 3. An example of error-invariant augmentation.

those clues collected from the Internet. Then, we annotate the ungrammatical sentences without clues collected from the Internet. Additionally, we propose an error-invariant augmentation technique to substitute named entities in the parallel data with similar ones, further enhancing the model's capability to correct native Chinese grammatical errors. Finally, we convert the parallel data into instructions, which are then utilized for fine-tuning LLMs. Detailed explanations of these steps are provided in the following subsections.

3.1   Hybrid Dataset Construction

ChatGPT-generated Data. As shown in the first lines of Table 1, the grammatical errors with clues are easy to detect and correct by recognizing the specific clues. For example, *"more than"* and *"about"* are used together leading to **redundant component**, *"The cause"* and *"caused by"* are used together leading to **structural confusion**, and *"prompting"* and *"pace"* are used together leading to **improper collocation**. Conversely, we can construct the ungrammatical sentences by inserting these cues into grammatical sentences. Thanks to the strong capabilities of ChatGPT, we can instruct ChatGPT to generate the ungrammatical sentences that meet our requirements by providing these clues collected from public websites[2]. An example is as shown in Fig. 2.

Human-annotated Data. Some types of native ungrammatical errors are hard to recognize, as shown in the last three lines of Table 1. We can find that those ungrammatical sentences are fluent and with no obvious clues of grammatical errors can help us to recognize them. For these types of grammatical errors, we mainly collected ungrammatical sentences from publicly available websites[3] and then manually annotated them.

---

[2] https://wenku.baidu.com.
[3] https://tiku.baidu.com/.

Table 2. Components of an instruction.

Instruction	{Task Suffix} Human:{Task Description} {Input} Assistant :{Output}
Task Suffix	A chat between a curious human and an artificial intelligence assistant. The assistant gives helpful, detailed, and polite answers to the human's questions
Task Description	Evaluate this sentence for grammar mistake
Input	*Ungrammatical sentence*
Output	*Grammatical sentence*

Table 3. Statistic of the dataset.

Dataset	Number	Percentage of Different Grammatical Errors (%)					
		ChatGPT-generated			Human-annotated		
		RC	SC	IC	IWO	IL	MC
training set	1061	23.54	28.25	13.70	6.50	13.18	15.07
validating set	500	–	–	–	–	–	–

3.2 Error-invariant Data Augmentation

To prioritize the model's focus on native grammar errors and improve its robustness, we have devised an error-invariant augmentation method, as shown in Fig. 3. Native Chinese grammatical errors are often subtle and infrequently found in the position of named entities. To address this, we adopt a strategy of substituting the named entities in the parallel data with similar ones[4]. By employing this augmentation method, the model can concentrate on identifying unchanged errors rather than specific nouns, thereby improving its performance in correcting subtle and imperceptible grammar errors.

3.3 Instruction Tuning

Instruction tuning [16,21] has emerged as the mainstream approach for fine-tuning LLMs by providing explicit instructions to enhance model comprehension. In this paper, we followed this mainstream trend and fine-tuned LLMs with instruction tuning. Instruction details are as shown in Table 2, which mainly consists of four components.

1. **Task suffix**: This component guides LLMs to assume the role of an AI assistant.
2. **Task description**: Here, the specific task that LLMs are required to accomplish is outlined.

---

[4] https://github.com/chatopera/Synonyms

3. **Input**: This corresponds to ungrammatical sentences that are used as input during the fine-tuning process.
4. **Output**: This represents grammatical sentences, which serve as the expected output during fine-tuning.

Table 4. Details of hyper-parameters.

Backbone	phoenix-inst-chat-7b
Max length	256
Optimizer	AdamW
Batch size	64
Epoch	1
Learning rate	2e–5
Lr schedule type	Linear
Warmup steps	5

4 Experiments

4.1 Datasets

We constructed a total of 1061 parallel data samples for training, and the data statistics are provided in Table 3. Roughly 35% of the data were manually annotated, while the remaining 65% were generated using ChatGPT. To evaluate the performance of our model, we utilized the validating set available on the NLPCC2023 SharedTask1 website[5], which consists of 500 parallel data samples. We report the model's performance on this validating set for all the experiments conducted.

4.2 Metrics

The evaluation of a grammatical error correction system relies on the extent to which its proposed corrections or edits align with the gold-standard edits [11]. In line with previous research [10,26], we adopt the word-level and char-level MaxMatch (M2) Scorer [3] for evaluation[6]. This scorer computes Precision, Recall, and $F_{0.5}$ scores, comparing the gold edit set with the system edit set.

4.3 Hyper-parameters

The models are implemented in PyTorch using the Huggingface Transformers[7]. We used phoenix-inst-chat-7b[8] [2] as the backbone. We set the max sequence

---

[5] https://github.com/masr2000/NaCGEC.
[6] https://github.com/HillZhang1999/MuCGEC/tree/main/scorers/ChERRANT.
[7] https://huggingface.co/.
[8] https://huggingface.co/FreedomIntelligence/phoenix-inst-chat-7b.

length to 256. The model is trained with the AdamW optimizer, where the batch size and epoch are set to 64 and 3, respectively. We set the learning rate and the schedule type of learning rate to 2e-5 and 'linear', respectively. The warmup step is set to 5. The hyper-parameters are shown in Table 4.

Table 5. Performance comparison between GrammarGPT and the SOTA baseline.

Model	#Param.	Data	Data size	Word-level			Char-level		
				Prec	Rec	$F_{0.5}$	Prec	Rec	$F_{0.5}$
S2S_BART	375M	Lang8 HSK	1.2M	22.31	10.14	17.99	22.13	9.66	17.59
S2S_BART	375M	Ours	1061	21.08	10.54	17.57	22.09	10.62	18.16
GrammarGPT	7B	Ours	1061	**42.42**	**16.87**	**32.56**	**46.67**	**18.58**	**35.84**

Table 6. Ablation study of our method.

Data		Word-level			Char-level		
		Prec	Rec	$F_{0.5}$	Prec	Rec	$F_{0.5}$
w/o Augmentation	human-annotated	12.20	1.51	5.04	13.89	1.48	5.19
	ChatGPT-generated	30.38	7.21	18.49	30.86	7.35	18.83
	Hybrid dataset	41.76	11.45	27.30	44.32	11.50	28.22
w/ Augmentation	human-annotated	15.46	4.52	10.42	16.48	4.44	10.68
	ChatGPT-generated	43.75	6.33	20.04	44.90	6.49	20.56
	Hybrid dataset	42.42	16.87	32.56	46.87	18.58	35.84

4.4 Experimental Results

To validate the effectiveness of our method, we conducted a comparison between our GrammarGPT and the state-of-the-art (SOTA) baseline, S2S_BART [26]. S2S_BART utilizes Chinese BART as the pre-trained model and fine-tunes it on the Lang8 [28] and HSK [23] datasets, which consist of approximately 1.2 million parallel data samples. We also fine-tuned S2S_BART on the hybrid dataset that we constructed, and the results are presented in Table 5.

Remarkably, we observed that S2S_BART trained on our 1k hybrid dataset achieved 17.57 and 18.16 $F_{0.5}$ on Word-level and Char-level separately, which is comparable to that baseline model using the 1.2M data from foreign language speakers. We attribute this to the significant discrepancy between the grammatical errors made by foreign language speakers and native Chinese speakers, making it challenging to effectively improve the performance of native CGEC by relying solely on data from foreign language speakers. These results further highlight the effectiveness of our method in constructing a hybrid dataset that contains native Chinese grammatical errors.

Furthermore, our GrammarGPT exhibited substantial improvement with only about 1k data samples for fine-tuning, achieving 32.56 and 35.84 $F_{0.5}$, respectively. It is almost double the performance of baseline models, showcasing the remarkable potential of open-source LLMs in native CGEC.

4.5 Ablation Study

In our analysis of the impact of our contributions, namely the construction of a hybrid dataset and the error-invariant augmentation method, we present the results in Table 6.

Notably, the model trained on ChatGPT-generated data consistently outperforms that trained the human-annotated data, irrespective of whether data augmentation is applied. We attribute this observation to two primary reasons. First, the quantity of human-annotated data is smaller than the data generated by ChatGPT due to the high cost of human annotation. Second, grammatical errors without clues are more challenging to correct.

Additionally, our hybrid dataset demonstrates the potential for enhancing the performance of native CGEC. This finding substantiates the effectiveness of our approach in constructing the hybrid dataset consisting of native Chinese grammatical errors.

Moreover, by employing the error-invariant augmentation method, we observe our model trained on hybrid dataset has significant improvements in Recall and $F_{0.5}$ metrics but only minor improvements in Precision. It indicates that our augmentation technique enhances the model's ability to detect grammatical errors by forcing the model to pay more attention to grammar errors in the augmentation data.

5 Conclusion

In this paper, we introduce GrammarGPT, an open-source Language Model (LLM) specifically designed for native Chinese grammatical error correction. We first construct a hybrid dataset containing approximately 1k parallel data samples. It comprises both ChatGPT-generated data and human-annotated data for dealing with grammatical errors with and without clues. Additionally, we introduced an error-invariant augmentation method to improve the model's capabilities in native Chinese grammatical error correction by forcing the model to pay more attention to grammar errors in the augmentation data. Finally, we further fine-tune the open-source large-scale language model on the constructed dataset, and experimental results and in-depth analysis demonstrate the effectiveness of our GrammarGPT in native Chinese grammatical error correction.

Acknowledgement. This work is supported by the National Natural Science Foundation of China (Grant No. 62271432) and the Guangdong Provincial Key Laboratory of Big Data Computing, The Chinese University of Hong Kong, Shenzhen (Grant No. B10120210117).

References

1. Chen, F., Feng, Y.: Chain-of-thought prompt distillation for multimodal named entity and multimodal relation extraction. ArXiv preprint arXiv:2306.14122 (2023)
2. Chen, Z., et al.: Phoenix: democratizing ChatGPT across languages. arXiv preprint arXiv:2304.10453 (2023)
3. Dahlmeier, D., Ng, H.T.: Better evaluation for grammatical error correction. In: Proceedings of the 2012 Conference of the North American Chapter of the Association for Computational Linguistics: Human Language Technologies, pp. 568–572. Association for Computational Linguistics, Montréal, Canada, June 2012. https://aclanthology.org/N12-1067
4. Fang, T., et al.: Is ChatGPT a highly fluent grammatical error correction system? A comprehensive evaluation. arXiv preprint arXiv:2304.01746 (2023)
5. Hinson, C., Huang, H.H., Chen, H.H.: Heterogeneous recycle generation for Chinese grammatical error correction. In: Proceedings of the 28th International Conference on Computational Linguistics, pp. 2191–2201 (2020)
6. Ho, N., Schmid, L., Yun, S.Y.: Large language models are reasoning teachers. arXiv preprint arXiv:2212.10071 (2022)
7. Katsumata, S., Komachi, M.: stronger baselines for grammatical error correction using a pretrained encoder-decoder model. In: Proceedings of the 1st Conference of the Asia-Pacific Chapter of the Association for Computational Linguistics and the 10th International Joint Conference on Natural Language Processing, pp. 827–832 (2020)
8. Li, J., et al.: Sequence-to-action: grammatical error correction with action guided sequence generation. Proc. AAAI Conf. Artif. Intell. **36**(10), 10974–10982 (2022)
9. Liang, D., et al.: BERT enhanced neural machine translation and sequence tagging model for Chinese grammatical error diagnosis. In: Proceedings of the 6th Workshop on Natural Language Processing Techniques for Educational Applications, pp. 57–66. Association for Computational Linguistics (2020)
10. Ma, S., et al.: Linguistic rules-based corpus generation for native Chinese grammatical error correction. In: Findings of the Association for Computational Linguistics: EMNLP 2022, pp. 576–589 (2022)
11. Ng, H.T., Wu, S.M., Briscoe, T., Hadiwinoto, C., Susanto, R.H., Bryant, C.: The CoNLL-2014 shared task on grammatical error correction. In: Proceedings of the Eighteenth Conference on Computational Natural Language Learning: Shared Task, pp. 1–14 (2014)
12. Peng, B., Li, C., He, P., Galley, M., Gao, J.: Instruction Tuning with GPT-4. arXiv preprint arXiv:2304.03277 (2023)
13. Rao, G., Gong, Q., Zhang, B., Xun, E.: Overview of NLPTEA-2018 share task Chinese grammatical error diagnosis. In: Proceedings of the 5th Workshop on Natural Language Processing Techniques for Educational Applications, pp. 42–51 (2018)
14. Rao, G., Yang, E., Zhang, B.: Overview of NLPTEA-2020 shared task for chinese grammatical error diagnosis. In: Proceedings of the 6th Workshop on Natural Language Processing Techniques for Educational Applications, pp. 25–35 (2020)
15. Rothe, S., Mallinson, J., Malmi, E., Krause, S., Severyn, A.: A simple recipe for multilingual grammatical error correction. In: Proceedings of the 59th Annual Meeting of the Association for Computational Linguistics and the 11th International Joint Conference on Natural Language Processing (Volume 2: Short Papers), pp. 702–707 (2021)

16. Sanh, V., et al.: Multitask prompted training enables zero-shot task generalization. arXiv preprint arXiv:2110.08207 (2021)
17. Scao, T.L., et al.: Bloom: a 176B-parameter open-access multilingual language model. arXiv preprint arXiv:2211.05100 (2022)
18. Touvron, H., et al.: LLaMA: open and efficient foundation language models (2023)
19. Wang, P., Wang, Z., Li, Z., Gao, Y., Yin, B., Ren, X.: SCOTT: self-consistent chain-of-thought distillation. arXiv preprint arXiv:2305.01879 (2023)
20. Wang, X., et al.: InstructUIE: multi-task instruction tuning for unified information extraction. arXiv preprint arXiv:2304.08085 (2023)
21. Wei, J., et al.: Finetuned language models are zero-shot learners. arXiv preprint arXiv:2109.01652 (2021)
22. Yu, J., et al.: Taoli LLaMA. https://github.com/blcuicall/taoli (2023)
23. Zhang, B.: Features and functions of the HSK dynamic composition corpus. Int. Chin. Lang. Educ. **4**, 71–79 (2009)
24. Zhang, B., Yang, H., Liu, X.Y.: Instruct-FinGPT: financial sentiment analysis by instruction tuning of general-purpose large language models. arXiv preprint arXiv:2306.12659 (2023)
25. Zhang, H., et al.: HuatuoGPT, towards taming language model to be a doctor. arXiv preprint arXiv:2305.15075 (2023)
26. Zhang, Y., et al.: MuCGEC: a multi-reference multi-source evaluation dataset for Chinese grammatical error correction. In: Proceedings of the 2022 Conference of the North American Chapter of the Association for Computational Linguistics: Human Language Technologies, pp. 3118–3130 (2022)
27. Zhang, Y., et al.: NaSGEC: a multi-domain Chinese grammatical error correction dataset from native speaker texts. arXiv preprint arXiv:2305.16023 (2023)
28. Zhao, Y., Jiang, N., Sun, W., Wan, X.: Overview of the NLPCC 2018 shared task: grammatical error correction. In: Zhang, M., Ng, V., Zhao, D., Li, S., Zan, H. (eds.) NLPCC 2018. LNCS (LNAI), vol. 11109, pp. 439–445. Springer, Cham (2018). https://doi.org/10.1007/978-3-319-99501-4_41
29. Zhao, Z., Wang, H.: MaskGEC: improving neural grammatical error correction via dynamic masking. Proc. AAAI Conf. Artif. Intell. **34**(01), 1226–1233 (2020)

Evaluation Workshop: Multi-perspective Scientific Machine Reading Comprehension

Enhanced CGSN System for Machine Reading Comprehension

Liwen Zheng, Haoran Jia, Hongyan Xie, Xi Zhang, and Yuming Shang[✉]

Beijing University of Posts and Telecommunications, Beijing, China
{zhenglw,jiahaoran,zhangx,shangym}@bupt.edu.cn

Abstract. This paper introduces the system proposed by the "Guess Right or Not (Ours)" team for NLPCC 2023 Shared Task 2 (https://github.com/Yottaxx/NLP CC23_SciMRC)--Multi-perspective Scientific Machine Reading Comprehension. This task requires participants to develop a reading comprehension model based on state-of-the-art Natural Language Processing (NLP) and deep learning techniques to extract word sequences or sentences from the given scientific texts as answers to relevant questions. In response to this task, we use a fine-grained contextual encoder to highlight key contextual information in scientific texts that is highly relevant to the question. Besides, based on existing advanced model CGSN [7], we utilize a local graph network and a global graph network to capture global structural information in scientific texts, as well as the evidence memory network to further alleviate the redundancy issues by saving the selected result in the previous steps. Experiments show that our proposed model performs well on datasets released by NLPCC 2023, and our approach ranks 1st for SMRC Task 2 according to the official results.

Keywords: SMRC · Fine-grained Contextual Information · Global Structural Information

1 Introduction

Machine Reading Comprehension (MRC) is a task that involves answering questions about a given context paragraph, which enables machines to read and understand unstructured text. MRC is a rapidly growing field of research due to its potential for various enterprise applications, and it holds the potential to revolutionize the way humans interact with machines. For example, as shown in Fig. 1, search engines equipped with MRC techniques can directly output correct answers to questions rather than a series of related web pages, which can significantly enhance the efficiency of information retrieval.

Early MRC systems primarily relied on rule-based or machine learning techniques, which depended on manually crafted rules or features [1–3]. The drawbacks of these methods lie in their limited ability to comprehend contextual information and their

Supported by the Natural Science Foundation of China (No.61976026), the Fundamental Research Funds for the Central Universities.

reduced generalization capabilities. Therefore, researchers have been dedicated to studying deep learning-based approaches in recent years, and as deep learning continues to evolve, researchers primarily focus on two research paradigms: attention mechanisms-based methods and fine-tuning or optimization performed on pre-trained language models. For example, BiDAF (Bi-Directional Attention Flow) [4] utilizes a bidirectional attention mechanism to capture contextual information at different granularity levels. Gong H et al. [5] employ a pre-trained transformer model, such as BERT [6], to encode the joint contextual information of texts and questions.

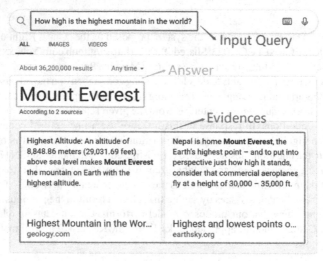

Fig. 1. An example of search engine Bing[1] with MRC.

Most of the current deep learning-based MRC methods still encounter challenges such as information loss during text vectorization and the long-distance semantic dependency. To tackle these issues, we initially focus on the embedding layer and conduct fine-grained context encoding on the input texts to prevent premature loss of essential feature information. Additionally, we leverage gating mechanisms to set up redundant filter, thereby further enhancing the refinement of vector representation. To capture long-distance semantic dependency information in scientific texts and problems effectively, we use the CGSN model [7], which employ local graph network and global graph network to capture both local semantic information and global contextual information separately, and establish long-range reasoning through iterative processes. Furthermore, the evidence memory network is utilized to store the selection results from previous steps and mitigate redundancy issues effectively.

In summary, our contributions are as follows:

- Following CGSN, we utilize local graph network and global graph network to enhance global structural contextual information.

---

[1] https://cn.bing.com/

- Based on CGSN, we propose a Fine-grained Contextual Encoder to highlight the most relevant features and eliminate redundant information.
- Our model achieves the first place in NLPCC 2023 shared task 2 on Scientific Machine Reading Comprehension (SMRC).

2 Related Work

Machine reading comprehension can be roughly categorized into four types: cloze tests, multiple choice, span extraction, and free answering [8]. This paper primarily focuses on the span extraction tasks. Due to limitations in dataset size, Traditional rule-based and machine learning-based methods exhibit poor performance and are impractical for deployment in practical applications. In recent years, researchers have discovered that methods based on deep neural networks excel in extracting contextual information, which results in significantly improved model performance compared to traditional methods [9].

MRC models based on deep learning techniques typically contain four steps [8]: embedding layer, feature extraction, question-text interaction, and answer prediction. Firstly, it is essential to convert the input natural language into vector representation. Match LSTM model [10] utilized word vectors to encode the input text. DocQA [11] and MPMRC [12] employed a combination of word embedding and character embedding techniques to extract the text representation vector. To capture contextual information, Zhang W et al. [13] integrated the dynamic text representation model ELMO to derive more precise text vectors. The encoding layer is primarily employed to extract key features that are highly relevant to questions from the input texts. Recurrent neural networks (RNNs) and variants are extensively utilized in machine reading comprehension tasks. To comprehensively incorporate both forward and backward information, bi-directional RNN networks are commonly employed in MRC [14, 16]. KAR model [15] utilized Bidirectional Long Short-Term Memory (BiLSTM) to extract contextual features. The interaction between questions and texts primarily relies on attention mechanisms to capture correlations and key features. To address the challenges posed by long-distance semantic dependencies, current methods predominantly employ self-attention mechanisms [19, 20]. R-Net model [17] introduced a gated self-attention mechanism to capture internal connections within texts, and Fastform model [18] utilized a multi-head self-attention mechanism for interaction. And finally, we aggregate information from all modules, make predictions, and output the final answer.

The adventure of pre-trained language models, such as BERT and XLnet [26], has revolutionized the intricate architecture of MRC models. It is now possible to achieve excellent results by solely fine-tuning these pre-trained language models. RoBERTa [21], ALBERT [22], and other models are all enhancements built upon BERT, which demonstrate remarkable performance in natural language processing tasks. Furthermore, methods based on pre-trained models have emerged as mainstream solutions for MRC tasks [23]. The length limitation of input texts in pre-trained models poses challenges for addressing long document reading comprehension tasks. Gong H et al. [5] employed reinforcement learning to enable the model to learn and determine the input length. They also utilized a loop mechanism to capture dynamic semantic information. Ding M et al. [24] drew inspiration from human cognitive processes and employed similar mechanisms to process long texts. Zhao J et al. [25] proposed a read-over-read method to alleviate the challenges associated with length limitations.

3 The Proposed Approach

3.1 Task Definition

Following CGSN, we take a question $Q = [q_1, q_2, ..., q_m]$ along with scientific texts $P = [p_1, p_2, ..., p_n]$ as input of MRC model, and the goal of our task to extract a free-form answer $A = [a_1, a_2, ..., a_l]$ for the input question from texts P, where m and n denotes the length of question and the number of paragraphs separately, $p_i = \left[w_i^1, w_i^2, ..., w_i^{k_i} \right] (1 \leq i \leq n)$ denotes paragraph i with the word length of k_i.

3.2 Model Structure

As shown in Fig. 2, our model is composed of four modules: fine-grained contextual encoder, local semantic extractor, global semantic extractor and memory network. Firstly, pre-trained Transformer encoder SciBERT [27] are utilized to encode the question-paragraph pair, and fine-grained contextual encoding is conducted to further refine and capture detailed information. Subsequently, local graph network is constructed at the token, sentence, paragraph, and texts levels. The information obtained at each granularity is then fed into the subsequent module to form the global graph network. The global information will feedback to enhance the local representation. Finally, at each time step, the memory network receives the enhanced local representation and the predicted logits, and updates the global graph paragraph nodes for the next step.

Fine-grained Contextual Encoder. We set the initial embedding of each question and paragraph as E_q and E_p, and utilize 2 layers of BiLSTM to obtain the fine-grained contextual information H_q and H_p.

$$H_q = BiLSTM\left(E_q\right) \tag{1}$$

$$H_p = BiLSTM\left(E_p\right) \tag{2}$$

The gating mechanism is employed to eliminate redundant information and capture semantic information that is highly relevant to the question.

$$H_p^q = Gate[H_q, H_p] \tag{3}$$

where H_p^q denotes the question-aware paragraph embedding.

Local Semantic Extractor. The local graph network is constructed by sub-graphs at four different granularity: token, sentence, paragraph, and texts. To initial the node representation, the question-aware paragraph embedding H_p^q will be fed into the Local Semantic Extractor. Token-level nodes h_t^{Local} are initialized by the corresponding token representation of H_p^q, and vector of sentence-level node h_s^{Local} can be calculated by the

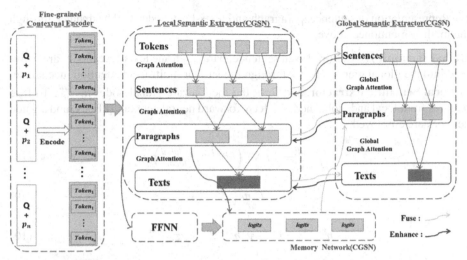

Fig. 2. The architecture of our proposed model. The Fine-grained Contextual Encoder is designed to highlight the most relevant features and eliminate redundant information, and the Local Semantic Extractor, Global Semantic Extractor and Memory Network proposed by CGSN are utilized to enhance global structural contextual information.

mean-pooling of h_t^{Local}. [CLS] of H_p^q can represent paragraph-level node h_p^{Local}, and texts-level nodes h_{text}^{Local} are initialized by the mean-pooling of h_p^{Local}.

The information propagation between sub-graphs in the unidirectional local graph network can only be implemented from low-level to high-level. By executing graph attention [28] sequentially between adjacent sub-graphs, it can finally capture fine-grained semantic information and local structural information in the input scientific texts. Taking sentence-level and paragraph-level sub-graphs as an example, the mathematical process of updating paragraph-level node h_p^o with sentence-level node h_s^o at time step o is as follows:

$$e_{sp} = \frac{\left(h_p^o W^Q\right)\left(h_s^o W^K\right)^T}{\sqrt{d_z}} \tag{4}$$

$$\alpha_{sp} = softmax_s\left(e_{sp}\right) = \frac{exp\left(e_{sp}\right)}{\sum_{i \in N_S} exp\left(e_{ip}\right)} \tag{5}$$

$$z_p^{head_x} = \sum_{s \in N_S} \alpha_{sp} h_s^o W^V \tag{6}$$

$$h_p^{o+1} = Cat\left[z_p^{head_1}, z_p^{head_2}, ..., z_p^{head_k}\right] \tag{7}$$

where e_{sp} denotes the attention coefficients between h_p^o and h_s^o, α_{sp} is the normalization of e_{sp}, $z_p^{head_x}$ denotes the output of the multi-head attention, W^Q, W^K, and W^V are the parameters of the query, key and value of attention mechanism, and h_p^{o+1} is the representation of paragraph-level node at time step $o + 1$, which is composed of the concatenation of the multi-head outputs.

Representation of sentence, paragraph and texts-level nodes will be updated through the method mentioned above.

Global Semantic Extractor. Local sentence, paragraph and texts-level nodes are delivered into the global graph network through the similar multi-head attention mechanism in **Local Semantic Extractor**, and form the local-aware global nodes h_{local}^{global}. To fuse features from local and global nodes, a feed-forward neural network (FFNN) and a gated network are employed.

$$z_f^{global} = FFNN\left(h^{global}, h_{local}^{global}\right) \tag{8}$$

$$\gamma = Gate\left(z_f^{global}\right) \tag{9}$$

$$h_f^{global} = (1 - \gamma)h^{global} + \gamma z_f^{global} \tag{10}$$

where h^{global} denotes the original global node representation, h_f^{global} denotes the updated global node representation.

To further extract global structure information and interaction information sufficiently, we employ cross attention mechanism between adjacent sub-graphs for m times.

Besides, to integrate the local and global information for more precise prediction, the global nodes are fed back to the local graph network, and multi-head attention mechanism is employed to obtain enhanced local graph nodes. We define L as the extraction loss:

$$L = -\frac{1}{n}\sum_{i=1}^{N}\sum_{j=1}^{N_i}[logP(y|h_p^{L \leftarrow G})] \tag{11}$$

where $h_p^{L \leftarrow G}$ represents the enhanced local node representation, and y denotes the predicted label of paragraph.

Memory Network. The enhanced local nodes and the prediction logits at time step o will be cached and utilized at time step $o + 1$ to mitigating the adverse effects of redundant information. Specifically, using prediction logits as the importance weights for paragraphs and performing feature fusion based on these weights can highlight important information while concealing redundant information.

4   Experiments

4.1   Dataset and Metric

We use the dataset released by NLPCC 2023 Shared task 2 to train and evaluate our MRC model, and we extract a portion of the training dataset to form a validation dataset. Table 1 shows the number of QA(question-answer) pairs in the given training and testing datasets. We use the "Free_form_answer" field as final answer and take F1 value as the evaluation metric following the official task guidelines.

Table 1. Size of QA pairs for the official datasets.

	# of Texts	# of QA pairs
Train	372	3278
Dev	120	1595
Test	147	1169

4.2 Experiment Settings

Our model is implemented based on PyTorch[2] and the hugging-face[3] framework. We use several pre-trained models, such as SciBERT[4], LED Encoder and BERT[5], and selected the pre-trained Transformer encoder SciBERT as the final initial encoder. To determine the optimal parameter settings, we conducted multiple sets of experiments with different batch size, epoch, learning rate, weight decay and warm-up proportion.

Table 2. Hyper-parameter setting.

Hyper-parameter	Value
Epoch num	5
Batch size	4
Optimizer	AdamW[31]
Learning rate	1e-5
Weight decay	0.01
Warm-up proportion	0.1
Max_token_len	256
Max_sentence_len	32
Max_paragraph_len	1
Local hop	4
Global hop	1

To limit the number of nodes in token-level, sentence-level, and paragraph-level subgraphs, we set the maximum number of nodes to 256, 32, and 1 respectively based on experimental results. Besides, following CGSN, we implied multi-hop graph attention in local and global graph network to capture global structural information and contextual information, and conducted experiments to determine the number of local hop and global hop. Some final training hyper-parameters are shown in Table 2.

---

[2] https://pytorch.org
[3] https://github.com/huggingface/transformers
[4] https://huggingface.co/allenai/scibert_scivocab_uncased
[5] https://huggingface.co/bert-base-uncased.

4.3 Baselines

To demonstrate the effectiveness of our model, we compare it with several existing methods, the specific description is listed as follows:

- LED [29]: LED is a method designed for long document question answering tasks, which utilize the pre-trained LED model [30] as answer generator. With the question and corresponding pre-selected evidences as input, the model trained with gold evidences and question-answer pairs will output the predicted answer for the input question.
- LED Encoder [30]: The large-scale pre-trained language models has achieved tremendous success in the field of natural language processing. we choose LED Encoder as backbone, which serves as the pre-trained encoder for the above LED model, and its involvement contributes to the final outstanding performance of LED on MRC.

4.4 Results and Analysis

Table 3 shows the top-4 official result of NLPCC 2023 Task 2. Our team "Guess Right or Not (Ours)" obtained a final evaluation score of 0.5459, and get the 1st place among 16 participating teams.

Table 3. Top-4 official result of NLPCC 2023 Task 2.

Team ID	System Name	Final Evaluation Score
1	Ours	0.5459
2	IMUNLP	0.4519
3	PIE	0.4181
4	OUC_NLP	0.3574

Table 4 shows the experimental results conducted on the Qasper [29] dataset. Comparison result with several typical baselines can validate the superiority of our method. As is shown in Table 4, our method achieves the best performance, which demonstrates the effectiveness of our solution to MRC task. Specifically, the fine-grained contextual information is highly important for understanding the semantic information of long texts, and the involvement of global structural information is also crucial in machine reading comprehension tasks. Moreover, evidence memory network also contributes to the improvement of the model performance.

Table 4. The experimental results of different models on Qasper dataset.

Model	F1 value
LED	51.50
LED Encoder	53.99
Our Method	54.37

5 Conclusion

In this paper, we design an MRC model based on the existing method CGSN, which employ a local graph network and a global graph network to capture local and global structural information in scientific texts. Besides, we propose a Fine-grained Contextual Encoder to highlight features relevant to questions and eliminate redundant information. Furthermore, we utilize various optimization strategies to optimize and improve the base model CGSN to achieve optimal performance on the NLPCC dataset. And according to the Official results of NLPCC 2023 shared task s on Scientific Machine Reading Comprehension make known that our solution takes the first place among all participants, which demonstrates the effectiveness of our solution to MRC task. However, there is still a long way for machine reading comprehension tasks, and how to extract more precise and interpretable answers remains an ongoing challenge that requires continuous and in-depth exploration.

References

1. Poon, H., Christensen, J., Domingos, P., et al.: Machine reading at the University of Washington. In: Proceedings of the NAACL HLT 2010 First International Workshop on Formalisms and Methodology for Learning by Reading, pp. 87–95 (2010)
2. Hirschman, L., Light, M., Breck, E., et al.: Deep read: a reading comprehension system. In: Proceedings of the 37th Annual Meeting of the Association for Computational Linguistics, pp. 325–332 (1999)
3. Riloff E, Thelen M.: A rule-based question answering system for reading comprehension testsIn. In: ANLP-NAACL 2000 Workshop: Reading Comprehension Tests as Evaluation for Computer-based Language Understanding Systems (2000)
4. Seo, M., Kembhavi, A., Farhadi, A., et al.: Bidirectional attention flow for machine comprehension. arXiv preprint arXiv:1611.01603 (2016)
5. Gong, H., Shen, Y., Yu, D., et al.: Recurrent chunking mechanisms for long-text machine reading comprehension. arXiv preprint arXiv:2005.08056 (2020)
6. Devlin, J., Chang, M.W., Lee, K., et al.: Bert: Pre-training of deep bidirectional transformers for language understanding. arXiv preprint arXiv:1810.04805 (2018)
7. Nie, Y., Huang, H., Wei, W., et al.: Capturing global structural information in long document question answering with compressive graph selector network. arXiv preprint arXiv:2210.05499 (2022)
8. Liu, S., Zhang, X., Zhang, S., et al.: Neural machine reading comprehension: methods and trends. Appl. Sci. **9**(18), 3698 (2019)
9. Gu, Y., Gui, X., Li, D., Shen, Y., Liao, D.: A review of machine reading comprehension based on neural networks. J. Softw. **31**(07), 2095–2126 (2020)

10. Wang S, Jiang J.: Machine comprehension using match-LSTM and answer pointer. arXiv preprint arXiv:1608.07905 (2016)
11. Clark C, Gardner M.: Simple and effective multi-paragraph reading comprehension. arXiv preprint arXiv:1710.10723 (2017)
12. Wang, Y., Liu, K., Liu, J., et al.: Multi-passage machine reading comprehension with cross-passage answer verification. arXiv preprint arXiv:1805.02220 (2018)
13. Zhang, W., Ren, F.: ELMo+ gated self-attention network based on BiDAF for machine reading comprehension. In: 2020 IEEE 11th International Conference on Software Engineering and Service Science (ICSESS), pp. 1–6 (2020)
14. Lee, H., Kim, H.: GF-Net: Improving machine reading comprehension with feature gates. Pattern Recogn. Lett. **129**, 8–15 (2020)
15. Wang, C., Jiang, H.: Explicit utilization of general knowledge in machine reading comprehension. arXiv preprint arXiv:1809.03449 (2018)
16. Ma, X., Zhang, J.: GSA-Net: gated scaled dot-product attention based neural network for reading comprehension. Automatika: časopis za automatiku, mjerenje, elektroniku, računarstvo i komunikacije, **61**(4), 643–650 (2020)
17. Wang, W., Yang, N., Wei, F., et al.: Gated self-matching networks for reading comprehension and question answering. In: Proceedings of the 55th Annual Meeting of the Association for Computational Linguistics (Volume 1: Long Papers), pp. 189–198 (2017)
18. Wu, C., Wu, F., Qi, T., et al.: Fastformer: additive attention can be all you need. arXiv preprint arXiv:2108.09084 (2021)
19. Shen, T., Zhou, T., Long, G., et al.: DiSAN: directional self-attention network for RNN/CNN-free language understanding. In: Proceedings of the AAAI Conference on Artificial Intelligence, vol. 32, issue 1 (2018)
20. Shaw, P., Uszkoreit, J., Vaswani, A.: Self-attention with relative position representations. arXiv preprint arXiv:1803.02155 (2018)
21. Liu, Y., Ott, M., Goyal, N., et al.: RoBERTa: a robustly optimized BERT pretraining approach. arXiv preprint arXiv:1907.11692 (2019)
22. Lan, Z., Chen, M., Goodman, S., et al.: ALBERT: a lite BERT for self-supervised learning of language representations. arXiv preprint arXiv:1909.11942 (2019)
23. Su, C., Fukumoto, F., Huang, X., et al.: DeepMet: a reading comprehension paradigm for token-level metaphor detection. In: Proceedings of the Second Workshop on Figurative Language Processing, pp. 30–39 (2020)
24. Zhao J, Bao J, Wang Y, et al.: RoR: Read-over-read for long document machine reading comprehension. arXiv preprint arXiv:2109.04780 (2021)
25. Ding, M., Zhou, C., Yang, H., et al.: Cogltx: applying BERT to long texts. Adv. Neural. Inf. Process. Syst. **33**, 12792–12804 (2020)
26. Yang, Z., Dai, Z., Yang, Y., et al.: XLNet: generalized autoregressive pretraining for language understanding. In: Advances in Neural Information Processing Systems (2019)
27. Beltagy, I., Lo, K., Cohan, A.: SciBERT: a pretrained language model for scientific text. arXiv preprint arXiv:1903.10676 (2019)
28. Veličković, P., Cucurull, G., Casanova, A., et al.: Graph attention networks. arXiv preprint arXiv:1710.10903 (2017)
29. Dasigi, P., Lo, K., Beltagy, I., et al.: A dataset of information-seeking questions and answers anchored in research papers. arXiv preprint arXiv:2105.03011 (2021)
30. Ainslie, J., Ontanon, S., Alberti, C., et al.: ETC: encoding long and structured inputs in transformers. arXiv preprint arXiv:2004.08483 (2020)
31. Kingma, D.P., Ba, J.: Adam: a method for stochastic optimization. arXiv preprint arXiv:1412.6980 (2014)

Scientific Reading Comprehension with Sentences Selection and Ranking

Jialei Chen[1], Weihua Wang[1,2,3(✉)], and Shuai Shao[1]

[1] College of Computer Science, Inner Mongolia University, Hohhot, China
32109166@mail.imu.edu.cn
[2] National and Local Joint Engineering Research Center of Intelligent Information Processing Technology for Mongolian, Hohhot, China
[3] Inner Mongolia Key Laboratory of Mongolian Information Processing Technology, Hohhot, China
wangwh@imu.edu.cn

Abstract. Scientific Machine Reading Comprehension (SMRC) aims to understand scientific long text by providing answers for the given questions. Most existing methods trend to answer the question using Transformer-based models. However, in the scientific domain, the original text is longer than the general domain. In this paper, we proposed a model that consists of a content retrieval module and a pre-trained model module. The content retrieval module finds the most semantically relevant sentences from the text and re-rank them. The seleted sentences and question will be input into the pre-trained model to get the answers. This model could overcome the length limitation of Transformer model length while achieving impressive results. Our model achieved 0.45 score of RougeL, resulting in the second place in the NLPCC2023 Shared Task2.

Keywords: Machine Reading Comprehension · Long Text Comprehension · Text retrieval · Pre-trained language model

1 Introduction

Machine Reading Comprehension (MRC) aims to enable machines to understand the content of texts, answer related questions, and provide accurate responses [1,2]. As a challenging research direction, MRC has gained significant interest from the research community due to its practical applications, such as question-answering dialogue systems [3,4]. The core challenge in MRC involves extracting pertinent information from a considerable amount of text, matching and reasoning with the information, and generating precise answers.

Scientific Machine Reading Comprehension (SMRC) is an extension of MRC specifically focused on comprehending and extracting text-specific information from scientific literature, academic papers, and other related texts to answer questions related to scientific knowledge [5]. NLPCC2023 Shared Task2 presents

F. Liu et al. (Eds.): NLPCC 2023, LNAI 14304, pp. 93–101, 2023.
https://doi.org/10.1007/978-3-031-44699-3_9

a multi-perspective scientific reading comprehension dataset that includes scientific papers and question-answering pairs from different perspectives. However, the substantial length of scientific papers presents a significant obstacle for reading comprehension.

To tackle the issue of lengthy texts in reading comprehension, we propose a simple retrieval and re-ranking method. Our approach is inspired by open-domain question-answering [6] and information retrieval techniques [7]. In the retrieval phase, our method treats sentences as fundamental text units and encodes them, along with the question, into two independent vector spaces using a bi-encoder. The encoded vector representations are then used to calculate cosine similarities, providing the K highest scoring sentences as candidate sets. In the subsequent re-ranking phase, a cross-encoder is employed to reorder combinations of the question and candidate sentences. The re-ordered sentences, along with the question, are input into a pre-trained model to generate the answer. This method effectively reduces text length, lowers computational costs, and captures relevant information scattered throughout long texts to answer questions.

Our retrieval and re-ranking pipeline significantly improves the baseline model by approximately 15 in terms of RougeL score on the NLPCC2023 Shared Task 2 dataset. The substantial enhancement in RougeL scores indicates that future research in scientific reading comprehension can benefit from the retrieval and re-ranking of text content that is more pertinent to the given questions.

2   Related Work

The QUALM system proposed by Lehnert [8] is an early MRC system, but due to its small scale, it has not been widely used. Hirschman [9] et al. proposed a bag-of-words technique that represents sentences with questions and context as sets of words and selects words that appear in both the question and the context as answers. Riloff [10] et al. designed a rule-based MRC system called Quarc, which contains different heuristic rules for different types of "wh" questions. Quarc also incorporates morphological analysis functions such as part-of-speech tagging, semantic categorization, and entity recognition. These works mainly rely on rule-based methods to solve MRC tasks. However, due to the lack of flexibility and the complexity of rule construction requiring expert knowledge, later works gradually shifted towards machine learning approaches. With the availability of large-scale benchmark datasets such as SQuAD [11], and Narrative QA [12], it became possible to tackle MRC tasks using deep neural architectures, providing a platform for evaluating the performance of MRC systems.

Subsequent work mainly focused on various attention-based interactions between passages and questions. Kadlec et al. [13] used Attention Sum, Dhingra et al. [14] used Gated attention, Wang et al. [15] used Self-matching, Cui et al. [16] used Attention over Attention, and Seo et al. [17] used Bi-attention. In our model, SentenceTransformer is used in the text retrieval part to calculate text similarity and to perform sentence ranking and retrieval based on the comparison of similarity between texts.

Recently, pre-trained language models (PrLMs) such as BERT [18], XLNet [19], and T5 [20] have achieved success in various natural language processing tasks. These powerful pre-trained encoders have demonstrated strong semantic encoding capabilities. Our model utilizes the T5 pre-trained model for encoding. These models typically consist of multiple layers of transformers, which encode sequences of limited length (e.g., 512). However, in some MRC tasks, input sequences may exceed the length limit. For example, documents in the Trivi-aQA dataset averagely contain 2,622 tokens. The SciMRC dataset used in this paper has an average of 6000 tokens per text. To handle documents with lengths far exceeding the input length of pre-trained models, it is common to split the documents into different segments and predict answers from each segment separately. The highest-scoring answer among these segments is selected as the final answer. Although this approach is simple, each part segmented from the document is treated independently, and the model fails to capture information that spans across text segments. Zhao et al. [21] predicted region answers from each block, compressed these answers into a new document, and then generated an answer. However, this two-step generation method inevitably introduces error propagation. Our model divides the text into individual sentences and selects sentences relevant to the question for answer generation. This approach only performs answer generation once, avoiding error propagation, and the sentence-level segmentation allows for finer extraction of textual information.

Regarding sentence retrieval, paragraph retrieval is an important step. Initially, TF/IDF-based sparse representation was used for retrieving supporting documents [22]. Lee et al. [23] introduced a supervised learning method that relies on BiLSTM to reorder paragraphs, while Wang et al. [24] trained a ranking system using reinforcement learning. The second approach to improve retrieval is by utilizing additional information such as Wikipedia or Wikidata graphs (Min et al. [25]; Asai et al. [26]). In our text retrieval, we use the Bi-encoder [27] approach for sentence selection, which is more efficient and performs better compared to previous methods.

3   Method

Our model draws inspiration from the human process of reading and comprehending lengthy texts. It focuses exclusively on the text content relevant to the given question. Our model comprises two components: the content retrieval model and the pre-trained model. The content retrieval model consists of two parts: retrieval and re-ranking, as depicted in Fig. 1. In the reading comprehension task, the scientific text is segmented into a collection of sentences. Both the sentence collection and the question collection are input into the content retrieval model. Specifically, for each question in the collection, a Bi-Encoder is employed to retrieve a candidate set from the sentence collection. Subsequently, re-ranking is performed to determine the sentence collection most semantically relevant to the given question. Finally, the question and the relevant sentence collection are fed into the pre-trained model for extracting the answer. This two-part model

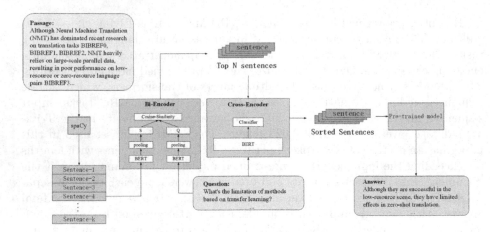

Fig. 1. The model consists of two parts: content retrieval and pre-trained model. The content retrieval part includes two steps: retrieval and re-ranking.

architecture efficiently retrieves and selects the most pertinent information for accurately answering the provided questions.

3.1 Retrieval Module

The retrieval component employs semantic search, which differs from traditional search methods reliant on lexical matching. Semantic search matches items based on their semantic information. The approach involves embedding all entries in the corpus, be it sentences, paragraphs, or documents, into a vector space. During the search process, the query is also embedded into the same vector space, and the closest embedding is identified from the corpus. These selected entries are expected to exhibit a high semantic overlap with the query. In our implementation, the sentence collection obtained by segmenting the articles in the dataset serves as the corpus, while the questions serve as queries for the semantic search process.

The bi-encoder is a commonly used model architecture in natural language processing tasks such as semantic search, sentence similarity calculation, and question-answering systems. It is designed to generate semantic vectors for text pairs. The bi-encoder architecture involves independently encoding the query text and candidate text (typically from a document collection or question-answer database) into two separate semantic vectors, without sharing parameters between them. The generation of semantic vectors follows an encoder-decoder structure. The encoder transforms an input text into a fixed-dimensional semantic vector that captures its semantic information. Similarity metrics such as cosine similarity or Euclidean distance can then be used to compute the similarity between two vectors. By utilizing the semantic vectors from the bi-encoder, it is possible to calculate similarity scores between queries and candidate texts in semantic search and find the most relevant texts to a query. The bi-encoder architecture is also applicable to tasks like sentence similarity calculation, where the semantic vectors of two sentences are compared to assess their similarity. The advantages of the bi-encoder architecture include high computational efficiency, as the encoder only needs to compute the semantic vectors once for each query, enabling efficient search and similarity calculations on large-scale text collections.

To input a collection of questions $Q = \{q_1, ...q_n\}$ and a collection of sentences $S = \{s_1, ...s_m\}$ into the bi-encoder, we obtain representations of the question and the sentence in the same vector space. Then, we calculate the semantic similarity between the question and the sentence using cosine similarity and select the top k highest cosine similarity scores as the retrieve candidates, where k is a hyperparameter.

3.2 Re-Ranking Module

Re-Rank is the process of rearranging the retrieve candidate sentences using a cross-encoder. The bi-directional encoder in the retrieval part captures some semantic information, but it mainly reduces the computational cost of traditional encoders in large-scale corpus matching.

The cross-encoder is a model architecture used to generate semantic vectors, which is employed in various natural language processing tasks such as text classification, sentence similarity calculation, and question-answering systems. Unlike the bi-encoder, the cross-encoder compares the combination of query and candidate texts when generating semantic vectors. It takes the query and candidate texts as input, processes them in the encoder, and generates an overall semantic vector representation. The design principle of the cross-encoder is to better capture the semantic relationship between queries and candidate texts. This can be achieved by using attention mechanisms, transformers, or other neural network structures. Compared to the bi-encoder, the cross-encoder model has higher computational costs because it requires encoding each query-candidate text pair. The semantic vectors generated by the cross-encoder can be used in text classification tasks to determine the degree of matching between queries and candidate texts or in sentence similarity calculation to assess the similarity between two sentences. In question-answering systems, the cross-encoder can compare the question with possible answer options to find the most relevant answer. The advantage of the cross-encoder lies in its ability to comprehensively consider the semantic relationship between queries and candidate texts, but it incurs higher computational costs due to the need for comparing every text pair. Therefore, in tasks requiring deeper semantic understanding, the cross-encoder model can provide more accurate matching and similarity calculation results.

4   Experiments

In this section, we introduce the dataset, baseline model, implementation details, evaluation metrics, and key results of this task.

4.1 Setuping

We implement sentence tokenization using Spacy, an open-source natural language processing (NLP) library designed for efficient text processing. Built on Python, Spacy provides a range of tools and functions for text processing.

The neural network is implemented using PyTorch, SentenceTransformer, and the HuggingFace Transformers library. For the content retrieval part, we employ the all-MiniLM-L6-v2 model from SentenceTransformer. This model is obtained by compressing a large pre-trained Transformer-based language model using knowledge distillation techniques, and it follows a bi-encoder architecture.

For the re-ranking part, we utilize the ms-marco-TinyBERT-L-2 model. This model is obtained by compressing a large pre-trained BERT-based language model using knowledge distillation techniques, and it follows a cross-encoder architecture.

For answer generation, we employ the T5-base model. During the training of the model, we set the learning rate to 1e–4, the batch size to 16, and train for 10 epochs. The maximum input length is set to 512, and the maximum output length is set to 128.

We implemented the model in PyTorch and trained it on a single NVIDIA A40 GPU with 48 GB VRAM. In our implementation, we set the hyperparameter k to 10, which means that we selected the top 10 most similar sentences from the article based on the bi-encoder and cosine similarity calculation.

4.2 Tasks and Datasets

We evaluate our model on the dataset provided by the NLPCC2023 ShareTask2. The training and validation sets consist of 592 data samples, where each sample contains five attributes: title, abstract, fulltext, figures, tables, and qas. These sets include a total of 4,873 question-answer pairs. The test set consists of 1,169 question-answer pairs.

4.3 Evaluation Metrics

We evaluated our model on the dataset provided by the NLPCC2023 ShareTask2. The training and validation sets consisted of 592 data samples, each containing five attributes: title, abstract, fulltext, figures, tables, and qas. These sets included a total of 4,873 question-answer pairs. The test set consisted of 1,169 question-answer pairs.

$$R_{lcs} = \frac{LCS(X,Y)}{m}$$

$$p_{lcs} = \frac{LCS(X,Y)}{n} \tag{1}$$

$$F_{lcs} = \frac{(1+\beta^2)R_{lcs}P_{lcs}}{R_{lcs} + \beta^2 P_{lcs}}$$

4.4   Main Results

The experimental results of our proposed model and the baseline model are shown in the table1. From the results, we can observe that our proposed model outperforms the baseline model significantly in various aspects, including Rouge and Bleu scores. Using RougeL as the evaluation metric, our model achieved a score of 45.

In order to further analyze the effectiveness of our model, we conducted ablation experiments to demonstrate the effectiveness of the content retrieval module. These experiments were performed on the train & validation dataset, which was divided into training, validation, and testing sets in an 8:1:1 ratio. The experimental parameters were kept consistent throughout, and we conducted experiments on both the t5-base and t5-small models.

As shown in the Table 2, when the content retrieval module was removed, the rougeL scores decreased by approximately 11.5 across different sizes of pre-training models. This indicates that by providing text content that is semantically relevant to the question, we are able to generate decent answers. The use of the entire text as input may prevent the model from focusing on the main content, resulting in noise instead.

Table 1. Experiment results on NLPCC2023 SharedTask2 dataset.

model	ROUGE-1	ROUGE-2	ROUGE-L	ROUGE-Lsum
Baseline	32.82	19.02	**30.58**	30.55
Ours	47.14	35.30	**45.18**	45.32

Table 2. Rouge&Bleu-score of ablation experiments for pre-trained models.

model	ROUGE-1	ROUGE-2	ROUGE-L	BLEU1	BLEU4
Baseline(T5-small)	28.64	15.31	**25.94**	17.24	6.18
Ours(T5-small)	39.49	27.37	**37.44**	12.22	6.01
Baseline(T5-base)	32.82	19.02	**30.58**	16.62	6.76
Ours(T5-base)	47.14	35.30	**45.18**	14.35	7.24

5   Conclusion

This paper introduces our model, which is capable of handling long-text scientific question-answering tasks. Our model can extract the sentences relevant to the question from long texts and effectively answer different questions based on these relevant sentences. Experimental results show that the model is able to identify and infer correct answers in long texts when facing different perspectives from beginners, students, and experts. The final model achieved the second-best results on the SciMRC dataset. It is important to note that although the SciMRC dataset is related to the field of science, our model is also suitable for other domains. For future work, we hope to improve the model's ability to compute the similarity between questions and text and enhance its ability to extract useful information from the text. We acknowledge that the selection of sentences by the model is crucial, as discarding sentences containing key information can significantly impact the model's results. Therefore, sentence selection becomes particularly critical for the model.

Acknowledgment. This work is supported by National Natural Science Foundation of China (Nos. 62066033, 61966025); Inner Mongolia Applied Technology Research and Development Fund Project (Nos. 2019GG372, 2020PT0002, 2022YFDZ0059); Inner Mongolia Natural Science Foundation (2020BS06001). We are grateful for the useful suggestions from the anonymous reviewers.

References

1. Chen, D.: Neural Reading Comprehension and Beyond. Stanford University, Stanford (2018)
2. Hermann, K.M., et al.: Teaching machines to read and comprehend. In: Advances in Neural Information Processing Systems, vol. 28 (2015)
3. Wen, T.H., et al.: A network-based end-to-end trainable task-oriented dialogue system. arXiv preprint arXiv:1604.04562 (2016)
4. Chen, H., Liu, X., Yin, D., Tang, J.: A survey on dialogue systems: Recent advances and new frontiers. ACM SIGKDD Explor. Newsl. **19**(2), 25–35 (2017)
5. Zhang, X., Zheng, H., Nie, Y., Huang, H., Mao, X.L.: SCIMRC: multi-perspective scientific machine reading comprehension. arXiv preprint arXiv:2306.14149 (2023)
6. Chen, D., Yih, W.T.: Open-domain question answering. In: Proceedings of the 58th Annual Meeting of the Association for Computational Linguistics: Tutorial Abstracts, pp. 34–37 (2020)
7. Manning, C.D.: An Introduction to Information Retrieval. Cambridge University Press, Cambridge (2009)
8. Lehnert, W.G.: The Process of Question Answering. Yale University, New Haven (1977)
9. Hirschman, L., Light, M., Breck, E., Burger, J.D.: Deep read: a reading comprehension system. In: Proceedings of the 37th Annual Meeting of the Association for Computational Linguistics, pp. 325–332 (1999)
10. Riloff, E., Thelen, M.: A rule-based question answering system for reading comprehension tests. In: ANLP-NAACL 2000 Workshop: Reading Comprehension Tests as Evaluation for Computer-Based Language Understanding Systems (2000)
11. Rajpurkar, P., Zhang, J., Lopyrev, K., Liang, P.: Squad: 100,000+ questions for machine comprehension of text. arXiv preprint arXiv:1606.05250 (2016)
12. Joshi, M., Choi, E., Weld, D.S., Zettlemoyer, L.: TriviaQA: a large scale distantly supervised challenge dataset for reading comprehension. arXiv preprint arXiv:1705.03551 (2017)
13. Kadlec, R., Schmid, M., Bajgar, O., Kleindienst, J.: Text understanding with the attention sum reader network. arXiv preprint arXiv:1603.01547 (2016)
14. Dhingra, B., Liu, H., Yang, Z., Cohen, W.W., Salakhutdinov, R.: Gated-attention readers for text comprehension. arXiv preprint arXiv:1606.01549 (2016)

15. Wang, W., Yang, N., Wei, F., Chang, B., Zhou, M.: Gated self-matching networks for reading comprehension and question answering. In: Proceedings of the 55th Annual Meeting of the Association for Computational Linguistics (Volume 1: Long Papers), pp. 189–198 (2017)
16. Cui, Y., Chen, Z., Wei, S., Wang, S., Liu, T., Hu, G.: Attention-over-attention neural networks for reading comprehension. arXiv preprint arXiv:1607.04423 (2016)
17. Seo, M., Kembhavi, A., Farhadi, A., Hajishirzi, H.: Bidirectional attention flow for machine comprehension. arXiv preprint arXiv:1611.01603 (2016)
18. Devlin, J., Chang, M.W., Lee, K., Toutanova, K.: Bert: pre-training of deep bidirectional transformers for language understanding. arXiv preprint arXiv:1810.04805 (2018)
19. Yang, Z., Dai, Z., Yang, Y., Carbonell, J., Salakhutdinov, R.R., Le, Q.V.: XLNet: generalized autoregressive pretraining for language understanding. In: Advances in Neural Information Processing Systems, vol. 32 (2019)
20. Raffel, C., et al.: Exploring the limits of transfer learning with a unified text-to-text transformer. J. Mach. Learn. Res. **21**(1), 5485–5551 (2020)
21. Zhao, J., et al.: ROR: read-over-read for long document machine reading comprehension. arXiv preprint arXiv:2109.04780 (2021)
22. Chen, D., Fisch, A., Weston, J., Bordes, A.: Reading wikipedia to answer open-domain questions. arXiv preprint arXiv:1704.00051 (2017)
23. Lee, J., Yun, S., Kim, H., Ko, M., Kang, J.: Ranking paragraphs for improving answer recall in open-domain question answering. arXiv preprint arXiv:1810.00494 (2018)
24. Wang, S., et al.: R 3: reinforced ranker-reader for open-domain question answering. In: Proceedings of the AAAI Conference on Artificial Intelligence, vol. 32 (2018)
25. Min, S., Chen, D., Zettlemoyer, L., Hajishirzi, H.: Knowledge guided text retrieval and reading for open domain question answering. arXiv preprint arXiv:1911.03868 (2019)
26. Asai, A., Hashimoto, K., Hajishirzi, H., Socher, R., Xiong, C.: Learning to retrieve reasoning paths over wikipedia graph for question answering. arXiv preprint arXiv:1911.10470 (2019)
27. Yi, X., et al.: Sampling-bias-corrected neural modeling for large corpus item recommendations. In: Proceedings of the 13th ACM Conference on Recommender Systems, pp. 269–277 (2019)

Overview of NLPCC Shared Task 2: Multi-perspective Scientific Machine Reading Comprehension

Xiao Zhang, Heqi Zheng, Yuxiang Nie, and Xian-Ling Mao[✉]

School of Computer Science and Technology, Beijing Institute of Technology, Beijing, China
maoxl@bit.edu.cn

Abstract. In this report, we give an overview of the shared task about multi-perspective scientific machine reading comprehension at the 12th CCF Conference on Natural Language Processing and Chinese Computing (NLPCC 2023). Scientific machine reading comprehension (SMRC) aims to understand scientific texts through interactions with humans by given questions. In this task, questions about scientific texts include perspectives from beginners, students and experts. It requires different levels of understanding of scientific texts. We describe the task, the corpus, the participating teams and their results.

Keywords: Machine reading comprehension · Multi-perspective · NLPCC 2023

1 Instruction

In today's fast-paced world, there are countless articles and information created around the world every day in the news field, self-media field and even technology field. Therefore, it is impossible to fully digest every article for us. Machine Reading Comprehension (MRC) can help us understand this information more quickly and obtain useful information from it. Based on machines' ability to understand natural language, MRC can extract relevant content from a large amount of information based on the questions we ask and make answers after understanding the content in a short time.

Scientific machine reading comprehension (SMRC) aims to understand scientific texts through interactions with humans by given questions. The ability of machines to understand and make sense of scientific texts is crucial for many applications such as scientific research [1,4,8], education [2,5] and industry [3,7,11]. With the increasing amount of scientific literature being produced, the need [6,9,10] for machines to understand these texts is becoming more pressing.

2   The Task

As far as we know, there is only one dataset [6] focused on exploring full-text scientific machine reading comprehension, which is proposed to improve MRC models in seeking information from specific papers with questions. However, the dataset has ignored the fact that different readers may have different levels of understanding of the text, and only includes single-perspective question-answer pairs from annotators whose background is NLP, which leads to a lack of consideration of different perspectives, especially for beginner's and expert's perspectives. Different perspectives correspond to different types of problems, which requires different levels of understanding. It will help us analyze and explore machine reading comprehension from a more comprehensive perspective. Therefore in NLPCC 2023, we offer a multi-perspective scientific machine reading comprehension task.

3   The Dataset

The provided dataset is referred as the SciMRC corpus in the following. It contains a training set, a validation set, and a test set. For the training set, it contains a large set of scientific papers from top conferences in natural language processing (e.g. ACL, EMNLP, NAACL, etc.) as well as corresponding human-written question-answer pairs (QA pairs) and their evidence paragraphs/figures/tables, which denotes the specific information in the paper that can support the answer to the question. The data is used for machine reading comprehension on scientific papers. The training and validation datasets include 4,873 QA pairs with their evidence while the test set contains 1,169 QA pairs with their evidence. As shown in Table 1, we collect QA pairs from different perspectives (i.e. BEGINNERS, STUDENTS, EXPERTS) to enhance the diversity of the data in the SciMRC and calculate the average of the paper length, the figure/table number, the question length and the evidence sentence number for each perspective.

Table 1. Representative features from SciMRC categorized by different perspectives

Type	Paper	Figure/Table	Question		Evidence
PERSPECTIVE	Avg Paper Length	Avg Figure/Table Number	Avg Question Length	Avg Answer Length	Avg Evidence Sentence Number
BEGINNERS	3725.6	5.32	10.0	17.2	1.39
STUDENTS			9.8	11.7	1.08
EXPERTS			22.4	95.9	4.56
ALL			11.0	21.8	1.56

3.1   Data Format

The training data contains a file and a directory, one file for the scientific papers with evidence and the other directory contains images and tables. In the training file, each json item contains six fields: "id" "title" "abstract" "full_text" "qas" and "figures_and_tables".

For evaluation, every line (in the json format) contains a paper with its question and the answer and evidence are absent. Each submission must contain a single json file with the name `answer.json`, with each key corresponding to a question id in the test set and its value is the answer to the question.

All files are encoded in UTF-8.

Obtaining the Dataset: You may download the training data from https://drive. google.com/file/d/1ewbgZOy6CEpjzoVxnkQPPVItj6yslUi1/ view?usp=sharing. The test data is available at https://drive.google.com/file/ d/1N2fVmr-InkIA8rdEoXrtIj6ENmDaGkrw/view.

Use of the Data: You are free to use the data for research purpose and please cite the dataset paper with the following bib entry (Tables 2 and 3).

```
@article{zhang2023scimrc,
  title={SciMRC: Multi-perspective Scientific Machine Reading
  Comprehension},
  author={Zhang, Xiao and Zheng, Heqi and Nie, Yuxiang and Huang,
  Heyan and Mao, Xian-Ling},
  journal={arXiv preprint arXiv:2306.14149},
  year={2023}
}
```

Table 2. A total of 16 teams from the global industrial and academic sectors are participating in our competition

Team ID	System Name
1	Evay Info AI Team
2	Dependency Graphs For Reading Comprehension
3	OUC_NLP
4	Langdiaozheyang
5	Emotional damage
6	Mirror
7	huawei_tsc_zeus
8	Lastonestands
9	cisl-nlp
10	CUHK_SU
11	its666
12	zutnlp-wujiahao
13	MPSMRC_cup
14	IMU_NLP
15	Nicaiduibudui
16	PIE

4   Evaluation Metric

In this paper, we utilized RougeL as our evaluation metric. RougeL is a commonly used metric for assessing the quality of text summarization systems. It measures the overlap between the generated summary and a reference summary using the longest common subsequence (LCS) algorithm. RougeL computes the length of the LCS between the two summaries and normalizes it by the length of the reference summary. This metric allows us to quantitatively evaluate the performance of our summarization system based on the similarity and coverage of the generated summaries compared to the reference summaries. The formula for RougeL can be expressed as:

$$\mathcal{R}_{LCS} = \frac{LCS(Prediction, Golden)}{len(Golden)} \tag{1}$$

$$\mathcal{P}_{LCS} = \frac{LCS(Prediction, Golden)}{len(Prediction)} \tag{2}$$

$$\mathcal{F}_{LCS} = \frac{(1 + \beta^2)\mathcal{R}_{LCS}\mathcal{P}_{LCS}}{\mathcal{R}_{LCS} + \beta^2\mathcal{P}_{LCS}} \tag{3}$$

5   Participating Teams

A total of 16 teams from the global industrial and academic sectors are participating in our competition.

6   Evaluation Results

The teams were ranked based on their performance in the evaluation, and the final scores represent their respective achievements. The team 'Nicaiduibudui' secured the top position with a score of 0.5459, followed by 'IMUNLP' with a score of 0.4519. 'PIE' and 'OUC_NLP' also performed well, obtaining scores of 0.4181 and 0.3574, respectively."

Table 3. Final Leaderboard

Team ID	System Name	Final Score
1	Nicaiduibudui	0.5459
2	IMUNLP	0.4519
3	PIE	0.4181
4	OUC_NLP	0.3574

7   Conclusion

We had a total of 16 teams participating in the competition and 4 of them submitted their final results. Each team developed their own system for the task at hand. The evaluation of the systems was performed using the RougeL metric, which is a widely used measure for assessing the quality of text summarization. In the field of machine reading, there are still significant challenges to overcome, but there is also considerable room for future development.

Acknowledgments. We thank the colleagues from Beijing Institute of Technology, especially the DataHammer research group to write potential questions for scientific papers. The annotation of the Multi-perspective Scientific Machine Reading Comprehension dataset is supported by National Key R&D Plan (No. 2020AAA0106600) and National Natural Science Foundation of China (No. 62172039). We also thank the participants for their valuable feedback and outstanding results.

References

1. Beltagy, I., Lo, K., Cohan, A.: SciBERT: a pretrained language model for scientific text. In: Proceedings of the 2019 Conference on Empirical Methods in Natural Language Processing and the 9th International Joint Conference on Natural Language Processing (EMNLP-IJCNLP), pp. 3615–3620. Association for Computational Linguistics, Hong Kong, China, November 2019. https://doi.org/10.18653/v1/D19-1371, http://aclanthology.org/D19-1371
2. Bianchi, N., Giorcelli, M.: Scientific education and innovation: From technical diplomas to university stem degrees. Microeconometric Studies of Education Markets (Topic), ERN (2019)
3. Bruches, E., Tikhobaeva, O., Dementyeva, Y., Batura, T.: TERMinator: a system for scientific texts processing. In: Proceedings of the 29th International Conference on Computational Linguistics, pp. 3420–3426. International Committee on Computational Linguistics, Gyeongju, Republic of Korea, October 2022. www.aclanthology.org/2022.coling-1.302
4. Cachola, I., Lo, K., Cohan, A., Weld, D.: TLDR: extreme summarization of scientific documents. In: Findings of the Association for Computational Linguistics: EMNLP 2020, pp. 4766–4777. Association for Computational Linguistics, November 2020. https://doi.org/10.18653/v1/2020.findings-emnlp.428, www.aclanthology.org/2020.findings-emnlp.428
5. de la Chica, S., Ahmad, F., Martin, J.H., Sumner, T.R.: Pedagogically useful extractive summaries for science education. In: International Conference on Computational Linguistics (2008)
6. Dasigi, P., Lo, K., Beltagy, I., Cohan, A., Smith, N.A., Gardner, M.: A dataset of information-seeking questions and answers anchored in research papers. In: Proceedings of the 2021 Conference of the North American Chapter of the Association for Computational Linguistics: Human Language Technologies, pp. 4599–4610 (2021). www.aclanthology.org/2021.naacl-main.365/
7. Erera, S., et al.: A summarization system for scientific documents. In: Proceedings of the 2019 Conference on Empirical Methods in Natural Language Processing and the 9th International Joint Conference on Natural Language Processing

(EMNLP-IJCNLP): System Demonstrations, pp. 211–216. Association for Computational Linguistics, Hong Kong, China, November 2019. https://doi.org/10.18653/v1/D19-3036, www.aclanthology.org/D19-3036

8. Marie, B., Fujita, A., Rubino, R.: Scientific credibility of machine translation research: a meta-evaluation of 769 papers. In: Proceedings of the 59th Annual Meeting of the Association for Computational Linguistics and the 11th International Joint Conference on Natural Language Processing (Volume 1: Long Papers), pp. 7297–7306. Association for Computational Linguistics, August 2021. https://doi.org/10.18653/v1/2021.acl-long.566, www.aclanthology.org/2021.acl-long.566

9. Sadat, M., Caragea, C.: SciNLI: a corpus for natural language inference on scientific text. In: Proceedings of the 60th Annual Meeting of the Association for Computational Linguistics (Volume 1: Long Papers), pp. 7399–7409. Association for Computational Linguistics, Dublin, Ireland, May 2022. https://doi.org/10.18653/v1/2022.acl-long.511, www.aclanthology.org/2022.acl-long.511

10. Wadden, D., et al.: Fact or fiction: verifying scientific claims. In: Proceedings of the 2020 Conference on Empirical Methods in Natural Language Processing (EMNLP), pp. 7534–7550. Association for Computational Linguistics, November 2020. https://doi.org/10.18653/v1/2020.emnlp-main.609, www.aclanthology.org/2020.emnlp-main.609

11. Zulfiqar, S., Wahab, M.F., Sarwar, M.I., Lieberwirth, I.: Is machine translation a reliable tool for reading German scientific databases and research articles? J. Chem. Inf. Model. **58**(11), 2214–2223 (2018)

Evaluation Workshop: Math Word Problem Solving

A Numeracy-Enhanced Decoding
for Solving Math Word Problem

Rao Peng🆔, Chuanzhi Yang🆔, Litian Huang🆔, Xiaopan Lyu🆔, Hao Meng🆔,
and Xinguo Yu$^{(\boxtimes)}$🆔

Faculty of Artificial Intelligence in Education, Central China Normal University,
Wuhan 430079, China
{pr3250,canola,litianhuang,menghao}@mails.ccnu.edu.cn
{xiaopan.lyu,xgyu}@ccnu.edu.cn

Abstract. Deep neural models have achieved promising progress in
solving Math Word Problems (MWPs) recently. This paper presents
a deep neural solver by adopting numeracy-enhanced decoding to promote the performance of expressions generation. It leverages numerical
properties to enhance the capabilities of the decoder, primarily focusing on two aspects: token embedding and target prediction. For token
embedding, this paper proposes a numeracy-enhanced token embedding
method, which fuses the explicit numerical feature with the contextual
feature for number tokens, enabling the decoder to perceive numerical
properties during the inference. For target prediction, this paper proposes a dynamic target prediction method, which utilizes a numerical
attention network to identify the mathematical category of the problem
and adaptively invokes category-aware parameter matrices to generate
diverse expressions for different problems. Experimental results demonstrate that the proposed method not only achieves competitive performance on the Chinese MWP dataset but also achieves state-of-the-art
results on the NLPCC Shared Task 3 dataset.

Keywords: Math Word Problem · Numeracy-enhanced Decoding ·
Token Embedding · Dynamic Target Prediction

1 Introduction

The research on solving MWP can be traced back to around the 1960s and holds
two significant implications: for the field of artificial intelligence and the field of
education [2,6]. In recent years, with the advancement of deep learning techniques, the focus of MWP research has primarily revolved around the sequence-
to-sequence framework [21]. This framework takes problem text sequences as
input and tokenized equations sequences as output. Numerous important works
have been dedicated to optimizing the encoder to obtain more effective semantic representations or reconstructing the decoder to make it more in line with

The original version of this chapter was revised: Chinese characters in Table 1 and
Table 3 of the paper are not displayed correctly. The correction to this chapter is
available at https://doi.org/10.1007/978-3-031-44699-3_38

ⓒ The Author(s), under exclusive license to Springer Nature Switzerland AG 2023, corrected publication 2023
F. Liu et al. (Eds.): NLPCC 2023, LNAI 14304, pp. 111–122, 2023.
https://doi.org/10.1007/978-3-031-44699-3_11

mathematical logic reasoning [13,23,25,26]. Leveraging the powerful knowledge transfer ability of pre-trained models, recent efforts have started exploring methods to enhance the solving performance of pre-trained models [5,9,10,17].

Despite the remarkable progress of pre-trained models in solving MWPs, there are still two main issues during the decoding stage. Firstly, the embedding of the number placeholder mainly captures contextual information from the problem, lacking the numerical properties to constrain the decoding. Secondly, the target prediction relies on a static vocabulary generated from the training samples, rendering the model unable to solve problems that involve extra symbols not present in the training set.

Regarding the first issue, existing work primarily focuses on the representation of numbers during the encoding phase [12,20,26]. MWP-BERT introduces a series of pre-training objectives related to numeracy, establishing connections between contextual representations and numerical properties [9]. However, the numerical properties play a more important role in the decoding process. For example, in the problem "The first number is 10, the second number is 15, what is their difference?", a tree-decoder may correctly predict the operator "−" for "their difference," but it cannot determine whether "10" or "15" should be the left child, resulting in an incorrect prediction of "−5" (as the calculation of negative numbers is beyond the scope of primary MWP). To address this issue, this paper proposes a numeracy-enhanced embedding method for the decoder. First, the explicit numerical features that can influence the decoding are summarized. Then, these features are fused with the context feature generated by the encoder to construct a new embedding for numbers. It enables the decoder to leverage explicit numerical features during the inference.

For the second issue, most works build the target vocabulary following [20,23], which includes operators (+, −, *, /, ^) and constants (3.14, 1, etc., appearing in the training set) that are context-independent, as well as number placeholders that are context-dependent. However, in practical education cases, problems may require extra operators or constants for solving. For example, the "Euclidean algorithm" needs to be used to "find the greatest common divisor of two numbers," which cannot be simply represented using the existing expression vocabulary. Furthermore, some problems involve the use of additional constants to address perturbations within the problem, such as the constant "1000" used in unit conversion problems. To tackle this issue, a numeracy-enhanced target prediction method is proposed. It firstly utilizes a numerical attention network to identify the category of the problem, and then adaptively invokes parameter matrices tailored to the identified category, thereby enabling the decoder to generate diverse expressions for different problems.

In summary, this work proposes a numeracy-enhanced decoding method for the pre-trained solving model, incorporating a token embedding method that allows the decoder to perceive the explicit numerical features during inference, and a dynamic prediction method that enables the decoder adaptively to generate a diverse expression for a different problem.

The contributions of this paper are summarized as follows:

1. This work proposes numeracy-enhanced decoding to improve the MWP-solving models. It incorporates numerical properties during the token embedding and target prediction of the decoder, achieving competitive performance on both the Chinese MWP benchmark and the Shared Task 3.
2. It introduces a numeracy-enhanced token embedding method, which builds explicit numerical features for each number placeholder and fuses it with contextual features, enabling the decoder to perceive numerical properties during the inference.
3. It introduces a numeracy-enhanced target prediction method, which utilizes a numerical attention network to identify the category of the problem and dynamically invokes category-aware parameter matrices, enabling the decoder to generate diverse expressions for different problems.

2 Related Work

The field of MWP solving has witnessed a series of transformative evolutions [7,18,21,24]. Recently Seq2Seq model has been widely adopted to solve MWP and achieve remarkable progress [21,23,26]. A significant milestone in this journey is the advent of pre-trained models for solving MWP [5,8,9,17]. These models gained language understanding ability and external knowledge through pre-training before conducting MWP-solving tasks, thus having significant advantages in performance [10].

Numeracy often refers to the attention to numerical understanding and manipulation [9]. This is especially important in tasks such as word representation learning, where the comprehension of numerical values and their interrelations can play a significant role [14]. Furthermore, attention has been given to MWP solving, where the focus is shifted from number value to the problem context of numbers by replacing numbers with symbolic placeholders [21,23]. Recent studies found that numerical properties can affect the generation of expressions, and some methods have been proposed to enable encoders to establish associations between numeracy and context, with a representative study being MWP-BERT [9]. Despite the attention given to numeracy encoding, the influence on decoding has received less exploration.

The development of decoding methods for MWP solving has been developed for several years [13,21,23]. The tree-decoder [23] significantly improved the performance of solving models and has since been widely applied in pre-trained solving models [8,9]. However, one of the issues with these decoders is that they use static candidate vocabulary during target prediction, limiting their ability to generate diverse expressions for a broader range of problems. To overcome this limitation, some studies, including DOL [18] and MathQA [1], have employed neural-symbolic decoding to generate formal language. These works demonstrated the effectiveness of Seq2Seq models in solving diverse problems by expanding the symbolic system.

Building upon these findings, this work explores the significance of numeracy on decoding, leveraging it to improve the token embedding and target prediction of the decoder, aiming to enhance the performance of the pre-trained solving model.

3 Methodology

3.1 Problem Statement

In the sequence-to-sequence solving framework, an MWP consists of a natural language description text P and an expression E represented as a string. In the input part, the problem text can be tokenized into a sequence $P = \{w_1, w_2, w_3, \ldots\}$ of length m, where a subset $n_P \subseteq P$ is used to describe the number list of the problem text. In the output part, the equation E is usually constructed based on a symbol vocabulary V (also known as Output-Lang) following certain arithmetic rules. The symbol vocabulary typically includes a number list n_P for numbers appearing in problems, as well as general operators V_{op} and constants V_{con}. The number list n_P can be transformed through number mapping [23], which replaces the numbers in the problem with unified placeholders while preserving the original numerical values and their positions in P. V_{op} contains common operators $(+, -, *, /, \char`^)$, while V_{con} includes commonly used constant values (such as 3.14, 1, 2, etc.) required for calculations.

3.2 Basic Model Description

In this study, a PLM-encoder from MWP-BERT [10] is utilized along with a Tree-decoder from GTS [23] as the basic model. The encoder utilizes a deep pre-trained network to transform the text P of the problem t into a representation matrix $Z \in \mathbb{R}^{m \times h}$, where m is the length of the character sequence and h is the dimension of the hidden features.

$$Z = \text{PLM\_encoder}(P) \tag{1}$$

The representation vector z_i in Z corresponding to the token w_i will be used in the decoding process, where i is the location of the tokens in P.

At the decoding stage, both the input and output of the decoder are in the form of prefix expressions. The initial goal vector q_0 is obtained by applying mean pooling to the output vectors Z of the encoder.

$$q_0 = \text{MeanPool}(Z) \tag{2}$$

For the t-th step during the iteration, the goal vector q_t is generated following the Top-Down Decomposition [23]. A context vector o_t is calculated based on the attention function. The goal vector q_t and the context vector o_t are then used in a scoring function $\text{Score}(\cdot)$ to compute the predicted score for each token embedding $e(y)$. The predicted token $\hat{y}$ for the current step is determined by selecting the token with the highest probability after applying the softmax function to the scores.

$$o_t = \text{Attn}\,(q_t, Z) \tag{3}$$

$$\text{prob}\,(y \mid q_t, o_t, P) = \frac{\text{Score}\,(y \mid q_t, o_t, e)}{\sum_i \text{Score}\,(y_i \mid q_t, o_t, e)} \tag{4}$$

$$\hat{y} = \text{argmax}\,(\text{prob}\,(y \mid q_t, o_t, P)) \tag{5}$$

This work primarily focuses on improving the token embedding and target prediction of the decoder, while no changes are made to the encoder. The details of the improvements are explained in Sect. 3.3 and Sect. 3.4 that follow.

3.3   A Numeracy-Enhanced Token Embedding

Following the existing works, the contextual representation $z_{\text{loc}(y|P)}$ generated by the encoder can be reused as the token embedding $e(y|P)$, where $\text{loc}(y|P)$ is the location index of the number y in n_P:

$$e(y \mid P) = z_{\text{loc}(y|P)} \quad \text{if } y \in n_p \tag{6}$$

Before MWP-BERT, the token embedding of numbers typically relied solely on the context of the numbers in the problem text. MWP-BERT introduced three pre-training objectives that allowed the encoder to perceive the relationship between context and numeracy properties. This paper suggests that numeracy properties can also be used to constrain the decoding process. Based on this viewpoint, the paper proposes five numeracy features that can influence the decoding process:

- Numerical type feature f_t: The numerical type is the most prominent feature of a number. Numbers are categorized into five types: integer, decimal, fraction, percentage, and other, with each type corresponding to a different feature value.
- The numerical magnitude influences the order of the numbers under certain operators in an expression. Some works encode this feature by using a graph encoder [11,22,26], instead, this work assigns numerical features based on descending order of numbers.
- Numerical units present the measurement scale of a number in the problem. A method similar to [16] is employed to extract the units and assign the same feature value to numbers with the same unit.
- Numerical ratio features f_r: The numerical ratio feature indicates whether a numerical value plays the role of a "ratio" in the problem. For example, "On a map with a scale of 1:500", "1" and "500" are both ratio values. The numerical ratio feature is represented as a binary value.
- Numerical digit feature f_d: The digit feature is important for problems involving digit knowledge, such as Divide 812 by 4, how many digits are in the quotient, and in which position is the highest digit?" This work marks the maximum digit of a number as the digital feature.

Any number that appears in the number list n_P can be explicitly encoded into a 5-dimensional feature vector e_N using the aforementioned features:

$$e^N = [f_t, f_m, f_u, f_r, f_d] \qquad (7)$$

This feature vector is concatenated with the original token embedding $e(y \mid P)$ and then passed through a fully-connected layer to obtain a numeracy-enhanced token embedding e':

$$e'(y \mid P) = \sigma \left(W_f \left(\text{concat} \left[z_{loc(y|P)} : e_y^N \right] \right) \right) \text{ if } y \in n_p \qquad (8)$$

where W_f is trainable matrix parameters used to fuse the contextual features and numerical features for a number token.

3.4   A Numeracy-Enhanced Target Prediction

In this section, a method is proposed to improve the target prediction of the decoder by utilizing enhanced numerical features. Specifically, an analysis of the experimental dataset was conducted, and four additional mathematical categories beyond the "general" problem were identified. Each category is accompanied by a category-specific operator or constant vocabulary, as depicted in Table 1.

Table 1. The category-specific vocabulary for the different mathematical categories

Mathematical Category	Problem Sample	Operator Vocabulary	Constant Vocabulary
General	甲数是48, 比乙数的3倍多6, 乙数是多少?	+, -, *, /, ^	1, 2
Number	8和6的最小公倍数是多少?	GCD(n1,n2), LCM(n1,n2), MOD(n1,n2), IDV(n1,n2)	-
Unit	江军做了20道计算题, 错了2道, 正确率是多少?	-	10, 100, 1000
Time	小明21时睡觉, 第2天早上7时起床, 小明睡了多少小时?	-	60, 12, 24, 30, 31, 365
Geometry	已知圆的周长为6.28, 那么圆的面积是多少?	-	3.14, 3, 4, 6, 180

In Table 1, the vocabulary corresponding to each mathematical category is presented, along with a textual example for each category. The categories and their samples are derived from the dataset used in the experiment. To distinguish the categories, a numerical attention network is proposed, which predicts the mathematical category of a problem.

$$\varepsilon_i = v_a \cdot \tanh\left(W_a \cdot [q_0 : e'(y_i \mid P)]\right) \text{ for } y_i \in n_p \tag{9}$$

$$a_i = \frac{\exp(\varepsilon_i)}{\sum_{j=1}^{k} \exp(\varepsilon_j)} \tag{10}$$

$$c = \sigma(W_b(\sum_{i=1}^{k} a_i \cdot e'(y_i \mid P)) + \beta_b) \tag{11}$$

where v_a, W_a, W_b and β_b are all trainable parameters, and e' is the numeracy-enhanced embedding of number tokens obtained in the last section. The attention network utilized the attention weights between the goal vector q_0 and the enhanced features e' of all numbers, to identify the mathematical category to which a given problem belongs.

Furthermore, the embedding matrices of operators and constants were expanded to ensure alignment with the vocabulary.

$$e(y \mid P, c) = \begin{cases} [M_{\text{op}}(y) : M_{\text{op}}^c(y)] & \text{if } y \in V_{\text{op}} \\ [M_{\text{con}}(y) : M_{\text{con}}^c(y)] & \text{if } y \in V_{\text{con}} \end{cases} \tag{12}$$

where M_{op}^c and M_{con}^c represent two sets of trainable embedding matrices corresponding to problem category c, and their lengths are aligned with the additional vocabulary.

In the prediction of the decoder, this work adjusts the scoring function Score($\cdot$) of the original tree decoder. Specifically, two sets of trainable parameters, W_{score}^c and α^c, are assigned to different categories c, and the scoring function adaptively calls different parameter sets based on c, enabling the generation tailored to the corresponding output vocabulary:

$$\text{Score}(y \mid q_t, o_t, e, c) = \alpha^c \tanh\left(W_{\text{score}}^c \left[q_t, o_t, e(y \mid P), c\right]\right) \tag{13}$$

$$\text{prob}(y \mid q_t, o_t, P, c) = \frac{\text{Score}(y \mid q_t, o_t, e, c)}{\sum_i \text{Score}(y_i \mid q_t, o_t, e, c)} \tag{14}$$

3.5 Training Objective

In the training stage, the training set $D = P_i, E_i$ is provided, where E_i represents the prefix tree structure of the expression and serves as the ground truth for each step of prediction. Consequently, the loss function for training can be computed as follows:

$$p(E \mid P) = \prod_{t=1}^{l} \text{prob}(y_t \mid q_t, o_t, P, c) \tag{15}$$

$$\text{Loss} = \sum_{(E,P) \in \mathbb{D}} \log(p(E \mid P)) \tag{16}$$

where l denotes the size of the expression E.

4   Experiments

In this section, the datasets and the baselines used in the experiment are first introduced. Then, all models are evaluated, and the results are analyzed. Finally, a case study on Shared Task 3 is presented for comparison.

4.1   Implementation Details

In this work, the Chinese-RoBERTa-wwm [3] is used as the pre-trained encoder. The model is fine-tuned on an NVIDIA RTX4090 card. The model was trained for 100 epochs with a batch size of 64. Adam optimizer is applied with an initial learning rate of 5e-5 and the dropout rate is set to 0.5. A 5-beam search was used in the test.

4.2   Datasets

In the training process, two datasets were utilized: Math23k and Ape-Clean. An overview of the training datasets is provided below:

- **Math23k** [21] is the most commonly-used Chinese dataset in MWP solving. It contains 23,162 problems including 21,162 training problems, 1,000 validation problems and 1,000 testing problems. This dataset also serves as the training set for the NLPCC·Shared Task 3.
- **Ape-clean** [9] is a high-quality Chinese dataset constructed from Ape-210k. Since some problems in Ape210k have extra obstacles for MWP solving, Ape-clean can be used for the fully-supervised learning setting. It contains 81,225 MWPs with 79,388 training problems and 1,837 testing problems. For training the proposed model, Ape-clean is combined with the training set of Math23k.

All models are evaluated on the Math23k test dataset and the Val dataset sourced from NLPCC Shared Task 3[1] (The test set of the task was not analyzed, as it only provided the true answers of the validation set). In the evaluation, the performance of models trained solely on Math23k and models trained on a larger joint training set (Ape-Clean+Math23k) was analyzed.

4.3   Baselines

The model is compared with the following baselines, including the state-of-the-art models:

- **LoRA+LLaMa7b** is a popular two-stage model that uses the LoRA algorithm [4] to fine-tune the basic LLaMa model [19] for general content generation tasks. "Please output the expression for the following math problem" is used as the instruction for this model.

---

[1] http://tcci.ccf.org.cn/conference/2023/taskdata.php.

- **MWP-flan-T5** is a pre-trained language model, and a fine-tuning setting similar to Generate & Rank is adapted for this study. The base model used is T5-PEGASUS [15], with a total of 275 million parameters, a maximum training length of 512, a batch size of 96, and a learning rate of 10e−4.
- **Generate & Rank** [17] designs a multi-task learning framework for adapting BART in MWP solving.
- **MWP-BERT (A&D)** [9,10] originally used BERT and RoBERTa as the backbone of the encoder and constructed 6 additional tasks to pre-train the model. Subsequently, an improved version of MWP-BERT (A&D) was proposed based on analysis identification and solution discrimination, achieving state-of-the-art performance.

4.4   Evaluation and Results

In this work, answer accuracy is used as the evaluation metric for both the proposed model and baseline comparisons, following the methodology of most related works. This metric refers to the percentage of correctly solved problems in a given dataset. The model is first compared with the baselines using two training strategies. The first strategy is to train the models solely on the Math23k train dataset, and the second one employs a joint training set that combines the Math23k and Ape-clean datasets. The corresponding results for both training strategies are measured on the testing set of Math23k and validation set from Shared Task, and are all presented in Table 2.

Table 2. Comparison of answer accuracy (%) between models solely trained on the Math23K and models trained on a joint dataset combined from Ape-clean and Math23k

	Solely Trained on Math23K		Joint Training Set	
	Math23K	Shared Task 3	Math23K	Shared Task 3
LoRA+LLaMa7b	70.5	20.3	76.7	25.3
MWP-flan-T5	80.3	24.5	82.4	29.6
Generate & Rank	85.4	28.7	90.1	36.2
MWP-BERT (A&D)	**85.6**	29.8	91.5	39.8
Our model	**85.6**	**32.2**	**91.6**	**43.1**

There are some interesting findings that can be concluded from the experiment results: Firstly, the results from Tables 2 demonstrate a significant improvement in the solving accuracy of all pre-trained models as the training data scale increases, and our model achieves competitive results on the Chinese MWP dataset. Secondly, the proposed model exhibits a more pronounced improvement compared to the baseline on Shared Task 3. This is primarily attributed to the fact that the Shared Task involves a greater variety of complex MWPs in comparison to Math23k, and these problems necessitate the application of the proposed decoding method for a successful solution. Thirdly, despite the ability of popular LLM-based models such as GPT, T5, LLaMa, etc., to quickly adapt to different generation tasks, their performance is inferior to specialized solving models in the Chinese MWP solving task such as MWP-BERT.

4.5 Case Study

In this section, the output from our model is shown and compared to the baseline model MWP-BERT (A&D) in Table 3. In the first two cases, the baseline model generated incorrect expressions and negative value answers during decoding. In contrast, our model achieved correct expressions and answers by incorporating numerical feature constraints during decoding. The baseline model lacked the time-related constant "12" and the unit-related constant "100" in the third and fourth cases, and failed to generate the correct expressions. Similarly, in the last two cases, the absence of integer division and least common multiple operators led to wrong answers. Contrastingly, our model, employing dynamic target prediction, generated accurate expressions and results.

Table 3. Comparison of output between our model and baseline on different cases

Problem Text	Answer	MWP-BERT	Our model
分针从12走到6，经过了多少分？	30	$x = 12 * (6 - 12) = -72$	$x = 60 * (12 - 6)/12 = 30$
生产一批零件，师傅做要6小时，徒弟做要10小时，当师徒合作，完成任务时，师傅比徒弟多生产了240个，这批零件共多少个？	960	$x = 240/(6 - 10) * (10 + 6) = -960$	$x = 240/(10 - 6) * (10 + 6) = 960$
一列火车每小时行95千米，它从上午6时跑到下午4时，他跑了多少千米？	950	$x = 95 * 6 = 570$	$x = 95 * ((12 - 6) + 4) = 950$
甲数是10.0，比乙数多2.0，甲数比乙数多多少%？	25	$x = 2/(10 - 2) = 0.25$	$x = 2/(10 - 2) * 100 = 25$
妈妈带50元去超市，买了3瓶料酒，每瓶8元，然后用剩下的钱买奶粉，每袋12元，最多可以买多少袋？	2	$x = (50 - 3 * 8)/12 = 2.1666$	$x = \text{IDV}((50 - 3 * 8), 12) = 2$
有一批故事书，无论是20人分，还是30人分都少2本，这一批故事书最少有多少本？	58	$x = 20 * 30 - 2 = 598$	$x = \text{LCM}(20, 30) - 2 = 58$

5   Conclusion

In this work, a numeracy-enhanced decoding approach for solving MWPs is proposed, which comprises a token embedding method and a target prediction method. On the input side of the decoder, explicit numerical features of numbers are fused with contextual information to obtain numeracy-enhanced embeddings for all numbers, enabling the decoding process to perceive the constraints imposed by numerical properties. On the output side of the decoder, a classifier is utilized to predict the problem category, dynamically invoking category-specific parameter matrices and vocabulary, enabling the model to generate diverse arithmetic expressions. Experimental results demonstrate the proposed method achieves competitive performance on the Chinese MWP and the highest accuracy on Shared Task 3.

However, most MWP research, including this work, has primarily focused on MWPs that can be formulated as equations. In contrast, the Shared Task includes numerous MWPs that cannot be easily formulated as equations. These problems may require a new solving paradigm. Therefore, the MWP community should prioritize exploring new solving paradigms, rather than seeking marginal benchmark improvements solely through network structure enhancements.

Acknowledgments. This work is partially supported by the General Program of the National Natural Science Foundation of China (Grant No: 61977029) and the China Postdoctoral Science Foundation (Grant No: 2023M731245).

References

1. Amini, A., Gabriel, S., Lin, S., Koncel-Kedziorski, R., Choi, Y., Hajishirzi, H.: MathQA: towards interpretable math word problem solving with operation-based formalisms. In: Proceedings of the 2019 Conference of the North American Chapter of the Association for Computational Linguistics: Human Language Technologies, pp. 2357–2367 (2019)
2. Bobrow, D.G.: A question-answering system for high school algebra word problems. In: Proceedings of the 1964 Fall Joint Computer Conference, pp. 591–614 (1964)
3. Cui, Y., Che, W., Liu, T., Qin, B., Yang, Z.: Pre-training with whole word masking for Chinese BERT. IEEE/ACM Trans. Audio Speech Lang. Process. **29**, 3504–3514 (2021)
4. Hu, E.J., et al.: LoRA: low-rank adaptation of large language models. arXiv:2106.09685 (2021)
5. Jie, Z., Li, J., Lu, W.: Learning to reason deductively: math word problem solving as complex relation extraction. In: Proceedings of the 60th Annual Meeting of the Association for Computational Linguistics, pp. 5944–5955 (2022)
6. Kintsch, W., Greeno, J.G.: Understanding and solving word arithmetic problems. Psychol. Rev. **92**, 109 (1985)
7. Kushman, N., Artzi, Y., Zettlemoyer, L., Barzilay, R.: Learning to automatically solve algebra word problems. In: Proceedings of the 52nd Annual Meeting of the Association for Computational Linguistics, pp. 271–281 (2014)
8. Li, Z., et al.: Seeking patterns, not just memorizing procedures: contrastive learning for solving math word problems. In: Findings of the Association for Computational Linguistics, NAACL 2022, pp. 2486–2496 (2022)
9. Liang, Z., et al.: MWP-BERT: numeracy-augmented pre-training for math word problem solving. In: Findings of the Association for Computational Linguistics, NAACL 2022, pp. 997–1009 (2022)

10. Liang, Z., Zhang, J., Zhang, X.: Analogical math word problems solving with enhanced problem-solution association. arXiv:2212.00837 (2022)
11. Lin, X., et al.: Learning relation-enhanced hierarchical solver for math word problems. IEEE Trans. Neural Netw. Learn. Syst. (2023, early access)
12. Lin, X., et al.: HMS: a hierarchical solver with dependency-enhanced understanding for math word problem. In: Proceedings of the 35th AAAI Conference on Artificial Intelligence, pp. 4232–4240 (2021)
13. Liu, Q., Guan, W., Li, S., Kawahara, D.: Tree-structured decoding for solving math word problems. In: Proceedings of the 2019 Conference on Empirical Methods in Natural Language Processing, pp. 2370–2379 (2019)
14. Mor, G., Ankit, G., Jonathan, B.: Injecting numerical reasoning skills into language models. In: Proceedings of the 58th Annual Meeting of the Association for Computational Linguistics, pp. 946–958 (2020)
15. Raffel, C., et al.: Exploring the limits of transfer learning with a unified text-to-text transformer. J. Mach. Learn. Res. **21**, 5485–5551 (2020)
16. Roy, S., Roth, D.: Unit dependency graph and its application to arithmetic word problem solving. In: Proceedings of the 31st AAAI Conference on Artificial Intelligence, pp. 3082–3088 (2017)
17. Shen, J., et al.: Generate & rank: a multi-task framework for math word problems. In: Findings of the Association for Computational Linguistics, EMNLP 2021, pp. 2269–2279 (2021)
18. Shi, S., Wang, Y., Lin, C.Y., Liu, X., Rui, Y.: Automatically solving number word problems by semantic parsing and reasoning. In: Proceedings of the 2015 Conference on Empirical Methods in Natural Language Processing, pp. 1132–1142 (2015)
19. Touvron, H., et al.: LLaMA: open and efficient foundation language models. arXiv arXiv:2302.13971 (2023)
20. Wang, L., Wang, Y., Cai, D., Zhang, D., Liu, X.: Translating a math word problem to an expression tree. In: Proceedings of the 2018 Conference on Empirical Methods in Natural Language Processing, pp. 1064–1069 (2018)
21. Wang, Y., Liu, X., Shi, S.: Deep neural solver for math word problems. In: Proceedings of the 2017 Conference on Empirical Methods in Natural Language Processing, pp. 845–854 (2017)
22. Wu, Q., Zhang, Q., Wei, Z.: An edge-enhanced hierarchical graph-to-tree network for math word problem solving. In: Findings of the Association for Computational Linguistics, EMNLP 2021, pp. 1473–1482 (2021)
23. Xie, Z., Sun, S.: A goal-driven tree-structured neural model for math word problems. In: Proceedings of the 28th International Joint Conference on Artificial Intelligence, pp. 5299–5305 (2019)
24. Yu, X., Wang, M., Gan, W., He, B., Ye, N.: A framework for solving explicit arithmetic word problems and proving plane geometry theorems. Int. J. Pattern Recognit. Artif. Intell. **33**, 1940005:1–1940005:21 (2019)
25. Zhang, J., et al.: Teacher-student networks with multiple decoders for solving math word problem. In: Proceedings of the 29th International Joint Conference on Artificial Intelligence, pp. 4011–4017 (2020)
26. Zhang, J., et al.: Graph-to-tree learning for solving math word problems. In: Proceedings of the 58th Annual Meeting of the Association for Computational Linguistics, pp. 3928–3937 (2020)

Solving Math Word Problem
with Problem Type Classification

Jie Yao, Zihao Zhou, and Qiufeng Wang[✉]

School of Advanced Technology, Xi'an Jiaotong-Liverpool University, Suzhou, China
{Jie.Yao22,Zihao.Zhou22}@student.xjtlu.edu.cn, Qiufeng.Wang@xjtlu.edu.cn

Abstract. Math word problems (MWPs) require analyzing text descriptions and generating mathematical equations to derive solutions. Existing works focus on solving MWPs with two types of solvers: tree-based solver and large language model (LLM) solver. However, these approaches always solve MWPs by a single solver, which will bring the following problems: (1) Single type of solver is hard to solve all types of MWPs well. (2) A single solver will result in poor performance due to over-fitting. To address these challenges, this paper utilizes multiple ensemble approaches to improve MWP-solving ability. Firstly, We propose a problem type classifier that combines the strengths of the tree-based solver and the LLM solver. This ensemble approach leverages their respective advantages and broadens the range of MWPs that can be solved. Furthermore, we also apply ensemble techniques to both tree-based solver and LLM solver to improve their performance. For the tree-based solver, we propose an ensemble learning framework based on ten-fold cross-validation and voting mechanism. In the LLM solver, we adopt self-consistency (SC) method to improve answer selection. Experimental results demonstrate the effectiveness of these ensemble approaches in enhancing MWP-solving ability. The comprehensive evaluation showcases improved performance, validating the advantages of our proposed approach. Our code is available at this url: https://github. com/zhouzihao501/NLPCC2023-Shared-Task3-ChineseMWP.

Keywords: Math Word Problem · Ensemble Learning · Bert2Tree · Large Language Model

1 Introduction

Math word problems (MWPs) are primarily solved by analyzing the text description of the problem and automatically generating mathematical equations to derive the solution, as illustrated in Table 1(a). Initially, the solver extracts the problem's text description and applies pre-processing techniques, including semantic parsing. Subsequently, leveraging the processed text description, the solver examines the mathematical logic relationships with the associated concepts and generates the relevant mathematical equations. Finally, by utilizing the generated equations, the solver obtains the corresponding answers.

J. Yao and Z. Zhou—Equal contribution.

© The Author(s), under exclusive license to Springer Nature Switzerland AG 2023
F. Liu et al. (Eds.): NLPCC 2023, LNAI 14304, pp. 123–134, 2023.
https://doi.org/10.1007/978-3-031-44699-3_12

Table 1. Examples of math word problem

(a) General MWP:
Text: Dingding has read 180 pages of a book and has 150 pages left to read. How many pages are there in this book?
Equation: x = 180 + 150
Answer: 330
(b) Law Finding MWP:
Text: Find the pattern and fill in the numbers. 2, 6, 10, __ , 18
Equation: x = 14
Answer: 14
(c) Unit Conversion MWP:
Text: The ratio of bean paste to white sugar is 2:1. Now there are 450 grams of white sugar, how many kilograms of bean paste are needed?
Equation: x = 450 * 2 ÷ 1000
Answer: 0.9

In recent years, a multitude of natural language processing (NLP) techniques have emerged to tackle MWPs [1], encompassing advancements in semantic parsing and deep learning. Semantic parsing serves as a powerful approach to decompose the textual content of a math problem into structured representations, facilitating the generation of corresponding mathematical expressions [8,14]. Numerous methodologies have been proposed for semantic parsing, spanning rule-based and statistical methods. With the boom of deep learning, the research on solving MWPs has recently made great progress. For example, tree-based models [19,21] as well as large language models (LLM) [16,18,22] have been extensively exploited to deal with MWPs, and increase the accuracy of prediction significantly.

However, these approaches always solve MWPs by a single solver, which usually brings the following two problems. (1) Single type of solver is hard to solve all types of MWPs well. For example, the tree-based solver is unable to solve some types of MWPs like law finding problems (e.g., Table 1(b)) because it relies on combining numbers into MWP and operators (+-*/) to get an answer equation, while the LLM solver is unable to solve complex MWPs due to lacking calculation ability. (2) A single solver tends to result in poor performance due to over-fitting.

To address these challenges, we adopt the following two approaches. (1) To combine the abilities of the tree-based solver and the LLM solver, we propose a problem type classifier. Specifically, we define some heuristic rules to divide MWP types into two categories. One is for LLM solver such as law finding problems and unit conversions problems (e.g., Table 1(c)), and the other is for tree-based solver. (2) To avoid over-fitting and improve the performance of the

LLM solver and tree-based solver, we apply ensemble techniques to both of them. For the tree-based solver, we propose an ensemble learning framework based on ten-fold cross-validation and voting mechanism. In the LLM solver, we adopt the self-consistency (SC) method to select the most appropriate answer and enhance the model's overall performance. Figure 1 shows an overview of our method (Ensemble-MWP). Firstly, the problem type classifier assigns each MWP to one category. Then the corresponding solver (either the tree-based or LLM solver) will process the MWP to obtain a preliminary result. Lastly, we adopt a post-processing method to obtain the final answer. In summary, our contributions are as follows:

- We propose a problem type classifier to combine the abilities of both the tree-based solver and the LLM solver. To the best of our knowledge, this is the first effort to integrate them.
- We propose an ensemble learning framework based on ten-fold cross-validation and voting mechanism for the MWP solver.
- Experimental results demonstrate the effectiveness of these ensemble techniques in enhancing the ability to solve MWPs.

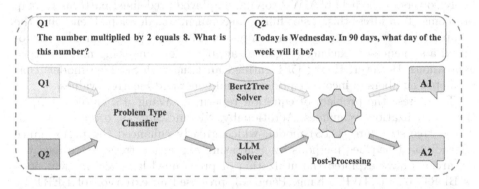

Fig. 1. Overview of Ensemble-MWP. The **Problem Type Classifier** assigns each MWP to either the **Bert2Tree solver** or the **LLM solver** based on a set of predefined rules. Once the classification is determined, the respective solver is employed to process the MWP and generate a preliminary result. The obtained result undergoes further **Post-processing** to derive the final answer

2   Related Work

2.1   Ensemble Learning

Ensemble learning has gained popularity for its ability to enhance predictive performance by combining multiple models. Bagging, a widely adopted ensemble learning technique, aims to reduce learner variation by training multiple samples using the same learning algorithm. Lin [11] conducted a study demonstrating the effectiveness of bagging methods in improving the performance of NLP models. The ten-fold cross-validation we adopt when dividing the dataset using the bagging technique.

Stacking represents another powerful ensemble learning technique, involving the combination of several weak learners using meta-learners. These weak learners are trained independently, and their predictions are then employed as input for the meta-learner, which makes the final decision. Nunes [12] conducted a study utilizing stacking in a document classification task, showcasing its efficacy. We use a problem type classifier that allows the different solvers to play to their strengths.

Moreover, ensemble learning has shown promise in enhancing deep learning models in NLP. Kim [7] conducted a study where they employed an ensemble approach to improve the text classification performance of Convolutional Neural Networks (CNNs). The SC method we utilize in LLM solver is more like a self-ensemble, acting on a single language model.

2.2   Tree-Based MWP Solver

Early solvers in the field of MWP solving employed predefined patterns to map problems. To address this, a slot-filling mechanism was developed, enabling the mapping of problems into equation templates using slots [2–4]. Wang [17] introduced a sequence-to-sequence (Seq2Seq) approach for generating mathematical expressions. However, Huang [5] identified an issue with Seq2Seq models that predicted numbers in incorrect positions and generated incorrect values.

To address the problem of equation repetition, Wang [15] employed equation normalization techniques. Additionally, Xie and Sun [19] proposed a goal-driven tree structure (GTS) model, which greatly enhanced the performance of traditional Seq2Seq methods by generating expression trees. More recently, researchers have explored the utilization of pre-trained language models, such as BERT [6], in MWP solving. Peng [13] proposed an extension of BERT by incorporating numerical information into the input sequence, thereby enhancing the power of BERT in handling MWPs. In this paper, we adopt the sequence-to-tree approach with bert (**Bert2Tree**) to solve MWPs, leveraging its improved performance over traditional methods.

2.3   LLM Solver

In recent years, LLMs have showcased their remarkable capabilities in the field of NLP. Wei's [22] research explored the emerging capabilities of LLMs in solving MWPs through step-by-step reasoning, leveraging cues derived from the chain-of-thought (CoT) [18]. Without avoiding the greedy decoding strategy in the CoT, wang [16] proposed the SC method, which allowed multiple inference paths to reach the correct answer for complex reasoning tasks. In this work, we utilize ChatGLM-6B [20] as our LLM solver.

3   Research Methodology

Fig. 1 shows the overview of our method (Ensemble-MWP), which contains four main components: problem type classifier, Bert2Tree solver, LLM solver, and post-processing stage. Firstly, the problem type classifier assigns each MWP to either the tree-based solver or the LLM solver. Once the classification is determined, the respective solver is employed to process the MWP and generate a preliminary result. Lastly, the final result is obtained through a post-processing block. In the following, we will describe more details of each component.

3.1   Problem Type Classifier

In our proposed problem type classifier, we integrate the Bert2Tree solver and the LLM solver. The main objective of the classifier is to categorize the MWPs in the dataset into two categories. The first category comprises MWPs that can be effectively solved by the Bert2Tree solver. Consequently, these MWPs are directed to the Bert2Tree solver for further processing. The second category consists of MWPs that are beyond the capabilities of the Bert2Tree solver. For this category, we utilize the LLM solver to handle them.

The classification process is guided by specific heuristic rules to identify particular problem types. For instance, problems involving unit conversions (e.g., centimeters, decimeters, meters), law finding, and decimal point transformations are categorized as MWPs that the Bert2Tree solver is unable to solve. As a result, these specific problem types are directed to the LLM solver, which is better equipped to address them. By employing these heuristic rules, we effectively determine the appropriate solver for each MWP based on its characteristics.

3.2   Bert2Tree Solver

Model Structure: As illustrated in Fig. 2, the Bert2Tree model is employed to solve the MWP. Firstly, we input the question text into the Bert2Tree model. Secondly, the model encodes the question text and generates the corresponding equation tree. Thirdly, we calculate $8 \div 2 = 4$ according to the equation tree. Finally, the Bert2Tree model returns the answer of 4.0.

For the structure of Bert2Tree, we adopt BERT as our encoder, we represent the question Q as a sequence of T tokens: $Q = [q_1, q_2, ..., q_T]$ and the process of encoding is

$$[h_1^q, h_2^q, ..., h_T^q] = BERT\left([q_1, q_2, ..., q_T]\right), \tag{1}$$

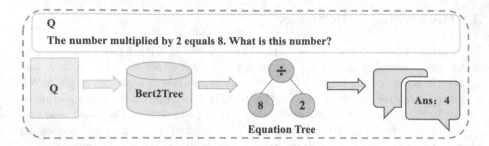

Fig. 2. The process of Bert2Tree solver. The MWP is fed into the **Bert2Tree model**, which performs a comprehensive analysis of the MWP text. Bert2Tree generates an **equation tree** that accurately captures the underlying mathematical structure of the problem. By extracting the mathematical expression from the tree, the model is able to compute the answer

where h_i^q represents the embedding of token q_i from the encoder. At last, the representation of question is H^Q:

$$H^Q = [h_1^q, h_2^q, ..., h_T^q]. \tag{2}$$

Then, we use a TreeDecoder to generate equation tree ET according to H^Q: $ET = [et_1, et_2, ..., et_n]$, where n is the length of the pre-order of equation tree, it can be written as:

$$[et_1, et_2, ..., et_n] = TreeDecoder\left(H^Q\right). \tag{3}$$

Finally, calculate the equation tree can get the final **Answer**:

$$Answer = Calculate\left(ET\right). \tag{4}$$

Ten-Fold Cross-Validation: In this paper, we use a ten-fold cross-validation method to avoid overfitting and improve the generalization performance of the model. We break the dataset into 10 equal parts randomly: $D_0 - D_9$. In the first model, D_9 is used as the validation set, and the remaining 9 parts are used as the training set to train the model and make predictions on the validation set. The accuracy of the model on the validation set is calculated and recorded. For the next 9 models, a different copy of the data is used as the validation set each time, and the remaining 9 copies are used as the training set. Finally, we get the accuracy of the 10 sets of models to evaluate the performance of the models.

Voting Mechanism: In the process of improving the answer accuracy, we use the voting mechanism of ensemble learning to improve the probability of predicting the correct answer. When predicting the answer to the problem, there are two cases in our voting mechanism: (1) Different models have different predictions, so we first choose the one with the most occurrences among the models as the final answer. (2) In cases where we have an equal number of voting results, we compare the sum of the accuracy of the validation sets of the models with the same prediction results, we set the accuracy of validation sets as the **confidence score** and select the one with the largest sum of confidence score as the final answer.

MWP-Bert and Data Augmentation: To further improve the ability of the Bert2tree solver, we use better encoder and data augmentation strategies. For the encoder, we use MWP-Bert [10], an MWP-specific pre-training language model. For data augmentation, we use Li's strategies [9]. They generate new MWPs by knowledge-guided entity replacement and logic-guided problem reorganization.

3.3 LLM Solver

In this paper, we utilize ChatGLM-6B as our LLM solver. To improve the performance of ChatGLM-6B, we use the Chain-of-Thought and Self-Consistency techniques.

Chain-of-Thought (CoT): The LLM solver relies primarily on the widely adopted CoT prompting [18], which has gained popularity in recent years. Few chain of thought demonstrations provided as exemplars in prompting can significantly improve the ability of large language models to perform complex reasoning. Specifically, we provide 8 MWPs in prompt and manually annotate detailed CoT for each MWP example. This enables the solver to acquire a comprehensive understanding of the problem-solving process and develop the capacity to apply logical thinking to mathematical challenges.

Self-Consistency (SC) Method: In the LLM solver, we leverage the SC [16] method as an integral component of our approach. It samples a diverse set of reasoning paths instead of only taking the greedy one and then selects the most consistent answer by marginalizing out the sampled reasoning paths. Specifically, we generated 20 answers for each MWP. By incorporating the SC method into our LLM solver, we enhance the accuracy and robustness of the generated solutions, enabling more reliable and effective MWP solving.

3.4 Post-processing

Upon obtaining results from both models, an additional step is carried out to process the answers using uniform rules, leading to the derivation of the final results. This post-processing stage plays a crucial role in improving the accuracy rate by applying specific rules to refine the answers. For example, one common rule involves retaining only two digits after the decimal point, ensuring precision and consistency in the results. Additionally, certain rules may involve omitting trailing zeros, eliminating any unnecessary redundancy or ambiguity in the final answers. These tailored rules provide a systematic approach to refine and standardize the answers, addressing any potential inconsistencies or inaccuracies generated by the individual models.

4   Experiments

4.1   Dataset Setting

We adopt Math23K [17] as our training dataset, which comprises 23,162 MWP examples. To ensemble Bert2Tree models, we use ten-fold cross-validation and obtain ten models. Each model's training dataset consists of 20,844 MWP examples, and the remaining 2,316 examples are included in the validation dataset. To evaluate our proposed Ensemble-MWP, we conduct experiments on a validation set of the NLPCC2023 Shared Task3 completion[1], which consists of 1,200 MWP examples. It is challenging to solve these MPWs because they have a low overlap of lexicon and templates with the Math23K dataset. We call these samples **Challenging Examples**, which make the models more difficult to generalize from the patterns and relationships seen in the training data.

4.2   Experimental Settings

To compare the model performance, we adopt the answers' accuracy as our evaluation metric, which is calculated by comparing the predicted answer with the correct answer. The higher the accuracy, the better the effect of the model or method used. For the baseline MPW solver, we adopt Bert2Tree [19] without voting mechanism and LLM solver [20] without SC as our baseline model in the experiments.

4.3   Experimental Results

Bert2Tree Solver: Through ten-fold cross-validation, we obtain the accuracy of each model, allowing us to compare the accuracy of different models. The results are shown in Table 2, where we can see that the accuracy ranges from 23.2% to 25.2%. Furthermore, we adopt MWP-Bert and Data augmentation on each Bert2Tree solver. In Table 3, we compared the accuracy of the model with and without the voting mechanism. We observed that when we used the voting mechanism, the accuracy improved from 24.1% to 26%. These results demonstrate that the voting mechanism is useful in solving MWPs correctly. When comparing Table 2 and 4, we see that the accuracy of the ten models are all improved when using MWP-BERT and data augmentation. It shows that using a domain-specific pre-trained language model like MWP-BERT and data augmentation can lead to better performance. As shown in Table 5, the accuracy was further improved by 2.8% when using the voting mechanism. It indicates that our voting mechanism is also efficient in stronger models.

---

[1] https://github.com/2003pro/CNMWP/tree/main/data.

Table 2. The performance of ten Bert2Tree solvers

Model (BERT)	M_0	M_1	M_2	M_3	M_4	M_5	M_6	M_7	M_8	M_9
Accuracy (%)	23.9	24.8	23.9	23.2	23.8	24.4	23.4	24.4	23.8	25.2

Table 3. Comparison of different methods. The accuracy of the baseline is the average of the ten models' accuracy in Table 2. The accuracy of the VoteMWP is the accuracy achieved by using the voting mechanism

Methods (BERT)	Baseline	**VoteMWP**
Accuracy (%)	24.1	**26.0**

Table 4. The performance of 10 Bert2tree solvers with MWP-Bert and data augmentation (DA)

Model (MWP-BERT+DA)	M_0	M_1	M_2	M_3	M_4	M_5	M_6	M_7	M_8	M_9
Accuracy (%)	25.8	25.8	26.1	26.6	25.4	24.5	26.1	24.3	25.6	25.5

Table 5. Comparison of different methods. The accuracy of the baseline is the average of the ten models' accuracy in Table 4. The accuracy of the VoteMWP is the accuracy achieved by using the voting mechanism

Methods (MWP-BERT+DA)	Baseline	**VoteMWP**
Accuracy (%)	25.6	**28.4**

LLM Solver: As we can see in Table 6, after incorporating the CoT prompting technique, the LLM solver initially achieves an accuracy rate of 5%. With the addition of the SC method, the accuracy rate of the LLM solver significantly improves to 9.17%. This enhancement demonstrates the effectiveness of integrating the SC method, as it directly contributes to the improved performance and reliability of the LLM solver in solving MWPs.

Problem Type Classifier: In our comparative analysis, we evaluate the performance of the Bert2Tree solver, the LLM solver, and the Ensemble-MWP solver. The results demonstrate that the integrated Ensemble-MWP solver achieves significantly higher accuracy compared to the individual solvers in Table 7.

By combining the strengths of multiple solvers and leveraging ensemble techniques, our integrated Ensemble-MWP solver offers improved capabilities in solving MWPs. The collaborative nature of the ensemble approach allows for the aggregation of insights and decision-making from multiple solvers, resulting in enhanced accuracy.

Table 6. Comparison of different methods in the LLM Solver. CoT prompting is used in the LLM solver, and we add the SC method later

Methods	CoT	**CoT + SC**
Accuracy (%)	5.00	**9.17**

Table 7. Comparison of different MWP Solvers. Three MWP Solvers: Bert2Tree Solver, LLM Solver, Ensemble-MWP

Solvers	Bert2Tree	LLM	**Ensemble-MWP**
Accuracy (%)	28.4	9.17	**33.1**

4.4 Case Study

In Fig. 3, we present a real case of Ensemble-MWP to illustrate the challenges faced when using a single solver. When both questions are inputted into a single solver, whether it is the Bert2Tree solver or the LLM solver, it is impossible to answer both questions correctly. However, by employing Ensemble-MWP, we utilize a problem type classifier that assigns each problem to the appropriate solver, resulting in accurate and reliable solutions for both questions. Through this ensemble approach, the final correct results are obtained, overcoming the limitations of using a single solver for multiple math word problems.

Q1	Bert2Tree: 24 ✓	**Problem Type**	**Final Result**
One factor is 6, the other factor is 4, what is the product?	LLM: 16 ✗	Bert2Tree	24 ✓
Q2	Bert2Tree: 27 ✗	**Problem Type**	**Final Result**
Find the pattern and fill in the numbers. 1, 3, 9, 27, __, 243.	LLM: 81 ✓	LLM	81 ✓

Fig. 3. Two cases solved by Ensemble-MWP

5   Conclusion and Future Work

In this paper, we propose an ensemble technique to enhance the capability of the MWP solver. By combining the strengths of the Bert2Tree solver and the LLM solver, we significantly improve the overall MWP-solving performance. Our approach capitalizes on the unique advantages offered by each solver, resulting in a novel and effective solution. Within the Bert2Tree solver, we introduce a ten-fold cross-validation and voting mechanism to further enhance the model's robustness and reliability. Through multiple iterations of cross-validation, we rigorously evaluate the performance of the solver on different subsets of the data. The integration of the voting mechanism ensures robust decision-making by considering the collective insights of the model's predictions. These enhancements not only improve the accuracy of the Bert2Tree solver but also bolster its resilience to handle diverse MWPs effectively.

In the future, our goal is to develop an automatic classifier that can proficiently identify the appropriate solver for MWPs. This innovative approach aims to alleviate the reliance on predefined rules, consequently enhancing the robustness of the system. By leveraging machine learning techniques, the classifier will autonomously categorize MWPs, assigning them to the most suitable solver based on their unique characteristics.

Acknowledgments. This research was funded by National Natural Science Foundation of China (NSFC) no.62276258, Jiangsu Science and Technology Programme (Natural Science Foundation of Jiangsu Province) no. BE2020006-4, Xi'an Jiaotong-Liverpool University's Key Program Special Fund no. KSF-E-43.

References

1. Bobrow, D.G.: Natural language input for a computer problem solving system (1964). www.api.semanticscholar.org/CorpusID:56584838
2. Bobrow, D.G.: A question-answering system for high school algebra word problems. In: Proceedings of 1964 Fall Joint Computer Conference, Part I, pp. 591–614 (1964)
3. Dellarosa, D.: A computer simulation of children's arithmetic word-problem solving. Behav. Res. Methods Instr. Comput. **18**(2), 147–154 (1986)
4. Fletcher, C.R.: Understanding and solving arithmetic word problems: a computer simulation. Behav. Res. Methods Instr. Comput. **17**(5), 565–571 (1985)
5. Huang, D., Liu, J., Lin, C.Y., Yin, J.: Neural math word problem solver with reinforcement learning. In: Proceedings of the 27th International Conference on Computational Linguistics, pp. 213–223 (2018)
6. Kenton, J.D.M.W.C., Toutanova, L.K.: Bert: pre-training of deep bidirectional transformers for language understanding. In: Proceedings of NAACL-HLT, vol. 1, p. 2 (2019)
7. Kim, Y., Jernite, Y., Sontag, D., Rush, A.: Character-aware neural language models. In: Proceedings of the AAAI Conference on Artificial Intelligence, vol. 30 (2016)
8. Koncel-Kedziorski, R., Hajishirzi, H., Sabharwal, A., Etzioni, O., Ang, S.D.: Parsing algebraic word problems into equations. Trans. Assoc. Comput. Linguistics **3**, 585–597 (2015)
9. Li, A., Xiao, Y., Liang, J., Chen, Y.: Semantic-based data augmentation for math word problems. In: Database Systems for Advanced Applications: 27th International Conference, DASFAA 2022, Virtual Event, April 11–14, 2022, Proceedings, Part III, pp. 36–51. Springer (2022)
10. Liang, Z., Zhang, J., Wang, L., Qin, W., Lan, Y., Shao, J., Zhang, X.: Mwp-bert: numeracy-augmented pre-training for math word problem solving. arXiv preprint arXiv:2107.13435 (2021)

11. Lin, S., Kung, Y., Leu, F.: Predictive intelligence in harmful news identification by bert-based ensemble learning model with text sentiment analysis. Inf. Process. Manag. **59**(2), 102872 (2022)
12. Nunes, R.M., Domingues, M.A., Feltrim, V.D.: Improving multilabel text classification with stacking and recurrent neural networks. In: Silva, T.H., Dorini, L.B., Almeida, J.M., Marques-Neto, H.T. (eds.) WebMedia '22: Brazilian Symposium on Multimedia and Web, Curitiba, Brazil, November 7–11, 2022, pp. 117–122. ACM (2022)
13. Peng, S., Yuan, K., Gao, L., Tang, Z.: Mathbert: A pre-trained model for mathematical formula understanding. arXiv preprint arXiv:2105.00377 (2021)
14. Shi, S., Wang, Y., Lin, C.Y., Liu, X., Rui, Y.: Automatically solving number word problems by semantic parsing and reasoning. In: Proceedings of the 2015 Conference on Empirical Methods in Natural Language Processing, pp. 1132–1142. Association for Computational Linguistics, Lisbon, Portugal, September 2015
15. Wang, L., Wang, Y., Cai, D., Zhang, D., Liu, X.: Translating a math word problem to an expression tree. arXiv preprint arXiv:1811.05632 (2018)
16. Wang, X., et al.: Self-consistency improves chain of thought reasoning in language models. arXiv preprint arXiv:2203.11171 (2022)
17. Wang, Y., Liu, X., Shi, S.: Deep neural solver for math word problems. In: Proceedings of the 2017 Conference on Empirical Methods in Natural Language Processing, pp. 845–854 (2017)
18. Wei, J., Wang, X., Schuurmans, D., Bosma, M., Xia, F., Chi, E., Le, Q.V., Zhou, D., et al.: Chain-of-thought prompting elicits reasoning in large language models. Adv. Neural. Inf. Process. Syst. **35**, 24824–24837 (2022)
19. Xie, Z., Sun, S.: A goal-driven tree-structured neural model for math word problems. In: Ijcai. pp. 5299–5305 (2019)
20. Zeng, A., et al.: Glm-130b: An open bilingual pre-trained model. arXiv preprint arXiv:2210.02414 (2022)
21. Zhou, Z., Ning, M., Wang, Q., Yao, J., Wang, W., Huang, X., Huang, K.: Learning by analogy: Diverse questions generation in math word problem. In: Findings of the Association for Computational Linguistics: ACL 2023, pp. 11091–11104. Association for Computational Linguistics, Toronto, Canada, July 2023. www.aclanthology.org/2023.findings-acl.705
22. Zoph, B., et al.: Emergent abilities of large language models. TMLR (2022)

Consistent Solutions for Optimizing Search Space of Beam Search

Yehui Xu, Sihui Li, Chujun Pu, Jin Wang, and Xiaobing Zhou$^{(\boxtimes)}$

School of Information Science and Engineering, Yunnan University, Kunming, China
zhouxb@ynu.edu.cn

Abstract. Research on math word problems has made significant advancements due to the emergence of language models. Large language models have excelled in a variety of reasoning tasks. Still, due to the demand for low costs, research on the upper bound of small language models in reasoning tasks and the limitation of the knowledge they can accommodate has drawn attention. In line with previous work on math word problems, we discover that models that only learned a single solution lacked reasoning ability during the decoding process, further exacerbating the error accumulation caused by exposure bias that will fail generalization. To tackle this problem, we suggest using the commutative property to generate a consistent solution set for each data in the training set. Then, we use it as additional training data to optimize the search space in beam search. On this foundation, we will go into great detail about how consistent solutions training affects the work process of beam search. In addition, we found significant differences between models trained using consistent solutions and those trained without consistent solutions, so the model ensemble technique is applied to improve model performance. In the NLPCC-2023 shared task 3, our model ultimately ranks fourth with an accuracy of 23.66%.

Keywords: Math Word Problem · Consistent Solutions · Beam Search

1 Introduction

Since the advent of pre-trained language models (PLMs), the enhancement in model performance on knowledge-intensive tasks like arithmetic reasoning and common sense reasoning has been attributed to the ability of semantic representation and the acquisition of knowledge learned implicitly by PLMs trained on pre-training tasks. The math word problem (MWP), as an important branch task in arithmetic reasoning, has attracted the attention of many scholars. Large language models (LLMs) such as GPT-4 [1] achieve SOTA on reasoning tasks, but training them is extremely expensive. Thus, exploring the upper bound of the capability of small language models and the limitation of the knowledge they can accommodate is a more crucial issue.

Numerous scholars have made outstanding contributions to previous work on MWP. Still, typically they only use one solution to each question in the training set, which will further damage generalization performance by exacerbating

© The Author(s), under exclusive license to Springer Nature Switzerland AG 2023
F. Liu et al. (Eds.): NLPCC 2023, LNAI 14304, pp. 135–146, 2023.
https://doi.org/10.1007/978-3-031-44699-3_13

136   Y. Xu et al.

Table 1. The example of consistent solutions

Text(W)	小李由乡里到县城办事每小时行4.0千米，到预定到达时间时，离县城还有1.5千米，如果小李每小时走5.5千米，到预定到达时间时，又会多走4.5 千米. 乡里距县城多少千米？ Xiao Li travels 4.0 km per hour from the village to the county seat to handle affairs. At the scheduled arrival time, he was still 1.5 km away from the county seat. If Xiao Li travels 5.5 km per hour, he will travel an additional 4.5 km by the scheduled arrival time. How many kilometers is the distance from the village to the county seat?
Solution 1(S^1)	$+, \times, \div, +, 4.5, 1.5, -, 5.5, 4.0, 4.0, 1.5$
Solution 2(S^2)	$+, \times, \mathbf{4.0}, \div, +, 4.5, 1.5, -, 5.5, 4.0, 1.5$
Final Answer(A)	17.5

the error accumulation of ingrained exposure bias in the generative model [2]. To address this, we propose utilizing the addition commutative and multiplication commutative properties to generate consistent solutions for each question in the training set. These consistent solutions are equivalent, as shown in Table 1. Training the model with consistent solutions can optimize the search space of beam search, reducing the error accumulation in exposure bias exacerbated by training with only one solution. This is due to the fact that consistent solutions can give the model the information to enhance reasoning abilities in the decoder, i.e., there may be a number of reasonable options available at each time step as opposed to using a single ground truth in a single solution, forcing the model to generate an optimal sequence of a solution according to the different ground truths from consistent solutions, which can be regarded as a disguised approximation strategy to not using ground truth in training. In testing, this will encourage model learning to adjust to circumstances without ground truth.

In addition, a significant distinction is found between models trained with consistent solutions and those without, based on comparing results on the validation set. The intuitive approach is to use this difference combined with the model ensemble technique to improve the accuracy of the test set.

To sum up, our main contributions are as follows:

1. We use the consistent solutions generated by using the commutative property to replace the single solution when training the model and explain how the consistent solutions optimize the search space of beam search.

2. We utilize two models, one trained with consistent solutions and one trained without consistent solutions, to further improve the model's performance with the model ensemble.

We achieve fourth place in the NLPCC-2023 shared task 3 with an accuracy of 23.66% on the test set. The specific ranking is shown in Table 2. Our system name is "Tsingriver". Our codes are available at Github[1].

[1] http://github.com/vincent-hyx/NLPCC2023.

Table 2. The ranking of the NLPCC-2023 shared task on Math Word Problem. Only the top five results are shown in the table. A total of 18 teams participated in the task, of which 7 teams submitted the results

Rank	System Name	Score(Acc)
1	Mimic Solver	45.83
2	Lagrange	29.75
3	Rush up	24.08
4	**Tsingriver**	**23.66**
5	BLCU-LCClab	22.58

2   Related Work

Parsing-based methods and rule-based methods attempt expression templates that summarize various problems from data, but the generalization performance is only moderately effective [3–6]. More researchers have concentrated their efforts on considering MWP as a generative task and continuing to optimize it since the invention of the seq2seq model. The seq2seq model is used as a baseline model on the proposed Chinese MWP dataset math23k [7].

In terms of decoder architecture, to adapt to the characteristics of generated solutions in MWP, many scholars have proposed tree-structured decoder [8–10], among which GTS [10] is considered a strong baseline model. Pointer networks utilized to enhance tree-structured decoder are impacted by machine translation model [11,12].

To improve the semantic representation of the encoder, graph convolutional networks are applied to capture relationships between quantities in math problems [13]. Similarly, the dependency parsing of hierarchical structure as semantic information is fused into an encoder to enhance the representation of the GTS model.

From the standpoint of deep reinforcement learning, the generative model could be considered a policy network employing the policy gradient algorithm to optimize the model's capacity for generation [14].

With the emergence of pre-trained language models like BERT [15], the MWP tasks have been switched to the generative model named bert2tree, with BERT and GTS Decoder as the backbone. Subsequent research improves model performance on more detailed issues, such as strengthening the model's awareness of numerical values through auxiliary or extra pre-training tasks [16–18], utilizing contrastive learning to increase the accuracy of solving the problem with similar solutions [19], and incorporating multilingual settings to boost generalization [20].

Inspired by the generative adversarial network (GAN), another mainstream method in the MWP problem employs the ranker network as a discriminator to score the answers in the candidate set generated by the generator. In order to better enhance representation through generative adversarial training, sampling candidate sets has become an important issue. Two methods to generate additional candidate answers, including adding tree-based disturbance to real labels [21] or using the diversity of solutions [22], both demonstrate the importance of using effective data augmentation for sampling.

In addition to regarding MWP as a generating task, the method combining deductive reasoning to treat MWP as an extraction task also shows excellent performance [23].

To sum up, inspired by the diversity of consistent solutions [22], in order to optimize the search space of the decoder, we use the commutative property to obtain the consistent solutions set for each problem and use it directly as training data to fine-tune the generative model consisting of the Mengzi encoder [24] and GTS decoder. Finally, we found significant differences between models trained using consistent solutions and those trained without consistent solutions, so the model ensemble technique is applied to improve model performance (Fig. 1).

3 Proposed System

3.1 Problem Statement

Given a data (W, S, A) from dataset $\mathcal{D}$, we denote the background and the question as the input $W = \{w_1, w_2, ..., w_n\}$ with length n, while the generated solution $S = \{s_1, s_2, ..., s_m\}$ following the pre-order traversal ordering is calculated to derive final answer A. Next, we define that S consisting of V_{num}, V_{op} and V_{con}, where $V_{num} = \{n_1, n_2, ..., n_l\}$ is variable-length set containing all the numerical quantities involved in W. $V_{op} = \{+, -, \times, \div, \wedge\}$ and $V_{con} = \{1, \pi\}$ denote the operators and the constant values that could be used in the solution, respectively. With number mapping [7], the elements among V_{num} transformed to $[NUM1], [NUM2], .., [NUMl]$ will be recognized by the encoder as a special token to encode all tokens in W uniformly.

Given W and S from $\mathcal{D}$ in the training stage, we first encode W using a pre-trained model, and then we extract the state H_{en} of the last hidden layer to represent W, which can be indicated as follows:

$$H_{en} = Encoder(W). \tag{1}$$

the conditional probability $p(S|W)$ can be decomposed as

$$p(S|W) = \prod_{i=1}^{m} p(s_i|h_i, H_{en}), \tag{2}$$

where h_i uniformly denote the i-th hidden state containing q_i and c_i used in GTS decoder [10]. At the beginning of decoding, q_1 is the vector of $[CLS]$ token from all the hidden state H_{en} and c_i is always derived by calculating attention between H_{en} and q_i. The objective is to minimize the negative log-likelihood of $\mathcal{D}$:

$$\mathcal{L} = \sum_{(W,S)\in\mathcal{D}} -\log p(S|W). \tag{3}$$

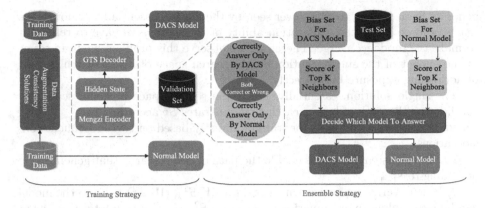

Training Strategy   Ensemble Strategy

Fig. 1. On the left is the training strategy with consistent solutions, and on the right is the ensemble strategy

3.2 Consistent Solutions

During the training stage, the teaching forcing mechanism will force the ground truth of the previous time step as the reasoning premise of the current time step. To simplify the decoding process and highlight the role of the ground truth of the previous time step, we can regard it as a Markov Decision Process. When using GTS decoder as an illustration, the conditional probability p_i^1 and p_i^2 can be expressed as follows:

$$
p_i^1 = \begin{cases} p(s_i^1|s_{i-1}^1), & \text{if } s_i^1 \text{ is left child} \\ p(s_i^1|s_{i-j}^1, ..., s_{i-1}^1), & \text{if } s_i^1 \text{ is right child} \end{cases}
\tag{4}
$$

$$
p_i^2 = \begin{cases} p(s_i^2|s_{i-1}^2), & \text{if } s_i^2 \text{ is left child} \\ p(s_i^2|s_{i-j}^2, ..., s_{i-1}^2), & \text{if } s_i^2 \text{ is right child} \end{cases}
\tag{5}
$$

where s_i^1 and s_i^2 denotes the prediction in current time step i, s_{i-1}^1 from solution 1 S^1 indicates the ground truth in previous time step i-1 and s_{i-j}^1 is parent node of s_i^1. Assumes s_{i-1}^2 is another ground truth from solution 2 S^2. For instance, 4.0 in S^1 and ÷ in S^2 both could be ground truth at the third time step as shown in Table 1. Let's use the left child node as an example to make the explanation more straightforward.

Considering only S^1 is used in training, the model would maximize the conditional probability p_i^1 in Eq. 4. However, in testing, if s_{i-1}^1 isn't selected and s_{i-1}^2 appear in the path of beam search, the specific predicted token of s_i^2 could be wrong even resulting error accumulation due to the conditional probability p_i^2 never seen by the model. Thus, the beam search algorithm will be invalid for searching consistent solutions except S^1, resulting in performance loss manifested as insufficient reasoning ability during decoding.

It is worth emphasizing that the insufficient reasoning ability is caused by the complete dependence on the only ground truth S^1, simultaneously failing to generate S^2 according to s^2_{i-1} never seen by the model. Essentially, although the teaching force limits the exploration ability of the model, we have to rely on it to make the model converge. Therefore, we observe this problem again in terms of the impact of the single solution on the search space of beam search instead of addressing exposure bias directly.

The single solution, essentially, limits the search space of beam search by invalidating the path of beam search that generates S^2 according to s^2_{i-1}. Thus, we adopt consistent solutions for training directly based on two subsequent considerations:

1) The consistent solutions enable the path of beam search that generates S^2 according to s^2_{i-1}.

2) When overfitting occurs with the data (W, S^1), (W, S^2) fed into the model can be regarded as an examination to generate S^2 and s^2_{i-1} simulates the output of the model used to predict the next token in testing, which is a disguised approximation strategy to not using ground truth in training.

Ideally, all the consistent solutions to each data should be sampled as training data to address this problem. But the cost of manually labeling all consistent solutions is relatively expensive. Thus, only the addition commutative property and the multiplication commutative property are utilized to generate consistent solutions. The experimental examples and figures for optimizing the search space of beam search are offered in Sect. 4.4.

3.3   Model Ensemble

The data distribution with respect to $\mathcal{D}$ is defined as $\mathcal{P}_{\mathcal{D}}(W)$, and a data $(W_1, S^1_1) \sim \mathcal{P}_{\mathcal{D}}(W)$. Next, We denote $\mathcal{D}^*$ as the dataset augmented through consistent solutions, corresponding to the data distribution $\mathcal{P}_{\mathcal{D}^*}(W)$. Thus, W_1 with t solutions and $(W_1, S^t_1) \sim \mathcal{P}_{\mathcal{D}^*}(W)$.

The model with parameters θ trained on the data distribution $\mathcal{P}_{\mathcal{D}}(W)$ is denoted as M_θ and the model with parameters θ^* trained on $\mathcal{P}_{\mathcal{D}^*}(W)$ denoted as M_{θ^*}. A significant distinction between models trained with consistent solutions and those without is found based on comparing results on the validation set. Thus, we attempt to utilize two models combined model ensemble to improve performance. To start with, construct bias sets for M_θ and M_{θ^*}. We define that B_{M_θ} as bias set involving W can be answered correctly by M_θ only, and $B_{M_{\theta^*}}$ as bias set involving W can be answered correctly by M_{θ^*} only. They can be described as follows:

$$B_\theta = \{W | W \in R(M_\theta(\cdot)), W \in E(M_{\theta^*}(\cdot))\}, \tag{6}$$

$$B_{\theta^*} = \{W | W \in R(M_{\theta^*}(\cdot)), W \in E(M_\theta(\cdot))\}, \tag{7}$$

where $R(\cdot)$ and $E(\cdot)$ are indicating functions. $R(\cdot)$ and $E(\cdot)$ indicate the problem from the validation set answered correctly and incorrectly, respectively.

Given a new $\hat{W}$, B_θ and $B_{\theta*}$, the encoder with parameters θ, uniformly, is used to derive the $[CLS]$ vector corresponding to $\hat{W}$ and the $[CLS]$ vector set corresponding to B_{M_θ} and $B_{M_{\theta*}}$ separately.

$$CLS_{\hat{W}} = Encoder_\theta(\hat{W}) \tag{8}$$

$$CLS_{B_\theta} = Encoder_\theta(B_\theta) \tag{9}$$

$$CLS_{B_{\theta*}} = Encoder_\theta(B_{\theta*}) \tag{10}$$

Next, we calculate cosine similarity between $CLS_{\hat{W}}$ and each element in CLS_{B_θ} and take the top k $[CLS]$ vector from CLS_{B_θ} denoted as $CLS_{B_\theta}^i$ according to cosine similarity in descending order. Similarly, we perform the same operation between $CLS_{\hat{W}}$ and $CLS_{B_{\theta*}}$ as described above. Final, we respectively calculate the score of $\hat{W}$ on two bias sets as follows:

$$Score_{B_\theta} = \frac{1}{k} \sum_{i=1}^{k} sim(CLS_{\hat{W}}, CLS_{B_\theta}^i), \tag{11}$$

$$Score_{B_{\theta*}} = \frac{1}{k} \sum_{i=1}^{k} sim(CLS_{\hat{W}}, CLS_{B_{\theta*}}^i), \tag{12}$$

where $sim(\cdot)$ indicates cosine similarity. $\hat{W}$ will be solved by M_θ if $Score_{B_\theta} > Score_{B_{\theta*}}$, otherwise by $M_{\theta*}$.

4   Experiment

4.1   Dataset

Experiments are conducted on the challenging dataset from NLPCC-2023 shared task 3, a well-annotated MWP dataset in Chinese. The training, validation, and test sets include 23162, 1200, and 1200 data, respectively.

Due to the commutative property being used to generate additional consistent solutions for each problem in the training set if their solution is commutative, the number of data in the training set is 48,103. Each question in the training set has a corresponding solution, whereas the validation and test sets only contain the final answer. This is a minor distinction between the training, validation, and test sets. Thus, the accuracy of the final answer serves as the evaluation metric in NLPCC-2023 shared task 3.

4.2   Implementation Details

In the training phase, we use AdamW [25] to optimize our models and tune hyperparameters based on the validation set results. In the hyperparameter setting, it is appropriate to set the learning rate at 8e-5 for the model trained without consistent solutions and 4e-5 for the model trained with consistent solutions. We recommend setting the rest of the hyperparameters involving warmup

Table 3. All results on the validation set. ✔ and ✘ indicate the model trained with or without consistent solutions

Model	Consistent Solutions	Acc.
Ernie2tree	✘	23.3
mBART	✘	19.0
mBART	✔	21.1
Mengzi2tree	✘	25.8
Mengzi2tree	✔	26.3
Model Ensemle	-	29.4

steps, dropout rate, hidden size, embedding size, and beam size at 3000, 0.5, 768, 128, and 3, respectively.

In the ensemble phase, we start with a statistical analysis of the results of two models on the validation set. Although the accuracy of the validation set for the two models is only marginally different, a detailed analysis of the answers of the models on particular questions reveals significant differences in that 37 problems are answered correctly only by M_θ and 62 problems are answered correctly only by M_{θ^*}. Thus, we utilize it to improve performance based on the hypothesis that the consistent distribution on validation and testing sets.

4.3 Experimental Results

Due to only one submission for the test set being allowed, we display all results on the validation set in Table 3. And the submission for the test set is shown in Table 2.

We experimented with two PLMs that work better in a Chinese context. In addition to comparing results from the end-to-end generative model to fine-tuning, mBART, used in previous work, is also added to our experiment.

Ernie-3.0-Base [26]. AutoRegressive and AutoEncoder networks are creatively combined for pre-training in ERNIE 3.0 by including semantic tasks like entity prediction, judging sentence causality, and reconstructing article sentence structure.

Mengzi-Bert-Base [24]. Mengzi encoder is a pre-trained model on 300G Chinese corpus. Masked language modeling(MLM), part-of-speech(POS) tagging and sentence order prediction(SOP) are used to train.

mBART [27]. With earlier methods concentrating just on the encoder, decoder, or reconstructing portions of the text, mBART is the first method to pre-train the complete sequence-to-sequence model by denoising full texts in multilingual setting.

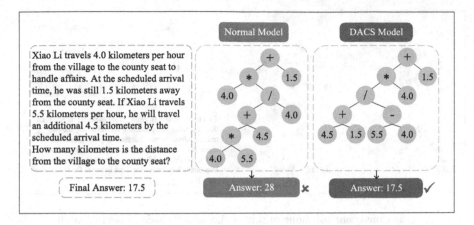

Fig. 2. Solution on two models. The DACS Model indicates the model trained with consistent solutions, while the Normal Model is trained without consistent solutions

4.4 Case Study

Solution on Models. The compared example from the validation set is fed into the Mengzi2tree with and without consistent solutions. The solution output is shown in Fig. 2.

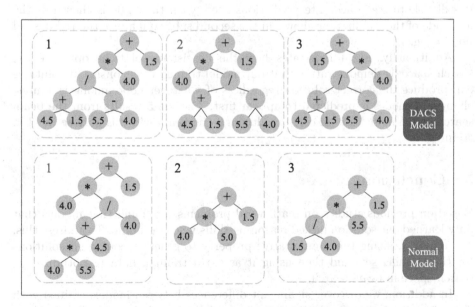

Fig. 3. The results of beam search on two models. The beam search result from the model trained with consistent solutions is shown above the red dashed line (Color figure online)

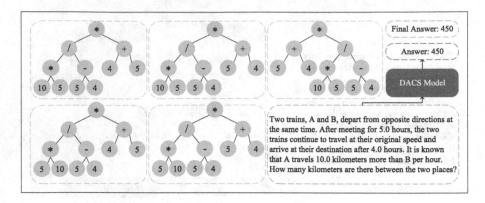

Fig. 4. Consistent solutions optimize the search space of beam search

When the left and right sub-nodes of the "∗" are interchangeable, selecting the "4.0" as the left node first, the model that has not been trained with consistent solutions cannot deduce the correct solution and the final answer. We will display the results of the beam search from the model trained with consistent solutions in the following subsection.

Optimization on Search Space. The model trained with consistent solutions is still able to make accurate predictions even when the "4.0" is chosen as the left node of the "∗" first, as shown in the second subgraph above the red dashed line in Fig. 3.

Additionally, Fig. 4 illustrates how the consistent solutions optimize the search space by demonstrating that our model trained with consistent solutions can produce the correct solution regardless of whatever node among the interchangeable nodes is predicted to appear first. The top 5 results from the beam search of the model are all correct, although the beam width is only set at 3 in training.

5   Conclusion

Based on previous studies on math word problems, we found that models that only learned one solution lacked reasoning skills when decoding. To address this, we suggest utilizing the commutative property to generate consistent solutions for the training set, and then using it as extra training data to optimize the search space in beam search.

In addition, we discover significant differences between models trained with and without consistent solutions, so the model ensemble is applied to improve performance. For future research, we will focus on exploring the optimization of search space with adversarial training and reinforcement learning.

References

1. OpenAI. Gpt-4 technical report. arXiv preprint arXiv:2303.08774 (2023)
2. Lee, S., Lee, D.B., Hwang, S.J.: Contrastive learning with adversarial perturbations for conditional text generation. In: International Conference on Learning Representations (2021)
3. Bakman, Y.: Robust understanding of word problems with extraneous information. arXiv preprint math/0701393 (2007)
4. Roy, S., Vieira, T., Roth, D.: Reasoning about quantities in natural language. Trans. Assoc. Comput. Linguistics 3, 1–13 (2015)
5. Liang, C.-C., Hsu, K.-Y., Huang, C.-T., Li, C.-M., Miao, S.-Yu., Su, K.-Y.: A tag-based English math word problem solver with understanding, reasoning and explanation. In: Proceedings of the 2016 Conference of the North American Chapter of the Association for Computational Linguistics: Demonstrations, pp. 67–71, June 2016
6. Hosseini, M.J., Hajishirzi, H., Etzioni, O., Kushman, N.: Learning to solve arithmetic word problems with verb categorization. In: Proceedings of the 2014 Conference on Empirical Methods in Natural Language Processing (EMNLP), pp. 523–533, October 2014
7. Wang, Y., Liu, X., Shi, S.: Deep neural solver for math word problems. In: Proceedings of the 2017 Conference on Empirical methods in Natural Language Processing, pp. 845–854, September 2017
8. Liu, Q., Guan, W., Li, S., Kawahara, D.: Tree-structured decoding for solving math word problems. In: Proceedings of the 2019 Conference on Empirical Methods in Natural Language Processing and the 9th International Joint Conference on Natural Language Processing (EMNLP-IJCNLP), pp. 2370–2379, November 2019
9. Wang, Y., Lee, H.-Y., Chen, Y.-N.: Tree transformer: integrating tree structures into self-attention. In Proceedings of the 2019 Conference on Empirical Methods in Natural Language Processing and the 9th International Joint Conference on Natural Language Processing (EMNLP-IJCNLP), pp. 1061–1070, November 2019
10. Xie, Z., Sun, S.: A goal-driven tree-structured neural model for math word problems. In: Proceedings of the Twenty-Eighth International Joint Conference on Artificial Intelligence, IJCAI-19, pp. 5299–5305, 7 2019
11. Lin, X., Huang, Z., Zhao, H., Chen, E., Liu, Q., Wang, H., Wang, S.: Hms: A hierarchical solver with dependency-enhanced understanding for math word problem. Proceedings of the AAAI Conference on Artificial Intelligence 35(5), 4232–4240 (2021)
12. Kim, B., Ki, K.S., Lee, D., Gweon, G.: Point to the expression: solving algebraic word problems using the expression-pointer transformer model. In: Proceedings of the 2020 Conference on Empirical Methods in Natural Language Processing (EMNLP), pp. 3768–3779, November 2020
13. Zhang, J., et al.: Graph-to-tree learning for solving math word problems. In: Proceedings of the 58th Annual Meeting of the Association for Computational Linguistics, pp. 3928–3937, July 2020
14. Huang, D., Liu, J., Lin, C.-Y., Yin, J.: Neural math word problem solver with reinforcement learning. In: Proceedings of the 27th International Conference on Computational Linguistics, pp. 213–223, August 2018
15. Devlin, J., Chang, M.-W., Lee, K., Toutanova, K.: BERT: pre-training of deep bidirectional transformers for language understanding. In: Proceedings of the 2019 Conference of the North American Chapter of the Association for Computational

Linguistics: Human Language Technologies, Volume 1 (Long and Short Papers), pp. 4171–4186, June 2019

16. Qin, J., Liang, X., Hong, Y., Tang, J., Lin, L.: Neural-symbolic solver for math word problems with auxiliary tasks. In: Proceedings of the 59th Annual Meeting of the Association for Computational Linguistics and the 11th International Joint Conference on Natural Language Processing, pp. 5870–5881, August 2021

17. Wu, Q., Zhang, Q., Wei, Z., Huang, X.: Math word problem solving with explicit numerical values. In: Proceedings of the 59th Annual Meeting of the Association for Computational Linguistics and the 11th International Joint Conference on Natural Language Processing, pp. 5859–5869, August 2021

18. Liang, Z., Zhang, J., Wang, L., Qin, W., Lan, Y., Shao, J., Zhang, X.: MWP-BERT: Numeracy-augmented pre-training for math word problem solving. In: Findings of the Association for Computational Linguistics: NAACL 2022, pp. 997–1009 (2022)

19. Li, Z., Zhang, W., Yan, C., Zhou, Q., Li, C., Liu, H., Cao, Y.: Seeking patterns, not just memorizing procedures: Contrastive learning for solving math word problems. In: Findings of the Association for Computational Linguistics: ACL 2022, pp. 2486–2496 (2022)

20. Tan, M., Wang, L., Jiang, L., Jiang, J.: Investigating math word problems using pretrained multilingual language models. In: Proceedings of the 1st Workshop on Mathematical Natural Language Processing, pp. 7–16, December 2022

21. Shen, J., Yin, Y., Li, L., Shang, L., Jiang, X., Zhang, M., Liu, Q.: Generate & rank: A multi-task framework for math word problems. In: Findings of the Association for Computational Linguistics: EMNLP 2021, pp. 2269–2279 (2021)

22. Liang, Z., Zhang, J., Wang, L., Wang, Y., Shao, J., Zhang, X.: Generalizing math word problem solvers via solution diversification. In: Proceedings of the AAAI Conference on Artificial Intelligence, 37, pp. 13183–13191, 06 2023

23. Jie, Z., Li, J., Lu, W.: Learning to reason deductively: math word problem solving as complex relation extraction. In: Proceedings of the 60th Annual Meeting of the Association for Computational Linguistics, pp. 5944–5955, May 2022

24. Zhang, Z., et al.: Towards lightweight yet ingenious pre-trained models for chinese. arXiv preprint arXiv:2110.06696 (2021)

25. Loshchilov, I., Hutter, F.: Decoupled weight decay regularization. In: International Conference on Learning Representations, May 2019

26. Sun, Y., et al.: Ernie 3.0: Large-scale knowledge enhanced pre-training for language understanding and generation. arXiv preprint arXiv:2107.02137, 2021

27. Liu, Y., et al.: Multilingual denoising pre-training for neural machine translation. Trans. Assoc. Comput. Linguistics 8, 726–742 (2020)

Evaluation Workshop: Conversational Aspect-Based Sentiment Quadruple Analysis

Improving Conversational Aspect-Based Sentiment Quadruple Analysis with Overall Modeling

Chenran Cai[1,2], Qin Zhao[1,2], Ruifeng Xu[1,2(✉)], and Bing Qin[1]

[1] Harbin Institute of Technology (Shenzhen), Shenzhen 518000, China
22s151167@stu.hit.edu.cn, {zhaoqin,xuruifeng}@hit.edu.cn,
qinb@ir.hit.edu.cn
[2] Guangdong Provincial Key Laboratory of Novel Security Intelligence Technologies,
Shenzhen 518000, China

Abstract. In this paper, we describe the experimental schemes of Team HLT-base for NLPCC-2023-Shared-Task-4 Conversational Aspect-based Sentiment Quadruple Analysis (ConASQ). Different from the aspect-based sentiment quadruple analysis task, the ConASQ task requires modeling the relationship between different utterances in context. Previous works commonly apply the attention mechanism (*e.g.*, self-attention, transformer) to model the interaction of different utterances after extracting the feature of each utterance. However, this approach may not capture the interaction of different utterances effectively with a single self-attention layer or a transformer layer. To address this issue, we propose a simple and efficient method in this paper. Specially, we concatenate all utterances as a single sentence and feed this sentence into the pre-trained model, which can better construct the representation of utterances from scratch. Then, we utilize different mask matrices to model the features of dialogue threads, speakers, and replies. Finally, we apply the gird-tagging method to quadruple extraction. Extensive experimental results show that our proposed framework outperforms other competitive methods and achieves 2nd performance in the ConASQ competition.

Keyword: Conversation Aspect-based Sentiment Quadruple

1 Introduction

Aspect-based sentiment analysis (ABSA) is a fine-grained sentiment analysis task that aims to identify the aspects of the entities in the text and determine the sentiment polarity for each identified aspect. There are different subtasks of ABSA, such as Aspect Term Extraction (ATE) [11,24], Aspect Term Sentiment Analysis (ATSA) [14,18], Aspect Sentiment Triplet Extraction (ASTE) [2,21,22], and Aspect Category Opinion Sentiment (ACOS) [1]. These subtasks involve different sentiment elements and their relations, such as the aspect term, aspect category, opinion term, and sentiment polarity. For example, given the sentence *"The food was delicious but the service was terrible."*, ATE will identify *"food"* and *"service"* as aspect terms, ATSA will assign *"positive"* to *"food"* and *"negative"* to *"service"*, ASTE will extract (*"food"*, *"delicious"*, *"positive"*) and (*"service"*, *"terrible"*, *"negative"*) as triplets, and ACOS will extract (*"food"*, *"quality"*, *"delicious"*, *"positive"*) and (*"service"*, *"general"*, *"terrible"*, *"negative"*) as quadruples.

To expand the application of ABSA, [10] proposes the conversational aspect-based sentiment quadruple analysis task (DiaASQ) and manually annotates a large-scale DiaASQ dataset. DiaASQ aims to detect the fine-grained sentiment quadruple of (`target`, `aspect`, `opinion`, `sentiment`) given a conversation text. Previous works [10] employ the attention mechanism (*e.g.*, self-attention, transformer) to model the interaction of different utterances after extracting the feature of each utterance. However, relying on a single self-attention layer or a transformer layer is insufficient to effectively model the interaction of different utterances, since the parameters of the newly added self-attention layer or transformer layer are randomly initialized. To address this issue, we propose a simple and efficient method in this paper. Specially, we concatenate all utterances in dialogue as a single sentence and feed this sentence into the pre-trained model, which can better construct the representation of utterances from scratch. Then, we utilize different mask matrices to model the features of dialogue threads, speakers, and replies, which can obtain the multi-view feature. Finally, we apply the fused multi-view features to accomplish the conversational aspect-based sentiment quadruple analysis task and apply the gird-tagging method to quadruple extraction. The main contributions of this paper are summarized as follows:

- We formulate the Conversational Aspect-based Sentiment Quadruple Analysis (ConASQ) task as the end-to-end quadruple prediction task and propose a simple and efficient framework to solve the ConASQ task, which improves the ConASQ task with overall modeling.
- Extensive experimental results show that our proposed framework outperforms other competitive methods and wins second place in the ConASQ competition.

2   Related Work

2.1   Aspect-Based Sentiment Analysis

Aspect-based sentiment analysis (ABSA) is a fine-grained sentiment analysis task, which can be decomposed into term extraction task (*e.g.*, aspect term and opinion term) [11,24] and classification task (*e.g.* category classification and sentiment classification) [14,18]. However, solving a single ABSA task fails to meet the needs in practical settings. To deal with this problem, recent studies gradually focus on the compound ABSA tasks such as aspect-opinion pair extraction [5], end-to-end ABSA [8,25], and aspect sentiment triplet extraction [2,21,22]. These tasks are similar in that they contain multiple subtasks. For example, the end-to-end ABSA consists of two subtasks, aspect term extraction, and aspect sentiment classification. [22] applied the pre-trained sequence-to-sequence model BART to solve the aspect sentiment triplet extraction task and achieved state-of-the-art performance. Moreover, there some works propose the aspect sentiment quadruple extraction task, such as Aspect-Category-Opinion-Sentiment (ACOS) [1] and Aspect Sentiment Quad Prediction (ASQP) [26].

Although the above methods can handle multiple subtasks and achieve good performance, they cannot utilize the dialogue data because these tasks and approaches are all based on a single sentence.

2.2 Dialogue Sentiment Analysis

Dialogue Sentiment Analysis is the task of identifying and extracting the sentiments expressed by the speakers in dialogue, which can enable various applications such as dialogue sentiment classification [19], multimodal conversational search [12,23], multimodal emotion recognition in Conversation [3,9]. It is a challenging task because dialogues are dynamic and interactive, which means that the opinions and sentiments of the speakers may change over time or depend on the context and the interlocutor. Most existing methods [6,16] commonly employ pre-trained models followed by fine-tuning and modeling the interaction of different utterances to accomplish the Dialogue Sentiment Analysis task and achieve superior performance.

In terms of existing research efforts, their dialogue-level opinion mining focus on coarse granularity. In contrast, fine-grained sentiment analysis in conversations is more valuable and practical.

2.3 Dialogue Aspect-Based Sentiment Analysis

Dialogue Aspect-based Sentiment Analysis is a novel task that aims to extract fine-grained opinions from dialogues, which is more challenging than traditional Aspect-based Sentiment Analysis (ABSA) because it requires understanding the context and coherence of dialogues, as well as handling multiple speakers and topics. [15] propose the task of conversational aspect sentiment analysis (CASA) that can provide useful fine-grained sentiment information for dialogue understanding and planning. Besides, they also construct the CASA dataset, which contains 3,000 chit-chat dialogues (27,198 sentences) with fine-grained sentiment information, including all sentiment expressions, their polarities, and the corresponding target mentions. However, the CASA dataset may not capture the comprehensive picture of the opinion status, as it lacks some key elements (*e.g.*, aspect).

To address this issue, [10] construct a new Conversational Aspect-based Sentiment Quadruple Analysis (DiaASQ) dataset, which covers four types of fine-grained sentiment information (*i.e.*, target, aspect, opinion, and sentiment). Moreover, the DiaASQ dataset is more complex and challenging than the CASA dataset, as one aspect term may have multiple sentiments associated with it in different utterances.

3 Task Introduction

3.1 Task Definition

Given a dialogue context $T = \{t_1, t_2, ..., t_n\}$ and its correlated reply record $R = \{r_1, r_2, ..., r_n\}$, where r_i denote i^{th} utterance reply to r_i^{th}. Each $t_i = \{w_1, w_2, ..., w_m\}$ denote i-th utterance text and m is the length of t_i. The reply record R reflects the hierarchical tree structure of t_i in T. Based on the input T and R, ConASQ aims to extract all possible (target, aspect, opinion, sentiment) quadruples, denoted as $Q = \{g, a, o, p\}_{k=1}^{K}$. The target g_k, aspect a_k or opinion o_k term is a sub-string of the utterance text t_i. The sentiment p_k $\in \{$ pos, neg, other $\}$ is a category label.

3.2 Evaluation Metric

To evaluate the performance, the ConASQ competition employs two metrics: micro-F1 score and iden-F1 score. The F1 score is computed using precision and recall, which are calculated as follows:

$$Precision = \frac{TP}{TP + FP}, \tag{1}$$

$$Recall = \frac{TP}{TP + FN}, \tag{2}$$

$$F1 = \frac{2 \times Precision \times Recall}{Precision + Recall}, \tag{3}$$

where TP represents true positives, FP represents false positives, TN represents true negatives, and FN represents false negatives. Specifically, when computing the micro-F1 score, TP corresponds to the number of predicted quadruples (*i.e.*, (target, aspect, opinion, sentiment)) that match exactly with those in the gold set. Conversely, for the iden-F1 score, TP counts the number of times the triplets (target, aspect, opinion) in the prediction match those in the golden set. The FP and FN also differ in the two settings. In order to better measure the performance of the model, the ConASQ competition applies the average of the two evaluation metrics as the final evaluation indicator.

$$\text{Avg. F1} = \frac{1}{2}(\text{micro-F1} + \text{iden-F1}). \tag{4}$$

4 Methodology

4.1 Overall Architecture

Figure 1 illustrates the overall architecture of our framework for the conversational aspect-based sentiment quadruple task, which contains three main components: (1) *Text representation module*, which aims to model the relationship

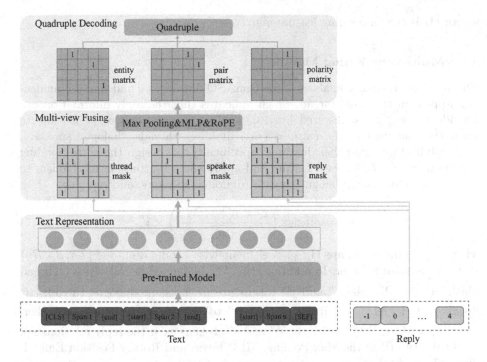

Fig. 1. The architecture of our framework on the conversational aspect-based sentiment quadruple task

of different utterances in dialogue and extract each token feature; (2) *Multi-view Interaction module*, which aims to obtain the different dialogue-specific feature (*i.e.*, dialogue threads, speakers and reply); (3) *Decoding module*, which adopts the fused feature to classify the pre-trained labels and decode the quadruple.

4.2 Text Representation Module

Given a dialogue context $T = \{t_1, t_2, ..., t_n\}$, which contains n utterances. To model the interaction of n utterances, we concatenate them into a sentence. Specially, we add two special tokens (*i.e.*, [start] and [end]) to distinguish the different utterances. In addition, due to the nature of the pre-trained language model, we keep the first and last tokens as [CLS] and [SEP] respectively. Compared with using the pre-trained language model to extract the feature of each utterance, our method better models the relationship between utterances, which is helpful for extracting the quadruple.

$$S = [[\text{CLS}], t_1, [\text{end}], [\text{start}], t_2, [\text{end}], ..., [\text{start}], t_n, [\text{SEP}]]. \quad (5)$$

Then, we utilize the pre-trained language model (*e.g.*, DeBERTa-v2 [7]) as the text encoder to map each token into a d_w-dimensional embedding:

$$\mathbf{H}_t = \text{DeBERTa-v2}(S), \quad (6)$$

where $\mathbf{H}_t$ is the embedding feature matrix.

4.3   Multi-view Fusing Module

Through our statistical analysis of the ConASQ dataset, we find that all quadru-ples appear in the same thread, which indicates that the reply information can provide the key cues. Inspired by [10], we introduce a multi-view module to learn the dialogue-specific features (*i.e.*, dialogue threads, dialogue speakers, and replying) and fuse their features. Specifically, we design the corresponding attention mask $\mathbf{M}^c$ for each feature and apply the self-attention mechanism to extract the features of dialogue threads, dialogue speakers, and replying.

$$\mathbf{T}_c = \text{softmax}\left(\frac{Q \times K^\top \odot \mathbf{M}^c}{\sqrt{d_h}}\right) \times V, \tag{7}$$

where Q, K and V all are $\mathbf{H}_t$, $\odot$ is element-wise production, $c \in \{Th, Sp, Rp\}$ and $\frac{1}{\sqrt{d_h}}$ is scaling factor. In addition, the $\mathbf{M}^c$ is defined as follows: (*i*) Thread Mask: $\mathbf{M}_{ij}^{Th} = 1$ if the ith and j^{th} tokens are in the same dialogue thread; (*ii*) Speaker Mask: $\mathbf{M}_{ij}^{Sp} = 1$ if the ith and j^{th} tokens are from the same speaker; (*iii*) Reply Mask: $\mathbf{M}_{ij}^{Rp} = 1$ if the ith and j^{th} tokens exist the reply relationship.

Then, we utilize the Max-Pooling, MLP layer, and Rotary Position Embed-ding [17] to obtain the final feature representation:

$$\mathbf{F} = \text{MLP}\left(\text{Max-Pooling}\left(\mathbf{T}_{Th}, \mathbf{T}_{Sp}, \mathbf{T}_{Rp}\right)\right)\mathcal{R}, \tag{8}$$

where $\mathcal{R}$ is a positioning matrix parameter.

4.4   ConASQ Classification Module

In our framework, we decompose the ConASQ task label into three type labels (*i.e.*, entity boundary labels, entity pair labels, and sentiment polarity labels). We utilize the fused representation $\mathbf{F}$ to calculate the score between any token pair and predict the probability distribution of entity boundary labels, entity pair labels, or sentiment polarity labels. Finally, we apply the cross-entropy loss function to calculate loss:

$$y = \text{softmax}((\mathbf{F})^T \times \mathbf{F}), \tag{9}$$

$$\mathcal{L}_k = -\frac{1}{G \cdot N^2} \sum_{g=1}^{G} \sum_{i=1}^{N} \sum_{j=1}^{N} \alpha^k y_{ij}^k \log\left(\boldsymbol{y}_{ij}^k\right), \tag{10}$$

where $k \in \{$ ent, pair, pol $\}$, N is the total token length in a dialogue, G is the total training data, y_{ij}^k is ground-truth label, and $\boldsymbol{y}_{ij}^k$ is the prediction. For decoding the process, we follow the previous works [10] and apply grid-tagging to according $\boldsymbol{y}_{ij}^k$ to decode the quadruple. Due to these three label types being

Table 1. Statistics of ConASQ dataset.

Lang	Set	Dialogue	Utterance	Speaker	Target	Aspect	Opinion	Quadruple
CH	total	1,000	7,452	4,991	8,308	6,572	7,051	5,742
	train	800	5,947	3,986	6,652	5,220	5,622	4,607
	valid	100	748	502	823	662	724	577
	test	100	757	503	833	690	705	558
EN	total	1,000	7,452	4,991	8,264	6,434	6,933	5,514
	train	800	5,947	3,986	6,613	5,109	5,523	4,414
	valid	100	748	502	822	644	719	555
	test	100	757	503	829	681	691	545

imbalanced, thus we apply a tag-wise weighting vector α^k to counteract this. During the training phase, we combine all three loss functions for training the entire framework.

$$\mathcal{L}_f = \mathcal{L}_{\text{ent}} + \beta \mathcal{L}_{\text{pair}} + \eta \mathcal{L}_{\text{pol}} . \tag{11}$$

5 Experiments

In this section, we present the experimental setup and the results of our framework on the ConASQ dataset.

5.1 Dataset

The ConASQ dataset consists of posts and replies about electronic products, especially mobile phones, on Sina Weibo. The dataset structures the posts into conversation trees based on the reply relation and contains 1000 dialogues, each with up to 10 sentences. [10] also translate original Chinese corpus into English and project the annotation to obtain a parallel corpus. The ConASQ dataset is randomly split into the train, valid, and test sets with a ratio of 8:1:1. Table 1 shows more statistics.

5.2 Experimental Settings

For the text feature extraction module, we employ the Erlangshen-DeBERTa-v2-320M-Chinese model[1] [7] and the Roberta-Large model[2] [13] as the feature extractors of our framework for Chinese and English ConASQ datasets, respectively. Besides, we utilize [unused1] and [unused2] as the special token of [start] and [end], respectively.

---

[1] https://huggingface.co/IDEA-CCNL/Erlangshen-DeBERTa-v2-320M-Chinese.
[2] https://huggingface.co/roberta-large.

156   C. Cai et al.

Table 2. Performance comparison of the baseline methods on Chinese ConASQ dataset. We highlight the best score in each column in bold, and the second-best score with underline. The results of baselines with † are retrieved from [10].

Methods	Micro			Iden		
	P(%)	R(%)	F1(%)	P(%)	R(%)	F1(%)
CRF-Extract-Classify†	-	-	8.81	-	-	9.25
SpERT†	-	-	13.00	-	-	14.19
ParaPhrase†	-	-	23.27	-	-	27.98
Span-ASTE†	-	-	32.21	-	-	30.85
DiaASQ†	-	-	<u>34.94</u>	-	-	<u>37.51</u>
Ours	45.77	40.68	**43.07**	49.19	43.73	**46.30**

For the hyper-parameters of our framework, β and η are set to 5 and 3. In experiments, we use different learning rate settings on two datasets. For the Chinese ConASQ dataset, the learning rate for the text representation module is 6e-4 and for the other parts is 1e-5. For the English ConASQ dataset, the learning rate for the text representation module is 1e-3 and for the other parts is 2e-5. Our framework uses AdamW as the optimizer and is trained for 20 and 15 epochs on Chinese and English ConASQ datasets, respectively. All experiments are conducted as Tesla V100.

5.3 Comparision Models

Following [10], we utilize the same comparison methods and apply the following baselines.

– CRF-Extract-Classify [1], which adopts a three-stage system for the ACOS dataset and retrofits it to further support target term extraction.
– SpERT [4], which utilizes a span-based transformer for joint extraction of entity and relation and modifies it to support triple-term extraction and polarity classification.
– Span-ASTE [20], which is a span-based approach for triplet ABSA extraction and adapts to the DiaASQ task by editing the last stage of SpanASTE to enumerate triplets.
– ParaPhrase [26], which is a generative seq-to-seq model for quadruple ABSA extraction and modifies the model outputs to fit the DiaASQ task.
– DiaASQ [10], which is an end-to-end solution based on the grid-tagging method for the DiaASQ task.

5.4 Main Results

We conduct experiments on the conversational aspect-based sentiment quadruple task, which are shown in Table 2 and 3, respectively. We can draw the following conclusions.

Table 3. Performance comparison of the baseline methods on English ConASQ dataset. We highlight the best score in each column in bold, and the second-best score with underline. The results of baselines with † are retrieved from [10].

Methods	Micro			Iden		
	P(%)	R(%)	F1(%)	P(%)	R(%)	F1(%)
CRF-Extract-Classify†	-	-	11.59	-	-	12.80
SpERT†	-	-	13.07	-	-	13.38
ParaPhrase†	-	-	24.54	-	-	26.76
Span-ASTE†	-	-	26.99	-	-	28.34
DiaASQ†	-	-	<u>33.31</u>	-	-	<u>36.80</u>
Ours	41.69	34.50	**37.75**	44.79	37.06	**40.56**

(1) Our framework significantly outperformers the other baselines on the conversational aspect-based sentiment quadruple datasets of Chinese and English. For example, in terms of Micro-F1, our framework outperforms CRF-Extract-Class by 34.26% and 26.16%, SpERT by 30.07% and 24.68%, ParaPhrase by 19.80% and 13.21%, Span-ASTE by 10.86% and 10.76%, and DiaASQ by 8.07% and 4.44% on two datasets, respectively. The reason is that our framework effectively models the relationship between different utterances, thus effectively improving the performance of our framework on the ConASQ task.

(2) We observe that the performance of our framework on Chinese ConASQ dataset is significantly better than that on the English dataset. The reason is that the English ConASQ dataset is translated from the Chinese dataset, which introduces bias.

Table 4. Ablation Study.

Methods	Micro			Iden		
	P(%)	R(%)	F1(%)	P(%)	R(%)	F1(%)
ZH						
Ours	**45.77**	**40.68**	**43.07**	**49.19**	**43.73**	**46.30**
w/o overall modeling	44.27	40.14	42.11	47.43	43.01	45.11
w/o RoPE	30.66	40.50	34.90	33.51	44.27	38.15
EN						
Ours	**41.69**	**34.50**	**37.75**	**44.79**	37.06	**40.56**
w/o overall modeling	39.81	31.19	34.98	43.56	34.13	38.27
w/o RoPE	25.95	33.76	29.35	29.20	**37.89**	33.01

5.5 Ablation Study

We also conduct the ablation study for our proposed framework, which is shown in Table 4. First, we perform ablation experiments on the way of modeling the different utterances. In our framework, we apply the overall modeling method, which concatenates all utterances into a single sentence and feeds it into the pre-trained model. *w/o overall modeling* directly applies the pre-trained model to extract the feature of each utterance. From the results, we observe that overall modeling outperformers single utterance modeling (*i.e., w/o overall modeling*). This is because the latter does not account for the deep modeling of the relationship between different utterances in dialogue. In addition, we conduct experiments on Rotary Position Embedding (RoPE). Removing RoPE (*i.e., w/o RoPE*) leads to performance degradation. This is because RoPE captures the overall relative distance between utterances in the dialogue. Such distance information can facilitate better discourse understanding.

Table 5. The online result of the conversational aspect-based sentiment quadruple task.

Rank	Team	Chinese		English		Avg. F1
		Micro-F	Iden-F	Micro-F	Iden-F	
1	PAssion	43.00	46.20	38.32	44.06	42.89
2	**HLT-base (Ours)**	42.13	44.97	37.75	40.56	41.35
3	540 go	40.80	44.26	38.20	40.92	41.05
4	Prophet	39.50	45.17	37.08	41.42	40.79
5	DUTIR_914	42.09	45.62	35.54	38.76	40.50
6	Werkzeug	41.08	44.68	35.21	40.30	40.32
7	Go Go Go	41.79	44.47	34.97	39.88	40.28
8	Mobu	40.88	43.86	36.04	39.84	40.15
9	RookieGoAhead	40.08	43.61	34.33	39.50	39.38
10	megrlcigyht	38.17	41.86	33.46	38.13	37.91
11	TUA1	33.69	40.79	29.48	32.43	34.10
12	POLab	35.58	41.97	5.36	12.06	23.74
13	GSAPL	7.25	8.43	33.21	37.11	21.50

5.6 Online Results

We report the online results of our framework in Table 5. Our framework shows a very convincing performance. We achieve second place in the conversational aspect-based sentiment quadruple task, which fully demonstrates the effectiveness of our framework.

6   Conclusion

In this paper, we present a framework to solve the conversational aspect-based sentiment quadruple task, where the key point is to model the interaction of different utterances. To address this issue, we propose a simple and efficient method in this paper. Specifically, we concatenate all utterances as a single sentence and feed this sentence into the pre-trained model, which can better construct the representation of utterances from scratch. As a result, our team ranks 2nd in this ConASQ competition, which demonstrates the effectiveness of the proposed framework. Moreover, we conduct ablation analysis experiments and find that each module of our framework is effective and contributes to the final performance.

Acknowledgment. This research was supported in part by the National Natural Science Foundation of China (62006062, 62176076), the Guangdong Provincial Key Laboratory of Novel Security Intelligence Technologies (2022B1212010005), Natural Science Foundation of Guangdong (2023A1515012922), and Shenzhen Foundational Research Funding JCYJ20220818102415032.

References

1. Cai, H., Xia, R., Yu, J.: Aspect-category-opinion-sentiment quadruple extraction with implicit aspects and opinions. In: Proceedings of the 59th Annual Meeting of the Association for Computational Linguistics and the 11th International Joint Conference on Natural Language Processing (Volume 1: Long Papers), pp. 340–350. Association for Computational Linguistics, Online, August 2021
2. Chen, Z., Huang, H., Liu, B., Shi, X., Jin, H.: Semantic and syntactic enhanced aspect sentiment triplet extraction. In: Proceedings of ACL Findings, pp. 1474–1483 (2021)
3. Chudasama, V., Kar, P., Gudmalwar, A., Shah, N., Wasnik, P., Onoe, N.: M2fnet: multi-modal fusion network for emotion recognition in conversation. In: Proceedings of the IEEE/CVF Conference on Computer Vision and Pattern Recognition, pp. 4652–4661 (2022)
4. Eberts, M., Ulges, A.: Span-based joint entity and relation extraction with transformer pre-training. In: ECAI 2020, pp. 2006–2013. IOS Press (2020)
5. Gao, L., Wang, Y., Liu, T., Wang, J., Zhang, L., Liao, J.: Question-driven span labeling model for aspect–opinion pair extraction. In: Proceedings of AAAI, vol. 35, pp. 12875–12883 (2021)
6. Ghosal, D., Majumder, N., Poria, S., Chhaya, N., Gelbukh, A.: Dialoguegcn: a graph convolutional neural network for emotion recognition in conversation. In: Proceedings of the 2019 Conference on Empirical Methods in Natural Language Processing and the 9th International Joint Conference on Natural Language Processing (EMNLP-IJCNLP), pp. 154–164 (2019)
7. He, P., Liu, X., Gao, J., Chen, W.: Deberta: decoding-enhanced bert with disentangled attention. In: International Conference on Learning Representations
8. Hu, M., Peng, Y., Huang, Z., Li, D., Lv, Y.: Open-domain targeted sentiment analysis via span-based extraction and classification. In: Proceedings of ACL, pp. 537–546 (2019)

9. Lee, J., Lee, W.: CoMPM: context modeling with speaker's pre-trained memory tracking for emotion recognition in conversation. In: Proceedings of the 2022 Conference of the North American Chapter of the Association for Computational Linguistics: Human Language Technologies, pp. 5669–5679. Association for Computational Linguistics, Seattle, United States, July 2022

10. Li, B., et al.: Diaasq: a benchmark of conversational aspect-based sentiment quadruple analysis (2023)

11. Li, X., Bing, L., Li, P., Lam, W., Yang, Z.: Aspect term extraction with history attention and selective transformation. In: Proceedings of IJCAI, pp. 4194–4200 (2018)

12. Liao, L., Long, L.H., Zhang, Z., Huang, M., Chua, T.S.: Mmconv: an environment for multimodal conversational search across multiple domains. In: Proceedings of the 44th International ACM SIGIR Conference on Research and Development in Information Retrieval, pp. 675–684 (2021)

13. Liu, Y., et al.: Roberta: a robustly optimized bert pretraining approach. arXiv preprint arXiv:1907.11692 (2019)

14. Phan, M.H., Ogunbona, P.O.: Modelling context and syntactical features for aspect-based sentiment analysis. In: Proceedings of ACL, pp. 3211–3220 (2020)

15. Song, L., Xin, C., Lai, S., Wang, A., Su, J., Xu, K.: Casa: conversational aspect sentiment analysis for dialogue understanding. J. Artif. Intell. Res. **73**, 511–533 (2022)

16. Song, X., Huang, L., Xue, H., Hu, S.: Supervised prototypical contrastive learning for emotion recognition in conversation. In: Proceedings of the 2022 Conference on Empirical Methods in Natural Language Processing, pp. 5197–5206. Association for Computational Linguistics, Abu Dhabi, United Arab Emirates, December 2022

17. Su, J., Lu, Y., Pan, S., Wen, B., Liu, Y.: Roformer: enhanced transformer with rotary position embedding (2021)

18. Sun, C., Huang, L., Qiu, X.: Utilizing bert for aspect-based sentiment analysis via constructing auxiliary sentence. In: Proceedings of NAACL, pp. 380–385 (2019)

19. Wang, J., et al.: Sentiment classification in customer service dialogue with topic-aware multi-task learning. In: Proceedings of the AAAI Conference on Artificial Intelligence, vol. 34, pp. 9177–9184 (2020)

20. Xu, L., Chia, Y.K., Bing, L.: Learning span-level interactions for aspect sentiment triplet extraction. In: Proceedings of the 59th Annual Meeting of the Association for Computational Linguistics and the 11th International Joint Conference on Natural Language Processing (Volume 1: Long Papers), pp. 4755–4766. Association for Computational Linguistics, Online, August 2021

21. Xu, L., Li, H., Lu, W., Bing, L.: Position-aware tagging for aspect sentiment triplet extraction. In: Proceedings of EMNLP, pp. 2339–2349 (2020)

22. Yan, H., Dai, J., Ji, T., Qiu, X., Zhang, Z.: A unified generative framework for aspect-based sentiment analysis. In: Proceedings of the 59th Annual Meeting of the Association for Computational Linguistics and the 11th International Joint Conference on Natural Language Processing (Volume 1: Long Papers), pp. 2416–2429. Association for Computational Linguistics, Online, August 2021

23. Ye, C., Liao, L., Feng, F., Ji, W., Chua, T.S.: Structured and natural responses co-generation for conversational search. In: Proceedings of the 45th International ACM SIGIR Conference on Research and Development in Information Retrieval, pp. 155–164 (2022)

24. Yin, Y., Wei, F., Dong, L., Xu, K., Zhang, M., Zhou, M.: Unsupervised word and dependency path embeddings for aspect term extraction. In: Proceedings of IJCAI, pp. 2979–2985 (2016)

25. Zhang, W., Deng, Y., Li, X., Bing, L., Lam, W.: Aspect-based sentiment analysis in question answering forums. In: Proceedings of EMNLP Findings, pp. 4582–4591 (2021)
26. Zhang, W., Deng, Y., Li, X., Yuan, Y., Bing, L., Lam, W.: Aspect sentiment quad prediction as paraphrase generation. In: Proceedings of the 2021 Conference on Empirical Methods in Natural Language Processing, pp. 9209–9219, November 2021

Conversational Aspect-Based Sentiment Quadruple Analysis with Consecutive Multi-view Interaction

Yongquan Lai[2,3], Shixuan Fan[1,2], Zeliang Tong[1,2], Weiran Pan[1,2],
and Wei Wei[1,2(✉)]

[1] Cognitive Computing and Intelligent Information Processing (CCIIP) Laboratory,
School of Computer Science and Technology, Huazhong University of Science and
Technology, Wuhan, China
{fanshixuan,tongzeliang,panwr,weiw}@hust.edu.cn
[2] Joint Laboratory of HUST and Pingan Property and Casualty Research (HPL),
Wuhan, China
[3] Ping An Property and Casualty Insurance Company of China, Ltd., Wuxi, China
laiyongquan932@pingan.com.cn

Abstract. With the development of information technology, the
increasing amount of content on the web has made aspect-based sentiment analysis an essential tool for extracting information about emotional states. However, most of the existing work focuses on a single
text, while little attention is paid to the task of sentiment analysis in
complex texts such as dialogues, in which the quadruple of target-aspect-
opinion-sentiment may appear in different speakers during one conversation thread. In this paper, we proposed a novel framework that was built
by a Chinese pre-trained language model and a grid tagging classifier.
In addition, we use multi-view interaction with three consecutive multi-
head attention modules to improve the performance and robustness of
our model. Besides, based on the excellent performance of the Chinese
pre-training model, the English version is transferred from the final Chinese weights to achieve cross-lingual transfer. To improve the generalization ability of the model, cross-validation is used to select the best
one. Our model ranks first on track 4 of the NLPCC-2023 shared task
on conversational aspect-based sentiment quadruple analysis. Our code
is publicly available at https://github.com/Joint-Laboratory-of-HUST-
and-PAIC/nlpcc2023-shared-task-diaASQ.

Keywords: Pre-trained language model · Attention · Cross-validation

1 Introduction

Sentiment analysis is one of the most active research areas in natural language
processing [11]. In recent years, due to the surge of user feedback information

---

Y. Lai and S. Fan—Contribute equally to this paper.

F. Liu et al. (Eds.): NLPCC 2023, LNAI 14304, pp. 162–173, 2023.
https://doi.org/10.1007/978-3-031-44699-3_15

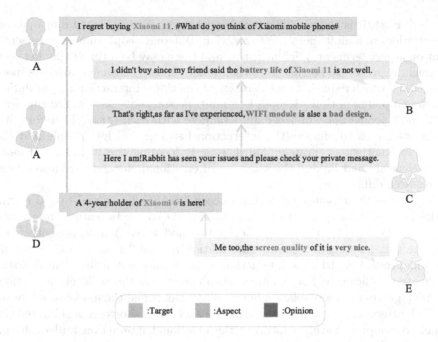

Fig. 1. An example data of the conversational aspect-based sentiment quadruple analysis (DiaASQ). In this dialogue, three quadruples appear, which are (*'Xiaomi 11'*, *'WIFI module'*, *'bad design'*, *'negative'*), (*'Xiaomi 11'*, *'battery life'*, *'not well'*, *'negative'*) and (*'Xiaomi 6'*, *'screen quality'*, *'very nice'*, *'positive'*).

about goods, social events, news, and other content on social media, the research of this task has attracted wide attention [16]. In linguistics, the sentiment elements of text are mainly composed of several parts: aspect term, aspect entity, opinion term, and sentiment polarity [19]. Based on the above linguistic background, relevant researchers have formally proposed a formal definition of aspect-based sentiment analysis (ABSA) [4], which the sentiment polarity was directed by an entity or aspect, not the whole sentence. Because different tasks have different combinations of elements extracted, the ABSA task was divided into a number of subtasks with different goals [21].

Compared to the single text piece, dialogue text usually contains more information, including the background, context, characteristics and relationship of the speaker [10], which are all unique challenges in the task of dialogue sentiment analysis and have a huge influence on emotional tendencies. Therefore, there is an urgent need to design a conversational aspect-based sentiment quadruple analysis framework, which aims to detect the fine-grained sentiment quadruple of target-aspect-opinion-sentiment. In this task, for a given data, our goal is to extract all the sentiment quadruples appeared in the dialogue. For example in Fig. 2, there are three sentiment quadruples that appeared in the dialogue. Although some scholars have made great efforts in the past, there is still a large degree of distortion in conversational aspect-based sentiment quadruple extraction [13]. First, it is always difficult to model the characteristics of multi-person conversations in a multi-person conversation. Different people may express sentiment on aspect terms at different times, and there may be a time delay between sentiment expressions. So this non-synchronicity makes sentiment analysis more challenging, which requiring consideration of emotional interaction and evolution at different points in time. Second, in a multi-person conversation, the emotions of different people may influence and compete with each other. Therefore, it's significant for us to analyze the interaction between multiple people and the impact of emotions accurately. Third, exactly locating the boundary of emotional elements and linking the same set of emotional elements are also one of the research difficulties.

To address those issues, Li et al. proposed DiaASQ [9], an end-to-end neural model for sentiment quadruple analysis. DiaASQ conducts feature interaction at three different views (i.e., speaker, reply, and thread) independently, and uses the max-pooling to aggerate information from different views. We argue this independent multi-view interaction manner may not utilize the dialogue information sufficiently. For example, when conducting thread-level interaction, DiaASQ ignores the reply relation between utterances and the model is not aware of which utterances come from the same speaker. Such shortcomings limited the model to comprehensively capturing the emotional interaction and evolution during the dialogue.

To this end, we introduce a novel multi-view interaction module consisting of three consecutive multi-head attention layers. Specifically, we first conduct the feature interaction between tokens from the same speaker to model the emotional state of each speaker. Then we conduct feature interaction between utterances and their corresponding replies to model the local emotional interaction. Finally, we allow tokens in the same thread to interact with each other to generate dialogue-specific features. This hierarchical feature interaction architecture allows us to aggregate emotional information from the local single speaker to the global multi-round dialogue and we experimentally proved this method brings a considerable performance improvement.

We also utilize other modules to further improve the model performance. To better adapt the Chinese data, we use macbert [3] as the encoder, which is pre-trained on a large corpus of Chinese text. And the English version model is transferred from the final Chinese weights to achieve cross-lingual transfer. In addition, we use k-fold validation to select the best models and ensemble them by weight averaging. The main contributions of this work are summarized as follows:

1. We deployed hierarchical feature interaction from the three levels of speaker, reply, and thread successively, and carries out multi-granularity feature interaction from local to global.
2. We use macbert as the encoder in order to better adapt to Chinese data. At the same time, the English model is fine-tuned on the basis of the Chinese model, and the effect is improved through cross-language interaction.

3. We experimental show that our method achieves state-of-the-art results on the conversational aspect-based sentiment quadruple analysis. The ablation study also proves the effectiveness of each component.

2   Related Works

2.1   Aspect Sentiment Triplet Extraction

As a compound ABSA task, the aspect sentiment triplet extraction (ASTE) task attempts to extract sentiment triplets from a given sentence that tell us what the opinion goal is, what its emotional tendency is, and why that emotion is expressed via opinion terms. Researchers have done several valuable attempts in ASTE task. Peng et al. [12] first proposed a two-stage pipeline model to extract the triplet of sentiment elements, which extract sentiment elements and construct aspect-opinion pairs separately. However, the pipeline method ignore the interaction between sentiment elements and commonly suffer from error propagation. So Wu et al. [17] extend the grid tagging scheme (GTS) applied to other ABSA task to predict sentiment triplets, while this methods rely on the interaction between word pairs. Xu et al. [18] proposed a span-level interaction model that explicitly considers the interaction between the span of the entire Aspect Term and Opinion Term. Their approach significantly improves the performance, especially on sentiment triplets which contain multi word targets or opinions. In order to further improve the model effect, Chen et al. [2] design a span-level bidirectional network, which includes a span separation loss to ensure that spans containing shared tokens have distinct representations.

Unlike the task that needs to be solved in this article, the ASTE task blurs the boundary between aspect term and aspect entity, and this article needs to accurately distinguish the two based on their differences.

2.2   Emotion Recognition in Conversation

As an extension of the basic task of sentiment analysis, conversational sentiment analysis has attracted wide attention in the field of natural language processing, and many researchers have focused on related research work [13]. Because dialogue is a dynamic process in which the emotional expression between participants influences and evolves. Therefore, it is necessary to focus on the emotional interaction of the participants in the dialogue and the evolution of emotions, rather than simply viewing the dialogue separately. Hazarika et al. [7] propose a conversational memory network that incorporates audio, visual, and textual features to capture dependencies between speakerstried and model the historical conversation information of people in the conversation. Ghosal et al. [6] proposed a graph-based convolutional neural network for emotion recognition in conversation, which used the relationship graph in the conversation to simulate the propagation and influence of emotion. Hu et al. [8] designed multiple rounds of reasoning modules to extract and integrate emotional cues, which fully understand the conversational context from a cognitive perspective.

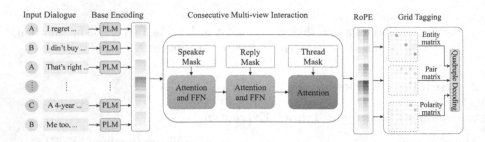

Fig. 2. Architecture of the model. The input dialogue for both languages are encoded by the same encoder, namely Macbert-large [3], and the output of the encoder is fed into three consecutive attention modules, as shown in the figure. The first two attention modules contain multi-head attention and feed-forward network (FFN), and they capture speaker and reply relations using speaker mask and reply mask respectively.

The task of emotion recognition in conversation needs to fully consider the context information, which can reveal the transfer process of emotion in dialogue by modeling the context, that is, the transmission and influence of emotion. The method mentioned above can be widely applied in this task to better distinguish different aspects of emotion and improve the accuracy of conversational aspect-based sentiment quadruple extraction.

3 Methodology

Our model is an improvement over the DiaASQ model [9], and the architecture is shown in Fig. 1.

3.1 Task Definition

Given a multi-user dialogue context $\mathcal{D} = \{u_1, \cdots, u_n\}$ with the corresponding replying record $l = \{l_1, \cdots, l_n\}$ of utterances, where l_i denotes that i-th utterance response to l_i utterance and each utterance u_i is composed by m length words w_j, denoted as $u_i = \{w_1, \cdots, w_m\}$. Based on $\mathcal{D}$ and l, the ABSA task aims to extract all target-aspect-opinion-sentiment quadruples, denoted as $Q = \{t, a, o, p\}_{k=1}^{K}$, where the target t, aspect a, opinion o are a sub-string of the dialogue context, separately, and the sentiment p is a category label $\in \{pos, neg, other\}$.

Following previous work [9], we split the ABSA task into three subtasks, namely *entity boundary, entity pair and sentiment polarity*. For *entity boundary* subtask, we use *tgt*, *asp*, and *opi* label to mark the head and tail of target, aspect, and opinion in the dialogue context. *Entity pair* subtask aims to use *h2h* (head-to-head) and *t2t* (tail-to-tail) labels to link different types of terms together as a combination (t, a, o). *Sentiment polarity* subtask is a sentiment classification task and we assign the category label (*i.e.* pos, neg, other) between the heads and tails of target and opinion terms.

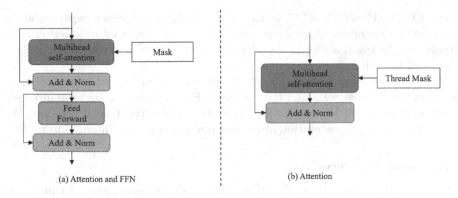

(a) Attention and FFN   (b) Attention

Fig. 3. Attention modules used in our method. The attention module is composed of multi-head attention and feed-forward network (FFN). The multi-head attention is the same as the one in the transformer [15], and the FFN (for the first two attention modules in 1) is a two-layer MLP with GELU activation. (Color figure online)

3.2 Base Encoding

We use macbert [3] as the pretrained language model (PLM) for both English and Chinese encoders. The macbert modifies the masked language model (MLM) task as a language correction manner to mitigate the discrepancy of the pre-training and fine-tuning stage. The output of the last attention module is fed into the RoPE and grid tagging modules as in the DiaASQ implementation [9].

$$u_i' = < [CLS], w_1, \cdots, w_m, [SEP] >, \tag{1}$$

$$H_i = h_{cls}, h_1, \cdots, h_m, h_{sep} = \text{PLM}(u_i'), \tag{2}$$

where h_m is the contextual representation of word w_m.

3.3 Consecutive Multi-view Interaction

In order to capture the deep interaction between different views, we design a consecutive multi-view interaction module, which captures the correlation in different views respectively through three consecutive attention layers. The first two attention modules consist of multi-head attention and feed-forward network(FFN) [15], shown in Fig. 3(a), capturing speaker and reply relations by using speaker mask and reply mask respectively.

$$H' = \text{Masked-Att}(Q, K, V, M^o)$$
$$= \text{Softmax}(\frac{(Q^T \cdot K) \odot M^o}{\sqrt{d}}) \cdot V, \tag{3}$$

$$H^o = \text{FFN}(H')$$
$$= \max(0, H'W_1 + b_1)W_2 + b_2, \tag{4}$$

where $\boldsymbol{Q}{=}\boldsymbol{K}{=}\boldsymbol{V}{=}\boldsymbol{H} \in \mathbb{R}^{N \times d}$ is the whole dialogue sequence representation obtained by pre-trained language model, and $\odot$ is element-wise production. The o represent the token interaction under different views respectively, *i.e.* speaker, reply, and thread.

The last attention module (in blue) contains a multi-head attention only, shown in Fig. 3(b), as we found that adding FFN degrades the performance (see ablation study), and thread mask is used to capture the thread relation. We denote the dialog representation after continuous multi-view interaction as $\boldsymbol{H}^f$.

3.4   Quadruple Decoding

First, we utilize multiple MLP layers with unshared parameters to map the dialogue context representations into multiple tag spaces respectively.

$$\boldsymbol{v}_i^r = \mathrm{MLP}^r(\boldsymbol{h}_i^f), \tag{5}$$

where $r \in \{tgt, \cdots, h2h, \cdots, pos, \cdots, \epsilon_{ent}, \cdots\}$ indicates a specific label and ϵ_{ent} denotes the non-relation label in the entity boundary matrix.

In order to help the model understand the dialogue context order, following previous work [9], we fuse the rotation position embedding (RoPE) [14] with the dialogue representation as the input of the quadruple decoding. RoPE can model the relative positional distance between tokens, which can be formalized as follows:

$$\boldsymbol{h}_i^r = \boldsymbol{\mathcal{R}}(\theta, i)\boldsymbol{v}_i^r, \tag{6}$$

where $\boldsymbol{\mathcal{R}}(\theta, i)$ is a positioning matrix parameterized by θ and the absolute index i of $\boldsymbol{v}_i^r$.

For entity boundary subtask, we compute the dot product similarity between tokens as a label score s_{ij}^r, and use softmax to compute the probabilities p_{ij}^r of multiple labels. Other subtasks also get label probabilities through the same method.

$$s_{ij}^r = (\boldsymbol{h}_i^r)^T \boldsymbol{h}_j^r,$$
$$p_{ij}^{ent}, p_{ij}^{tgt}, p_{ij}^{asp}, p_{ij}^{opi} = \mathrm{Softmax}([s_{ij}^{\epsilon_{ent}}; s_{ij}^{tgt}; s_{ij}^{asp}; s_{ij}^{opi}]), \tag{7}$$

During model training, we use the commonly used cross-entropy loss function for each subtask.

$$\mathcal{L}_k = -\frac{1}{G \cdot N^2} \sum_{g=1}^{G} \sum_{i=1}^{N} \sum_{j=1}^{N} \boldsymbol{\alpha}^k \, y_{ij}^k \log(p_{ij}^k), \tag{8}$$

where $k \in \{ent, pair, pol\}$ indicates one of subtasks, and $\boldsymbol{\alpha}^k$ is the label weight to alleviate the problem of label imbalance in the dataset. The final loss $\mathcal{L}$ is the weighted sum of three subtask losses:

$$\mathcal{L} = \mathcal{L}_{ent} + \beta\mathcal{L}_{pair} + \eta\mathcal{L}_{pol}, \tag{9}$$

where $\mathcal{L}_{ent}, \mathcal{L}_{pair}$, and $\mathcal{L}_{pol}$ represent the losses of the three subtasks, namely entity boundary, entity pair and sentiment polarity, separately. β and η are specify hyperparameters.

Table 1. Data statistics.

		Dialogue				Items		Pairs			Quadruples		
		Dia.	Utt.	Spk.	Tgt.	Asp.	Opi.	Pair_{t-a}	Pair_{t-o}	Pair_{a-o}	Quad.	Intra.	Cross
ZH	Total	1,000	7,452	4,991	8,308	6,572	7,051	6,041	7,587	5,358	5,742	4,467	1,275
	Train	800	5,947	3,986	6,652	5,220	5,622	4,823	6,062	4,297	4,607	3,594	1,013
	Valid	100	748	502	823	662	724	621	758	538	577	440	137
	Test	100	757	503	833	690	705	597	767	523	558	433	125
EN	Total	1,000	7,452	4,991	8,264	6,434	6,933	5,894	7,432	4,994	5,514	4,287	1,227
	Train	800	5,947	3,986	6,613	5,109	5,523	4,699	5,931	3,989	4,414	3,442	972
	Valid	100	748	502	822	644	719	603	750	509	555	423	132
	Test	100	757	503	829	681	691	592	751	496	545	422	123

3.5 Training Strategy

Cross Validation and Model Fusion. We randomly split the training data into 5 folds, and train the model on each fold. For each fold, we select the best model on the validation set and use the weight for model fusion. The model fusion is done by averaging the weights of the selected models. Note that we only select the top 3 models among the 5 folds, as we found that using more models degrades the performance.

Language Transfer from Chinese to English. We found that transfer learning from Chinese to English is effective, and we use the following method to transfer the model from Chinese to English. First, we train the model on Chinese data using cross-validation and model fusion(as described above). Then we use the fused Chinese model to initialize the parameters of the English model. Finally, the English model is trained as usual. We found that this method is more effective than training the model from scratch on English data.

Sentiment Correction by Rules. We extract the apsect-opinion pairs from the training set and build the rules based on the pairs. We keep the top 512 pairs both positive and negative sentiments. We remove the pairs that appear in both positive and negative sentiments, resulting in 426 pairs for both negative and postive and both. The numbers of pairs for both languages are the same probably because the english dataset is directly translated from the chinese dataset. These pairs are used to correct the sentiment prediction in a simple manner: if the pair appears in the prediction, we change the corresponding sentiment to the sentiment of the pair.

4   Experiment

4.1   Experimental Settings

Dataset. DiaASQ [9] is a mobile phone field conversational aspect-based sentiment quadruple analysis dataset, collected from Weibo. Each conversation originates from a root post, and multiple speakers participate in replying to predecessor posts. Multiple threads and multiple turns of conversation form a tree structure. The statistical information of the dataset is shown in Table 1.

Table 2. Main results on the offline test set. The best results are in bold.

Method	Chinese		English		Avg. F1
	Micro F1	Iden.F1	Micro F1	Iden.F1	
CRF-Extract-Classify	8.81	9.25	11.59	12.80	10.61
SpERT	13.00	14.19	13.07	13.38	13.41
ParaPhrase	23.27	27.98	24.54	26.76	25.64
Span-ASTE	27.42	30.85	26.99	28.34	28.40
DiaASQ	34.94	37.51	33.31	36.80	35.64
Ours	**43.00**	**46.20**	**38.32**	**44.06**	**42.90**

Evaluation Metrics. Following previous works [9], we evaluate all methods on quadruple extraction, using *micro F1* and *identification F1* as metrics respectively. *Micro F1* measures the whole quadruple, including the sentiment polarity and *identification F1* does not distinguish the polarity.

Alternative Baselines. Following previous work [9], we select **CRF-Extract Classify** [1], **SpERT** [5], **Span-ASTE** [18], **ParaPhrase** [20] and **DiaASQ** [9] as baselines, where DiaASQ is the official baseline of the track 4 of the NLPCC-2022 shared task.

Implementation Details. We take the Chinese-macbert-large [3] as the pretrain language model for the Chinese and English datasets. Throughout the experiments, we use Adam optimizer, where the initial learning rate is 1e-6. In order to prevent overfitting, the dropout rate is fixed at 0.2. Specify hyperparameters β and η are set to 3.

4.2   Main Comparisons

All evaluation results under automatic metrics are reported in 2. We can observe that, among all models, our method achieves the best results in evaluation metrics. Compared with the official baseline, our method improves by 8.06%, 8.69%, 5.01%, and 7.26% on the micro F1 and identification F1 evaluation metrics for

Chinese and English datasets, respectively. Compared with the official baseline model (DiaASQ), the performance improvement of our solution mainly comes from a stronger pre-training model, more sufficient feature interaction, and our training strategy. Our approach also achieves the best result in the DiaASQ competition.

Table 3. Ablation results

	Chinese		English		Avg. F1
	Micro-F1	Iden-F1	Micro-F1	Iden-F1	
DiaASQ	34.94	37.51	33.31	36.80	35.64
w/o PLM	14.21	17.55	15.68	19.57	16.75
Ours	43.00	46.20	38.32	44.06	42.90
w/o PLM	17.52	21.33	16.97	20.28	19.03
w DiaASQ PLM	40.46	42.80	35.76	41.65	40.17
w max pooling	41.79	43.55	36.05	41.20	40.65
w all ffn	42.19	44.68	36.57	42.27	41.43
w/o k-fold	41.21	43.12	36.35	42.72	40.85
w/o trans	41.22	43.87	36.83	41.43	40.84
w/o rule	42.82	45.93	37.89	43.77	42.60

4.3   Ablation Study

In order to verify the effectiveness of each optimization we made to the official baseline (DiaASQ), we conducted detailed comparison experiments. The experimental results are shown in Table 3.

For **pre-trained language model**, we design two variants: removing the pre-trained model entirely, using only randomly initialized word2vec (w/o PLM), and using a pre-trained language model consistent with the baseline model (w DiaASQ PLM). We can observe that different pre-trained language models have a greater impact on performance, and the version without PLM drops significantly, proving the important role of pre-trained language models in modeling semantic relevance.

For **methodology**, we replaced the multi-view deep interaction module with multi-view interaction max-pooling in the official baseline model (w max pooling), and the average F1 on the Chinese and English datasets dropped by 1.93% and 2.56%, respectively. This proves that multi-view deep interaction has a strong ability to aggregate information from different views, which is beyond the reach of the max pooling in the baseline method. We also add ffn layer for the thread view in consecutive multi-view interaction module (w all ffn), and the average F1 dropped by 0.47%.

For **training strategy**, we remove k-fold model fusion (w/o k-fold), language transfer (w/o trans), and rule-based sentiment correction (w/o rule), separately.

The performers of three variants of our method decrease by 2.05%, 2.06% and 0.29% in the average F1 metric respectively, which demonstrates the importance of model ensemble and cross-lingual learning to further improve model performance and stability.

5   Conclusion

In this paper, we use a Chinese pre-trained language model and grid tagging schema as backbone to tackle the problem of conversational aspect-based sentiment quadruple analysis. We deploy a multi-view interaction module consisting of three consecutive multi-head attention layers to aggregate emotional information from the local single speaker to the global multi-round dialogue. Besides, the English version model is transferred from the final Chinese weights and k-fold validation is used to improve the model performance. Finally, our proposed framework received second place in the NLPCC 2023 task 4, with an average F1 score of 42.89%. Although exciting improvements over the baseline DiaASQ model appear, our results show that the conversational aspect-based sentiment quadruple analysis is still challenging, which needs further consideration and discussion.

Acknowledgments. This work was supported in part by the National Natural Science Foundation of China under Grant No. 62276110, in part by CCF-AFSG Research Fund under Grant No. RF20210005, and in part by the fund of Joint Laboratory of HUST and Pingan Property & Casualty Research (HPL). The authors would also like to thank the anonymous reviewers for their comments on improving the quality of this paper.

References

1. Cai, H., Xia, R., Yu, J.: Aspect-category-opinion-sentiment quadruple extraction with implicit aspects and opinions. In: Proceedings of the 59th Annual Meeting of the Association for Computational Linguistics and the 11th International Joint Conference on Natural Language Processing (Volume 1: Long Papers), pp. 340–350 (2021)
2. Chen, Y., Keming, C., Sun, X., Zhang, Z.: A span-level bidirectional network for aspect sentiment triplet extraction. In: Proceedings of the 2022 Conference on Empirical Methods in Natural Language Processing, pp. 4300–4309. Association for Computational Linguistics, Abu Dhabi, United Arab Emirates, December 2022. https://aclanthology.org/2022.emnlp-main.289
3. Cui, Y., Che, W., Liu, T., Qin, B., Wang, S., Hu, G.: Revisiting pre-trained models for Chinese natural language processing. In: Proceedings of the 2020 Conference on Empirical Methods in Natural Language Processing: Findings. pp. 657–668. Association for Computational Linguistics, Online, November 2020. https://www.aclweb.org/anthology/2020.findings-emnlp.58
4. Do, H.H., Prasad, P.W., Maag, A., Alsadoon, A.: Deep learning for aspect-based sentiment analysis: a comparative review. Expert Syst. Appl. **118**, 272–299 (2019)

5. Eberts, M., Ulges, A.: Span-based joint entity and relation extraction with transformer pre-training. In: ECAI 2020, pp. 2006–2013. IOS Press (2020)
6. Ghosal, D., Majumder, N., Poria, S., Chhaya, N., Gelbukh, A.: Dialoguegcn: a graph convolutional neural network for emotion recognition in conversation. In: Proceedings of the 2019 Conference on Empirical Methods in Natural Language Processing and the 9th International Joint Conference on Natural Language Processing (EMNLP-IJCNLP), pp. 154–164 (2019)
7. Hazarika, D., Poria, S., Zadeh, A., Cambria, E., Morency, L.P., Zimmermann, R.: Conversational memory network for emotion recognition in dyadic dialogue videos. In: Proceedings of NAACL-HLT, pp. 2122–2132 (2018)
8. Hu, D., Wei, L., Huai, X.: Dialoguecrn: contextual reasoning networks for emotion recognition in conversations. In: Proceedings of the 59th Annual Meeting of the Association for Computational Linguistics and the 11th International Joint Conference on Natural Language Processing (Volume 1: Long Papers), pp. 7042–7052 (2021)
9. Li, B., et al.: Diaasq: a benchmark of conversational aspect-based sentiment quadruple analysis. arXiv preprint arXiv:2211.05705 (2022)
10. Majumder, N., Poria, S., Hazarika, D., Mihalcea, R., Gelbukh, A., Cambria, E.: Dialoguernn: an attentive RNN for emotion detection in conversations. In: Proceedings of the AAAI Conference on Artificial Intelligence, vol. 33, pp. 6818–6825 (2019)
11. Pang, B., Lee, L., et al.: Opinion mining and sentiment analysis. Found. Trends Inf. Retrieval 2(1–2), 1–135 (2008)
12. Peng, H., Xu, L., Bing, L., Huang, F., Lu, W., Si, L.: Knowing what, how and why: a near complete solution for aspect-based sentiment analysis. In: Proceedings of the AAAI Conference on Artificial Intelligence, vol. 34, pp. 8600–8607 (2020)
13. Poria, S., Majumder, N., Mihalcea, R., Hovy, E.: Emotion recognition in conversation: research challenges, datasets, and recent advances. IEEE Access 7, 100943–100953 (2019)
14. Su, J., Lu, Y., Pan, S., Wen, B., Liu, Y.: Roformer: Enhanced transformer with rotary position embedding. CoRR abs/2104.09864 (2021), arxiv.org/abs/2104.09864
15. Vaswani, A., et al.: Attention is all you need. Advances in neural information processing systems 30 (2017)
16. Vinodhini, G., Chandrasekaran, R.: Sentiment analysis and opinion mining: a survey. Int. J. 2(6), 282–292 (2012)
17. Wu, Z., Ying, C., Zhao, F., Fan, Z., Dai, X., Xia, R.: Grid tagging scheme for aspect-oriented fine-grained opinion extraction. In: Findings of the Association for Computational Linguistics: EMNLP 2020, pp. 2576–2585 (2020)
18. Xu, L., Chia, Y.K., Bing, L.: Learning span-level interactions for aspect sentiment triplet extraction. In: Proceedings of the 59th Annual Meeting of the Association for Computational Linguistics and the 11th International Joint Conference on Natural Language Processing (Volume 1: Long Papers), pp. 4755–4766 (2021)
19. Zhang, L., Wang, S., Liu, B.: Deep learning for sentiment analysis: a survey. Wiley Interdisciplinary Rev. Data Mining Knowl. Discovery 8(4), e1253 (2018)
20. Zhang, W., Deng, Y., Li, X., Yuan, Y., Bing, L., Lam, W.: Aspect sentiment quad prediction as paraphrase generation. In: Proceedings of the 2021 Conference on Empirical Methods in Natural Language Processing, pp. 9209–9219 (2021)
21. Zhang, W., Li, X., Deng, Y., Bing, L., Lam, W.: A survey on aspect-based sentiment analysis: tasks, methods, and challenges. IEEE Trans. Knowl. Data Eng. (2022)

A Model Ensemble Approach for Conversational Quadruple Extraction

Zijian Tu, Bo Zhang, Chuchu Jiang, Jian Wang$^{(\boxtimes)}$, and Hongfei Lin

School of Computer Science and Technology,
Dalian University of Technology, Dalian 116024, Liaoning, China
{tuzj,zhangbo1998,chuchu}@mail.dlut.edu.cn, {wangjian,hflin}@dlut.edu.cn

Abstract. Fine-grained sentiment analysis of dialogue text is crucial for the model to understand the conversational participants' viewpoints and provide accurate responses in generating replies. Unfortunately, in the field of conversational opinion mining, coarse-grained dialogue emotion analysis remains the mainstream approach, despite being unable to meet the actual needs in some specific scenarios such as customer service question and answer system. This work focuses on conversational aspect-based sentiment quadruple analysis, which aims to detect the sentiment quadruple of target-aspect-opinion-sentiment in a dialogue. In this study, we mainly extract triplets and judge the unique sentiment, which is determined by the target and opinion terms together. For this purpose, we fine-tune the pre-trained language models using the DiaASQ dataset. We optimize the rotation positional information embedding by combining the actual length of the dialogue text and use adversarial training to enhance the model's performance and robustness. Finally, We use beam search ensemble algorithm to improve the entire triplet extraction system's performance. Our system achieved an average F1 score 40.50 that ranked second in the Chinese dataset and fifth in the general dataset for the Conversational Aspect-based Sentiment Quadruple Analysis shared task at NLPCC-2023.

Keywords: conversational quadruple extraction · fine-grained sentiment analysis · beam search ensemble algorithm

1 Introduction

Aspect-based sentiment analysis has become a popular technique in natural language processing to identify people's opinions and attitudes towards products or services by analyzing the sentiment of the text [1]. However, traditional sentiment analysis techniques often fail to capture the conversational flow of a dialogue or conversation. Conversations are complex and dynamic, where different speakers may have different viewpoints and emotions towards distinct aspects of the target, making it crucial to perform fine-grained sentiment analysis of dialogue text. In certain specific scenarios, such as a customer service question

F. Liu et al. (Eds.): NLPCC 2023, LNAI 14304, pp. 174–184, 2023.
https://doi.org/10.1007/978-3-031-44699-3_16

and answer system, it is insufficient to solely identify the emotions expressed by consumers during a conversation. It becomes more important to identify the specific viewpoints of consumers regarding different aspects of the product in order to effectively address post-sales issues and provide better assistance. However, coarse-grained dialogue emotion analysis remains the mainstream approach in the field of conversational opinion mining. It appears that despite incorporating dialogue into the fine-grained sentiment analysis (DiaASQ) [2], the model's actual performance is still subpar.

Our work focuses on conversational aspect-based sentiment quadruple analysis (CASQA), which aims to detect the sentiment quadruple of target-aspect-opinion-sentiment in a dialogue. As shown in Fig. 1, our task involves extracting triples such as 'Apple','power consumption' and 'can't hold' from multiple rounds of dialogue among four speakers who are discussing the various aspects of the iPhone's performance. The extracted triples like 'Apple', 'power consumption' and 'can't hold' will then be evaluated for negative emotional polarity. The Corresponding aspect-based quadruples extracted in this dialogue fragment are shown in the Table 1. CASQA enables us to identify sentiment with respect to the specific aspects and opinions expressed in the conversation and provides a more accurate understanding of the conversation's sentiment.

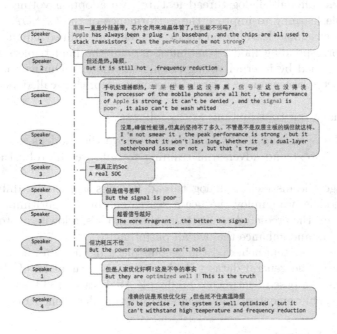

Fig. 1. Illustration of CASQA task

On the basis of the model and data set provided by DiaASQ, We achieved CASQA task by extracting triplets that judge the unique sentiment, which is determined by the target and opinion terms together.

Table 1. Corresponding aspect-based quadruples

Target	Aspect	Opinion	Sentiment
Apple	performance	strong	pos
Apple	signal	poor	neg
Apple	optimized	well	pos
Apple	power consumption	can't hold	neg

Our method is divided into two stages: (1) We first utilized a Neural Network Intelligence tool to search for hyperparameters that would lead to optimal performance of the model. Then we optimize the rotation positional information embedding (Roformer) [3] by combining the actual length of the dialogue text. Based on the discovered hyper-parameters, we fine-tuned the model using the Chinese-English dataset provided by DiaASQ. After gradient back-propagation, the adversarial training FGM method [4]is used to improve the performance and robustness of the model. (2) Multiple pre-trained language models ensemble. We have trained several models that perform well in the field of ABSA for enhancing the understanding of the DiaASQ task. Given that different models may learn different dialog thread features, we adopts a voting mechanism and ensemble learning to improve the performance of the CASQA system [5]. We perform ensemble learning on the 5 different pre-trained language models to obtain corresponding model combinations, and the final triplets prediction results is obtained by internal voting among the models. During the ensemble learning process, we propose a model ensemble algorithm called beam search ensemble.

In summary, our contributions are as follows:

- We use the optimized RoPE to further improve the model's understanding of dialog context and adversarial training to improve the robustness of the model.
- To leverage the distinctive dialog thread features learned by different pre-trained models, we employ the beam search ensemble algorithm. This algorithm merges the predicted results from these models, allowing us to integrate their insights and enhance the overall performance.
- Our proposed system achieved the second place in the Chinese dataset and fifth place in the general dataset during the final evaluation of the Conversational Aspect-based Sentiment Quadruple Analysis shared task at NLPCC-2023. This achievement strongly demonstrates the effectiveness of our method.

2   Related Work

From the traditional approach of text-level sentiment analysis to the more comprehensive fine-grained analysis that encompasses opinion mining through the prediction of various elements, including aspect terms, sentiment polarity, opinion terms, aspect categories, and targets. The growing popularity of open-domain dialogue systems, particularly ChatGPT, has given rise to increased interest in sentiment analysis of integrated conversations.

Zhao et al. [6] and Wu et al. [7] proposed an end-to-end method to solve the task of Pair-wise Aspect and Opinion Terms Extraction and a multi-task learning framework based on shared spans, where the terms are extracted under the supervision of span boundaries. Peng et al. [8] proposed a two-stage framework to extract aspect sentiment triplet. The first stage predicts what, how and why in a unified model, and then the second stage pairs up the predicted what (how) and why from the first stage to output triplets. Knoester et al. [9] proposed work extends a state-of-the-art model for ABSA with the methodology of Domain Adversarial Training to create a deep learning adaptable cross-domain structure. This improves the generalization and robustness of the model. Li et al. [2] constructed a large-scale high-quality DiaASQ dataset which contains both Chinese and English version. They bridged the gap between fine-grained sentiment analysis and conversational opinion mining by developing a neural model which shows huge wins on the cross-utterance quadruple extraction. However, their systems have limited understanding of the entity, aspect, and sentiment triples in multi-turn dialogues. In contrast, our optimized rotational position embedding enables our model to better comprehend the relationships between triples across the conversation context. Additionally, our proposed model integration method leverages multiple perspectives to enhance the accuracy of triplet extraction in the model's multi-turn conversation flow.

3 Methodology

3.1 Triplets Extraction Model

Based on tree-structured parzen estimator (TPE), a classic Bayesian optimization algorithm, we obtain a preliminary range of hyperparameters suitable for different models. On various long text benchmark datasets, Su et al. [3] proposed Rotary Position Embedding(RoPE). By using RoPE, various valuable properties can be achieved, such as the ability to flexibly adjust sequence length, a reduction in the strength of inter-token dependencies at greater relative distances, and the potential to enhance the linear self-attention mechanism with relative position encoding. Consistent superior performance in comparison to alternative methods has been demonstrated through their experiences. Our task is to integrate the dialog into the tree-like dialogue replying structure. Since our context length is shorter than the long text dataset on Roformer, we modify the weight of the rotation positional information embedding.

$$\begin{cases} \boldsymbol{p}_{i,2t} & = \sin\left(10000^{-wei*2t/d}\right) \\ \boldsymbol{p}_{i,2t+1} = \cos\left(10000^{-wei*2t/d}\right) \end{cases} \tag{1}$$

in which wei is the RoPE embedding weight that we adjusted and $p_{i,2t}$ is the $2t^{th}$ element of the d-dimensional vector p_i.

FGM is an adversarial training method, applying adversarial perturbations to word embeddings. Suppose the word embedding vector is s, and the model conditional probability of y given s as $p(y|s; \theta)$, where θ are the parameter of the classifier, N is the number of labeled examples. Then the adversarial perturbation r_{adv} on s as

$$r_{\mathrm{adv}} = -\epsilon g/\|g\|_2 \,\mathrm{where}\, g = \nabla_s \log p(y \mid s; \boldsymbol{\theta}). \tag{2}$$

The adversarial loss is computed as

$$\boldsymbol{L}_{\mathrm{adv}}(\boldsymbol{\theta}) = -\frac{1}{N} \sum_{n=1}^{N} \log p(y_n \mid s_n + r_{\mathrm{adv},n}; \boldsymbol{\theta}) \tag{3}$$

Based on the above optimization strategy, we add 100 dialogue verification sets to the training set to train the model, and finally get the best performance of a single model. The structure of our system is shown in Fig. 2.

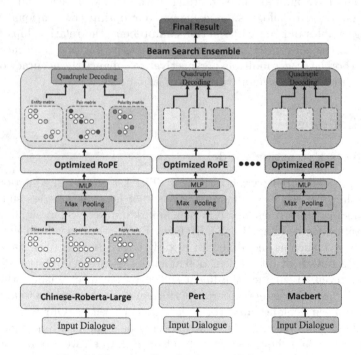

Fig. 2. The overall architecture of the system

3.2   Models Selection

In this section, we conducted experiments using several powerful Aspect-Based Sentiment Analysis (ABSA) systems that have been verified on classic ABSA tasks, as reported in [10]. To encode the dialogue text for our task, we trained both the English and Chinese versions of these models separately.

BERT [11] was the first pre-trained language model that used a large-scale corpus, and has led to significant performance improvements in many downstream natural language processing tasks. In recent years, several improved Chinese pre-trained language models based on BERT have emerged, including the Chinese versions of RoBERTa-wwm [12], PERT [13], and MacBERT [14].

RoBERTa-wwm is a Chinese pre-trained language model based on RoBERTa that uses a whole-word masking strategy and other pre-training techniques to improve performance.

PERT takes a different approach to pre-training by replacing the Masked Language Model (MLM) with a word order prediction task, where the model is presented with randomly shuffled text and tasked with predicting the original word order. This approach has been shown to improve the performance of pre-trained models.

MacBERT improves upon the pre-training technique of RoBERTa by incorporating a synonym masking strategy. This strategy aims to reduce the gap between pre-training and fine-tuning phases, and has demonstrated effective performance improvements in Chinese pre-trained language models.

These models were selected for their proven efficacy in ABSA tasks and were separately trained for Chinese and English language inputs.

3.3   Ensemble Model

As the number of distinct models continues to increase, finding the optimal combination of models quickly becomes computationally expensive to model with traditional methods. To overcome this challenge, we propose a beam search ensemble algorithm for model fusion. This algorithm incorporates improvements to the beam search approach, enabling a more efficient convergence to the optimal combination. As shown in Fig. 3, we use beam search ensemble algorithm to get the final result.

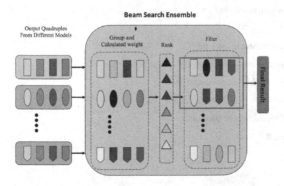

Fig. 3. The details of the beam search ensemble

180   Z. Tu et al.

One key issue with traditional model fusion is the distribution of voting weight amongst the models. In our algorithm, we have effectively addressed this issue by considering the performance of each model and reducing any bias that may arise from poorly performing models. By doing so, the algorithm ensures that only models with good performance are given more significant voting weight, and thus produce optimal results.

Our proposed algorithm is superior in terms of generalization ability when compared to other existing model fusion methods. In addition, the algorithm reduces time complexity significantly and allows for single model voting. This approach fully considers the strengths of each model, and effectively updates the voting weight to produce the best possible results. Overall, the beam search ensemble algorithm can combine the prediction results of all models to obtain more accurate prediction results. As follows.

Beam search ensemble algorithm to merge distinct predicted results

Input: models_data: a list of multiple model predictions

output: final_data

set **k**: the most likely number of emotions to be selected in each identifier combination

set threshold **t** ,define empty dictionary: ensembled_data, define empty lists: final_data, beam

1: **for** data in models_data **do**

2:       **for** doc in data **do**

3:             **for** triplet in doc['triplets'] **do**

4:                   identifier=(doc['doc_id'],)+tuple(triplet[:-3])

5:                   ensembled_data[identifier].append(triplet[-3])

6:             **end for**

7:       **end for**

8: **end for**

9: **for** identifier, predictions in ensembled_data.items() **do**

10:   counter = a statistical emotion counter

11:   **for** prediction in predictions **do**

12:       counter[prediction] += 1

13:   **end for**

15:   **if** the counter length >= 1 **do**

16:   beam_sum =the sum of emotional counts in beam

17:   *emotion*_weight = count / beam_sum

18:       **if** *emotion*_weight >= threshold **t do**

19:       add quadruple to **final_data**

20:       **end if**

21:   **end if**

22:**end for**

In this process, the calculation of the importance weight is to calculate the relative weight of each emotion in proportion through the number of occurrences of each emotion in the prediction result of the statistical model, and then filter the prediction result according to the threshold. Compared with the voting method, the beam search ensemble algorithm can better deal with the situation where there are fewer identifiers and the emotional distribution is unbalanced, and it can better control the misjudgment rate while improving the prediction effect.

4   Experiments

4.1   Dataset and Evaluation Index

The DiaASQ dataset includes 1000 dialogues in both Chinese and English languages. It is split into a training set, a verification set, and a test set at a ratio of 8:1:1 for each language. Since the data was originally in Chinese, and the English data set was translated from it, there is some degree of noise in the English data, which accounts for the lower F1 scores of the model on the English data set compared to the Chinese data set. As a result, improving the model's performance on the English data set proves to be more challenging. Since our main focus is on quadruple extraction, we primarily measure the performance using micro F1 and identification F1 scores. The micro F1 score considers the entire quad, including the sentiment polarity. On the other hand, the identification F1 score, as described in Barnes et al. [15], does not differentiate between different polarities in the evaluation.

4.2   Results and Analysis

To evaluate the effectiveness of the optimization techniques we applied to our models, we first selected RoBERTa-large, the most effective pre-trained language model, and conducted a single-model comparison experiment on both the Chinese and English test sets. Next, we compared each baseline model to the model incorporating all of our improvements. In the end, we will employ the beam search ensemble algorithm to obtain the best possible prediction result by leveraging the various models optimized for optimal performance. +FGM means that adversarial training modules are added to the +optimized RoPE, +verification sets means that model training is further trained with verification sets on the basis of the first two and +all means using all of the above strategies at the same time. The ablation experiments are shown in Table 2.

Table 2 demonstrates that incorporating optimized RoPE into the DiaASQ baseline results in an improvement of 1.02% and 0.87% for the roberta-large model in both Chinese and English datasets. This highlights the effectiveness of adjusting the weight of the positional embedding information based on the length of the conversation and its ability to enhance the model's context comprehension. Additionally, the adversarial training process that accumulates both the original

Table 2. The F1 of different models on the Chinese and English test set

Model	Chinese			English		
	Micro-F1	Iden-F1	Avg. F1	Micro-F1	Iden-F1	Avg. F1
DiaASQ (baseline)	34.94	37.51	36.23	33.31	36.8	35.06
roberta-large	36.24	42.78	38.31	33.67	37.3	34.69
+optimized RoPE	38.35	42.72	39.33	34.74	37.96	35.55
+FGM	38.50	42.92	39.51	34.82	38.08	35.65
+verification sets	39.23	43.85	$41.54_{+5.32}$	35.13	38.55	$36.84_{+1.79}$
roberta-base	33.7	40.02	36.86	31.68	35.96	33.82
+all	35.74	44.26	**40.00**	32.74	37.2	**34.97**
bert-large	33.17	39.33	36.25	31.29	35.41	33.35
+all	35.53	43.9	**39.715**	32.67	36.98	**34.83**
Pert	31.28	38.66	34.37	/	/	/
+all	34.64	42.83	**38.135**	/	/	/
Macbert	33.05	40.79	36.92	/	/	/
+all	35.39	43.85	**39.62**	/	/	/
beam search ensemble(ours)	42.09	45.62	$\textbf{43.855}_{+7.63}$	35.54	38.76	$\textbf{37.15}_{+2.10}$

gradient and the adversarial gradient can mitigate overfitting and improve the model's robustness. After including a verification set consisting of 100 dialogues in the training data, the average F1 score for the Chinese dataset increased by 2.03% in the Roberta-large model, while that of the English dataset increased by 1.21%. This suggests that the dataset is of high quality, and that the amount of data plays a significant role in limiting the performance of the models. We applied the aforementioned optimization techniques to other Bert-based models, and observed improvement in their performance. Considering the different features learned by each model and the nuances of their predicted quadruples, we utilized the beam search ensemble algorithm to merge the predictions of multiple models in the Table 2, assign weights to each of them, sort them, and screen out the quadruples with weights greater than the threshold t. The final result showed an increase of 7.63% compared to the baseline. Furthermore, when compared to the optimal model, the beam search ensemble algorithm demonstrated an improvement of 2.31%.

5   Conclusion

In this paper, we propose a model ensemble approach for conversational quadruple extraction. We initiated our efforts to enhance the task's performance by optimizing the RoPE positional information embedding. Subsequently, we employed adversarial training techniques to further boost the model's robustness and generalization capabilities. Additionally, we expanded the training dataset and further improved the model's F1 scores for both Chinese and English test set. We then trained several models using these optimization strategies and identified the best results using the beam search ensemble algorithm. Experimental results on the NLPCC2023 Shared Task4 DiaASQ dataset demonstrate the effectiveness of our method and the necessity of the rotation positional information embedding module and using beam search ensemble algorithm to integrates correct predictions from distinct models.

References

1. Liu, B., Zhang, L.: A survey of opinion mining and sentiment analysis. In: Mining Text Data, pp. 415–463. Springer (2012)
2. Li, B., Fei, H.: Diaasq: a benchmark of conversational aspect-based sentiment quadruple analysis. CoRR abs/2211.05705 (2022)
3. Su, J., Lu, Y.: Roformer: enhanced transformer with rotary position embedding. CoRR abs/2104.09864 (2021)
4. Miyato, T., Dai, A.M.: Adversarial training methods for semi-supervised text classification. In: 5th International Conference on Learning Representations, ICLR 2017, Toulon, France, April 24–26, 2017, Conference Track Proceedings. OpenReview.net (2017)
5. Cui, S., Han, Y.: A two-stage voting-boosting technique for ensemble learning in social network sentiment classification. Entropy **25**(4), 555 (2023)
6. Zhao, H., Huang, L.: Spanmlt: a span-based multi-task learning framework for pair-wise aspect and opinion terms extraction. In: Proceedings of the 58th Annual Meeting of the Association for Computational Linguistics, ACL 2020, Online, July 5–10, 2020, pp. 3239–3248 (2022)
7. Wu, S., Fei, H.: Learn from syntax: improving pair-wise aspect and opinion terms extraction with rich syntactic knowledge. In: Zhou, Z. (ed.) Proceedings of the Thirtieth International Joint Conference on Artificial Intelligence, IJCAI 2021, Virtual Event / Montreal, Canada, 19–27 August 2021, pp. 3957–3963 (2021)
8. Peng, H., Xu, L.: Knowing what, how and why: a near complete solution for aspect based sentiment analysis. In: The Thirty-Fourth AAAI Conference on Artificial Intelligence, AAAI 2020, The Thirty-Second Innovative Applications of Artificial Intelligence Conference, IAAI 2020, The Tenth AAAI Symposium on Educational Advances in Artificial Intelligence, EAAI 2020, New York, NY, USA, February 7–12, 2020, pp. 8600–8607. AAAI Press (2020)
9. Knoester, J., Frasincar, F.: Domain adversarial training for aspect-based sentiment analysis. In: Web Information Systems Engineering - WISE 2022–23rd International Conference, Biarritz, France, November 1–3, 2022, Proceedings. LNCS, vol. 13724, pp. 21–37 (2022)
10. Li, Z., Zou, Y.: Learning implicit sentiment in aspect-based sentiment analysis with supervised contrastive pre-training. In: Proceedings of the 2021 Conference on Empirical Methods in Natural Language Processing, EMNLP 2021, Virtual Event/Punta Cana, Dominican Republic, 7–11 November, 2021, pp. 246–256. Association for Computational Linguistics (2021)
11. Devlin, J., Chang, M.: BERT: pre-training of deep bidirectional transformers for language understanding. In: Proceedings of the 2019 Conference of the North American Chapter of the Association for Computational Linguistics: Human Language Technologies, NAACL-HLT 2019, Minneapolis, MN, USA, June 2–7, 2019, Volume 1 (Long and Short Papers), pp. 4171–4186 (2019)

12. Liu, Y., Ott, M.: Roberta: A robustly optimized BERT pretraining approach. CoRR abs/1907.11692 (2019)
13. Cui, Y., Yang, Z.: PERT: pre-training BERT with permuted language model. CoRR abs/2203.06906 (2022)
14. Cui, Y., Che, W.: Revisiting pre-trained models for Chinese natural language processing. In: Findings of the Association for Computational Linguistics: EMNLP 2020, Online Event, 16–20 November 2020. Findings of ACL, vol. EMNLP 2020, pp. 657–668
15. Barnes, J., Kurtz, R.: Structured sentiment analysis as dependency graph parsing. In: Proceedings of the 59th Annual Meeting of the Association for Computational Linguistics and the 11th International Joint Conference on Natural Language Processing, ACL/IJCNLP 2021, (Volume 1: Long Papers), Virtual Event, August 1–6, 2021

Enhancing Conversational Aspect-Based Sentiment Quadruple Analysis with Context Fusion Encoding Method

Xisheng Xiao, Jiawei Chen, Qianer Li, Peijie Huang$^{(\boxtimes)}$, and Yuhong Xu

College of Mathematics and Informatics, South China Agricultural University,
Guangzhou, China
pjhuang@scau.edu.cn

Abstract. Aspect-based sentiment analysis (ABSA) has been a hot research topic due to its ability to fully exploit people's opinions through social media texts. Compared with analyzing sentiment in short texts, conversational aspect-based sentiment quadruple analysis, also known as DiaASQ, aiming to extract the sentiment quadruple of target-aspect-opinion-sentiment in a dialogue, is a relatively new task that involves multiple speakers with varying stances in a conversation. Conversations are longer than ordinary texts and have richer contexts, which can lead to context loss and pairing errors. To address this issue, this work proposes a context-fusion encoding method based on conversation threads and lengths to integrate the speech of different speakers, enabling the model to better understand conversational context and extract cross-utterance quadruples. Experimental results have demonstrated that the proposed method achieves an average F1-score of 42.12% in DiaASQ, which is 6.48% higher than the best comparative model, indicating superior performance.

Keywords: Conversational aspect-based sentiment quadruple analysis · Context fusion · Conversational opinion mining

1 Introduction

In recent years, many people have shared their opinions and reviews on the internet through various social media platforms. Fully mining information from these texts can provide significant help in improving products and increasing efficiency, making aspect-based sentiment analysis (ABSA) [1–3] a popular research direction. ABSA is a task that aims to detect fine-grained sentiment towards specific aspects of targets. Initially, ABSA only focused on aspect terms and sentiment polarities [4–6]. Later, researchers gradually realized the importance of two other key factors that influence sentiment polarity judgments: opinion terms and categories [2]. Depending on the different elements of interest, various ABSA tasks have been proposed, including pair extraction tasks (e.g. aspect-opinion pair extraction, AOPE [7]), triple ABSA tasks (e.g. aspect sentiment triplet extraction, ASTE [8,9]), and quadruple ABSA tasks (e.g. aspect sentiment quad prediction, ASQP [10,11]).

© The Author(s), under exclusive license to Springer Nature Switzerland AG 2023
F. Liu et al. (Eds.): NLPCC 2023, LNAI 14304, pp. 185–196, 2023.
https://doi.org/10.1007/978-3-031-44699-3_17

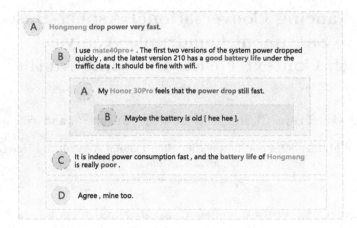

Fig. 1. Illustration of the conversational aspect-based sentiment quadruple analysis. We can extract the following four target-aspect-opinion-sentiment quadruples from this dialog: ('Hongmeng', 'drop power', 'very fast', 'neg'), ('mate40pro+', 'battery life', 'good', 'pos'), ('Honor 30Pro', 'power drop', 'fast', 'neg'), and ('Hongmeng', 'battery life', 'poor', 'neg').

The aforementioned research has been based on short texts such as comments. However, conversational texts are also a significant category in social media, and conducting sentiment analysis on these texts is equally meaningful. To perform fine-grained sentiment analysis on conversational texts, aspect-based sentiment quadruple analysis [12], also known as DiaASQ, has been proposed. As shown in Fig. 1, conversational texts have a natural special structure. Firstly, a conversation consists of multiple participants who may have different stances and views [13]. Secondly, the elements of sentiment quadruples may come from multiple sentences, which we refer to as cross-utterance quadruples. Finally, As the conversation progresses, the topic tends to shift gradually. These characteristics pose new challenges for modeling sentiment analysis on conversational texts.

To address the problem of DiaASQ, Li et al. [12] proposed a new model that used the thread, speaker, and reply views to model the conversation. Their model encodes each utterance separately using pre-trained language models (PLMs) [14], and then models the global information relying on self-attention mechanisms [15] and masking methods. This approach, however, can not fully utilize the powerful contextual modeling capabilities of PLMs, resulting in the loss of some interactive information between adjacent utterance pairs. Therefore, we propose a context-fusion encoding method for DiaASQ, which models the contextual information of the entire thread's speech, rather than model each sentence separately, performing better in extracting cross-utterance quadruples. Meanwhile, we treat extremely short conversations as a whole for context encoding. Furthermore, we incorporate regularized dropout [16] and fast gradient method [17] to improve the robustness of the model.

In summary, the main contributions of this work could be summarized as follows: (1) proposing a context-fusion encoding method that allows the model to better understand context and extract cross-utterance quadruples; (2) incorporating regularized dropout and fast gradient method into the model to enhance its performance; (3) the experimental results have demonstrated that the proposed method achieves an average F1-score of 42.12% in DiaASQ, which is 6.48% higher than the best comparative model, indicating superior performance.

2   Related Work

In this section, we will provide an overview of related work that focuses on sentiment analysis of short texts and the shared task.

2.1   Aspect-Based Sentiment Quadruples Extraction

In the field of aspect-based sentiment analysis (ABSA) for short texts, aspect sentiment quad prediction (ASQP), also referred to as aspect-based sentiment quadruple extraction, has been an active research area [2,3]. Cai et al. [10] were the pioneers to investigate the ABSA quadruple extraction task, with a focus on implicit aspects or opinions. They introduced two new datasets with sentiment quadruple annotations and constructed a series of pipeline baselines by combining existing models to benchmark the task. Zhang et al. [11] proposed a paraphrase modeling strategy to predict sentiment quadruples end-to-end. They transformed the original quadruple prediction task into a text generation problem and solved it using a Seq2Seq modeling paradigm. This approach enabled the full utilization of label semantics, i.e., the meaning of sentiment elements. Later methods have further formalized the task as generating opinion trees [18,19] or structured schema [20].

2.2   Conversational Aspect-Based Sentiment Quadruple Analysis

Conversational aspect-based sentiment quadruple analysis [12] was a new task, and previous work did not consider how to extract sentiment quadruples from conversation text. The shared task provided a model that used a novel labeling scheme based on the grid-tagging method [8], which divided the labeling task into three sub-tasks: detections of entity boundary, entity pair, and sentiment polarity. Compared to pipeline models that required extract-filter-matching processes [10], this approach reduced error propagation and accumulation. Additionally, compared to seq-to-seq approaches [11], it avoided exposure bias. The model first extracted the contextual representation of the sentence through an encoding layer. Then, it proposed a multi-view interaction layer that constructed Thread Mask, Speaker Mask, and Reply Mask, combined with a multi-head self-attention mechanism [15] to strengthen the awareness of the dialogue discourse. Finally, it fused the Rotary Position Embedding (RoPE) [21] and calculated the score between any token pair in terms of the label.

3   Methodology

In this section, we will provide a detailed description of our method. Our model structure is shown in Fig. 2. Overall, we propose a context-fusion encoding method based on the thread and conversation length in the stage of context characterization. We will introduce the adversarial training strategy and regularization technique strategy we used as well.

3.1   Task Introduction

The goal of conversational aspect-based sentiment quadruple analysis is to extract the target-aspect-opinion-sentiment quadruple from conversational texts. The target, aspect, and opinion are continuous words extracted from sentences, and these elements may come from different sentences, referred to as cross-utterance. The sentiment polarity can be classified into three categories: positive, negative, and neutral, based on the extracted three elements. As shown in Fig. 1, a conversation starts from a root post. All subsequent posts are child or grandchild posts of this root post. The so-called thread refers to the subtree derived from the root node of the conversation tree. We treat the root post as a separate thread. Target denotes a particular object(e.g. product or service), while aspect denotes a specific attribute or component of the target. In contrast, category is a broader concept that refers to the class to which the aspect belongs. An opinion term often takes the form of an adjective that conveys the speaker's evaluation of the aspect. For instance, as shown in Fig. 1, the aspect of "battery life" related to the target "mate40pro+" is mentioned.

Specifically, we represent each dialog as a training sample $D = \{u_1, ..., u_n\}$ with the corresponding replies $r = \{l_1, ..., l_n\}$ of utterances, where l_i denotes i^{th} utterance reply to l_i^{th} utterance. To maintain generality, we consider u_1 as root utterance. $t_k = \{u_i, u_{i+1}, ..., u_j\}(1 \le i \le j \le n)$ represents k-th thread where l_i equal to 1 and $\{l_{i+1}...l_j\} \in \{i, i+1, ..., j-1\}$. Each $u_i = \{w_1, ..., w_{m_i}\}$ denotes i-th utterance text and m_i is the length of utterance of u_i. DiaASQ aims to extract all possible $(target, aspect, opinion, sentiment)$ quadruples, denoted as $Q = \{t, a, o, p\}$ where $\{t, a, o\}$ is the sub-string of dialogue D and $p \in \{pos, neg, other\}$.

3.2   Context Fusion Encoding with Adversarial Training

Thread Fusion. Usually, a dialogue consists of multiple rounds and involves multiple speakers, presenting a complex hierarchical structure. As reported in [12], around 22% of cross-utterance quadruples exist in the Chinese and English datasets. If context encoding is only performed on individual utterance, on the one hand, the outstanding performance of PLMs [14] can not be fully utilized; on the other hand, there is no interaction between different utterances, undoubtedly resulting in the loss of contextual information. Therefore, we propose a contextual fusion method based on thread, which we call "thread fusion", and use PLMs to better model multiple speakers and different utterances. The method

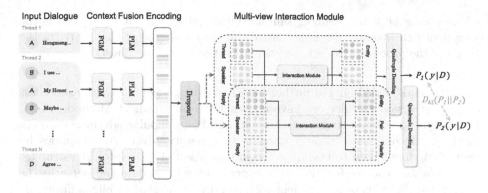

Fig. 2. The overall framework of the proposed method.

merges the utterances in the same thread of conversation into a dialogue segment and treats each segment as a whole for contextual representation encoding.

$$t'_k = < [cls], u_i, [sep], u_{i+1}, [sep], ..., [sep], u_j, [sep] >, \tag{1}$$

$$TH_k = h_{cls}, H_i, h_{sep}, ..., h_{sep}, H_j, h_{sep} = \text{PLMs}(t'_k), \tag{2}$$

where $u_i, ..., u_j$ are the utterances of k-th thread t_k , $[cls]$ and $[sep]$ are the special tokens in PLMs, H_i and TH_k means the contextual representation of i-th utterance and k-th thread. We found that the contents discussed in the same thread often have relevance, while the relationships between different threads are relatively weak. This is also the motivation for our proposed thread fusion.

Dialog Fusion. After further analysis of the dataset, it is discovered that some threads in certain conversations are very short in length, containing incomplete quadruples and little information, resulting making no predictions from model. As shown in Table 1, the average length of threads is around 28, with the shortest thread containing only 3 words. Naturally, we consider additional processing for these particularly short threads, by merging them into longer texts. In addition, the maximum length of threads in the Chinese dataset is 257 words, with the longest conversation containing 462 words. It is not applicable to all conversations, as some long conversations may exceed the maximum acceptable length of PLMs. Moreover, long conversations are usually more informative and may introduce noise to the model if merged together.

Taking into account the above two points, we propose treating certain conversations with a length less than a threshold value τ as a whole, and using a PLMs to obtain its global context information. The representation of whole dialog DH can be constructed as follow:

$$D' = < [cls], u_1, [sep], u_2, [sep], ..., [sep], u_n, [sep] >, \tag{3}$$

$$DH = \begin{cases} h_{cls}, H_1, h_{sep}, ..., H_n, h_{sep} = \text{PLMs}(D'), & \text{if } \sum_{i=1}^{n} m_i \leq \tau, \\ TH_1 || TH_2 || ... || TH_k, & \text{else}, \end{cases} \tag{4}$$

where dialog D' is one training sample connected by $[cls]$ and $[sep]$, m_i is the length of i-th utterance, τ is a controllable hyperparameter that restricts the scope of the processing object, and the operation of "$||$" is concat.

Adversarial Training. For further improving the performance and robustness of context fusion encoder, we have chosen the Fast Gradient Method (FGM) [17] as our adversarial training technique. FGM is a popular adversarial attack method, which is used in deep learning to generate adversarial examples by perturbing input data to maximize the loss function of the model. It calculates the gradient of the loss function with respect to the input data and perturbs the data in the direction of the gradient with a certain magnitude while maintaining a maximum norm constraint. The perturbations r_{adv} can be defined as:

$$r_{adv} = \epsilon \cdot g/\|g\|_2 \text{ where } g = \nabla_s L(D, y), \tag{5}$$

where ϵ is a hyperparameter limiting the size of adversarial perturbations r_{adv}.

3.3 Quadruple Decoder

Multi-view Interaction. Following Li et al. [12], we construct attention masks M^c and use multi-head self-attention [15] to extract three types of features: dialogue threads, speakers, and reply, where $c \in \{Th, Sp, Rp\}$ and the corresponding values represent thread mask, speak mask and speaker mask, respectively:

$$H^c = \text{Masked-Att}\left(Q, K, V, M^c\right) = \text{Softmax}(\frac{\left(Q^T \cdot K\right) \odot M^c}{\sqrt{d}}) \cdot V, \tag{6}$$

where $Q = K = V = DH$ is the representation of whole dialogue. Thread mask $M_{ij}^{Th} = 1$ if the ith and j^{th} token belong to the same dialogue thread; speaker mask $M_{ij}^{Sp} = 1$ if the ith and j^{th} token are derived from the same speaker; and reply mask $M_{ij}^{Rp} = 1$ if the two utterances containing the ith and j^{th} token respectively have a replying relation.

To better guide discourse understanding, the model fuses the Rotary Position Embedding (RoPE) [21] into token representations, which can dynamically encode the relative distance globally between tokens at the dialogue level. And then the score s_{ij}^r indicating the probability of relation label r between w_i and w_j can be calculated as:

$$s_{ij}^r = (R(\theta, i)v_i^r)^T (R(\theta, j)v_j^r), \tag{7}$$

where $R(\theta, i)$ is a positioning matrix parameterized by θ and the absolute index i of v_i^r.

Regularization. Inspired by Liang et al. [16], we improve quadruple decoder using Regularized Dropout (R-Drop), an unsupervised contrastive loss, as the regularization technique. By utilizing the probabilistic nature of the dropout layer, the model's predictions vary each time. R-Drop passes each training data sample through the model twice, and then uses Kullback-Leibler (KL) divergence to constrain the results of the two predictions, which can be defined by the following formula:

$$\mathcal{L}_{KL} = \frac{\alpha}{2} \left[\mathcal{D}_{KL} \left(\mathcal{P}_1^w(y \mid D) \| \mathcal{P}_2^w(y \mid D) \right) + \mathcal{D}_{KL} \left(\mathcal{P}_2^w(y \mid D) \| \mathcal{P}_1^w(y \mid D) \right) \right], \quad (8)$$

where $\mathcal{P}_1^w(y \mid D)$ and $\mathcal{P}_2^w(y \mid D)$ are two distributions of model predictions, α is the coefficient weight to control $\mathcal{L}_{KL}$.

3.4 Learning

The training loss $\mathcal{L}_d$ of the sum of each subtask can be defined as:

$$\mathcal{L}_k = -\frac{1}{G \cdot N^2} \sum_{g=1}^{G} \sum_{i=1}^{N} \sum_{j=1}^{N} \alpha^k y_{ij}^k \log \left(p_{ij}^k \right), \quad (9)$$

$$\mathcal{L}_d = \mathcal{L}_{\text{ent}} + \beta \mathcal{L}_{\text{pair}} + \eta \mathcal{L}_{\text{pol}}, \quad (10)$$

where $k \in \{$ ent, pair, pol $\}$ indicates a subtask defined by Li [12], N is the total token length in a dialogue, and G is the total training data instances. y_{ij}^k is ground-truth label, p_{ij}^k is the prediction. A tag-wise weighting hyperparameters α^k is applied to counteract the imbalance among label types, where $\alpha^{pair} = \beta$ and $\alpha^{pol} = \eta$ are determined by dataset and experimental tuning. The finally loss $\mathcal{L}$ with the loss of R-Drop is:

$$\mathcal{L} = \mathcal{L}_d^1 + \mathcal{L}_d^2 + \mathcal{L}_{KL}, \quad (11)$$

where $\mathcal{L}_d^1$ and $\mathcal{L}_d^2$ represent the loss obtained from the model predicting the same sample twice.

4 Experiment

4.1 Datasets and Metrics

Datasets. The corpus consists of posts and comments collected from Weibo, the largest Chinese social media platform. The datasets include both Chinese and English, with the English dataset being translated from the Chinese dataset [12]. As shown in Fig. 1, a dialogue starts from a root post and is composed of replies from multiple speakers. Each reply to the root post is considered as a thread. From a data structure perspective, the multi-thread and multi-turn dialogue forms a tree structure, where each subtree of the root node is a thread. This data structure provides clear information about the target of each sentence's reply, which benefits the model's understanding of context a lot.

The data statistics of datasets are shown in Tables 1. From Table 1, we can see that the English dataset is, on average, slightly longer than the Chinese dataset. The length difference between the shortest and longest samples is very large, regardless of whether it is an utterance, thread, or dialogue.

Metrics. The task of DiaASQ uses exact F1 as the metric, and a sample will be viewed as false unless it matches all four elements exactly. Therefore, the task uses micro F1 and identification F1 [22] respectively for measurements, where micro F1 measures the whole quad, including the sentiment polarity. In contrast, identification F1 does not distinguish the polarity, and is more suitable for evaluating the model's boundary prediction ability and entity matching ability. Finally, the evaluation criterion for the competition is the average of the four indicators of the Chinese and English datasets.

4.2   Experiment Setting

Due to the similarity in content between the Chinese and English datasets, after initial parameter search, we used the same parameter settings for both datasets. We set the maximum epoch to 30 and trained the model with an early stopping mechanism. The batch size was 1, and evaluation was performed every 100 steps. The initial learning rate was set to 1e-5, and we applied a dropout rate of 0.1 to the intermediate layer. We set the weight α in R-Drop as 1e-4. For the dialogue length threshold τ, we experimented with several different values, including 128, 192, 256, and 512. As shown in Table 1, 512 is already longer than all of dialogues. Following prior work, we used Chinese-Roberta-wwm-base [23] and Roberta-Large [24] as our base encoders for the Chinese and English datasets, respectively.

4.3   Baseline System

We mainly compared some of the latest models of short-text ABSA and dialogue ABSA, as shown below:

- **CRF-Extract-Classify** [10]. A three-stage system (extract, filter, and combine) proposed for the sentence-level quadruple ABSA.
- **SpERT** [25]. A model for joint extraction of entity and relation based on a span-based transformer. The model was slightly modified to support triple-term-extraction and polarity classification.
- **Span-ASTE** [26]. A span-based approach for triplet ABSA extraction. Similarly, it was change to be compatible with the DiaASQ task by editing the last stage of SpanASTE to enumerate triplets.
- **ParaPhrase** [11]. A generative seq-to-seq model for the quadruple ABSA extraction. The model outputs are modified to adapt to DiaASQ task.
- **DiaASQ$_{MTV}$** [12]. A model to solve the problem of DiaASQ benchmark, which encoding the utterance separately.

Table 1. Statistics on the length of utterance, thread, and dialog in the testset. 'Utt.', 'Thd.', and 'Dia.' respectively refer to utterance, thread, and dialog.

	ZH			EN		
	Utt.	Thd.	Dia.	Utt.	Thd.	Dia.
Avg. Len.	28.88	56.50	218.65	30.56	59.78	231.34
Max. Len.	142	257	462	156	258	481
Min. Len.	3	4	76	3	3	85

Table 2. Performance of the context fusion encoding method in both main experiments and ablation experiments. 'T-Fusion' represents the thread fusion method, and 'D-Fusion$_{128}$' represents the dialog fusion method with a dialogue length threshold of $\tau=128$.

Model	ZH		EN		Avg.
	Micro	Iden.	Micro	Iden.	
CRF-Extract-Classify	8.81	9.25	11.59	12.80	10.61
SpERT	13.00	14.19	13.07	13.28	13.39
ParaPhrase	23.27	27.98	24.54	26.76	25.64
Span-ASTE	27.42	30.85	26.99	28.34	28.40
DiaASQ$_{MTV}$	34.94	37.51	33.31	36.80	35.64
Ours	**42.79**	**45.58**	**38.52**	**41.60**	**42.12**
w/o FGM, R-Drop	39.96	42.60	35.08	40.13	39.44
w/o D-Fusion$_{128}$	40.80	44.26	38.20	40.92	41.05
w/o T-Fusion	42.57	44.55	38.51	40.93	41.64

4.4   Results and Analysis

Main Experiment. Table 2 presents the main results of our experiments, demonstrating that our model outperforms all the models with which it is compared. Our best model incorporates thread fusion encoding and dialog fusion encoding with $\tau=128$ and it is trained using FGM and R-Drop. The DiaASQ$_{MTV}$ scores an average of 35.64% on the English and Chinese datasets, while our method exceeds it by approximately 6.48%. This result demonstrates the effectiveness of our approach and theory. Generally, the scores on the Chinese dataset are higher than those on the English dataset.

We also conducted some ablation experiments. First, to verify the effectiveness of context fusion method and eliminate the interference of FGM and R-Drop, we removed these two modules and obtained an average score of 39.44%. Although this score is worse than the main model, it is still 3.8% higher than DiaASQ$_{MTV}$, further demonstrating that the context fusion method we proposed can help with the context encoding of the model.

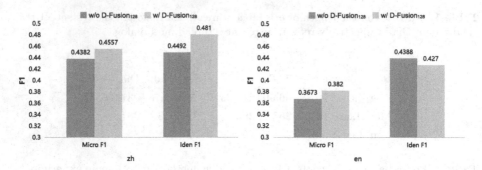

Fig. 3. The comparison of the model with and without D-Fusion$_{128}$ method on the dialog which length less than 128.

In another ablation experiment, we verified whether thread fusion and dialog fusion respectively played a role. The model achieves Average F1 of 41.05% when removed dialog fusion, while achieves 41.64% when removed the thread fusion. We also can find out that dialog fusion had a greater effect than thread fusion. This result was somewhat unexpected, as dialog fusion only processes some short conversations, while thread fusion is effective for all conversations. One possible explanation we propose is that the effect of thread fusion is to improve the accuracy of quadruple extraction within the same thread, whereas many quadruples may not only be cross-utterance but also cross-thread. For cross-thread sentences, dialog fusion can have a greater effect.

In the above experiments, our team achieved the third place in the NLPCC 2023 shared task 4 by obtaining an average score of 41.05% without using the dialog fusion method which is denoted as D-Fusion$_{128}$. In fact, our theoretical best score of 42.12%, which could have achieved a higher ranking, was not submitted due to the competition's limit of three submission attempts.

4.5 Effectiveness of Dialog Fusion

It is believe that the reason why dialog fusion improves the score is that the model enhances its ability to understand the context of short dialogues. To further verify this, we first identified all sentences with a dialogue length of less than 128 and then compared the model's F1 scores on these sentences before and after adding D-Fusion$_{128}$. The results are shown in Fig. 3. After adding D-Fusion$_{128}$, the micro F1 and identification F1 scores on the Chinese dataset increased by 1.75% and 3.18% respectively, while the micro F1 score on the English dataset increased by 1.47%. These results support our hypothesis. However, the identification F1 score on the English dataset decreased, indicating that the model's prediction performance for English boundaries deteriorated after concatenating the dialogues. This may be due to the fact that the English dataset are generally longer than the Chinese dataset (as shown in Table 1) and that English has WordPiece mechanism in PLMs, making the text longer and harder to locate. Overall, this indicates that dialog fusion does improve the accuracy of the model in understanding and modeling the context of short dialogues. We also experiment different threshold τ for further validation and as the τ increased, there was an overall downward trend in the average score, which is consistent with our hypothesis.

5 Conclusion

This work proposes a context fusion method to enhance the performance of conversational aspect-based sentiment quadruple analysis. Firstly, utterances within the same thread are merged through thread fusion, enabling the model to simultaneously model context information from multiple speakers. Then, dialog fusion is applied to some particularly short dialogues to obtain global information, which effectively improves the model's performance on shorter dialogues. Through experiments, we conclude that concatenating the entire text of long dialogues actually leads to negative effects. Our model achieved an average F1 score of 42.12%, which is 6.48% higher than the DiaASQ$_{MTV}$, indicating the effectiveness of our approach.

Acknowledgements. This work was supported by Natural Science Foundation of Guangdong Province (No. 2021A1515011864) and National Natural Science Foundation of China (No. 71472068).

References

1. Phan, H.T., Nguyen, N.T., Hwang, D.: Aspect-level sentiment analysis: a survey of graph convolutional network methods. Inform. Fusion **91**, 149–172 (2023)
2. Zhang, W., Li, X., Deng, Y., Bing, L., Lam, W.: A survey on aspect-based sentiment analysis: tasks, methods, and challenges. CoRR (2022)
3. Liu, B.: Sentiment analysis and opinion mining. Synth. Lect. Hum. Lang. Technol. **5**(1), 1–167 (2012)
4. Li, R., Chen, H., Feng, F., Ma, Z., Wang, X., Hovy, E.: Dual graph convolutional networks for aspect-based sentiment analysis. In: ACL-IJCNLP (2021)
5. Zhang, Z., Zhou, Z., Wang, Y.: Ssegcn: syntactic and semantic enhanced graph convolutional network for aspect-based sentiment analysis. In: NAACL-HLT (2022)
6. Zhou, Y., Liao, L., Gao, Y., Jie, Z., Lu, W.: To be closer: learning to link up aspects with opinions. In: EMNLP (2021)
7. Chen, S., Liu, J., Wang, Y., Zhang, W., Chi, Z.: Synchronous double-channel recurrent network for aspect-opinion pair extraction. In: ACL (2020)
8. Wu, Z., Ying, C., Zhao, F., Fan, Z., Dai, X., Xia, R.: Grid tagging scheme for end-to-end fine-grained opinion extraction. In: EMNLP (2020)
9. Xu, L., Li, H., Lu, W., Bing, L.: Position-aware tagging for aspect sentiment triplet extraction. In: EMNLP (2020)
10. Cai, H., Xia, R., Yu, J.: Aspect-category-opinion-sentiment quadruple extraction with implicit aspects and opinions. In: ACL-IJCNLP (2021)
11. Zhang, W., Deng, Y., Li, X., Yuan, Y., Bing, L., Lam, W.: Aspect sentiment quad prediction as paraphrase generation. In: EMNLP (2021)

12. Li, B., et al.: Diaasq: A benchmark of conversational aspect-based sentiment quadruple analysis. In: Findings of ACL (2023)
13. Koolagudi, S.G., Rao, K.S.: Emotion recognition from speech: a review. Inter. J. Speech Technol. **15**, 99–117 (2012)
14. Devlin, J., Chang, M.-W., Lee, K., Toutanova, K.: Pre-training of deep bidirectional transformers for language understanding. In: NAACL-HLT, Bert (2019)
15. Vaswani, A., et al.: Attention is all you need. In: NIPS (2017)
16. Liang, X., et al.: R-drop: regularized dropout for neural networks. In: NeurIPS (2021)
17. Miyato, T., Dai, A.M., Goodfellow, I.: Adversarial training methods for semi-supervised text classification. In: ICLR (2017)
18. Bao, X., Wang, Z., Jiang, X., Xiao, R., Li, S.: Aspect-based sentiment analysis with opinion tree generation. In: IJCAI (2022)
19. Mao, Y., Shen, Y., Yang, J., Zhu, X., Cai, L.: Seq2path: generating sentiment tuples as paths of a tree. In: Findings of ACL (2022)
20. Lu, Y.: Unified structure generation for universal information extraction. In: ACL (2022)
21. Jianlin, S., Yu, L., Pan, S., Murtadha, A., Wen, B., Liu, Y.: Roformer: enhanced transformer with rotary position embedding. CoRR (2021)
22. Barnes, J., Kurtz, R., Oepen, S., Øvrelid, L., Velldal, E.: Structured sentiment analysis as dependency graph parsing. In: ACL/IJCNLP (2021)
23. Cui, Y., Che, W., Liu, T., Qin, B., Yang, Z.: Pre-training with whole word masking for Chinese bert. IEEE/ACM Trans. Audio Speech Lang. Process. **29**, 3504–3514 (2021)
24. Liu, Y., et al.: Roberta: a robustly optimized bert pretraining approach. CoRR (2019)
25. Eberts, M., Ulges, A.: Span-based joint entity and relation extraction with transformer pre-training. In: ECAI (2020)
26. Lu, X., Chia, Y.K., Bing, L.: Learning span-level interactions for aspect sentiment triplet extraction In: ACL/IJCNLP (2021)

Evaluation Workshop: Chinese Medical Instructional Video Question Answering

A Unified Framework for Optimizing Video Corpus Retrieval and Temporal Answer Grounding: Fine-Grained Modality Alignment and Local-Global Optimization

Shuang Cheng[1,2,3], Zineng Zhou[1,2,3], Jun Liu[1,2,3], Jian Ye[1,2,3(✉)], Haiyong Luo[1,2,3], and Yang Gu[1,2,3]

[1] Institute of Computing Technology, Chinese Academy of Sciences, Beijing, China
{chengshuang22s,zhouzineng22s,liujun22s,jye,yhluo,guyang}@ict.ac.cn
[2] University of Chinese Academy of Sciences, Beijing, China
[3] Beijing Key Laboratory of Mobile Computing and Pervasive Device, Beijing, China

Abstract. Present advancements in digital content have resulted in an enhanced interest in video understanding. The Temporal Answer Grounding in Video Corpus (TAGVC) aims to pinpoint the visual response within an extensive array of untrimmed instructional videos using language-based questions. This research explores TAGVC, a notably complex task involving an intricate combination of skills including video retrieval and comprehension, visual answer localization, and collaboration between vision and language, posing challenges greater than the initial Temporal Answer Grounding in a Single Video (TAGSV). This paper outlines a novel approach to tackling such challenges, proposing a Fine-grained Modality Alignment and Local-Global Optimization Framework(FMALG) for TAGVC. By combining the strengths of visual and textual predictions, this system offers a resilient solution. The fine-grained modality alignment is used to understand each video segment's context succinctly. In addition, the local-global optimization technique is implemented to learn the global retrieval capabilities and visualize answer localization. The subtitle quality is also improved using OpenAI's ChatGPT. The efficacy of the proposed methods is evidenced through extensive experiments, where we achieved first place on track 3 and second place on track 2.

Keywords: Video Question Answering · Video-grounded · Visual Answer Localization

1 Introduction

The rapid proliferation of digital content, particularly in the form of videos, has led to a surge in research interest in the field of video understanding. This is

S. Cheng, Z. Zhou and J. Liu—Equal contribution

further fueled by the increasing demand for efficient and effective methods to retrieve and comprehend information from large-scale video corpora. This paper focuses on a novel task in this domain, namely Temporal Answer Grounding in Video Corpus (TAGVC), which aims to locate the visual answer in a large collection of untrimmed instructional videos using a natural language question.

The TAGVC task is a complex one, requiring a range of skills including the interaction between vision and language, video retrieval, passage comprehension, and visual answer localization. It presents a higher level of difficulty than the initial Temporal Answer Grounding in a Single Video (TAGSV), or Visual Answer Localization (VAL), because it demands the precise retrieval of the target video from a substantial video corpus and the accurate localization of the visual answer corresponding to this target video.

Our research is inspired by the work of [1], who introduced the TAGVC task and proposed a cross-modal contrastive global-span (CCGS) method, jointly training the video retrieval and visual answer localization subtasks in an end-to-end manner. Their method has shown impressive results in terms of video retrieval and answer localization, outperforming other competitive methods in the field. In addition, we also draw insights from the work of [2], who proposed a joint training method for dense passage retrieval and passage re-ranking, named MutualSL. Their method has shown significant improvements in the retrieval performance, which is a crucial aspect of the TAGVC task.

However, despite the advancements made by these studies, there are still several limitations that need to be addressed. For example, current TAGVC methods, including visual and textual predictors, encounter substantial disparities between the visual and text-based modalities. The visual predictor struggles with continuous clip prediction due to the frequent changing of video scenes and semantics to the question. On the other hand, the textual predictor, if the video lacks subtitle information for a long clip, this clip cannot be located. These limitations highlight the need for a more robust and comprehensive approach to the TAGVC task.

In response to these challenges, we propose a novel method that leverages the strengths of both visual and textual predictors while mitigating their weaknesses. We introduce a Fine-grained Modality Alignment and Local-Global Optimization Framework for TAGVC. Initially, we divide the video into subtitle-based segments, each having a succinct context for fine-grained modality alignment. Secondly, We have implemented the Local-Global Optimization technique, using three types of loss functions to independently learn the capabilities of global retrieval and visual answer localization. In addition, we utilize OpenAI's ChatGPT to enhance the quality of subtitles and streamlining their length. This approach aids in more efficient, parallel training, and also mitigates the effects of subtitle truncation.

Our comprehensive experiments demonstrate the effectiveness of our proposed methods, which achieved first place on track 3 and second place on track 2 in testB.

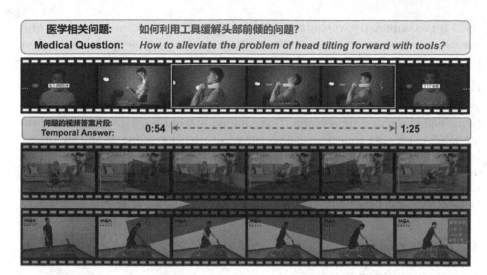

Fig. 1. Illustration of the video corpus visual answer localization in the medical instructional video.

2 Related Work

2.1 Video Question Answering

Video question answering (VideoQA) represents a blossoming research area, witnessing rapid advancements in datasets and methodologies. Tapaswi et al. [3] introduced the MovieQA dataset and extended memory networks to the VideoQA realm. Subsequent research [4,5] introduced sophisticated memory architectures to optimize interaction across different modalities. Jang et al. [6] presented the TGIF-QA dataset, combining deep appearance and motion features with spatial and temporal attention for precise question answering.

Recent multi-modal VideoQA studies [7,8] have augmented VideoQA with spatio-temporal annotations and have called for intelligent systems that can retrieve relevant moments and detect referenced visual concepts concurrently. These research efforts substantiate that temporal annotations linked to questions enhance both the accuracy and interpretability of QA models. Further investigations [9,10] have incorporated captions as supplementary input sources and developed a modality weighting strategy to improve question answering performance. However, these studies overlooked the potential of the correlation between frames and subtitles, which can act as guidance to enhance language and video understanding within VideoQA models.

2.2 Temporal Natural Language Localization in Video

Temporal natural language localization (TNLL) in videos primarily aims to locate natural languages temporally within videos. The existing TNLL works

[11–14] predominantly employ top-down models, with predefined temporal proposals and focus on creating robust multi-modal interaction modules to select
the proposal most relevant to the language query.

Weakly supervised TNLL tasks are also well-studied. The method proposed
by Bojanowski et al. [15] contemplates the task of synchronizing a video with
a set of temporally ordered sentences, leveraging temporal ordering as additional constraint and supervision. Text-Guided Attention [16–18] suggests learning joint visual-text embeddings and using the attention scores as the alignment
between video frames and the query. In comparison, Lin et al. [19] devised a top-
down proposal generation module combined with a semantic completion module
to measure the semantic similarity between proposals and queries, refining the
alignment scores of top-selected proposals.

3   Methodology

3.1   Problem Definition

The objective of the Chinese Medical Instructional Video Question Answering
track3, Temporal Answer Grounding in Video Corpus (TAGVC), is to provide a
comprehensive solution for addressing medical or health-related question (Q) by
utilizing a corpus of Chinese medical instructional videos ($V_C = \{V_1, V_2, ..., V_n\}$)
and their corresponding subtitles ($S_C = \{S_1, S_2, ..., S_n\}$, $S_i = \{T_1, T_2, ..., T_r\}$).
Here, n denotes the number of videos in the corpus, and r denotes the number of subtitle segments. The primary objective is to determine accurately the
starting and ending timepoints ($[\hat{V}_s, \hat{V}_e]$) within the most relevant video (V^*)
for the given answer. This research aims to improve the accuracy and efficiency
in extracting relevant information from medical instructional videos to facilitate
effective question-answering in the Chinese medical domain, specifically within
a large video corpus.

3.2   Data Preprocess

During the data analysis, it was discovered that the dataset contained a significant number of low-quality subtitles filled with numerous typos. Additionally,
the video subtitles tended to be excessively long, causing the GPU to run out
of memory during the training process. To address these issues, we introduce
the Few-Shot based ChatGPT optimization method, which aims to improve the
quality of subtitles. This method involves providing prompts such as examples of
subtitle optimization, preprocessing tasks, and executing the Few-Shot learning
strategy to bolster ChatGPT's abilities. By adopting this approach, we efficiently
reduce the length of subtitles, resulting in concise text that accurately captures
the essence and key information. Moreover, the language model automatically
corrects errors, including spelling, grammar, and semantic inconsistencies, leading to an overall enhancement in quality. The prompt we employ is structured
as follows:

Help me simplify the contents of each dictionary whose key is 'text' in the following list. It is imperative to retain the content unchanged while significantly reducing the word count. Additionally, ensure that the list structure remains unaltered.
Example:
1. 使用频率最高→高频使用
2. 髋关节在人体主要负责承重→髋关节主要负责承重
Output should adhere to the following format:
1. 'raw'→ 'modified'
2. ...
Lists:
{text}

Prompt 1: Few-Shot ChatGPT

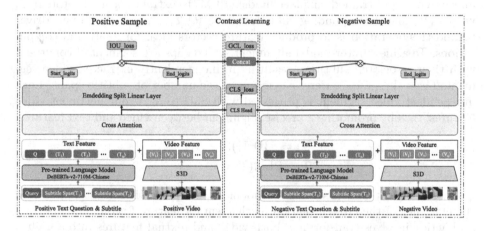

Fig. 2. Overview of proposed Fine-grained Modality Alignment and Local-Global Optimization Framework.

The benefits of this approach encompass the transformation of lengthy subtitles into concise texts while preserving their inherent meaning. Furthermore, it enhances the quality and accuracy through automated error correction, including spelling, grammar, and semantic inconsistencies. Finally, the Few-Shot-based optimization method enables ChatGPT to exhibit robust adaptability in handling long sentences, extracting key information, and minimizing information loss. Ultimately, this method offers a practical solution for subtitle generation, significantly enhancing convenience and efficiency in the process.

3.3 Overall Architecture

Shown in Fig. 2, The proposed FMALG is a Contrastive Learning structure with five components: video corpus sampling, feature extraction, cross-modal fusion, global spanning matrix, and two specific modules - global span comparison learning and global span predictor. The video corpus sampling stage creates positive and negative samples for comparison training. Feature extraction extracts fine-grained video and text features by pre-trained model and achieving precise modality alignment. Through cross-modal fusion, the cross-attention mechanism merges the text and video modalities, comprehensively integrating the data. A global spanning matrix is then constructed by partitioning the fused information with positional embedding. This matrix facilitates efficient utilization of information, enabling analysis and comparison of global characteristics. Ultimately, these modules enhance retrieval and grounding results, maximizing the effectiveness and efficiency of FMALG.

Fine-Grained Cross-Modal Alignment. Building on the foundation of the baseline method [1], a preexisting visual model, specifically S3D [20], works in unison with a pre-trained language model (PLM) to extract feature vectors from videos (V) and corresponding subtitles $(\mathbf{T} = [Q, T_1, ..., T_r])$. The main driver behind this operation is to produce feature vectors ideal for analytical computations. To achieve inter-modal alignment, video clips are segmented congruent with their associated subtitles, resulting in independently extracted video segments $(\mathbf{V} = [V_1, ..., V_r])$. Here, r symbolizes the number of subtitle spans. Each independent video segment is processed with S3D to draw out pertinent video features, thereby promoting a precise alignment between video and text features.

$$\mathbf{V_i} = \text{S3D}(V_i), i \in [1, r]$$
$$\mathbf{T} = \text{PLM}(T) \tag{1}$$

In subsequent phases of our methodology, we place significant reliance on the efficiency of the cross-attention mechanism for feature fusion. The first pivotal action involves transforming both video and textual features into a unified output, $\mathbf{F}_{joint}$, utilizing the Cross-Attention (CA) mapping function. The CA function, optimized during the previous alignment stage, takes video features, $\mathbf{F}_{video} = [\mathbf{V_1}, ..., \mathbf{V_r}]$, and text features, $\mathbf{F}_{text} = T$, as input variables as articulated in the equation:

$$\mathbf{F}_{joint} = \text{CA}(\mathbf{F}_{video}, \mathbf{F}_{text}) \tag{2}$$

The Cross-Attention mapping function amalgamates these dynamic representations, producing a coherent output, $\mathbf{F}_{joint}$, that effectively bridges the inherent disparities between the video and textual domains.

Local-Global Optimization. Our model's video retrieval and localization capabilities are enhanced by the application of Local-Global Optimization within the training process, offering effective supervision at diverse stages. Particularly, both positive and negative video samples are transformed into feature cross-modal interactions, denoted respectively as $\mathbf{F}_{joint}^{positive}$ and $\mathbf{F}_{joint}^{negative}$. Subsequently, these features are bifurcated into positive and negative samples by the CLS Head. To compute the aggregate CLS_{loss} for video retrieval, we employ Cross-Entropy loss founction. The retrieval performance of the model can be reinforced by adhering to the baseline of Global-span Contrastive Learning, denoted as GCL_{loss}.

Furthermore, in the visual answer localization task, we continue to employ the baseline approach. This involves transferring the features through the Embedded Split Linear Layer (ESLayer), which results in the generation of start and end probabilities for the video response. The Intersection Over Union (IOU) loss is then computed using Cross-Entropy, denoted as IOU_{loss}.

The incorporation and concurrent optimization of these components give rise to the final loss function, predicated on the local-global approach. This can be encapsulated by the following equation:

$$Loss = CLS_{\text{loss}} + GCL_{\text{loss}} + IOU_{\text{loss}} \qquad (3)$$

4   Experimental Evaluation

4.1   Dataset and Evaluation Metrics

We conducted experiments for the NLPCC Shared Task 5, which provides Chinese medical instructional videos sourced from YouTube[1]. The dataset comprises of 1628 videos, out of which 1228 are assigned to the Train and Dev set. Each video contains multiple question-answer pairs, each pair uniquely matched and annotated by experts with medical training. To select the optimal model, we divided the dataset into the Train and Valid set with a ratio of 90% and 10%, respectively.

The leaderboard evaluation methodology incorporates both Intersection over Union (IoU) and mean IoU (mIoU), computed as the average IoU across all test samples.

4.2   Experiment Settings

In this study, we have evaluated the impact of text feature extraction, visual feature extraction, data preprocessing schemes, Fine-Grained Cross-Modal Alignment (FG-MA) and a Local-Global Optimization (LGO) policy on the Visual Answer Localization task. The experimental results summarized in Table 1, Table 2 and Table 3 provide insights into the performance of various methods, which can be analyzed in the following sections.

Text and Visual Feature Setting. Table 1 primarily discusses the experimental results of utilizing different text and visual feature extraction methods for Temporal Answer Grounding in Video Corpus (TAGVC). The baselines performances are from the DeBERTa-v2-320M as the text feature extractor and I3D as the visual feature extractor.

---

[1] https://github.com/cmivqa/NLPCC-2023-Shared-Task-5.

When comparing other text feature extraction models, DeBERTa-v2-710M-Chinese [21] demonstrates a consistent superior result over the RoBERTa-Chinese-large [22] model and baseline model - with mean scores on valid and test sets that exceed their counterparts. This suggests that DeBERTa-v2-710M-Chinese has a superior capability in extracting and understanding features from the text source, which is crucial for the TAGVC task. As for the video feature extraction methods, it is noted that when S3D is applied in conjunction with the text feature extractors, it consistently outperforms the I3D method. Employing S3D with DeBERTa-v2-710M-Chinese again resulted in the greatest results. This indicates not only the supremacy of the S3D feature extractor in dealing with visual information, but also the promising performance of the DeBERTa model in cross-modal tasks.

Table 1. Experimental results obtained from distinct backbone networks. RoBERTa and DeBERTa refer to RoBERTa-Chinese-large and DeBERTa-v2-710M-Chinese, respectively.

Method	Valid Set				A Test Set			
	R@1	R@10	R@50	Average	R@1	R@10	R@50	Average
Baseline	0.2217	0.3681	0.4777	0.3558	0.1947	0.3397	0.4409	0.3291
Text Feature Setting								
RoBERTa + I3D	0.2104	0.3445	0.4594	0.3381	0.1787	0.3236	0.4295	0.3106
DeBERTa + I3D	0.2352	0.3798	0.4864	0.3671	0.2106	0.3583	0.4457	0.3382
Visual Feature Setting								
Baseline + S3D	0.2269	0.3724	0.4817	0.36	0.1999	0.3436	0.4498	0.3311
RoBERTa + S3D	0.2156	0.3488	0.4634	0.3412	0.1839	0.3277	0.4386	0.3157
DeBERTa + S3D	0.2404	0.3841	0.4902	0.3716	0.2156	0.3629	0.4564	0.3416

Data Preprocess Setting. This study meticulously analyses the impact of various data preprocessing techniques on Temporal Answer Grounding in Video Corpus (TAGVC). Techniques such as Data Clean, Hard Caption and Few-Shot ChatGPT (FSC), along with an integrated DC+HC+FSC approach, are used to optimize captions and refine data set quality.

As depicted in Table 2, implementing these data preprocessing methods significantly improves performance in both the validation and the test sets. The combination of DC, HC, and FSC yielded the most favourable results, validating the potency of comprehensive data preprocessing techniques in enhancing TAGVC. Methodologically, this research adopts an elaborate evaluation that varies one variable at a time to document its sequential effects - a strategy pivotal in distinguishing the unique influence of each component.

Commencing with a baseline feature extractor, the improvements in performance are evident with each successive preprocessing method. The initiation of Data Clean increases the average performance from 0.3625 in the validation set to 0.3318 in the test set. The subsequent inclusion of Hard Caption and

FSC yields additional enhancements. Remarkably, the combined DC+HC+FSC strategy results in a pronounced boost to 0.3998 and 0.352 averages for the validation and test sets, respectively. The pattern reemerges when the language feature extractor is switched to DeBERTa-v2-710M-Chinese, with the combined use of DC, HC, and FSC leading to the highest average performance of 0.4093 and 0.3776 in the validation and test sets, respectively.

Table 2. The impact of data preprocessing schemes on Temporal Answer Grounding in Video Corpus (TAGVC). Notably, the first and second experimental groups utilized the baseline and DeBERTa-v2-710M-Chinese models as their language feature extractors, respectively. Furthermore, each subsequent experiment incorporated the S3D model for video feature extraction.

Method	Valid Set				A Test Set			
	R@1	R@10	R@50	Average	R@1	R@10	R@50	Average
Based on Baseline in which S3D are used for visual feature extractor								
+Data Clean	0.2316	0.3758	0.4801	0.3625	0.2017	0.3426	0.4512	0.3318
+Hard Caption	0.2524	0.3974	0.5042	0.3847	0.2196	0.3475	0.4592	0.3421
+Few-Shot ChatGPT	0.2501	0.4015	0.4938	0.3818	0.2154	0.3423	0.4606	0.3394
+DC+HC+FSC	0.2752	0.4029	0.5214	0.3998	0.2256	0.3569	0.4736	0.352
Based on DeBERTa-v2 and S3D								
+DataClean	0.2519	0.3912	0.4983	0.3804	0.2242	0.3662	0.4649	0.3518
+Hard Caption	0.2647	0.4041	0.5137	0.3942	0.2374	0.3806	0.4757	0.3646
+Few-Shot ChatGPT	0.2623	0.4082	0.5031	0.3912	0.2331	0.3751	0.4868	0.365
+DC+HC+FSC	0.2874	0.4096	0.5308	0.4093	0.2433	0.3897	0.4998	0.3776

Model Setting. Table 3 elucidates the influence of Fine-Grained Cross-Modal Alignment (FG-MA) and a Local-Global Optimization (LGO) policy on the Visual Answer Localization task performance.

A perceptible augmentation in the R@K values is discernible following LGO implementation, evident across both validation and test sets. This consistent improvement bolsters the argument for LGO's potential in performance enhancement. The integration of FG-MA escalates this further, amplifying performance across both sets under evaluation. Such tangible improvements underscore the pivotal role of fine-grained alignment between differing modalities, thereby aligning with the findings of previous studies [23]. This insinuates that fostering granular-level connections promotes increased benefits.

When incorporated within the intricate architecture of DeBERTa-v2-710M-Chinese along with S3D, the LGO policy and FG-MA collectively actuate more profound advancements. Such improvements can be attributed to the sophisticated representations proffered by contemporary models, which likely expedite the optimization policy and alignment strategy in tapping performance enhancement potential further.

Table 3. The influence of Fine-Grained Cross-Modal Alignment (FG-MA) and a Local-Global Optimization (LGO) policy on the Visual Answer Localization task.

Method	Valid Set				A Test Set			
	R@1	R@10	R@50	Average	R@1	R@1	R@1	Average
Based on Baseline and data preprocese								
+ LGO	0.2778	0.4161	0.5362	0.41	0.2266	0.3757	0.4837	0.362
+ FG-MA	0.2789	0.4172	0.5373	0.4111	0.2277	0.3768	0.4848	0.3631
+ LGO + FG-MA	0.3029	0.4517	0.5716	0.4421	0.2487	0.3913	0.4991	0.4283
Based on DeBERTa-v2-710M-Chinese, S3D and data preprocese								
+ LGO	0.2987	0.4623	0.5989	0.4533	0.2489	0.3919	0.4999	0.3802
+ FG-MA	0.3089	0.4694	0.6035	0.4606	0.2501	0.3998	0.491	0.3803
+ LGO + FG-MA	0.3483	0.5168	0.6367	0.5006	0.2641	0.3964	0.5042	0.4554

5 Conclusion

In conclusion, our research introduces the Fine-grained Modality Alignment and Local-Global Optimization Framework (FMALG), which effectively addresses the complexities of TAGVC. A range of experiments were conducted to evaluate the impact of various feature extraction techniques, data preprocessing schemes, and model settings. Remarkably, the DeBERTa-v2-710M-Chinese and S3D models emerged as the most effective means of text and visual feature extraction, respectively. Using a combination of sophisticated data preprocessing techniques resulted in significant performance improvements. We also observed tangible enhancements in task performance when utilizing Fine-Grained Cross-Modal Alignment and a Local-Global Optimization policy. Our proposed FMALG framework, validated through comprehensive evaluations, secured top rankings in testB, thus illustrating the potential of our approach and its significance in advancing video understanding. Extensive experimental evaluations have demonstrated the effectiveness of the proposed FMALG, securing it leading rankings in testB (first place on track 3, second place on track 2). These findings underscore the potential of our approach and contribute significantly towards the advancement of video understanding. As refinement of this framework continues, it is anticipated to make substantial contributions to the video comprehension domain.

Acknowledgment. The research work is supported by National Key R&D Program of China (No.202 2YFB3904700), Key Research and Development Program of in Shandong Province (2019JZZY020102), Key Research and Development Program of Jiangsu Province (No.BE2018084), Industrial Internet Innovation and Development Project in 2021 (TC210A02M, TC210804D), Opening Project of Beijing Key Laboratory of Mobile Computing and Pervasive Device.

References

1. Li, B., Weng, Y., Sun, B., Li, S.: Learning to locate visual answer in video corpus using question. In: ICASSP 2023–2023 IEEE International Conference on Acoustics, Speech and Signal Processing (ICASSP), pp. 1–5 (2023)
2. Weng, Y., Li, B.: Visual answer localization with cross-modal mutual knowledge transfer. In: ICASSP 2023–2023 IEEE International Conference on Acoustics, Speech and Signal Processing (ICASSP), pp. 1–5 (2023)
3. Tapaswi, M., et al.: Understanding stories in movies through question-answering. In: CVPR pp. 4631–4640 (2016)
4. Na, S., Lee, S., Kim, J., Kim, G.: A read-write memory network for movie story understanding. In: ICCV, pp. 677–685. IEEE Computer Society (2017)
5. Kim, J., Ma, M., Kim, K., Kim, S., Yoo, C.D.: Progressive attention memory network for movie story question answering. In: CVPR, pp. 8337–8346 (2019)
6. Jang, Y., Song, Y., Yu, Y., Kim, Y., Kim, G.: Tgif-qa: toward spatio-temporal reasoning in visual question answering. In: CVPR, pp. 2758–2766 (2017)
7. Lei, J., Licheng, Y., Bansal, M., Berg, T.L.: Localized, compositional video question answering. In: EMNLP, Tvqa (2018)
8. Lei, J., Yu, L., Berg, T.L., Bansal, M.: Tvqa+: spatio-temporal grounding for video question answering. In: ACL (2020)
9. Kim, H., Tang, Z., Bansal, M.: Dense-caption matching and frame-selection gating for temporal localization in videoqa. In: ACL (2020)
10. Kim, J., Ma, M., Pham, T.X., Kim, K., Yoo, C.D.: Modality shifting attention network for multi-modal video question answering. In CVPR. IEEE (2020)
11. Gao, J., Sun, C., Yang, Z., Nevatia, R.: Tall: temporal activity localization via language query. In: ICCV, pp. 5267–5275 (2017)
12. Hendricks, L.A., Wang, O., Shechtman, E., Sivic, J., Darrell, T., Russell, B.C.: Localizing moments in video with natural language. In: ICCV, pp. 5804–5813. IEEE Computer Society (2017)
13. Yuan, Y., Mei, T., Zhu, W.: To find where you talk: temporal sentence localization in video with attention based location regression. In: AAAI, pp. 9159–9166. AAAI Press (2019)
14. Ma, Z., Ye, J., Yang, X., Liu, J.: Hcld: a hierarchical framework for zero-shot cross-lingual dialogue system. In: Proceedings of the 29th International Conference on Computational Linguistics, pp. 4492–4498 (2022)
15. Bojanowski, P., et al.: Weakly-supervised alignment of video with text. In: ICCV, pp. 4462–4470. IEEE Computer Society (2015)
16. Mithun, N.C., Paul, S., Roy-Chowdhury, A.K.: Weakly supervised video moment retrieval from text queries. In: CVPR, pp. 11592–11601. Computer Vision Foundation/IEEE (2019)
17. Liu, J., Cheng, S., Zhou, Z., Gu, Y., Ye, J., Luo, H.: Enhancing multilingual document-grounded dialogue using cascaded prompt-based post-training models. In: Proceedings of the Third DialDoc Workshop on Document-grounded Dialogue and Conversational Question Answering, Toronto, Canada, pp. 44–51. Association for Computational Linguistics (July 2023)
18. Ma, Z., Liu, Z., Ye, J.: Sldt: sequential latent document transformer for multilingual document-based dialogue. In: Proceedings of the Third DialDoc Workshop on Document-grounded Dialogue and Conversational Question Answering, pp. 57–67 (2023)

19. Lin, Z., Zhao, Z., Zhang, Z., Wang, Q., Liu, H.: Weakly-supervised video moment retrieval via semantic completion network. In: AAAI, pp. 11539–11546. AAAI Press (2020)
20. Xie, S., Sun, C., Huang, J., Tu, Z., Murphy, K.: Rethinking spatiotemporal feature learning: Speed-accuracy trade-offs in video classification. In: Proceedings of the European Conference on Computer Vision (ECCV), pp. 305–321 (2018)
21. Zhang, J., et al.: Fengshenbang 1.0: Being the foundation of chinese cognitive intelligence. CoRR, abs/ arXiv: 2209.02970 (2022)
22. Cui, Y., et al.: Pre-training with whole word masking for chinese bert. arXiv preprint arXiv:1906.08101 (2019)
23. Zhao, Z., Guo, L., He, X., Shao, S., Yuan, Z., Liu, J.: Mamo: masked multimodal modeling for fine-grained vision-language representation learning. arXiv preprint arXiv:2210.04183 (2022)

A Two-Stage Chinese Medical Video Retrieval Framework with LLM

Ningjie Lei[1], Jinxiang Cai[1], Yixin Qian[1], Zhilong Zheng[1], Chao Han[1,3],
Zhiyue Liu[2,3], and Qingbao Huang[1,3(✉)]

[1] School of Electrical Engineering, Guangxi University, Nanning, Guangxi, China
[2] School of Computer, Electronics and Information, Guangxi University, Nanning, Guangxi, China
[3] Guangxi Key Laboratory of Multimedia Communications and Network Technology, Nanning, China
{leiningjie,keeplucky}@st.gxu.edu.cn
qbhuang@gxu.edu.cn

Abstract. With the increasing popularity of online videos, research on video corpus retrieval (VCR) has made significant progress. However, existing VCR models have not performed well in the medical field due to the unique characteristics of medical VCR task. Specifically, the open-ended queries used in medical VCR are more challenging compared to image-caption style queries, and the long duration of medical videos poses a great burden on model retrieval efficiency. To address these challenges, we propose a two-stage framework based on GPT-3.5 and cross-modal contrastive global-span (CCGS) for medical video VCR (termed GPT-CMR). In the first stage, we leverage the powerful natural language processing capabilities of the large language model (LLM) GPT-3.5 to improve retrieval efficiency. In the second stage, we use CCGS model to further enhance retrieval accuracy. Additionally, we developed a CCGS-VCR Analyzer to leverage the characteristics of the CCGS model's output without additional training costs. According to the official result, our method achieve first place in Track 2 of the NLPCC 2023 Task 5 competition. Experiments show that our method has retrieval efficiency and accuracy far exceeding the official baseline.

Keywords: Video corpus retrieval · Large language model · Cross-modal contrastive global-span

1 Introduction

In recent years, the rise of online videos has fundamentally changed the way people acquire knowledge and access information [12,24]. However, in the case of medical videos, individuals often lack the necessary medical expertise to effectively navigate the vast array of resources available on the internet. Therefore, it is highly meaningful to explore a video retrieval system that can assist people in efficiently and accurately obtaining targeted medical videos.

F. Liu et al. (Eds.): NLPCC 2023, LNAI 14304, pp. 211–220, 2023.
https://doi.org/10.1007/978-3-031-44699-3_19

Video Corpus Retrieval (VCR) is a complex task that requires a deep understanding of both language and video. The majority of current VCR datasets, such as MSVD [2], ActivityNet [7] and MSR-VTT [25] consist of short video clips accompanied by a few queries. These queries are often in the form of image captions like "a dog is running in the grass." However, in the medical video domain, the goal of Video Corpus Retrieval is to retrieve target videos based on open-ended queries like "How can I ease my neck pain?" This demands models with a more profound comprehension of the videos. Medical videos also tend to be longer, with an average duration of 388.68 s in the proposed medical video dataset by [6]. Open-ended problems and extended video duration require models with robust overall capabilities. Models that prioritize efficient reasoning, such as the dual-tower structure utilized in [17], may not be well-suited for medical video retrieval. While span-based models like [13] have shown good performance, they suffer from low reasoning efficiency.

To address the aforementioned challenges, we present a two-stage retrieval-rerank framework aimed at improving both reasoning efficiency and accuracy. In the first stage, we utilized large language model [1] GPT-3.5 due to its excellent performance in natural language processing tasks to generate video summaries based on video subtitles. As the length of the summary is much shorter than that of the subtitles, we can use pretrained language models [4,9,11,21] like RoBERTa [16] for efficient retrieval. However, due to the loss of local key text information during the process of subtitles conversion into summarizes, further reranking was necessary to improve retrieval accuracy. In the second stage, we made the following enhancements to the cross-modal contrastive global-span (CCGS) model [13] : (1) We designed a CCGS-VCR Analyzer for the VCR task that leverages the characteristics of the CCGS model's output without training cost. This CCGS-VCR Analyzer utilizes a simulated annealing algorithm [10] to weigh the position and quantity sequences to obtain the final prediction sequence; (2) To address the scarcity of training samples in medical video datasets, we employed projected gradient descent(PGD) [19] for adversarial training to improve model robustness.

In summary, our contributions include:

- To balance efficiency and accuracy for Chinese medical long video retrieval, we designed a two-stage retrieval-rerank framework using GPT-3.5 and CCGS. To the best of our knowledge, we are the first to attempt using large language model to assist with the retrieval of Chinese medical videos.
- In this study, we propose a novel CCGS-VCR Analyzer without training cost specifically designed for the VCR task that leverages the output characteristics of the CCGS model. The results of the ablation experiments demonstrate the effectiveness of the CCGS-VCR Analyzer.
- Our solution achieve first place in Track 2 of the NLPCC 2023 Task 5 competition, with significantly improved retrieval accuracy and efficiency compared to the official baseline.

2   Related Work

With the growing popularity of online videos, VCR task has emerged as a crucial research topic in the field of multimodal learning. With the expansion of pre-training data such as Laion-400m [23] and Laion-5b [22] and the emergence of contrastive learning [8], multimodal pre-training models [3,14,15] such as CLIP [20] have gained prominence in video retrieval due to their robust image-text matching capabilities. Typically, clip-based method [18] utilize the CLIP model for image-text encoding, followed by cosine similarity calculation to generate the output. One advantage of this approach is that visual features can be computed beforehand and stored as vectors, enabling efficient inference by encoding the query and computing cosine similarity with the visual feature vectors. However, although effective for short videos and image-caption queries, this method may not be suitable for lengthy medical videos with open-ended queries.

Li et al. [13] developed the CCGS method for medical video retrieval to tackle the challenge of lengthy medical videos. The CCGS method first extracts features to obtain positive and negative pairs of video samples, and then feeds them into a language model along with their corresponding positive subtitle samples to extract text features. The resulting text feature pairs are then fused with visual feature pairs through cross-modal fusion, which generates a Global-span Matrix that is used for prediction purposes. Although CCGS achieve good results on the MedVidCQA dataset [6], its inference efficiency is limited by the long input subtitles. In the domain of natural language processing, text retrieval tasks usually follow a retrieval-rerank two-stage framework, which includes initial sorting using simple methods like the dual-tower model proposed by [5] in the retrieval stage to ensure efficiency and more complex methods in the rerank stage to improve retrieval accuracy. Works within such a framework have demonstrated good retrieval efficiency and accuracy. Additionally, previous studies like [1] have showcased the remarkable ability of large language models for text-related tasks such as Text Summarization.

3   The Proposed Approach

3.1   Task Definition

Formally, Video Corpus Retrieval(VCR) task comprises a set of queries $Q = \{q_1, q_2, q_3, q_4, ..., q_k\}$ and a video corpus $V = \{v_1, v_2, v_3, ..., v_4\}$, where k denotes the total number of queries and n represents the number of videos in the video corpus. Each query q corresponds to a unique video v, while each video may correspond to multiple queries. The primary objective of the VCR task is to accurately identify the specific video v that corresponds to each query q.

3.2   Method

Figure 1 illustrates our two-stage framework comprising retrieval and rerank stages. The retrieval stage employs GPT-3.5 and RoBERTa [16] for preliminary

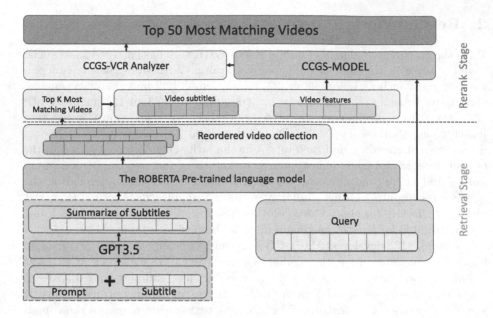

Fig. 1. The overall framework of GPT-CMR.

retrieval ranking, while the rerank stage utilizes the CCGS model [13] in conjunction with an CCGS-VCR Analyzer that we developed to selectively reorder the results obtained from the retrieval stage.

Retrieval Stage. We utilized GPT-3.5 to generate a video summary from the subtitles of a single video. To do so, we used a manually crafted prompt that instructed the model to retain key information for ease of retrieval tasks. We then combined this prompt with the video subtitles and input it into GPT-3.5 to produce the video summary. The output of this process is a new video corpus $V = \{v_1 : s_1; v_2 : s_2; v_3 : s_3; ...; v_n : s_n\}$, where v_i denotes the video ID and s_i represents the corresponding video summary. Subsequently, we concatenated each query q_i in the set $Q=\{q_1, q_2, q_3, q_4, ..., q_k\}$ with every video summary s_i in V to construct the $Input_i=\{q_i + s_1, q_i + s_2, q_i + s_3, ..., q_i + s_n\}$ for RoBERTa [16]. This input was employed to generate $P_i=\{v_1 : p_1, v_2 : p_2, v_3 : p_3, ..., v_n : p_n\}$, where p_i signifies the probability score of each video in V given the query q_i. Finally, we sorted the P_i in descending order based on P_i values, which enabled us to rank the videos in V according to their relevance to the queries in Q.

Rerank Stage. After the first stage, each query can retrieve a list of video ID sorted in descending order by their relevance score. For instance, let $R_i = \{v_7, v_1, v_{15}, ..., v_q\}$ represent such a list. In this stage, we select the top k videos from R_i and feed them, along with their corresponding subtitles and video features, into the CCGS model [13]. To improve robustness against adversarial attacks, we incorporate PGD [19] perturbations into the text embedding layer of the CCGS model during training.

CCGS-VCR Analyzer. Considering that the CCGS model [13] is a span-based model, we have designed a CCGS-VCR Analyzer for the VCR task based on the characteristics of the CCGS model's output. For example, let's assume that the original prediction obtained from CCGS is $Predict_{orig}=[video_1 : segment_1, video_3 : segment_2, video_3 : segment_{24}, video_3 : segment_{15}, video_2 : segment_{28}]$. For the assessment of $Predict_{orig}$, a comprehensive analysis can be conducted from two perspectives: positional order and segment count. Positional order refers to the relative position of a video within $Predict_{orig}$. A higher position indicates greater relevance to the query. As such, we can generate $Predict_{pos}=[video_1, video_3, video_2]$ by organizing the videos in $Predict_{orig}$ based on their positional order. Similarly, the frequency of appearance of a video within $Predict_{orig}$ is indicative of its relevance to the query. Thus, we can generate $Predict_{num}=[video_3, video_1, video_2]$ by organizing the videos in $Predict_{orig}$ based on their frequency of appearance.

Finally, we will calculate the weighted sum of $Predict_{pos}$ and $Predict_{num}$ to obtain the final prediction, which is defined as:

$$Prediction = \alpha * Predict_{pos} + \beta * Predict_{num} \qquad (1)$$

where the parameters α and β are obtained through a simulated annealing algorithm [10] with the overall metric on the validation set as the optimization target.

4 Experiments

4.1 Dataset and Evaluation

We utilized Chinese Medical Instructional Video Question Answering(CMIVQA) dataset, which was released by NLPCC 2023 Shared Task 5, to assess the effectiveness of our method. Table 1 presents the composition of the training and testing datasets in CMIVQA, as well as the average video length. During training, we randomly selected four hundred samples from the training set to use as the validation set. To evaluate the system's performance, we used R@1, R@10, R@50, MRR, and overall value as metrics, where overall is the sum of R@1, R@10, R@50, and MRR. In addition, to explore reasoning efficiency, we will also calculate the average reasoning time for each query, which is the total reasoning time divided by the number of queries.

4.2 Experimental Settings

All of our experiments were conducted on a single NVIDIA 3090 GPU. The training process consisted of retrieval and rerank stages, and the detailed parameters can be found in Table 2. In terms of experimental settings, we considered both retrieval accuracy and efficiency. To investigate the best retrieval accuracy, we selected the top 150 of the retrieval stage as the input for the rerank stage in the comparative and ablation experiments. To evaluate the impact of our framework on retrieval accuracy while improving efficiency, the retrieval stage's top k values were set to top 5, top 10, top 20, top 50, top 100, and top 150, respectively. Retrieval accuracy and average search time were then computed on the test set.

Table 1. Composition of the CMIVQA Dataset.

Dataset	Videos	QA pairs	Vocab Nums	Question Avg. Len	Video Avg. Len
Train	1,228	2,937	3125	17.16	263.3
Test	200	492	2171	17.81	242.4

Table 2. Main hyper-parameter setting

Retrieval stage		Rerank stage	
Epoch num	100	Epoch num	30
Batch size	32	Batch size	1
Optimizer	AdamW	Optimizer	AdamW
Learning rate	3e-6	Learning rate	1e-5
Weight decay	0.01	PGD ϵ/α	1/0.3

4.3   Results and Discussions

To assess the efficacy of our framework, we conducted ablation experiments and compared our method with the official baseline and CCGS [13]. The detailed experimental results are documented in Table 3. We carried out a comparison between our framework and the baseline model in terms of retrieval efficiency and retrieval accuracy under the condition of top k=top 10 to demonstrate its superiority, as presented in Fig. 2. Moreover, we investigated the influence of retrieval efficiency on retrieval accuracy using our method by testing different values of top k separately, and the results are outlined in Table 4 and Fig. 3.

Table 3. Comparison experiment and ablation experiment results. The experimental results of the official baseline were obtained from official, while the experimental parameters of CCGS were consistent with GPT-CMR's reranking stage, except for the absence of PGD.

Model	R@1	R@10	R@50	MRR	Overall
Official baseline	0.3943	0.5366	0.6423	0.4412	2.0144
CCGS	0.4012	0.8024	0.8696	0.4991	2.5723
GPT-CMR(Ours)	**0.5764**	**0.8391**	**0.9431**	**0.6710**	**3.0296**
W/o Analyzer	0.5163	0.8374	0.9431	0.6323	2.9290

From the results, it is evident that our proposed GPT-CMR framework outperformed all other models in every metric. When compared to the official baseline, GPT-CMR presented significant improvements across all metrics. Furthermore, when compared to CCGS, GPT-CMR demonstrated enhancements across all metrics, especially with 17.52% increase in R@1, indicating superior retrieval accuracy performance.

The last row of Table 4 presents the ablation experiment results of GPT-CMR after removing CCGS-VCR Analyzer. We used simulated annealing algorithm [10] to optimize the overall value as the optimization objective on the validation set and determined the weights in formula (1) to be α =0.9 and β=0.1. From the ablation experiment results, it can be seen that removing CCGS-VCR Analyzer led to a significant decrease in both R@1 and MRR, indicating the effectiveness of CCGS-VCR Analyzer.

Furthermore, we evaluated the retrieval efficiency and accuracy of GPT-CMR, CCGS, and the official baseline by setting top k as top 10, and the comparative results are depicted in Fig. 2. As shown in Fig. 2(a), although the retrieval accuracy decreased after reducing top k from top 150 to top 10, GPT-CMR still outperformed all baseline models in overall retrieval accuracy. Additionally, as seen in Fig. 2(b), the retrieval time of GPT-CMR was significantly faster than that of all baseline models.

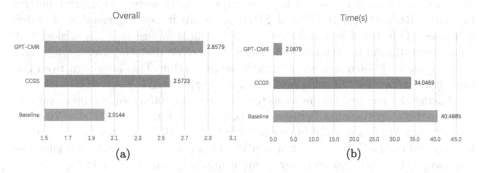

(a)   (b)

Fig. 2. Experimental results of retrieval efficiency time. Figure 2(a) shows the comparison of the Overall metrics between GPT-CMR and other models under the top 10 condition, with the horizontal axis indicating the Overall value. Figure 2(b) shows the comparison of retrieval time, with the horizontal axis representing the average retrieval time of queries in seconds.

Table 4. The retrieval metrics and retrieval time results of GPT-CMR under different top k conditions.

Top k	R@1	R@5	R@10	R@50	MRR	time(s)
top 5	0.5609	0.7296	0.7825	0.8699	0.6455	1.3076
top 10	0.5508	0.7744	0.7886	0.8719	0.6465	2.0879
top 20	0.5569	0.7886	0.8089	0.8719	0.6568	4.2988
top 50	0.5565	0.7906	0.8292	0.8719	0.6590	11.8995
top 100	0.5535	0.7947	0.8321	0.9021	0.6627	23.6831
top 150	0.5764	0.7947	0.8391	0.9429	0.6710	34.1863

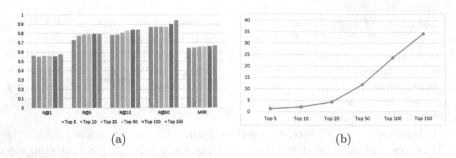

Fig. 3. The experimental results under different top k conditions. Figure 3(a) shows the statistics of retrieval accuracy under different values of k, while Fig. 3(b) illustrates the trend of retrieval time under different values of k.

From the experimental results in Table 4, it can be observed that the increase of k value has a small impact on R@1 before $k=150$. However, the overall metrics including R@5, R@10, R@50 and MRR show an increasing trend as k value increases. This trend is more evident in Fig. 3(a) where there is a slow but steady growth. As for retrieval efficiency, it is clear that the average retrieval time significantly increases with an increase in k value. This is evident from the line chart in Fig. 3(b) showing an overall increasing trend.

Taking the comparison between top 10 and top 100 as an example, we can observe that top 100 only increases by 0.0027% in terms of R@1 compared to top 10, and MRR also only improves by 0.0162%. However, the retrieval time for top 100 is 11.343 times that of top 10. This phenomenon indicates that the improvement in retrieval accuracy brought about by the increase in top k is not proportional to the decrease in retrieval efficiency.

In addition, in terms of the R@5 metric, there is a significant improvement of 4.48% in accuracy when comparing top 10 to top 5. However, the retrieval time for top 10 is only 0.7803 s longer than that of top 5. Therefore, selecting a reasonable top k can achieve decent retrieval accuracy on the basis of fast retrieval efficiency.

5   Conclusion

In this paper, we propose a two-stage framework called GPT-CMR (Chinese Medical Video Retrieval with CCGS and GPT-3.5) for medical VCR task. To improve the efficiency of medical video retrieval, we use the large language model GPT-3.5 in the first stage to generate video summaries based on the video subtitles, which are then used for initial retrieval. In the second stage, we employ CCGS [13] in conjunction with CCGS-VCR Analyzer to rerank the top k retrieval results obtained in the first stage. This process yields the final retrieval results. Comparative experiments demonstrate the superiority of GPT-CMR in terms of retrieval accuracy and time efficiency. Ablation experiments also confirm the effectiveness of the CCGS-VCR Analyzer. Furthermore, the retrieval accuracy and efficiency of GPT-CMR can be impacted by varying values of top k. To address this, we conducted an analysis of GPT-CMR's performance using different top k values. Our data analysis indicates that GPT-CMR can maintain excellent retrieval accuracy while sustaining efficient retrieval performance.

We believe that there are some directions for future exploration. Firstly, there is a need to explore more effective ways of leveraging large language models to improve the performance of the VCR task. While we have attempted to generate video summaries to assist in VCR, other techniques such as keyword-based retrieval can also be explored. Secondly, given that the GPT-CMR model heavily relies on textual information, there is a pressing need to investigate how audio and visual information can be integrated more effectively to assist in VCR tasks. Finally, although GPT-CMR has demonstrated notable progress in terms of retrieval efficiency compared to baseline models, it still falls short of meeting the requirements of practical applications. As such, further research is necessary to enhance retrieval efficiency.

Acknowledgments. This work was supported by the Guangxi Natural Science Foundation (No. 2022GXNSFAA035627), Guangxi Natural Science Foundation Key Project (Application No. 2023JJD170015), National Natural Science Foundation of China (62276072), Guangxi Scientific and Technological Bases and Talents Special Projects (guikeAD23026213 and guikeAD23026230), Innovation Project of Guangxi Graduate Education, and the Open Research Fund of Guangxi Key Laboratory of Multimedia Communications and Network Technology.

References

1. Brown, T., et al.: Language models are few-shot learners. Adv. Neural. Inf. Process. Syst. **33**, 1877–1901 (2020)
2. Chen, D., Dolan, W.B.: Collecting highly parallel data for paraphrase evaluation. In: Proceedings of the 49th Annual Meeting of the Association for Computational Linguistics: Human Language Technologies, pp. 190–200 (2011)
3. Chen, Y.-C., et al.: UNITER: universal image-text representation learning. In: Vedaldi, A., Bischof, H., Brox, T., Frahm, J.-M. (eds.) ECCV 2020. LNCS, vol. 12375, pp. 104–120. Springer, Cham (2020). https://doi.org/10.1007/978-3-030-58577-8_7
4. Dong, L., et al.: Unified language model pre-training for natural language understanding and generation. In: Advances in Neural Information Processing Systems 32 (2019)
5. Gao, W., et al.: Deep retrieval: learning a retrievable structure for large-scale recommendations. arXiv preprint arXiv:2007.07203 (2020)
6. Gupta, D., Attal, K., Demner-Fushman, D.: A dataset for medical instructional video classification and question answering. Sci. Data **10**(1), 158 (2023)
7. Heilbron, F.C., Escorcia, V., Ghanem, B., Niebles, J.C.: Activitynet: a large-scale video benchmark for human activity understanding. In: 2015 IEEE Conference on Computer Vision and Pattern Recognition (CVPR), pp. 961–970. IEEE (2015)
8. Jaiswal, A., Babu, A.R., Zadeh, M.Z., Banerjee, D., Makedon, F.: A survey on contrastive self-supervised learning. Technologies **9**(1), 2 (2020)

9. Kenton, J.D.M.W.C., Toutanova, L.K.: Bert: Pre-training of deep bidirectional transformers for language understanding. In: Proceedings of naacL-HLT, vol. 1, p. 2 (2019)
10. Kirkpatrick, S., Gelatt, C.D., Jr., Vecchi, M.P.: Optimization by simulated annealing. Science **220**(4598), 671–680 (1983)
11. Lewis, M., et al.: Bart: denoising sequence-to-sequence pre-training for natural language generation, translation, and comprehension. In: Proceedings of the 58th Annual Meeting of the Association for Computational Linguistics, pp. 7871–7880 (2020)
12. Li, B., Weng, Y., Sun, B., Li, S.: Towards visual-prompt temporal answering grounding in medical instructional video. arXiv preprint arXiv:2203.06667 (2022)
13. Li, B., Weng, Y., Sun, B., Li, S.: Learning to locate visual answer in video corpus using question. In: ICASSP 2023–2023 IEEE International Conference on Acoustics, Speech and Signal Processing (ICASSP), pp. 1–5. IEEE (2023)
14. Li, J., Li, D., Xiong, C., Hoi, S.: Blip: bootstrapping language-image pre-training for unified vision-language understanding and generation. In: International Conference on Machine Learning, pp. 12888–12900. PMLR (2022)
15. Li, J., Selvaraju, R., Gotmare, A., Joty, S., Xiong, C., Hoi, S.C.H.: Align before fuse: vision and language representation learning with momentum distillation. Adv. Neural. Inf. Process. Syst. **34**, 9694–9705 (2021)
16. Liu, Y., et al.: Roberta: a robustly optimized bert pretraining approach. arXiv preprint arXiv:1907.11692 (2019)
17. Lu, W., Jiao, J., Zhang, R.: Twinbert: distilling knowledge to twin-structured compressed bert models for large-scale retrieval. In: Proceedings of the 29th ACM International Conference on Information & Knowledge Management, pp. 2645–2652 (2020)
18. Luo, H., et al.: Clip4clip: an empirical study of clip for end to end video clip retrieval and captioning. Neurocomputing **508**, 293–304 (2022)
19. Madry, A., Makelov, A., Schmidt, L., Tsipras, D., Vladu, A.: Towards deep learning models resistant to adversarial attacks. Stat. **1050**, 4 (2019)
20. Radford, A., et al.: Learning transferable visual models from natural language supervision. In: International Conference on Machine Learning, pp. 8748–8763. PMLR (2021)
21. Raffel, C., et al.: Exploring the limits of transfer learning with a unified text-to-text transformer. J. Mach. Learn. Res. **21**(1), 5485–5551 (2020)
22. Schuhmann, C., et al.: Laion-5b: an open large-scale dataset for training next generation image-text models. Adv. Neural. Inf. Process. Syst. **35**, 25278–25294 (2022)
23. Schuhmann, C., et al.: Laion-400m: open dataset of clip-filtered 400 million image-text pairs. In: NeurIPS Workshop Datacentric AI. No. FZJ-2022-00923, Jülich Supercomputing Center (2021)
24. Weng, Y., Li, B.: Visual answer localization with cross-modal mutual knowledge transfer. In: ICASSP 2023–2023 IEEE International Conference on Acoustics, Speech and Signal Processing (ICASSP), pp. 1–5. IEEE (2023)
25. Xu, J., Mei, T., Yao, T., Rui, Y.: Msr-vtt: a large video description dataset for bridging video and language. In: Proceedings of the IEEE Conference on Computer Vision and Pattern Recognition, pp. 5288–5296 (2016)

Improving Cross-Modal Visual Answer Localization in Chinese Medical Instructional Video Using Language Prompts

Zineng Zhou[1,2,3], Jun Liu[1,2,3], Shuang Cheng[1,2,3], Haiyong Luo[1,2,3](✉),
Yang Gu[1,2,3], and Jian Ye[1,2,3]

[1] Institute of Computing Technology, Chinese Academy of Sciences, Beijing, China
{zhouzineng22s,liujun22s,chengshuang22s,guyang,jye}@ict.ac.cn
[2] University of Chinese Academy of Sciences, Beijing, China
[3] Beijing Key Laboratory of Mobile Computing and Pervasive Device, Beijing, China
yhluo@ict.ac.cn

Abstract. The growing popularity of video content for acquiring knowledge highlights the need for efficient methods to extract relevant information from videos. Visual Answer Localization (VAL) is a solution to this challenge, as it identifies video clips that can provide answers to user questions. In this paper, we explore the VAL task using the Chinese Medical instructional video dataset as part of the CMIVQA track1 shared task. However, VAL encounters difficulties due to differences between visual and textual modalities. Existing VAL methods use separate video and text encoding streams, as well as cross encoders, to align and predict relevant video clips. To address this issue, we adopt prompt-based learning, a successful paradigm in Natural Language Processing (NLP). Prompt-based learning reformulates downstream tasks to simulate the masked language modeling task used in pre-training, using a textual prompt. In our work, we develop a prompt template for the VAL task and employ the prompt learning approach. Additionally, we integrate an asymmetric co-attention module to enhance the integration of video and text modalities and facilitate their mutual interaction. Through comprehensive experiments, we demonstrate the effectiveness of our proposed methods, achieving first place in the CMIVQA track1 leaderboard with a total score of 0.3891 in testB.

Keywords: VAL · Prompt · Cross-modal fusion · Data pre-processing

1 Introduction

The emergence of video content has led people to increasingly adopt video formats for acquiring knowledge. However, due to the typically lengthy nature of video clips, extracting knowledge from them can be a time-consuming and tedious process. Therefore, finding efficient methods to retrieve relevant information from videos is important.

Z. Zhou, J. Liu and S. Cheng—Equal contribution.

© The Author(s), under exclusive license to Springer Nature Switzerland AG 2023
F. Liu et al. (Eds.): NLPCC 2023, LNAI 14304, pp. 221–232, 2023.
https://doi.org/10.1007/978-3-031-44699-3_20

Visual Answer Localization (VAL) is an emerging task that corresponds to this issue. Its objective is to identify the video clips that can answer the user's question. The process of VAL involves analyzing the visual and subtitle components of a video to identify segments that contain relevant information. Recently, a new task temporal answer localization in the Chinese Medical instructional video is proposed. The datasets for this task have been collected from high-quality Chinese medical instructional channels on the YouTube website. These datasets have been manually annotated by medical experts. In this paper, we explored the VAL task in Chinese Medical dataset, which is the shared task in CMIVQA track1.

The VAL task presents challenges due to significant disparities between the visual and textual modalities [1]. Previous research has been conducted in related tasks like video segment retrieval [2] and video question answering [3]. However, it does not work well to directly transfer these methods due to difference in tasks [4]. Existing VAL methods typically employ a two-stream model to separately encode video and text, and utilize a cross encoder to align the modalities [4,5]. They then use cross-modal representations to predict the relevant video clips. The effectiveness of these methods relies on pre-trained language models, such as Deberta, but there is a noticeable discrepancy between the finetuning process of the VAL task and the pre-training of language models. The pre-training phase utilizes Masked Language Modeling, while the downstream VAL tasks involve token prediction.

We adopt language prompt to resolve this issue. Prompt-based learning is a novel paradigm in NLP that has achieved great success. In contrast to the conventional "pre-train, finetune" paradigm that involves adapting pre-trained models to downstream tasks through objective engineering, the "pre-train, prompt predict" paradigm reformulates the downstream tasks to simulate the masked language modeling task optimized during the original pre-training, utilizing a textual prompt. This paradigm aligns the downstream tasks more closely with the pre-training tasks, thereby enabling better retention of acquired knowledge. Notably, under low-resource conditions, it surpasses the "pre-train, finetune" paradigm, and has demonstrated promising results across various NLP tasks, including Question Answering and Text Classification.

In our work, we developed a prompt template for the VAL task and utilized the prompt learning approach. To enhance the integration of video and text modalities, we employ an asymmetric co-attention module to foster their mutual interaction. Our comprehensive experiments demonstrate the effectiveness of our proposed methods, which achieved the first place on the leaderboard on CMIVQA track1 with a total score of 0.3891 in testB.

2   Related Work

2.1   Visual Answer Localization

Visual answer localization is an important task in cross-modal understanding [4,5]. This task involves identifying the video clips that correspond to the user's query [6]. The current methods in(VAL) primarily employ sliding windows to generate multiple segments and rank them based on their similarity to the query. Alternatively, some methods use a scanning-and-ranking approach. They sample candidate segments through the sliding window mechanism and integrate the query with each segment representation using a matrix operation Some approaches directly predict the answer without the need for segment proposals [7]. In the latest work [5,8], the subtitle and query are inputted into a pretrained language model. Subsequently, a cross encoder is utilized to interact with the visual modality. In this paper, we utilize the prompt technique to improve the model's comprehension of the task, achieving this by employing a prompt to transform VAL into a MLM task.

2.2 Prompt Based Learning

Prompt-based learning is an emerging strategy that enables pre-trained language models to adapt to new tasks without additional training, or by training only a small subset of parameters. The manual prompt involves creating an intuitive template based on human understanding. The early use of prompts in pre-trained models can be traced back to GPT-1/2 [9,10]. These studies demonstrated that by designing suitable prompts, language models (LMs) could achieve satisfactory zero-shot performance in various tasks, including sentiment classification and reading comprehension. Subsequent works [11–13] further explored the use of prompts to extract factual or commonsense knowledge from language models (LMs). PET [14] is a semi-supervised training technique that rephrases the input in completion format using a prompt to enhance the model's comprehension of the task. It subsequently annotates the unsupervised corpus with multiple models tailored to single prompts, and ultimately trains the classifier on the enlarged corpus. And our approach is inspired by the ideas introduced in the PET technique.

3 Method

This section begins with the presentation of our data preprocessing approach, which aims to reduce noise in the model inputs. Subsequently, we will introduce our novel model architecture, emphasizing the significant components of prompt construction and cross-modal fusion. Ultimately, we will provide a detailed explanation of our loss design and training techniques.

3.1 Task Formalization

The Chinese Medical Instructional Video Question-Answering task aims to provide a comprehensive solution by addressing medical or health-related question (Q) in conjunction with Chinese medical instructional video (V) and their corresponding set of subtitles $(S = [T_i]_{i=1}^{r})$, where r denotes the number of subtitle spans. The primary objective is to accurately determine the start and end time-points of the answer $[\hat{V}_s, \hat{V}_e]$ within the video V.

This task endeavors to develop advanced algorithms and systems capable of comprehending questions posed in Chinese medical instructional videos and effectively retrieving the corresponding answers. Moreover, it incorporates a subtitle timeline table (STB) that precisely maps each subtitle span to its corresponding timeline span in the subtitle set S. By functioning as a Look-up $Table$, this timeline table facilitates seamless mapping between frame span timepoints $[\hat{V}_s, \hat{V}_e]$ and accurate target answers $[V_s, V_e]$, thereby ensuring the provision of accurate target answers. Ultimately, the task can be mathematically represented as:

$$\left[\hat{V}_s, \hat{V}_e\right] = \mathrm{f}(Q, V, S) \tag{1}$$

$$[V_s, V_e] = \mathrm{STB}(\left[\hat{V}_s, \hat{V}_e\right]) \tag{2}$$

3.2   Data Preprocess

Before inputting the data into the model, a comprehensive data analysis was conducted. It was discovered that the subtitle information provided in the dataset was incomplete, as certain videos lacked subtitles. Upon closer examination, it was determined that the absence of subtitles was primarily attributed to the lack of audio subtitles (soft subtitles) in these videos.

However, it was observed that the video content itself contained subtitles, referred to as hard subtitles. In order to address this issue, Optical Character Recognition (OCR)[1] technology was employed to extract the subtitle text from the videos and supplement the missing captions. Additionally, for cases where subtitle information lacked both hard and soft subtitles, the corresponding subtitle was filled with a space. This method was implemented to enhance the integrity of the data.

3.3   Model Architecture

In this shared task, a novel method (MutualSL) [5] is employed as the baseline, demonstrating superior performance compared to other state-of-the-art (SOTA) approaches across various public VAL datasets. To further enhance the VAL capability for Chinese medical videos, an extended version of the baseline method is utilized by integrating prompts that activate powerful language comprehension and representation capabilities offered by large-scale language models for downstream tasks. Additionally, asymmetric co-attention [15] is incorporated to improve the model's cross-modal interaction capability.

The structure of the model is depicted in Fig. 1. During the initial stage, diverse feature extractors are employed to extract representations from both the input text and video frame sequences. Subsequently, the model combines

---

[1] https://github.com/YaoFANGUK/video-subtitle-extractor.

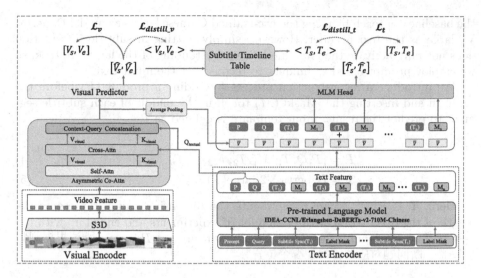

Fig. 1. The proposed cross-modal prompt model comprises separate feature extractors for video and text. Video features are enriched through Asymmetric Co-Att and the Visual Predictor, yielding $[\hat{V}_s, \hat{V}_e]$ predictions. Text and video features are combined using MLM Head and a broadcast mechanism, resulting in $[\hat{T}_s, \hat{T}_e]$ predictions. The final outcome considers four losses, with $< V_s, V_e >$ as the pseudo-label generated by text for video, and $< T_s, T_e >$ as the pseudo-label generated by video for text.

asymmetric co-attention with both video features and text-query features. To facilitate cross-modal interaction, the model employs a broadcast mechanism to combine the deep video features extracted by Asymmetric Co-Attn with the text features extracted by Deberta-V2-large [16] resulting in the final fused features being text-based. Finally, both the fused textual features and visual features are individually processed by their corresponding Predictors to obtain the final result.

Visual Feature Extraction. In contrast to the baseline model, we use separable 3D CNN (S3D) [17] pretrained on Kinetic 400 [18], which has better integration of spatial-temporal features and enhanced generalization capability, to extract video features instead of Two-Stream Inflated 3D ConvNets (I3D) [19]. Specifically, first, we extract video keyframes from video V using FFmpeg, and then S3D extracts video features from the video frames:

$$\mathbf{V} = \text{S3D}(V) \tag{3}$$

Here, $\mathbf{V} \in \mathbb{R}^{k \times d}$, where d represents the dimension and k represents the length of the video.

Text Input Template. The main objective of text encoder is to provide us with high-quality question and subtitle information representation. we still follow the baseline approach by using the pre-trained Chinese language model Deberta-V2-large as the text encoder. However, simply putting in subtitle information does not fully activate the large model's understanding of the language task, so we employ prompt-based techniques to reconstruct the input text.

We introduce a reconstruction process by adding a prompt (P) before the problem and inserting the [Mask] (M) token in the middle of each subtitle segment to predict the result. Input template is defined as T

$$T = \{P, Q, T_1, M_1, T_2, M_2, ..., T_n, M_n\} \tag{4}$$
$$\mathbf{T} = \text{Deberta-V2-large}(T) \tag{5}$$

Here, $\mathbf{T} \in \mathbb{R}^{n \times d}$, where d represents the dimension and n represents the length of the text. We went through a lot of experiments and ended up with the best performing prompt templates. Finally Our prompt P is set as "请根据视频和字幕判断问题对应的答案在哪个位置".

Cross-Modal Fusion. To improve the semantic representation of video features and capture interactions between visual and textual information, we employ asymmetric co-attention. This mechanism consists of three components: a self-attention (SA) layer, a cross-attention (CA) layer, and the Context-Query Concatenation (CQA).

In the self-attention layer, the video features $\mathbf{V}$ extracted by S3D are utilized to capture internal dependencies within the visual information. This process yields enhanced visual features, denoted as $\mathbf{V}_{\text{visual}}^{SA}$, and attention keys, represented as $\mathbf{K}_{\text{visual}}^{SA}$.

$$\mathbf{V}_{\text{visual}}^{\text{SA}}, \mathbf{K}_{\text{visual}}^{\text{SA}} = \text{LN}(\text{SA}(\mathbf{V})) \tag{6}$$

Next, we incorporate textual features $\mathbf{Q}_{\text{textual}}$ obtained from the prompt and question into the visual features. The cross-attention layer plays a crucial role in integrating these textual features with the visual features $\mathbf{V}_{\text{visual}}^{SA}$ and $\mathbf{K}_{\text{visual}}^{SA}$. This integration facilitates the fusion of information from both modalities, enabling a comprehensive understanding of the video content. The output of the cross-attention layer is represented as $\mathbf{V}_{\text{visual}}^{CA}$ and $\mathbf{K}_{\text{visual}}^{CA}$, capturing the cross-modal interactions and enriching the semantic representation of the visual features.

$$\mathbf{V}_{\text{visual}}^{CA}, \mathbf{K}_{\text{visual}}^{CA} = \text{LN}(\text{CA}(\mathbf{V}_{\text{visual}}^{SA}, \mathbf{K}_{\text{visual}}^{SA})) \tag{7}$$

Finally, the outputs of the cross-attention layer, $\mathbf{V}_{\text{visual}}^{CA}$ and $\mathbf{K}_{\text{visual}}^{CA}$, along with the textual features $\mathbf{Q}_{\text{textual}}$, are concatenated and fed into the Context-Query Concatenation layer. This layer combines the contextual information from the video and the query, resulting in a text-aware video representation, $\mathbf{V}_{\text{visual}}^{CQA}$, that captures the interplay between visual and textual elements.

$$\mathbf{V}_{\text{visual}}^{CQA} = \text{Conv1d}(\text{Concat}[\mathbf{Q}_{\text{textual}}, \mathbf{V}_{\text{visual}}^{CA}, \mathbf{K}_{\text{visual}}^{CA}]) \tag{8}$$

Regarding the textual modality, we employ global averaging to pool the visual features $\mathbf{V}_{\text{visual}}^{CQA}$, resulting in the representation $\overline{V}_{\text{visual}}^{CQA}$. Finally, we combine $\overline{V}_{\text{visual}}^{CQA}$ with $\mathbf{T}_{\text{Deberta}}$ extracted by the Deberta-v2 model through summation to obtain the ultimate output of the textual features $\overline{\mathbf{T}}$.

$$\overline{V}_{\text{visual}}^{CQA} = \text{AvgPool}(\mathbf{V}_{\text{visual}}^{CQA}) \tag{9}$$

$$\overline{\mathbf{T}} = \{\overline{V}_{\text{visual}}^{CQA} + \mathbf{T}_{Deberta}^{i}\}_{i=1}^{n} \tag{10}$$

Visual Predictor. To address the current task, we adhere to the Visual Predictor approach established by the baseline, which includes separate start and end predictors. Each predictor is composed of a unidirectional LSTM model and a FNN. The $\mathbf{V}_{\text{visual}}^{CQA}$) features are inputted into the LSTM model, followed by the utilization of the feedforward layer to calculate the logarithm of the predicted time point logits $\{\hat{\mathbf{V}}_{\mathbf{s}}, \hat{\mathbf{V}}_{\mathbf{e}}\}$, encompassing both the start and end time points.

$$\hat{\mathbf{V}}_{\mathbf{s}} = \text{FNN}(\text{LSTM}_{\text{start}}(\mathbf{V}_{\text{visual}}^{CQA})) \tag{11}$$

$$\hat{\mathbf{V}}_{\mathbf{e}} = \text{FNN}(\text{LSTM}_{\text{end}}(\mathbf{V}_{\text{visual}}^{CQA})) \tag{12}$$

Prompt-Based Prediction. Figure 2 illustrates the "prompt,predict" paradigm. Our Input template is T with n "[mask]" tokens. We aim to predict the category words "始" and "末" using the textual prompt T. This process is similar to masked language modeling during the pre-training stage. Let $\mathbf{T}_s$ represent the probability of the "始" token and $\mathbf{T}_e$ represent the probability of the "末" token of all mask. Additionally, $[\hat{T}_s, \hat{T}_e]$ represent the probabilities of the ground truth being predicted as "始" and "末", respectively.

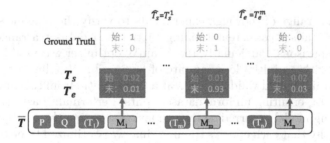

Fig. 2. Illustration of the "prompt, predict" paradigm.

Loss Function. In order to optimize the logits of the Visual Predictor and the Prompt-based Prediction, we utilize the Cross-Entropy function (CE). To enhance the model's robustness, we employ a subtitle timeline Look-up Table, which generates pseudo-labels $\langle V_s, V_e \rangle$ for videos based on text prediction results and $\langle T_s, T_e \rangle$ for texts based on video prediction results. Additionally, we introduce the rdrop loss to further improve the model's robustness and enhance its generalization capabilities.

Finally, our loss function is defined as follows:

$$\mathcal{L}_{\text{total}} = \mathcal{L}_{\text{v}} + \mathcal{L}_{\text{t}} + \mathcal{L}_{\text{distill\_v}} + \mathcal{L}_{\text{distill\_t}} + \beta \times \mathcal{L}_{\text{Rdrop}} \qquad (13)$$

The loss terms are defined as follows: $\mathcal{L}_{\text{v}}$ represents the loss between the predicted video features and the true labels, $\mathcal{L}_{\text{distill\_v}}$ represents the loss between the predicted video features and the pseudo labels, $\mathcal{L}_{\text{t}}$ represents the loss between the predicted text features and the true labels, $\mathcal{L}_{\text{distill\_t}}$ represents the loss between the predicted text features and the pseudo labels, and $\mathcal{L}_{\text{Rdrop}}$ represents the loss of rdrop. Additionally, β represents the weight of the rdrop loss.

4   Experiments

4.1   Dataset and Metrics

NLPCC Shared Task 5 involves a dataset of 1628 Chinese Medical Instructional Videos with annotated question-answer pairs tied to video sections and divided into training (2936 examples) and two test sets (491 and 510 examples). This dataset, sourced from YouTube's Chinese medical channels and annotated by experts, includes videos, audios, and both types of Chinese subtitles. The data extraction process converts everything to Simplified Chinese.

Performance is evaluated using two metrics: Intersection over Union (IoU) and mean IoU (mIoU) [20], assessing video frame localization as a span prediction task. The examination includes "$R@n, IoU = \mu$" and "$mIoU$", with experiments using $n = 1$ and $\mu \in 0.3, 0.5, 0.7$ for evaluation.

4.2   Experiment Details

We executed a range of thorough experiments to verify the pipeline's efficiency. All tests maintained consistent training tactics and dataset arrangements for accurate comparisons. Particularly, the AdamW optimizer was used in our training regimen with an initial learning rate of 8e-6 and a 10% linear warmup. We divided the training and validation sets at a 0.9:0.1 ratio from the officially given annotated data, ensuring uniform dataset splits. Performance assessment of the top-performing model occurred on the validation set using the official testA sets. It is noteworthy that each epoch's training time was optimized to be only 30 min.

4.3   Experimental Results and Analysis

In this study, we have evaluated the impact of text feature extraction, visual feature extraction, data preprocessing schemes, asymmetric co-attention model setting and prompt setting on the Visual Answer Localization task. The experimental results summarized in Table 1 and Table 2 provide insights into the performance of various methods, which can be analyzed in the following sections.

Table 1. Impact of text and visual feature extraction, and data preprocessing schemes on Visual Answer Localization task performance. Visual Feature setting is based on DeBERTa-v2-710M-Chinese; Data Preprocess setting is based on DeBERTa-v2-710M-Chinese and S3D.

Method	Valid Set				TestA Set			
	IoU = 0.3	IoU = 0.5	IoU = 0.7	mIoU	IoU = 0.3	IoU = 0.5	IoU = 0.7	mIoU
Baseline	60.52	43.13	26.58	43.41	56.71	40.65	23.58	40.28
Text Feature Setting								
Macbert-large	62.86	45.30	25.73	44.63	57.37	40.93	22.06	40.12
RoBERTa-large	58.74	42.07	27.90	41.57	55.74	40.07	19.12	38.31
DeBERTa-v2	**62.37**	**44.93**	**27.64**	**44.98**	**56.92**	**41.13**	**23.54**	**40.53**
Visual Feature Setting								
+ S3DG	61.64	43.25	26.81	43.90	56.63	40.55	23.81	40.33
+ Resnet151	59.14	42.49	25.99	42.54	52.10	40.49	23.12	38.57
+ S3D	**62.68**	**44.34**	**29.06**	**45.36**	**56.68**	**41.34**	**25.52**	**41.18**
Data Preprocess Setting								
+ Soft Caption	62.83	44.40	29.09	45.44	57.03	41.49	25.56	41.36
+ Hard Caption	63.70	44.88	29.30	45.96	57.86	42.03	25.69	41.86
+ Both Caption	**64.17**	**45.13**	**29.42**	**46.24**	**58.18**	**42.17**	**25.71**	**42.02**

Text Feature Setting. Among Chinese-Mac- bert-large [21], Chinese-RoBERTa-large [22], and DeBERTa-v2-710M-Chinese [16], we observe that the DeBERTa-v2-710M-Chinese model performs the best in IoU scores and mIoU for Valid Set and TestA Set, surpassing the baseline model. This proves its superior effectiveness in text feature extraction for the Visual Answer Localization task.

Visual Feature Setting. When evaluating different visual feature extraction schemes, we find that incorporating S3D into the DeBERTa-v2-710M model yields the highest mIoU on the Valid Set (45.36) and shows consistent improvement in the TestA Set (41.18), exceeding the baseline by 1.2%. This demonstrates S3D's suitability compared to S3DG and Resnet151, which scored lower than the baseline, showcasing their lower efficacy in visual feature extraction.

Data Preprocess. The blend of soft and hard caption extraction schemes outperforms the baseline model in mIoU scores for Valid Set (46.24) and TestA Set (42.02), substantiating the benefit of using audio and OCR-based techniques for caption extraction. A combination of both techniques results in the biggest improvement, hinting the advantage of using both audio and visual information to improve model performance in Visual Answer Localization tasks.

Model Evaluation. When examining the impact of different model settings, adding the Asy-Co-Att mechanism results in a significant improvement in performance across all IoU thresholds on both the validation and TestA sets, as compared to the baseline De-S3D-DP model. This indicates the mechanism effectively captures visual-textual interactions and refines video feature semantics.

While the addition of Rdrop also improves upon the base model, it doesn't provide the same significant gains as Asy-Co-Att. However, combining Asy-Co-Att and Rdrop attains the best performance, highlighting their complementary benefits.

Table 2. Impact of Model Settings and Prompt Configurations on De-S3D-DP for Visual Answer Localization. De-S3D-DP denotes the method which separately employs DeBERTa-v2-710M-Chinese and S3D models to extract textual and visual modality features, and optimizes the text through the use of both soft and hard subtitles. Asy-Co-Att refers to the asymmetric co-attention mechanism. Both (A&R) indicates that both the Asy-Co-Att and RDrop methods are employed simultaneously.

Method	Valid Set				TestA Set			
	IoU = 0.3	IoU = 0.5	IoU = 0.7	mIoU	IoU = 0.3	IoU = 0.5	IoU = 0.7	mIoU
De-S3D-DP	64.17	45.13	29.42	46.24	58.18	42.17	25.71	42.02
Model Setting								
+ Asy-Co-Att	65.61	46.23	34.29	48.71	60.17	43.53	26.98	43.56
+ Rdrop	64.87	46.11	31.07	47.35	60.61	42.72	25.43	42.92
+ **Both(A&R)**	**67.28**	**48.01**	**35.14**	**50.14**	60.08	**44.57**	**27.43**	**44.03**
Text Prompt Setting Based on best method								
+ Prompt$_1$	65.10	52.64	37.15	51.63	60.25	45.49	27.19	44.31
+ **Prompt$_2$**	**66.14**	**54.03**	**39.20**	**53.12**	**60.82**	**46.94**	**27.71**	**45.16**

Text Prompt Setting. We analyzed two prompt configuration schemes: Prompt$_1$, which constructs text input without a [Mask] (M) token for predictions; and Prompt$_2$, which includes the [Mask] (M) token for downstream prediction. Prompt$_2$ performs better across all IoU thresholds and datasets. This consistency with the pretraining task seems to enhance the model's Visual Answer Localization abilities.

In summary, our analysis indicates that certain pre-trained language models (e.g., Macbert-large) and data preprocessing techniques (e.g., combining soft and hard captions) can significantly improve the performance of the Visual Answer Localization task. Besides, based on the De-S3D-DP model above, the results in Table 2 suggest that incorporating both the Asy-Co-Att mechanism and Rdrop method, along with the Prompt$_2$ configuration, leads to the most significant improvements in performance for the Visual Answer Localization task.

5 Conclusion

This research is dedicated to the challenge of gleaning pertinent information from videos through Visual Answer Localization (VAL). Our focus was the VAL task, utilizing the Chinese Medical instructional video dataset in the CMIVQA track1 shared task. The inability of existing methods to effectuate a smooth transfer from related tasks is recognized. To surmount these challenges, the Prompt-based learning paradigm from Natural Language Processing (NLP) was employed by us. This approach recalibrates downstream tasks to emulate the masked language modeling task employed during pre-training. A prompt template customized for the VAL task was developed and the prompt learning approach institutionalized. Furthermore, an asymmetric co-attention module was initiated to augment the integration of video and text data.

The efficiency of our methods was illustrated by our experiments, culminating in us achieving the topmost place on the CMIVQA track1 leaderboard, with an aggregate score of 0.3891 in testB. Prompt-based learning is proven to hold superiority over traditional pre-training and fine-tuning methods, especially under low-resource conditions. To conclude, our research propels VAL techniques forward and lays out functional solutions for valuing knowledge from videos.

Acknowledgement. This work was supported in part by the National Key Research and Development Program under Grant 2020YFB2104200 the National Natural Science Foundation of China under Grant 62261042 and 62002026, the Key Research Projects of the Joint Research Fund for Beijing Natural Science Foundation and the Fengtai Rail Transit Frontier Research Joint Fund under Grant L221003, the Strategic Priority Research Program of Chinese Academy of Sciences under Grant XDA28040500, and the Key Research and Development Project from Hebei Province under Grant 21310102D.

References

1. Zhang, H., Sun, A., Jing, W., Zhou, J.T.: Temporal sentence grounding in videos: a survey and future directions. arXiv preprint arXiv:2201.08071 (2022)
2. Tang, H., Zhu, J., Liu, M., Gao, Z., Cheng, Z.: Frame-wise cross-modal matching for video moment retrieval. IEEE Trans. Multimedia **24**, 1338–1349 (2021)
3. Lei, J., Yu, L., Bansal, M., Berg, T.L.: TVQA: localized, compositional video question answering. arXiv preprint arXiv:1809.01696 (2018)
4. Li, B., Weng, Y., Sun, B., Li, S.: Towards visual-prompt temporal answering grounding in medical instructional video. arXiv preprint arXiv:2203.06667 (2022)
5. Weng, Y., Li, B.: Visual answer localization with cross-modal mutual knowledge transfer. In: ICASSP 2023-2023 IEEE International Conference on Acoustics, Speech and Signal Processing (ICASSP), pp. 1–5. IEEE (2023)
6. Anne Hendricks, L., Wang, O., Shechtman, E., Sivic, J., Darrell, T., Russell, B.: Localizing moments in video with natural language. In: Proceedings of the IEEE International Conference on Computer Vision, pp. 5803–5812 (2017)
7. Zhang, H., Sun, A., Jing, W., Zhou, J.T.: Span-based localizing network for natural language video localization. arXiv preprint arXiv:2004.13931 (2020)
8. Li, B., Weng, Y., Sun, B., Li, S.: Learning to locate visual answer in video corpus using question. In: ICASSP 2023-2023 IEEE International Conference on Acoustics, Speech and Signal Processing (ICASSP), pp. 1–5. IEEE (2023)
9. Radford, A., Narasimhan, K., Salimans, T., Sutskever, I., et al.: Improving language understanding by generative pre-training (2018)
10. Radford, A., Jeffrey, W., Child, R., Luan, D., Amodei, D., Sutskever, I., et al.: Language models are unsupervised multitask learners. OpenAI Blog **1**(8), 9 (2019)
11. Petroni, F., et al.: Language models as knowledge bases? arXiv preprint arXiv:1909.01066 (2019)

12. Talmor, A., Elazar, Y., Goldberg, Y., Berant, J.: oLMpics-on what language model pre-training captures. Trans. Assoc. Comput. Linguist. **8**, 743–758 (2020)
13. Liu, J., Cheng, S., Zhou, Z., Gu, Y., Ye, J., Luo, H.: Enhancing multilingual document-grounded dialogue using cascaded prompt-based post-training models. In: Proceedings of the Third DialDoc Workshop on Document-grounded Dialogue and Conversational Question Answering, Toronto, Canada, pp. 44–51. Association for Computational Linguistics (2023)
14. Schick, T., Schütze, H.: Exploiting cloze questions for few shot text classification and natural language inference. arXiv preprint arXiv:2001.07676 (2020)
15. Li, C., et al.: mPLUG: effective and efficient vision-language learning by cross-modal skip-connections. arXiv preprint arXiv:2205.12005 (2022)
16. Zhang, J., et al.: Fengshenbang 1.0: being the foundation of Chinese cognitive intelligence. CoRR, abs/2209.02970 (2022)
17. Xie, S., Sun, C., Huang, J., Tu, Z., Murphy, K.: Rethinking spatiotemporal feature learning: speed-accuracy trade-offs in video classification. In: Proceedings of the European Conference on Computer Vision (ECCV), pp. 305–321 (2018)
18. Kay, W., et al.: The kinetics human action video dataset. arXiv preprint arXiv:1705.06950 (2017)
19. Carreira, J., Zisserman, A.: Quo vadis, action recognition? A new model and the kinetics dataset. In: Proceedings of the IEEE Conference on Computer Vision and Pattern Recognition, pp. 6299–6308 (2017)
20. Gupta, D., Attal, K., Demner-Fushman, D.: A dataset for medical instructional video classification and question answering. Sci. Data **10**(1), 158 (2023)
21. Cui, Y., Che, W., Liu, T., Qin, B., Wang, S., Hu, G.: Revisiting pre-trained models for Chinese natural language processing. In: Proceedings of the 2020 Conference on Empirical Methods in Natural Language Processing: Findings, pp. 657–668. Association for Computational Linguistics (2020)
22. Cui, Y., Che, W., Liu, T., Qin, B., Yang, Z.: Pre-training with whole word masking for Chinese BERT. arXiv preprint arXiv:1906.08101 (2019)

Overview of the NLPCC 2023 Shared Task: Chinese Medical Instructional Video Question Answering

Bin Li[1], Yixuan Weng[2], Hu Guo[1], Bin Sun[1], Shutao Li[1(✉)], Yuhao Luo[1],
Mengyao Qi[1], Xufei Liu[1], Yuwei Han[1], Haiwen Liang[1], Shuting Gao[1],
and Chen Chen[1]

[1] College of Electrical and Information Engineering, Hunan University, Changsha,
China
{libincn,hu_guo,sunbin611,shutao_li,lyh1643023251}@hnu.edu.cn
[2] National Laboratory of Pattern Recognition Institute of Automation, Chinese
Academy Sciences, Beijing, China

Abstract. In this paper, we present an overview of the NLPCC 2023
shared task, named Chinese Medical Instructional Video (CMIVQA),
which includes three sub-tracks: temporal answer grounding in a single video, video corpus retrieval, and temporal answer grounding in
video corpus. The CMIVQA datasets containing the videos, audios, and
corresponding subtitles are made public, and the corresponding labels
are manually annotated by medical experts. Details of the shared task,
datasets, evaluation metrics, and final results will be provided in order.
We hope this shared task can provide more insights into the first-aid,
medical emergency, or medical education.

Keywords: Chinese medical instructional video · Video question
answering · Video retrieval · Temporal answer grounding

1 Introduction

The Multi-modal Video Question Answering (MVQA) is one of the key techniques to building a multi-modal human-robot interaction system [1,2], and has
long[1] received much attention in the Artificial Intelligence (AI) fields for many
years [3–5]. The traditional MVQA technique can be mainly divided into two
types, i.e., multiple choice [6] or sentence generation [7], which can provide users
with information-enriched textual feedback. However, the MVQA is not enough

---

[1] Official Website: https://cmivqa.github.io/.

This work is supported by the National Natural Science Fund of China (62221002,
62171183), the Hunan Provincial Natural Science Foundation of China (2022JJ20017),
and in part by the CAAI-Huawei MindSpore Open Fund. This work will also be used
on MindSpore.
B. Li and Y. Weng—These authors contribute this work equally.

F. Liu et al. (Eds.): NLPCC 2023, LNAI 14304, pp. 233–242, 2023.
https://doi.org/10.1007/978-3-031-44699-3_21

for people to accomplish a particular task with a series of step-by-step procedures, as the textual feedbacks are too plain to perform the act [8]. For example, when asking "How to examine lymph nodes in the head and neck?", you may fail to act according directly to the textual answer obtained from the MVQA.

Recently, a new task named temporal answer grounding (TAG) has been proposed [9] to solve this problem. Different from the MVQA, the TAG technique is more efficient and effective [10], as it can provide more intuitive video clips for people to accomplish a particular task with a question. The video with the corresponding verbal explanations is the more intuitive and effective feedback for people to perform the answer steps [11]. However, current research mainly focuses on TAG tasks in English-oriented medical instructional videos, while few studies concentrate on the Chinese. Besides, the TAG task is defined in the given single video, which means that the target answer can be easily found within the video clips. This does not comply with real-world scenarios, where people sometimes need to search for the answer through multiple video corpus [12].

In order to promote the development of related TAG technologies in the Chinese field and explore more applications suitable for Chinese real-world medical instructional scenarios, we proposed the first Chinese Medical Instructional Video Question Answering (CMIVQA) challenge. Specifically, we built the competition datasets from high-quality Chinese medical instructional channels on the YouTube website, where the questions and the corresponding labels are manually annotated by medical experts. The whole tasks include three tracks: (1) Temporal Answer Grounding in Singe Video (TAGSV), (2) Video Corpus Retrieval (VCR), and (3) Temporal Answer Grounding in Video Corpus (TAGVC). The first track TAGSV is similar to the traditional TAG task, which requires the participants to find the most relevant video clips given a single Chinese video. The second VCR and third TAGVC can be viewed as different pipelines of the TAG technique in a large video corpus. The ultimate goal for this shared task is to develop a system that can provide temporal answer video segments for a first-aid, medical emergency, or medical education within multiple video corpus.

2   Task Introduction

2.1   Definition of Each Track

This CMIVQA shared task contains 3 tracks:

1. Temporal Answer Grounding in Singe Video: given a medical or health-related question and a single untrimmed Chinese medical instructional video, this track aims to locate the temporal answer (start and end time points) within the video. As can be seen from the Fig. 1, when given a Chinese medical-related question "如何利用工具缓解头部前倾的问题?" (How to alleviate the problem of head tilting forward with tools ?) in a single video, the goal of this track is to locate to most related temporal answer span (0:54 s-1:25 s) that can answer this question.

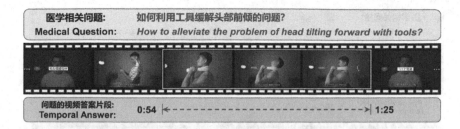

Fig. 1. Introduction of the Temporal Answer Grounding in Singe Video track

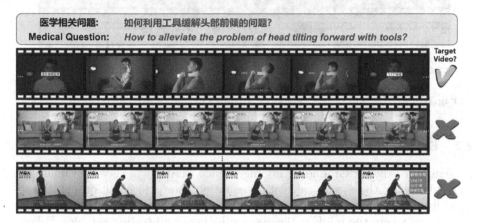

Fig. 2. Introduction of the Video Corpus Retrieval track

2. Video Corpus Retrieval: given a medical or health-related question and a large collection of untrimmed Chinese medical instructional videos, this track aims to find the most relevant video corresponding to the given question in the video corpus. As shown in Fig. 2, when given a Chinese medical-related question "如何利用工具缓解头部前倾的问题?" (How to alleviate the problem of head tilting forward with tools ?) in the video corpus, the aim of this track is to find the most related video as the target video. Intuitively, the video content of the first one is more related with the given medical question.

3. Temporal Answer Grounding in Video Corpus: given a text question and a large collection of untrimmed Chinese medical instructional videos, this track aims at finding the matching video answer span within the most relevant video corresponding to the given question in the video corpus. As shown in Fig. 3, when given a Chinese medical-related question "如何利用工具缓解头部前倾的问题?" (How to alleviate the problem of head tilting forward with tools ?) in the video corpus, the ultimate goal is to locate the most relevant video segments within the given video corpus. The predicted answer should be 0:54 s-1:25 s.

236   B. Li et al.

Fig. 3. Introduction of the Temporal Answer Grounding in Video Corpus track

2.2 Evaluation Metrics

1. Temporal Answer Grounding in Singe Video (TAGSV): we will evaluate the results using the metric calculation equation shown in equation (1). Specifically, we use Intersection over Union (IoU), and mIoU as the evaluation metrics, where the mIoU is the average IoU over all testing samples. Following the previous work [8], we adopt "R@n, IoU $= \mu$", and "mIoU" as the evaluation metrics, which treat localization of the video frames in the video as a span prediction task. The "R@n, IoU $=\mu$" denotes the Intersection over Union (IoU) of the predicted temporal answer span compared with the ground truth span, where the overlapping part is larger than "μ" in top-n retrieved moments. The "mIoU" is the average IoU over the samples. In this track, we use n = 1 and $\mu \in$ 0.3, 0.5, 0.7 to evaluate the TAGSV results. The main ranking of this track is based on the **mIoU** score, and other metrics in this track are also provided for further analysis.

$$\text{IOU} = \frac{A \cap B}{A \cup B}$$
$$mIOU = \left(\sum_{i=1}^{N} \text{IOU}_i \right) / N \tag{1}$$

where A and B represent different spans, and $\sum_{i=1}^{N} \text{IOU}_i$ represent IoU = 0.3/0.5/0.7 respectively, N=3.

2. Video Corpus Retrieval (VCR): following the pioneering work [13], we adopt the video retrieval metric like "R@n" for evaluation. Specifically, we adopt the n=1, 10, and 50 to denote the recall performance of the video retrieval. The Mean Reciprocal Rank (MRR) score to evaluate the Chinese medical

instructional video corpus retrieval track, which can be calculated as follows.

$$MRR = \frac{1}{|V|} \sum_{i=1}^{|V|} \frac{1}{\text{Rank}_i} \tag{2}$$

where the $|V|$ is the number of the video corpus. For each testing sample V_i, the Rank_i is the position of the target ground-truth video in the predicted list. In this track, the main ranking of this track is based on the **Overall** score. The Overall score is calculated by averaging the R@1, R@10, R@50 and MRR scores, which is shown as follows.

$$\text{Overall} = \frac{1}{|M|} \sum_{i=1}^{|M|} \frac{1}{\text{Value}_i} \tag{3}$$

where the $|M|$ is the number of the evaluation metrics. Value_i is the i-th metric in the above metrics (R@1, R@10, R@50 and MRR), $|M|$=4.

3. Temporal Answer Grounding in Video Corpus (TAGVC): we kept the Intersection over Union (IoU) metric similar to the Track 1, the retrieval indexes "R@n, n=1/10/50" and MRR similar to Track 2 for further analysis. The "R@n, IoU = 0.3/0.5/0.7" is still used, where we assign the n = 1, 10, 50 for evaluation. The index of mean IoU in video retrieval subtask, i.e., "R@1/10/50—mIOU", is also adopted for measuring the average level of participating model's performance. In this track, the main ranking of this track is based on the **Average** score. The Average score is calculated by averaging the R@1—mIoU, R@10—mIoU, R@50—mIoU scores, which is shown as follows, where the $|M'| = 3$.

$$\text{Average} = \frac{1}{|M'|} \sum_{i=1}^{|M'|} \frac{1}{\text{Value}_i} \tag{4}$$

2.3 Dateset

The videos for this competition are crawled from the Chinese medical instructional channels on the YouTube website, where the subtitles (in Chinese) are transcribed from the corresponding video. The question and corresponding temporal answer are manually labeled by annotators with the medical background. Each video may contain several question-answer pairs, where each question corresponds to a unique answer. The dataset is split into a training set, a validation set, and a test set. During the competition, the test set along with the true "id" data number is not available to the public. The Fig. 4 shows the dataset examples for the CMIVQA shared task. The "id" is the sample number which is used for the video retrieval track. The "video_id" means the unique ID from YouTube. The "question" item is written manually by the medical experts. The "start and end second" represent the temporal answer from the corresponding

```
array ⊟[
  object ⊟{
    "id": number 60,
    "video_id": string "L8wKeHJANR0",
    "question": string "如何使用弓箭步来缓解膝关节痛？",
    "start_second": number 840,
    "end_second": number 906,
  },
  object ⊟{
    "id": number 61,
    "video_id": string "L8wKeHJANR0",
    "question": string "如何双手叉腰站立膝盖微蹲来缓解膝关节痛？",
    "start_second": number 840,
    "end_second": number 906,
  }...
]
```

Fig. 4. Overview of the competition datasets

Table 1. Details of the datasets in NLPCC shared task 5

Dataset	Videos	QA pairs	Vocab Nums	Question Avg. Len	Video Avg. Len
Train & Dev	1228	2937	3125	17.16	263.3
Test A	200	492	2171	17.81	242.4
Test B	200	511	2234	17.48	310.9

video. As a result, our final goal is to retrieve the target video ID from the test corpus, and then locate the visual answer.

All the Train & Dev files include videos, audio, and the corresponding subtitles. The video and the corresponding audio come from Youtube Chinese medical channel, which is obtained by using Pytube tools[2]. The subtitles are generated from the Whisper[3], which contains Simplified Chinese and Traditional Chinese tokens. In order to unify the character types of questions and subtitles, we converted all the questions and subtitles into simplified Chinese. As shown in Table 1, the whole datasets contain 1,628 videos, where the QA pairs are 3,940. We also report the vocabulary numbers in Simplified Chinese and Traditional Chinese, the averaged question length and the average video length. The Test A&B set and baseline are released at the website[4] for further comparison.

---

[2] https://github.com/pytube/.
[3] https://github.com/openai/whisper.
[4] https://github.com/WENGSYX/CMIVQA_Baseline/.

3   Baseline Methods

In this section, we will introduce our baseline methods in the three tracks in this shared task in order.

3.1   Baseline Method for Track 1

Inspired by the work [11], we adopt a crossmodal mutual knowledge transfer span localization (MutualSL) method for track 1. MutualSL shares both visual predictor and textual predictor, so the semantic knowledge understanding can be better performed between cross-modalities. Also, a one-way dynamic loss function is used to dynamically adjust the proportion of knowledge transfer.

In the experiments, we followed the original hyper-parameter settings Specifically, we set all the dimensions to 1024 and use the AdamW optimizer for training, where lr = 1e−5. We use PyTorch in three A100 GPUs for experiments, where the batch size = 4 and training epoch = 15.

3.2   Baseline Method for Track 2 and 3

We use the cross-modal contrastive global-span (CCGS) method [13] to perform tracks 2 and 3. Specifically, we adopt the global-span contrastive learning to sort the positive and negative span points in the video corpus. Contrastive learning can differentiate the positive and negative samples during video retrieval for track 2. Also, we use the global-span predictor with the element-wise cross-modal fusion to locate the final visual answer for the track 3.

For the experiments, we use the DeBerta-V3 [14] to encode the texts, and then calculate the logits for all videos. We sort all the logits and select the highest prediction interval as the final result. We set d = 768 and optimize the loss function via the AdamW optimizer with lr = 1e−5. As for the hyper-parameter, we follow the original work. The hidden size d is set to 768. We use DeBERTa-v3-base as the pre-trained language model (with a limited maximum length of 1300). We use PyTorch in two A100 GPUs for experiments, where the batch size = 1 and training epoch = 15.

4   Evaluation Results

There is a total of 26 teams registered for the NLPCC 2023 Shared Task 5. Since the competition adopts a double-list leaderboard, the final result should be the result of leaderboard B. During the run of Leaderboard A, a total of 13 teams submitted their results. During the run of leaderboard B, a total of 9 teams submitted their results. We then give a brief introduction to the representative systems designed by **nsddd** for track 1, **DSG-1** for track 2, and **nsddd** for track 3 (Tables 2 and 3).

For the track 1, to overcome the disparities between the visual and textual modalities, the nsddd team proposed to adopt the prompt-based learning to finish this track. Specifically, they develop a prompt template tailored for the VAL

240   B. Li et al.

Table 2. Final Results of the track 1

Rank	Team ID	R@1,IoU = 0.3	R@1,IoU = 0.5	R@1,IoU = 0.7	mIoU(R@1)
1	nsddd	0.5557	0.3894	0.2239	0.3891
2	Ditto	0.5284	0.3816	0.2290	0.3866
3	HLT-base	0.5245	0.3562	0.2524	0.3794
4	辣子鸡丁队	0.5205	0.3679	0.2368	0.3788
5	WAN	0.5284	0.3738	0.2368	0.3782
6	Mote	0.5068	0.3581	0.2446	0.3768
7	Ditto	0.4912	0.3542	0.1879	0.3596
8	Baseline Method	0.4990	0.3738	0.2133	0.3592

Table 3. Final Results of the track 2

Rank	Team ID	R@1	R@10	R@50	MRR	Overall
1	DSG-1	0.5225	0.7613	0.8982	0.6118	2.7938
2	nsddd	0.5342	0.7241	0.8239	0.5916	2.6738
3	Weilan	0.4540	0.7143	0.8395	0.5472	2.5550
4	HLT-base	0.4853	0.6497	0.6986	0.5373	2.3709
5	Baseline Method	0.3249	0.4403	0.5427	0.3641	1.6720

Table 4. Final Results of the track 3

Rank	Team ID	R@1|mIoU	R@10|mIoU	R@50|mIoU	Average
1	nsddd	0.2346	0.4368	0.5631	0.4115
2	DSG-1	0.2221	0.3799	0.4773	0.3598
3	HLT-base	0.2090	0.3854	0.4513	0.3486
4	Baseline Method	0.1431	0.2642	0.3560	0.2545

task and leverage prompt learning to align the semantic information between the downstream pre-training. Additionally, they employ an asymmetric co-attention module to enhance the integration and interaction between the video and text modalities. To further improve the robustness of their model, they introduce r-drop [15] strategy. Moreover, in terms of data pre-processing, they utilize Optical Character Recognition (OCR) to extract video hard captions, thereby reducing data noise (Table 4).

For the track 2, the DSG-1 team proposed a two-stage retrieval-rerank framework. In the first stage, they utilized the large language model gpt-3.5 [16] to generate video summaries based on video subtitles and then use RoBERTa [17] for efficient retrieval. In the second stage, they designed a CCGS-VCR Analyzer for the VCR task that leverages the characteristics of the CCGS model's output without training cost. And, they employed projected gradient descent (PGD) [18] strategy for adversarial training to improve model robustness.

For the track 3, the nsddd team proposed to leveraging visual cues that are contextually relevant to the given question, utilizing the explicit semantic information embedded in text patterns. To extract subtitle information and facilitate retrieval and prediction, they employ the DeBERTa-v2-710M-Chinese pre-trained language model [19] as our backbone network. In order to enhance the robustness and performance of the model, they introduce various techniques during the training process, including data cleaning, pre-processing, and subtitle optimization based on Few-Shot ChatGPT[5] and contrastive loss.

5   Conclusion

This paper briefly introduced the overview of the NLPCC 2023 Shared Task 5: Chinese Medical Instructional Video Question Answering (CMIVQA). We proposed the new task CMIVQA containing three sub-tracks, Temporal Answer Grounding in Singe Video (TAGSV), Video Corpus Retrieval (VCR), and Temporal Answer Grounding in Video Corpus (TAGVC). Then, we introduced the datasets used in the whole competition. Finally, we reported the evaluation results of all three tracks. Despite the promising results of these competitors, the overall system is still not applicable for real application. There is still a long way to the instructional temporal answering grounding in video corpus. In short, we believe our new tasks can lead to more interesting insights for applications in multi-modal fields.

References

1. Song, Q., Sun, B., Li, S.: Multimodal sparse transformer network for audio-visual speech recognition. IEEE Trans. Neural Networks Learn. Syst., 1–11 (2022)
2. Buch, S., Eyzaguirre, C., Gaidon, A., Wu, J., Fei-Fei, L., Niebles, J.C.: Revisiting the" video" in video-language understanding. In: Proceedings of the IEEE/CVF Conference on Computer Vision and Pattern Recognition, pp. 2917–2927 (2022)
3. Li, B., et al.: More but correct: Generating diversified and entity-revised medical response. arXiv preprint arXiv:2108.01266 (2021)
4. Li, B., Weng, Y., Xia, F., Sun, B., Li, S.: VPAI_Lab at MedVidQA 2022: a two-stage cross-modal fusion method for medical instructional video classification. In: Proceedings of the 21st Workshop on Biomedical Language Processing, pp. 212–219, Dublin, Ireland, May 2022. Association for Computational Linguistics
5. Jabeen, S., Li, X., Amin, M.S., Bourahla, O., Li, S., Jabbar, A.: A review on methods and applications in multimodal deep learning. ACM Trans. Multimed. Comput. Commun. Appl. 19(2s), 1–41 (2023)
6. Rogers, A., Gardner, M., Augenstein, I.: QA dataset explosion: a taxonomy of NLP resources for question answering and reading comprehension. ACM Comput. Surv. 55(10), 1–45 (2023)
7. Yang, A., Miech, A., Sivic, J., Laptev, I., Schmid, C.: Just ask: learning to answer questions from millions of narrated videos. In: Proceedings of the IEEE/CVF International Conference on Computer Vision, pp. 1686–1697 (2021)

---

[5] https://chat.openai.com/chat.

8. Gupta, D., Attal, K., Demner-Fushman, D.: A dataset for medical instructional video classification and question answering. Sci. Data **10**(1), 158 (2023)
9. Gupta, D., Demner-Fushman, D.: Overview of the medvidqa 2022 shared task on medical video question-answering. In: Proceedings of the 21st Workshop on Biomedical Language Processing, pp. 264–274 (2022)
10. Li, B., Weng, Y., Sun, B., Li, S.: Towards visual-prompt temporal answering grounding in medical instructional video. arXiv preprint arXiv:2203.06667 (2022)
11. Weng, Y., Li, B.: Visual answer localization with cross-modal mutual knowledge transfer. In: ICASSP 2023–2023 IEEE International Conference on Acoustics, Speech and Signal Processing (ICASSP), pp. 1–5 (2023)
12. Neo, S.-Y., Ran, Y., Goh, H.-K., Zheng, Y., Chua, T.-S., Li, J.: The use of topic evolution to help users browse and find answers in news video corpus. In: Proceedings of the 15th ACM International Conference on Multimedia, pp. 198–207 (2007)
13. Li, B., Weng, Y., Sun, B., Li, S.: Learning to locate visual answer in video corpus using question. In ICASSP 2023–2023 IEEE International Conference on Acoustics, Speech and Signal Processing (ICASSP), pp. 1–5 (2023)
14. He, P., Gao, J., Chen, W.: Debertav 3: improving deberta using electra-style pre-training with gradient-disentangled embedding sharing. arXiv preprint arXiv:2111.09543 (2021)
15. Lijun, W., et al.: R-drop: regularized dropout for neural networks. Adv. Neural. Inf. Process. Syst. **34**, 10890–10905 (2021)
16. Brown, T., et al.: Language models are few-shot learners. Adv. Neural Inf. Process. Syst. **33**, 1877–1901 (2020)
17. Liu, Y., et al.: Roberta: a robustly optimized bert pretraining approach. arXiv preprint arXiv:1907.11692 (2019)
18. Gupta, H., Jin, K.H., Nguyen, H.Q., McCann, M.T., Unser, M.: CNN-based projected gradient descent for consistent ct image reconstruction. IEEE Trans. Med. Imaging **37**(6), 1440–1453 (2018)
19. He, P., Liu, X., Gao, J., Chen, W.: Deberta: decoding-enhanced bert with disentangled attention. arXiv preprint arXiv:2006.03654 (2020)

Evaluation Workshop: Chinese Few-Shot and Zero-Shot Entity Linking

Improving Few-Shot and Zero-Shot Entity Linking with Coarse-to-Fine Lexicon-Based Retriever

Shijue Huang[1,2], Bingbing Wang[1,2], Libo Qin[3], Qin Zhao[1,2], and Ruifeng Xu[1,2(✉)]

[1] Harbin Institute of Technology (Shenzhen), Shenzhen 518000, China
{22S051040,bingbing.wang}@stu.hit.edu.cn,
{zhaoqin,xuruifeng}@hit.edu.cn
[2] Guangdong Provincial Key Laboratory of Novel Security Intelligence Technologies, Shenzhen 518000, China
[3] School of Computer Science and Engineering, Central South University, Changsha, China
lbqin@csu.edu.cn

Abstract. Few-shot and zero-shot entity linking focus on the tail and emerging entities, which are more challenging but closer to real-world scenarios. The mainstream method is the "retrieve and rerank" two-stage framework. In this paper, we propose a coarse-to-fine lexicon-based retriever to retrieve entity candidates in an effective manner, which operates in two layers. The first layer retrieves coarse-grained candidates by leveraging entity names, while the second layer narrows down the search to fine-grained candidates within the coarse-grained ones. In addition, this second layer utilizes entity descriptions to effectively disambiguate tail or new entities that share names with existing popular entities. Experimental results indicate that our approach can obtain superior performance without requiring extensive finetuning in the retrieval stage. Notably, our approach ranks the 1st in NLPCC 2023 Shared Task 6 on Chinese Few-shot and Zero-shot Entity Linking.

Keywords: Entity linking · Few-shot and zero-shot learning

1 Introduction

Entity linking is a crucial task in natural language processing that involves associating an ungrounded mention in text with its corresponding entity in a knowledge base, thereby facilitating language understanding. Entity linking serves as a fundamental component for various downstream applications, including question answering [4], knowledge base completion [13,20], text generation [10] and end-to-end task-oriented dialogue system [11]. However, existing entity linking systems face challenges when dealing with newly created or tail entities that share names with popular entities. To address this challenge, the few-shot and zero-shot entity linking task has been proposed, aiming to enhance models' ability to accurately link against the less popular and emerging entities [8].

F. Liu et al. (Eds.): NLPCC 2023, LNAI 14304, pp. 245–256, 2023.
https://doi.org/10.1007/978-3-031-44699-3_22

Recent research on few-shot and zero-shot entity linking task has primarily employed a "retrieve and rerank" two-stage framework, owing to the vast number of entities present in knowledge bases. In this framework, the first stage involves selecting candidate entities for a given mention, while the second stage reranks these candidates and selects the most probable entity. Specifically, Logeswaran et al. [8] explore deep cross-attention within candidate rerank stage. Wu et al. [16] adopt a BERT architecture based two-stage approach for the zero-shot linking. And to leverage additional information from entity embeddings, Xu et al. [17] consider entities as input tokens and introduce a LUKE-based cross-encoder in the reranking stage. Moreover, Xu et al. [18] enhance the dual encoder model in the retrieve stage by incorporating the Wikidata type system as an auxiliary supervision task. And they also release a new benchmark in Chinese.

In this paper, we propose a coarse-to-fine lexicon-based retriever that improves the few-shot and zero-shot entity linking in an effective manner. Specifically, our proposed approach consists of two layers of lexicon-based retriever. In the first layer, two separate BM25 models [12], namely the AT-BM25 and KB-BM25, are employed to retrieve coarse-grained candidate entities based on the entity names from the alias table and the knowledge base, respectively. Subsequently, in the second layer, another BM25 model called Description-BM25 is introduced to retrieve fine-grained candidates from the previously obtained coarse-grained candidates by leveraging the entity descriptions. This step utilizes the entity description as detailed context to disambiguate tail entities that share names with existing popular entities. To further refine the retrieved candidates, we employ a BERT-based dual-encoder for reranking. Finally, we propose an ensemble method to aggregate the results of the reranker with the outputs from the three BM25 models in the coarse-to-fine lexicon-based retriever. This ensemble approach ensures more robust predictions.

Experimental results demonstrate significant improvement of our coarse-to-fine lexicon-based retriever, even without extensive finetuning in retrieve stage. Notably, our approach achieves the 1st place in NLPCC 2023 Shared Task 6.

The main contributions of our work are summarized as follows:

- We propose a coarse-to-fine lexicon-based retriever based on BM25 to improve few-shot and zero-shot entity linking, which offers a solution to mitigate the computational burden while improving retrieve accuracy.
- We introduce an ensemble method to aggregate the results from both retrieve and rerank stage, resulting in more robust predictions.
- Empirical results and analyses indicate the effectiveness of our approach in few-shot and zero-shot entity linking. And our approach ranks the 1st in NLPCC 2023 Shared Task 6.

2 Related Work

Entity Linking. Entity linking (EL) refers to the task of associating mentions with entries in a designated database or dictionary of entities. In order to achieve accurate and efficient identification of target entities from extensive knowledge bases (KBs), most entity linking systems adopt a two-stage approach known as "retrieve and rerank". This contains a retriever that retrieves candidate entities from the knowledge base, followed by a reranker that reorders the candidates and selects the most probable entity. In traditional entity retrieval, existing methods typically rely on simple techniques such as frequency information [19] or sparse-based models [12] to quickly retrieve a small set of candidate entities. For the ranking stage, neural networks have been widely utilized to calculate the relevance score between mentions and entities [3,7].

Recently, the emergence of pre-trained language models (PLMs) has led to their extensive adoption in both retrieve and rerank stages of entity linking. For instance, Logeswaran et al. [8] employ a cross-encoder architecture and introduce deep cross-attention in the candidate ranking stage, demonstrating significance of attention between the mention-context pairs and entity descriptions. Wu et al. [16] explore a BERT-based two-stage approach for zero-shot linking. Xu et al. [17] leverage additional information encoded in entity embeddings by considering entities as input tokens in the rerank stage, proposing an entity-enhanced cross-encoder based on LUKE. Wiatrak et al. [14] propose a proxy-based metric learning loss coupled with an adversarial regularizer, providing an efficient alternative to conduct hard negative sampling in candidate retrieve stage. In comparison to these existing works, our approach do not need large-scale fine-tuning for candidate retrieval, effectively reducing computational overhead while maintaining effectiveness.

Few-Shot and Zero-Shot Entity Linking. Entity linking on temporally evolving knowledge bases (KBs) presents a formidable challenge in zero-shot settings. To address this, Hoffart et al. [5] introduce a method for entity linking on emerging entities, particularly dealing with the ambiguity surrounding their names. More recently, Logeswaran et al. [8] propose the zero-shot entity linking task to evaluate the generalization capability of entity linking systems, making minimal assumptions. They also release an English zero-shot entity linking dataset. In the context of Chinese entity linking, Xu et al. [18] introduce a challenging multi-domain benchmark that utilizes Wikidata as the KB. In contrast to most of the existing works, our research focuses specifically on few-shot and zero-shot entity linking in the Chinese language.

3   Methodology

In this section, we introduce our approach for few-shot and zero-shot entity linking. Given a knowledge base E consisting of entities, each characterized by a name e_i and a description d_i. The objective of this task is to determine the most suitable entity for a given mention m_i within a document doc_i.

Our approach follows the "retrieve and rerank" two-stage framework. In the retrieve stage, we propose a coarse-to-fine lexicon-based retriever that efficiently

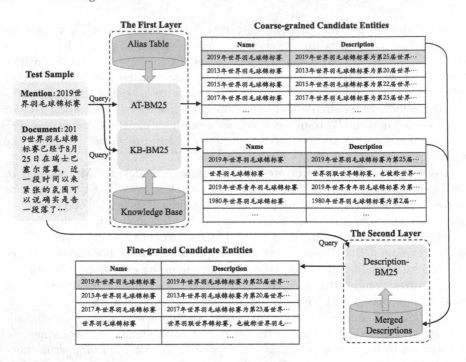

Fig. 1. The architecture of coarse-to-fine lexicon-based retriever, where the first layer contains `AT-BM25` and `AT-BM25` to retrieve coarse-grained candidate entities from alias table and knowledge base. And the second layer utilizes the `Description-BM25` to obtain fine-grained candidate entities from coarse-grained ones.

retrieves candidate entities without the need for time-consuming large-scale fine-tuning (Sect. 3.1). In the rerank stage, we adopt a BERT-based dual-encoder to reevaluate the retrieved candidate entities and select the most appropriate entity (Sect. 3.2). Finally, we introduce an ensemble method to combine the results obtained from both stages, thereby producing more robust predictions (Sect. 3.3).

3.1   Coarse-to-Fine Lexicon-Based Retriever

The overall architecture of our proposed coarse-to-fine lexicon-based retriever is illustrated in Fig. 1. It contains two layers to retrieve candidate entities in a coarse-to-fine manner.

The First Layer (Coarse Stage). Given a text sample (m_i, doc_i), an entity set $E = \{e_i, d_i\}_{i=1}^N$, and an alias table $AT = \{m_j, e_j\}_{j=1}^M$ that defines the probability of a mention m_j linking to an entity e_j, we construct the retriever in two layers. In the first layer, we employ two separate BM25 models, namely `AT-BM25` and `KB-BM25`. The `AT-BM25` model uses the entity names in the alias table as the corpus, while the KB-BM25 model utilizes that in the knowledge base. By treating the mention m_i in the test sample as a query, we utilize these two models to retrieve coarse-grained candidate entities as follows:

$$D_{AT} = \{m_j, m_j \in AT\}, \tag{1}$$

$$D_{KB} = \{e_i, e_i \in E\}, \tag{2}$$

$$Cand_{AT} = \text{AT-BM25}(m_i, D_{AT}), \tag{3}$$

$$Cand_{KB} = \text{KB-BM25}(m_i, D_{KB}), \tag{4}$$

where D_{AT} and D_{KB} are the corpus to build AT-BM25 and KB-BM25, respectively; $Cand_{AT}$ and $Cand_{KB}$ are the retrieved coarse-grained candidate entities from alias table and knowledge base.

The Second Layer (Fine Stage). To further disambiguate the tail entities based on the detailed mention context, we treat the document doc_i of the test sample as query and merge the obtained coarse-grained candidate entities $Cand_{AT}$ and $Cand_{KB}$ into a non-repeated set $Cand_1$. We then introduce the second layer BM25 model, called Description-BM25, which utilizes the descriptions from the obtained coarse-grained candidate entities as the corpus. This step retrieves the fine-grained candidate entities as follows:

$$Cand_1 = Cand_{AT} \cup Cand_{KB}, \tag{5}$$

$$D_{des} = \{d_i, d_i \in Cand_1\}, \tag{6}$$

$$Cand_2 = \text{Description-BM25}(doc_i, D_{des}), \tag{7}$$

where $Cand_1$ are the merged coarse-grained candidate entities; D_{des} is the union of descriptions from $Cand_1$, which is used to build Description-BM25; $Cand_2$ is the obtained fine-grained candidate entities.

3.2 BERT-Based Dual Encoder

To rerank the obtained coarse-grained candidate entities and get the most proper entity, we follow previous works [1,16] to train a BERT-based dual encoder. This approach offers scalability benefits, as the entity embeddings can be pre-computed and stored, allowing for fast retrieval and similarity score computation using dot product. Figure 2 illustrates the architecture of the BERT-based dual encoder. Given a document $\{x_1, x_2, ...x_n\}$ with n tokens, where a mention $m = \{x_i, x_{i+1}, ...x_j\}$ is present, the input sequence for the mention is constructed as follows:

$$X_1 = \text{[CLS]}\, x_1, ..., x_{i-1}\,\text{[unused0]}\, x_i, ..., x_j\,\text{[unused1]}\, x_{j+1}, ..., x_n\,\text{[SEP]}, \tag{8}$$

where [unused0] and [unused1] are are special tokens stand of mention start and end, respectively. Following Humeau et al. [6], we feed the input sequence

of the mention into the BERT encoder [2] to obtain the representation of the
[CLS] token in the last layer:

$$y_m = \text{BERT}(X_1), \tag{9}$$

where y_m is the representation of given mention.

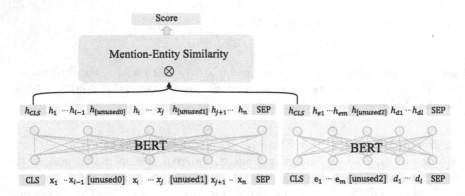

Fig. 2. The architecture of BERT-based dual-encoder. Two BERT encoders are
employed to encode the mention within context and the entity-description pair separately. And the mention-entity similarity is computed by dot product.

For a given entity e, which includes the entity name $\{e_1, ..., e_m\}$ and description $\{d_1, ..., d_l\}$, the input sequence is created by concatenating the entity name
and description:

$$X_2 = [\text{CLS}] \ e_1, ..., e_m \ [\text{unused2}] \ d_1, ..., d_l \ [\text{SEP}], \tag{10}$$

where [unused2] is a special token to separate the entity name and description.
Similar to the mention encoding approach, we feed the input sequence of entity
into the BERT encoder to obtain the representation of the entity:

$$y_e = \text{BERT}(X_2), \tag{11}$$

where y_e is the representation of entity.

Finally, the score of the mention and entity pair is calculated as the dot
product of their representations:

$$s(m, e) = y_m \cdot y_e \tag{12}$$

Optimization. We apply the standard cross-entropy loss to train the BERT-
based dual encoder:

$$\mathcal{L} = -\frac{1}{N} \sum_{n=1}^{N} y_n \cdot log\hat{y_n}, \tag{13}$$

where N is the number of total samples, y_n is the golden label, and $\hat{y_n}$ is the
predicted distribution.

Inference. During the inference phase, we utilize the BERT-based dual encoder to rerank the combination of coarse-grained and fine-grained candidate entities $(Cand_1 \cup Cand_2)$ in the retrieval stage to avoid missing retrievals and error propagation. Moreover, to enhance computational efficiency, we pre-compute $\boldsymbol{y}_e$ for each $e \in E$ and store all the entity embeddings.

3.3 Ensemble Method

Due to we focus on entity linking in few-shot and zero-shot scenarios, where a majority of the entity mentions are either unseen or only a few of them are encountered during training. This could introduce a bias in the rerank stage, because there is a huge gap between the training set and the few-shot and zero-shot test set. To mitigate this bias, we propose an ensemble method that leverages information from both the retrieve and rerank stages, aiming to enhance the robustness of predictions.

To achieve this, we employ an ensemble strategy that combines four results obtained from the retrieve and rerank stages, include:

– The top-ranked result from the `AT-BM25` retrieval process;
– The top-ranked result from the `KB-BM25` retrieval process;
– The top-ranked result from the `Description-BM25` retrieval process;
– The top-ranked prediction from the BERT-based dual encoder;

In our ensemble strategy, the final predicted result is determined by considering above four predicted results. If two or more results are identical, we select the same result as the final prediction. In cases where the four predicted results differ, we choose the output from the BERT-based dual encoder as the final prediction. Additionally, there may has a unique 2:2 situation arising during voting. In this case, we opt for the prediction that incorporates the result derived from the BERT-based dual encoder.

4 Experiments

4.1 Data

Hansel Dataset. Hansel [18] is a benchmark dataset for few-shot and zero-shot entity linking in simplified Chinese. The training set of Hansel is derived from Wikipedia and the test set consists of Few-Shot (FS) and Zero-Shot (ZS) settings. The FS setting focuses on tail entity linking, while the ZS setting aims to evaluate the zero-shot generalization to emerging and tail entities. The dataset statistics are presented in Table 1.

Knowledge Base. In order to reflect the realistic scenario of knowledge bases evolving over time, the Hansel dataset divides Wikidata entities into two sets, namely the Known and New sets, based on two historical dumps:

Table 1. Statistics of the Hansel dataset.

	# Mentions			# Documents			# Entities		
	In-KB	NIL	Total	In-KB	NIL	Total	E_{known}	E_{new}	Total
Train	9.89M	–	9.89M	1.05M	–	1.05M	541K	–	541K
Validation	9,677	–	9,677	1,000	–	1,000	6,323	–	6,323

- Known Entities (E_{known}) are Wikidata entities from the dump on August 13, 2018. And our models are trained using E_{known} as the knowledge base.
- New Entities (E_{new}) refer to Wikidata entities from the dump on March 15, 2021, which are not present in E_{known}. These entities are added to Wikidata between 2018 and 2021 and unseen during training on the 2018 data, representing a zero-shot setting.

Alias Table. For both E_{known} and E_{new}, Hansel constructs an alias table by extracting information from Wikipedia dated March 1, 2021. And this table is generated by parsing Wikipedia's internal links, redirections, and page titles.

4.2 Experimental Settings

In the retrieve stage, we use rank-BM25[1] implementation of BM25 algorithm for the coarse-to-fine lexicon-based retriever. And the number of retrieved candidate entities for `AT-BM25`, `KB-BM25` and `Description-BM25` are all set 10.

In the rerank stage, our model is implemented using the Huggingface Library [15], with `bert-base-chinese` as backbone model for the BERT-based dual encoder. We use AdamW [9] to optimize the parameters of model. Due to the large amount of training data, the training epoch is set to 1 and the batch size is set 384. The learning rate is set $5e^{-5}$. And the max sequence length of mention and entity are both set 128. All experiments are conducted on Tesla V100 GPUs.

4.3 Main Results

The evaluation metric employed in is accuracy, and the evaluation results on test set are provided by the organizers. The main results in shown in Table 2, our approach achieves 1st place in NLPCC 2023 Shared Task 6 on Chinese Few-shot and Zero-shot Entity Linking.

It is evident from the results that our approach significantly outperforms the systems ranked second and third, with an accuracy advantage of 9.06% and 15.96%, respectively. This notable improvement can be attributed as follows:

- The proposed coarse-to-fine lexicon-based retriever can accurately retrieve candidate entities, which plays a crucial role in our overall approach and forms a solid foundation for subsequent processes.

---

[1] https://github.com/dorianbrown/rank_bm25.

Table 2. The results for NLPCC 2023 Shared Task 6.

System name	Accuracy
Ours	0.6915
ITNLP	0.6009
YNU-HPCC	0.5319

Table 3. The performance of three used lexicon-based retriever. The r@1, r@5 and r@10 represent the top-1 recall, top-5 recall and top-10 recall, respectively.

Retriever	r@1	r@5	r@10
AT-BM25	0.5232	0.8245	0.8626
KB-BM25	0.4846	0.6015	0.6614
Description-BM25	0.3891	0.6904	0.8341

- The utilization of a BERT-based dual encoder allows for effective reranking of candidate entities, thereby enhancing the final prediction result.
- Our proposed ensemble method effectively combines the information from both retrieve and rerank stages to disambiguate entities, which bridges the gap between training and few-shot or zero-shot test setting.

4.4 Performance of Retrieve Stage

In order to gain a deeper understanding of how our coarse-to-fine lexicon-based retriever improves few-shot and zero-shot entity linking, we present a comprehensive analysis of the retrieve stage's performance. Specifically, we retrieve 10 candidate entities for all BM-25 models and report the recall at the top-1, top-5, and top-10 levels on the test set.

The results are illustrated in Table 3. We can have the following observations: Firstly, the AT-BM25 model achieves the best performance across all metrics, indicating that the prior knowledge contained in the alias table significantly benefits the few-shot and zero-shot entity linking. We speculate that this improvement stems from the fact that newly created or tail mentions in the test set may share similar names with certain aliases.

Secondly, the KB-BM25 model exhibits the poorest performance. This observation aligns with our expectations since most mentions do not strictly match entity names in the knowledge base. However, the results obtained from the KB-BM25 model still contribute because mentions link accurately when they match entity names in the knowledge base.

Lastly, the Description-BM25 model does not exhibit significant disambiguation as expected. We attribute this to the limited maximum length of the context, which is imposed by computational resource constraints, thereby impacting the disambiguation of tail entities. Nonetheless, Description-BM25 model provides an alternative perspective by retrieving candidate entities based on descriptions, thus also enhancing the final prediction.

Table 4. The ablation study.

System name	Accuracy
Ours	0.6915
w/o Ensemble	0.6791
w/o AT-BM25	0.6713
w/o KB-BM25	0.6791
w/o Description-BM25	0.6769

4.5 Ablation Study

In order to validate the effectiveness of our proposed coarse-to-fine lexicon-based retriever, we conducted an ablation study by individually removing the ensemble method and the AT-BM25, KB-BM25, and Description-BM25.

The results are presented in Table 4. We can observe that when we remove the ensemble method, the accuracy drops 1.24%. This suggest that the ensemble method can aggregate useful information form both retrieve and rerank stages, which results in more robust prediction.

And it can be observed that upon removing AT-BM25, KB-BM25, and Description-BM25, the accuracy decreased by 2.02%, 1.24%, and 1.46%, respectively. This observation provides evidence that all the employed BM25 models in our coarse-to-fine lexicon-based retriever contribute positively to the task of few-shot and zero-shot entity linking. Furthermore, the combination of these models leads to the retrieval of more accurate candidate entities.

5   Conclusion

In this paper, we present a novel approach for improving few-shot and zero-shot entity linking through a coarse-to-fine lexicon-based retriever. Our proposed method adopts the widely-used "retrieve and rerank" framework, consisting of two stages: the coarse-to-fine lexicon-based retriever for retrieving candidate entities, and a BERT-based dual encoder for reranking the candidate entities. Moreover, we address the learning bias during the training phase of rerank stage by employing an ensemble method that combines information from both retrieve and rerank stages. The experimental results and analyses verify the effectiveness of our approach, which achieves the 1st ranking in the NLPCC 2023 Shared Task 6 on Chinese Few-shot and Zero-shot Entity Linking.

Acknowledgements. This research was supported in part by the National Natural Science Foundation of China(62006062, 62176076), the Guangdong Provincial Key Laboratory of Novel Security Intelligence Technologies(2022B1212010005), Natural Science Foundation of Guangdong(2023A1515012922), and Key Technologies Research and Development Program of Shenzhen JSGG20210802154400001.

References

1. Botha, J.A., Shan, Z., Gillick, D.: Entity linking in 100 languages. In: Proceedings of the 2020 Conference on Empirical Methods in Natural Language Processing (EMNLP), pp. 7833–7845. Association for Computational Linguistics, Online (2020). https://doi.org/10.18653/v1/2020.emnlp-main.630. https://aclanthology.org/2020.emnlp-main.630

2. Devlin, J., Chang, M.W., Lee, K., Toutanova, K.: BERT: pre-training of deep bidirectional transformers for language understanding. In: Proceedings of the 2019 Conference of the North American Chapter of the Association for Computational Linguistics: Human Language Technologies, Minneapolis, Minnesota (Volume 1: Long and Short Papers), pp. 4171–4186. Association for Computational Linguistics (2019). https://doi.org/10.18653/v1/N19-1423. https://aclanthology.org/N19-1423

3. Fang, Z., Cao, Y., Li, Q., Zhang, D., Zhang, Z., Liu, Y.: Joint entity linking with deep reinforcement learning. In: The World Wide Web Conference, WWW 2019, pp. 438–447. Association for Computing Machinery, New York (2019). https://doi.org/10.1145/3308558.3313517

4. Févry, T., Baldini Soares, L., FitzGerald, N., Choi, E., Kwiatkowski, T.: Entities as experts: sparse memory access with entity supervision. In: Proceedings of the 2020 Conference on Empirical Methods in Natural Language Processing (EMNLP), pp. 4937–4951. Association for Computational Linguistics, Online (2020). https://doi.org/10.18653/v1/2020.emnlp-main.400. https://aclanthology.org/2020.emnlp-main.400

5. Hoffart, J., Altun, Y., Weikum, G.: Discovering emerging entities with ambiguous names. In: Proceedings of the 23rd International Conference on World Wide Web, WWW 2014, pp. 385–396. Association for Computing Machinery, New York (2014). https://doi.org/10.1145/2566486.2568003

6. Humeau, S., Shuster, K., Lachaux, M.A., Weston, J.: Poly-encoders: architectures and pre-training strategies for fast and accurate multi-sentence scoring. In: International Conference on Learning Representations (2020). https://openreview.net/forum?id=SkxgnnNFvH

7. Kolitsas, N., Ganea, O.E., Hofmann, T.: End-to-end neural entity linking. In: Proceedings of the 22nd Conference on Computational Natural Language Learning, Brussels, Belgium, pp. 519–529. Association for Computational Linguistics (2018). https://doi.org/10.18653/v1/K18-1050. https://aclanthology.org/K18-1050

8. Logeswaran, L., Chang, M.W., Lee, K., Toutanova, K., Devlin, J., Lee, H.: Zero-shot entity linking by reading entity descriptions. In: Proceedings of the 57th Annual Meeting of the Association for Computational Linguistics, Florence, Italy, pp. 3449–3460. Association for Computational Linguistics (2019). https://doi.org/10.18653/v1/P19-1335. https://aclanthology.org/P19-1335

9. Loshchilov, I., Hutter, F.: Decoupled weight decay regularization. In: International Conference on Learning Representations (2019). https://openreview.net/forum?id=Bkg6RiCqY7

10. Puduppully, R., Dong, L., Lapata, M.: Data-to-text generation with entity modeling. In: Proceedings of the 57th Annual Meeting of the Association for Computational Linguistics, Florence, Italy, pp. 2023–2035. Association for Computational Linguistics (2019). https://doi.org/10.18653/v1/P19-1195. https://aclanthology.org/P19-1195

11. Qin, L., Xu, X., Che, W., Zhang, Y., Liu, T.: Dynamic fusion network for multi-domain end-to-end task-oriented dialog. In: Proceedings of the 58th Annual Meeting of the Association for Computational Linguistics, pp. 6344–6354. Association for Computational Linguistics, Online (2020). https://doi.org/10.18653/v1/2020.acl-main.565. https://aclanthology.org/2020.acl-main.565

12. Robertson, S., Zaragoza, H.: The probabilistic relevance framework: BM25 and beyond. Found. Trends® Inf. Retrieval **3**(4), 333–389 (2009). https://doi.org/10.1561/1500000019

13. Shen, W., Wang, J., Han, J.: Entity linking with a knowledge base: issues, techniques, and solutions. IEEE Trans. Knowl. Data Eng. **27**(2), 443–460 (2015). https://doi.org/10.1109/TKDE.2014.2327028

14. Wiatrak, M., Arvaniti, E., Brayne, A., Vetterle, J., Sim, A.: Proxy-based zero-shot entity linking by effective candidate retrieval. In: Proceedings of the 13th International Workshop on Health Text Mining and Information Analysis (LOUHI), Abu Dhabi, United Arab Emirates (Hybrid), pp. 87–99. Association for Computational Linguistics (2022). https://aclanthology.org/2022.louhi-1.11

15. Wolf, T., et al.: Huggingface's transformers: state-of-the-art natural language processing (2020)

16. Wu, L., Petroni, F., Josifoski, M., Riedel, S., Zettlemoyer, L.: Scalable zero-shot entity linking with dense entity retrieval. In: Proceedings of the 2020 Conference on Empirical Methods in Natural Language Processing (EMNLP), pp. 6397–6407. Association for Computational Linguistics, Online (2020). https://doi.org/10.18653/v1/2020.emnlp-main.519. https://aclanthology.org/2020.emnlp-main.519

17. Xu, Z., Chen, Y., Shi, S., Hu, B.: Enhancing entity linking with contextualized entity embeddings. In: Lu, W., Huang, S., Hong, Y., Zhou, X. (eds.) NLPCC 2022. LNCS, vol. 13552, pp. 228–239. Springer, Cham (2022). https://doi.org/10.1007/978-3-031-17189-5_19

18. Xu, Z., Shan, Z., Li, Y., Hu, B., Qin, B.: Hansel: a Chinese few-shot and zero-shot entity linking benchmark, pp. 832–840. Association for Computing Machinery, New York (2023). https://doi.org/10.1145/3539597.3570418

19. Yamada, I., Shindo, H., Takeda, H., Takefuji, Y.: Joint learning of the embedding of words and entities for named entity disambiguation. In: Proceedings of the 20th SIGNLL Conference on Computational Natural Language Learning, Berlin, Germany, pp. 250–259. Association for Computational Linguistics (2016). https://doi.org/10.18653/v1/K16-1025. https://aclanthology.org/K16-1025

20. Zhang, C., et al.: Feature engineering for knowledge base construction. IEEE Data Eng. Bull. (2014)

Overview of NLPCC 2023 Shared Task 6: Chinese Few-Shot and Zero-Shot Entity Linking

Zhenran Xu[1], Zifei Shan[2], Baotian Hu[1(✉)], and Min Zhang[1]

[1] Harbin Institute of Technology, Shenzhen, China
xuzhenran@stu.hit.edu.cn, {hubaotian,zhangmin2021}@hit.edu.cn
[2] Tencent, Shenzhen, China
zifeishan@tencent.com

Abstract. Entity Linking (EL) is the task of grounding a textual mention in context to a corresponding entity in a knowledge base. However, current EL systems demonstrate a popularity bias, significantly underperforming on tail and emerging entities. To this end, we organize NLPCC 2023 Shared Task 6, i.e., Chinese Few-shot and Zero-shot Entity Linking, which aims at testing the generalization ability of Chinese EL systems to less popular and newly emerging entities. The dataset for this task is a human-calibrated and multi-domain Chinese EL benchmark with Wikidata as KB, consisting of few-shot and zero-shot test sets. There are 22 registered teams and 13 submissions in total, and the highest accuracy is 0.6915. The submitted approaches focus on different aspects of this problem and use diverse techniques to boost the performance. All relevant information can be found at https://github.com/HITsz-TMG/Hansel/tree/main/NLPCC.

Keywords: Entity Linking · Few-shot Learning · Zero-shot Learning

1 Introduction

Entity Linking (EL) is the task of grounding a textual mention in context to a corresponding entity in a Knowledge Base (KB). It is a fundamental component for many downstream applications, such as Question Answering [3,5,6], KB Completion [10,13] and Dialogue [2].

An unresolved challenge in EL is to accurately link against emerging and less popular entities. The **Zero-Shot Entity Linking** problem was presented by Logeswaran et al. [8], aiming at linking mentions to entities unseen during training. In our continuously evolving world, new entities (such as "2022 Winter Olympics" in Fig. 1) emerge, so the generalization ability to emerging entities is essential for the evaluation of EL systems. On the other hand, Chen et al. [1] raised a common popularity bias in EL, i.e. EL systems significantly underperform on tail entities that share names with popular entities. Figure 2 shows

F. Liu et al. (Eds.): NLPCC 2023, LNAI 14304, pp. 257–265, 2023.
https://doi.org/10.1007/978-3-031-44699-3_23

Entities in training set from 2018-08-13 dump

Test example corresponding to emerging entities

Fig. 1. Zero-shot setting. Models are trained with a previous Wikipedia dump, and tested on newly emerging entities.

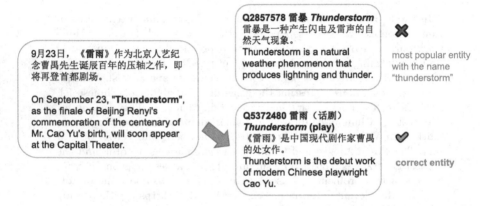

Fig. 2. Few-shot setting. The correct entity is not the most popular by the mention.

an example. Current state-of-the-art EL systems (e.g., mGENRE [4]) tend to choose the most popular entity that shares the same mention text. Intuitively, we name the challenge to resolve tail entities as **Few-Shot Entity Linking**, as most of them have only a few number of training examples. Despite the aforementioned studies, non-English resources for zero-shot and few-shot EL are seldom available, hindering progress for these challenges across languages.

To prompt the research in Chinese EL, we organize the **Chinese Few-shot and Zero-shot Entity Linking** task and provide a human-calibrated and challenging EL dataset, i.e., Hansel. Hansel consists of few-shot and zero-shot test sets, with a Wikipedia-based training set. The few-shot slice is collected from a multi-stage matching and annotation process. A core property of this slice is that all mentions are ambiguous and "hard" [11], where the ground-truth entity is not the most popular by the mention. The zero-shot slice is collected from a searching-based process. Given a new entity's description, annotators find corresponding mentions and adversarial examples with web search engines over

Table 1. Statistics of the Hansel dataset. We break down the number of distinct entities by whether the entity is in E_{new}.

	# Mentions	# Documents	# Entities		
			E_{known}	E_{new}	Total
Train	9.88M	1.05M	541K	–	541K
Validation	9,674	1,000	6,320	–	6,320
Hansel-FS	4,000	3,986	3,375	–	3,375
Hansel-ZS	4,000	3,998	968	2,880	3,848

diverse domains. To the best of our knowledge, Hansel is the first non-English EL dataset focusing on emerging and tail entities.

In total, we receive 22 team registrations and 13 submissions. We use accuracy as the evaluation metric, and top-3 teams achieved 0.6915, 0.6009, and 0.5319 separately. The best performing team solves the proposed task by striking a balance among sparse and dense retrieval methods, suggesting that future work may explore the combination of lexical and semantic similarity.

2   Dataset

A set of **entities** E in Knowledge Base (KB) is provided. We assume that each entity has a name and a description. Given an input text document $D = \{s_1, \ldots, s_d\}$ and a list of **mentions** with spans: $M_D = \{m_1, \ldots, m_n\}$, the task of **Entity Linking (EL)** is to output mention-entity pairs: $\{(m_i, e_i)\}_{i \in [1,n]}$, where each corresponding entity e_i is an entry in KB.

We publish an EL dataset for simplified Chinese (zh-hans), named Hansel. The training set is processed from Wikipedia. The test set contains Few-Shot (FS) and Zero-Shot (ZS) slices, focusing respectively on tail entities and emerging entities. Both test sets contain mentions from diverse documents, with the ground truth entity ID annotated. Dataset statistics are shown in Table 1.

2.1   Knowledge Base

To reflect temporal evolution of the knowledge base, we split Wikidata entities into **Known** and **New** sets using two historical dumps:

Known Entities (E_{known}) refer to Wikidata entities in 2018–08–13 dump. All our models are trained with E_{known} as KB.

New Entities (E_{new}) refer to Wikidata entities in 2021–03–15 dump that do not exist in E_{known}. Intuitively, entities in E_{new} were newly added to Wikidata between 2018 and 2021 thus never seen when training on 2018 data, thus considered as a zero-shot setting.

Entity Filtering. We filter Wikidata entities to get a clean KB: we remove all instances of disambiguation pages, templates, categories, modules, list pages,

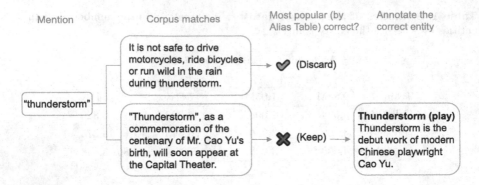

Fig. 3. Annotation process for the Few-Shot dataset, with a translated example in Hansel-FS. We first match aliases against the corpora to generate potential mentions, then judge whether the most popular entity (AT@1) is the correct entity. We only keep cases where AT@1 is incorrect, and then annotate the correct entity.

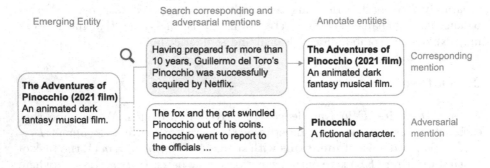

Fig. 4. Annotation process for the Zero-Shot dataset, with a translated example in Hansel-ZS. Given a new entity, we search on the Web for a corresponding mention, and a few mentions that share the same mention text but refer to different entities.

project pages, Wikidata properties, as well as their subclasses. For the scope of our work, we further constrain to entities with Chinese Wikipedia pages. After filtering, there are roughly 1M entities in E_{known} and 57K entities in E_{new}.

Alias Table. An alias table defines the prior probability of a text mention m linking to an entity e, i.e. $P(e|m)$, estimated as follows:

$$P(e|m) = \frac{count(m, e)}{count(m)}, \tag{1}$$

where $count(m)$ denotes the number of anchor texts with the surface form m in Wikipedia; $count(m, e)$ denotes the number of anchor texts with the surface form m pointing to the entity e. We extract an alias table *AT-base* from Wikipedia 2021–03–01 by parsing Wikipedia internal links, redirections and page titles.

2.2 Few-Shot Evaluation Slice

For the Few-Shot (FS) test set, we collect human annotations in three Chinese corpora: LCSTS [7], covering short microblogging texts, SohuNews and TenSite-News [12], covering long news articles.

Matching. The FS slice is collected based on a matching-based process as illustrated in Fig. 3. We first use *AT-base* to match against the corpora to generate potential mentions, then randomly sample for human annotation. Note that we only match ambiguous mentions with at least two entity candidates in E_{known}, and keep limited examples per mention word for better diversity.

Annotation. Human annotation was performed on more than 15K examples with 15 annotators. For each example, annotators first modify the incorrect mention boundary, or remove the example if it is not an entity mention. Then, they select the referred entity from candidate entities given by *AT-base*. For each candidate, annotators have access to its description (first paragraph in Wikipedia) and Wikipedia link. If the candidate with the highest prior (AT@1) is correct, then the example is discarded. 75% of examples are dropped in this step. If none of the candidates are correct, the annotator find the correct Wikipedia page for the entity through search engines.

There are 3,000 examples in Hansel-FS after quality control, and Fig. 2 shows an example. In order to prevent shortcuts that could unfairly enhance the performance on Hansel-FS (e.g., simply choosing the candidate with the second highest prior), we add 1,000 adversarial examples where AT@1 is the correct entity. Therefore, as Table 1 shows, the FS slice has 4,000 mentions from 3,986 documents, covering 3,375 diverse entities. Domains are news (51.3%) and social media (48.7%).

2.3 Zero-Shot Evaluation Slice

Collecting a Zero-Shot (ZS) slice is challenging, due to the difficulty to find occurrences of new entities on a fixed text corpus, especially when the corpus has no hyperlink structure. To address this challenge, we design a data collection scheme by searching entity mentions across the Web given an entity description.

Searching-Based Annotation. The process is shown in Fig. 4 with an annotation example. Given the title, description and aliases of an entity in E_{new}, annotators search the Internet[1] for a corresponding mention and collect the mention context. They further seek 1 or 2 adversarial examples by searching for a same or similar mention referring to a different entity. Such ambiguous mentions introduce more diversity on this dataset. Figure 2 shows another example and its adversarial mention in the ZS slice.

As Table 1 shows, the ZS slice has 4,000 mentions from 3,998 documents, covering 3,848 diverse entities. Domains are news (38.9%), social media (15.8%), and other articles such as E-books and commerce (45.3%) for ZS slice.

---

[1] To facilitate searching, we provide annotators with pre-filled search query templates in an annotation tool, such as Google queries with entity names and target domains.

Table 2. An example and its adversarial mention collected by annotators in Hansel-ZS. The mentions are wrapped with [E1] and [/E1].

Mention 1	2019 年 [E1] 上海大师赛 [/E1] 举行了男单正赛的抽签仪式。今年进入网球名人堂的李娜与获得男单正赛外卡的张之臻 …
Translation	The draw of men's singles competition was held in 2019 **[E1] Shanghai Masters [/E1]**. Na Li, who entered the Tennis Hall of Fame …
Entity 1	2019年上海大师赛^{Q69355546}：2019年上海大师赛为第12届上海大师赛，是ATP世界巡回赛1000大师赛事的其中一站 …
Translation	2019 Shanghai Masters^{Q69355546}: The 2019 Shanghai Masters was the 12th edition of the Shanghai ATP Masters 1000 …
Mention 2	#2020斯诺克世锦赛# 交手记录 … 2019年 [E1] 上海大师赛 [/E1] 半决赛：奥沙利文10-6威尔逊 …
Translation	#2020 World Snooker Championship# Match Record … 2019 **[E1] Shanghai Masters [/E1]** Semi-final: O'Sullivan 10–6 Wilson …
Entity 2	2019年斯诺克上海大师赛^{Q66436641}：2019年世界斯诺克·上海大师赛属于2019年9月9日－15日在上海富豪环球东亚酒店举行 …
Translation	2019 Shanghai Snooker Masters^{Q66436641}: The 2019 World Snooker Shanghai Masters took place at the Regal International …
Analysis	During data collection, Entity 1 (entity in E_{new}) was provided. The annotator found Mention 1 via Web search, as well as an adversarial Mention 2 with the same phrase ("Shanghai Masters"), referring to a tennis tournament and a snooker tournament respectively

3   Evaluation Results

In total, 22 teams registered for this shared task and we received 13 submissions. Other than the final submission, we also provided 4 additional submission opportunities and released the test results to help the participated teams improve their system. In the result submission phase, participants are **not** given whether the example is from the zero-shot slice or the few-shot slice. We adopt the accuracy on the test set (i.e., a total of 8K examples in Hansel-FS and Hansel-ZS) as the evaluation metric.

3.1   Evaluation Systems

The submitted approaches focus on different aspects of this shared task and use diverse techniques to boost the performance. Here we briefly introduce the solutions of top-3 teams.

– *Oops!*: The team proposes a coarse-to-fine lexicon-based retriever to retrieve entity candidates in two layers. The first layer retrieves coarse-grained candidates by leveraging entity names, while the second layer narrows down the search to fine-grained candidates within the coarse-grained ones. This second layer utilizes entity descriptions to effectively disambiguate tail or new entities that share names with existing popular entities.

- *ITNLP*: The team applies a "retrieve-and-rerank" two-stage approach to tackle the entity linking problem. The first stage uses an alias table to retrieve candidates based on mention texts. The second stage uses a cross-encoder based on ERNIE [14] to re-rank candidates, leveraging fine-grained mention-entity interaction.
- *YNU-HPCC*: The team uses Elastic Search to retrieve candidates, and then encodes mention contexts and entity descriptions with Sentence-BERT [9]. The final prediction is based on the similarity of sentence embeddings.

3.2 Submission Results

In Table 3, we present the test results of the entity linking systems in Sect. 3.1. From the results on Hansel-ZS, all systems show strong transferability on emerging entities, indicating the zero-shot capability of two-stage "retrieve-and-rerank" methods. Comparing the overall results of FS (i.e., tail entities) and FS-adv (i.e., head entities), we observe that the tail entities are harder to disambiguate than the head ones. The team *Oops!* strikes a balance between head and tail entities, thus achieving the 1st place in the shared task. We hypothesize that the retrieval stage in *Oops!* is critical for its state-of-the-art performance, as its retrieval stage ensembles entities from alias table, sparse and dense retrievers.

Table 3. Results on the Hansel dataset. We break down the results on the few-shot slice, the zero-shot slice and the adversarial examples.

	Hansel-FS		Hansel-ZS		Overall
	FS	FS-adv	ZS	ZS-adv	
Oops!	**0.4457**	**0.9170**	0.8163	**0.8290**	**0.6915**
ITNLP	0.3070	0.6960	**0.8173**	0.7380	0.6009
YNU-HPCC	0.2107	0.7090	0.7357	0.7070	0.5319

4 Conclusion

In this paper, we present a comprehensive overview of the NLPCC 2023 Shared Task 6: Chinese Few-shot and Zero-shot Entity Linking. Current entity linking (EL) systems demonstrate a popularity bias, significantly underperforming on tail and emerging entities. In this shared task, we propose the first Chinese few-shot and zero-shot EL benchmark, which aims at testing the generalization ability of Chinese EL systems to less popular and newly emerging entities. We received 13 submissions from 22 registered teams. The best performing team solves the proposed task by striking a balance among sparse and dense retrieval methods, suggesting that future work may explore the combination of lexical and semantic similarity. There is still large room for system improvement on this task, and we call for more EL research on less popular entities.

Acknowledgement. This work is jointly supported by grants: This work is jointly supported by grants: Natural Science Foundation of China (No. 62006061 and 82171475), Strategic Emerging Industry Development Special Funds of Shenzhen (No.JCYJ20200109113403826).

References

1. Chen, A., Gudipati, P., Longpre, S., Ling, X., Singh, S.: Evaluating entity disambiguation and the role of popularity in retrieval-based NLP. In: Proceedings of the 59th Annual Meeting of the Association for Computational Linguistics and the 11th International Joint Conference on Natural Language Processing (Volume 1: Long Papers), pp. 4472–4485. Association for Computational Linguistics (2021). https://doi.org/10.18653/v1/2021.acl-long.345, https://aclanthology.org/2021.acl-long.345
2. Curry, A.C., et al.: Alana v2: entertaining and informative open-domain social dialogue using ontologies and entity linking. Alexa Prize Proceedings (2018)
3. De Cao, N., Aziz, W., Titov, I.: Question answering by reasoning across documents with graph convolutional networks. In: Proceedings of the 2019 Conference of the North American Chapter of the Association for Computational Linguistics: Human Language Technologies, Volume 1 (Long and Short Papers), pp. 2306–2317. Association for Computational Linguistics, Minneapolis, Minnesota (2019)
4. De Cao, N., et al.: Multilingual autoregressive entity linking. Trans. Assoc. Comput. Linguist. **10**, 274–290 (2022)
5. Févry, T., Baldini Soares, L., FitzGerald, N., Choi, E., Kwiatkowski, T.: Entities as experts: sparse memory access with entity supervision. In: Proceedings of the 2020 Conference on Empirical Methods in Natural Language Processing (EMNLP), pp. 4937–4951. Association for Computational Linguistics (2020). https://doi.org/10.18653/v1/2020.emnlp-main.400, https://www.aclweb.org/anthology/2020.emnlp-main.400
6. Guu, K., Lee, K., Tung, Z., Pasupat, P., Chang, M.W.: REALM: retrieval-augmented language model pre-training. In: Proceedings of the 37th International Conference on Machine Learning. PMLR, Vienna, Austria (2020). https://proceedings.icml.cc/static/paper_files/icml/2020/3102-Paper.pdf
7. Hu, B., Chen, Q., Zhu, F.: LCSTS: a large scale Chinese short text summarization dataset. In: Proceedings of the 2015 Conference on Empirical Methods in Natural Language Processing, pp. 1967–1972. Association for Computational Linguistics, Lisbon, Portugal (2015). https://doi.org/10.18653/v1/D15-1229, https://www.aclweb.org/anthology/D15-1229
8. Logeswaran, L., Chang, M.W., Lee, K., Toutanova, K., Devlin, J., Lee, H.: Zero-shot entity linking by reading entity descriptions. In: Proceedings of the 57th Annual Meeting of the Association for Computational Linguistics, pp. 3449–3460. Association for Computational Linguistics, Florence, Italy (2019). https://doi.org/10.18653/v1/P19-1335, https://www.aclweb.org/anthology/P19-1335
9. Reimers, N., Gurevych, I.: Sentence-BERT: sentence embeddings using Siamese BERT-networks. In: Proceedings of the 2019 Conference on Empirical Methods in Natural Language Processing and the 9th International Joint Conference on Natural Language Processing (EMNLP-IJCNLP), pp. 3982–3992. Association for Computational Linguistics, Hong Kong, China (2019). https://doi.org/10.18653/v1/D19-1410, https://aclanthology.org/D19-1410

10. Shen, W., Wang, J., Han, J.: Entity linking with a knowledge base: issues, techniques, and solutions. IEEE Trans. Knowl. Data Eng. **27**(2), 443–460 (2014)
11. Tsai, C.T., Roth, D.: Cross-lingual wikification using multilingual embeddings. In: Proceedings of the 2016 Conference of the North American Chapter of the Association for Computational Linguistics: Human Language Technologies, pp. 589–598. Association for Computational Linguistics, San Diego, California (2016). https://doi.org/10.18653/v1/N16-1072, https://www.aclweb.org/anthology/N16-1072
12. Wang, C., Zhang, M., Ma, S., Ru, L.: Automatic online news issue construction in web environment. In: Proceedings of the 17th International Conference on World Wide Web, pp. 457–466 (2008)
13. Zhang, C., Ré, C., Sadeghian, A., Shan, Z., Shin, J., Wang, F., Wu, S.: Feature engineering for knowledge base construction. IEEE Data Eng. Bull. (2014). http://arxiv.org/1407.6439arxiv.org/abs/1407.6439
14. Zhang, Z., Han, X., Liu, Z., Jiang, X., Sun, M., Liu, Q.: ERNIE: enhanced language representation with informative entities. In: Proceedings of the 57th Annual Meeting of the Association for Computational Linguistics, pp. 1441–1451. Association for Computational Linguistics, Florence, Italy (2019)

Evaluation Workshop: Chinese Essay Discourse Coherence Evaluation

Two-Stage Topic Sentence Extraction for Chinese Student Essays

Yuwu Dong[1,2], Feiran Zheng[1,2], Hongyu Chen[1,2], Yizhou Ding[1,2],
Yifan Zhou[1,2], and Hao He[1,2(✉)]

[1] MoE Key Lab of Artificial Intelligence, AI Institute, Shanghai Jiao Tong
University, Shanghai, China
{dongyuwu,zfrzfrnzbnzb,hongyuchen,dingyizhou,
y.f.zhou10132,hehao}@sjtu.edu.cn
[2] State Key Lab of Advanced Optical Communication System and Network,
Shanghai Jiao Tong University, Shanghai, China

Abstract. In this paper, we present the method proposed by our team
for Track 2 of NLPCC 2023 Shared Task 7, which focuses on the extraction of paragraph-level and whole essay topic sentences in middle school
student essays. This paper proposes a two-stage topic sentence extraction framework for each paragraph and the whole essay. In the first stage,
we extract topic sentences for each paragraph, considering local semantic and contextual aspects. In the second stage, we derive the text topic
sentence for the whole essay from the extracted paragraph-level topic
sentences. Compared with the one-stage method, the two-stage method
which can focus on the local semantic information of paragraphs related
to the task has advantages in paragraph and full-text topic sentence
extraction. Comparative experiments show that the extraction performance of the fine-tuned two-stage topic sentence extraction framework
surpasses the few-shot large language models (GPT-3.5 et al.). The final
comprehensive index also achieved the first-place result in this track.

Keywords: Topic sentences extraction · Information extraction ·
Automated essay evaluation

1 Introduction

Evaluation Chinese middle school student essays is a time-consuming and
resource-intensive task. Therefore, employing an automated essay scoring system
to assist in the evaluation process can significantly enhance efficiency. NLPCC
2023 Shared Task 7 presents a natural language understanding task focusing
on the logical structure and coherence of Chinese essays. Specifically, Track 2
aims to extract paragraph-level topic sentences for each paragraph and one topic
sentence from whole essays written by middle school students.

Inspired by [4,7,14] use of a multi-stage approach to NLP, this paper proposes a two-stage method for extracting topic sentences that target the local information within student essays and the concept of pseudo-paragraph for the text sequence elements which are semantically the same paragraph and do not contain the topic sentence. In the first stage, the topic sentences of all paragraphs are extracted. During this stage, the model focuses on the semantic and contextual aspects at the paragraph level, including the themes and arguments within each paragraph. In the second stage, the topic sentences for the entire essay are extracted from the text sequence of topic sentences derived from the paragraphs, facilitating the effortless acquisition of the whole essay's topic sentences. As the topic sentence extraction process in these two stages only involves the content of specific paragraphs or text sequence of sentences within the essay, we refer to it as a two-stage topic sentence extraction that targets the local information of the essays. Universal Information Extraction (UIE) model is employed as the text sequence extraction model in each stage.

The main contributions of our work in this paper are as follows:

1. **Proposal of a Two-Stage Topic Sentence Extraction Method:** We propose a feasible approach to extract topic sentences from student essays, introducing the concept of Two-Stage Topic Sentence Extraction. This approach allows us to specifically target the paragraph-level information within the essay's paragraphs and extract topic sentences accordingly.
2. **Analysis of Paragraphs and Topic Sentences in Student Essays:** We prove through data that there are a certain number of paragraphs that do not contain topic sentences and propose the concept of pseudo-paragraph. These confirmed results provide valuable guidance for designing suitable methods and strategies.
3. **Performance Analysis:** We evaluate the performance of our method on a Chinese essay dataset, including comparisons with the GPT [10,13] of LLMs. The results show that our method achieves effective outcomes and obtains the first-place result in Track 2.

2   Related Work

Extracting a specific sentence from a text sequence involves the task of information extraction (IE) in natural language processing (NLP). IE refers to the extraction of desired structured information from text, which is a subfield of NLP. Deep learning methods [2,3] often divide IE into multiple subtasks of different types and model each subtask using neural classifiers, such as Named Entity Recognition (NER), Relation Extraction (RE), Event Extraction (EE), and others.

Currently, the most effective method for NER is fine-tuning a pre-trained language model like BERT [5] based on specific tasks to achieve accurate extraction. RE can be categorized into two different modes including the traditional pipeline approach [20] and the end-to-end approach [9,17,19]. For EE, the most effective method also utilizes BERT and often involves joint training with other tasks such as NER and RE [6,16,18]. Lu proposed the UIE model adopted a unified structure generation approach to model various IE tasks using structured extraction language and leverages the capability of remote text structure supervision for pre-training structure generation [8].

To extract the sentences from the text sequence, Pujari proposed a two-stage framework for extracting sentences with opinions from a given news article [11]. It utilized the naive Bayes classifier to assign scores in the first stage and used prior probability to sort to obtain sentences with opinions. Similarly, Deng proposed a new two-stage automatic text summarization that is based on keyword sentence screening in the first stage and based on sentence summarization in the second stage [4].

In the case of sentence extraction from a text segment, the NER task can be utilized by replacing the named entities with the desired text sequence. We utilized the NER extraction task and two-stage method to extract paragraph topic sentences and full-text topic sentences.

3 Task Definition and Approach

3.1 Task Definition

In the process of Chinese middle school student essay scoring, the extraction of essay topic sentences is indispensable. Track 2 of NLPCC 2023 Shared Task 7 focuses on extracting paragraph-level and full-text-level topic sentences from each essay. Every essay contains topic sentences which are primarily manifested in two aspects: 1) Each paragraph of the essay has a topic sentence that reflects the central idea of the paragraph; 2) The essay as a whole also has a topic sentence that reflects the central idea of the essay. Track 2 transforms the evaluation process of the essay's topic sentences into an IE task in NLP, aiming to extract both paragraph-level and full-text-level topic sentences from the essay.

The dataset used in this paper is jointly constructed by East China Normal University and Microsoft. It consists of Chinese essays written by middle school students, and the topic sentences have been annotated by annotators. The annotations include the topic sentences of each paragraph and the topic sentence of the whole essay.

3.2 Approach

The topic sentence extraction model mainly used in this paper is the UIE model [8] proposed by Lu et al. In this chapter, the UIE model and its principle are mainly introduced. In addition, the most important methods used in our experiments will be introduced in this chapter.

UIE Principle. The UIE model [8] is a unified framework for a text-to-structure generation that can model four different IE tasks. It decomposes the transformation from text to structured format into two atomic operations: Spotting and Associating. Spotting involves determining the positions of desirable spans while associating specifies the semantic roles between different spans. The UIE model's spotting abilities are primarily utilized in this paper, and the associating mechanism is not utilized as it doesn't require specifying semantic roles between different spans.

Regarding the output of the UIE model, it employs a structural extraction language (SEL). SEL includes *Spot Name* and *Asso Name* for each structure, where *Spot Name* represents the key information segments to be extracted, and *Asso Name* represents the information segments associated with the upper-level *Spot Name*.

For the input of the UIE model, the authors propose a structural schema instructor (SSI) to specify the desired output structure. SSI utilizes the prompt mechanism to control which types of information should be spotted and associated. The tokens form the structural schema instructor represented by s. Assuming the text sequence to be extracted is represented by x, the entire UIE model's input and output are expressed by the formula $y = UIE(s \oplus x)$. Here, y represents the structured extraction language sequence, which corresponds to the final IE results with *Spot Name* and *Asso Name*.

Regarding the structure of the UIE model, it utilizes the encoder and decoder of the transformer [15]. As shown in Eq. 1 and Eq. 2, the structural schema instructor s and the text sequence to be extracted x are input to the transformer encoder. The encoder outputs hidden layer information H. In addition to including the hidden layer information H from the encoder, the transformer encoder input also includes the decoder state h_i^d previously output by the decoder.

$$H = Encoder(s_1, ..., s_{|s|}, x_1, ..., x_{|x|}) \tag{1}$$

$$y_i, h_i^d = Decoder([H; h_1^d, ..., h_{i-1}^d]) \tag{2}$$

The resulting sequence y_i is the SEL expression representing the information extraction output.

Sentence Extraction Methods. The most crucial aspect of this paper is the use of the UIE model structure as the primary IE model for extracting topic sentences from Chinese essays written by middle school students. The schema is designed for *paragraph topic sentences* and *full-text topic sentences*. The paper conducted multiple experiments using the UIE model, including both one-stage and two-stage methods (see Fig. 1).

One-Stage Method and the Use of UIE. In the one-stage method, a schema with two spot names, *paragraph topic sentences* and *full-text topic sentence*, is designed, without including an asso name. This method involves placing *paragraph topic sentences* and *full-text topic sentences* in the same schema structure and fine-tuning the UIE model with the text sequence to be extracted. In other words, a single UIE model is trained using a schema that includes both *paragraph topic sentences* and *full-text topic sentence* spot names to directly extract

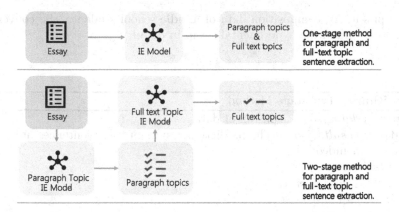

Fig. 1. The schematic diagrams of the one-stage method topic sentence extraction and two-stage method topic sentence extraction.

topic sentences from the entire essay. The extraction results include several paragraph topic sentences and one overall text topic sentence. Therefore, the entire process requires training only one UIE model to perform the extraction of both paragraph and overall text topic sentences.

Two-Stage Method and the Use of UIE. In the two-stage method, unlike the one-stage method, two UIE models with the same structure but different weight parameters are used. In other words, the two-stage method involves designing separate schemas for *paragraph topic sentences* and *full-text topic sentences*. Therefore, two UIE models with the same structure but different weight parameters are employed. There are two steps involved in this method: 1) extracting topic sentences of different paragraphs and 2) extracting topic sentences of the full text. The first step involves extracting topic sentences for each paragraph of the Chinese essay. This step uses a schema with the spot name *paragraph topic sentences*. Thus, if the Chinese essay has N paragraphs, ideally, N paragraph topic sentences will be extracted. According to the official documentation and our observed statistical analysis (details will be provided in the 4 section), the overall text topic sentence can be generated from the paragraph topic sentences. In other words, the overall text topic sentence is derived from the topic sentences of each paragraph in the essay. Therefore, the second step is to design a schema with the spot name *full-text topic sentence*. The text sequence to be extracted is the result of the successful extraction of paragraph topic sentences from the first step. Refer to Algorithm 1 for more details of the two-stage method for extracting topic sentences.

4   Experiments

This chapter mainly introduces the definition of model evaluation indicators related to the experiment, the analysis and statistics of characters and paragraph topics in the composition data of middle school students, the conversion of data format, and the experimental setup in detail.

Algorithm 1: Two-stage Method

Input : $data\_json$ - Jsons all of data
Output: $results\_json$ - The prediction results of topic sentences are included

1   $results\_json \leftarrow [];$
2   **for** $data \in data\_json$ **do**
3   **if** $length(data['Text']) = 0$ **then**
4   **continue;**
5   **end**
6     $paragraph\_topics \leftarrow [];$
7     $res\_paras \leftarrow para\_model(data['Text']);$
8   **for** $res \in res\_paras$ **do**
9   **if** $'ParagraphTopic'$ **in** res **and** $length(res['ParagraphTopic'])$ >0 **then**
10   append $res['ParagraphTopic'][0]['text']$ to $paragraph\_topics$
11   **end**
12   **end**
13   **if** $length(paragraph\_topics) = 0$ **then**
14       $res\_fulltext \leftarrow$ $fulltext\_model(\text{join\_with\_separator}(data['Text'],'\#\#\#'));$
15   **end**
16   **else**
17       $res\_fulltexts \leftarrow$ $fulltext\_model(\text{join\_with\_separator}(paragraph\_topics,'\#\#\#'));$
18   **end**
19     $Full\_textTopic \leftarrow None;$
20     $res \leftarrow res\_fulltexts[0]$
21   **if** $'FulltextTopic'$ **in** res **and** $length(res['FulltextTopic']) >0$ **then**
22   sort $res['FulltextTopic']$ by descending order of $'probability'$
23       $Full\_textTopic \leftarrow res['FulltextTopic'][0]['text'];$
24   **end**
25   **if** $Full\_textTopic = None$ **and** $length(paragraph\_topics) >0$ **then**
26       $Full\_textTopic \leftarrow paragraph\_topics[-1];$
27   **end**
28     $result \leftarrow \{'ID' : data['Id'],' ParagraphTopic' : paragraph\_topics,' Full-textTopic' : Full\_textTopic\}$ append $result$ to $results\_json$;
29   **end**
30   **return** $results\_json$

4.1   Evaluation Metrics

The evaluation of Chinese essay topic sentence extraction mainly focuses on several aspects. These include the accuracy, recall, precision, and F1 score of paragraph-level and full-text-level topic sentence extraction. The accuracy of paragraph-level topic sentence extraction (ParaAcc) is defined as the number of correctly extracted paragraph-level topic sentences as shown in Eq. 3, denoted as $P_{correct}$, divided by the total number of labeled paragraph-level topic sentences, denoted as P_{label}. From the perspective of recall, the accuracy of paragraph-level topic sentence extraction is also equivalent to its recall (ParaRec). The precision of paragraph-level topic sentence extraction (ParaPre) is defined as the $P_{correct}$ divided by the total number of predicted paragraph-level topic sentences, denoted as P_{infer}, as shown in Eq. 5. As for its F1 score (ParaF1), it is defined as the harmonic mean of precision and recall as shown in Eq. 7. Similarly, the accuracy, recall, precision, and F1 score of full-text-level topic sentences follow the same principle as paragraph-level topic sentences, as shown in Eq. 4,6 and 8. The final accuracy (FinalAcc) combines the weighted sum of paragraph-level topic accuracy and full-text-level topic accuracy as shown in Eq. 9.

$$ParaRec = ParaAcc = \frac{P_{correct}}{P_{label}} \tag{3}$$

$$FullRec = FullAcc = \frac{F_{correct}}{F_{label}} \tag{4}$$

$$ParaPre = \frac{P_{correct}}{P_{infer}} \tag{5}$$

$$FullPre = \frac{F_{correct}}{F_{infer}} \tag{6}$$

$$ParaF_1 = \frac{2 \times ParaRecll \times ParaPre}{ParaRec + ParaPre} \tag{7}$$

$$FullF_1 = \frac{2 \times FullRecll \times FullPre}{FullRec + FullPre} \tag{8}$$

$$FinalAcc = 0.3 \times ParaAcc + 0.7 \times FullAcc \tag{9}$$

4.2   Data Analysis

The dataset for Track 2 focuses on the task of topic sentence extraction. The training and validation sets consist of 50 and 10 Chinese essays, respectively, with annotations for both paragraph-level and full-text-level topic sentences. We utilize this annotated dataset of 60 essays to train and evaluate our model, and subsequently test its performance on a test set containing 5,000 essays.

Each data instance in the dataset represents a complete essay that has been divided into paragraphs as shown in the raw data in 2. The content of the essay is represented by a list, where different elements of the list indicate paragraph divisions in the original text. However, these divisions do not necessarily indicate separate paragraphs. As shown in Fig. 3, although the three lines are different elements of the *Text* list, they actually represent the content of the same paragraph, which contains only one topic sentence. If there is an element in the *Text* list that is semantically a paragraph with other structurally adjacent elements but does not contain a text sequence of topic sentences, it is called a *pseudo-paragraphs*.

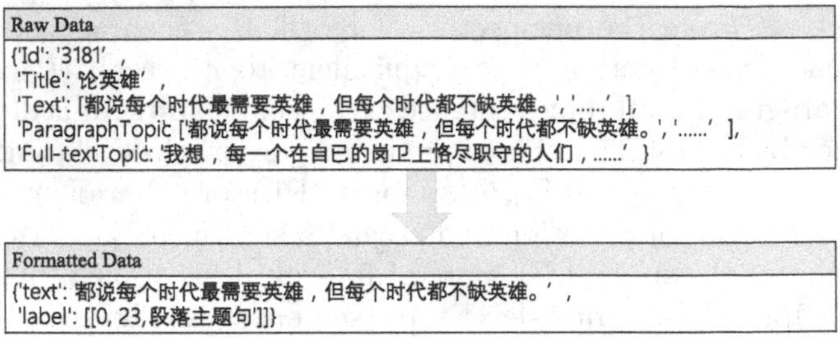

Fig. 2. Data format conversion at the paragraph-level.

Based on our statistical analysis, it was found that 8% of the data instances in the training set have a mismatch between the number of topic sentences and the number of annotated paragraphs provided in the data. According to the official information and data analysis, this discrepancy can be attributed to the following factors: 1) Some text sequences are different elements of the *Text* list but semantically belong to the same paragraph in the original text. These elements of the *Text* contain only one topic sentence, as shown in Fig. 3. This situation accounts for 2% of the training set. 2) As mentioned in the guideline, some paragraphs do not have an explicit topic sentence. As shown in the example in Fig. 4, this instance is an independent paragraph in the training set but lacks an annotated paragraph-level topic sentence. This scenario accounts for 6% of the training set. During model training and prediction, we handle these cases of pseudo-paragraphs without clear topic sentences or actual topic sentences by setting appropriate thresholds.

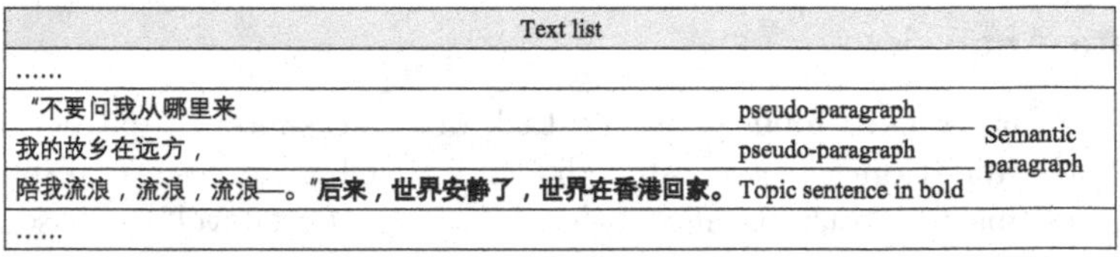

Fig. 3. An example of a semantic paragraph with a pseudo-paragraph.

Finally, based on our analysis of the 50 essays in the training set, we found that the token length distribution ranges from 600 to 1014, with an average

Text list
......
在路上，他还不停的问我："小姨你说那种蚂蚁会不会变成小精灵晚上帮我赶走那些坏人。""会的，会的。"他听了我的回答高兴的一蹦一跳。
......
银溪流云轻梳妆，微风岸，碧如簪，黑瓦白墙，烟雨红尘淡。流水含情自吟唱，思忆长，梦江南。
......

Fig. 4. An example of paragraphs with no explicit paragraph topic.

length of 713 tokens. The average number of paragraphs per essay is 6.76, assuming that different elements of the list represent semantically different paragraphs in the essay.

4.3 Data Format Conversion

We employ the UIE model for information extraction. To transform the original data structure into the desired structure for our model, as shown in Fig. 3, we convert the raw data into the format that includes the starting and ending indices of the labeled sequence, along with the corresponding label (Spot Name). This format is applied to both the training and validation sets. This conversion allows us to obtain the data format suitable for fine-tuning the model.

4.4 Experiment Settings

The training and validation sets of 60 data instances were combined and randomly split into training and validation sets in a 5:1 ratio. All subsequent experimental schemes were conducted using the new training and validation sets, including two sets of primary approaches along with some experiments using GPT language models as controls.

For the one-stage approach, the first step involved converting the format of the training and validation sets. During the format conversion process, the paragraphs of each article were connected using the ### token to create a single essay, enabling the model to perceive the global semantic information. Furthermore, the starting and ending indices of each topic sentence annotation were considered in relation to the entire essay. The model used was *uie-base*, with a learning rate of 1e−5, batch size of 16, and training epochs set to 100. The model with the highest F1 score on the validation set in 100 epochs was selected as the optimal model.

Regarding the two-stage approach, all parameter configurations remained the same as in the one-stage approach. The key difference lies in the design of the two-stage approach, which utilizes two separate models to capture the relationship between paragraph topic sentences and full-text topic sentences. The training and prediction of the model in the stage of full-text topic sentence extraction are slightly different. 1) During training, the input content for the model extracting full-text topic sentences consists of the concatenation of labeled paragraph-level topic sentences, with the ### token used as the connector. 2) During model prediction, the full-text topic sentence extraction model utilizes the paragraph topic sentences predicted by the first-stage model. During model training and prediction, we deal with these pseudo-paragraphs without explicit topic sentences or actual topic sentences by setting an appropriate threshold.

Pre-trained LLMs such as the GPT family have made great achievements in the field of NLP [1,10,12]. For the experiments using GPT large language models, the GPT-3.5-turbo and GPT-4-0314 versions were selected[1]. For the GPT-3.5-turbo experiment, both zero-shot and three-shot prompts were used. The GPT-4-0314 experiment utilized a three-shot prompt. All three experiments with GPT models also employed the two-stage method, and the text sequence extracted from the full-text topic sentences in the second stage is the annotated data rather than the predicted data in the first stage in order to compare with the two-stage method implemented by UIE.

4.5   Results and Analysis

Table 1. Experimental results of different methods on the new validation set. The equality of Precision, Recall, and F1 metrics for the GPT series of large language models is due to the fact that the number of topic sentences predicted by the model and the number of topic sentences labeled are equal.

Method	Precision		Recall		F1	
	ParaPre	FullPre	ParaRec	FullRec	ParaF1	FullF1
One-stage(UIE)	64.93		63.29		64.10	
Two-stage(UIE)	**71.67**	54.55	**68.25**	60.00	**69.92**	57.14
Two-stage(GPT-3.5 0-shot)	1.59	0	1.59	0	1.59	0
Two-stage(GPT-3.5 3-shot)	31.75	30.00	31.75	30.00	31.75	30.00
Two-stage(GPT-4 3-shot)	38.10	30.00	38.10	30.00	38.10	30.00

Based on our experiments, the optimal models of our one-stage method and the optimal models of the two-stage method with different steps yield the results shown in Table 1 on the validation set. We observed that the first stage of the two-stage approach for paragraph topic extraction outperforms the one-stage method. Therefore, for the task of extracting topic sentences from paragraphs, the model trained specifically for paragraph extraction performs better than the model trained to extract paragraph topics from the entire document. Regarding the GPT series of large language models, we discovered that the performance in experiments related to GPT falls short of the effectiveness achieved by the two-stage method utilized by UIE.

---

[1] https://platform.openai.com/docs/api-reference/introduction.

Table 2. Our method ranked first on the final test set of 5000 instances, where * represents the test result of the other team's models or methods.

Model	ParaAcc	FullAcc	FinalAcc	ParaSimilarity	FullSimilarity
Model1*	**62.61**	33.33	42.12	85.20	79.16
Model2*	**62.61**	23.81	35.45	85.20	76.11
One-stage(Ours)	59.44	23.58	34.34	86.41	66.97
Two-stage(Ours)	61.27	**34.92**	**42.82**	**87.34**	**80.37**

Based on the predictions of our two models on a test dataset comprising 5000 instances, the predicted results were submitted to the official evaluation for scoring. The performance of our two proposed models, as well as two models from another team on the test dataset, is presented in Table 2. It can be observed that our two-stage approach for extracting full-text-level topic sentences outperforms the other models, resulting in the highest final accuracy score. Compared with the one-stage method, the two-stage method which can focus on the local semantic information of paragraphs related to the task has advantages in paragraph and full-text topic sentence extraction. Furthermore, in terms of paragraph-level topic sentence similarity and document-level topic sentence similarity, the predictions of our two-stage model also surpass those of the other models. Considering the overall rankings, our models achieved the highest scores and ranks first.

5   Conclusion

In this paper, we present a two-stage topic extraction approach by UIE that focuses on local information within paragraphs. The concept of pseudo-paragraph is proposed by this paper for the elements which are semantically the same paragraph and do not contain the topic sentence. Additionally, we conduct comparative experiments among the latest and most advanced GPT models that are prevalent in the current research community. Our approach which ultimately achieves the first position on the leaderboard with an advantage provides evidence of its effectiveness. However, there is some room for further improvement such as conducting threshold adjustment experiments in the pseudo-paragraph topic sentence determination and exploring the use of more sophisticated IE models during the two-stage process.

References

1. Bang, Y., et al.: A multitask, multilingual, multimodal evaluation of ChatGPT on reasoning, hallucination, and interactivity. arXiv preprint arXiv:2302.04023 (2023)
2. Bengio, Y., Ducharme, R., Vincent, P.: A neural probabilistic language model. In: Advances in Neural Information Processing Systems, vol. 13 (2000)
3. Collobert, R., Weston, J., Bottou, L., Karlen, M., Kavukcuoglu, K., Kuksa, P.: Natural language processing (almost) from scratch. J. Mach. Learn. Res. **12**(ARTICLE), 2493–2537 (2011)

4. Deng, Z., Ma, F., Lan, R., Huang, W., Luo, X.: A two-stage Chinese text summarization algorithm using keyword information and adversarial learning. Neurocomputing **425**, 117–126 (2021). https://doi.org/10.1016/j.neucom.2020.02.102
5. Devlin, J., Chang, M.W., Lee, K., Toutanova, K.: BERT: pre-training of deep bidirectional transformers for language understanding. arXiv preprint arXiv:1810.04805 (2018)
6. Lin, Y., Ji, H., Huang, F., Wu, L.: A joint neural model for information extraction with global features. In: Proceedings of the 58th Annual Meeting of the Association for Computational Linguistics, pp. 7999–8009 (2020)
7. Liu, J., Xu, Y., Zhao, L.: Automated essay scoring based on two-stage learning. ArXiv abs/1901.07744 (2019)
8. Lu, Y., et al.: Unified structure generation for universal information extraction. arXiv preprint arXiv:2203.12277 (2022)
9. Luan, Y., Wadden, D., He, L., Shah, A., Ostendorf, M., Hajishirzi, H.: A general framework for information extraction using dynamic span graphs. arXiv preprint arXiv:1904.03296 (2019)
10. Ouyang, L., et al.: Training language models to follow instructions with human feedback. In: Advances in Neural Information Processing Systems, vol. 35, pp. 27730–27744 (2022)
11. Pujari, R., Desai, S., Ganguly, N., Goyal, P.: A novel two-stage framework for extracting opinionated sentences from news articles. arXiv preprint arXiv:2101.09743 (2021)
12. Qin, C., Zhang, A., Zhang, Z., Chen, J., Yasunaga, M., Yang, D.: Is ChatGPT a general-purpose natural language processing task solver? arXiv preprint arXiv:2302.06476 (2023)
13. Radford, A., Narasimhan, K., Salimans, T., Sutskever, I.: Improving language understanding by generative pre-training (2018)
14. Song, W., Zhang, K., Fu, R., Liu, L., Liu, T., Cheng, M.: Multi-stage pre-training for automated Chinese essay scoring. In: Conference on Empirical Methods in Natural Language Processing (2020)
15. Vaswani, A., et al.: Attention is all you need. In: Advances in Neural Information Processing Systems, vol. 30. Curran Associates, Inc. (2017)
16. Wadden, D., Wennberg, U., Luan, Y., Hajishirzi, H.: Entity, relation, and event extraction with contextualized span representations. arXiv preprint arXiv:1909.03546 (2019)
17. Zeng, X., Zeng, D., He, S., Liu, K., Zhao, J.: Extracting relational facts by an end-to-end neural model with copy mechanism. In: Proceedings of the 56th Annual Meeting of the Association for Computational Linguistics (Volume 1: Long Papers), pp. 506–514 (2018)
18. Zhang, T., Ji, H., Sil, A.: Joint entity and event extraction with generative adversarial imitation learning. Data Intell. **1**(2), 99–120 (2019)
19. Zheng, S., Wang, F., Bao, H., Hao, Y., Zhou, P., Xu, B.: Joint extraction of entities and relations based on a novel tagging scheme. arXiv preprint arXiv:1706.05075 (2017)
20. Zhong, Z., Chen, D.: A frustratingly easy approach for entity and relation extraction. arXiv preprint arXiv:2010.12812 (2020)

Multi-angle Prediction Based on Prompt Learning for Text Classification

Zhengyu Ju[1], Zhao Li[1,2(✉)], Shiwei Wu[3], Xiuhao Zhao[3], and Yiming Zhan[3]

[1] Qilu University of Technology (Shandong Academy of Sciences), Jinan, China
[2] Shandong Computer Science Center (National Supercomputer Center in Jinan),
Jinan, China
`liz@sdas.org`
[3] Evay Info, Jinan, China
`{wushw,zhanym}@sdas.org`

Abstract. The assessment of Chinese essays with respect to text coherence using deep learning has been relatively understudied due to the lack of large-scale, high-quality discourse coherence evaluation data resources. Existing research predominantly focuses on characters, words, and sentences, neglecting automatic evaluation of Chinese essays based on articles' coherence. This paper aims to research automatic evaluation of Chinese essays based on articles' coherence by leveraging some data from LEssay, a Chinese essay coherence evaluation dataset jointly constructed by the CubeNLP laboratory of East China Normal University and Microsoft. The coherence of Chinese essays is primarily evaluated based on two big aspects: 1. The smoothness of logic (the appropriateness of using related words, and the appropriateness of logical relationship between contexts) 2. The reasonableness of sentence breaks (how well punctuation is used and how well the sentence is structured). Therefore, in this paper, we adopt prompt learning and cleverly design a multi-angle prediction prompt template that can realize the assessment of the coherence of Chinese essay from four angles. During the inference stage, the prediction of the coherence of Chinese essays is obtained through the multi-angle prediction template and voting mechanism. Notably, the proposed method demonstrates excellent results in the NLPCC2023 Shared-Task7 Track1.

Keywords: Prompt learning · Multi-angle prediction · Voting mechanism

1 Introduction

The difficulty of automatic coherence evaluation for Chinese essays using artificial intelligence (AI) is marked by a dearth of extensive labeled data specifically dedicated to evaluating the coherence of Chinese essays. Consequently, there exists a notable research gap in the classification of the coherence degree of Chinese essays within the AI-based Chinese essay assessment techniques.

F. Liu et al. (Eds.): NLPCC 2023, LNAI 14304, pp. 281–291, 2023.
https://doi.org/10.1007/978-3-031-44699-3_25

With rapid rise of large language models (LLMs) such as T5 [13] and GPT-3 [1], etc. Researchers have found that pre-trained language models (PLMs) yield remarkable outcomes in various downstream tasks encompassing text classification, question answering, and knowledge graph. Through in-depth research, it has been discerned that since LLMs are trained with a large amount of data in the pre-training stage, they have acquired rich knowledge [3, 11].

For text classification problem, based on this finding, researchers have proposed the utilization of the fine-tuning approach to mine and make use of the knowledge of PLMs acquired in pre-training stage, wherein a classifier is appended to a PLM to enable the adaptation of the PLM to a downstream task. However, the effectiveness of fine-tuning in capturing the knowledge gained by PLMs during pre-training is limited in scenarios characterized by sparse training data, such as few-shot and zero-shot scenarios. Such limitations become particularly evident in real-world settings. For instance, when evaluating the coherence of Chinese essays, the practical challenge of the lack of discourse coherence evaluation resources has persistently hindered progress.

In light of the lack of massive labeled data, researchers have recently proposed the adoption of prompt learning to effectively mine and leverage the knowledge acquired during the pre-training phase of PLMs. Prompt learning has emerged as a promising approach in which the text classification problem can be converted into a cloze problem by using [MASK] token and prompt characters, when dealing with text classification task. The cloze problem format closely aligns with the pre-training task of PLMs, leading to enhanced stimulation of PLMs and obtaining the knowledge of PLMs acquired during pre-training better. The final prediction is achieved through the application of answer engineering which is another research content of prompt learning. For instance, in the case of predicting the coherence of an article, a prompt template is defined as follows: "<TEXT>这篇文章的连贯程度? <MASK>". Here, the <TEXT> placeholder is replaced by an article's text, resulting in a new input. It will be introduced into a PLM. Assuming the coherence category is labeled as "excellent coherence", the [MASK] token is most likely to be filled with words from the words set that represents "excellent coherence". The mapping from the words set representing categories to the corresponding classes is referred to as the verbalizer [6], serving as an effective mechanism to bridge the regression values of PLMs and the final prediction regression values which can identify which category the input belongs to directly.

In this paper, we aim to automate the classification of coherence of Chinese essays by leveraging prompt learning. A small amount of labeled data in LEssay is used in our study.

Merely employing the prompt template "<TEXT>这篇文章的连贯程度? <MASK>" and treating it as a conventional text classification problem fail to realize the particularity of assessing coherence of Chinese articles. Therefore, this simplistic approach is inadequate in achieving reliable coherence predictions.

The assessment of coherence of Chinese essays encompasses four crucial aspects: the use of related words, the logical relationship between contexts, the use of punctuation, and the sentence structure. Based on such particularity, in this paper, we will design a prompt template that can predict the coherence of Chinese articles from the four angles respectively. By doing so, we move beyond the simplistic notion of treating coherence assessment as a mere text classification task, and we can obtain more comprehensive knowledge from PLMs.

In scenarios characterized by limited annotated data, such as the few-shot scenario, updating the parameters of randomly initialized model components becomes challenging. However, we contend that the extensive knowledge acquired by PLMs during the pre-training stage is often sufficient to address downstream task, without the need to introduce additional parameters or randomly initialized model components to help PLM make predictions. In this paper, we propose the utilization of prompt learning to mine and leverage the knowledge of PLMs. The primary objective of our proposed method is to construct a prompt template that serves as the vital link between PLMs and downstream task and enables effective and comprehensive mining of PLM knowledge through this template construction better. The construction of the prompt template constitutes the focal point of prompt learning research. Meanwhile, our proposed method does not introduce supplementary model components. We design a multi-angle prediction prompt template carefully to realize the comprehensive acquisition and utilization of the knowledge acquired by PLMs in the pre-training stage well. Furthermore, we craft the training and inference modes of the model in a thoughtful manner to ensure accurate predictions in coherence classification for essays.

In this paper, the procedure of our proposed method can be outlined as follows: (1) Given that Chinese articles are basically long text, it is feasible to gain the coherence of essays by analyzing a portion of the text, each Chinese essay's text is sliced and evenly segmented into two parts, effectively leveraging the semantic information within the text and augmenting the amount of trainable supervised data to a certain extent. (2) A multi-angle prediction prompt template is devised specifically, capable of generating coherence prediction from each assessment angle. (3) During the model training stage, the prompt template is integrated with the original input sequence. The wrapped input sequence is then introduced to a PLM, utilizing a mapping mechanism to obtain multiple [MASK] regression values, The loss values between these multiple regression values and the ground truth are strictly calculated, and model optimization is achieved by minimizing the sum of these loss values. (4) In the inference stage, multiple [MASK] regression values are obtained using the same approach employed during training. Subsequently, a voting mechanism is employed to facilitate the prediction of article coherence.

This paper makes several key contributions, which can be summarized as follows:

- Making use of the special properties of Chinese text, slice the article into two equal length text, which alleviates the problem of less supervised data available for training to a certain extent.
- Conduct prompt engineering for prompt learning, involving the design of a prompt template tailored for multi-angle prediction to facilitate comprehensive coherence assessment of Chinese essays.

- Devise a rigorous training mechanism that ensures strict model optimization, coupled with the astute utilization of a voting mechanism to realize the inference of the coherence of Chinese essays.
- In NLPCC2023 SharedTask7 Track1, the proposed method has demonstrated outstanding performance, substantiating the effectiveness of the proposed method.

2   Related Work

2.1   BERT

BERT [4], introduced by Google in 2018, is a pre-trained language model that employs a deep bidirectional Transformer [15] architecture as its core component. This model has attained state-of-the-art (SOTA) performance across various Natural Language Processing (NLP) tasks.

2.2   Prompt Learning

The advent of LLMs and the recognition that the extensive knowledge is acquired by PLMs during the pre-training phase have spurred a burgeoning development in prompt learning [9]. Prompt learning has emerged as a more effective approach than fine-tuning, particularly in few-shot scenario and zero-shot scenario. Promisingly, prompt learning has found application in a wide range of downstream tasks of NLP, including but not limited to Text Classification [14], Natural Language Understanding [10], Relationship Extraction [2,5]. Notably, this methodology has exhibited noteworthy predictive performance in these downstream tasks of NLP.

2.3   Prompt Engineering

Prompt engineering plays a pivotal role in prompt tuning. As evidenced in the preceding example, prompt characters and [MASK] token are used to construct a prompt template. We denoted the template as $f_{prompt}(\cdot)$. The original input sequence $x = (x_0, x_1, ...x_N)$ is integrated into the template to form a cloze input form $f_{prompt}(x)$, we can bridge the gap between PLMs and downstream tasks by this way.

   Prompt engineering methods encompass two primary approaches: manual template design and automatic template construction. The former entails the expertise and experience of designers who possess specialized knowledge in the domain that the used dataset related to. Skillfully crafting a template through manual designing can yield excellent outcomes, particularly in zero-shot scenarios. On the other hand, automatic template construction methods, such as prompt mining [7], prompt paraphrasing, continuous prompt [12], mitigate the need for manual intervention. These approaches can train template using limited data to make accurate prediction.

3   Task Definition

The objective of this task is to construct a multi-angle prediction prompt template and use the template to comprehensively acquire and utilize the knowledge acquired by PLMs in the pre-training stage to accurately predict the coherence classification of Chinese essays in scenario of having limited annotated data available for model training and verification. The coherence classification results are categorized into three levels, namely 2 (excellent coherence), 1 (moderate coherence), and 0 (incoherence).

4   Method

This section will delineate the proposed approach, encompassing several key components: (1) supervised data preprocessing; (2) prompt characters design and template construction; (3) overview of model operation flow; (4) model training and inference.

4.1   Supervised Data Preprocessing Module

The raw input to the model is text which is a metadata of LEssay. Given that the majority of the input text is long text, it is observed that the coherence of an article can be assessed by analyzing a portion of the text, rather than having to consider the whole article. Therefore, we employ slicing operation, dividing the original input sequence $x = (x_1, x_2, ...x_N)$ into two input sequences $x_a = (x_1, ...x_{\frac{N}{2}}), x_b = (x_{\frac{N}{2}+1}, x_{\frac{N}{2}+2}, ...x_N)$ evenly. This approach partially mitigates the issue of having too little supervised data available for training.

4.2   Prompt Characters Design and Template Building Module

Prompt character design plays a pivotal role in the prompt engineering process. By carefully selecting prompt characters that are relevant to the specific task and dataset, we can elicit and utilize knowledge of PLMs better.

Given the unique nature of this task that we can evaluate the coherence of an essay from four specific assessment angles, we design four groups of prompt characters to represent four assessment angles, including "关联词使用恰当程度？", "上下文之间逻辑关系情况？", "标点符号使用情况？", "句子结构情况？", which is referred to as $T0, T1, T2, T3$.

A prompt template, designed to realize multi-angle prediction, has been devised cleverly by using four groups of prompt characters: "$< TEXT >< T0 >< MASK >< T1 >< MASK >< T2 >< MASK >< T3 >< MASK >$". This template enables the coherence prediction of Chinese essays base on four distinct assessment angles. Each <MASK> token will make prediction based on the coherence assessment angle in front of the <MASK> respectively.

4.3   Overview of Model Operation Flow

The PLM utilized in this study is denoted as M. After the slicing operation, the input sequence is divided into two parts. Let us assume that the input sequence after slicing is represented as $original\_input = (x_1, x_2, ..., x_n)$. As shown in Fig. 1, The model input sequence $original\_input$ is integrated with the multi-angle prediction prompt template defined in Sect. 4.2, yielding a new input sequence x_p, $x_p =< original\_input >< T0 >< MASK >< T1 >< MASK >< T2 ><$ $MASK >< T3 >< MASK >$. The integrated input sequence x_p is then introduced into the pre-trained language model M. The regression value of MLM Head of M is obtained finally.

$$logits = M(x_p) \tag{1}$$

where $logits \in \mathbb{R}^{n \times vocab\_size}$, n is the max sequence length of input sequence. $vocab\_size$ is vocabulary length of M.

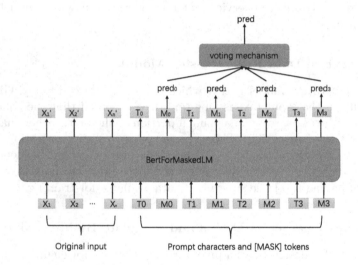

Fig. 1. Model architecture diagram

In order to realize the mapping between the PLM's vocabulary and the answer space, we design a mapping mechanism $f : \nu \longmapsto \gamma$, Where ν is the words set representing classes, γ is the set of classes. We define $\nu_2 = \{$"好"$\}$, $\nu_1 = \{$"一般"$\}$, $\nu_0 = \{$"差"$\}$, $\gamma = \{0, 1, 2\}$. $U_{y \in \gamma} \nu_y = \nu$. The probability that [MASK] is predicted as class y:

$$p(y\|x_p) = p([MASK] = a\|x_p), a \in \nu_y \tag{2}$$

The value of $p([MASK] = a\|x_p)$ is the $[tokenizer.encode(a)]$-th value of $logits$ in the [MASK], ν_k is the words set that represent class k.

For an input sequence, we can get four probability vectors because the template we designed has four [MASK] tokens, which is the reason why the template we design can realize multi-angle prediction.

4.4 Training and Inference

Training. Following the approach described in Sect. 4.3, the x of the sliced data $\{x:\ original\ input,\ label:\ y\}$ is combined with the multi-angle prediction prompt template to generate the new input sequence x_p. Subsequently, x_p is introduced into M and the proposed mapping mechanism is employed to obtain the probability vector of [MASK] tokens respectively.

$$p_{pi} = [p_{pi}(y = 0|x_p), p_{pi}(y = 1|x_p), p_{pi}(y = 2|x_p)], i = 0, 1, 2, 3 \qquad (3)$$

where p_{pi} represents the probability vector of i-th [MASK] when x_p is introduced into our proposed model, $p_{pi}(y = m|x_p)$ represents the probability that class m is predicted in the i-th [MASK] when x_p is introduced into our proposed model.

Hence, when the proposed model receives an input sequence x_p, it generates a vector at each [MASK] position, denoted as p_{p0}, p_{p1}, p_{p2}, p_{p3}, which represent the probability vectors based on four assessment angles respectively, then we can calculate the loss:

$$loss_0 = BCE\_Loss\,(p_{p0}, label) \qquad (4)$$

$$loss_1 = BCE\_Loss\,(p_{p1}, label) \qquad (5)$$

$$loss_2 = BCE\_Loss\,(p_{p2}, label) \qquad (6)$$

$$loss_3 = BCE\_Loss\,(p_{p3}, label) \qquad (7)$$

$$loss = loss_0 + loss_1 + loss_2 + loss_3 \qquad (8)$$

Inference. For the raw input sequence to be predicted $x = (x_1, x_2, ...x_N)$, two input sequences can be obtained after slicing operation. We note sliced input sequence as $x_a = \left(x_1, ... x_{\frac{N}{2}}\right)$, $x_b = (x_{\frac{N}{2}+1}, x_{\frac{N}{2}+2}, ...x_N)$. Two input sequences are introduced into our proposed model respectively. And we will get $P_a = [p_{a0}, p_{a1}, p_{a2}, p_{a3}]^{\top}$, $P_b = [p_{b0}, p_{b1}, p_{b2}, p_{b3}]^{\top}$, P_m represents the combined tensor of the regression values of the sliced input sequence x_m at the four [MASK] positions, $P_m \in \mathbb{R}^{4 \times 3}$. p_{kj} represents the regression vector of the input sequence x_k at the j-th [MASK] token, $p_{kj} \in \mathbb{R}^{1 \times 3}$. As a result, For the original input sequence $x = (x_0, x_1, ...x_N)$, we can calculate the regression value.

$$P_x = [M_{x0}, M_{x1}, M_{x2}, M_{x3}]^{\top} = P_a + P_b \qquad (9)$$

$$P_a + P_b = [p_{a0} + p_{b0}, p_{a1} + p_{b1}, p_{a2} + p_{b2}, p_{a3} + p_{b3}]^{\top} \qquad (10)$$

where M_{xj} is the regression vector of input sequence x in j-th [MASK] token.

Compute the index of the maximum value of each [MASK] regression vector's elements, they are the prediction results of the coherence classification relative to the four coherence classification assessment angles respectively.

$$pred_0 = argmax\,(M_{x0}) \qquad (11)$$

$$pred_1 = argmax\,(M_{x1}) \qquad (12)$$

$$pred_2 = argmax\,(M_{x2}) \tag{13}$$

$$pred_3 = argmax\,(M_{x3}) \tag{14}$$

By employing a voting mechanism, the final prediction for the coherence level of a Chinese article is determined by selecting the index that was predicted the most times among the four assessment angles.

$$num_i = num\_of\,(pred_j == i)\,, i = 0,1,2;\, j = 0,1,2,3 \tag{15}$$

$$pred = argmax\,(num_i) \tag{16}$$

where i represents the index of class and $pred_j$ represents the predicted value of the j-th criterion. The final predicted value $pred$ is the index that the category was predicted the most times.

5   Experiment

In this section, we will demonstrate the effectiveness of the proposed method based on some of data from LEssay.

5.1   Dataset

To evaluate the effectiveness of the proposed method, we conducted experiments using some of data from the LEssay, which is utilized in the NLPCC2023 Shared-Task7 Track1. It is specifically designed for evaluating the coherence of Chinese articles. Our experimental data consists of 50 Chinese essays for training, 10 Chinese essays for validation, and 5,000 Chinese essays for testing. The coherence of the Chinese essays can be classified into three categories: 2 (excellent coherence), 1 (moderate coherence), and 0 (incoherence).

5.2   Baseline

Fine-Tuning. Fine-tuning adds a [CLS] token at the beginning of the original input sequence and then feeding it into a PLM. To predict the classification results, a classifier composed of a linear layer is added to the last layer of the PLM to predict the classification results.

P-Tuning. P-tuning [10] is an automatic method for constructing prompt templates to facilitate downstream task prediction. This approach employs custom prompt embedding to obtain preliminary prompts and uses MLP and LSTM to further process prompts, resulting in the final prompts for a template. P-tuning has demonstrated excellent performance in both few-shot and fully-supervised settings.

5.3   Implementation Details

For all our experiments, we employ $bert-base-chinese$ as our PLM. The epoch is 50. We use AdamW [8] as the model optimizer and the learning rate is set to 2e-5. Loss values are calculated by BCE loss function. During the training phase, we set the batch size to 2, while for verification and testing, the batch size is set to 8.

5.4   Main Results

During the testing phase, we employed precision (P), recall (R), and Macro-F1 (F1) to evaluate the effectiveness of our proposed model. The specific results of our proposed method and baseline are shown in Table 1.

Table 1. Experiment results on NLPCC2023 SharedTask7 Track1 dataset

Model	P	R	F1
Fine-tuning	34.78	34.48	29.15
P-tuning	34.12	33.36	33.36
Ours	**36.26**	**37.10**	**35.77**

In both Fine-tuning and P-tuning, randomly initialized parameters are introduced to assist in model prediction. In few-shot setting, due to the scarcity of adequate labeled data, it becomes challenging to optimize these randomly initialized parameters effectively. From Table 1, it can also be observed that the proposed method is better than Fine-tuning and P-tuning in terms of precision, recall and Macro-F1. Furthermore, the Macro-F1 is 6.62% higher than Fine-tuning and 2.41% higher than P-tuning, respectively.

5.5   Analyze

To further assess the effectiveness of our proposed method, we conducted a series of ablation experiments as follows: 1. Randomly initialize 4 prompt tokens to replace the prompt characters used in our proposed method, it means that we use $< TEXT >< T0 >< MASK >< T1 >< MASK >< T2 ><MASK >< T3 >< MASK >$ as prompt template, where $< T0 >, < T1 >$, $< T2 >, < T3 >$ are initialized randomly. 2. Remove four groups of prompt characters, which means that it uses $< TEXT >< MASK >< MASK ><MASK >< MASK >$ as prompt template. 3. The prompt characters still use four essay coherence evaluation criteria, but it only uses one $< MASK >$. Consequently, the prompt template used is $< TEXT >< T0 >< T1 >< T2 ><T3 >< MASK >$, indicating the absence of multi-angle prediction. 4. Use one $< MASK >$ and no prompt character is added, which means that it uses $< TEXT >< MASK >$ as prompt template. 5. The slicing operation is not used. The specific results are shown in Table 2.

Table 2. Ablation experiment results

Model	P	R	F1
Ours	**36.26**	37.10	**35.77**
Initialize the prompt tokens at random	35.44	**38.29**	33.77
Without prompt characters	33.70	34.29	24.27
With prompt characters and one [MASK]	33.15	32.92	28.47
Without prompt characters and with one [MASK]	36.20	36.78	34.56
Without slicing operation	35.13	35.44	33.71

In comparison to our proposed method, the ablation experiments involving random initialization of prompt tokens and the removal of prompt characters (ablation experiments 1 and 2) result in a reduction of 2% and 11.5% in Macro-F1, respectively. These experiments serve as the evidence of the fact that we cannot optimize randomly initialized parameters effectively in few-shot setting and the effectiveness of our proposed prompt characters design method, which utilizes the four angles of essay coherence evaluation criteria as prompt characters. In comparison to the proposed method, the ablation experiments involving the use of prompt characters but only one [MASK] token for prediction, and the use of only one [MASK] token without prompt characters (ablation experiments 3 and 4) result in a reduction of 7.3% and 1.21% in Macro-F1, respectively. These findings provide evidence for the effectiveness of our proposed multi-angle prediction template, which utilizes multiple [MASK] tokens to predict the results from multiple assessment angles, as well as the utilization of the voting mechanism. The ablation experiment involving the removal of the slicing operation (ablation experiment 5) results in a decrease of 2.06% in Macro-F1, compared to the approach using the proposed slicing operation as described in the paper. This observation provides further evidence for the effectiveness of our use of the slicing operation to alleviate the problem of lacking a substantial amount of supervised training data.

6   Conclusion

In this paper, we present a novel deep learning approach to address the task of coherence classification of Chinese essays. We propose a unique multi-angle prediction prompt template construction method. Our approach employs four distinct criteria of evaluating the coherence of Chinese essays to be prompt characters set. Additionally, we introduce a [MASK] token following each group of prompt characters, allowing for the prediction bases on the corresponding assessment angle. To ensure effective training, we establish rigorous mechanisms that require accurate predictions for each [MASK] token. During inference, we leverage a voting mechanism to obtain the final coherence classification prediction for Chinese essays. We also apply a slicing operation to all texts to mitigate the challenge of limited training data. The proposed method achieves excellent results in NLPCC2023 SharedTask7 Track1, which proves the effectiveness of the proposed method. In theory, even when we scale with larger datasets, we can still employ the template used in the paper. By leveraging a substantial amount of supervised data to optimize prompt and other parameters better, we can achieve more accurate multi-angle predictions. When we need predict the coherence of other forms of text and if the text can also be evaluated from multiple angles, we can construct prompt templates following the method proposed in the paper and implement the final prediction using a voting mechanism. In theory, this approach can yield favorable results in the scenario.

Acknowledgments. This work was supported by Improvement of Innovation Ability of Small and Medium Sci-tech Enterprises Program (No. 2023TSGC0182) and Tai Shan Industry Leading Talent Project.

References

1. Brown, T., et al.: Language models are few-shot learners. Adv. Neural. Inf. Process. Syst. **33**, 1877–1901 (2020)
2. Chen, X., et al.: Adaprompt: adaptive prompt-based finetuning for relation extraction. arXiv preprint arXiv:2104.07650 (2021)
3. Davison, J., Feldman, J., Rush, A.M.: Commonsense knowledge mining from pretrained models. In: Proceedings of the 2019 Conference on Empirical Methods in Natural Language Processing and the 9th International Joint Conference on Natural Language Processing (EMNLP-IJCNLP), pp. 1173–1178 (2019)
4. Devlin, J., Chang, M.W., Lee, K., Toutanova, K.: Bert: pre-training of deep bidirectional transformers for language understanding. arXiv preprint arXiv:1810.04805 (2018)
5. Han, X., Zhao, W., Ding, N., Liu, Z., Sun, M.: Ptr: prompt tuning with rules for text classification. AI Open **3**, 182–192 (2022)
6. Hu, S., et al.: Knowledgeable prompt-tuning: Incorporating knowledge into prompt verbalizer for text classification. arXiv preprint arXiv:2108.02035 (2021)
7. Jiang, Z., Xu, F.F., Araki, J., Neubig, G.: How can we know what language models know? Trans. Assoc. Comput. Linguistics **8**, 423–438 (2020)
8. Kingma, D.P., Ba, J.: Adam: A method for stochastic optimization. arXiv preprint arXiv:1412.6980 (2014)
9. Liu, P., Yuan, W., Fu, J., Jiang, Z., Hayashi, H., Neubig, G.: Pre-train, prompt, and predict: a systematic survey of prompting methods in natural language processing. ACM Comput. Surv. **55**(9), 1–35 (2023)
10. Liu, X., et al.: GPT understands, too. arXiv preprint arXiv:2103.10385 (2021)
11. Petroni, F., Rocktäschel, T., Lewis, P., Bakhtin, A., Wu, Y., Miller, A.H., Riedel, S.: Language models as knowledge bases? arXiv preprint arXiv:1909.01066 (2019)
12. Qin, G., Eisner, J.: Learning how to ask: querying LMS with mixtures of soft prompts. arXiv preprint arXiv:2104.06599 (2021)
13. Raffel, C., et al.: Exploring the limits of transfer learning with a unified text-to-text transformer. J. Mach. Learn. Res. **21**(1), 5485–5551 (2020)
14. Schick, T., Schütze, H.: Exploiting cloze questions for few shot text classification and natural language inference. arXiv preprint arXiv:2001.07676 (2020)
15. Vaswani, A., et al.: Attention is all you need. Advances in neural information processing systems 30 (2017)

Overview of the NLPCC 2023 Shared Task: Chinese Essay Discourse Coherence Evaluation

Hongyi Wu[1]([✉]), Xinshu Shen[1], Man Lan[1,2]([✉]), Xiaopeng Bai[3], Yuanbin Wu[1,2], Aimin Zhou[1,2], Shaoguang Mao[4], Tao Ge[4], and Yan Xia[4]

[1] School of Computer Science and Technology, East China Normal University, Shanghai, China
{hongyiwu,xinshushen}@stu.ecnu.edu.cn, {mlan,ybwu,amzhou}@cs.ecnu.edu.cn
[2] Shanghai Institute of AI for Education, East China Normal University, Shanghai, China
[3] Department of Chinese Language and Literature, East China Normal University, Shanghai, China
xpbai@zhwx.ecnu.edu.cn
[4] Microsoft Research Asia, Beijing, China
{shaoguang.mao,tage,yanxia}@microsoft.com

Abstract. In this paper, we present an overview of the Chinese Essay Discourse Coherence Evaluation task in the NLPCC 2023 shared tasks. We give detailed descriptions of the task definition and the data for training as well as evaluation. We also summarize the approaches investigated by the participants of this task. Such approaches demonstrate the state-of-the-art of discourse coherence evaluation for Chinese essay. The data set and evaluation tool used by this task is available at https://github.com/cubenlp/NLPCC-2023-Shared-Task7.

Keywords: Discourse Coherence · Topic Sentence Extraction · Discourse Relation Recognition

1 Introduction

Discourse coherence, a key aspect in natural language processing (NLP), is of paramount importance in various tasks, including essay grading in academic contexts. Despite its significance, discourse coherence, especially in Chinese, has not been extensively studied due to the lack of comprehensive and annotated datasets [2,4,11].

To address this limitation, we have organized a competition focusing on discourse coherence in Chinese essay assessment. A significant feature of our competition is the utilization of the newly constructed LEssay dataset, developed by the CubeNLP laboratory of East China Normal University in collaboration with Microsoft Research Asia. This dataset was designed to promote and assess the development of AI techniques for evaluating discourse coherence in Chinese

F. Liu et al. (Eds.): NLPCC 2023, LNAI 14304, pp. 292–301, 2023.
https://doi.org/10.1007/978-3-031-44699-3_26

essays, marking the first instance of employing such a robust dataset in a competition revolving around discourse coherence in Chinese essays [3,5].

The main objective of our competition is to foster the development of innovative techniques for assessing discourse coherence in essays-an integral facet of text quality. A total of 21 teams registered for the competition, and seven of them submitted their final results, demonstrating a robust and engaging participation in our initiative. Our competition comprises four tracks: `Coherence Evaluation` (**CE**), `Text Topic Extraction` (**TTE**), `Paragraph Logical Relation Recognition` (**PLRR**), and `Sentence Logical Relation Recognition` (**SLRR**). Each track aims at addressing a specific aspect of discourse coherence and text quality. The multifaceted LEssay dataset, which serves as the backbone for all these tracks, adds a unique dimension to our competition, challenging the teams to delve into the intricate complexities of discourse coherence in the real-world scenario of Chinese essay evaluation.

Our key contribution resides in bridging the gap in the available resources for discourse coherence in Chinese through the LEssay dataset. This provides an opportunity to evaluate the performance of participating teams using real-world texts, thereby adding to the complexity and diversity of tasks usually encountered in coherence studies [6,9].

This overview paper is organized as follows: Sect. 2 provides a detailed description of the competition; Sect. 3 introduces the LEssay dataset and its annotation guidelines; Sect. 4 discusses the employed evaluation metric; Sect. 5 presents various approaches undertaken by the participating teams; Sect. 6 discloses the final results, and Sect. 7 concludes the paper.

2   Competition Tracks and Task Definitions

The competition was organized into four tracks, each examining a distinct facet of discourse coherence. This structure not only allowed for a comprehensive evaluation of the essays but also encouraged participants to consider the interconnected nature of the different aspects of text coherence. Figure 1 provides a visual representation of these four tracks in the context of essay evaluation.

2.1   Coherence Evaluation (CE)

Description and Definition. Coherence, referring to the logical and smooth flow of ideas in a text, is a fundamental aspect of effective writing. This track encourages participants to detect and assess the coherence in middle school student essays. It explores how discourse structure and logical composition contribute to the overall coherence of a text. Participants are to evaluate the coherence of an essay on a three-level scale: 2 for excellent, 1 for moderate, and 0 for poor coherence. The assessment focuses on two elements: logical flow and sentence break appropriateness.

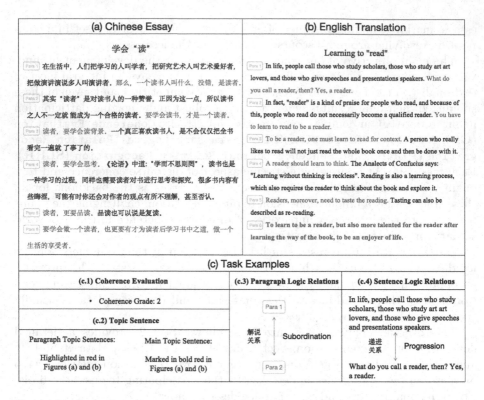

Fig. 1. A schematic representation of the four competition tracks with respect to the components of discourse coherence in an essay. It depicts the interaction between the tracks, emphasizing the comprehensive approach to evaluating essay coherence.

2.2 Text Topic Extraction (TTE)

Description and Definition. The organization of content in a text heavily influences its coherence. Each paragraph generally contains a central idea, embodied in a topic sentence. The extraction of these topic sentences is essential for assessing the structural quality and coherence of the text. In this track, participants are to identify the topic sentence of each paragraph and one overarching topic sentence for the entire essay.

2.3 Paragraph Logical Relation Recognition (PLRR)

Description and Definition. The logical relations between paragraphs are crucial in text understanding and information extraction, providing insights into the quality, coherence, and structure of a text. This track aims to evaluate the capacity of participants to recognize these relations in middle school student essays. Participants are to identify the logical relationship between two ordered paragraphs from a composition, based on provided definitions and examples of logical relationships.

2.4 Sentence Logical Relation Recognition (SLRR)

Description and Definition. The logical relations between sentences are integral to the evaluation of the coherence, fluency, and overall logical structure of a text. This track seeks to assess participants' abilities in classifying and understanding the logical relationships between sentences, such as cause-effect, comparison, and chronology. Participants are to determine the type of logical relation between two consecutive sentences from an essay, based on provided definitions and examples.

3 Dataset Description

In this section, we discuss the characteristics and distribution of the dataset used in our study. This dataset comprises a rich set of Chinese essays written by middle school students. For each task, the dataset was split into training, development, and testing subsets. We also encourage participants to leverage complementary resources for enhancing their training.

3.1 Dataset Overview

As shown in Table 1, the granularity of the text varies across different tasks, ranging from the whole essay to individual sentences. We have meticulously curated these data, ensuring they accurately represent middle school writing. Besides, we encourage participants to leverage data from other sources to enhance their training.

During the testing phase, we provide a substantial number of Chinese essays as test data. To maintain the highest quality and accuracy of the competition, we meticulously review a portion of the test set, providing constructive feedback to participants.

Table 1. Data statistics of the four tasks. Each task has its specific granularity, which is reflected in the size of the training, development, and testing subsets.

	Textual granularity	Train Set	Dev Set	Test Set
Track 1	Essay	50	10	5000
Track 2	Essay	50	10	5000
Track 3	Paragraph	100	20	5000
Track 4	Sentence	450	50	10000

3.2 Annotation Process

Our dedicated team of annotators, comprising language students and expert reviewers, underwent extensive training before initiating the annotation process. The dataset was divided into five distinct groups to ensure efficient and consistent annotation. This rigorous process, involving the grading of discourse coherence, the identification of topic sentences, and the Portraits of discourse relations, spanned three months and culminated in the production of a high-quality annotated dataset.

To maintain the quality of the annotated data, we measured Inter-Annotator Agreement (IAA) across various tasks, such as identifying discourse coherence score, primary topic sentence, paragraph and sentence relation. We achieved IAAs of 65.53%, 78.90%, 94.33%, and 94.26% across the four tasks, respectively, thereby validating the reliability and consistency of our annotations.

3.3 Dataset Distribution

As a case study, we present the distribution of coherence scores in the Track 1 data. Figure 2 illustrates the percentage of essays that were assigned each coherence grade across different genres. This visual representation underscores the diversity of the dataset and the varied proficiency levels of the middle school students' writings.

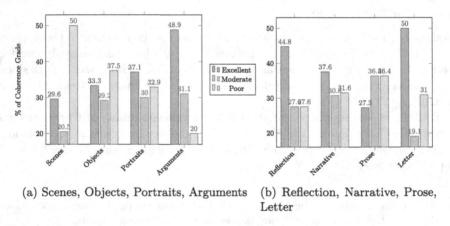

(a) Scenes, Objects, Portraits, Arguments   (b) Reflection, Narrative, Prose, Letter

Fig. 2. Distribution of coherence grades across different genres, represented as bar plots. This graph demonstrates the diverse proficiency levels of middle school students' writings across different genres.

We believe this comprehensive dataset description will help the participants to gain a better understanding of the tasks and support their efforts in developing effective models. Specific data formats and additional details are provided in the competition's technical manual and data specification document[1], to avoid cluttering the paper with excessive details.

---

[1] https://github.com/cubenlp/NLPCC-2023-Shared-Task7/blob/main.

4   Evaluation Metrics

In this work, we employ several evaluation metrics across the shared tasks, including precision (P), recall (R), accuracy, and the Macro-F1 score (F_1). Precision is defined as the ratio of correctly identified instances to the total number of identified instances. Recall is defined as the ratio of correctly identified instances to the total number of instances labeled in the ground truth. The F1-score, often used in tasks involving binary or multi-class classification, is the harmonic mean of precision and recall, calculated using the formula: $F_1 = \frac{2PR}{P+R}$.

For the tasks of Coherence Evaluation (CE), Paragraph Logical Relation Recognition (PLRR), and Sentence Logical Relation Recognition (SLRR), we employ P, R, and F_1 as metrics to evaluate the effectiveness of coherence or logical relationship identification.

On the other hand, the task of Text Topic Extraction (TTE) uses accuracy as the metric to evaluate the effectiveness of extracting paragraph and overall topics from the text. Specifically, paragraph theme sentence accuracy $(ParaAcc)$ is defined as the ratio of accurately identified paragraph theme sentences to the total number of paragraph theme sentences. Similarly, overall theme sentence accuracy $(FullAcc)$ is defined as the ratio of accurately identified overall theme sentences to the total number of overall theme sentences. The comprehensive evaluation accuracy is a weighted sum of $ParaAcc$ and $FullAcc$, calculated as $0.3 * ParaAcc + 0.7 * FullAcc$.

5   Participated Systems

In total, seven teams submitted 48 entries, with each team being allowed to submit at most one entry per track per day. Table 2 shows the detailed information about the participating teams.

Table 2. The detailed information of participants.

System	Organization	Participating Tracks
EssayFlow	Peking University	Track 1
Evay Info AI Team	Shandong Computer Science Center	Track 1
Ouchnai	National Open University	Track 1/2/3/4
CLsuper	Guangdong University of Foreign Studies	Track 1
Wuwuwu	Shanghai Jiao Tong University	Track 2/3/4
Lrt123	Beijing Normal University	Track 3
BLCU_teamworkers	Beijing Language and Culture University	Track 3/4

5.1   Track 1. Coherence Evaluation (CE)

The aim of this track was to evaluate the coherence of text from both a global and local perspective. Notably, this was a common approach used by many of the participating teams. **EssayFlow** utilized the pre-trained model[2] as a backbone,

---
[2] https://huggingface.co/hfl/chinese-roberta-wwm-ext.

then proposed a hierarchical classification model that integrates punctuation information, and further developed a multi-tower framework for cross-domain adaptation to enhance performance in low-resource settings. The **Evay Info AI Team**, on the other hand, deployed a prediction system based on four perspectives, with a voting mechanism to provide a comprehensive coherence evaluation [3]. Lastly, **Ouchnai** leveraged a combination of a local coherence discriminative model and a punctuation correction model, both fine-tuned on BERT [1], to extract features from the text. A GBRT, with linguistically-informed constraints, was employed to map these features into a final global coherence score.

5.2   Track 2. Text Topic Extraction (TTE)

In this track, **Ouchnai** developed two token classification models for paragraph-level and overall topic sentence extraction. On the other hand, **Wuwuwu** proposed a two-stage topic sentence extraction approach tailored for student essays, which first identifies topic sentences from each paragraph, considering the semantic and contextual aspects at a paragraph level, and then distills a global topic sentence from this sequence of paragraph topic sentences, utilizing the UIE model [8] for information extraction in both stages.

5.3   Tracks 3 & 4: Paragraph-Level and Sentence-Level Logical Relation Recognition (PLRR & SLRR)

For these tracks, **wuwuwu** utilized relevant data from the Discovery dataset [10], translated it into Chinese and augmented the respective category in their training set. They employed a self-training strategy, progressively increasing the size of the training set. Given the label imbalance, they expanded each category in steps of 10%, 12%, etc., selecting the model with the highest precision on the validation set at each step. Besides, **Ouchnai** leveraged a sequence classification approach for logical relation recognition, fine-tuning a BERT-based model pretrained on TED-CDB dataset [7] for improved task-specific performance.

6   Results

A comprehensive analysis of the results presented in Tables 3, 4, and 5 revealed the robust performance of several methods across the four tracks.

In the Coherence Evaluation (Track 1), the multi-tower framework and hierarchical classification model, as demonstrated by **EssayFlow**, provided superior outcomes, suggesting the efficacy of these techniques in evaluating the coherence of texts. At the same time, the four-perspective prediction system deployed by the **Evay Info AI Team** also yielded competitive results, underlining the effectiveness of multiple evaluation perspectives in text coherence assessment.

Table 3. Results for Track 1: Coherence Evaluation

Team Name	Organization	P	R	F_1	Acc
EssayFlow	Peking University	**38.50**	**43.54**	32.54	**43.99**
Evay Info AI Team	Shandong Computer Science Center	35.64	35.70	**35.61**	36.05
Ouchnai	National Open University	36.38	41.32	33.22	34.92
CLsuper	Guangdong University of Foreign Studies	34.13	34.28	32.80	32.88

In Text Topic Extraction (Track 2), both **Ouchnai** and **Wuwuwu** presented strong performance, with **Ouchnai** having a slight edge. This demonstrates the feasibility and effectiveness of their respective strategies, such as a two-stage topic sentence extraction process and a token classification model, in textual topic extraction.

Table 4. Results for Track 2: Text Topic Extraction

Team Name	Organization	$ParaAcc$	$FullAcc$	$FinalAcc$
Wuwuwu	Shanghai Jiao Tong University	61.27	**34.92**	**42.82**
Ouchnai	National Open University	**62.61**	33.33	42.12

When moving towards logical relation recognition, both at the paragraph-level (Track 3) and sentence-level (Track 4), the sequence classification approach adopted by **Ouchnai** showed remarkable superiority. The high precision and recall rates achieved by **Ouchnai** reflect the strength of pre-training and fine-tuning methodologies, particularly when using BERT-based models. Meanwhile, the performance of **Wuwuwu** accentuates the utility of self-training and dataset augmentation strategies in tackling challenges posed by label imbalance.

Table 5. Results for Track 3: Paragraph Logical Relation Recognition (PLRR) and Track 4: Sentence Logical Relation Recognition (SLRR)

Team Name	Organization	Track 3: PLRR				Track 4: SLRR			
		P	R	F_1	Acc	P	R	F_1	Acc
Ouchnai	National Open University	**54.66**	**52.45**	**52.16**	**71.03**	**36.63**	**36.36**	**34.38**	**53.95**
Wuwuwu	Shanghai Jiao Tong University	29.26	28.98	28.77	46.97	23.49	25.37	23.67	39.94
Lrt123	Beijing Normal University	28.19	30.26	27.54	48.81	–	–	–	–
BLCU_teamworkers	Beijing Language and Culture University	27.17	27.65	25.95	48.73	7.55	6.30	6.32	18.35

In sum, the findings from the competition reveal that a combination of pre-training and fine-tuning methodologies appears highly effective across these tasks. Alongside, other approaches, such as multi-tower frameworks, hierarchical models, diverse evaluation perspectives, and dataset augmentation also exhibit their respective merits. These insights contribute to future research and applications in the field of automated essay evaluation.

7   Conclusions

This paper provides the overview of the Chinses Essay Discourse Coherence (CEDC) shared task in NLPCC 2023. We release a high-quality Chinese learner corpus and briefly introduce participants' methods. The final results show that it is still a challenging task which deserves more concern.

Acknowledgements. We appreciate the support from National Natural Science Foundation of China with the Main Research Project on Machine Behavior and Human Machine Collaborated Decision Making Methodology (72192820 & 72192824), Pudong New Area Science & Technology Development Fund (PKX2021-R05), Science and Technology Commission of Shanghai Municipality (22DZ2229004) and Shanghai Trusted Industry Internet Software Collaborative Innovation Center.

References

1. Devlin, J., Chang, M., Lee, K., Toutanova, K.: BERT: pre-training of deep bidirectional transformers for language understanding. In: Burstein, J., Doran, C., Solorio, T. (eds.) Proceedings of the 2019 Conference of the North American Chapter of the Association for Computational Linguistics: Human Language Technologies, NAACL-HLT 2019, Minneapolis, MN, USA, June 2–7, 2019, Volume 1 (Long and Short Papers), pp. 4171–4186. Association for Computational Linguistics (2019). https://doi.org/10.18653/v1/n19-1423
2. Farag, Y., Yannakoudakis, H., Briscoe, T.: Neural automated essay scoring and coherence modeling for adversarially crafted input. In: Proceedings of the 2018 Conference of the North American Chapter of the Association for Computational Linguistics: Human Language Technologies, Volume 1 (Long Papers), pp. 263–271. Association for Computational Linguistics, New Orleans, Louisiana (2018). https://doi.org/10.18653/v1/N18-1024, aclanthology.org/N18-1024
3. Flansmose Mikkelsen, L., Kinch, O., Jess Pedersen, A., Lacroix, O.: DDisCo: a discourse coherence dataset for Danish. In: Proceedings of the Thirteenth Language Resources and Evaluation Conference, pp. 2440–2445. European Language Resources Association, Marseille, France (2022). http://aclanthology.org/2022.lrec-1.260
4. Guan, J., Mao, X., Fan, C., Liu, Z., Ding, W., Huang, M.: Long text generation by modeling sentence-level and discourse-level coherence. In: Zong, C., Xia, F., Li, W., Navigli, R. (eds.) Proceedings of the 59th Annual Meeting of the Association for Computational Linguistics and the 11th International Joint Conference on Natural Language Processing, ACL/IJCNLP 2021, (Volume 1: Long Papers), Virtual Event, August 1–6, 2021. pp. 6379–6393. Association for Computational Linguistics (2021). https://doi.org/10.18653/v1/2021.acl-long.499
5. Lai, A., Tetreault, J.: Discourse coherence in the wild: a dataset, evaluation and methods. In: Proceedings of the 19th Annual SIGdial Meeting on Discourse and Dialogue, pp. 214–223. Association for Computational Linguistics, Melbourne, Australia (2018). https://doi.org/10.18653/v1/W18-5023, http://aclanthology.org/W18-5023
6. Lin, Z., Ng, H.T., Kan, M.: Automatically evaluating text coherence using discourse relations. In: Lin, D., Matsumoto, Y., Mihalcea, R. (eds.) The 49th Annual Meeting

of the Association for Computational Linguistics: Human Language Technologies, Proceedings of the Conference, 19–24 June, 2011, Portland, Oregon, USA, pp. 997–1006. The Association for Computer Linguistics (2011), aclanthology.org/P11-1100/

7. Long, W., Webber, B., Xiong, D.: TED-CDB: a large-scale Chinese discourse relation dataset on TED talks. In: Proceedings of the 2020 Conference on Empirical Methods in Natural Language Processing (EMNLP), pp. 2793–2803. Association for Computational Linguistics, Online (2020). https://doi.org/10.18653/v1/2020.emnlp-main.223, aclanthology.org/2020.emnlp-main.223

8. Lu, Y., et al.: Unified structure generation for universal information extraction. In: Muresan, S., Nakov, P., Villavicencio, A. (eds.) Proceedings of the 60th Annual Meeting of the Association for Computational Linguistics (Volume 1: Long Papers), ACL 2022, Dublin, Ireland, May 22–27, 2022, pp. 5755–5772. Association for Computational Linguistics (2022). https://doi.org/10.18653/v1/2022.acl-long.395

9. Shrivastava, D., Mishra, A., Sankaranarayanan, K.: Modeling topical coherence in discourse without supervision. CoRR abs/1809.00410 (2018). arxiv.org/abs/1809.00410

10. Sileo, D., de Cruys, T.V., Pradel, C., Muller, P.: Mining discourse markers for unsupervised sentence representation learning. In: Burstein, J., Doran, C., Solorio, T. (eds.) Proceedings of the 2019 Conference of the North American Chapter of the Association for Computational Linguistics: Human Language Technologies, NAACL-HLT 2019, Minneapolis, MN, USA, June 2–7, 2019, Volume 1 (Long and Short Papers), pp. 3477–3486. Association for Computational Linguistics (2019). https://doi.org/10.18653/v1/n19-1351

11. Xiong, H., He, Z., Wu, H., Wang, H.: Modeling coherence for discourse neural machine translation. In: The Thirty-Third AAAI Conference on Artificial Intelligence, AAAI 2019, The Thirty-First Innovative Applications of Artificial Intelligence Conference, IAAI 2019, The Ninth AAAI Symposium on Educational Advances in Artificial Intelligence, EAAI 2019, Honolulu, Hawaii, USA, January 27 - February 1, 2019, pp. 7338–7345. AAAI Press (2019). https://doi.org/10.1609/aaai.v33i01.33017338

Improving the Generalization Ability in Essay Coherence Evaluation Through Monotonic Constraints

Chen Zheng[1,2]([✉]), Huan Zhang[1], Yan Zhao[1], and Yuxuan Lai[1,2]

[1] The Open University of China, Beijing, China
{zhengchen,zhanghuan,zhaoyan,laiyx}@ouchn.edu.cn
[2] Engineering Research Center of Integration and Application of Digital Learning Technology, Ministry of Education, Beijing, China

Abstract. Coherence is a crucial aspect of evaluating text readability and can be assessed through two primary factors when evaluating an essay in a scoring scenario. The first factor is logical coherence, characterized by the appropriate use of discourse connectives and the establishment of logical relationships between sentences. The second factor is the appropriateness of punctuation, as inappropriate punctuation can lead to confused sentence structure. To address these concerns, we propose a coherence scoring model consisting of a regression model with two feature extractors: a local coherence discriminative model and a punctuation correction model. We employ gradient-boosting regression trees as the regression model and impose monotonicity constraints on the input features. The results show that our proposed model better generalizes unseen data. The model achieved third place in track 1 of NLPCC 2023 shared task 7. Additionally, we briefly introduce our solution for the remaining tracks, which achieves second place for track 2 and first place for both track 3 and track 4.

Keywords: Automated Essay Scoring · Discourse Coherence · Monotonic Constraints

1 Introduction

Discourse coherence refers to the degree to which the various components of a discourse are logically interconnected and contribute to a clear and meaningful message [1]. Analyzing coherence can greatly benefit numerous natural language processing tasks, such as text generation [2], summarization [3] and essay scoring [4,5].

In essay scoring tasks, there are many dimensions to measure the student's language proficiency, such as lexical sophistication, grammatical errors, content coverage and discourse coherence [6]. Since coherence is a key property of a well-written essay, coherence assessment plays an essential role in the task.

In this work, we argue that two key aspects should be considered when evaluating the coherence of an essay. The first aspect is the logical coherence between sentences. The content of the essay should demonstrate a clear progression of ideas, with sentences and paragraphs closely connected and unfolding in logical order. Factors that may negatively impact the logical coherence between sentences include the improper use of discourse connectives and a lack of logical relationships between contexts. The second aspect is the appropriateness of punctuation. Proper punctuation is essential for clarifying the structure and organization of the essay. It can help establish logical connections between sentences, making the text easier to understand. Inappropriate punctuation can lead to confusion and disrupt the smooth flow of the text.

In this work, we propose a feature-based coherence-scoring model framework. We employ two feature extractors to tackle the two essential aspects of coherence. Specifically, the first feature extractor is a local discriminative model [7], while the second is a punctuation correction model [8]. The local discriminative model takes two or three consecutive sentences as input and generates a probability estimate of the local coherence of the sequence. We separated the essay into successive sentences, taking each one as input for the model. Following the inference, we obtained the ratio of coherent sequences to the total number of sequences. The punctuation correction model examines the essay's punctuation usage and explicitly focuses on identifying redundant, missing, and misused commas and periods.

Following feature extractors, we propose employing a regression model to map features onto a final global coherence score. A simple yet transparent model for combining features is linear regression. However, when the patterns in the data exhibit non-linear relationships, alternative models such as random forest regression, gradient-boosted regression trees (GBRT), and neural networks offer superior performance compared to linear regression. A non-linear model may be prone to overfitting the data and negatively impacting the validity of automated scores. To address this issue, we enforce regulations on the input features to maintain linguistically-informed monotonicity, thereby enhancing scoring transparency and improving the model's generalization ability.

Consequently, we present a scoring model that utilizes GBRT and incorporates monotonic constraints on the input features. We assume that the input feature, the ratio of locally coherent sequences to the total sequence of the essay, demonstrates a positive correlation with global coherence. Thus, we apply an increasing constraint to this feature. Furthermore, we assume that the feature of the number of redundant, missing, and misused commas and periods negatively correlates with global coherence. Hence, we impose a decreasing constraint on these features.

In summary, our contributions are as follows:

– We proposed a novel coherence scoring model consisting of a scorer with two feature extractors, i.e. a local discriminative model and a punctuation correction model. We showed that a local discriminative model with a more extended contextual input performs better than just consecutive pairs of sentences on the subsequent scoring tasks.

- We implement linguistically-informed monotonicity constraints on the input features to enhance the generalization ability in scoring essay coherence.
- Experiments on the LEssay dataset demonstrate the effectiveness of our proposed methods, and we achieved third place on track 1 from NLPCC2023 shared task 7.

In the last of this paper, we will briefly overview our solution for the remaining tracks from NLPCC 2023 shared task 7. The code is available at https://github.com/chernzheng/nlpcc2023_shared_task7_ouchnai_solutions.

2   Related Works

Coherence Modeling. The early development of models for coherence analysis was influenced by lexical cohesion [9], which refers to sharing identical or semantically related words in nearby sentences. Reference [10] introduced the concept of lexical chains and demonstrated that the number and density of lexical chains correlated with the topic structure. Reference [11] introduced the TextTiling algorithm revealing that sentences or paragraphs within a subtopic exhibit higher cosine values than those in neighbouring subtopics. Reference [12]'s LSA Coherence method pioneered the use of embeddings in studying coherence between sentences.

Modern neural representation-learning coherence models [7,13,14] incorporate insights from early unsupervised coherence models for learning sentence representations and assessing their transformations between adjacent sentences. These models are designed to differentiate between natural and unnatural discourses based on deep neural networks.

Automated Chinese Essay Scoring. Reference [15] implemented LDA to score Chinese essays. Reference [16] enhanced the accuracy of Chinese AES by recognizing beautiful sentences and incorporating them as literary features. Reference [17] assessed the organizational score of high school argumentative essays. Reference [18] investigated cross-prompt holistic scoring on four distinct essay sets, with articles in each dataset responding to a distinct prompt. Reference [19] proposed a multi-task learning framework for the Chinese AES and an inter-sequence attention mechanism to enhance information interaction between the different trait tasks.

3   Method

The architecture of our coherence scoring model is presented in Fig. 1. The model consists of three components: a local discriminative model, a punctuation correction model, and a scorer. The local discriminative model is employed to evaluate the local coherence of consecutive sentences of the essay. The punctuation correction model is utilized to identify the inappropriateness of punctuation usage. The scorer maps the features extracted from the above two models into a final coherence score of the essay.

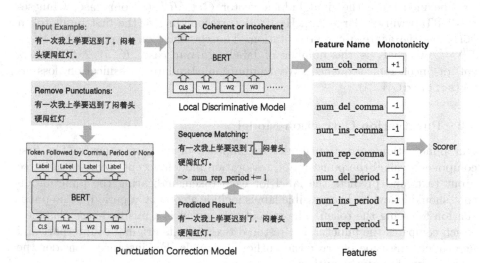

Fig. 1. The figure shows the architecture of our coherence scoring model. The punctuation correction model outputs six features: num_del_comma, num_ins_comma, num_rep_comma, num_del_period, num_ins_period, and num_rep_period, which enforced decreasing constraints on the subsequent scoring process. The local discriminative model output one feature: num_coh_norm, which enforces an increasing constraint.

3.1   Local Discriminative Model

Our local discriminative model is similar to that of Ref. [7], but we employ BERT as an encoder and treat the problem as a text classification task. Reference [7] proposed a scoring model to differentiate between consecutive sentence pairs in the training corpus, which are assumed to be coherent, and constructed incoherent ones. We extend the input sequence to three consecutive sentences rather than just two sentences and compare the different context lengths on the performance of subsequent scoring tasks.

For the case of sentence pairs, the input sequence is represented as [CLS] + Sentence A + [SEP] + Sentence B, where segment embeddings distinguish between the two sentences. For an essay with n sentences, s_i is the i-th sentence. We construct negative training samples by replacing one of the sentences, s_i or s_{i+1}, with another sentence, s_j $(j \neq i, i+1)$, from the same essay. The trained model denoted as **LD-Bisent**).

For the case of three sentences, the input sequence is set as [CLS] + Sentence A + Sentence B + Sentence C without using a special token [SEP] to separate them. We randomly substitute one sentence, s_i, s_{i+1} or s_{i+2}, by s_j ($j \neq i, i + 1, i+2$) from the same essay as the negative training sample. The trained model denoted as **LD-Trisent**).

The model use the final hidden vector $C \in R^H$ (in our case, Chinese-RoBERTa-wwm-ext-large [20], H=1024) corresponding to the first input token [CLS] as the aggregate representation. The classification layer weights $W \in R^{K \times H}$, where K is the number of labels. In our case, $K = 2$ for coherent or incoherent sequence. We compute a standard classification loss as $\log(\mathtt{softmax}(CW^T))$.

3.2   Punctuation Correction Model

Our punctuation correction model is composed of two components. The first component, called the punctuation restoration model, accepts punctuation-free input texts and predicts the label for each token, indicating the punctuation that should follow it. The possible labels include a comma, a period, or no punctuation following the token. The second component is a misused-case classifier, which compares the punctuation-restored text with its original counterpart and determines the type of error the author has made. For instance, consider the sentence written by the author:

有一次我上学要迟到了。闷着头硬闯红灯。

(I ran late for school one day and recklessly charged through the red light.)
To begin with, we remove the punctuation, resulting in the sentence

有一次我上学要迟到了闷着头硬闯红灯

Next, we input this sentence into the punctuation restoration model. The model predicts that the token '了' should be followed by a comma, the token '灯' should be followed by a period, and no punctuation following the rest of the token. Consequently, the punctuation-restored sentence becomes

有一次我上学要迟到了，闷着头硬闯红灯。

Subsequently, the misused-case classifier aligns the punctuation-restored sentence with its original counterpart and identifies that a comma has been erroneously used after the token '了'.

The punctuation restoration model is built upon a token classification model. We remove all punctuation marks from the original text and then pass it through a BERT encoder to obtain the final hidden vector for each input token $T_i \in R^H$. The probability of the token i belonging to one of the labels $\{0, 1, 2\}$ is computed as $\mathtt{softmax}(S \cdot T_i)$, where $S \in R^{K \times H}$ is the set of weights to be learned of the final layer. Here, label 0 signifies that the token is not followed by punctuation, label 1 indicates a comma follows it, label 2 indicates it is followed by a period, and $K = 3$ is the number of labels.

The misused-case classifier uses a sequence-matching algorithm to compare the punctuation-restored texts with their original counterparts. We then count the instances of redundant, missing, and misused punctuation in the essay. For the sake of simplicity, all colons within the dataset are transformed into commas.

Semicolons, question marks, and exclamation marks are replaced with periods while disregarding other punctuations.

3.3 Scorer

The scorer takes extracted features from the above two models as input. The one feature is the ratio of coherent sequences to the total number of sequences in the essay (num_coh_norm). Additional features are the number of redundant, missing, and misused commas (num_del_comma, num_ins_comma, and num_rep_comma) and the period counterparts (num_del_period, num_ins_period, and num_rep_period).

We employ the abovementioned features as input and utilize a GBRT scorer with monotonic constraints to map these features into a final global coherence score. We impose a decreasing constraint for all features extracted from the punctuation correction model because these features characterize the inappropriateness of punctuation. For feature $x_i \in \{$num_del_comma, num_ins_comma, num_rep_comma, num_del_period, num_ins_period, num_rep_period$\}$, the model satisfies

$$\text{GBRT}(x_1, \ldots, x_i, \ldots, x_n) \geq \text{GBRT}(x_1, \ldots, x_i', \ldots, x_n) \tag{1}$$

whenever $x_i \leq x_i'$. We impose an increasing constraint for feature $x_j =$ num_coh_norm because the feature captures the local coherence between adjacent sentences. It satisfies

$$\text{GBRT}(x_1, \ldots, x_j, \ldots, x_n) \leq \text{GBRT}(x_1, \ldots, x_j', \ldots, x_n) \tag{2}$$

whenever $x_j \leq x_j'$.

We compare our proposed scoring model against two regression models: a linear model and a random forest model. We also compare the performance of our model with different configurations, i.e. the scorer with or without monotonic constraints and the local discriminative model with different context lengths.

4 Experiments

4.1 Datasets

LEssay Dataset. The LEssay dataset consists of four sub-datasets corresponding to four tasks. All tasks are related to the coherence evaluation of Chinese student essays. The first sub-dataset is dedicated to the task of global coherence evaluation. It includes a training set of 50 essays, a verification set of 10 essays, and a test set of 5,000 essays. All of these essays are written in Chinese by middle school students and assessed for their coherence on three levels: excellent, moderate, and poor. The remaining three sub-datasets are allocated to the topic sentence extraction, paragraph and sentence logical relation recognition tasks, respectively.

These four tasks are interconnected, and a model trained on one sub-dataset can potentially contribute to another task. However, in this study, a global coherence scoring model will be trained only by the first sub-dataset and two external datasets. These external datasets, including the Chinese essay dataset for pre-training [18] and the IWSLT 2012-zh dataset for punctuation restoration [21], will be utilized to train the feature extractors for the scoring model. The global coherence scores of the first sub-dataset will be used to train the scorer.

Chinese Essay Dataset for Pre-training. The dataset comprises 93,002 essays authored by Chinese students in grades 7 to 12, covering various topics and genres, such as narrative, argumentative, and expository essays.

We utilized the dataset for training the local discriminative model. In practice, we excluded essays with the lowest rating (assigned rating 1) due to poor writing quality. For the remaining essays, we divided each into consecutive sentence pairs or triple sentences, assuming their coherence. And we constructed incoherent sentences, as described in Sect. 3.1. We generated 4.3 million positive and equal negative training samples for the LD-Bisent. We also prepared 3.1 million positive and equal negative training samples for the LD-Trisent.

IWSLT2012-Zh Dataset. The dataset consists of 150k lines of sentences in Chinese from TED talk transcripts. We only predict commas and periods. The question marks are converted to periods for simplicity.

4.2   Experimental Settings

We use the pre-trained Chinese-RoBERTa-wwm-ext-large model to fine-tune the local discriminative and punctuation correction models. For the random forest scorer, we set the number of trees in the forest to 30 and maintained the other parameters at their default values. For the GBRT scorers, we configure the number of boosted gradients to 30, with a maximum tree depth for base learners of 4. The learning rate is set to 1, and all other parameters are left at their default values.

We use precision, recall, and macro F1-score to evaluate the effectiveness of coherence identification. The precision is calculated by dividing the number of correctly identified coherence types (excellent, moderate, and poor) by the total number of identified coherence types. The recall is determined by dividing the number of correctly identified coherence types by the total number of coherence types as labelled.

4.3   Results

Table 1 presents the results of each regression model. In the experiment, we used the LD-Trisent feature extractor in linear and random forest regressions.

Table 1. Comparison of regression models

Model	Precision	Recall	Macro F1
Linear Regression	35.55	48.44	25.57
Random Forest Regression	38.86	23.44	28.74
GBRT (Bi-sent)	33.41	34.10	31.82
GBRT w/ MC (Bi-sent)	36.98	23.02	26.67
GBRT (Tri-sent)	35.77	36.26	34.52
GBRT w/ MC (Tri-sent)	37.28	39.90	33.02

Our findings suggest that the GBRT model with monotonic constraint using LD-Trisent (GBRT w/ MC (Tri-sent)) performs better in terms of precision and recall compared to the same model without enforcing monotonic constraint (GBRT (Tri-sent)). Furthermore, this model demonstrates improvements in precision, recall, and macro F1 score compared to the same model using LD-Bisent (GBRT w/ MC (Bi-sent)) and LD-Bisent without enforcing monotonic constraint (GBRT (Bi-sent)). Additionally, this model exhibits superior performance in macro F1 score compared to both linear and random forest regressions.

Our results show that training local coherence models to predict longer contexts than just consecutive pairs of sentences can result in better performance on subsequent scoring tasks, which agrees with the previous study on discourse representation [22].

5   Our Solution to the Remaining Tracks from NLPCC2023 Shared Task7

5.1   Text Topic Extraction (Track 2)

This task aims to identify the topic sentence for each paragraph and one overall topic sentence for a given middle school student essay.

In our approach, we employ two token classification models to identify both paragraph-level and overall topic sentences. The first model accepts the essay title connected to a paragraph as input. For each token, it outputs a label indicating whether the token belongs to the topic sentences of the paragraph (designated as a key token). The topic sentences of each paragraph are determined by the ratio of key tokens to the total number of tokens within the sentence. We select the sentence with the highest ratio as the topic sentence for that paragraph. The model is fine-tuned on Chinese-RoBERTa-wwm-ext-large.

The second model is similar to the first, but the input is a sequence that sequentially connects the essay title to all paragraph's topic sentences. We assume that the overall topic sentence is one of the paragraph topic sentences and determine it by calculating the ratio of key tokens to the total number of tokens within each paragraph topic sentence. We select the sentence with the highest ratio as the overall topic sentence. The second model is fine-tuned on the first model.

The evaluation results are shown in Table 2. Our approach achieved second place in Track 2.

Table 2. The result of text topic extraction.

Team	Para. Acc.	Full Acc.	Final Acc.	Para. Simi.	Full Simi.
wuwuwu	61.27	34.92	42.82	87.34	80.37
Ours	62.61	33.33	42.12	85.20	79.16

5.2   Paragraph Logical Relation Recognition (Track 3)

The task aims to determine the logical relationship between the two consecutive paragraphs of an essay. The logical relationship includes co-occurrence, inversion, explanatory and superior-subordinate relationships.

Our approach regards the paragraph-level logical relation recognition task as a sequence classification problem. Specifically, we process a pair of paragraphs as input, and the model determines the logical relationship between these paragraphs. Considering the similarity between this task and sentence-level logical relation recognition, we chose to fine-tune the model trained for track 4.

The evaluation results for track 3 are shown in Table 3. Our approach achieved first place in the track.

Table 3. The results of paragraph-level logical relation recognition.

Team	Precision	Recall	Macro F1
Ours	54.66	52.45	52.16
wuwuwu	29.26	28.98	28.77
Lrt123	28.19	30.26	27.54
BLCU_teamworkers	27.17	27.65	25.95

5.3   Sentence Logical Relation Recognition (Track 4)

The task is comparable to the previous task. Nonetheless, the logical relationships are sentence-based and include 12 different relationships.

We employ a two-stage training approach for our classification model. In the first stage, we utilize an external dataset, TED-CDB [23], to pre-train the model based on Chinese-RoBERTa-wwm-ext-large. In the subsequent stage, we fine-tune the pre-trained model on the current dataset to enhance its performance for the given task.

The evaluation results for track 4 are shown in Table 4. Our approach achieved first place in the track.

Table 4. The results of sentence-level logical relation recognition.

Team	Precision	Recall	Macro F1
Ours	36.63	36.36	34.38
wuwuwu	23.49	25.37	23.67
BLCU_teamworkers	7.55	6.30	6.32

6 Conclusion and Future Work

In this study, we present a scoring model to assess the global coherence of Chinese student essays. This scoring model incorporates two feature extractors: a local coherence discriminative model and a punctuation correction model. Furthermore, we employed a GBRT model with linguistically-informed monotonicity constraints to convert features into a final global coherence score.

Our findings suggest that the enforced regulations on the features improved the model's generalization capability, and a local discriminative model with a context extending beyond consecutive sentence pairs can achieve better performance in scoring tasks.

For future research, we will incorporate the features of paragraph-level coherence into the scoring model. The current model considers sentence-level coherence by introducing a local discriminative model. But the global coherence characterized by logical relationships between paragraphs is equally important for coherence evaluation. By incorporating paragraph-level coherence features, we can further enhance the performance of the scoring model and provide a more accurate assessment.

Acknowledgements. This work is supported by NSFC (62206070), the Innovation Fund Project of the Engineering Research Center of Integration and Application of Digital Learning Technology, Ministry of Education (1221014, 1221052), and National Key R&D Program of China (2021YFF0901005).

References

1. Jurafsky, D., Martin, J. H.: Speech and Language Processing, 3rd edn. (Draft of Jan 7, 2023) (2023)

2. Huang, L., Ye, Z., Qin, J., Lin, L., Liang, X.: GRADE: automatic graph-enhanced coherence metric for evaluating open-domain dialogue systems. In Proceedings of the 2020 Conference on Empirical Methods in Natural Language Processing (EMNLP), pp. 9230–9240 (2020)
3. Christensen, J., Soderland, S., Etzioni, O.: Towards coherent multi-document summarization. In Proceedings of the 2013 Conference of the North American Chapter of the Association for Computational Linguistics: Human Language Technologies, pp. 1163–1173 (2013)
4. Miltsakaki, E., Kukich, K.: Evaluation of text coherence for electronic essay scoring systems. Nat. Lang. Eng. **10**(1), 25–55 (2004)
5. Burstein, J., Tetreault, J., Andreyev, S.: Using entity-based features to model coherence in student essays. In: Human Language Technologies: The 2010 Annual Conference of the North American Chapter of the Association for Computational Linguistics, pp. 681–684 (2010)
6. Cahill, A., Evanini, K.: Natural language processing for writing and speaking. In: Handbook of Automated Scoring, pp. 69–92. Chapman and Hall/CRC, Boca Raton (2020)
7. Xu, P., et al.: A cross-domain transferable neural coherence model. In: Proceedings of the 57th Annual Meeting of the Association for Computational Linguistics, pp. 678–687 (2019)
8. Zhang, H., et al.: PaddleSpeech: an easy-to-use all-in-one speech toolkit. In: Proceedings of the 2022 Conference of the North American Chapter of the Association for Computational Linguistics: Human Language Technologies: System Demonstrations, pp. 114–123 (2022)
9. Halliday, M. A. K., Hasan, R.: Cohesion in English (No. 9). Routledge (1976)
10. Morris, J., Hirst, G.: Lexical cohesion computed by thesaural relations as an indicator of the structure of text. Comput. Linguist. **17**(1), 21–48 (1991)
11. Hearst, M.A.: Text Tiling: segmenting text into multi-paragraph subtopic passages. Comput. Linguist. **23**(1), 33–64 (1997)
12. Foltz, P.W., Kintsch, W., Landauer, T.K.: The measurement of textual coherence with latent semantic analysis. Discourse Process. **25**(2–3), 285–307 (1998)
13. Li, J., Li, R., Hovy, E.: Recursive deep models for discourse parsing. In: Proceedings of the 2014 Conference on Empirical Methods in Natural Language Processing (EMNLP), pp. 2061–2069 (2014)
14. Mesgar, M., Strube, M.: A neural local coherence model for text quality assessment. In: Proceedings of the 2018 Conference on Empirical Methods in Natural Language Processing, pp. 4328–4339 (2018)
15. Zhang, M., Hao, S., Xu, Y., Ke, D., Peng, H.: Automated essay scoring using incremental latent semantic analysis. J. Softw. **9**(2), 429–436 (2014)
16. Fu, R., Wang, D., Wang, S., Hu, G., Liu, T.: Elegart sentence recognition for automated essay scoring. J. Chin. Inf. Process. **32**(6), 10 (2018)
17. Song, W., Song, Z., Liu, L., Fu, R.: Hierarchical multi-task learning for organization evaluation of argumentative student essays. In: IJCAI, pp. 3875–3881 (2020)
18. Song, W., Zhang, K., Fu, R., Liu, L., Liu, T., Cheng, M.: Multi-stage pre-training for automated Chinese essay scoring. In Proceedings of the 2020 Conference on Empirical Methods in Natural Language Processing (EMNLP), pp. 6723–6733 (2020)
19. He, Y., Jiang, F., Chu, X., Li, P.: Automated Chinese essay scoring from multiple traits. In: Proceedings of the 29th International Conference on Computational Linguistics, pp. 3007–3016 (2022)

20. Cui, Y., Che, W., Liu, T., Qin, B., Wang, S., Hu, G.: Revisiting pre-trained models for Chinese natural language processing. Findings Assoc. Comput. Linguist.: EMNLP **2020**, 657–668 (2020)
21. Federico, M., Cettolo, M., Bentivogli, L., Michael, P., Sebastian, S.: Overview of the IWSLT 2012 evaluation campaign. In: Proceedings of the International Workshop on Spoken Language Translation (IWSLT), pp. 12–33 (2012)
22. Iter, D., Guu, K., Lansing, L., Jurafsky, D.: Pretraining with contrastive sentence objectives improves discourse performance of language models. In: Proceedings of the 58th Annual Meeting of the Association for Computational Linguistics, pp. 4859–4870 (2020)
23. Long, W., Webber, B., Xiong, D.: TED-CDB: a large-scale Chinese discourse relation dataset on ted talks. In: Proceedings of the 2020 Conference on Empirical Methods in Natural Language Processing (EMNLP), pp. 2793–2803 (2020)

Task-Related Pretraining with Whole Word Masking for Chinese Coherence Evaluation

Ziyang Wang[1,2], Sanwoo Lee[1,3], Yida Cai[1,2], and Yunfang Wu[1,3(✉)]

[1] MOE Key Laboratory of Computational Linguistics, Peking University, Beijing, China
[2] School of Software and Microelectronics, Peking University, Beijing, China
[3] School of Computer Science, Peking University, Beijing, China
wuyf@pku.edu.cn

Abstract. This paper presents an approach for evaluating coherence in Chinese middle school student essays, addressing the challenges of time-consuming and inconsistent essay assessment. Previous approaches focused on linguistic features, but coherence, crucial for essay organization, has received less attention. Recent works utilized neural networks, such as CNN, LSTM, and transformers, achieving good performance with labeled data. However, labeling coherence manually is costly and time-consuming. To address this, we propose a method that pretrains RoBERTa with whole word masking (WWM) on a low-resource dataset of middle school essays, followed by finetuning for coherence evaluation. The WWM pretraining is unsupervised and captures general characteristics of the essays, adding little cost to the low-resource setting. Experimental results on Chinese essays demonstrate that this strategy improves coherence evaluation compared to naive finetuning on limited data. We also explore variants of their method, including pseudo labeling and additional neural networks, providing insights into potential performance trade-offs. The contributions of this work include the collection and curation of a substantial dataset, the proposal of a cost-effective pretraining method, and the exploration of alternative approaches for future research.

Keywords: Coherence evaluation · pretraining · low-resource · Chinese computing

1 Introduction

In Chinese National College Entrance Examination and Senior High School Entrance Examination, evaluating the writing quality of essays has been a time-consuming task whose results might lack consistency when evaluated by human raters. Previous essay assessment tasks have focused on leveraging linguistic features of essays, such as those related to rhetoric and idioms.

© The Author(s), under exclusive license to Springer Nature Switzerland AG 2023
F. Liu et al. (Eds.): NLPCC 2023, LNAI 14304, pp. 314–322, 2023.
https://doi.org/10.1007/978-3-031-44699-3_28

Coherence is a fundamental concept in essay assessment and is particularly useful to assess how well an essay is organized. Coherence can be broken down to the cohesion between sentences and the fluency of transitions between paragraphs. It plays a vital role in ensuring clarity, conciseness and fluency in an essay, which is also crucial in improving the overall writing quality.

While early works on coherence evaluation can trace back to entity grid model(Barzilay and Lapata 2008; Guinaudeau and Strube 2013), recent works (Farag and Yannakoudakis 2019; Mesgar and Strube 2018; Moon et al. 2019; Nguyen and Joty 2017) have focused on utilizing neural networks for modeling coherence with varied structures such as CNN, LSTM and transformers. These models have achieved noticeable performance when sufficient amount of labeled data is provided. As emphasized above, manually labeling the coherence of essays relies on expert knowledge, requiring significant amount of time and cost. Hence modeling coherence in a low-resource setting can be crucial in many real-world scenarios and applications. However, most previous coherence models assume sufficient labeled data available while the low-resource setting is less explored.

In this paper, we present our approach which pretrains RoBERTa with whole word masking (WWM) on Chinese middle school student essays collected from an external source. WWM is performed in an unsupervised way which adds little cost to the original low-resource setting. In addition, WWM is effective in capturing general characteristics of middle school essays. Subsequently, the pretrained RoBERTa is finetuned on a small set of training data for coherence evalutaion.

Though we pretrain RoBERTa, our method is easy-to-employ and universal across most of the transformer-based language models. Experiment results on Chinese essays written by middle school students provided by NLPCC2023 Shared Task7 demonstrates that this simple strategy can achieve a fair performance. We also illustrate the performance of some variants of our method including pseudo labeling and adding additional neural network on top of RoBERTa, which provides insights into potential methods that are likely to result in performance drop.

The contributions of this work are as follows:

- We collected and curated a substantial amount of middle school student essay data relevant to the task.
- We propose a simple yet effective pretraining method that comes with little additional cost under a low-resource setting.
- We carry out experiments on several methods beyond pretraining to provide future works with evidence on effective approach for coherence evaluation.

2   Related Work

For Coherence Evaluation, there had been several theories that characterize coherence(Asher and Lascarides 2003; Grosz et al. 1995; Mann and Thompson 1988). Inspired by the Centering Theory (Grosz et al. 1995), some early coherence evaluation models (Barzilay and Lapata 2008; Guinaudeau and Strube 2013) were proposed to distinguish a coherent from incoherent texts with the entity grid model.

Later works have designed neural network architectures for coherence modeling: the Neural Local Coherence Model (Nguyen and Joty 2017) which uses CNN to capture local coherence features in an essay; LSTM variants for modeling potentially longer coherence relationships (Farag and Yannakoudakis 2019; Mesgar and Strube 2018; Moon et al. 2019); multi-task learning which jointly trains Bi-LSTM to score coherence and predict the type of grammatical role (GR) of a dependent with its head. With transformer-based models becoming widespread across various NLP tasks, some recent works utilized transformer-based architectures for coherence evaluation. For instance, Jeon and Strube (Jeon and Strube 2022) proposed an entity-based neural local coherence model which encode an essay with XLNet.

Coherence evaluation can be incorporated into other tasks to boost the performance of the target task. One model for automated essay scoring (AES), for instance, can take coherence evaluation as one of its components for assessing organization score of an essay (He et al. 2022; Song et al. 2020), which greatly improves the effectiveness of essay scoring.

3   Method

When pretraining a language model, general corpora such as Chinese Wikipedia are typically used to capture the linguistic knowledge that is universal across various NLP tasks. However, essays written by middle school students might differ substantially from the corpora on which the language model is pretrained. In general, grammatical and logical errors are frequently found in those essays, which poses a gap between language models and the downstream coherence evaluation task for middle school students' essays.

To this end, we pretrain RoBERTa on middle school student essays with whole word masking (WWM) strategy so that RoBERTa has a better understanding of the general content and structure of the essays. Pretraining with WWM is performed in an unsupervised way, hence it could be easily adopted in our setting where little labeled examples are available. We choose whole word masking as it outperforms individual character masking in various Chinese NLP tasks (Cui et al. 2021).

Whole Word Masking (WWM) primarily changes the training data generation strategy during the pre-training phase. In simple terms, the original tokenization based on Word Piece would split a complete word into several subwords, and during the generation of training samples, these separated subwords would be randomly masked. In WWM, if some of the Word Piece subwords of a complete word are masked, then other parts belonging to the same word will also be masked, which means the whole word is masked.

It's important to note that the term "mask" here refers to different actions, such as replacing with [MASK], keeping the original vocabulary, or randomly replacing with another word. It is not limited to the case where a word is replaced with the [MASK] label.

Subsequently, we finetune the pretrained RoBERTa on the labeled dataset. Specifically, we add a linear classifier head on top of the [CLS] token representation produced by RoBERTa, and finetune the model with the standard cross entropy loss:

$$\mathcal{L}_{class} = \sum_{i=1}^{n} \sum_{c=1}^{|C|} p(y_c^{(i)}|x_c^{(i)}) \log q(y_c^{(i)}|x_c^{(i)}) \tag{1}$$

where $p(y_c^{(i)}|x_c^{(i)})$ and $q(y_c^{(i)}|x_c^{(i)})$ are the true and predicted probability of c-th class of i-th training instance, respectively.

4 Experiments

4.1 Dataset and Evaluation Metric

We carry out experiments on the dataset provided by NLPCC2023 Shared Task7 Track1: Coherence Evaluation[1] This dataset consists of Chinese essays written by middle school students, where the coherence of each essay is evaluated on a three-level scale of excellent, moderate and poor. Within the dataset, 60 essays are train set, while another 5000 essays serve as test set. The data statistics are shown in Table 1.

Table 1. Statistics of Coherence Evaluation dataset

	paragraphs/article	sentences/paragraph	words/paragraph	words/sentence
Median	6.0	2.0	68.0	27.0
90%ile	10.0	5.0	234.0	64.0
Mean	6.79	2.65	88.50	33.38
Maximum	49	42	1010	550

For pretraining dataset, we crawl essay data from website Lele Ketang[2] The Chinese essays are written by middle school students from 7 to 12 grade. We split the dataset during pretraining so that all data is utilized while also ensuring appropriate text length for the language model. This yielded approximately 200,000 essays. The statistics of the length of the above data is provided in Table 2.

The performances of our method and baselines are evaluated on macro precision(P), recall(R), F1-score(F1) and accuracy (acc). We perform 5-fold cross validation on training set, and report the test set performance of models that have best validation accuracies.

---

[1] https://github.com/cubenlp/NLPCC-2023-Shared-Task7.
[2] http://www.leleketang.com/zuowen/.

Table 2. Statistics of the length of the pretraining data

	Median	75th Percentile	90th Percentile	Average	Maximum	Minimum
Value	329.0	344.0	361.0	292.35	3563	50

4.2 Implementation Details

We implement our model with Pytorch and transformers library. For pre-training, We used the Roberta-chinese-wwm-ext-large as the baseline pre-trained model and trained it for 10 epochs using AdamW optimizer with default parameters. The batch size was set to 16 and the learning rate was set to 2e-5. The training was performed on two NVIDIA RTX 3090 GPUs. Next, we finetune the pretrained RoBERTa with the Adawm optimizer for 20 epochs. The learning rate was set to 1e-5 and the batch size was fixed at 8. All other parameters were set to their default values.

4.3 Baselines

We consider several variants of our method as baselines which we compare our proposed method against:

PFT our proposed method; pretraining on task-related data with WWM followed by finetuning.

PFT+HAN a hierarchical attention pooling network (HAN) on top of RoBERTa pretrained on task-related data; Attention pooling layer with RoBERTa map the essay into a sequence of paragraph representations, and another attention pooling layer maps paragraph representations into an essay representation for final classification. Punctuations in each paragraph are embedded as a single vector that is concatenated to the corresponding paragraph representation.

PFT+HAN+pseudo assign pseudo labels on unlabeled test set using PFT model, and augment original train set with pseudo dataset to train HAN.

Table 3. Performance comparison on the test set. Best results are in bold.

Model	Precision	Recall	F1	Accuracy
PFT	**38.50**	**43.54**	32.54	**43.99**
PFT+HAN	34.91	35.14	**34.83**	35.15
PFT+HAN+pseudo	33.68	32.20	28.46	38.78

5 Results

Experiment results are shown in Table 3. We can observe that even when provided with a small amount of labeled data, combining finetuning with the task-related pretraining is an efficient strategy which can outperform random guess by a large margin, achieving an accuracy of 43.99%. Contrary to our expectation, PFT experiences a big drop in its performance when it is added with an auxiliary hierarchical attention pooling network, reaching an accuracy of 35.15%. Augmenting PFT+HAN further with pseudo labeled test data slightly improves the accuracy (38.78%) yet it also worsens precision, recall and F1 of PFT+HAN. It shows that knowledge learnt from PFT is not good enough to transfer to the test set, since the pseudo-labeled dataset has a harmful effect on the PFT+HAN model. In short, both adding auxiliary network or pseudo-dataset to PFT have failed to make further improvements over a simple PFT.

6 Conclusion

Coherence is a fundamental concept in essay assessment in that it plays a vital role in ensuring clarity, conciseness and fluency of an essay. Due to the prohibitive cost for manually assigning coherence labels to essays, developing coherence models under low-resource settings is of importance in various real-world scenarios. In this paper, we propose an effective approach for Chinese coherence evaluation task. Specifically, we address the challenge of a small amount of labeled data through pretraining RoBERTa with a large amount of task-related data in an unsupervised manner and finetuning the pretrained model on labeled data.

Experiment results on the Chinese essays written by middle school students demonstrate that our simple approach can outperform a random guess by a large margin despite of limited amount of labeled data. In addition to the simplicity, our method is also applicable to transformer-based coherence evaluation models other than RoBERTa. However, both adding auxiliary network or pseudo-dataset to our original method had negative effects on the performance, indicating that more investigations are necessary to carefully design auxiliary network or self-training strategy.

Acknowledgement. This work is supported by the National Natural Science Foundation of China (62076008) and the Key Project of Natural Science Foundation of China (61936012).

Appendix

During the process of improving overall accuracy, we have also experimented with some new model architectures, including the Cross Task Grader model mentioned below.

PFT+HAN

We proposed a multi-layer coherence evaluation model, depicted in Fig. 1, which firstly utilized pre-trained RoBERTa to extract features from the articles, followed by an attention pooling layer. Then, we concatenated punctuation-level embeddings and passed them through another attention pooling layer. Finally, we obtained the ultimate coherence score by using a classifier.

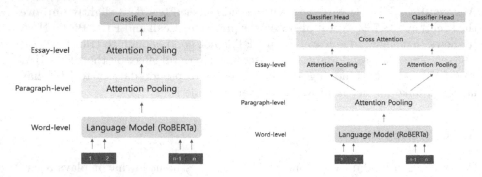

Fig. 1. PFT+HAN   **Fig. 2.** Cross Task Grader

Pre-trained Encoder. A sequence of words $s_i = \{w_1, w_2, \ldots, w_m\}$ is encoded with the pre-trained RoBERTa.

Paragraph Representation Layer. An attention pooling layer applied to the output of the pre-trained encoder layer is designed to capture the paragraph representations and is defined as follows:

$$m_i = tanh(W_m \cdot x_i + b_m) \tag{2}$$

$$u_i = \frac{e^{w_u \cdot m_i}}{\sum_{j=1}^{m} e^{w_u \cdot m_j}} \tag{3}$$

$$p = \sum_{i=1}^{m} u_i \cdot x_i \tag{4}$$

where W_m is a weights matrix, w_u is a weights vector, m_i is the attention vector for the i-th word, u_i is the attention weight for the i-th word, and p is the paragraph representation.

Essay Representation Layer. We incorporated punctuation representations to enhance the model's performance. We encoded the punctuation information for each paragraph, obtaining the punctuation representation pu_i for each paragraph. Then, we concatenated this representation pu_i with the content representation p_i of each paragraph:

$$c_i = concatenate(p_i, pu_i) \tag{5}$$

where c_i represents the representation of the concatenated i-th paragraph. Next, we use another layer of attention pooling to obtain the representation of the entire essay and is defined as follows:

$$a_i = tanh(W_a \cdot c_i + b_a) \tag{6}$$

$$v_i = \frac{e^{w_v \cdot a_i}}{\sum\limits_{j=1}^{a} e^{w_v \cdot a_j}} \tag{7}$$

$$E = \sum_{i=1}^{a} v_i \cdot c_i \tag{8}$$

where W_a is a weights matrix, w_v is a weights vector, a_i is the attention vector for the i-th paragraph, v_i is the attention weight for the i-th paragraph, and E is the essay representation.

Cross Task Grader

We also used Multi-task Learning(MTL) in our experiment, which is depicted in Fig. 2.

We used both target data and some pseudo-labeled essays from various grade and created a separate PFT+HAN model for each. To facilitate multi-task learning, we adopted the Hard Parameter Sharing approach, sharing the pre-trained encoder layer and the first layer of attention pooling among all the models.Additionally, we added a cross attention layer before the classifier.

Cross Attention Layer. After obtaining the essay representation, we added a cross attention layer to learn the connections between different essays, defined as follows:

$$A = [E_1, E_2, \ldots, E_N] \tag{9}$$

$$\alpha_j^i = \frac{e^{score(E_i, A_{i,j})}}{\sum\limits_{i}^{l} e^{score(E_i, A_{i,l})}} \tag{10}$$

$$P_i = \sum \alpha_j^i \cdot A_{i,j} \tag{11}$$

$$y_i = concatenate(E_i, P_i) \tag{12}$$

where A is a concatenation of the representations for each task $[E_1, E_2, \ldots, E_N]$, and α_j^i, is the attention weight. We then calculate attention vector P_i through a summation of the product of each weight α_j^i and $A_{i,j}$. The final representation y_i is a concatenation of E_i and P_i.

References

Asher, N., Lascarides, A.: Logics of Conversation. Cambridge University Press, Cambridge (2003)

Barzilay, R., Lapata, M.: Modeling local coherence: an entity-based approach. Comput. Linguist. **34**(1), 1–34 (2008)

Cui, Y., Che, W., Liu, T., Qin, B., Yang, Z.: Pre-training with whole word masking for Chinese BERT. IEEE/ACM Trans. Audio Speech Lang. Process. **29**, 3504–3514 (2021)

Farag, Y., Yannakoudakis, H.: Multi-task learning for coherence modeling. arXiv preprint arXiv:1907.02427 (2019)

Grosz, B.J., Joshi, A.K., Weinstein, S.: Centering: a framework for modelling the local coherence of discourse. Comput. Linguist. **21**(2), 203–225 (1995)

Guinaudeau, C., Strube, M.: Graph-based local coherence modeling. In: Proceedings of the 51st Annual Meeting of the Association for Computational Linguistics (Volume 1: Long Papers), pp. 93–103 (2013)

He, Y., Jiang, F., Chu, X., Li, P.: Automated Chinese essay scoring from multiple traits. In: Proceedings of the 29th International Conference on Computational Linguistics, pp. 3007–3016 (2022)

Jeon, S., Strube, M.: Entity-based neural local coherence modeling. In: Proceedings of the 60th Annual Meeting of the Association for Computational Linguistics (Volume 1: Long Papers), pp. 7787–7805 (2022)

Mann, W.C., Thompson, S.A.: Rhetorical structure theory: toward a functional theory of text organization. Text-interdisciplinary J. Study Discourse **8**(3), 243–281 (1988)

Mesgar, M., Strube, M.: A neural local coherence model for text quality assessment. In: Proceedings of the 2018 Conference on Empirical Methods in Natural Language Processing, pp. 4328–4339 (2018)

Moon, H.C., Mohiuddin, T., Joty, S., Chi, X.: A unified neural coherence model. arXiv preprint arXiv:1909.00349 (2019)

Nguyen, D.T., Joty, S.: A neural local coherence model. In: Proceedings of the 55th Annual Meeting of the Association for Computational Linguistics (Volume 1: Long Papers), pp. 1320–1330 (2017)

Song, W., Song, Z., Liu, L., Fu, R.: Hierarchical multi-task learning for organization evaluation of argumentative student essays. In: IJCAI, pp. 3875–3881 (2020)

Evaluation Workshop: Chinese Spelling Check

Towards Robust Chinese Spelling Check Systems: Multi-round Error Correction with Ensemble Enhancement

Xiang Li⬤, Hanyue Du⬤, Yike Zhao⬤, and Yunshi Lan$^{(\boxtimes)}$⬤

East China Normal University, Shanghai, China
{xiang.li,hydu,ykzhao}@stu.ecnu.edu.cn, yslan@dase.ecnu.edu.cn

Abstract. Chinese Spelling Check requires a system to automatically correct spelling errors in a sentence. There are diverse methods proposed to solve this task. A few methods improve the robustness of the model through data augmentation, but they have some weaknesses. Errors inserted randomly might disturb the real distribution of data. Moreover, different models may produce different results when predicting the same error sentence. Based on these intuitions, we develop a multi-round error correction method with ensemble enhancement, which is robust in solving Chinese Spelling Check challenges. Specifically, multi-round error correction follows an iterative correction pipeline, where a single error is corrected at each round, and the subsequent correction is conducted based on the previous results. Furthermore, we proposed two strategies of ensemble enhancement. For each predicted correction, results of multiple models are mutually authenticated by weighted voting and dominate voting. Experiments have proved the effectiveness of our system. It achieves the best performance on NLPCC 2023 CSC shared tasks. More analyses verify that both multi-round error correction and ensemble enhancement contribute to its good results. Our code is publicly available on GitHub.

Keywords: Chinese Spelling Check · Multi-round Error Correction · Ensemble

1 Introduction

Chinese[1] Spell Checking (CSC) is a challenging NLP task for detecting and correcting spelling errors in Chinese text, where the errors are mainly caused by phonological confusion and visual confusion [16]. It plays an important role in tasks in many downstream applications, such as speech recognition [8], Chinese grammar error correction, search engine [5,22], automatic essay scoring [2,19], and optical character recognition [1,27]. In the past decades, the techniques for CSC tasks have made great progress. Various methods have been well developed [17,30,33,35].

---

[1] https://github.com/Ashura5/MECEE.

© The Author(s), under exclusive license to Springer Nature Switzerland AG 2023
F. Liu et al. (Eds.): NLPCC 2023, LNAI 14304, pp. 325–336, 2023.
https://doi.org/10.1007/978-3-031-44699-3_29

Table 1. Example of Chinese spelling errors, where errors are marked in red.

Erroneous sentence	我买了一个花卷后就去付近的证卷公司开户了。
Target sentence	我买了一个花卷后就去附近的证券公司开户了。
Prediction (1)	我买了一个花券后就去附近的证券公司开户了。
Prediction (2)	我买了一个花卷后就去附近的证券公司开户了。

Despite significant progress in the methods for CSC tasks, there are few methods investigating on the robustness of CSC systems. In particularly, CRASPell [17] is proposed as a robust system to solve CSC challenge. This study synthesizes a single sentence with multiple errors by randomly inserting errors such that the augmented data could strengthen the training of the CSC model. Li and Zhang et al., [13] improves the robustness of the model by identifying the most vulnerable characters in a sentence and replacing them with characters in a confusion set to create adversarial examples. Both of these methods improve the robustness of the model through data augmentation, but they have weaknesses. Inserting errors randomly might disturb the real distribution of data and their effect is hard to control as they simply plays roles during data preparation.

Towards the robust CSC systems, intuitively, we find there may exist multiple errors in a sentence, which interfere with the context and thus affect the correction of the error. As illustrated in Table 1, the wrong word "证卷" affected the model's judgment of the "花卷", causing the mis-correction of the prediction (1). Moreover, as shown in Table 1, prediction (1) and (2) from different models may produce different results when predicting the same error sentence. Inspired from the traditional ensemble techniques [7,11,15], we comprehensively consider the results of each model through the ensemble strategies, and finally output the correct prediction, which also improves the robustness of the model.

Based on the above intuitions, we develop a multi-round error correction with ensemble enhancement, which is robust in solving CSC challenges. Specifically, multi-round error correction follows an iterative correction pipeline [38], where a single error is corrected at each round and the subsequent correction is conducted based on the presubsequent results. This procedure encourages the system to correct the most observable error at first, then the followup correction becomes easier. This can be considered as the implicit modeling of the dependency of the errors. Moreover, two strategies of ensemble enhancement are proposed. For each predicted correction, results of multiple models are authenticated mutually by weighted voting and dominate voting, which ensures the accuracy of the correction.

Experiments have proved that our system works effectively. It achieves the best performance on NLPCC 2023 CSC shared tasks, which results in 4.40, 76.03%, 48.04% and 58.88% on FPR, precision, recall and F1 score of correction, respectively. More analyses verify that both multi-round error correction and ensemble enhancement contribute its good results.

2 Related Work

CSC is a fundamental NLP task that aims to detect and correct the wrong characters in a Chinese sentence and has received a great amount of attention in the past few decades. The early methods for CSC tasks are template-based, which largely rely on hand-craft rules and dictionaries [10,21]. Later, a three-step strategy is developed for CSC challenge, where error detection, candidate generation, and candidate selection are performed in turn to convert a erroneous sentence into correct one [3,25,31]. In recent years, thanks to the emergence of neural network, a large number of neural network-based CSC methods have been proposed. SpellGCN [4] combines BERT with graph convolution network (GCN) [12] to construct two similarity graphs based on the relationship between pronunciation and shape, and merge them into a unique semantic space. REALISE [29] uses BERT and ResNet to capture textual and visual information respectively and fuse them to correct errors. Followup studies like PLOME [18], PHMOSpell [9], SCOPE [14] also leverage the multi-modal information of Chinese characters but design different model architectures to boost their performance in CSC tasks. However, these methods neglect the robustness of the system and are vulnerable to the noise of the training data and adversarial attacks.

Towards the robust CSC systems, two existing methods are developed. Specifically, Li and Zhang et al., [13] point out a CSC method can be easily attacked by adversarial training examples so they strength the model with task-specific pre-training strategies and the synthesized adversarial samples to improve the robustness of the model. To make the model robust to the contextual noise brought by typos, CRASPell [17] tries to generate a noisy context for each training instance, and then forces the correction model to produce similar output based on the original and noisy context. Different from the above methods, which propose data augmentation techniques to improve robustness, our system improve robustness by multi-round error correction and ensemble enhancement.

3 Our Approach

Our method follows an overall framework as shown in Fig. 1. The raw data is processed via a **Data Preparation** module, where non-Chinese and non-alphanumeric characters are removed from the data. Then a **Multi-round Error Correction Model** is conducted to correct the erroneous sentences based on the phonetics-enriched encoder with multiple rounds of single-error correction. This iterative procedure will stop when the confidence of a correction fails to exceed a threshold. Two strategies of **Ensemble Enhancement** are developed to integrate the corrected sentences generated from several correction models. The final prediction will be produced via further **Sentence Calibration** module. Next, we will describe each module in detail.

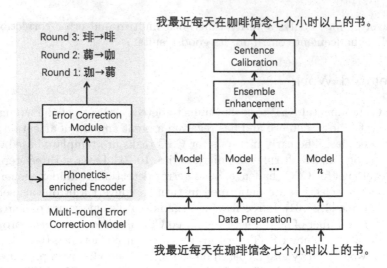

Fig. 1. Overall framework of our Chinese Spelling Check systems.

3.1 Data Preparation

To obtain a well-trained CSC system, we curated training dataset by collecting and processing data that are primarily used for Chinese Grammar Correction and Spelling Check. To make the data more suitable for the training of our system. We conduct data cleaning, which consists of the following two steps:

- **Character Standardization.** As the raw data contains both simplified and traditional Chinese characters, which leads to inconsistency to the training data. We convert the traditional Chinese characters into simplified Chinese characters.
- **Bad Case Filtering.** To further ensure the quality of training data, we filter out sentences containing non-Chinese or non-alphanumeric characters. We remove these sentence pairs with different lengths.

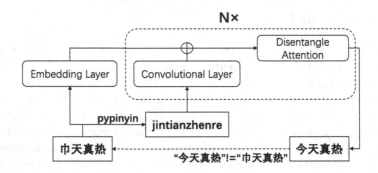

Fig. 2. Multi-round Error Correction

3.2   Multi-round Error Correction

Instead of correcting all the errors in a single sentence at once, we formulate the task as multiple rounds of error correction, which could implicitly model the dependency of errors and improve the robustness of the system. To this end, we propose multi-round error correction model as illustrated in Fig. 2. For each round, our model focuses on correcting the most observable error in the sentence. After that, the corrected sentence produced from the last round will be considered as the input of the next round. Until no confident corrected sentences are produced. Next, we introduce components in the model in detail.

Phonetics-Enriched Encoder. To encode the erroneous sentences, we adopt the phonetics-enriched encoder in DCN [26] to encode the erroneous sentence with the enriched phonetic information (referred to as Pinyin). For example, if our input is "巾天真热", we will also take its phonetic sequence "jin tian zhen re" as the enriched sequence. Specifically, we first convert the Chinese characters into vector representation via an embedding layer. Meanwhile, we use the pypinyin library[2] to get the pinyin of each Chinese character and the phonetic information is viewed as a sequence and encoded via a convolutional layerAfter that, we leverage a disentangled attention module [6] to fuse character and phonetic information together in order to strengthen the weight of phonetic encoding in the model to better solve the phonological errors.

Error Predictor. The encoder outputs the encoded representation for each characters in the sequence, we then use the Softmax function to transfer these hidden representations into probabilities. For each character in the sequence, we calculate the probability that it will be converted to each word in our dictionary. The position with the highest probability will be corrected first. For example, in the Table 1, the first round of error correction model will correct "珈" into "蒟", in the second round, the "蒟" error correction into "咖". At the last round, due to the correction of "咖", "琲" is successfully corrected into "啡". If this probability is greater than a threshold, we output the model's modification result this time and continue the next round of correction. Otherwise, we stop the iteration and return the predicted sentence. As a result, the correction process may repeat n times.

3.3   Two Strategies of Ensemble Enhancement

We train several multi-round correction models at the same time and ensemble their results to produce a more robust result. To enhance the robustness of the model and better collect the features of this spelling check dataset through the validation set, we propose the following two ensemble strategies for our system:

- **Weighted Voting.** Following traditional ensemble strategy [34], we assign a priori weight to each model and conduct correction via weighted voting. If a model suggests a modification for a character, the weight of that correction is

---

[2] https://github.com/mozillazg/python-pinyin.

increased by the weight of the model. If the final weight of the correction to certain character exceeds a certain threshold, the correction with the highest weight is applied to the sentence.

– **Dominant Voting.** The second strategy increases the power of the most confidence model. Instead of accumulating the weights, we let the model with the largest weight make the decision. If two models have made the same modification, we only keep the weight made by the model that is ranked higher. Compared with weighted voting, this strategy lets the model with the large weight dominate the voting.

Algorithm 1: Ensemble Enhancement

Input: input sentence $x^{(i)}$; output sentences from m models: $(\hat{y}_1^{(i)}, \hat{y}_2^{(i)}, ..., \hat{y}_m^{(i)})$;
weights of m models: $\{w_1, w_2, ..., w_m\}$
Initial: $\mathcal{E} \leftarrow \emptyset$; α
for $\hat{y}_j^{(i)} \in (\hat{y}_1^{(i)}, \hat{y}_2^{(i)}, ..., \hat{y}_m^{(i)})$ **do**
    for *each correction* $(a \rightarrow b)$ *from* $x^{(i)}$ *to* $\hat{y}_j^{(i)}$ **do**
        $\mathcal{E} \leftarrow \mathcal{E} \cup \{(a \rightarrow b)\}$
        Strategy 1) Compute the accumulative weights:
        $w_{(a \rightarrow b)} \leftarrow w_{(a \rightarrow b)} + w_j$ ▷ weighted voting
        Strategy 2) Remain the largest weight:
        $w_{(a \rightarrow b)} \leftarrow \max([w_{(a \rightarrow b)}, w_j])$ ▷ dominant voting
    end
end
for $(a \rightarrow b) \in \mathcal{E}$ **do**
    if $w_{(a \rightarrow b)} > \alpha$ *and* $(a \rightarrow b) = argmax(\{a \rightarrow *\})$ **then**
        Apply correction $(a \rightarrow b)$ to $x^{(i)}$ and obtain $\hat{y}^{*(i)}$
    end
end
Return: $\hat{y}^{*(i)}$

The detailed algorithm of these two ensemble strategies are displayed in Algorithm 1. It is worth noting that these two strategies are alternative for ensembling, we choose one strategy for all the erroneous sentences at one-time. Our overall ensembled system will be described in Sect. 4.2.

3.4 Sentence Calibration

To avoid false positive error correction which is caused by the multi-round correction and joint correction of multiple models, we conduct a simple sentence calibration. Specifically, we replace the tokens that are deemed as incorrect based on the multi-round error correction with symbol "[MASK]". Then we feed the masked sentence into Chinese-BERT which returns the joint probability of the prediction of the masked positions. We denote it as P_{pred}. P_{pred} indicates how fluency the prediction makes the sentence to be. We compare it with the joint probability of the original tokens of the masked positions, which is denoted as P_{orig}. If $P_{\text{orig}} > P_{\text{pred}}$, we believe the corrected sentence does not improve the original sentence and we directly use the original input as the prediction.

For example, $P_{\text{pred}} = 2.45$ of the predicted sentence "高先生便发动面馆的服务员一起将煮好的面送到路边给环卫工吃。" is lower than $P_{\text{pred}} = 3.04$ of the original input sentence "高先生便带动面馆的服务员一起将煮好的面送到路边给环卫工吃。". As a result, we abandon the correction made by our system.

4 Experiments

4.1 Datasets

For training, we augment the data with a variety of related datasets, including CGED [23,24], CTC2021 [36], HSK [32], Lang8 [37], MuCGEC [34], YACLC [28], SIGNHAN14, SIGNHAN15, hybrid and WANG27 [27]. These datasets cover a wide range of Chinese text sources, providing a comprehensive and diverse data pool for our system to learn.

Among them, CGED, CTC2021, WANG27, and HSK datasets are specifically designed for Chinese Grammar Error Correction tasks, providing a rich source of sentences with various types of errors. SIGNHAN14 and SIGNHAN15 datasets are derived from the Chinese handwriting recognition tasks, where errors in sentences are generally caused by the misuse of phonologically similar characters. We process the above datasets via data preparation steps mentioned in Sect. 3.1 and denote the cleaned training data from the shared tasks as **Cleaned Set**. Lang8, MuCGEC, and YACLC datasets are collections of CGEC challenges but the corpus is collected from the learners studying Chinese as a Foreigner Language (CFL), where. We follow the existing work [27] to synthesize some CSC data using the above CGEC dataset and denote them as **Augmented Set**. Eventually, our cleaned data and the augmented set for training contains around 1 million and 500,000 sentence pairs, respectively.

We follow the evaluation metrics in the shared tasks to measure the results. FPR is to measure the False Positive Rate at the sentence level. P_D, R_D and $F1_D$ are precision, recall and F1 score of error detection. P_C, R_C and $F1_C$ are precision, recall and F1 score of error correction.

4.2 Comparable Methods

We compare our overall system with its variants, which can be demonstrated as follows:

- **Base**: This is the traditional CSC model without multi-round correction, there is no ensemble is included. We train it with different training data set.
- **Multi-round**: This the single model of multi-round error correction, there is no ensemble is included. We also train it with different training data set.
- **Ensemble**: This is multi-round error correction model with ensemble enhancement. Specifically, we train three multi-round models with cleaned data, augmented data and all data. Then we use weighted voting strategy to ensemble their results. We further fine-tune another multi-round model with validation data provided in the shared task and ensemble the results via dominant voting.

- **Base**$_{SC}$, **Multi-round**$_{SC}$ **Ensemble**$_{SC}$: These are the base, multi-round and ensemble models featured with sentence calibration.

We also compare the results of our system on the test set with results from **Other Systems** on the leaderboard[3].

4.3 Implementation Details

For data preparation, we use the unicodedata module from Python's standard library for character set conversion, and use zhconv[4] for conversion between Simplified and Traditional Chinese.

For multi-round error correction, we employ BERT-base[5] as encoder. We use AdamW [20] as an optimizer for model training and fine-tuning. Referring to the PLOME [18], we set the learning rate to $5e-5$, the batch size to 64, and the maximum sentence length to 128. We use a server with a V100 32G GPU to run our code, and each model is trained for 3 epochs, with each epoch takes about 4 hours to run. We use 0.3 as the threshold for correction and the maximum number of iteration is set to 5.

For model ensembling, we used different random seeds for models using different datasets during the weighted voting stage, and trained two models for each, totaling six models. We assigned a weight of 1 to each model, and chose an ensemble threshold of 2. For dominate voting, we trained an additional model that overfits on the validation set. We assigned a weight of 1 to the results from the previous weighted voting, and a weight of 0.5 to the model trained on the validation set. After dominate voting, we obtained the final result of our model ensemble. All the hyper-parameters are set based on the best performance on the validation set.

4.4 Comparison with Other Systems

We display the results in Table 2. Our system achieves the best performance of $F1_D$ and $F1_C$ on the test set compared with other systems and rank first in the NLPCC 2023 shared CSC challenge. We believe this is because our overall architecture designed for CSC tasks is effective. For example, among the one thousand data entries in the validation set, we notice 500 of them have spelling errors. Out of them, 470 entries have one error, 29 entries have two errors, and 1 entry has three errors in a single sentence. Our design of correcting one error per round is more in line with the characteristics of this tasks. Besides this, ensemble and calibration are also important in achieving ggos results.

---

[3] https://github.com/Arvid-pku/NLPCC2023_Shared_Task8/tree/main.
[4] https://github.com/gumblex/zhconv.
[5] https://github.com/google-research/bert.

4.5 Comparison with Variants

We compare the results of our system and its variants, we have the following observations: (1) When we compare the same model trained on different data sets, we notice that due to the large size of our cleaned set, it can already help to train our system well. As the augmented data is synthesized by corpus from other tasks, adding the augmented set even deteriorates the performance of our model. (2) Our ensemble enhancement can significantly improve the performance. It balances and controls accuracy and recall by adjusting different thresholds. When the threshold is lower, the result has a higher recall rate but lower accuracy. When the threshold is higher, the result has higher accuracy but lower recall rate. (3) The post-processing of sentence calibration strategy can reduce FPR dramatically. However, we also notice that if the original prediction does not contain many false corrections, it may hurt the performance instead.

Table 2. Performance of the comparable methods.

Method	Dataset	FPR $\downarrow$	P_D $\uparrow$	R_D $\uparrow$	$F1_D$ $\uparrow$	P_C $\uparrow$	R_C $\uparrow$	$F1_C$ $\uparrow$
Evaluation on validation set								
Base	Cleaned set	7.20	66.91	34.65	45.66	57.82	29.94	39.45
Multi-round	Cleaned set	7.80	67.62	44.44	53.63	60.46	39.74	47.96
Multi-round$_{SC}$	Cleaned set	**4.40**	73.82	44.07	55.19	65.93	39.36	49.29
Base	Augmented set	10.60	57.74	33.71	42.57	47.74	27.87	35.19
Multi-round	Augmented set	11.80	58.55	**45.76**	51.37	50.84	39.74	44.61
Multi-round$_{SC}$	Augmented set	7.80	63.85	45.57	53.18	55.41	39.55	46.16
Base	All	9.40	58.39	30.13	39.75	46.72	24.11	31.81
Multi-round	All	10.60	58.27	40.49	47.78	49.86	34.65	40.89
Multi-round$_{SC}$	All	7.60	62.61	39.74	48.62	53.71	34.09	41.71
Ensemble	All	6.20	73.29	44.44	55.33	66.77	**40.49**	50.41
Ensemble$_{SC}$	All	4.60	**77.12**	44.44	**56.39**	70.26	**40.49**	**51.37**
Evaluation on test set								
Ensemble$_{SC}$	All	4.40	79.95	50.52	**61.92**	76.03	**48.04**	**58.88**
HW-TSC	–	5.96	78.77	**50.85**	61.80	73.9	47.7	57.98
GLN	–	4.00	81.97	47.15	59.87	78.36	45.07	57.23
Zhao jia	–	**1.92**	**85.92**	39.33	53.96	**79.05**	36.19	49.65

4.6 Case Study

For the example "大家欣系弱狂，奔走相告。", our multi-round error correction system first corrects the mistake to "大家欣系若狂，奔走相告。", and in the second round, it corrects it to "大家欣喜若狂，奔走相告。".

And for the example "骨头汤的主要成分是水，其它还包括脂肪、蛋白质、胆固醇等。", our multi-round error correction system outputs "骨头汤的主要成分是水，其它还包含脂肪、蛋白质、胆固醇等。", but actually both "包括" and "包含" are fine, so our sentence calibration module will delete the modification and finally output "骨头汤的主要成分是水，其它还包括脂肪、蛋白质、胆固醇等。".

However, for the example "杨洪基推掉的商演机会，他已经不记得有多少次了。", the model we trained using the cleaned set would modify it to "杨洪基推掉的上演机会，他已经不记得有多少次了。", but the model trained with the Augmented set and the entire dataset would not make any modifications. Through our weighted voting strategy, our model will not make any changes.

5 Conclusions

For the Chinese spelling check task, we developed a multi-round error correction approach with ensemble enhancement, which is a robust system. It achieves the best performance on NLPCC 2023 CSC shared tasks. More analyses verify that each component contributes to the good results.

Acknowledgments. This work was supported in part by Research Funds under National Natural Science Foundation of China (Grant No. 61977026), East China Normal University (Grant No. 2022ECNU-WHCCYJ-29, 2022ECNU-WHCCYJ-31), and Ministry of Education of China (Grant No. YHJC22ZD067).

References

1. Afli, H., Qiu, Z., Way, A., Sheridan, P.: Using SMT for OCR error correction of historical texts. In: Language Resources and Evaluation (2016)
2. Burstein, J., Chodorow, M.: Automated essay scoring for nonnative English speakers. In: Proceedings of a Symposium on Computer Mediated Language Assessment and Evaluation in Natural Language Processing - ASSESSEVALNLP 1999 (1999)
3. Chen, K.Y., Lee, H.S., Lee, C.H., Wang, H.M., Chen, H.H.: A study of language modeling for Chinese spelling check (2013)
4. Cheng, X., et al.: Spellgcn: Incorporating phonological and visual similarities into language models for Chinese spelling check. In: Proceedings of the 58th Annual Meeting of the Association for Computational Linguistics (2020)
5. Gao, J., Li, X., Micol, D., Quirk, C., Sun, X.: A large scale ranker-based system for search query spelling correction. In: International Conference on Computational Linguistics (2010)
6. He, P., Liu, X., Gao, J., Chen, W.: Deberta: decoding-enhanced BERT with disentangled attention. CoRR (2020)
7. Heafield, K., Lavie, A.: Combining machine translation output with open source: the carnegie mellon multi-engine machine translation scheme. In: The Prague Bulletin of Mathematical Linguistics, vol. 93 (2010)
8. Hinton, G., et al.: Deep neural networks for acoustic modeling in speech recognition: the shared views of four research groups. IEEE Signal Process. Mag. **29**, 82–97 (2012)

9. Huang, L., et al.: Phmospell: phonological and morphological knowledge guided Chinese spelling check. In: Proceedings of the 59th Annual Meeting of the Association for Computational Linguistics and the 11th International Joint Conference on Natural Language Processing (Volume 1: Long Papers) (2021)
10. Jiang, Y., et al.: A rule based Chinese spelling and grammar detection system utility. In: 2012 International Conference on System Science and Engineering (ICSSE) (2012)
11. Kantor, Y., et al.: Learning to combine grammatical error corrections. Cornell University - arXiv (2019)
12. Kipf, T., Welling, M.: Semi-supervised classification with graph convolutional networks. arXiv: Learning (2016)
13. Li, C., Zhang, C., Zheng, X., Huang, X.: Exploration and exploitation: two ways to improve Chinese spelling correction models. In: Proceedings of the 59th Annual Meeting of the Association for Computational Linguistics and the 11th International Joint Conference on Natural Language Processing (Volume 2: Short Papers) (2021)
14. Li, J., Wang, Q., Mao, Z., Guo, J., Yang, Y., Zhang, Y.: Improving Chinese spelling check by character pronunciation prediction: the effects of adaptivity and granularity (2022)
15. Lin, R., Ng, H.: System combination for grammatical error correction based on integer programming
16. Liu, C.L., Lai, M.H., Chuang, Y.H., Lee, C.Y.: Visually and phonologically similar characters in incorrect simplified Chinese words. In: International Conference on Computational Linguistics (2010)
17. Liu, S., et al.: CRASpell: a contextual typo robust approach to improve Chinese spelling correction
18. Liu, S., Yang, T., Yue, T., Zhang, F., Wang, D.: PLOME: pre-training with misspelled knowledge for Chinese spelling correction. In: Proceedings of the 59th Annual Meeting of the Association for Computational Linguistics and the 11th International Joint Conference on Natural Language Processing (Volume 1: Long Papers), pp. 2991–3000 (2021)
19. Lonsdale, D., Strong-Krause, D.: Automated rating of ESL essays. In: Proceedings of the HLT-NAACL 03 Workshop on Building Educational Applications Using Natural Language Processing (2003)
20. Loshchilov, I., Hutter, F.: Fixing weight decay regularization in ADAM. CoRR (2017)
21. Mangu, L., Brill, E.: Automatic rule acquisition for spelling correction. International Conference on Machine Learning (1997)
22. Martins, B., Silva, M.J.: Spelling correction for search engine queries. In: Advances in Natural Language Processing, pp. 372–383 (2004)
23. Rao, G., Gong, Q., Zhang, B., Xun, E.: Overview of nlptea-2018 share task Chinese grammatical error diagnosis. In: Proceedings of the 5th Workshop on Natural Language Processing Techniques for Educational Applications (NLPTEA-2018) (2018)
24. Rao, G., Yang, E., Zhang, B.: Overview of nlptea-2020 shared task for Chinese grammatical error diagnosis. In: Proceedings of the 6th Workshop on Natural Language Processing Techniques for Educational Applications (NLPTEA-2020) (2020)
25. Tseng, Y.H., Lee, L.H., Chang, L.P., Chen, H.H.: Introduction to SIGHAN 2015 bake-off for Chinese spelling check. In: Proceedings of the Eighth SIGHAN Workshop on Chinese Language Processing (2015)

26. Wang, B., Che, W., Wu, D., Wang, S., Hu, G., Liu, T.: Dynamic connected networks for Chinese spelling check. In: Findings of the Association for Computational Linguistics: ACL-IJCNLP 2021, pp. 2437–2446 (2021)
27. Wang, D., Song, Y., Li, J., Han, J., Zhang, H.: A hybrid approach to automatic corpus generation for Chinese spelling check. In: Proceedings of the 2018 Conference on Empirical Methods in Natural Language Processing, pp. 2517–2527 (2018)
28. Wang, Y., Kong, C., et al.: YACLC: a Chinese learner corpus with multidimensional annotation. CoRR (2021)
29. Xu, H., et al.: Read, listen, and see: leveraging multimodal information helps Chinese spell checking. Cornell University - arXiv (2021)
30. Yin, X., Hu, X., Wan, X.: Chinese spelling check with nearest neighbors (2022)
31. Yu, J., Li, Z.: Chinese spelling error detection and correction based on language model, pronunciation, and shape. In: Proceedings of The Third CIPS-SIGHAN Joint Conference on Chinese Language Processing (2014)
32. Zhang, B.: Features and functions of the HSK dynamic composition corpus. In: International Chinese Language Education, pp. 71–79 (2009). (in Chinese)
33. Zhang, X., Yan, H., Yu, S., Qiu, X.: SDCL: self-distillation contrastive learning for Chinese spell checking (2022)
34. Zhang, Y., et al.: MuCGEC: a multi-reference multi-source evaluation dataset for Chinese grammatical error correction. In: Proceedings of the 2022 Conference of the North American Chapter of the Association for Computational Linguistics: Human Language Technologies, pp. 3118–3130 (2022)
35. Zhao, G., Guo, Y., Xia, F., Ma, C.: A multimodal method for Chinese spelling correction. In: 2022 International Joint Conference on Neural Networks (IJCNN), pp. 01–07 (2022)
36. Zhao, H., Wang, B., Wu, D., Che, W., Chen, Z., Wang, S.: Overview of CTC 2021: Chinese text correction for native speakers. arXiv preprint arXiv:2208.05681 (2022)
37. Zhao, Y., Jiang, N., Sun, W., Wan, X.: Overview of the NLPCC 2018 shared task: grammatical error correction. In: Zhang, M., Ng, V., Zhao, D., Li, S., Zan, H. (eds.) Natural Language Processing and Chinese Computing, pp. 439–445 (2018)
38. Zhou, Z., Xv, X., Chen, Z., Han, W., Mu, Y., Zhang, J.: Chinese spelling check error correction system based on pinyin coding and multi-wheel error correction reasoning. Technical report (2022)

Overview of the NLPCC 2023 Shared Task: Chinese Spelling Check

Xunjian Yin[1,2,3]($\boxtimes$) (iD), Xiaojun Wan[1,2,3], Dan Zhang[4] (iD), Linlin Yu[4] (iD), and Long Yu[4] (iD)

[1] Wangxuan Institute of Computer Technology, Peking University, Beijing, China
{xjyin,wanxiaojun}@pku.edu.cn
[2] Center for Data Science, Peking University, Beijing, China
[3] The MOE Key Laboratory of Computational Linguistics, Peking University, Beijing, China
[4] Beijing Founder Electronics Co., Ltd., Beijing, China
{zhangdan,llyu,yulong}@founder.com.cn

Abstract. This paper provides an overview of the Chinese Spelling Check shared task 8, held at NLPCC 2023. The task aims to correct spelling errors in Chinese sentences, including homophonic errors, visually similar errors, and other types of errors found in Chinese news articles. We present the task's description, previous work related to Chinese Spelling Check, statistics on the provided dataset, evaluation results, and a summary of the submitted approaches. The dataset consists of 1k instances for development and 11k instances for evaluation, collected from publicly available news articles and books. The errors in the dataset were manually identified and labeled. A total of 47 teams registered for the task, with 12 teams submitting their results. The evaluation metric used is the F1 score, with the highest achieved score being 0.5888. The submitted approaches employ various techniques to enhance performance, each focusing on different aspects of the problem. For more information, please visit our official website.

Keywords: Chinese Spelling Check · Error Correction

1 Introduction

Spelling[1] errors are a common occurrence in both written text by individuals and in natural language processing tasks, posing significant challenges. These errors can have detrimental effects on the accuracy and clarity of the conveyed information. Consequently, numerous methods have been proposed to address the issue of spelling errors in various tasks, such as spelling check [3,4,24].

While English and other alphabetic languages have relatively fewer characters to manage, Chinese, being character-based, comprises a vast inventory of

---

[1] https://github.com/Arvid-pku/NLPCC2023_Shared_Task8.

F. Liu et al. (Eds.): NLPCC 2023, LNAI 14304, pp. 337–345, 2023.
https://doi.org/10.1007/978-3-031-44699-3_30

over 10,000 characters. Furthermore, a considerable portion of Chinese characters exhibit similarities, either in phonology or morphology, making them prone to being mistakenly replaced with other characters from the vocabulary. Correcting these errors can be particularly challenging [9,10,17]. To illustrate this point, consider the example shown in Table 1, where the original sentence contains three incorrect characters highlighted in red: the first error is a phonetic similarity mistake, as both 药 and 要 have the same pinyin pronunciation, "yao4"; the second error is a graphic similarity mistake between 堤 and 提: the third error is even more difficult to correct because it is necessary to know that in Chinese, when the object is a human being, "提高(improve)" is paired with "素质(ability)" rather than "品质".

Table 1. Examples of phonological similarity error and visual similarity error. The correct sentence means "We need to improve our abilities."

Wrong	我们 药(pinyin: *yao4*. "medicine")	堤(strokes: {土, 是}. "dyke")	高自身品质
Correct	我们 要(pinyin: *yao4*. "need")	提(strokes: {手, 是}. "improve")	高自身素质

According to Liu et al. [11], approximately 83% of Chinese spelling errors are attributed to phonetic similarity, 48% are caused by graphic similarity, and 35% involve both factors. So we need to train the model to improve its effectiveness on both of these errors. Numerous studies in the field of Chinese Spelling Check (CSC) have focused on incorporating phonetic and graphic information into neural models to learn the phonological or morphological relationships between characters [2,7,8,16,23]. However, the current state of these models and the effectiveness of the techniques employed in CSC remain unclear due to limited test sets and a lack of comprehensive evaluation and analysis. In addition, in practice, the third type of error is more difficult, so we also need to focus on evaluating the third type of error.

To facilitate a more thorough evaluation of the current advancements in Chinese spelling correction technology, in NLPCC2023, we have organized a shared task and introduced a new validation set and test set for participants. The provided dataset features a wider range of errors and presents more significant challenges, aiming to benefit the research community in this domain.

The dataset comprises 1,000 instances for development and 11,000 instances for evaluation, collected from publicly available news articles and books. Errors within the dataset were manually identified and labeled. A total of 47 teams registered for the task, with 12 teams submitting their results. The evaluation metric employed is the F1 score, with the highest achieved score reaching 0.5888. The submitted approaches encompass a variety of techniques aimed at enhancing performance, each focusing on different aspects of the problem.

2   Related Work

The field of Chinese Spelling Correction (CSC) has witnessed significant advancements in recent years. Various approaches have been proposed to tackle this task, leveraging state-of-the-art models and incorporating different linguistic and visual features. In this section, we review several notable works in the domain and discuss their contributions. FASpell [6] introduced the use of BERT as a denoising autoencoder for CSC. By training BERT on corrupted Chinese sentences and reconstructing the original sentences, FASpell achieved promising results in spelling correction. Another approach, Soft-Masked BERT [24], combined a Bi-GRU based detection network with a BERT based correction network. This hybrid architecture effectively detected errors and generated corrected spellings using BERT, leading to improved performance in CSC. To incorporate phonetic and graphic information into CSC models, SpellGCN proposed the utilization of graph convolutional networks on pronunciation and shape similarity graphs. By capturing the underlying relationships between characters based on their pronunciation and shape, SpellGCN aimed to enhance the accuracy of spelling correction [2]. Nguyen et al. [13] employed TreeLSTM to obtain hierarchical character embeddings as graphic information. This approach utilized the structural information within Chinese characters to enhance the representation learning process, ultimately improving CSC performance. REALISE [19] adopted a combination of Transformer [15] and ResNet5 [5] to separately capture phonetic and graphic information. By leveraging these two powerful architectures, REALISE aimed to better capture the distinctive features of Chinese characters, leading to enhanced spelling correction accuracy. In the case of PLOME [12], the authors chose to apply the GRU [1] to encode pinyin and stroke sequences. By effectively modeling the sequential patterns in pinyin and strokes, PLOME improved the ability to correct spelling errors in Chinese text. PHMOSpell [7] derived phonetic and graphic information from multi-modal pre-trained models, including Tacotron2 and VGG19. By leveraging the complementary strengths of these models, PHMOSpell aimed to enhance the representation learning process and achieve more accurate spelling correction. And InfoKNN-CSC [20] extends the standard CSC model by linearly interpolating it with a k-nearest neighbors model.

Despite the advancements in CSC models, the benchmarks and evaluation methods for this task remain inadequate. The commonly used datasets are the SIGHAN datasets [14,18,22], which were utilized in CSC campaigns conducted in 2013, 2014, and 2015. However, there is a need for more diverse and challenging datasets to evaluate the performance of CSC models accurately.

3   Dataset

3.1   Dataset Provided

The development dataset we provided consists of 1000 sentence pairs, encompassing both incorrect and correct sentences. This dataset serves as a valuable resource for participants to conduct local training and testing. In addition to utilizing our development dataset, participants are encouraged to augment their training data with other open-source datasets, such as SIGHAN13, SIGHAN14, SIGHAN15, Lang8, HSK, CGED, MuCGEC, YACLC, CTC2021[2], among others. These external datasets can provide further diversity and enhance the performance of their systems.

Furthermore, we employed a closed-source dataset comprising 11,000 sentence pairs with the same distribution as the development set. This closed-source dataset was exclusively used as a test set to evaluate the performance of all participants' systems.

The errors present in the original sentences can be categorized into three main types: Homophonic Spelling Errors, Visually Similar Errors, and Other Types. Table 2 illustrates examples of each error type encountered in our dataset.

Table 2. Examples of our datasets. There are three types of errors in our sentences.

	Input	Target
Homophonic Spelling Error	公司在处理技术、产品设计、检验检测等方面有着坚实的基础和出色的造诣，形成了较强的技术优式。	公司在处理技术、产品设计、检验检测等方面有着坚实的基础和出色的造诣，形成了较强的技术优势。
Visually Similar Error	严格落实"开喷淋、常冲洗、勤洒水"等防治措施。	严格落实"开喷淋、常冲洗、勤洒水"等防治措施。
Other Types	然而几个以前，张大妈还深陷在窨井盖爆炸的阴影中。	然而几个月前，张大妈还深陷在窨井盖爆炸的阴影中。
	老一辈科学家身上充沛着为科学而献身的可贵精神。	老一辈科学家身上充满着为科学而献身的可贵精神。

3.2 Analysis of SIGHAN Datasets

As mentioned in the previous work [21], SIGHAN datasets have been widely used as a test set in previous studies. However, they suffer from several critical drawbacks that need to be addressed:

1. Limited Size: The SIGHAN datasets are relatively small, with only a few thousand sentence pairs in the training set and approximately a thousand errors in each test set. This scarcity of data makes it challenging to train robust error correction models and effectively evaluate their performance. To compensate for this limitation, researchers have used confusion sets for data augmentation. However, due to the small dataset size, these confusion sets often cover the errors already present in the test sets, leading to evaluation results that may not accurately reflect the true error correction ability of the models.

---

[2] Please note that the references to external datasets have been hyperlinked for ease of access and reference.

2. Traditional Chinese vs. Simplified Chinese: The SIGHAN datasets use traditional Chinese, while most current research primarily focuses on simplified Chinese. Although tools like OpenCC[3] can convert traditional Chinese to simplified Chinese, some aspects of the data may not perfectly align with the conventions and usage of simplified Chinese.
3. Noisy Data: The SIGHAN datasets contain varying degrees of noise, including instances where errors are not properly corrected. This noise affects the reliability of the datasets and subsequently impacts the training and evaluation of error correction models.

These drawbacks of the SIGHAN datasets necessitate careful consideration and potential strategies to address them in order to foster more reliable and comprehensive error correction research. We therefore evaluated the participants' models using our own labeled test set.

4   Evaluation Metrics

The system's performance will be evaluated using the following metrics:

4.1   Detection Level

Detection precision is the percentage of detected errors that overlap with the standard detection answers. It is calculated by dividing the number of overlapping positions between the detected errors and the standard detection answers by the total number of detected errors.

Detection recall is the percentage of standard detection answers that overlap with the detected errors. It is calculated by dividing the number of overlapping positions between the detected errors and the standard detection answers by the total number of standard detection answers.

Detection F1-score is the harmonic mean of detection precision and recall.

4.2   Correction Level

Correction precision is the percentage of corrected characters that match the standard correction answers. It is calculated by dividing the number of corrected characters that match the standard correction answers by the total number of edited characters.

Correction recall is the percentage of corrected characters that match the standard correction answers. It is calculated by dividing the number of corrected characters that match the standard correction answers by the total number of standard correction answers.

Correction F1-score is the harmonic mean of correction precision and recall.

These evaluation metrics assess the AI model's ability to detect and correct spelling errors in textual content. They provide a comprehensive evaluation of the model's accuracy and efficiency in error identification and rectification. Higher scores indicate better model performance.

---

[3] https://github.com/BYVoid/OpenCC.

4.3 False Positive Rate

In consideration of real-world applications, we also include the **false positive rate** at the sentence level in our analysis. This metric measures the proportion of correctly formed sentences that are incorrectly altered by the model.

Table 3. Final evaluation results and rankings. The best results are in **bold**.

rank	team	char-detect-P	char-detect-R	char-detect-F1	char-correct-P	char-correct-R	char-correct-F1	sentence-FPR
1	GGbond	79.95	50.52	**61.92**	76.03	**48.04**	**58.88**	4.4
2	HW-TSC	78.77	**50.85**	61.8	73.9	47.7	57.98	5.96
3	GLN	81.97	47.15	59.87	78.36	45.07	57.23	4.0
4	Zhao Jia	**85.92**	39.33	53.96	**79.05**	36.19	49.65	1.92
5	RTX5090	75.14	39.41	51.7	69.63	36.52	47.91	3.4
6	TingZhiDui	74.87	43.37	54.92	62.79	36.37	46.06	5.32
7	CUHK_SU	79.48	33.0	46.64	76.98	31.96	45.17	**1.76**
8	CSCJXYZ	78.31	35.3	48.66	72.14	32.52	44.83	4.68
9	HHS	56.04	36.96	44.54	48.34	31.89	38.43	11.04
10	OUC_NLP	51.67	30.33	38.22	43.85	25.74	32.44	8.52
11	POLab	19.49	33.74	24.71	18.23	31.56	23.11	2.84
12	ZZUNLP	19.3	44.78	26.97	15.2	35.26	21.24	4.44

5 Evaluation

5.1 Results

A total of 47 teams registered for the shared task, and 12 of them submitted results that complied with the rules. The complete results and rankings can be found in Table 3. The highest F0.5 score achieved for correction was 0.5888, which is noticeably lower compared to the results obtained on the SIGHAN test set.

5.2 Result Analysis

The provided table (Table 3) presents the evaluation results and rankings of different teams' models. The evaluation metrics include precision (P), recall (R), and F1 score for both character detection (char-detect) and character correction (char-correct), as well as the false positive rate (FPR) at the sentence level. The rankings are based on the F1 score for character correction.

Character Detection. In terms of character detection performance, the team "Zhao Jia" achieved the highest precision (85.92%) among all the teams, demonstrating their ability to accurately identify incorrect characters in Chinese sentences. However, their recall (39.33%) was relatively low. The team "GGbond" obtained the highest F1 score (61.92%), demonstrating a good balance between precision (79.95%) and recall (50.52%). "HW-TSC" ranked second with a slightly lower F1 score (61.8%), but had the highest recall (50.85%) among all the teams, indicating that they were able to detect more incorrect characters.

Character Correction. For character correction, "Zhao Jia" achieved the highest precision (79.05%) and "GGbond" had the highest recall (48.04%). However, neither of these teams achieved the best balance between precision and recall, as indicated by their F1 scores. The team "GGbond" had the highest F1 score (58.88%), followed closely by "HW-TSC" (57.98%). Both teams demonstrated relatively good performance in correcting incorrect characters in Chinese sentences. Teams "GLN," "Zhao Jia," and "RTX5090" achieved comparable results in terms of F1 score for character correction, while the remaining teams had lower performance. It's worth noting that some teams with higher character detection performance did not necessarily exhibit superior character correction capabilities.

Sentence-Level False Positive Rate. The false positive rate (FPR) at the sentence level measures the rate of incorrectly identified incorrect characters within sentences. A lower FPR indicates better performance in avoiding false corrections. The team "CUHK_SU" achieved the lowest FPR (1.76%), demonstrating their ability to make accurate corrections with minimal false positives. "Zhao Jia" and "POLab" also achieved relatively low FPRs (1.92% and 2.84% respectively). It's important to strike a balance between identifying incorrect characters and avoiding false corrections, as high FPRs can negatively impact the overall quality of the spelling correction system.

Overall Performance. Based on the F1 score for character correction, the team "GGbond" achieved the best overall performance, ranking first in the evaluation. They demonstrated a good balance between precision and recall in detecting incorrect characters. "HW-TSC" and "GLN" obtained the second and third rankings, respectively.

In conclusion, the results from the evaluation highlight the teams' performance in character detection, character correction, and sentence-level false positive rate. The team "GGbond" consistently achieved top rankings in both character detection and correction, while "Zhao Jia" excelled in character detection precision and achieved the lowest false positive rate. These findings provide valuable insights into the strengths and weaknesses of different teams' models for Chinese spelling check.

5.3   Representative Systems

The majority of participants employed the technique of model ensemble, where they reproduced several current representative models and integrated them using various voting methods to obtain the final results.

One notable system is developed by Team GGbond, who proposed a robust multi-round error correction method with ensemble enhancement. Their approach follows an iterative correction pipeline, wherein each round focuses on correcting a specific error, and subsequent corrections are made based on the previous results. Additionally, they introduced two strategies for ensemble enhancement: weighted voting and dominant voting, which were utilized to obtain the final results.

Another noteworthy system is introduced by Team HW-TSC, who aimed to enhance the capabilities of two baseline models, namely MacBert and MDC-Spell. The researchers implemented several optimization strategies to improve the performance of these models. Furthermore, they employed model ensemble techniques by combining the outputs of both models. The optimization methods utilized in this study included data augmentation, language model ranking, and NER correction. These enhancements significantly contributed to the overall performance improvement of the system.

6   Conclusion

In conclusion, the Chinese Spelling Check shared task at NLPCC 2023 aimed to correct spelling errors in Chinese sentences. A total of 47 teams registered for the task, with 12 teams submitting their results for evaluation. The dataset consists of 1k instances for development and 11k instances for evaluation, collected from publicly available news articles and books. The highest achieved F1 score for spelling correction was 0.5888, obtained by the team GGbond. The submitted approaches utilized various techniques, including machine learning algorithms, neural networks, and linguistic rules, to enhance performance. For more information on the shared task, interested readers can visit the official website[4].

References

1. Bahdanau, D., Cho, K., Bengio, Y.: Neural machine translation by jointly learning to align and translate. arXiv preprint arXiv:1409.0473 (2014)
2. Cheng, X., et al.: SpellGCN: incorporating phonological and visual similarities into language models for Chinese spelling check. arXiv preprint arXiv:2004.14166 (2020)
3. Etoori, P., Chinnakotla, M., Mamidi, R.: Automatic spelling correction for resource-scarce languages using deep learning. In: Proceedings of ACL 2018, Student Research Workshop, pp. 146–152 (2018)
4. Guo, J., Sainath, T.N., Weiss, R.J.: A spelling correction model for end-to-end speech recognition. In: ICASSP 2019–2019 IEEE International Conference on Acoustics, Speech and Signal Processing (ICASSP), pp. 5651–5655. IEEE (2019)
5. He, K., Zhang, X., Ren, S., Sun, J.: Deep residual learning for image recognition. In: Proceedings of the IEEE Conference on Computer Vision and Pattern Recognition, pp. 770–778 (2016)
6. Hong, Y., Yu, X., He, N., Liu, N., Liu, J.: Faspell: a fast, adaptable, simple, powerful Chinese spell checker based on DAE-decoder paradigm. In: Proceedings of the 5th Workshop on Noisy User-generated Text (W-NUT 2019), pp. 160–169 (2019)

---

[4] https://github.com/Arvid-pku/NLPCC2023_Shared_Task8.

7. Huang, L., et al.: Phmospell: phonological and morphological knowledge guided Chinese spelling check. In: Proceedings of the 59th Annual Meeting of the Association for Computational Linguistics and the 11th International Joint Conference on Natural Language Processing (Volume 1: Long Papers). pp. 5958–5967 (2021)
8. Ji, T., Yan, H., Qiu, X.: SpellBert: a lightweight pretrained model for Chinese spelling check. In: Proceedings of the 2021 Conference on Empirical Methods in Natural Language Processing, pp. 3544–3551 (2021)
9. Jia, Z., Wang, P., Zhao, H.: Graph model for Chinese spell checking. In: Proceedings of the Seventh SIGHAN Workshop on Chinese Language Processing, pp. 88–92 (2013)
10. Kukich, K.: Techniques for automatically correcting words in text. ACM Comput. Surv. (CSUR) **24**(4), 377–439 (1992)
11. Liu, C.L., Lai, M.H., Tien, K.W., Chuang, Y.H., Wu, S.H., Lee, C.Y.: Visually and phonologically similar characters in incorrect Chinese words: analyses, identification, and applications. ACM Trans. Asian Lang. Inf. Process. (TALIP) **10**(2), 1–39 (2011)
12. Liu, S., Yang, T., Yue, T., Zhang, F., Wang, D.: Plome: pre-training with misspelled knowledge for Chinese spelling correction. In: Proceedings of the 59th Annual Meeting of the Association for Computational Linguistics and the 11th International Joint Conference on Natural Language Processing (Volume 1: Long Papers), pp. 2991–3000 (2021)
13. Nguyen, M., Ngo, G.H., Chen, N.F.: Domain-shift conditioning using adaptable filtering via hierarchical embeddings for robust Chinese spell check. arXiv preprint arXiv:2008.12281 (2020)
14. Tseng, Y.H., Lee, L.H., Chang, L.P., Chen, H.H.: Introduction to SIGHAN 2015 bake-off for Chinese spelling check. In: Proceedings of the Eighth SIGHAN Workshop on Chinese Language Processing, pp. 32–37 (2015)
15. Vaswani, A., et al.: Attention is all you need. In: Advances in neural Information Processing Systems, vol. 30 (2017)
16. Wang, B., Che, W., Wu, D., Wang, S., Hu, G., Liu, T.: Dynamic connected networks for Chinese spelling check. In: Findings of the Association for Computational Linguistics: ACL-IJCNLP 2021, pp. 2437–2446 (2021)
17. Wang, D., Tay, Y., Zhong, L.: Confusionset-guided pointer networks for Chinese spelling check. In: Proceedings of the 57th Annual Meeting of the Association for Computational Linguistics, pp. 5780–5785 (2019)
18. Wu, S.H., Liu, C.L., Lee, L.H.: Chinese spelling check evaluation at SIGHAN bake-off 2013. In: SIGHAN@ IJCNLP, pp. 35–42. Citeseer (2013)
19. Xu, H.D., et al.: Read, listen, and see: leveraging multimodal information helps Chinese spell checking. arXiv preprint arXiv:2105.12306 (2021)
20. Yin, X., Hu, X., Wan, X.: Chinese spelling check with nearest neighbors (2022)
21. Yin, X., Wan, X.: A comprehensive evaluation and analysis study for Chinese spelling check (2023)
22. Yu, L.C., Lee, L.H., Tseng, Y.H., Chen, H.H.: Overview of SIGHAN 2014 bake-off for Chinese spelling check. In: Proceedings of The Third CIPS-SIGHAN Joint Conference on Chinese Language Processing, pp. 126–132 (2014)
23. Zhang, R., et al.: Correcting Chinese spelling errors with phonetic pre-training. In: Findings of the Association for Computational Linguistics: ACL-IJCNLP 2021, pp. 2250–2261 (2021)
24. Zhang, S., Huang, H., Liu, J., Li, H.: Spelling error correction with soft-masked Bert. arXiv preprint arXiv:2005.07421 (2020)

Evaluation Workshop: User Feedback Prediction and Response Generation

User Preference Prediction for Online Dialogue Systems Based on Pre-trained Large Model

Chenyang Li[1,2], Long Zhang[1,2](✉), Qiusheng Zheng[1,2], Zhongjie Zhao[1,2], and Ziwei Chen[1,2]

[1] Zhongyuan University of Technology, Zhengzhou 450007, China
zhanglong@zut.edu.cn
[2] Henan Key Laboratory on Public Opinion Intelligent Analysis, Zhengzhou 450007, China

Abstract. Online conversation system user preference prediction can improve online conversation system to enhance the quality of the conversation. This paper design an online conversation quality preference assessment model for this problem from the novel perspective of pre-trained large model classification, which incorporates two pre-trained large model, BERT and Ernie, by analyzing data variability, using data enhancement and pseudo-labeling techniques and semi-supervised learning, to finally build our user preference prediction assessment model. The model was evaluated on the official dataset released by NLPCC-2023, and the KL value of the evaluation metric reached 0.9173, which represents the latest level in this research direction. Other features such as linguistic expressions in dialogues are not considered in this study for the time being, and the interpretability of the model needs to be further improved. By fusing pre-trained large model and performing semi-supervised learning, the resulting model are able to predict user preferences of online dialogue systems very well.

Keywords: Text Classification · Pre-trained Model · Data Augmentation · Pseudo-labeling · Model Fusion

1 Introduction

NLPCC released the shared task User Feedback Prediction and Response Generation in 2023, which focuses on predicting user preferences based on user feedback in online dialogue tasks to improve the quality of dialogue systems. Online conversation systems usually have a user feedback mechanism, such as like and dislike buttons. When a user is satisfied with the response, he/she can click the like button, and vice versa for the dislike button. The feedback signal represents the user's vote on the quality of the response and also represents his/her preference. It is a worthwhile direction to study and invest in how to use this signal to improve the quality of the conversation system. Based on this direction, NLPCC 2023 publishes tasks that rely on deep learning techniques to solve

Fund projects: Key Research Projects of Henan Higher Education Institutions (No.22B520054); Songshan Laboratory Pre-research Project (YYJC032022021); Natural Science Foundation of Zhongyuan University of Technology (2023MS021).

this problem. The dataset for this task was provided by XiaoMi AI Lab and consisted of 16,000 training sets, 2,000 test sets and 2,000 test sets. As shown in Table 1, each piece of data consists of a query and a reply, each reply contains multiple replies to correspond to the current query, and each reply contains the number of likes and dislikes for the current query-reply conversation. The goal of this task is mainly to predict the satisfaction probability of each query-reply in the test set. In evaluating the performance, KL scatter is mainly used as the evaluation criterion, i.e., the probability distribution of the test set is predicted and then compared with the true distribution of the test set.

There is currently no systematic research methodology in academia for the niche area of online dialogue quality preference assessment alone, and dialogue quality preference assessment is an important tool for improving online dialogue systems and enhancing dialogue quality. Research in this area currently suffers from several problems. First, it is difficult to understand the semantic meaning of dialogues and to understand user intentions, emotions and needs, so it is difficult to make correct assessments for complex scenarios; Second, it is difficult to use the information provided by the context in multi-round sessions, and cannot make full use of unstructured data to dynamically assess user preferences.

With the rapid development of deep learning, this paper designs online conversation quality preference assessment model from the new perspective of pre-trained big model classification for this problem, fuses two pre-trained big model, BERT and Ernie, and performs semi-supervised learning by analyzing data variability and using data enhancement and pseudo-labeling techniques to finally build our quality assessment model. The model was evaluated on the official dataset published by NLPCC, and the evaluation index reached a KL value of 0.9173, which represents the latest level in the direction of this research.

The narrative of this paper is structured as follows, with Section II providing a concise and comprehensive overview of related work and a brief description of our implementation approach. Section III describes the data set used in this model. Section IV describes in detail the data processing, model construction and experimental methods. Section V presents the experimental results and the analysis of the results. Section VI summarizes the work of this paper and presents the remaining problems and future directions in this field.

2 Related Work

Text classification has an important role in natural language processing and text mining, and predictive classification through continuous learning of text features is of great importance and research value in all aspects of research [1]. Traditional text classification is based on machine learning methods [2], including support vector machines, decision trees, and plain Bayes, but all of these methods only address the lexical level and cannot effectively learn and reflect the semantic relevance and deep semantic features between utterances.

In recent years, deep learning techniques have made remarkable progress in both computer vision and natural language processing. In natural language processing tasks, deep learning-based text classification model have received much attention and research, such as CNN [3, 4], RNN [5, 6], GNN [7], Attention [8], and pre-training model. They all show excellent results in natural language processing tasks such as text classification. In particular, pre-trained model are exposed to a large amount of text data during pre-training, so they can learn richer semantic information, and they also have higher accuracy and generalization ability in tasks such as text classification.

Semi-supervised learning is an emerging intelligent learning paradigm in recent years that uses unlabeled data to improve model performance [4], where traditional supervised learning methods require the use of labeled data for modeling. However, labeling training data in the real world can be costly or time-consuming. There are implicit costs associated with obtaining this labeling data from domain experts, such as limited time and financial resources. This is especially true for applications that involve learning with a large number of class labels and sometimes similarities. Semi-supervised learning (SSL) model can allow model to integrate some or all of the unlabeled data in their supervised learning to address this inherent bottleneck. The goal is to maximize the learning performance of the model with this newly labeled data while minimizing the cost of the labeled data.

3 Datasets

In this paper, we use the official public datasets published by NLPCC 2023, which is referred to as UFP in this paper. Online dialogue systems usually have a user feedback mechanism, where users can vote to express their preference for a dialogue, and this datasets collects information about users' votes, including the text of dialogue pairs (query, reply) and the number of likes and dislikes. The UFP datasets contains a training set, a validation set and a test set, and its detailed statistics are shown in Table 1.

Table 1. Statistics of the datasets.

Type	Query	Average Reply	Avg Like per Reply	Avg Dislike per Reply
train	16000	3.14	16.15	8.42
dev	2000	3.07	19.84	9.41
test	2000	3.16	30.57	12.19

4 Model Implementation

Figure 1 shows the general flow framework of our model implementation. Through analysis, it is found that this task is a logistic regression task, slightly different from the classification task, which requires the addition of a sigmoid activation function on top of the classification model as a way to output probabilities. We first pre-process the text content, then evaluate the current mainstream deep learning model, select the better-performing model as our baseline model, and finally enhance the KL metrics with pseudo-labeling, data augmentation, and model fusion.

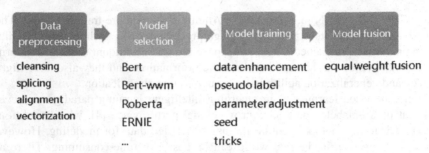

Fig. 1. Data pre-processing, training and post-processing process of the experiment.

4.1 Pre-training Large Model

Bert-wwm [9] is an upgraded version of Bert released by Harbin Institute of Technology and iFlytek, which mainly changes the training sample generation strategy of the original pre-training truncation. Compared to Bert, Bert-wwm is improved by replacing a complete word with a mask tag instead of an anagram. Chinese is different from English in that the smallest token in English is a word, while the smallest token in Chinese is a word. Words are composed of one or more words, and there is no obvious division between each word, and words contain more information. Compared to word-based masks, word-based masks enable the model to learn more semantic information.

The Ernie3.0 [10] model is a large-scale knowledge enhancement model incorporating autoregressive networks and self-coding networks, which is obtained by training on a corpus consisting of plain text and large-scale knowledge graphs. As shown in Fig. 2, the information sharing between structured knowledge and unstructured text is facilitated by inputting entity relationships of large-scale knowledge graphs and large-scale text data simultaneously into the pre-trained model for joint mask training, which substantially improves the model's ability to remember and reason about knowledge. In this way, Ernie is able to capture more subtle semantic distinctions and combine them with entity relationships in the knowledge graph to achieve more accurate classification.

When faced with complex tasks, multiple model may need to be trained jointly to achieve good results. Model fusion is a method of training multiple model and fusing them, aiming to outperform individual model by fusing their results. There are three commonly used model fusion methods. The first one is the voting method, which is applicable to classification tasks, i.e., voting on the prediction results of multiple learning model to determine the final result by minority rule, and also setting weights based on manual settings or based on model evaluation scores. The second is the averaging method, which is applicable to regression and classification tasks, i.e., averaging the predicted probabilities for the learned model. The third one is the cross-fusion method, the main idea is to divide the original training set into two parts first, for example, dividing the training set and the test set by 9:1. In the first round of training, multiple model are trained using the training set, and then predictions are made on the test set, and in the second round of training, the prediction results of the model on the test set after the first round of training are directly used as new features to continue to participate in the training.

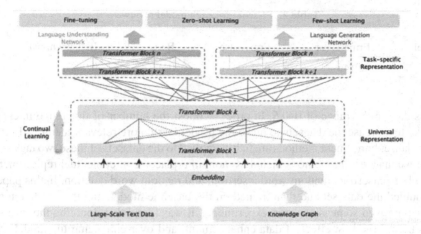

Fig. 2. Ernie3.0 structure diagram.

4.2 Data Pre-processing

After obtaining the training set, this paper first carried out the cleaning work and found that there were 55 replies with the content of nan in the training and validation sets, and we removed these 55 replies. Next write code to extract the content of the datasets, we put the query and the corresponding reply for the splicing operation, its input as text, for each reply the number of likes and dislikes, find the probability of liking as a label. The average length of these texts was 26, 75\% of the texts were under 31, and the maximum text length was 210. Since the maximum length that Ernie's pre-trained model can handle is 512, we choose a maximum length of 64 to truncate and patch the spliced text in order to allow the model to learn more features during training.

4.3 Model Selection

In order to be able to compare model differences under the same random conditions, experiments were conducted by fixing the random seed as 42. As shown in Table 2, we selected the current mainstream pre-trained model, including Bert, a variant model of Bert, and Ernie, and fine-tuned each model on this basis. Intuitively, the larger the network model, the deeper the layers, the more powerful the learning ability, so our Ernie model was chosen to test the 20-layer network structure of Ernie3.0-xbase, and the Ernie we propose later refers to Ernie3.0-xbase. After validation, we found that only two model, Bert-wwm and Ernie, exceeded the baseline of the task in the validation set, so we used these two model as the baseline model for our task.

4.4 Data Analysis and Data Enhancement

In this paper, we found that the officially provided datasets has uneven distribution through data analysis, and some tags correspond to a small amount of data. As shown in Fig. 3,we divide 0–1 into 10 intervals for all data labels, and the labels correspond

Table 2. F1 score for each model review.

Model	Ernie-xbase	Ernie-base	Bert	Bert-wwm-ext
F1	0.9146	0.9136	0.9118	0.9107

to less data in the range of 0–0.5. In order to boost the number of this range interval, we take to increase the datasets to make the model learn more relevant features. In this paper, data enhancement methods are firstly applied to the datasets of these two tags, and the data enhancement methods include synonym replacement, contextual replacement, homophone insertion, random word insertion, and random word deletion. In this paper, we doubled the data set and then trained on the baseline model, and the validation set scores improved somewhat. After experiments, it was found that doubling the data set has achieved the best effect of data enhancement, and over-enhancing the model will result in over-fitting. In this paper, the pseudo-labeling technique is also used to enhance the model effect. Pseudo-labeling comes from semi-supervised learning, the core idea of which is to improve model performance in a supervised process by drawing on unlabeled data, details of which are presented in Subsect. 4.5.

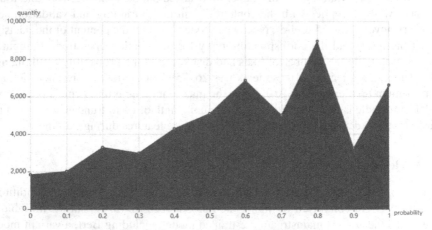

Fig. 3. Dataset probability distribution.

4.5 Semi-supervised Learning with Pseudo-labeling

The pseudo-label semi-supervised learning process is shown in Fig. 4. In this paper, the prediction results of the model on unlabeled test data are added to the training set [11], thus increasing the amount of data to enhance the model effect. Pseudo-labeling semi-supervised learning adds entropy regularization to the loss function, forcing the predicted classes to overlap less, which is justified and effective for the performance improvement of the model in this classification task [12]. On the one hand, according to the clustering hypothesis principle, points with higher classification probability are usually more likely to be in the same category, so their pseudo-labels can be used as plausible labels; On the other hand adding an entropy regularization term in the loss function allows to obtain information from unlabeled data within the framework of maximum a posteriori estimation. By minimizing the conditional entropy of the class probabilities of unlabeled data, low density separation between classes is promoted without any modeling of density, and information about the degree of overlap of the distribution of unlabeled data can be used to improve model performance through entropy regularization. This method is suitable for cases where the model accuracy is high. But still, in order to avoid the introduction of a large number of incorrect labels, which leads to the accumulation of error errors in layers when the model learns, this paper uses model alignment techniques to control the amount of incorrect labels introduced [13], by first performing prediction label probability scaling through temperature coefficients, i.e., amplifying the probability gap between the predicted label and the correct label, and later introducing uncertainty prediction confidence to select plausible pseudo-samples, and when the uncertainty is low, the prediction probability of the model can better reflect the accuracy of the prediction. Then we fine-tune both Bert and Ernie model and take the part of the data where the difference between the two predicted probability values is less than 0.1, the probabilities are averaged and then added to the training set for retraining. The number of pseudo-labels is close to 500 each time, which indicates that our datasets has added 500 data to the original number.

4.6 Model Fusion

After several rounds of pseudo-label training, the filtered pseudo-labels will get closer and closer, and eventually the model reaches a state of fit, at which time the subsequent pseudo-labeling methods are no longer able to improve the F1 value of the test set. So we used model fusion to further improve the F1 score. About model fusion, Prof. Zhihua Zhou's book on machine learning mentions that model fusion needs to be good and different, i.e., the more different the model are, the better the fusion effect. We add differentiation in two ways, one by using two different model, Bert and Ernie, and two by repartitioning the training and validation sets to change the model inputs. When using the two model to make predictions on the test set, the probabilities of each conversation are output, and then the probabilities predicted by the two model are made to sum in equal weights, resulting in the new probabilities predicted by the fusion of the model.

5 Experimental Results

As shown in Table 3, we present the final F1 values of 0.9173 for our two identified baseline model Bert-wwm and Ernie in the single model case, under the pseudo-labeling approach, and under the model fusion approach. Experiments demonstrate that data augmentation, pseudo-labeling and model fusion all improve the performance of our model to some extent. As shown in Table 4, the specific parameters of our model are demonstrated.

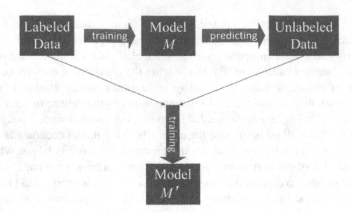

Fig. 4. Semi-supervised learning with pseudo-labeling.

Table 3. Model KL scores under data enhancement, pseudo-labeling and model fusion.

Models	Online KL Values
Ernie3.0	91.5053
+ Data Enhancement	91.6542
+ Pseudo-labeling	91.7163
+ Model Fusion	91.7368

Table 4. Model Parameters.

Models	Max_Len	Batch_Size	Seed	Epoch	Learning_Rate
Bert-wwm	64	32	42/43	5	2e-5
Ernie3.0	64	32	42/43	5	2e-5

6 Summary

Through extensive experiments, it was found that most of the model predicted similar results scores for this task dataset, and since the number of datasets in this task is not small, the data enhancement technique does not improve this task significantly. Instead, using the pseudo-labeling approach increases the size of the dataset, boosts the F1 score of the test set, and increases the generalizability of the model. After using the multi-round pseudo-labeling method, the pseudo-labeling derived from subsequent filtering hardly changes, resulting in no further performance improvement of the model. In this case, model fusion techniques can be used to take multiple model with large differences and learn different inputs separately, so that the knowledge learned among multiple model is as different as possible, which enables better integration of multiple model and improves performance.

For further optimization, for the overfitting problem in the training set, data balancing can be considered when dividing the training and validation sets. When using the pseudo-labeling method, a threshold judgment is attempted using the difference between the results predicted by the two model, and the results with smaller differences in predictions between the two model are selected and averaged and added to the training set as pseudo-labels. When using model fusion, multiple model can be trained first using a five-fold cross-validation method and then averaging the multiple predictions.

References

1. Minaee, S., Kalchbrenner, N., Cambria, E., Nikzad, N., Chenaghlu, M., Gao, J.: Deep learning based text classification: a comprehensive review. ACM Comput. Surv. (CSUR) **54**(3), 1–40 (2020)
2. Cheng, J.: Research and implementation of Chinese long text classification algorithm based on deep learning. Univ. Chinese Acad. Sci. (2020)
3. Wan, S., Lan, Y., Guo, J., Xu, J., Pang, L., Cheng, X.: A deep architecture for semantic matching with multiple positive sense representations. In: Proceedings of the AAAI Conference on Artificial Intelligence, vol. 30(1), p. 10 (2015)
4. Wang, Z., Hamza, W., Florian, R.: Bilateral multi-perspective matching for natural language senses. In: procedures of the twenty Sixth International Joint Conference on artistic intelligence. IJCAI-17, pp. 4144–4150 (2017)
5. Le, H.T., Cerisara, C., Denis, A.: Do convolutional networks need to be deep for text classification? https://doi.org/10.48550/arXiv.1707.04108 (2017)
6. Guo, B., Zhang, C., Liu, J., Ma, X.: Improving text classification with weighted word embeddings via a multi-channel text CNN model. Neurocomputing **363**, 366–374 (2019). https://doi.org/10.1016/j.neucom.2019.07.052
7. Yao, L., Mao, C., Luo, Y.: Graph revolutionary networks for text classification. Corr, abs/1809.05679 (2018)
8. Kim, S., Hyun Hong, J., Kang, I., Kwak, N.: Semantic sense matching with densely connected recurrent and co attentive information. Proc. AAAI Conf. Artif. Intell. **33**(01), 6586–6593 (2018)
9. Cui, Y., Che, W., Liu, T., Qin, B., Yang, Z.: Pre-Training with whole word masking for Chinese BERT. In: IEEE/ACM Transactions on Audio, Speech, and Language Processing, vol. 29, pp. 3504–3514 (2021)
10. Sun, Y., et al.: ERNIE 3.0: large-scale knowledge enhanced pre-training for language understanding and generation. ArXiv, abs/2107.02137 (2019)
11. Rizve, M.N., Duarte, K., Rawat, Y.S., Shah, M.: In defense of pseudolabeling: an uncertainty-aware pseudo-label selection framework for semisupervised learning. arxiv:2101.06329 (2021)
12. Lee, D.-H.: Pseudo-Label: the simple and efficient semi-supervised learning method for deep neural networks. In: ICMLW (2013)
13. Rizve, M.N., Duarte, K., Rawat, Y.S., Shah, M.: In defense of pseudo-labeling: an uncertainty-aware pseudo-label selection framework for semi-supervised learning. In: ICLR 2021: The Ninth International Conference on Learning Representations (2021)

Auto-scaling Distribution Fitting Network for User Feedback Prediction

Yuanyuan Cui[✉], Yanggang Lin, Bangyu Wu, Hao Chen, Bo Zeng,
and Xianchang Luo

NetEase Yidun AI Lab, Hangzhou, China
{hzcuiyuanyuan,hzlinyanggang,wubangyu,chenhao22,cengbo,
luoxianchang}@corp.netease.com

Abstract. The goal of User Feedback Prediction is to precisely estimate the probability that an AI generated response will be accepted by actual users. As the available dataset is collected from unknown online contributors in a case-wise manner, there are many annotation disagreements. The ground truth is moderately reliable, but not entirely trustworthy. In this paper, we propose an auto-scaling distribution fitting network to get out of this dilemma. Firstly, we use a smoothing coefficient to cope with any potential annotation errors, which control the confidence of a sample based on the number of annotators. Secondly, we add an automatic temperature scaling layer to rescale the logits output. It takes the contextual representation of reply sequence as input, and can effectively mitigate annotation disagreements stemming from individual biases. Besides, we employ soft cross entropy as our loss function to learn directly from the golden probability distribution. Our system achieves 2nd place in Track 1 of NLPCC 2023 Shared Task 9, with experimental results demonstrating its effectiveness.

Keywords: User Feedback Prediction · Annotation Disagreement · Temperature Scaling

1 Introduction

More and more evidence suggests that for NLP tasks which involve subjective judgments of human, a binary black-or-white golden ground truth exists only in imagination. This is particularly true when it comes to mature interactive AI products, as they are openly available for a large group of users with varying preferences, rather than a specific individual. For intelligent assistants like Xiao Ai and Siri, a reply highly appreciated by a user, maybe totally worthless to another one. Properly assessing these preferences could help AI generate high-quality replies which satisfy the majority, thereby improving the overall interactive experience.

The NLPCC 2023 Shared Task 9 provides an opportunity for researchers to further investigate the above challenge. In their online conversation system,

F. Liu et al. (Eds.): NLPCC 2023, LNAI 14304, pp. 358–365, 2023.
https://doi.org/10.1007/978-3-031-44699-3_32

users could click a "like" or "dislike" button to express personal attitude towards machine responses. Each item recorded by the user feedback mechanism consists of four parts: a query from user, a reply from AI, the number of "like" votes, and its "dislike" counterpart. This shared task includes two tracks: (1) Track 1 - Prediction of likes and dislikes; (2) Track 2 - Conversation generation based on likes and dislikes. In Track 1, given a (query, reply) pair, one needs to predict the distribution of annotations (*soft* label), rather than the majority of annotations (*hard* label).

Our system focused on Track 1. As the like/dislike votes are offered by a crowd of people, the records are actually rife with annotation disagreements. Researchers have demonstrated that these disagreements mainly stem from two sources [8]. Some ones are a result of annotation errors, namely *noise*. The others are caused by linguistically debatable items and annotator preference, namely *bias*. We have designed specific solutions to address both the two types of disagreements. Firstly, to tackle with inevitable noise, we adopt a modified learning target with smoothing coefficient. It tends to allocate more confidence to samples which have been voted by more users. Secondly, to extract valuable information from biases, we design an automatic temperature scaling layer. It can distinguish genuine ambiguous replies from those can be clearly judged by most people, thereby mitigating overfitting. Lastly, a CE soft loss function enables the model to learn directly from distributional representation instead of single hard assignment. Our auto-scaling distribution fitting network achieves 2nd place in the Track 1 of NLPCC 2023 Shared Task 9.

The main contributions of this work are three-fold, summarized as follows:

1. We explore solutions of user feedback prediction from the perspective of annotation disagreements.
2. Our smoothing coefficient can effectively mitigate the adverse impact of random noise in datasets with unfixed annotators.
3. Our automatic temperature scaling layer has the ability to adjust probability distribution based on the characteristics of the textual content.

2   Related Work

For contemporary Artificial Intelligence, a large portion of supervised datasets are constructed in a **crowd-souring** way. Annotating one certain instance by multiple persons is a common practice to reduce incorrect labels [1]. The subjective individual preferences will be implicitly encoded into the data, leading to evident crowd-disagreement [2]. There is growing awareness that crowd-disagreement is informative. Enforcing a single ground truth by averaging or majority voting will sacrifices the valuable nuances embedded in annotator's assessments. For NLP tasks which involve subjective judgments natively, such as sentiment analysis [3] and user feedback prediction, it is particularly necessary to model multiple perspectives [4].

Researchers have put forward a great deal of methods for training directly from data with disagreements without obtaining an aggregated label firstly. Some methods treat each annotation as a separate learning instance, and replicate or weight the samples according to the number of labels or some measure of disagreement [5]. Other multi-task methods are suitable for datasets in which the labeled records are traceable. Researchers train a model that jointly predicts the majority label and all the individual annotator's labels [6]. In the NLPCC Shared Task 9, annotations over different users are aggregated into a probabilistic distribution (soft label), so we could learn directly from that distribution using a modified soft loss function [7].

3   Main Methods

In this section, we will introduce our solution to the User Feedback Prediction Track. It consists of two parts, acting on target distribution and predicted distribution respectively.

3.1   Smoothing Coefficient

In the given dataset, there are no *hard* labels as absolute like or dislike. On the contrary, the inconsistent voting results of a group are regarded as a probability distribution. For a given query-reply with n_0 "likes" and n_1 "dislikes", a probability of "like" is computed based on the ratio:

$$p = n_0/(n_0 + n_1) \tag{1}$$

The Shared Task 9 assumes that all annotators are equally reliable. However, an item voted by 3 users is apparently less credible than the one voted by 30 users. Taking the number of voters into account is helpful to deal with noise-wise disagreements, which arise from annotation errors. We use a smoothing coefficient α to exert influence on soft labels, placing less confidence on the items without enough voters. For a given query-reply pair with n_0 "likes" and n_1 "dislikes", the target probability p is modified as:

$$p' = (\alpha + n_0)/(2\alpha + n_0 + n_1) \tag{2}$$

p' will degenerate back to Eq. 1 with $\alpha = 0$. It "likes" and "dislikes" are quantitatively equal, $p' = p = 0.5$. It ensures that the classification boundary won't shift. We set α to 0.75 as introduced in [9].

3.2   Automatic Temperature Scaling Layer

For intelligent assistants, there are no restrictions on user queries. But the machine replies are not entirely freely generated. A large proportion of them are fixed scripts. In average, each reply in the trainset are recorded 3.73 times, and only 18% of them are unique. Bias-wise disagreements are caused by the fact that some contents don't fit into mainstream preference, making them inherently vulnerable to personal idiosyncrasy of annotators, no matter what the queries are.

Reply Matters More. These disagreements can be measured quantitatively as the uncertainty of annotations. For a reply r_i, we calculated the mean value over all its occurrences regardless of different queries:

$$\sigma^2(\boldsymbol{r}_i) = \frac{1}{N_i} \sum_{j=1}^{N_i} \frac{n_{0_{ij}} * n_{1_{ij}}}{(n_{0_{ij}} + n_{1_{ij}})^2} \tag{3}$$

where N_i is the number of times that r_i appears in the trainset. Figure 1 shows the quantity of replies in each $\sigma^2(r)$ interval. The level of annotation disagreement is strongly relevant to the textual content. Some replies exhibit a high level, while others don't. Along this line of thought, we design a special temperature scaling layer. It facilitates the model to pay more attention on the reply and automatically rescale the output logits.

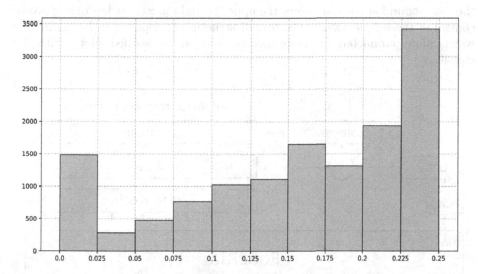

Fig. 1. Quantity of replies in each $\sigma^2(r)$ interval. The ones with more disagreements account for a larger proportion in the whole trainset

System Overview. Our base model is a pretrained large RoBERTa [14]. We formulate the shared task as dual-sentence text classification, and simply concatenate the pair of query and reply as input to the RoBERTa model:

$$\hat{\boldsymbol{x}}_i = [\text{CLS}] \text{ query sequence } [\text{SEP}] \text{ reply sequence } [\text{SEP}] \tag{4}$$

The representation corresponding to the [CLS] token is taken as the contextual representation for the entire sequence. It is then fed to a fully-connected layer to get the output logits $\boldsymbol{z}_i$.

Automatic Temperature Scaling. Temperature scaling is widely used in model distillation [10], which is a typical soft-target learning process. A single parameter T, named **temperature**, is inserted into the softmax activation function as follows:

$$f(\boldsymbol{x}_i) = \text{softmax}(\boldsymbol{z}_i/T) \tag{5}$$

A higher value of T will produce a softer probability distribution over classes. T is a hyper-parameter, which is manually set and kept frozen during training. It is shared by all samples and cannot fit into a certain one. Therefore, we turn to adopt matrix scaling and softplus activation function as introduced in [11]:

$$T_i = \text{softplus}(\boldsymbol{W}_{T_i}\boldsymbol{c}_i + b_{T_i}) \tag{6}$$

$$f(\boldsymbol{x}_i) = \text{softmax}(\boldsymbol{z}_i * T_i) \tag{7}$$

where $\boldsymbol{c}_i$ is a max-pooled contextual vector of the reply sequence. Softplus clamps the lower bound at zero and keeps the upper bound unrestricted, avoiding overly control of the output range. The overall structure is depicted in Fig. 2. In this way, scaling parameters are reply-specific, and can be learned jointly with the classifier.

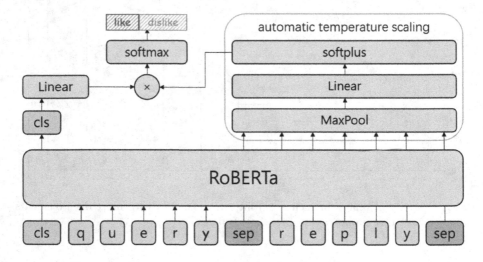

Fig. 2. RoBERTa model with an automatic temperature scaling layer

Soft Loss Function. Our model is trained with soft cross-entropy. It is derived from standard cross-entropy, the only difference being the use of soft labels instead of one-hot hard labels. Training with CE as a soft loss is especially suitable for datasets with a substantial number of annotations per item [12]. We have tested other well-known probability-comparing loss functions, such as MSE and KL. All of them are outperformed by CE by a narrow margin.

4 Experiments

4.1 Data Analysis and Evaluation Metric

In this task, a dataset of nearly 19,500 Chinese conversation samples[1] is officially provided and the overview statistics is shown in Table 1. Each sample contains one query and several replies. User feedback to each reply is record in detail, with the numbers of "likes" and "dislikes" collected separately.

Table 1. Statistics of the datasets (with "nan" filtered out).

Type	Queries	Length	Avg Replies	Avg Likes	Avg Dislikes	Replies	Length	Repetitions
train	15,977	6.2	3.1	19.8	9.4	13,441	15.3	3.7
dev	1,999	6.2	3.1	30.6	12.2	3,162	15.2	1.9
test	1,498	6.3	3.2	–	–	2,711	15.3	1.8

The final evaluation is ranked by Kullback-Leibler Divergence from predicted probability distribution to the ground truth. It's a soft metric for the similarity between two distributions. For the ith query, the corresponding sim_i is calculated as:

$$sim_i = \frac{1}{m_i} \sum_{j=1}^{m_i} \frac{1}{1 + p_{ij} \log(p_{ij}/q_{ij}) - (1 - p_{ij}) \log[(1 - p_{ij})/(1 - q_{ij})]} \quad (8)$$

where m_i is the number of replies belong to the ith query, p_{ij} is the golden probability and q_{ij} is the predicted value. Finally, to measure the overall divergence, compute an average score over the whole N queries in the dataset:

$$similarity = \frac{1}{N} \sum_{i=1}^{N} sim_i \quad (9)$$

4.2 Experimental Settings

We take three pretrained models as our baselines: a BERT-base[2] [13] model, a RoBERTa-base[3] [14] model and a RoBERTa-large[4] [14] model. In order to get a strong baseline, we pick up Roberta-large as the backbone network for further experiments.

Our learning rate is set to $2e^{-5}$ with a warm-up schedule. Models in base-scale are finetuned for 2,000 steps with a batch size of 80, and large-scale ones run longer to 3,500 steps with a smaller batch size of 30.

All the experimental results we reported are conducted on devset, except for the official ranking scores. In the formal evaluation phase, all retained models are ensembled to make a competitive submission.

---

[1] https://github.com/XiaoMi/nlpcc-2023-shared-task-9/.
[2] https://huggingface.co/bert-base-chinese.
[3] https://huggingface.co/hfl/chinese-roberta-wwm-ext.
[4] https://huggingface.co/hfl/chinese-roberta-wwm-ext-large.

4.3   Main Results

We conducted experiments on Track 1, which are shown in Table 2. Our baseline is a finetuned RoBERTa model. We compare the effectiveness of different probability comparing loss functions to choose the most suitable one. Though the official metric is similar to KL divergence, KL loss function don't perform better than CE as expected. MSE is the least effective one, due to the lack of log function as others. Following this experiment, we select CE as our default soft loss function for the given dataset.

As for smoothing coefficient, an overlarge α will destructively perturb the original probability distribution, while tiny one can not give full play to its role. The value of α depends on the noise level of the dataset and the number of annotators. As present in Table 1, each item in the trainset is voted 29.2 times (19.8 likes + 9.4 dislikes), an *alpha* of 0.75 occupies a proportion of about 5%.

Table 2. Performance comparison of various baselines and methods for Track 1. The adopted configuration in each group is highlighted in **bold**. The experiments of automatic temperature scaling utilize a default α of 0.75.

Models	KL-similarity		
Baseline	BERT-base	RoBERTa-base	RoBERTa-large
	91.06	90.99	**91.35**
Soft Loss Function	CE	MSE	KL
	91.35	91.23	91.33
w/ Smoothing Coefficient α	0.50	0.75	1.00
	91.33	**91.45**	91.28
w/ Automatic Temperature Scaling	MaxPool	AvgPool	CNN-3
	91.57	91.49	91.53

The automatic temperature scaling layer takes contextual representation of reply as input, and we have tried three methods to encode the variable-length sequence into a single vector. They are MaxPool, AvgPool and CNN (kernel size = 3). Maxpool is proved to be a simple but effective unit, with the most salient features abstracted. It surpasses AvgPool and CNN by 0.08 and 0.04 respectively.

4.4   Online Results

The final evaluation results on testset are released by the organizer. As shown in Table 3, our system achieves 2nd place in Track 1 of NLPCC 2023 Shared Task 9. Our performance is comparable to the 1st place team with a slight margin of -0.13. We get an advantage of 0.27 over the 3rd place team, due to the specific approaches to deal with annotation disagreements.

Table 3. Track 1 submission results.

Rank	System Name	Score
1	shidishimeidaidaiwo	92.13
2	dunnlp (ours)	**92.00**
3	zut	91.73

5   Conclusions

In this paper, we propose an auto-scaling distribution fitting network for user feedback prediction, which realizes excellent performance by utilizing annotation disagreements. It is composed of two modules, a smoothing coefficient for noise-wise disagreements and an automatic temperature scaling layer for bias-wise disagreements. Together with a CE soft loss function, our model is capable of achieving ballance between the group commonality and individual preference of different annotators. Our system is placed the 2nd in Track 1 of NLPCC 2023 Shared Task 9, which demonstrated its effectiveness.

References

1. Snow, R., O'Connor, B., Jurafsky, D., Ng, A.: Cheap and fast - but is it good? evaluating non-expert annotations for natural language tasks. ACL (2008)
2. Dumitrache, A., Aroyo, L., Welty, C.: A crowdsourced frame disambiguation corpus with ambiguity. ACL (2019)
3. Kian Kenyon-Dean, et al.: Sentiment analysis: it's complicated!. NAACL (2018)
4. Cabitza, F., Campagner, A., Basile, V.: Toward a perspectivist turn in ground truthing for predictive computing. AAAI (2023)
5. Sheng ,V.S., Provost, F., Ipeirotis. PG.: Get another label? improving data quality and data mining using multiple, noisy labelers. SIGKDD (2008)
6. Rodrigues. F., Pereira. F.: Deep learning from crowds. AAAI (2018)
7. Uma, A., Fornaciari, T., Hovy, D., Paun, S., Plank, B., Poesio, M.: Learning from disagreement: a survey. J. Artif. Intell. Res. **72**, 1385–1470 (2021)
8. Plank, B., Hovy, D., Søgaard. A.: Linguistically debatable or just plain wrong?. ACL (2014)
9. Ando, A., Kobashikawa, S., Kamiyama, H., Masumura, R., Ijima, Y., Aono. Y.: Soft-target training with ambiguous emotional utterances for DNN-based speech emotion classification. ICASSP (2018)
10. Hinton, G., Vinyals, O., Dean, J.: Distilling the knowledge in a neural Network. NIPS (2014)
11. Uma, A., Almanea, D., Poesio, M.: Scaling and disagreements: bias, noise and ambiguity. Front. Artif. Intell., Hum.-Centered AI (2022)
12. Uma, A., Fornaciari, T., Hovy, D., Paun, S., Plank, B., Poesio, M.: A case for soft-loss functions. AAAI (2020)
13. Devlin, J., Chang, M.W., Lee, Toutanova, K.: BERT: pretraining of deep bidirectional transformers for language understanding. EMNLP (2018)
14. Liu, Y., et al.: A robustly optimized BERT pretraining approach. ACL (2019)

Adversarial Training and Model Ensemble for User Feedback Prediciton in Conversation System

Junlong Wang[1], Yongqi Leng[2], Xinyu Zhai[1], Linlin Zong[1], Hongfei Lin[3], and Bo Xu[3(✉)]

[1] School of Software Technology, Dalian University of Technology, Dalian, China

[2] College of Intelligence and Computing, Tianjin University, Tianjin, China
[3] School of Computer Science and Technology, Dalian University of Technology, Dalian, China
xubo@dlut.edu.cn

Abstract. Developing automatic evaluation methods that are highly correlated with human assessment is crucial in the advancement of dialogue systems. User feedback in conversation system provides a signal that represents user preferences and response quality. The user feedback prediction (UFP) task aims to predict the probabilities of likes with machine-generated responses given a user query, offering a unique perspective to facilitate dialogue evaluation. In this paper, we propose a powerful UFP system, which leverages Chinese pre-trained language models (PLMs) to understand the user queries and system replies. To improve the robustness and generalization ability of our model, we also introduce adversarial training for PLMs and design a local and global model ensemble strategy. Our system ranks first in NLPCC 2023 shared Task 9 Track 1 (User Feedback Prediction). The experimental results show the effectiveness of the method applied in our system.

Keywords: User Feedback Prediction · Pre-trained Language Model · Adversarial Training · Model Ensemble

1 Introduction

Open-domain conversational system is designed to satisfy users' need [1] such as information support, communication, and entertainment, etc. Appraising the quality of the responses not only reflects the system's capability but also offers valuable insights for identifying areas that require further improvements [2]. In order to get the user's explicit satisfaction with the generated responses by machine, online conversation systems usually have a user feedback mechanism, such as like and dislike buttons, users can click the like button when they are satisfy with the response, and vice versa for the dislike button. These real-world feedback signal represents the user's vote on the quality of the response and also represents their preference. Based on this, we can study how to cater to user's preferences and improve the quality of the generated responses to obtain high likes.

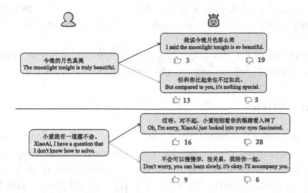

Fig. 1. Two examples from the evaluation task dataset.

In this paper, we focus on solving the problem of UFP in conversation system. Figure 1 present two examples from the evaluation task dataset, in the first example located in the upper half, we can see that the reply that praises the user and is more human-like receives positive feedback with high likes, while the reply that receives negative feedback with high dislikes appears repetitive and boring. In this task, we aim to predict the probabilities of likes given a query-reply pair (e.g., 3/22 and 13/16 for the first example). In order to better understand user preferences for response content in dialogue scenarios and objectively measure the quality of system responses, we conducted a study based on the real-world user feedback dataset from the dialogue system in NLPCC2023 shared task. In this work, we propose an effective UFP system that leverages a local and global ensemble of multiple Chinese PLMs, incorporating adversarial training for fine-tuning.

In the preprocessing phase, we perform purposeful data augmentation to expand the training data. Subsequently, we formulate the UFP task as a text regression problem and employ PLMs with Muti-Sample Dropout (MSD) [3] to locally approximate the ensemble of multiple models. Additionally, we introduce adversarial training [4] to substantially enhance the robustness of individual models.

In the end, we significantly improved the performance of our system by employing blending ensemble strategy, which integrates multiple independent models globally. The result shows that the Kullback-Leibler similarity score of the system proposed in this paper for UFP is 92.13, ranking the first, which indicates that the effectiveness and superiority of our system. The main contributions of this paper can be summarized as follows:

- We build our system based on the Chinese PLMs to learn the user satisfaction level for user queries and system replies in UFP task.

- We integrate adversarial training to effectively enhance the robustness of individual models and devise a local and global ensemble method, which significantly improves the performance of the UFP system.

- The final evaluation results show that our proposed system achieves the first place in the contest, which proves the effectiveness of our method.

2   Related Work

Due to the openness of content and the diversity of topics, it is challenging to evaluate the quality of responses in open domain dialogue systems. Existing automatic evaluation methods usually assess the response from language quality (Perplexity [5]), response diversity (DIST [6]), and relevance (BLEU [7]), they are easy to conduct but ineffective to reflect the dialogue quality [8]. Relatively, human evaluation is of high reliability but it tends to be very cost- and time-intensive. Therefore, researchers have made great efforts to find more reliable automatic evaluation methods that are highly correlated with human evaluation. USR [9] leveraged an unsupervised and reference-free method to approximate the specific scores rated by annotators. SelF-Eval [10] designed a self-supervised fine-grained dialogue evaluation model with a multilevel contrastive learning method. Sun et al. [11] proposed a user satisfaction annotation dataset for dialogue evaluation.

BERT-based [12] PLMs have facilitated the understanding of the relationship between context and response in dialogue evaluation tasks [13], and many improved Chinese PLMs from BERT have emerged in recent years. RoBERTa-wwm [14] use whole word masking strategy based on RoBERTa [15] . MacBERT [16] achieves significant results in Chinese NLP tasks through adopting masked language model as correction. ERNIE [17] strengthens representations by masking knowledge entities from the corpus. Moreover, in order to improve the performance of specific downstream tasks, many works have introduced adversarial training [18,19] for model to improve robustness to small, approximately worst case perturbations. Additionally, in many shared tasks, the winners integrate multiple models instead of using a single model [20,21]. Ensemble learning methods leverage multiple models to extract different features from the training data and then combine the prediction results through various strategies such as Bagging, Boosting, Stacking, Voting [22], and Blending, etc. Ensemble learning effectively reduces errors in individual models, and improves generalization ability.

3   Methodology

Our method is divided into two stages: (1) single text regression model training, where each query-reply pair in the training data is concatenated as input to the

Encoder to extract semantic information. Then, we apply MSD for local model integration, and a regression head is used for prediction. After gradient back-propagation, PGD adversarial training is employed to enhance the robustness of the model. Additionally, targeted data augmentation is applied based on the characteristics of the dataset. The architecture of our model is shown in Fig. 2. (2) multi-model ensemble, we globally integrate the models obtained from the first stage using the blending ensemble method.

3.1 Task Definition

Given a user query and system reply pair, our goal is to predict the probabilities of likes p_i for it, where $p_i \in [0, 1]$, and the computation of p_i is determined by the relative frequency of the term "like" within user feedback. Obviously, we can define UFP task as a regression problem.

3.2 Model Architecture

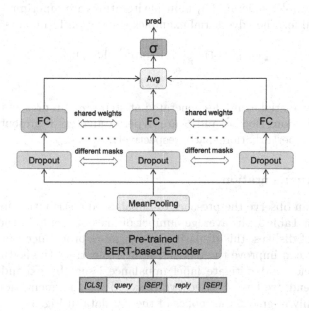

Fig. 2. The architecture of our model

Input Representation. For each query-reply pair, we concatenate the query and reply sentences into a text sequence in the following form:

$$\{[CLS], query, [SEP], reply, [SEP]\}$$

We utilize a BERT-based encoder to represent the input sequence. Subsequently, we apply the mean pooling to the output of the Encoder to obtain the sentence-level embedding.

Muti-Sample Dropout for Local Ensemble. Before the regression head, which consists of a fully connected layer and a sigmoid activation function, we employ MSD [3] as a regularization technique. Specifically, we incorporate multiple parallel dropout layers and they share the fully connected layer, then we can compute the average of the logits from these parallel samples. This module approximates the ensemble of multiple sub-models by averaging the predicted results obtained from different inputs, effectively enhancing the generalization ability of the model.

3.3 Adversarial Training

We introduce Projected Gradient Descent (PGD) [23], which is considered to be the best in first-order adversarial, to improve the robustness of the model in UFP task. PGD adopts a multi-iteration approach to obtain the optimal adversarial examples within a batch, in contrast to Fast Gradient Descent [18]. To be specific, the word embedding layer of the PLMs is attacked in each iteration. Finally, the adversarial examples generated by multiple iterations are superimposed to obtain the optimal value. The adversarial examples generation formula is as follows.:

$$e_{t+1} = \Pi_{e+s}(e_t + \alpha g(e_t)/\|g(e_t)\|_2) \tag{1}$$

$$g(e_t) = \nabla_e L(e_t, y) \tag{2}$$

where e_t is adversarial examples generated at step t, $g(\cdot)$ represents the gradient calculation function. Both α and S are hyperparameters representing step size and adversarial perturbation space, respectively.

3.4 Data Augmentation

In Fig. 3, we can observe the presence of imbalanced distribution in the dataset, and as show in Table 3, the average number of likes per reply in the training set is twice that of dislikes, this disparity is even more pronounced in the test set. Intuitively, we can improve the model's ability to extract the features of replies that users prefer and mitigate label imbalance issues by expanding high-like data. To this end, we have devised two targeted data augmentation strategies:

1-R: we only augment the replies of the *All* data in Fig. 3.

1-QR: based on **1-R**, we also expand the queries of the samples.

Specifically, for a query or a reply sentence, we randomly select one of four strategies to generate a pseudo sentence: *Back translation*[1], *Replacement with synonyms, Deletion words*, and *Exchange adjacent characters*.

---

[1] We implemented it by calling the Baidu Translation API:https://api.fanyi.baidu.com/api.

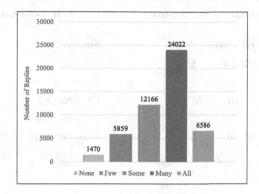

Fig. 3. The label distribution of the training set. *None* represents replies where all user feedbacks are dislike ($p_i = 0$), *Few* denotes $p_i \in (0, 0.3]$, *Some* denotes $p_i \in (0.3, 0.6)$, *Many* represents that $p_i \in [0.6, 1)$, and *All* represents replies where all user feedbacks are like ($p_i = 1$).

3.5   Blending for Global Ensemble

In order to integrate the learning ability of each model and improve the generalization ability of the final system, we use a blending ensemble strategy to integrate multiple models. For each model, we select the strategy that yield the best performance and utilize the predictions on the validation set by all fine-tuned models as features for the second stage, where we learn a new model to ensemble them. We employ linear regression method to learn the weights for model fusion, the final system is obtained by weighting the contributions of five individual models.

4   Experiments

As shown in Table 1, our system achieved the 1st place in the final official test set results. We conducted a three-stage experiment to prove the effectiveness of our method. First, we selected five effective PLMs to conduct a single-model comparison experiment on the validation set as baselines: RoBERTa[2] [16], ERNIE-3.0-xbase[3] [17], ERNIE-3.0-base[4] [17], MacBERT[5] [16], and MRC-RoBERTa[6]. We used the root mean square error loss and some main training hyper-parameters are shown in Table 2. Secondly, we conducted comparative experiments for each baseline model that incorporated all improvements, the results are show in Table 4. Finally, the model ensemble experiment was conducted.

---

[2] https://huggingface.co/hfl/chinese-roberta-wwm-ext-large.
[3] https://huggingface.co/nghuyong/ernie-3.0-xbase-zh.
[4] https://huggingface.co/nghuyong/ernie-3.0-base-zh.
[5] https://huggingface.co/hfl/chinese-macbert-large.
[6] https://huggingface.co/luhua/chinese_pretrain_mrc_roberta_wwm_ext_large.

Table 1. Final results of top-5 teams.

System name	KL-Score	Rank
Ours	**92.13**	**1**
dunnlp	92.00	2
zut	91.73	3
YNU-HPCC	91.63	4
HTDZNLP	91.40	5

Table 2. Hyper-parameter setting.

Setting	Value
Epoch num	8
Batch size	32
Optimizer	Adam
Learning rate	1e-5
Dropout num of MSD	5
Dropout rate of MSD	0.3

4.1 Dataset and Evaluation

The overview statistics of dataset is shown in Table 3. A query sentence may have multiple replies, and we consider a query-reply pair as a single sample.

Table 3. Statistics of the evaluation task dataset.

Item	train	val	test
# Query	16000	2000	2000
Avg # Reply	3.14	3.07	3.16
Avg # Like per Reply	16.15	19.84	30.57
Avg # Dislike per Reply	8.42	9.41	12.19

In this task, the evaluation metric is Kullback-Leible similarity score (KL-Score), for a gold and a prediction, the score is computed as:

$$
\begin{aligned}
Score1 &= gold \times log(gold) + (1 - gold) \times log(1 - gold) \\
Score2 &= gold \times log(pred) + (1 - gold) \times log(1 - pred) \\
KL\text{-}Score &= \frac{1}{1 + Score1 - Score2}
\end{aligned}
\tag{3}
$$

then, the average score of all replies for each query is calculated, and the final result is the average score across all queries.

4.2 Results and Analysis

(1) Among all the base models, ERNIE-xbase performs the best, while the smaller parameter-sized ERNIE-base also shows impressive performance. Moreover, ERNIE-xbase+PGD+1-QR achieves the best KL-Score of 91.590, demonstrating its powerful Chinese semantic understanding ability through knowledge enhanced pre-training methods.

Table 4. The KL-Score of different models on the validation set.

Method	RoBERTa	ERNIE-xbase	ERNIE-base	MacBERT	MRC-RoBERTa
Base	91.263	91.353	91.272	91.220	91.207
+MSD	91.289	91.353	91.281	91.053	91.420
+MSD+PGD	**91.485**	91.500	91.336	91.356	**91.584**
+MSD+PGD+1-R	85.469	91.583	**91.532**	91.356	91.384
+MSD+PGD+1-QR	94.363	**91.590**	91.503	**91.365**	91.374

Table 5. The KL-Score of model ensemble on the validation and test set.

Models	Val	Test
ERNIE-xbase+RoBERTa	91.730	92.038
ERNIE-xbase+RoBERTa+MacBERT	91.768	92.065
ERNIE-xbase+RoBERTa+MacBERT+ERNIE-base	91.802	92.127
ERNIE-xbase+RoBERTa+MacBERT+ERNIE-base+MRC-RoBERTa	**91.818**	**92.136**

(2) The MSD local ensemble method improves the performance of all models except MacBERT. Additionally, the experimental results highlight the effectiveness of PGD adversarial training, all models have shown remarkable performance improvement after the introduction of PGD, particularly with RoBERTa, which achieved a 0.196 improvement in terms of the KL-Score. MRC-RoBERTa with MSD and PGD achieves the second-best overall performance. This model is based on RoBERT-wwm pre-trained on a large-scale reading comprehension corpus, and we speculate that the UFP task can also be viewed as a reading comprehension task, where its strong reading comprehension ability effectively models the matching degree between queries and replies.

(3) We also experimented with two data augmentation strategies on each model, the results show that ERNIE-xbase and ERNIE-base achieved the best performance through the 1-QR and 1-R strategies, respectively, validating the effectiveness of our purposeful augmentation of high-like data.

(4) In terms of model ensemble, as shown in Table 5, the blending method for global integration significantly improves the performance of the UFP system. Furthermore, the system's performance is directly proportional to the number of models in the ensemble, demonstrating the power and scalability of the ensemble method.

5 Conclusion and Future Work

In this work, we define the UFP task as a text regression task that measures the quality of responses and understands user preferences in conversation system. We perform purposeful data augmentation and utilize PLMs to encode queries and replies, and introduce adversarial training and a local and global model

ensemble strategy to significantly improve the system's robustness and performance. Experimental results show the effectiveness of our proposed method, and
our system achieved first place in track 1 of the NLPCC 2023 Shared Task 9.
The effective UFP system demonstrates its applicability to dialogue evaluation
tasks. Moreover, it can be further extended to encompass various query-reply
matching tasks, facilitating the retrieval or generation of highly scored replies to
meet user requirements.

In the future, we will focus on mining the differences between replies with
different scores to the same query, to efficiently utilize user feedback as a super-
visory signal for designing models that are better suited for dialogue evaluation
tasks.

Acknowledgements.. This work was supported in part by the National Natural Sci-
ence Foundation of China under Grant Grant 62006034; in part by the Natural Science
Foundation of Liaoning Province under Grant 2021-BS-067; and in part by the Dalian
High-level Talent Innovation Support Plan under Grant 2021RQ056.

References

1. Shum, H., He, X., Li, D.: From Eliza to XiaoIce: challenges and opportunities with
   social chatbots. Front. Inf. Technol. Electron. Eng. **19**(1), 10–26 (2018). https://
   doi.org/10.1631/FITEE.1700826
2. Deriu, J., et al.: Survey on evaluation methods for dialogue systems. Artif. Intell.
   Rev. **54**(1), 755–810 (2021). https://doi.org/10.1007/s10462-020-09866-x
3. Inoue, H.: Multi-sample dropout for accelerated training and better generalization.
   arXiv preprint arXiv:1905.09788 (2019)
4. Goodfellow, I.J., Shlens, J., Szegedy, C.: Explaining and harnessing adversarial
   examples. arXiv preprint arXiv:1412.6572 (2014)
5. Bengio, Y., Ducharme, R., Vincent, P.: A neural probabilistic language model. In:
   Advances in Neural Information Processing Systems 13 (2000)
6. Li, J., Galley, M., Brockett, C., Gao, J., Dolan, B.: A diversity-promoting objective
   function for neural conversation models. arXiv preprint arXiv:1510.03055 (2015)
7. Papineni, K., Roukos, S., Ward, T., Zhu, W.-J.: BLEU: a method for automatic
   evaluation of machine translation. In: Proceedings of the 40th Annual Meeting of
   the Association for Computational Linguistics, pp. 311–318. (2002)
8. Liu, C.-W., Lowe, R., Serban, I.V., Noseworthy, M., Charlin, L., Pineau, J.: How
   not to evaluate your dialogue system: an empirical study of unsupervised evaluation
   metrics for dialogue response generation. arXiv preprint arXiv:1603.08023 (2016)
9. Mehri, S., Eskenazi, M.: USR: an unsupervised and reference free evaluation metric
   for dialog generation. arXiv preprint arXiv:2005.00456 (2020)
10. Ma, L., Zhuang, Z., Zhang, W., Li, M., Liu, T.: Self-Eval: self-supervised fine-
    grained dialogue evaluation. arXiv preprint arXiv:2208.08094 (2022)
11. Sun, W., et al.: Simulating user satisfaction for the evaluation of task-oriented
    dialogue systems. In: Proceedings of the 44th International ACM SIGIR Conference
    on Research and Development in Information Retrieval, pp. 2499–2506 (2021)
12. Devlin, J., Chang, M.-W., Lee, K., Toutanova, K.: BERT: pre-training of
    deep bidirectional transformers for language understanding. arXiv preprint
    arXiv:1810.04805 (2018)

13. Ye, Z., Lu, L., Huang, L., Lin, L., Liang, X.: Towards quantifiable dialogue coherence evaluation. arXiv preprint arXiv:2106.00507 (2021)

14. Cui, Y., Che, W., Liu, T., Qin, B., Yang, Z.: Pre-training with whole word masking for Chinese BERT. IEEE/ACM Trans. Audio, Speech, Lang. Process. **29**, 3504–3514 (2021)

15. Liu, Y., et al.: RoBERTa: a robustly optimized BERT pretraining approach. arXiv preprint arXiv:1907.11692 (2019)

16. Cui, Y., Che, W., Liu, T., Qin, B., Wang, S., Hu, G.: Revisiting pre-trained models for Chinese natural language processing. arXiv preprint arXiv:2004.13922 (2020)

17. Sun, Y., et al.: ERNIE 3.0: large-scale knowledge enhanced pre-training for language understanding and generation. arXiv preprint arXiv:2107.02137 (2021)

18. Miyato, T., Dai, A.M., Goodfellow, I.: Adversarial training methods for semi-supervised text classification. arXiv preprint arXiv:1605.07725 (2016)

19. Jiang, H., He, P., Chen, W., Liu, X., Gao, J., Zhao, T.: SMART: robust and efficient fine-tuning for pre-trained natural language models through principled regularized optimization. arXiv preprint arXiv:1911.03437 (2019)

20. Agrawal, S., Mamidi, R.: Lastresort at semeval-2022 task 4: towards patronizing and condescending language detection using pre-trained transformer based models ensembles. In: Proceedings of the 16th International Workshop on Semantic Evaluation (SemEval-2022), pp. 352–356 (2022)

21. Yu, W., Boenninghoff, B., Roehrig, J., Kolossa, D.: Rubcsg at semeval-2022 task 5: ensemble learning for identifying misogynous memes. arXiv preprint arXiv:2204.03953 (2022)

22. Sagi, O., Rokach, L.: Ensemble learning: a survey. Wiley Interdisc. Rev.: Data Min. Knowl. Discov. **8**(4), e1249 (2018)

23. Madry, A., Makelov, A., Schmidt, L., Tsipras, D., Vladu, A.: Towards deep learning models resistant to adversarial attacks. arXiv preprint arXiv:1706.06083 (2017)

Generating Better Responses from User Feedback via Reinforcement Learning and Commonsense Inference

Mingxiu Cai, Daling Wang[✉], Shi Feng, and Yifei Zhang

School of Computer Science and Engineering, Northeastern University, Shenyang, China

2201760@stu.neu.edu.cn, {wangdaling,fengshi,zhangyifei}@cse.neu.edu.cn

Abstract. Dialogue generation task is one of the popular research topics in the field of natural language processing. However, how to improve the quality of model generated responses with the user feedback in the dialogue generation task is still one of the difficulties in the research. In this paper, we propose a dialogue generation method based on user feedback by modeling the likeability of user feedback and optimizing the model by using Reinforcement Learning from Human Feedback (RLHF) techniques to generate more likeable responses to users. We also introduce commonsense inference to help the model better understand the knowledge context and user intent. Finally, we used contrastive search in the decoding stage to make the generated responses more diverse. To verify the effectiveness of the model, we conducted some experiments and compared our model with the baseline models. The experiment results show that our approach outperforms the baseline models in terms of automatic evaluation. The final evaluation results show that our model ranks 2nd in the NLPCC 2023 Shared Task 9 Track 2.

Keywords: Dialogue Generation · User Feedback · RLHF · Commonsense Inference · Contrastive Search

1 Introduction

Currently, human-machine dialogue systems have been widely used in many application areas, such as intelligent customer service and education. These applications increasingly require the generation of natural, fluent, personalized and diverse dialogues to improve user satisfaction. In addition, in the field of natural language processing, many researchers have invested a lot of time and work in trying to find a better way to implement dialogue generation tasks.

Among the dialogue generation techniques, the dialogue generation task of user feedback is an important application scenario, and the core of this task is how to generate natural, fluent and diverse dialogue responses based on user input and feedback. Currently, many researchers in this area have proposed various approaches for this task, forming a series of alternative development

F. Liu et al. (Eds.): NLPCC 2023, LNAI 14304, pp. 376–387, 2023.
https://doi.org/10.1007/978-3-031-44699-3_34

directions. Jaques et al. [1] propose a reinforcement learning multi-domain dialogue generation method based on user feedback to improve the generalization ability of the model. Gao et al. [2] use feedback data from social media to build a large-scale feedback prediction training dataset. To mitigate possible distortions between feedback and engagement, they transform the ranking problem into a comparison of response pairs involving a small number of confounding factors. Zhang et al. [3] explore the use of explicit and implicit steering-level user feedback to improve multiaction dialogue strategy learning, and the historical predictions of these feedbacks are cost effective to collect and faithful to real-world scenarios.

However, these approaches face certain challenges when dealing with user feedback to generate dialogue responses. User feedback data is not always accurate and difficult to normalize and preprocess [4]. For example, some users may provide only vague feedback without providing enough information. In this case, the model may not be able to understand the true intent of the user and thus fail to generate targeted responses. Therefore, it is worth exploring how to make use of the information hidden in user feedback to better generate dialogue responses. In addition, the approaches represented by generative models often have problems such as repetitive or incoherent responses.

In practical applications, it should often be centered on the user and continuously adjusted and optimized through user feedback, a process that provides useful references for improving the quality of generated responses. Based on this, we propose a dialogue generation method based on user feedback, which generates more likable responses by modeling the likability of user feedback and optimizing the model using Reinforcement Learning from Human Feedback (RLHF) techniques. At the same time, we introduce commonsense inference to help the model better understand the knowledge background and user intent. Finally, we use contrastive search in the decoding stage to make the generated responses more diverse. This approach can be adaptively adjusted and optimized based on user feedback, thus improving the quality of the model generated responses.

Our contributions are as follows:

- We propose a user feedback based dialogue generation method to improve the quality of automatically generated responses. We combine the RLHF approach to build a user feedback-based response generation model to optimize and adapt the quality of response generation.
- We introduce commonsense inference techniques into dialogue generation to better understand and interpret user intent through commonsense knowledge. Commonsense inference techniques can be used to model and analyze the state of the dialogue generation model to better understand the context, distinguish between different language styles, and more accurately match user intent with response sentences.
- We combine the decoding method of contrastive search to generate more diverse and fluent dialogue responses, improving the utility of the model. The experiment results show that our approach outperforms the baseline models in terms of automatic evaluation. Our model achieves 2nd in the NLPCC 2023 Shared Task 9 Track 2.

2   Related Work

2.1   Dialogue Generation

In recent years, dialogue generation methods based on pretrained models have gradually become the mainstream approaches in dialogue generation techniques. Such approaches are usually based on pretrained language models, which are optimized by fine tuning and other means to achieve the generative capability of dialogue systems. Dialogue generation methods based on pretrained models are usually implemented using the Encoder-Decoder structure, which converts dialogue history into a context vector representation and then generates dialogue responses by Decoder. However, this approach has some problems in generating diverse and personalized responses. Because the generation capability of the model is limited by the pretrained corpus, it may lead to generated responses that do not match the real needs of users and actual situations [5].

2.2   Dialogue Based on User Feedback

Model optimization using user feedback has become an effective approach in dialogue generation systems. Among them, RLHF is a widely used technique nowadays. Researchers record the readability, trustworthiness and relevance values of the responses. These values are then used as a reward signal to optimize the final responses, thus improving the quality of the responses [6]. RLHF can effectively use human dialogue information for optimization of the model, greatly improving the effectiveness of dialogue generation. Wu et al. use fine-grained human feedback as an explicit training signal [7]. They introduced fine-grained RLHF that can train and learn from fine-grained reward functions and integrate multiple reward models associated with different feedback types. Different from previous works, we use human liked scores and diversity scores as a combined reward to generate more likeable responses to users.

2.3   Commonsense Inference in Dialogue

Commonsense inference is a new technique that has been applied to the field of natural language processing in recent years. Commonsense inference models can understand natural language and provide commonsense explanations and relevant information using external knowledge bases [8] to better address the ambiguity and uncertainty of models in the dialogue generation process. Commonsense reasoning techniques can cope with complex scenarios brought about by dialogue environments, user speech, and other factors, enabling dialogue generation systems to better understand and answer user questions. Bosselut et al. [9] hypothesized that an important step in automatic commonsense completion is to develop generative models of common sense knowledge, and proposed communication Transformer- COMET, learning to use natural language generating rich and diverse descriptions of commonsense. In this work, we use COMET to generate commonsense inference sentences to help the model better understand the knowledge context and user intent.

3   Methodology

In this paper, we propose a dialogue generation model based on user feedback, as shown in Fig. 1. The model consists of three main stages: commonsense inference, RLHF and contrast search decoding. Commonsense inference is responsible for generating commonsense sentences to better understand the user's intention; RLHF is responsible for optimizing the model in response to user feedback; and contrastive search plays a role in the decoding stage, which enables the model to generate more diverse and fluent dialogue responses.

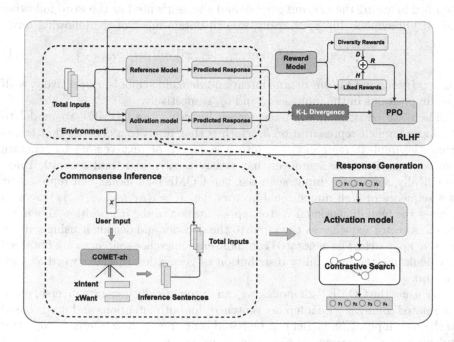

Fig. 1. The overall framework of our model.

3.1   Task Definition

The input to this task is a user query $X = \{x_1, x_2, x_3, \ldots, x_N\}$ and the output is an automatically generated response $Y = \{y_1, y_2, y_3, \ldots, y_T\}$, where x and y are the tokens, and N and T are the corresponding number of tokens. However, due to the different preferences of each individual, the generated responses may not meet the expectations of users. To improve the generated responses, this task introduces human subjective feedback $f = \{Like, Dislike\}$, where $Like$ and $Dislike$ are the user's like and dislike scores, respectively.

3.2   Commonsense Inference

Commonsense inference sentences, as implicit information for dialogue generation tasks, help generate richer and more reasonable dialogue responses. In this paper, we use COMET-zh[1], a BART-based generative language model, to generate commonsense inference sentences. The model uses the context and external knowledge from the training data to directly generate natural language commonsense inference sentences that conform to the grammar rules.

In the input, we use two special symbols, $xIntent$ and $xWant$, to represent the user's intention and need. Specifically, we represent the user's intention as the word following the $xIntent$ symbol and the user's need as the word following the $xWant$ symbol [10]. Specifically, we can obtain input of the following form:

$$X = \{x_1, x_2, \ldots, xIntent, x_{i_1}, \ldots, xWant, x_{i_2}, \ldots, x_N\} \tag{1}$$

where $xIntent$ and $xWant$ denote intent and demand symbols, respectively, with specific positions in the input as i_1 and i_2, respectively.

Then, we encode the input sentences by using the COMET-zh model to obtain an implicit representation h, which is then input to a decoder that transforms the implicit representation into a sequence of text vectors to generate commonsense inference sentences that satisfy the syntactic and semantic rules. Specifically, say for the input sentence, the COMET-zh model can represent it as a sequence of high dimensional vectors, i.e. $H = \{h_1, h_2, \ldots, h_n\}$, where h_i denotes the high dimensional vector representation of the ith position. Then, we take this vector sequence as the input to the decoder and decode it using autoregressive approach. The generated commonsense inference sentences are obtained by calculating the probability distribution of generating the next word at each position.

By using the COMET-zh model, we can automatically generate diverse, problem related commonsense inference sentences for both intentions and needs based on the user input. The model can be based on commonsense inference to better understand and interpret user intentions and needs.

3.3   RLHF

To make better use of human feedback, we employ a reinforcement learning with human feedback (RLHF) based approach to train the dialogue generation model. Specifically, we use a combination of a reference model and an activation model using KL divergence to prevent policy bias. Also, we combine a reward model for diversity scoring and human liked function scoring to update the model using a Proximal Policy Optimization (PPO) strategy.

Environment. We view the dialogue system as an environment in which our model receives user input and commonsense inference and then outputs the

---
[1] https://huggingface.co/svjack/comet-atomic-zh.

appropriate responses. Specifically, our model engages in dialogue with humans, and it needs to be able to predict appropriate responses while the user is inputting questions [11]. The state s of this environment can be represented as a tuple (X, Y), where X denotes the user's input and Y denotes the current response.

PPO. We use a PPO based policy optimization algorithm to train our dialogue generation model. Specifically, we use a combination of a reference model and an activation model. The reference model does not perform parameter updates when the policy is updated and is used as a reference for the policy. The activation model performs parameter updates using the PPO algorithm and is used for the actual policy generation. The DialoGPT model is chosen for both the reference model and the activation model.

For the reference and activation models, we use the KL divergence to measure the similarity between them. Specifically, we can define the KL divergence as:

$$D_{KL}(\pi_{ref}(\cdot|s)||\pi(\cdot|s)) = \mathbb{E}_{a \sim \pi_{ref}(\cdot|s)} \left[\log \frac{\pi_{ref}(a|s)}{\pi(a|s)} \right] \tag{2}$$

where $\pi_{ref}(\cdot|s)$ denotes the policy distribution of the reference model and $\pi(\cdot|s)$ denotes the policy distribution of the activation model. We use KL scatter to prevent the activation model from excessively deviating from the reference model and to make the policy update more robust.

In the strategy update phase, we update the strategy distribution of the activation model using the PPO algorithm [12], which is a strategy gradient-based algorithm that updates the strategy by applying the calculated superiority ratio to the inferiority ratio. Specifically, we can use the objective function of PPO expressed as:

$$L_\theta^{clip}(\tilde{\theta}) = \mathbb{E}_t \left[\min \left(r_t(\theta)\hat{A}_t(\theta, \tilde{\theta}), clip(r_t(\theta), 1 - epsilon, 1 + \epsilon)\hat{A}_t(\theta, \tilde{\theta}) \right) \right] \tag{3}$$

where $\tilde{\theta}$ denotes the old model parameters, and $\hat{A}_t(\theta, \tilde{\theta})$ denotes the superiority estimates generated using the current policy θ and the old policy $\tilde{\theta}$ at time step t, comparing the superiority using the truncation function $clip$ for restriction. $r_t(\theta)$ is the reward function that represents the degree of superiority or inferiority of the responses generated by the model under the current strategy.

Reward Model. In the reward model, we introduce a diversity scoring and a human like function scoring for evaluating the responses generated by the model. Specifically, we set a combined reward R, which can be expressed as a linear combination of diversity scoring and human liked function scoring:

$$R(s, a) = \alpha D_s(a) + \beta H_s(a) \tag{4}$$

where $D_s(a)$ denotes the diversity score between the model generated response a and the previously generated response, and $H_s(a)$ denotes how much humans like the response. α and β are hyperparameters that balance the contribution of the two scoring scores.

Specifically, the diversity score is calculated using word vectors and cosine similarity for measuring the similarity between different responses. We also introduce human liked scoring for measuring how close the model-generated responses are to natural human language interactions. Specifically, we denote the human liked function as $H_s(a)$, where s denotes the current state and a denotes the model generated responses. The function uses human preference feedback, which determines the score of each response and thus guides the learning of the model.

During model training, we continuously iterate the training using a policy optimization algorithm to continuously update the model's policy. Specifically, we use the PPO algorithm to update the policy parameters and update the model's response policy based on the combined reward R defined in the reward model to optimize the model's output.

3.4   Contrastive Search

Contrastive search decoding [13] is an emerging technique for text generation. It improves the quality of text generation by comparing the text sequences generated by different generation algorithms and filtering out the optimal results. In this model, we employ a contrastive search decoding technique to optimize the DialoGPT model as a reinforcement learning activation model in order to improve the quality and diversity of its dialogue generation.

Specifically, we used a combination of beam search and forced search for contrast search decoding. First, multiple alternative text sequences are generated using beam search, and then the optimal sequence is selected as the final output using the forced search method. Among them, the specific implementation of beam search and forced search can be expressed using the following equation:

$$x_t^{(k)} = \arg\max_{x \in V} \left(\log p(x|x_0^{(k)}, \ldots, x_t^{(k)}) + \lambda \frac{1}{t} \sum_{i=1}^{t} \log p(x_i^{(k)}|x_0^{(k)}, \ldots, x_t^{(k)}) \right) \quad (5)$$

where $x_t^{(k)}$ denotes the word selected at time step t for the kth alternative text sequence. V denotes the set of all alternative words. $p(x|x_0^{(k)}, \ldots, x_t^{(k)})$ is the probability distribution for computing the generated word x in the DialoGPT model. λ is the regularization factor to balance language fluency and diversity, which is regularized here by adding an N-gram language model.

4   Experiments

4.1   Dataset Description

We use the dataset published by NLPCC 2023 Shared Task 9 to evaluate the performance of our approach. The dataset collects user dialogue data from a real online dialogue system and stores all information during the dialogue, including user input and system responses, as well as feedback given by the user. The conversation data is labeled according to the user feedback, and each system response is marked with a "like" or "dislike" score. The data were then divided into training, validation and test sets in the ratio of 8:1:1 for training and evaluation of the deep learning models. Table 1 shows the number of sentences, responses, and average likes and dislikes for the train set, test set, and validation set, respectively.

Table 1. Statistics of NLPCC 2023 Shared Task 9 dataset.

Type	Query	Average Reply	Avg Like per Reply	Avg Dislike per Reply
train	16000	3.14	16.15	8.42
dev	2000	3.07	19.84	9.41
test	2000	3.16	30.57	12.19

4.2 Experimental Settings

We use the Adamw optimizer with a learning rate of 1e−5. The batch size is 16 and the number of training epochs is 25. We save checkpoints in each epoch and select the best checkpoint based on the performance of the validation set. We use the Pytorch deep learning framework to implement the model and train the model on two NVIDIA GeForce RTX 3090 GPUs.

4.3 Evaluation Metrics

We use the following automatic evaluation metrics to evaluate the performance of our model:

1. **PPL**: PPL (Perplexity) is a common metric used in language models. It is calculated by calculating the probability of each word for a given test data and using their geometric mean as the perplexity of the test set.
2. **Dist-1/2**: Dist-1/2 is a metric that measures the degree of similarity between model generation and reference responses. It is a metric based on edit distance and scores high if the generated responses are similar to the reference responses.
3. **BLEU**: BLEU is a commonly used conversation generation evaluation metric that can be used to evaluate the similarity between the generated responses and the reference responses. BLEU calculates a score by comparing the n-grams that appear in the reference responses with the n-grams that appear in the model-generated responses. It can consider several n-grams of different lengths simultaneously.

4.4   Baselines

To evaluate the performance of the model on these automatic evaluation metrics, four baselines were selected for comparison:

1. **BART-Chinese**: BART [14] is a Transformer-based sequence-to-sequence generation model, and BART-Chinese is a pre-trained model on Chinese corpus, which shows good generative power and naturalness in Chinese dialogue generation task.
2. **CDial-GPT2**: CDial-GPT2 [15] is a Chinese dialogue generation model based on GPT2 training. It uses open domain dialogue data for pretraining and performs well in a singleturn dialogue generation task, while obtaining good scores in both automatic and human evaluations.
3. **EVA2.0**: EVA2.0 [16] is a proposed model for dialogue generation tasks in Chinese contexts. It uses a multi-knowledge source information fusion technique based on dynamic knowledge graphs to fuse the extracted multi-source information to achieve more accurate answer generation.
4. **SimCTG**: SimCTG is a Chinese GPT-2 language model trained on the LCCC dataset and used for decoding by contrastive search. It is able to generate texts with more diversity and avoid generating repetitive responses.

4.5   Automatic Evaluation

Table 2 summarizes the results of our experiments for all models. The table shows the scores of each model on each metric, and the highest score for each metric is shown in bolded font.

Table 2. The automatic evaluation results.

Model	PPL	D-1	D-2	B-1	B-2	B-3	B-4
BART-Chinese	86.89	1.82	10.56	0.0918	0.1051	0.0911	0.0974
CDial-GPT2	45.90	2.55	11.29	0.1481	0.1502	0.1466	0.1396
EVA2.0	32.71	2.97	13.57	0.1828	0.1791	**0.1844**	0.1750
SimCTG	35.66	3.44	13.10	0.1677	0.1672	0.1608	0.1657
Ours	**27.12**	**3.72**	**15.54**	**0.1898**	**0.1879**	0.1748	**0.1776**

As can be seen from the table, our model performs the best on almost all metrics, especially in terms of Dist-2 and BLEU-2 scores. Our model scored 15.54 on Dist-2, which is much higher than the other models. In addition, our model scored the highest in BLEU-2 score (0.1879), while the other models scored between 0.105 and 0.179. The remarkable improvements increase on all metrics, which indicate the effectiveness of RLHF and commonsense inference, as well as contrastive search.

4.6   Ablation Study

We conducted an ablation study to verify the efficiency of each component of our model. Specifically, we designed three variants of our model: (1) w/o Comm: the commonsense inference knowledge component was removed and the input to the model was only user queries; (2) w/o RLHF: the reinforcement learning optimization model component was removed and the model was fine-tuned for training; (3) w/o Contr: the contrastive search component was removed and the top-p decoding approach was used. The results in Table 3 present that each component is beneficial to the final performance, which suggest commonsense inference knowledges are necessary for understanding the knowledge context and user intent. Furthermore, RLHF makes a contribution to the overall performance, which demonstrates RLHF can optimize and adapt the quality of response generation.

Table 3. The ablation study results.

Model	PPL	D-1	D-2	B-1	B-2	B-3	B-4
Ours	**27.12**	**3.72**	**15.54**	**0.1898**	**0.1879**	0.1748	**0.1776**
w/o Comm	29.51	3.54	14.19	0.1864	0.1821	0.1716	0.1748
w/o RLHF	29.83	3.29	13.97	0.1878	0.1841	**0.1805**	0.1737
w/o Contr	31.66	2.96	13.16	0.1779	0.1823	0.1728	0.1701

4.7   Online Evaluation

To better evaluate the performance of each model, the evaluation was also conducted by online evaluation. According to the task evaluation description, eight researchers with relevant experience were invited to evaluate how much each model was liked in the generated responses. A sample of 500 tests from the test set was selected for this evaluation. For each dialogue, each researcher evaluated the responses generated by each model separately and gave a score from 0 to 2, with a score of 2 indicating that the generated responses were very liked and a score of 0 indicating that the generated responses were very unliked. Table 4 shows the average score for each model on the manually evaluated metrics.

Table 4. The online evaluation results.

Model	Score
rank 1	1.656
rank 2 (Ours)	1.562
rank 3	1.409
rank 4	1.388
rank 5	1.214
rank 6	1.202

As can be seen from the Table 4, our model achieved the 2nd highest overall score (1.562) in the online evaluation, showing that our model is able to generate diverse, high-quality and liked responses from users.

5   Conclusions

In this paper, we propose a user feedback based dialogue generation method to improve the quality of machine generated automatic responses. First, we introduce the Reinforcement Learning from Human Feedback (RLHF) technique to improve the performance of the model in dialogue generation by including user feedback as part of the optimization objective function. Second, we used the commonsense inference technique to introduce knowledge inference into the dialogue model to improve the comprehension and response accuracy of the model. Finally, we use the decoding method of contrastive search to make the responses generation more diverse. The results of automatic evaluation experiments show that our approach outperforms the baseline model in terms of the quality and fluency of generated responses. Finally, our model received the 2nd place in NLPCC 2023 Shared Task 9 Track 2.

Acknowledgments. The work was supported by National Natural Science Foundation of China (62172086, 62272092).

References

1. Jaques, N., et al.: Human-centric dialog training via offline reinforcement learning. In: Proceedings of the 2020 Conference on Empirical Methods in Natural Language Processing, EMNLP 2020, Online, November 16–20, 2020, pp. 3985–4003 (2020)
2. Gao, X., Zhang, Y., Galley, M., Brockett, C., Dolan, B.: Dialogue response ranking training with large-scale human feedback data. In: Proceedings of the 2020 Conference on Empirical Methods in Natural Language Processing, EMNLP 2020, Online, November 16–20, 2020, pp. 386–395 (2020)
3. Zhang, S., et al.: Multi-action dialog policy learning from logged user feedback. arXiv preprint arXiv:2302.13505 (2023)
4. Ziegler, D.M., et al.: Fine-tuning language models from human preferences. arXiv preprint arXiv:1909.08593 (2019)
5. Wu, Z., Bi, W., Li, X., Kong, L., Kao, B.: Lexical knowledge internalization for neural dialog generation. In: Proceedings of the 60th Annual Meeting of the Association for Computational Linguistics (Volume 1: Long Papers), ACL 2022, Dublin, Ireland, May 22–27, 2022, pp. 7945–7958 (2022)
6. Liu, Z., Wang, H., Niu, Z.-Y., Wu, H., Che, W., Liu, T.: Towards conversational recommendation over multi-type dialogs. In: Proceedings of the 58th Annual Meeting of the Association for Computational Linguistics, ACL 2020, Online, July 5–10, 2020, pp. 1036–1049 (2020)
7. Wu, Z., et al.: Fine-grained human feedback gives better rewards for language model training. arXiv preprint arXiv:2306.01693 (2023)
8. Sap, M., et al.: Atomic: an atlas of machine commonsense for if-then reasoning. Proc. AAAI Conf. Artif. Intell. **33**, 3027–3035 (2019)

9. Bosselut, A., Rashkin, H., Sap, M., Malaviya, C., Celikyilmaz, A., Choi, Y.: COMET: commonsense transformers for automatic knowledge graph construction. In: Proceedings of the 57th Conference of the Association for Computational Linguistics, ACL 2019, Florence, Italy, July 28- August 2, 2019, Volume 1: Long Papers, pp. 4762–4779 (2019)

10. Sabour, S., Zheng, C., Huang, M.: CEM: commonsense-aware empathetic response generation. Proc. AAAI Conf. Artif. Intell. **36**, 11229–11237 (2022)

11. Sharma, A., Lin, I.W., Miner, A.S., Atkins, D.C., Althoff, T.: Towards facilitating empathic conversations in online mental health support: A reinforcement learning approach. In: Proceedings of the Web Conference 2021, pp. 194–205 (2021)

12. Schulman, J., Wolski, F., Dhariwal, P., Radford, A., Klimov, O.: Proximal policy optimization algorithms. arXiv preprint arXiv:1707.06347 (2017)

13. Su, Y., Lan, T., Wang, Y., Yogatama, D., Kong, L., Collier, N.: A contrastive framework for neural text generation. In: NeurIPS (2022)

14. Lewis, M., et al.: BART: denoising sequence-to-sequence pre-training for natural language generation, translation, and comprehension. In: Proceedings of the 58th Annual Meeting of the Association for Computational Linguistics, ACL 2020, Online, July 5–10, 2020, pp. 7871–7880 (2020)

15. Wang, Y., et al.: A large-scale Chinese short-text conversation dataset. In: Natural Language Processing and Chinese Computing: 9th CCF International Conference, NLPCC 2020, Zhengzhou, China, October 14–18, 2020, Proceedings, Part I 9, pp. 91–103. Springer (2020)

16. Yuxian, Gu., et al.: EVA2.0: investigating open-domain Chinese dialogue systems with large-scale pre-training. Mach. Intell. Res. **20**(2), 207–219 (2023)

Overview of the NLPCC 2023 Shared Task 9: User Feedback Prediction and Response Generation

Hanlin Teng[1], Hongda Sun[2], Wei Liu[1]([✉]), Shuang Dong[1], Rui Yan[2], Jian Luan[1], and Bin Wang[1]

[1] XiaoMi AI Lab, Beijing, China
{tenghanlin1,liuwei40,dongshuang1,luanjian,wangbin11}@xiaomi.com
[2] Gaoling School of Artificial Intelligence, Renmin University of China, Beijing, China
{sunhongda98,ruiyan}@ruc.edu.cn

Abstract. This paper presents an overview of user feedback prediction and response generation in the NLPCC 2023 shared task. We focus on how to utilize feedback data of user likes and dislikes to guide conversation response generation. The goal of this task is to predict accurate user preference and improve response quality to increase user likes. Participants need to integrate preference information into their models to generate responses that align with the user needs. In this paper, we summarize the key components of this task, including task description, dataset, evaluation metrics, participant methods, and final results. We also highlight the potential applications of incorporating like and dislike data in conversation generation.

Keywords: Conversation generation · User feedback · Response quality

1 Introduction

Recently, open-domain conversational AI systems have found wide-ranging applications. These applications increasingly demand the generation of fluent, personalized, and diverse conversations to enhance user satisfaction [1,2]. Among these conversation generation techniques, user feedback prediction and response generation stands out as a crucial application scenario. Firstly, assessing user preference accurately from a conversation is a crucial step in conversation systems, requiring the system to comprehend user intent and recognize which reply is more likely to be well-received by the user given a particular query [3]. Furthermore, improving the quality of generated responses based on user feedback is another core step in conversation systems. After receiving a user query, the system's primary objective is to produce responses that align as closely as possible with the user's preferences and needs, thereby enhancing the overall user experience and satisfaction [4,5].

© The Author(s), under exclusive license to Springer Nature Switzerland AG 2023
F. Liu et al. (Eds.): NLPCC 2023, LNAI 14304, pp. 388–395, 2023.
https://doi.org/10.1007/978-3-031-44699-3_35

Online conversation systems typically include a user feedback mechanism, such as like and dislike buttons, which allow users to express their satisfaction or dissatisfaction with the response they receive. This feedback signal not only represents the user's vote on the quality of the response, but also reflects their preferences. Therefore, it is important to explore how this signal can be leveraged to enhance the quality of the conversation system.

In this paper, we construct a new online conversation dataset for the task of user feedback prediction and response generation, which contains two tracks:

- Track 1: Prediction of likes and dislikes: Given a (query, reply) pair, predict the probabilities of likes, dislikes.
- Track 2: Conversation generation based on likes and dislikes: Incorporate like and dislike data into conversation generation to improve response quality and obtain high likes.

Teams are allowed to participate in one or multiple tracks. Eventually, 25 teams registered, 8 teams submitted Track 1 results, and 6 teams submitted Track 2 results. We separately describe the task and the dataset of each track in Sect. 3 and 4, and analyze the submission results in detail in Sect. 5.

2 Related Work

Predicting user feedback has gained significant attention due to its relevance in user satisfaction and conversation system improvement. Traditional methods use supervised learning techniques and feature engineering to capture the contextual information. However, these methods may lack the ability to capture complex patterns in user feedback [6]. Recently, deep learning techniques, such as recurrent neural networks [7] and attention mechanisms [8], have been applied to better capture contextual dependencies. Additionally, the integration of pre-trained language models like BERT [9] has shown promising results in understanding user preference using feedback information.

Generating contextually appropriate and engaging responses is also a key component of conversational AI systems. Early research in this field involved statistical language models like n-grams and sequence-to-sequence models, which struggled with long-range dependencies and fluency issues [10]. Recent advancements in natural language generation have been largely driven by the Transformer-based model architecture, which have proven to be highly effective in response generation tasks, enabling self-attention mechanisms to capture global context and produce coherent and contextually relevant responses [8]. To incorporate user feedback into response generation, researchers have explored various methods. Reinforcement learning has emerged as an effective technique for response generation based on user feedback [11]. The model first generates a response and then receives reward signals based on how well the response aligns with user feedback. It enables the system to learn from user interactions and iteratively improve the generated responses, increasing the likelihood of generating satisfactory replies [12].

3   Task Description

The competition aims to improve the quality of replies and get more likes by incorporating like and dislike data into conversation generation. As dialogue systems evolve, it becomes crucial to fine-tune the generated responses taking into account user preferences. This competition asks contestants to use like and dislike data and incorporate it into dialogue generation models to generate more user-friendly responses.

3.1   Track 1: Prediction of Likes and Dislikes

In the online conversation system, for a user query q_i, there are multiple replies $r_{i1}, r_{i2}, \cdots, r_{i,n_i}$ can be collected. Meanwhile, for each reply r_{ik}, a user will choose to click "like" or "dislike" as feedback on whether the reply is satisfactory. Therefore, the goal of the user feedback prediction task is to predict the Bernoulli distribution of clicking likes or dislikes. In other words, given each query-reply pair (q_i, r_{ik}), the probability $p_{ik} \in [0, 1]$ of clicking "like" is mainly to be estimated.

3.2   Track 2: Conversation Generation Based on Likes and Dislikes

The dataset consists of rows where each row represents a user query directed towards the dialogue chatbot. These queries serve as explicit expressions of users' questions, requests, or concerns during their interactions with the system. Participants are required to submit their results with the same number of rows as the test dataset. Each row should contain the reply results corresponding to the query.

Participants are expected to utilize the provided data from track 1 to fine-tune their dialogue models and generate responses that are more likely to be well-received by users. To assess the popularity or likability of the generated replies, multiple reviewers or assessors will be gathered. They will evaluate and assign a favorability score to each response. This evaluation process aims to capture the overall user satisfaction and identify responses that resonate positively with users.

4   Dataset Description

The dataset is collected from Xiao Ai's log. Since it is based on real user feedback, it can objectively reflect the user preference for the system replies. We eliminated a large number of queries with unclear semantics, and retained the queries with sufficient user feedback. We finally randomly selected 20,000 cases as the data of Track 1, and split them into training/validation/test set according to the ratio of 8:1:1. We additionally extracted 500 unique conversation cases as the test set of Track 2.

We expect that the participants can grasp the user preferences in the conversation data in Track 1, and complete the task of user preference prediction. Based on the above results, the dialogue system is required to make more accurate replies to meet the needs of users.

```
{
    "query": "你喜欢听什么歌",
    "replies": [
        {
            "reply": "你喜欢什么，小爱就喜欢什么",
            "dislike": 3,
            "like": 2
        },
        {
            "reply": "你知道的，我什么歌都喜欢。😊",
            "dislike": 2,
            "like": 3
        },
        {
            "reply": "你知道的，我什么歌都喜欢。",
            "dislike": 4,
            "like": 6
        },
        {
            "reply": "亲爱哒，最喜欢的还是土嗨土嗨的那种，热闹啊！",
            "dislike": 2,
            "like": 4
        },
        {
            "reply": "受你影响，品味现在和你差不多了。",
            "dislike": 47,
            "like": 146
        },
```

Fig. 1. An example of multiple replies and their corresponding likes and dislikes based on a given query.

5   Results

5.1   Evaluation Metrics

The overview statistics of the dataset are presented in Table 1. A query sentence may have multiple replies, and a query-reply pair is considered as a single sample.

Table 1. Data statistics.

Type	Query #	Average Reply #	Avg Like # per Reply	Avg Dislike # per Reply
train	16,000	3.14	16.15	8.42
dev	2,000	3.07	19.84	9.41
test	2,000	3.16	30.57	12.19

In Track 1, participants are required to provide a preference ratio for each sample in the test set. In order to evaluate the difference between the predicted distribution and the ground truth distribution, we use the KL-Score as a metric to assess the participants' performance. The formulas for computing the KL-Score are:

$$Score1 = gold \times \log(gold) + (1 - gold) \times \log(1 - gold)$$
$$Score2 = gold \times \log(pred) + (1 - gold) \times \log(1 - pred)$$
$$KL - Score = \frac{1}{1 + Score1 - Score2}$$

where *gold* is the gold value and *pred* is the predicted value. The KL-Score measures the similarity between the gold value and the prediction in the given task.

For track 2, the evaluation is performed using manual assessment to achieve a better evaluation of each model's performance. The evaluation is conducted through an online assessment method to ensure accuracy and consistency. Eight researchers with relevant experience were invited to assess the popularity of generated responses for each model. A set of 500 test samples was selected from the test dataset for this evaluation. For each dialogue, each researcher individually evaluated the responses generated by each model and assigned a score ranging from 0 to 2, where 2 indicated a highly popular response and 0 indicated a highly unpopular response.

Then, the average score of all replies for each query is calculated, and the final result is the average score across all queries.

5.2   Participants

A total of 9 teams participated in this shared task and we received over 50 submissions. In addition to the final submission, we require up to one submission per day and publish test results to help participating teams improve the system. We provide leaderboards for both tracks in Tables 2 and 3 for a comprehensive overview of the submissions. We rank participants based on the highest scores in their submissions. Overall, the number and quality of submissions during the testing process has increased. In addition, most participants achieved better grades in their latest submissions than in previous submissions.

5.3   Main Results

The full score of track 1 is 100 points. The best team in track 1 has a score of 92.13. There is not much difference between the top two scores, while the other teams still have a lot of room for improvement. The full score of track 2 is 2 points. The best team in track 2 scored 1.656. Due to the use of ChatGPT, the score was higher than other teams. The second-placed team scored 1.562, which is based on the open source model. Based on the introduction of reinforcement learning and other technologies.

In track 1, where the maximum score is 100 points, the top-performing team achieved an impressive score of 92.13. The margin between the scores of the top two teams is minimal, indicating their close competition. However, there is still substantial room for improvement among the remaining teams.

Table 2. Track 1 Team Leaderboard.

Rank	Team	Score
1	师弟师妹带带我	92.13
2	dunnlp	92.00
3	zut	91.73
4	YNU-HPCC	91.63
5	HTDZNLP	91.4
6	666	91.24
7	Tryourbest classification	90.94
8	little_spice	90.72

In track 2, the highest possible score is 2 points. The leading team in track 2 achieved an impressive score of 1.656, thanks to their utilization of Chat-GPT. This team had a significant advantage over other participants. The second-ranked team earned a score of 1.562 by implementing advanced techniques like reinforcement learning in addition to leveraging open-source models.

Table 3. Track 2 Team Leaderboard.

Rank	Team	Score
1	YNU-HPCC	1.656
2	Devs	1.562
3	little_spice	1.409
4	666	1.388
5	ZUT	1.214
6	HTDZNLP	1.202

6 Conclusion

In this paper, we provide a comprehensive overview of NLPCC2023 Shared Task 9: User Feedback Prediction and Response Generation. Evaluating the quality of a chatbot is a challenging task, and the traditional binary evaluation using 0 and 1 has several limitations. In this shared task, we constructed a dataset with likes and dislikes based on the logs of XiaoAi, a leading chatbot in China. The real data labels derived from XiaoAi's interactions offer valuable insights for research purposes. We received experimental results from 9 participating teams, and we will review the reports of the top-performing teams and summarize the strengths of each system. Excellent reports showcased the utilization of advanced techniques such as model fusion, Projected Gradient Descent, and reinforcement learning. These attempts indicate that there is still significant room for improvement in the systems of this task. We encourage further research on how to effectively utilize human feedback.

References

1. Roller, S., et al.: Recipes for building an open-domain chatbot. In: Proceedings of the 16th Conference of the European Chapter of the Association for Computational Linguistics: Main Volume, pp. 300–325 (2021)
2. Kottur, S., Moura, J., Lee, S., Batra, D.: Natural language does not emerge 'naturally' in multi-agent dialog. In: Proceedings of the 2017 Conference on Empirical Methods in Natural Language Processing, pp. 2962–2967 (2017)
3. Zhang, S., Dinan, E., Urbanek, J., Szlam, A., Kiela, D., Weston, J.: Personalizing dialogue agents: I have a dog, do you have pets too? In: Proceedings of the 56th Annual Meeting of the Association for Computational Linguistics (Volume 1: Long Papers), pp. 2204–2213 (2018)
4. Ashfaq, M., Yun, J., Shubin, Yu., Loureiro, S.M.C.: I, chatbot: modeling the determinants of users' satisfaction and continuance intention of AI-powered service agents. Telematics Inform. **54**, 101473 (2020)
5. Serban, I.V., et al.: A deep reinforcement learning chatbot. arXiv preprint arXiv:1709.02349 (2017)
6. Ritter, A., Cherry, C., Dolan, W.B.: Data-driven response generation in social media. In: Proceedings of the Conference on Empirical Methods in Natural Language Processing, pp. 583–593 (2011)
7. Medsker, L.R., Jain, L.C.: Recurrent neural networks. Des. Appl. **5**(64–67), 2 (2001)
8. Vaswani, A., et al.: Attention is all you need. In: Advances in Neural Information Processing Systems, vol. 30 (2017)
9. Devlin, J., Chang, M.-W., Lee, K., Toutanova, K.: Bert: pre-training of deep bidirectional transformers for language understanding. In: Proceedings of NAACL-HLT, pp. 4171–4186 (2019)
10. Sordoni, A., et al.: A neural network approach to context-sensitive generation of conversational responses. In: Proceedings of the 2015 Conference of the North American Chapter of the Association for Computational Linguistics: Human Language Technologies, pp. 196–205 (2015)

11. Li, J., Monroe, W., Ritter, A., Jurafsky, D., Galley, M., Gao, J.: Deep reinforcement learning for dialogue generation. In: Proceedings of the 2016 Conference on Empirical Methods in Natural Language Processing, pp. 1192–1202 (2016)
12. Li, X., Chen, Y.-N., Li, L., Gao, J., Celikyilmaz, A.: Investigation of language understanding impact for reinforcement learning based dialogue systems. arXiv preprint arXiv:1703.07055 (2017)

Evaluation Workshop: Learn to Watch TV: Multimodal Dialogue Understanding and Response Prediction

Multimodal Dialogue Understanding via Holistic Modeling and Sequence Labeling

Chenran Cai[1,2], Qin Zhao[1,2], Ruifeng Xu[1,2(✉)], and Bing Qin[1]

[1] Harbin Institute of Technology (Shenzhen), Shenzhen 518000, China
crcai1023@gmail.com, {zhaoqin,xuruifeng}@hit.edu.cn, qinb@ir.hit.edu.cn
[2] Guangdong Provincial Key Laboratory of Novel Security Intelligence Technologies,
Shenzhen 518000, China

Abstract. This paper introduces the experimental schemes of Team HLT-base for the NLPCC-2023-Shared-Task-10 Learn to Watch TV: Multimodal Dialogue Understanding and Response Prediction (MDUG) competition. In this paper, we focus on two subtasks of multimodal dialogue understanding: the dialogue scene identification task and the dialogue session identification task. To solve these subtasks, we propose a simple and efficient multimodal framework, where two points are taken into account: *i.e.*, modeling the interaction of different utterances and effectively fusing the information of different modalities. For the former, we concatenate all utterances into a single sentence and feed it into the pre-trained model; for the latter, we use a transformer layer to fuse the multimodal features. Extensive experiments show that our proposed framework achieves state-of-the-art (SOTA) performance compared with other competitive methods, and ranks 1st in both subtasks (*i.e.*, track1: dialogue scene identification and track2: dialogue session identification) in the MDUG competition.

Keywords: Multimoal dialogue understand · Sequence labeling

1 Introduction

Dialogue understanding [9,22] is a fundamental task in natural language processing that aims to extract semantic information from natural language utterances in a dialogue context. Dialogue understanding can enable various applications such as dialogue systems [2,20], question answering [7,12], information retrieval [3,15], and summarization [5]. However, most of the existing research on dialogue understanding focuses on the textual modality, ignoring the rich information that can be conveyed by other modalities such as speech, vision, and gesture. Multimodal dialogue understanding [13,27] is an emerging research area that aims to leverage multimodal information to enhance dialogue understanding and enable new applications that require multimodal interaction. For example, [1] extends the visual question answering task to a dialogue setting and applies the multiturn video question answering dataset (*i.e.*, AVSD), which is constructed from

F. Liu et al. (Eds.): NLPCC 2023, LNAI 14304, pp. 399–411, 2023.
https://doi.org/10.1007/978-3-031-44699-3_36

the human activity dataset. However, existing studies are not suitable for open-domain conversations and real scenes due to the short duration and single content feature of the video question answering dataset.

To solve these challenges, NLPCC-2022-Shared-Task-10 designs the Multimodal Dialogue Understanding and Generation (MDUG) competition, which constructs a large-scale multi-modal dialogue dataset based on 1859 TV episodes to facilitate open-domain multimodal dialogue understanding. Moreover, for long video understanding, this completion proposes two fundamental subtasks: multimodal dialogue scene identification task and multimodal dialogue session identification task. Specifically, the former aims to detect the boundaries of dialogue scenes in movies and TV series, which are viewed as the minimal semantic units of a video. The latter aims to detect the boundaries of dialogue sessions. The difference is that session topic shift at the discourse level is a common phenomenon in dialogue scenes, which means that there may be multiple sessions in one dialogue scene.

However, there are two problems while solving these tasks: (i) Each sample contains multiple utterances. Thus, we first require seeking ways to model the interaction of different utterances. (ii) Due to the multimodal nature of these two tasks, effectively fusing the information of different modalities is another problem. In this paper, we propose a simple and efficient multimodal framework that tackles both problems. For the former, we concatenate all utterances into a single sentence and feed it into the pre-trained model; for the latter, we use a transformer layer to fuse the multimodal features. Finally, we apply the fused multimodal features to accomplish the multimodal dialogue understanding task. Extensive experiments show that our proposed framework achieves state-of-the-art (SOTA) performance compared with other competitive methods, and ranks 1st in both subtasks (*i.e.*, track1: dialogue scene identification task and track2: dialogue session identification task) in the MDUG competition. The main contributions of this paper are summarized as follows:

- We formulate the multimodal understanding task as the sequence labeling task and utilize the same framework to complete these two tasks by addressing two related problems (*i.e.*, modeling the interaction of different utterances and effectively fusing the information of different modalities).
- The proposed framework outperforms other competitive methods and achieves SOTA performance, as evidenced by extensive experimental results.

2   Related Work

2.1   Multimodal Dialogue Scene Identification

Multimodal Dialogue Scene Identification is the task of detecting the boundaries of dialogue scenes in movies and TV series. A dialogue scene is a continuous sequence of utterances that occur in the same spatial and temporal context. This task is a crucial component of multimodal dialogue understanding, which aims to develop open-domain dialogue systems that can utilize visual and textual information from long videos. By segmenting the videos into meaningful units, this task can facilitate dialogue analysis and response generation, as well as video retrieval and summarization. [10] first constructs a large-scale movie understanding dataset MovieNet, which contains 1,100 movies and 42 K scene boundaries annotations. Based on this dataset, some supervised learning-based methods [10,14] achieve great success in the video scene segmentation task. Moreover, [23] proposed an effective Self-Supervised Learning framework to learn better shot representations from unlabeled long-term videos. However, MovieNet is annotated from sequences of shots that are extracted by [16], which results in coarse shot boundaries and imprecise scene labels. To address this shortage, [21] build a large-scale multimodal dialogue dataset based on 1859 TV episodes and manually annotated the dialogue scene boundaries to facilitate open-domain multimodal dialogue understanding.

2.2   Multimodal Dialogue Session Identification

Topic shift at the discourse level is a common phenomenon in dialogue scenes, which makes the dialogue context rather important for dialogue understanding. In recent years, there has been a lot of work [24,26] on the task of dialogue topic segmentation, which aims to divide the dialogue into topically coherent segments. Some existing works treat dialogue topic segmentation as a topic-tracking problem [11,19]. However, these methods are impractical for open-domain dialogue, as it requires a list of pre-defined categories that cover different topics. Therefore, to overcome this limitation, [21] formulates dialogue topic segmentation as an extension of text segmentation [6,25,26] and construct a large-scale multimodal dialogue dataset with manual annotations of dialogue session boundaries, which is called the multimodal dialogue session identification task.

3   Task Introduction

3.1   Task Definition

Given a dialogue context $T = \{t_1, t_2, ..., t_N\}$ and its correlated video clip $V = \{v_1, v_2, ..., v_N\}$ as input where N is the length of dialogue, the dialogue scene identification and dialogue session identification tasks aim to classify each text and video clip pair $\{t_i, v_i\}$ into pre-defined categories ($i.e.$, 0, 1). In this paper, we formulate these two tasks as a sequence labeling task. Let $Y = \{y_1, y_2, ..., y_n\}$ be the correlated sequence labels, $y_i \in \mathcal{Y}$, and $\mathcal{Y}$ is the pre-defined label set ($i.e.$, 0, 1).

The scene label is either 0 or 1, indicating whether the current turn belongs to the same scene as the previous turn (0) or starts a new scene (1). Similarly, the session label is either 0 or 1, indicating whether the current turn continues the same topic as the previous turn (0) or switches to a new topic (1).

3.2   Evaluation Metric

Dialogue scene identification and dialogue session identification tasks are evaluated using the Accuracy value that is calculated as follows:

$$\text{Accuracy} = \frac{TP + TN}{TP + TN + FP + FN}, \tag{1}$$

where TP represents true positives, FP represents false positives, TN represents true negatives, and FN represents false negatives. In detail, the dialogue scene identification task labels the short video that concludes a dialogue scene as the positive instance. Likewise, the dialogue session identification task labels the utterance that terminates a dialogue session as the positive instance. Besides, this competition adopts the F1 scores as an auxiliary metric to prevent the influence of unbalanced label distribution. The calculation equation is shown as follows:

$$Precision = \frac{TP}{TP + FP}, \tag{2}$$

$$Recall = \frac{TP}{TP + FN}, \tag{3}$$

$$\text{F1} = \frac{2 \times Precision \times Recall}{Precision + Recall}. \tag{4}$$

In order to better measure the performance of the model, the competition applies the average of Accuracy score and F1 score as the final evaluation indicator.

$$\text{final result} = \frac{1}{2}(\text{Accuracy} + \text{F1}). \tag{5}$$

4   Methodology

4.1   Overall Architecture

Figure 1 illustrates the overall architecture of our framework for the dialogue scene identification task and dialogue session identification task, which contain the three main components: (1) *Text representation module*, which aims to model the relationship of different utterances in the entire dialogue and extract each utterance feature; (2) *Image representation module*, which aims to obtain the image feature correlated with the utterances; (3) *Multimodal fusing and classification module*, which first utilizes the transformer layer to fuse the text and image features. Then this module adopts the fused feature to implement the sequence label (*i.e.*, dialogue scene identification task and dialogue session identification task).

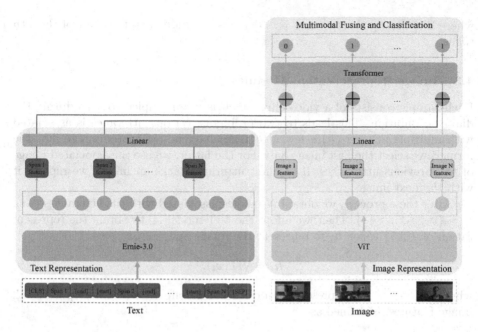

Fig. 1. The architecture of our framework on the dialogue scene identification task and dialogue session identification task

4.2 Text Representation Module

Given a dialogue context $T = \{t_1, t_2, ..., t_N\}$, which contains N utterances. To model the interaction of N utterances, we concatenate them into a sentence. Specially, we add two special tokens (*i.e.*, [start] and [end]) to distinguish the different utterances. In addition, due to the nature of the pre-trained language model, we keep the first and last tokens as [CLS] and [SEP] respectively. Compared with using the pre-trained language model to extract the feature of each utterance, this method better models the relationship between utterances, which is helpful for scene and session identifications.

$$S = [[\text{CLS}], t_1, [\text{end}], [\text{start}], t_2, [\text{end}], ..., [\text{start}], t_N, [\text{SEP}]]. \quad (6)$$

Then, we utilize the pre-trained language model (*i.e.*, Ernie-3.0 [18]) as the text encoder to map each token into a d_w-dimensional embedding. To extract the feature of each utterance, we apply the one [CLS] and N-1 [start] tokens as features of N utterances:

$$\mathbf{H}_t = \text{Ernie-3.0}(S), \quad (7)$$

where $\mathbf{H}_t \in \mathbb{R}^{N \times d_w}$ is the embedding feature matrix of one [CLS] and N-1 [start]. To unify the dimensions of representations between different modalities, we feed the text representation $\mathbf{H}_t$ into a trainable linear projection:

$$T = \text{Linear}(\mathbf{H}_t), \quad (8)$$

where $\boldsymbol{T} = [\boldsymbol{t}_1, \boldsymbol{t}_2, \cdots, \boldsymbol{t}_N]$, $\boldsymbol{t}_i \in \mathbb{R}^{d_h}$ denotes the hidden state vector of the i-th token.

4.3   Image Representation Module

Each sample consists of a video clip, which is downsampled to 3 fps during the dialogue duration. This leads to two problems: (i) one utterance is associated with multiple images; (ii) a few utterances have no associated image. For the former, we select the first image only. For the latter, we use the associated image of the previous utterances. If the first utterance lacks an image, we replace it with the next image.

After these process, we obtain N images associated with the utterances (*i.e.*, $V = \{v_1, v_2, ..., v_N\}$). Then, we adopt the ViT model [4] to obtain the representation of [CLS] token $\boldsymbol{h}_i$ to represent the image v_i:

$$\boldsymbol{h}_i = \text{ViT}(v_i), \tag{9}$$

where $\boldsymbol{h}_i \in \mathbb{R}^{d_v}$. The representation of the video clip V, which incorporates all image features, is defined as

$$\mathbf{H}_v = [\boldsymbol{h}_1, \boldsymbol{h}_2, \cdots, \boldsymbol{h}_N], \tag{10}$$

where N is the number of images. To reduce memory usage and run time, we save the $\mathbf{H}_v$ feature, which means we do not fine-tune the ViT model. Subsequently, we employ a trainable linear projection to map $\mathbf{H}_v$ to d_h-dimensional:

$$V = \text{Linear}(\mathbf{H}_v), \tag{11}$$

where $V = [\boldsymbol{v}_1, \boldsymbol{v}_2, \cdots, \boldsymbol{v}_N]$, $\boldsymbol{v}_i \in \mathbb{R}^{d_h}$ denotes the hidden state vector of the i-th video image.

4.4   Multimodal Fusing and Classification Module

We sum the text representation $\boldsymbol{T}$ and image representation $\boldsymbol{V}$. Then, we apply a transformer layer to fuse them. Subsequently, we feed the fused feature representation into a linear layer to predict the probability distribution of scene labels or session labels. It is worth noting that dialogue scene identification and dialogue session identification are using the same framework to solve. Finally, we apply the cross-entropy loss function to calculate loss $\mathcal{L}_f$:

$$\mathbf{F} = \text{trans}(\boldsymbol{T} + \boldsymbol{V}), \tag{12}$$

$$\boldsymbol{y}^f = \text{softmax}(\mathbf{F} \cdot \boldsymbol{W} + \boldsymbol{b}), \tag{13}$$

$$\mathcal{L}_f = -\frac{1}{N} \sum_{i=1}^{N} y_i \log\left(\boldsymbol{y}_i^f\right), \tag{14}$$

where $y_i \in \mathbb{R}^{|\mathcal{Y}|}$ is the ground truth and $|\mathcal{Y}| = 2$ is the size of the pre-defined label set. To alleviate the imbalance between these two label types, we utilize a tag-wise weighting vector to counteract this. During the training phase, we utilize $\mathcal{L}_f$ with a weight factor to train the entire framework.

Table 1. Statistics of MDUG dataset

Split	Dialogue clips	Utterances	Dialogue scenes	Dialogue sessions
train	40K	100M	56K	106K
valid	1,955	50K	3,202	6,331
test	666	17K	945	1,802

5 Experiments

5.1 Dataset

The competition dataset consists of 40,006, 1955, and 666 dialogue clips in the train, valid, and test sets, respectively. The number of utterances in each set is 1,000,079, 50,032, and 16,749, respectively. The videos and dialogues for this task are crawled from online American TV series and split into train, valid, and test sets. Each sample comprises a series of dialogue utterances associated with the video clip (downsampled to 3fps) during the dialogue duration. Each clip is converted to the "jpg" format for further modeling. Table 1 shows more statistics.

5.2 Experimental Settings

For the text feature extraction module, we employ Ernie-3.0-xbase-zh[1] [18] model to embed each token as a 1024-dimensional embedding. For the image feature extraction module, we utilize vit-base-patch16-224[2] [4] to embed each image as a 768-dimensional embedding. The trainable linear projections map both text and image features into 1024-dimensional embeddings.

The hyper-parameters of our framework are as follows: the ratio of weight loss with label 0 to weight loss with label 1 is 1:5 and the number of transformer layers is 1. In the experiments, we use different learning rate for different modules. For the text representation module, the learning rate is $1e\text{-}5$. For the multimodal fusing and classification module, the learning rate is $6e\text{-}5$. It is worth noting that we fix the parameters of the ViT model for the image representation module. Moreover, to reduce the running time, we only use 5000 data samples for training. All experiments are conducted as Tesla V100.

---

[1] https://huggingface.co/nghuyong/ernie-3.0-xbase-zh.
[2] https://huggingface.co/google/vit-base-patch16-224.

Table 2. Performance comparison of the variants methods on MDUG dataset for subtask 1: dialogue scene identification. We highlight the best score in each column in bold, and the second-best score with underline

Models	Acc (%)	P (%)	R (%)	F1 (%)	final result
Random Mode	50.79	6.29	**49.71**	11.16	30.98
RoFormer-chinese-base [17] (2021)	90.54	<u>26.92</u>	30.33	<u>28.52</u>	<u>59.53</u>
Erlangshen-Longformer-330M [28] (2022)	**93.24**	16.42	2.11	3.74	48.49
Erlangshen-DeBERTav2-320M [28] (2022)	90.93	26.17	25.14	25.65	58.29
Ours	<u>91.35</u>	**30.77**	<u>31.19</u>	**30.98**	**61.17**

Table 3. Performance comparison of the variants methods on MDUG dataset for subtask 2: dialogue session identification. We highlight the best score in each column in bold, and the second-best score with underline

Models	Acc(%)	P(%)	R(%)	F1(%)	final result
Random Mode	50.57	11.59	**48.92**	18.75	34.66
RoFormer-chinese-base [17] (2021)	84.75	37.04	<u>44.16</u>	<u>40.29</u>	62.52
Erlangshen-Longformer-330M [28] (2022)	80.93	18.54	18.75	18.64	49.79
Erlangshen-DeBERTav2-320M [28] (2022)	86.69	**42.11**	30.01	39.96	<u>63.32</u>
Ours	**86.50**	<u>41.99</u>	41.50	**41.74**	**64.12**

5.3   Comparision Models

We utilize different Chinese pre-trained language models to replace the backbone of our framework as the baseline methods. Since we concatenate all utterances in the context, the text input length exceeds 512. Therefore, we choose some pre-trained models that can handle 1024 tokens. The following are the baselines we use.

- Erlangshen-Longformer-330M[3] [28], which adopts an attention mechanism that scales linearly with sequence length, allowing it to process documents of thousands of tokens or longer and to handle long sequences of up to 4,096 tokens.
- RoFormer-chinese-base[4] [17], which is a BERT-like autoencoding model with rotary position embeddings that are a type of relative position embeddings that can handle long sequences without increasing the memory consumption.
- Erlangshen-DeBERTa-v2-320M-Chinese[5] [8], which is a natural language processing model that improves on BERT and RoBERTa models using two novel techniques: disentangled attention and enhanced mask decoder.

---

[3] https://huggingface.co/IDEA-CCNL/Erlangshen-Longformer-330M.
[4] https://huggingface.co/junnyu/roformer-chinese-base.
[5] https://huggingface.co/IDEA-CCNL/Erlangshen-DeBERTa-v2-320M-Chinese.

5.4   Main Results

We conduct the main experiments on dialogue scene identification and dialogue session identification tasks, which are shown in Table 2 and 3, respectively. We compare the performance of pre-trained language models (*i.e.*, RoFormer, Long-former, and Debertav2) and draw the following conclusions.

Table 4. Ablation Study

Models	Acc(%)	P(%)	R(%)	F1(%)	final result
dialogue scene identification					
Ours	91.35	**30.77**	**31.19**	**30.98**	**61.17**
w/o image	91.26	26.97	23.70	25.23	58.24
w/o text	90.91	23.37	20.25	21.70	56.30
w/o weighted loss	**93.76**	48.81	5.95	10.61	52.18
w/o holistic modeling	91.73	25.88	17.66	20.99	56.36
dialogue session identification					
Ours	86.50	41.99	41.50	**41.74**	**64.12**
w/o image	86.08	40.60	**41.96**	41.27	63.67
w/o text	81.35	23.99	27.66	25.70	53.53
w/o weighted loss	**89.07**	**61.82**	16.34	25.85	57.46
w/o holistic modeling	84.80	34.95	35.35	35.15	59.97

(1) We can find that the random method has an accuracy rate of less than 50%, but a high recall rate. This is because the label distribution of the MDUG dataset is imbalanced. Due to this imbalance phenomenon, we focus on the F1 metric, which reflects the model capabilities more accurately and affects the final results more significantly.

(2) Our framework significantly outperformers the other baselines on both the dialogue scene identification and the dialogue session identification datasets. For example, in terms of F1, our framework (*i.e.*, Ernie-3.0-xbase-zh) surpasses RoFormer-chinese-base by 2.46% and 1.45%, Erlangshen-Longformer-330M by 27.24% and 23.10%, and Erlangshen-DeBERTav2-320M by 5.33% and 1.78% on two datasets, respectively. These show that Ernie-3.0-xbase-zh has a better ability to model different utterances in context, which may be due to Ernie-3.0-xbase-zh being a large-scale knowledge-enhanced pre-trained model for language understanding.

(3) For the poor performance of Erlangshen-Longformer-330M, we consider that it is caused by the extreme imbalance of labels that prevents the Longformer from overfitting these datasets, resulting in low recall and F1 scores for the Longformer.

5.5   Ablation Study

We also conduct the ablation study for the proposed method, which is presented in Table 4. The results reveal that our framework achieves the best performance when combining image and text features, which suggests that both components are beneficial. Compared with removing image (*i.e.*, *w/o image*), removing text (*i.e.*, *w/o text*) leads to more performance degradation. This shows that the text is crucial for our framework.

Table 5. Online results on the dialogue scene identification task

Rank	Team name	Acc(%)	F1(%)	final result
1	HLT-base	**88.70**	**27.57**	**58.14**
2	noobyj	83.39	21.41	52.40

Table 6. Online results on the dialogue session identification task

Rank	Team name	Acc(%)	F1(%)	final result
1	HLT-base	**87.24**	**38.42**	**62.83**
2	noobyj	83.89	24.21	54.05

Furthermore, we perform ablation experiments on weighted loss. In our framework, we set the weight factor of cross-entropy loss to 1:5 according to the distribution proportion of labels (*i.e.*, the ratio of weight loss with label 0 to weight loss with label 1 is 1:5). *w/o weighted loss* sets the weight factor of cross-entropy loss to 1:1. From the results, we can find that the weight factor 1:5 outperforms the weight factor 1:1 (*i.e. w/o weighted loss*). This shows that the weight factor of cross-entropy loss can effectively alleviate the influence of imbalanced labels.

Moreover, we also conduct experiments on the way of modeling the different utterances. In our framework, we apply the holistic modeling method, which concatenates all utterances into a single sentence and feeds it into the pre-trained model. *w/o holistic modeling* applies the pre-trained model to extract the feature of each utterance. From the results, we observe that holistic modeling significantly outperformers single utterance modeling (*i.e.*, *w/o holistic modeling*). This is because the latter does not account for the deep modeling of the relationship between different utterances in context.

5.6   Online Results

We report the online results of our framework in Table 5 and 6. Our framework shows a very convincing performance. We achieve first place in both the dialogue scene identification and the dialogue session identification subtasks, which fully demonstrates the effectiveness of our framework.

6   Conclusion

In this paper, we mainly propose a simple and efficient framework to achieve a better multimodal dialogue understanding. The framework simultaneously solves the multimodal dialogue understanding for track1: dialogue scene identification and track2: dialogue session identification, where two points are taken into account (*i.e.*, modeling the interaction of different utterances and fusing the information of different modalities). As a result, our team wins both subtasks in this MDUG competition, which demonstrates the effectiveness of the proposed framework. Moreover, we conduct ablation analysis experiments and find that each module of our proposal is effective and contributes to the final performance.

Acknowledgment. This research was supported in part by the National Natural Science Foundation of China (62006062, 62176076), the Guangdong Provincial Key Laboratory of Novel Security Intelligence Technologies(2022B1212010005), Natural Science Foundation of Guangdong (2023A1515012922), and Shenzhen Foundational Research Funding JCYJ20210324115614039.

References

1. Alamri, H., et al.: Audio visual scene-aware dialog. In: Proceedings of the IEEE/CVF Conference on Computer Vision and Pattern Recognition, pp. 7558–7567 (2019)
2. Black, E., Hunter, A.: An inquiry dialogue system. Auton. Agent. Multi-Agent Syst. **19**, 173–209 (2009)
3. Cai, D., Wang, Y., Liu, L., Shi, S.: Recent advances in retrieval-augmented text generation. In: Proceedings of the 45th International ACM SIGIR Conference on Research and Development in Information Retrieval, pp. 3417–3419 (2022)
4. Dosovitskiy, A., et al.: An image is worth 16×16 words: transformers for image recognition at scale. In: International Conference on Learning Representations
5. Fang, Y., et al.: From spoken dialogue to formal summary: an utterance rewriting for dialogue summarization. In: Proceedings of the 2022 Conference of the North American Chapter of the Association for Computational Linguistics: Human Language Technologies, pp. 3859–3869 (2022)
6. Galley, M., McKeown, K., Fosler-Lussier, E., Jing, H.: Discourse segmentation of multi-party conversation. In: Proceedings of the 41st Annual Meeting of the Association for Computational Linguistics, pp. 562–569 (2003)
7. Hao, T., Li, X., He, Y., Wang, F.L., Qu, Y.: Recent progress in leveraging deep learning methods for question answering. Neural Comput. Appl. **34**, 2765–2783 (2021). https://doi.org/10.1007/s00521-021-06748-3

8. He, P., Liu, X., Gao, J., Chen, W.: DeBERTa: Decoding-enhanced BERT with disentangled attention. In: International Conference on Learning Representations
9. He, W., et al.: Unified dialog model pre-training for task-oriented dialog understanding and generation. In: Proceedings of the 45th International ACM SIGIR Conference on Research and Development in Information Retrieval, pp. 187–200 (2022)
10. Huang, Q., Xiong, Yu., Rao, A., Wang, J., Lin, D.: MovieNet: a Holistic Dataset for Movie Understanding. In: Vedaldi, A., Bischof, H., Brox, T., Frahm, J.-M. (eds.) ECCV 2020. LNCS, vol. 12349, pp. 709–727. Springer, Cham (2020). https://doi.org/10.1007/978-3-030-58548-8_41
11. Khan, O.Z., Robichaud, J.P., Crook, P.A., Sarikaya, R.: Hypotheses ranking and state tracking for a multi-domain dialog system using multiple ASR alternates. In: Sixteenth Annual Conference of the International Speech Communication Association (2015)
12. Kwiatkowski, T., et al.: Natural questions: a benchmark for question answering research. Trans. Assoc. Comput. Linguist. 7, 453–466 (2019)
13. Liao, L., Ma, Y., He, X., Hong, R., Chua, T.S.: Knowledge-aware multimodal dialogue systems. In: Proceedings of the 26th ACM International Conference on Multimedia, pp. 801–809 (2018)
14. Rao, A., et al.: A local-to-global approach to multi-modal movie scene segmentation. In: Proceedings of the IEEE/CVF Conference on Computer Vision and Pattern Recognition, pp. 10146–10155 (2020)
15. Seltzer, J., Cheng, K., Zong, S., Lin, J.: Flipping the script: inverse information seeking dialogues for market research. In: Proceedings of the 45th International ACM SIGIR Conference on Research and Development in Information Retrieval, pp. 3380–3383 (2022)
16. Sidiropoulos, P., Mezaris, V., Kompatsiaris, I., Meinedo, H., Bugalho, M., Trancoso, I.: Temporal video segmentation to scenes using high-level audiovisual features. IEEE Trans. Circ. Syst. Video Technol. 21(8), 1163–1177 (2011)
17. Su, J., Lu, Y., Pan, S., Wen, B., Liu, Y.: RoFormer: enhanced transformer with rotary position embedding (2021)
18. Sun, Y., et al.: ERNIE 3.0: large-scale knowledge enhanced pre-training for language understanding and generation. arXiv preprint arXiv:2107.02137 (2021)
19. Takanobu, R., et al.: A weakly supervised method for topic segmentation and labeling in goal-oriented dialogues via reinforcement learning. In: IJCAI, pp. 4403–4410 (2018)
20. Valizadeh, M., Parde, N.: The AI doctor is. In: A survey of task-oriented dialogue systems for healthcare applications. In: Proceedings of the 60th Annual Meeting of the Association for Computational Linguistics (Volume 1: Long Papers), pp. 6638–6660 (2022)
21. Wang, Y., Zhao, X., Zhao, D.: Overview of the NLPCC 2022 shared task: multimodal dialogue understanding and generation. In: In: Lu, W., Huang, S., Hong, Y., Zhou, X. (eds.) Natural Language Processing and Chinese Computing: 11th CCF International Conference, NLPCC 2022, Guilin, China, September 24–25, 2022, Proceedings, Part II, vol. 13552, pp. 328–335. Springer, Cham (2022). https://doi.org/10.1007/978-3-031-17189-5_29
22. Wu, H., Xu, K., Song, L., Jin, L., Zhang, H., Song, L.: Domain-adaptive pretraining methods for dialogue understanding. In: Proceedings of the 59th Annual Meeting of the Association for Computational Linguistics and the 11th International Joint Conference on Natural Language Processing (Volume 2: Short Papers), pp. 665–669. Association for Computational Linguistics, Online (Aug 2021)

23. Wu, H., et al.: Scene consistency representation learning for video scene segmentation. In: Proceedings of the IEEE/CVF Conference on Computer Vision and Pattern Recognition, pp. 14021–14030 (2022)

24. Xia, J., et al.: Dialogue topic segmentation via parallel extraction network with neighbor smoothing. In: Proceedings of the 45th International ACM SIGIR Conference on Research and Development in Information Retrieval, pp. 2126–2131 (2022)

25. Xing, L., Carenini, G.: Improving unsupervised dialogue topic segmentation with utterance-pair coherence scoring. arXiv preprint arXiv:2106.06719 (2021)

26. Xu, Y., Zhao, H., Zhang, Z.: Topic-aware multi-turn dialogue modeling. In: Proceedings of the AAAI Conference on Artificial Intelligence, vol. 35, pp. 14176–14184 (2021)

27. Zhang, H., Liu, M., Gao, Z., Lei, X., Wang, Y., Nie, L.: Multimodal dialog system: relational graph-based context-aware question understanding. In: Proceedings of the 29th ACM International Conference on Multimedia, pp. 695–703 (2021)

28. Zhang, J., et al: Fengshenbang 1.0: Being the foundation of Chinese cognitive intelligence (2023)

Overview of the NLPCC 2023 Shared Task 10: Learn to Watch TV: Multimodal Dialogue Understanding and Response Generation

Yueqian Wang[1], Yuxuan Wang[1,2], and Dongyan Zhao[1,2,3](✉)

[1] Wangxuan Institute of Computer Technology, Peking University, Beijing, China
{wangyueqian,zhaody}@pku.edu.cn, wyx@stu.pku.edu.cn
[2] Center for Data Science, AAIS, Peking University, Beijing, China
[3] Artificial Intelligence Institute of Peking University, Beijing, China

Abstract. In this paper, we present an overview of NLPCC 2023 Shared Task 10, Multimodal Dialogue Understanding and Response Generation, which includes four sub-tasks: dialogue scene identification, dialogue session identification, dialogue response retrieval, and dialogue response generation. A bilingual multi-modal dialogue dataset consisting of 100M utterances was made public for the shared task. This dataset contains 119K dialogue scene boundaries and 62K dialogue session boundaries annotated manually. This paper presents details of this shared task, dataset, evaluation metric and evaluation results.

Keywords: multi-modal dialogue · dialogue scene identification · dialogue session identification

1 Introduction

Building open-domain dialogue systems [5,30,39,43] has long been an aim of artificial intelligence. Recently, neural-based open-domain dialog systems are of growing interest [9,19,33,42,43], most of which are trained on large-scale datasets to learn a response conditioned on the textual contexts. One emerging area is multi-modal dialogue system. [6] first extended Visual Question Answering (VQA) [1,8,22,44] to dialogue setting. In this problem, questions about a given image are positioned in a multi-turn dialogue where each dialogue turn is a question-answer pair. [2] introduced a multi-turn video question answering dataset. Focusing on daily chat, [23,36] proposed an open-domain dialogue dataset extracted from movies, TV series and their corresponding subtitles. Thanks to these large-scale corpora, numerous approaches have shown remarkable performance in building multi-modal dialogue agents [13,16–18,20,37]. However, existing works perform much worse on open-domain dialogue datasets than QA-style datasets.

F. Liu et al. (Eds.): NLPCC 2023, LNAI 14304, pp. 412–419, 2023.
https://doi.org/10.1007/978-3-031-44699-3_37

Compared to images and short videos, movies and TV series contain richer historical, cultural and regional background knowledge. Besides, these story-based long videos have more complicated structures. Imagine you are watching the TV series *Friends*: In a museum, Ross is chatting with Carol about her marriage. Suddenly the camera turns and Ross begins to enjoy coffee with his friends in the Central Perk Cafe. Such a dramatic change of scenes is common in movies to exhibit a person's life in a few hours. Therefore, movies and TV series understanding is much more difficult than homemade video understanding, and directly using movies or TV series with their corresponding subtitles to train an open-domain dialogue system may not be the best option. In terms of temporal structure, movies and TV series are composed of scenes, where each scene is a sequence of semantically related continuous shots. The shots are captured by a camera that operates for an uninterrupted period of time, so they are usually visually continuous. A scene can be viewed as the smallest semantic unit of a movie.

For the above reasons, video scene segmentation is a fundamental step for understanding long videos such as movies. There are lots of studies [3,4,10, 25,27–29] about video scene segmentation, most of which adopt unsupervised approaches such as clustering or dynamic programming. [14] first constructed a large-scale movie understanding dataset *MovieNet*, with 318 movies in the dataset annotated with scene boundaries. Following this work, some supervised learning-based works [14,26] achieved great progress in video scene segmentation. However, MovieNet is annotated from sequences of shots that are extracted by [31], and are not precise enough. Besides, most previous works do not consider language modality, which is crucial for high-level video understanding.

In a dialogue scene, topic shift at the discourse-level is a common phenomenon. Continuing with the previous example, in the Central Perk Cafe, Ross talks about almost everything with his friends while the visual background is always a big orange couch. In such a situation, the dialogue context plays an important role in dialogue understanding. However, tracking all previous utterances is unnecessary and not feasible, since this consumes large computational resources and may introduce noise. Therefore capturing related topic-aware clues at the discourse-level is essential for dialogue understanding.

Dialogue Topic Segmentation (DTS) segments the dialogue into topically coherent pieces and has attracted lots of attention in recent years. Existing works regard DTS as a topic-tracking problem [15,34]. However, it is almost impossible to have a list of pre-defined categories that distinguish different topics in an open-domain dialogue. Hence, following another line of research, we process the DTS as an extension of text segmentation [7,11,32,40,41]. Due to the lack of sufficient annotated corpus, almost all previous work chose to use unsupervised methods. And recent datasets [41] can not reflect the effectiveness of the proposed methods due to the lack of a vast variety of dialogue topics.

To solve the above-mentioned challenges, we construct a large-scale multimodal dialogue dataset based on 1859 TV episodes. We manually annotated the dialogue scene and dialogue session boundaries to facilitate open-domain multimodal dialogue understanding and generation. Figure 1 shows some examples of the dataset. In NLPCC 2023 Shared Task 10, 10 teams registered for the shared task, 3 teams submitted the final results, but one of the 3 teams withdrew its submissions and report after the submission deadline, so results of the remaining 2 teams are reported.

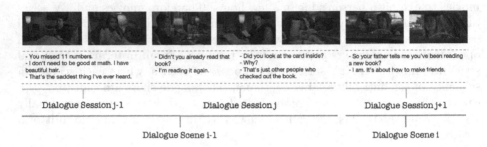

Fig. 1. Examples from our dataset. Only a few of the most relevant frames are displayed here. As shown above, the discourse contents in a scene can be vary greatly.

2 Task Description

We divide the multi-modal dialogue understanding and generation task into two phases: multi-modal context understanding and response generation. Specifically, in the multi-modal context understanding stage, we need to determine whether the dialogue topic or the video scene has changed. In the response generation stage, the ultimate goal is to generate a response that is coherent with the dialogue context and relevant to the video context. In summary, NLPCC 2023 Shared Task 10 includes four sub-tasks: (1) dialogue scene identification, (2) dialogue session identification, (3) dialogue response retrieval, and (4) dialogue response generation. Formally, we denote a multi-modal dialogue clip as (V, U), where $U = \{u_1, \ldots, u_N\}$ denotes the dialogue clip with each u_i denotes the i-th dialogue utterance. N is the number of dialogue utterances in a multi-modal dialogue clip. $V = \{v_1, \ldots, v_N\}$ serve as a video clip with v_i denoting as the i-th short video paired with u_i.

2.1 Dialogue Scene Identification

Following the previous definition of scene [14, 26, 27], a scene is a semantic unit where a certain activity takes place among a certain group of characters. The environment in a scene may change as the story goes on, thus traditional visual-cue-based approaches can not solve this problem well. Considering this attribute, we did not formulate a scene as a sequence of shots as in previous work. Instead, we formulate a dialogue scene as a short video sequence $[v_1, \ldots, v_{L_s}]$, where L_s

is the length of a dialogue scene. Then the dialogue scene identification sub-task can be formulated as a binary classification problem. Specifically, given a multi-modal dialogue clip (V, U), one is asked to predict a sequence $[o_1, \ldots, o_N]$, where $o_i \in \{0, 1\}$ denotes whether the i-th short video v_i is the start of a new dialogue scene.

2.2 Dialogue Session Identification

Dialogue session [32], also referred to as dialogue topic [7,40,41], is a topically related semantic unit in a conversation. Similar to monologue text segmentation, given a dialogue in the form of a sequence of utterances, one is asked to find the topic boundaries between utterances. Similar to the dialogue scene identification sub-task, the i-th utterance u_i is annotated with a binary label $y_i \in \{0, 1\}$ indicating whether u_i is the start of a new dialogue session.

2.3 Dialogue Response Retrieval

This setting is similar to dialogue response generation in Sect. 2.4, but a list of 15 candidates are given, and participants need to choose one answer from the candidates. The candidates are chosen as follows: 1 ground truth answer, 2 utterances from the same clip, 6 utterances from other clips in the same episode, and 6 utterances from other episodes.

2.4 Dialogue Response Generation

The dialogue response generation sub-task is formulated as follows: given the previous $N - 2$ utterances in a dialogue clip $C = \{u_1, \ldots, u_{N-2}\}$ with video clip V as context and the $(N-1)$-th utterance as query, the goal is to generate the response u_N. In this sub-task, N is set to 5, and all examples in the test set must meet the following conditions: (1) all N utterances are in the same scene, and (2) the CLIP-Score [12] of (u_N, v_N) is above the average score of all utterances in the dataset. If you are interested in the full data of the test set, please refer to [38].

3 Dataset Description

We construct the dataset on 335 TV series with 1859 videos in total. Compared with movies, TV shows contain fewer artistic expressions and monologues. We carefully selected the TV series to keep the high quality and generality of our dataset. Specifically, we remove the animations to make the video close to real-life scenarios. We also screen documents or talk shows that contain a large number of monologues. In addition, the selected TV series include almost all genres. The bilingual subtitles come from subtitle groups, thus most of the Chinese subtitles are human translations. We manually align the TV series with its subtitles.

To provide a high-quality dataset to support this shared task, we have made a great effort to manually annotate dialogue scenes and session boundaries. We segment the TV episode into a sequence of short videos, each short video is aligned with a dialogue utterance. Annotators watch these short videos to see if there are scene transitions or session transitions in them. We find that multimodal information greatly improves the efficiency of annotators. In the end, we randomly sampled 5% annotation results of every annotator for validation. If there are more than 5% boundaries being wrong labeled, all the results of the annotator are asked to be re-annotated. We repeat this procedure for three turns. After that, we segment the TV series episode into 90-second clips. As a result, we got 43K multi-modal dialogue clips, 1.1M utterances, 63K dialogue scene boundaries, and 119K dialogue session boundaries. We split our dataset to train:valid:test with 20:1:1. In the test set, sub-task 1&2 and sub-task 3&4 use different clips to prevent answer leakage. More statistics are shown in Table 1.

Table 1. Statistics of our dataset

Split	dialogue clips	utterances	dialogue scenes	dialogue sessions
Training data	40K	1M	56K	106K
Validation data	1,955	50K	3,202	6,331
Test data	1,934	50K	3,284	6,949

4 Results

We report accuracy and F1 for sub-task 1&2, accuracy for sub-task 3, BLEU-4 [24], ROUGE-L [21] and CIDEr [35] for sub-task 4. The overall results are shown in Table 2.

Results of NLPCC 2022 Shared Task 4 are also listed in Table 2. Note that these results are only for reference and can not be compared fairly to the results in NLPCC 2023, as their test sets are different.

Table 2. Evaluation results

Team ID	Task 1		Task 2		Task 3	Task 4		
	Acc	F1	Acc	F1	Acc	Bleu-4	Rouge-L	CIDEr
noobyj	0.834	0.214	0.839	0.242	**0.314**	–	–	–
TerenceCai	**0.887**	**0.276**	**0.872**	**0.384**	–	–	–	–
Random	0.508	0.112	0.505	0.188	0.062	0.000	0.000	0.000
Results of NLPCC 2022 Shared Task 4								
LingJing	0.939	0.182	0.878	0.289	–	–	-	–
Eastwood	–	–	0.723	0.398	–	–	–	–

5   Conclusion

This paper briefly introduces the overview of the NLPCC 2023 Shared Task 10: Multi-modal Dialogue Understanding and Response Generation. We introduce a large-scale video-grounded dialogue dataset with detailed annotations. Based on this dataset we propose four benchmarks for multi-modal dialogue understanding and generation. We believe our new benchmarks can lead to interesting insights into designing better multi-modal dialogue systems.

References

1. Agrawal, A., et al.: VQA: visual question answering. Int. J. Comput. Vision **123**, 4–31 (2015)
2. AlAmri, H., et al.: Audio visual scene-aware dialog. In: 2019 IEEE/CVF Conference on Computer Vision and Pattern Recognition (CVPR), pp. 7550–7559 (2019)
3. Baraldi, L., Grana, C., Cucchiara, R.: A deep siamese network for scene detection in broadcast videos. In: Proceedings of the 23rd ACM International Conference on Multimedia (2015)
4. Chasanis, V., Likas, A.C., Galatsanos, N.P.: Scene detection in videos using shot clustering and sequence alignment. IEEE Trans. Multimedia **11**, 89–100 (2009)
5. Colby, K.M., Weber, S., Hilf, F.D.: Artificial paranoia. Artif. Intell. **2**, 1–25 (1971)
6. Das, A., et al.: Visual dialog. In: Proceedings of the IEEE Conference on Computer Vision and Pattern Recognition, pp. 326–335 (2017)
7. Galley, M., McKeown, K., Fosler-Lussier, E., Jing, H.: Discourse segmentation of multi-party conversation. In: ACL (2003)
8. Gao, H., Mao, J., Zhou, J., Huang, Z., Wang, L., Xu, W.: Are you talking to a machine? dataset and methods for multilingual image question. In: NIPS (2015)
9. Gao, J., Galley, M., Li, L.: Neural approaches to conversational AI. ArXiv abs/1809.08267 (2019)
10. Han, B., Wu, W.: Video scene segmentation using a novel boundary evaluation criterion and dynamic programming. In: 2011 IEEE International Conference on Multimedia and Expo, pp. 1–6 (2011)
11. Hearst, M.A.: Text tiling: segmenting text into multi-paragraph subtopic passages. Comput. Linguistics **23**, 33–64 (1997)
12. Hessel, J., Holtzman, A., Forbes, M., Le Bras, R., Choi, Y.: CLIPScore: a reference-free evaluation metric for image captioning. In: Proceedings of the 2021 Conference on Empirical Methods in Natural Language Processing, pp. 7514–7528. Association for Computational Linguistics, Online and Punta Cana, Dominican Republic (2021). https://doi.org/10.18653/v1/2021.emnlp-main.595, https://aclanthology.org/2021.emnlp-main.595
13. Hori, C., et al.: End-to-end audio visual scene-aware dialog using multimodal attention-based video features. In: ICASSP 2019–2019 IEEE International Conference on Acoustics, Speech and Signal Processing (ICASSP), pp. 2352–2356. IEEE (2019)
14. Huang, Q., Xiong, Y., Rao, A., Wang, J., Lin, D.: MovieNet: a holistic dataset for movie understanding. ArXiv abs/2007.10937 (2020)
15. Khan, O.Z., Robichaud, J.P., Crook, P.A., Sarikaya, R.: Hypotheses ranking and state tracking for a multi-domain dialog system using multiple ASR alternates. In: INTERSPEECH (2015)

16. Le, H., Chen, N.F., Hoi, S.: Learning reasoning paths over semantic graphs for video-grounded dialogues. In: International Conference on Learning Representations (2021)
17. Le, H., Sahoo, D., Chen, N., Hoi, S.C.: Bist: bi-directional spatio-temporal reasoning for video-grounded dialogues. In: Proceedings of the 2020 Conference on Empirical Methods in Natural Language Processing (EMNLP), pp. 1846–1859 (2020)
18. Le, H., Sahoo, D., Chen, N.F., Hoi, S.C.H.: Multimodal transformer networks for end-to-end video-grounded dialogue systems. In: ACL (2019)
19. Li, J., Monroe, W., Shi, T., Jean, S., Ritter, A., Jurafsky, D.: Adversarial learning for neural dialogue generation. In: EMNLP (2017)
20. Li, Z., Li, Z., Zhang, J., Feng, Y., Niu, C., Zhou, J.: Bridging text and video: a universal multimodal transformer for video-audio scene-aware dialog. arXiv preprint arXiv:2002.00163 (2020)
21. Lin, C.Y.: Rouge: a package for automatic evaluation of summaries. In: Text summarization branches out, pp. 74–81 (2004)
22. Malinowski, M., Fritz, M.: A multi-world approach to question answering about real-world scenes based on uncertain input. In: NIPS (2014)
23. Meng, Y., et al.: OpenViDial: a large-scale, open-domain dialogue dataset with visual contexts. ArXiv abs/2012.15015 (2020)
24. Papineni, K., Roukos, S., Ward, T., Zhu, W.J.: Bleu: a method for automatic evaluation of machine translation. In: Proceedings of the 40th annual meeting on association for computational linguistics, pp. 311–318. Association for Computational Linguistics (2002)
25. Protasov, S., Khan, A., Sozykin, K., Ahmad, M.: Using deep features for video scene detection and annotation. SIViP **12**, 991–999 (2018)
26. Rao, A., et al.: A local-to-global approach to multi-modal movie scene segmentation. In: 2020 IEEE/CVF Conference on Computer Vision and Pattern Recognition (CVPR), pp. 10143–10152 (2020)
27. Rasheed, Z., Shah, M.: Scene detection in hollywood movies and tv shows. In: 2003 IEEE Computer Society Conference on Computer Vision and Pattern Recognition, 2003. Proceedings. 2, II-343 (2003)
28. Rotman, D., Porat, D., Ashour, G.: Optimal sequential grouping for robust video scene detection using multiple modalities. Int. J. Semantic Comput. **11**, 193–208 (2017)
29. Rui, Y., Huang, T.S., Mehrotra, S.: Exploring video structure beyond the shots. In: IEEE International Conference on Multimedia Computing and Systems (Cat. No.98TB100241), Proceedings, pp. 237–240 (1998)
30. Shum, H., He, X., Li, D.: From Eliza to XiaoIce: challenges and opportunities with social chatbots. Front. Inf. Technol. Electron. Eng. **19**, 10–26 (2018)
31. Sidiropoulos, P., Mezaris, V., Kompatsiaris, Y., Meinedo, H., Bugalho, M.M.F., Trancoso, I.: Temporal video segmentation to scenes using high-level audiovisual features. IEEE Trans. Circuits Syst. Video Technol. **21**, 1163–1177 (2011)
32. Song, Y., et al.: Dialogue session segmentation by embedding-enhanced texttiling. ArXiv abs/1610.03955 (2016)
33. Sordoni, A., et al.: A neural network approach to context-sensitive generation of conversational responses. In: NAACL (2015)
34. Takanobu, R., et al.: A weakly supervised method for topic segmentation and labeling in goal-oriented dialogues via reinforcement learning. In: IJCAI (2018)
35. Vedantam, R., Lawrence Zitnick, C., Parikh, D.: Cider: consensus-based image description evaluation. In: Proceedings of the IEEE Conference on Computer Vision and Pattern Recognition, pp. 4566–4575 (2015)

36. Wang, S., Meng, Y., Li, X., Sun, X., Ouyang, R., Li, J.: OpenViDial 2.0: a larger-scale, open-domain dialogue generation dataset with visual contexts. ArXiv abs/2109.12761 (2021)
37. Wang, S., et al.: Modeling text-visual mutual dependency for multi-modal dialog generation. ArXiv abs/2105.14445 (2021)
38. Wang, Y., Zheng, Z., Zhao, X., Li, J., Wang, Y., Zhao, D.: VSTAR: a video-grounded dialogue dataset for situated semantic understanding with scene and topic transitions (2023)
39. Weizenbaum, J.: Eliza-a computer program for the study of natural language communication between man and machine. Commun. ACM **9**, 36–45 (1966)
40. Xing, L., Carenini, G.: Improving unsupervised dialogue topic segmentation with utterance-pair coherence scoring. In: SIGDIAL (2021)
41. Xu, Y., Zhao, H., Zhang, Z.: Topic-aware multi-turn dialogue modeling. In: AAAI (2021)
42. Zhao, T., Zhao, R., Eskénazi, M.: Learning discourse-level diversity for neural dialog models using conditional variational autoencoders. In: ACL (2017)
43. Zhou, L., Gao, J., Li, D., Shum, H.Y.: The design and implementation of XiaoIce, an empathetic social chatbot. Comput. Linguist. **46**(1), 53–93 (2020)
44. Zhu, Y., Groth, O., Bernstein, M.S., Fei-Fei, L.: Visual7W: grounded question answering in images. In: 2016 IEEE Conference on Computer Vision and Pattern Recognition (CVPR), pp. 4995–5004 (2016).

Correction to: A Numeracy-Enhanced Decoding for Solving Math Word Problem

Rao Peng⑩, Chuanzhi Yang⑩, Litian Huang⑩, Xiaopan Lyu⑩,
Hao Meng⑩, and Xinguo Yu⑩

Correction to:
Chapter "A Numeracy-Enhanced Decoding for Solving Math Word Problem" in: F. Liu et al. (Eds.): *Natural Language Processing and Chinese Computing*, LNAI 14304, https://doi.org/10.1007/978-3-031-44699-3_11

The original version of this paper Chinese characters in Table 1 and Table 3 of the paper are not displayed correctly. This has been corrected.

The updated original version of this chapter can be found at
https://doi.org/10.1007/978-3-031-44699-3_11

Author Index

F. Liu et al. (Eds.): NLPCC 2023, LNAI 14304, pp. 421–429, 2023.
https://doi.org/10.1007/978-3-031-44699-3

Printed in the United States
by Baker & Taylor Publisher Services